CW00409266

1 MONTH OF FREE READING

at
www.ForgottenBooks.com

By purchasing this book you are eligible for one month membership to ForgottenBooks.com, giving you unlimited access to our entire collection of over 1,000,000 titles via our web site and mobile apps.

To claim your free month visit:
www.forgottenbooks.com/free159951

ISBN 978-0-365-20423-7
PIBN 10159951

CONCISE DICTIONARY

OF THE

HOLY BIBLE.

BY REV. JAMES COVEL, JUNIOR.

DESIGNED FOR THE USE OF SUNDAY SCHOOL TEACHERS
AND FAMILIES.

WITH MAPS AND NUMEROUS FINE ENGRAVINGS.

NEW-YORK:
PUBLISHED BY G. LANE & P. P. SANDFORD,
For the Sunday School Union of the Methodist Episcopal Church,
at the Conference Office, 200 Mulberry-street.

J. Collord, Printer.
1843.

PREFACE

TO

DICTIONARY OF THE BIBLE.

THE DICTIONARY, which is now presented to the reader, is the result of the most careful and patient investigation. The author, of course, has been indebted to various sources for materials ; but all the articles, with few exceptions, have been sent to the press in manuscript ; and, during two years past, all the time which could in justice be spared from other duties has been exclusively devoted to the preparation of this work.

In most Dictionaries of the Bible, a large proportion of the matter consists of *Scripture narrative*. But Bibles are too numerous, and their contents too well understood by that class of persons who read Bible Dictionaries, to render such details necessary.

The object of this work is simply to explain and illustrate the meaning of this precious book ; and no name or term occurring in the Bible has been omitted, respecting which any thing could be ascertained which was judged important in the accomplishment of this object, or which would seem to be desirable in a work of this kind. I have derived great assistance from works which would not be likely to fall in the way of common readers. Such as Gesenius's Hebrew and English Lexicon, translated from the Latin.

This invaluable work is purely a philological work ; and although it rarely presents any allusion to theological sentiments, no student of the Bible should be without it.

The Greek and English Lexicon of the New Testament, by Dr. Robinson, the translator of Gesenius.

This work bears in every page marks of integrity, learning, and diligence. In both of the above-named works, attention has been given to the interpretations of difficult passages ; and therefore the two together form a good commentary on the original Scriptures. Besides, Dr. Jahn's Biblical Archæology, Robinson's Calmet, the Biblical Repository, the works of Professor Stuart, Dr. A. Clarke, Burckhardt, Macknight, Watson, and others, have been constantly at hand. Geographical articles have received particular attention ; no fact is stated but on the latest and best authority, and on which the reader may depend. The references are all made in every article for the purpose of illustration ; and no article should be considered as read until every passage is examined.

Respecting the engravings, the reader may rely on their accuracy also. No *pains* or *expense* has been spared to procure those which are correct ; and they are executed by one of the best artists in our country.

The division and accentuation of the words have been carefully attended to ; and, in some instances, they have been respelled, as a guide to their correct pronunciation.

In the pronunciation, observe the following rules :—

1. When a vowel is followed by an accent, it has the long sound, as A'bel, but otherwise, the short sound as Ad'am.

3. Every final *i*, marked as a distinct syllable, has the long sound as a'i, Hu-sha-i.

3. Ch is pronounced like k, as Che'bar, except in cherub, cherubim, Rachel, Chittim.

4. G is hard before e, and i, as Gehazi, Gideon.

New-York, July 6, 1898.

BIBLICAL DICTIONARY.

AARON, (*A'ron,*) the son of Amram and Joch'e-bed, of the tribe of Levi. Aaron was three years older than his brother Moses; and in effecting the deliverance of the Hebrews we find them constantly associated. During the march of the children of Israel through the wilderness, Aaron and his sons were appointed by God to exercise for ever the office of priests in the tabernacle.

After the tabernacle was built, Moses consecrated Aaron to the high priesthood with the holy oil, and invested him with his priestly robes, —his garments "of glory and beauty." Two miraculous interpositions confirmed him in his office of high priest, as of Divine appointment. The first was the destruction of Ko'rah, who sought that office for himself, and of the two hundred and fifty Levites who supported his pretensions, Num. xvi. The second was the blossoming of Aaron's rod, which was designed "to cause the murmurings of the Israelites against him to cease."

Aaron married E-lish'e-ba, the daughter of Amminadab,

of the tribe of Judah, by whom he had four sons, Na'-dab and Abi'hu, E-le-a'zar and Ith'a-mar, Ex. vi, 23. The first two were killed by fire from heaven, as a punishment for presuming to offer incense with strange fire in their censers, Lev. x, 1, 2. From the two others the succession of high priests was continued in Israel.

The account of the death of Aaron is peculiarly solemn and affecting. As he and Moses, in striking the rock at Meribah, Num. xvi, had not honoured God by a perfect obedience and faith, he in his wrath declared unto them that they should not enter into the promised land. Soon after, the Lord commanded Moses, "Take Aaron, and Eleazar his son, and bring them up to Mount Hor; and strip Aaron of his garments,"—his splendid pontifical vestments,— "and put them upon Eleazar his son; and Aaron shall be gathered unto his people, and shall die there." In Deuteronomy it is said that Aaron died at Mo-se'ra; because that was the name of the district in which Mount Hor was situated.

ABB 6 ABI

AARONITES, Priests who served the sanctuary, of the family of Aaron.

AB, in the Hebrew chronology, the eleventh month of the civil year, and the fifth of the ecclesiastical year, which began with Ni'san. This month answered to the moon of July, comprehending part of July and of August, and contained thirty days.

A-BAD'DON, Heb. corresponding to *Apollyon*, Gr. hat is, *Destroyer*, is represented, Rev. ix, 11, as king of the locusts, and the angel of the bottomless pit.

A-BA'NA. Probably a branch of the Barrady, or Chrysor'rhoas, which derives its source from the foot of Mount Lib'a-nus, eastward. Perhaps the Pharpar is the same with Oron'tes, the most noted river of Syr'ia, which rises a little to the north or north-east of Damascus, 2 Kings v, 12.

AB'A-RIM, mountains east of Jordan, over against Jericho, on the northern border of Moab, within the limits of the tribe of Reuben.

AB'BA, a Syr'i-ac word, which signifies *father*. The learned Mr. Selden, from the Babylonian Ge-mar'a, has proved that slaves were not allowed to use the title abba in addressing the master of the family to which they belonged. This may serve to illustrate Rom. viii, 15, and Gal. iv, 6. St. Paul and St. Mark added to it when writing to foreigners the explanation, *father*.

A-BED'NE-GO, the Chaldee name given by the king of Babylon's officer to Aza-ri'ah, one of Daniel's companions, Dan. i, 7. This name imports the servant of Nago, or Nego, which is supposed to signify the sun, or morning star.

A'BEL. The second son of Adam and Eve, and born probably in the second or third year of the world, and was killed about the year of the world, 139.

A'BEL-MIS'RA-IM, the floor of Atad, beyond the river Jordan, where Joseph, his brethren, and the Egyptians mourned for the death of Jacob, Gen. l, 11.

A'BEL-SHIT'TIM, a city situate in the plains of Moab, beyond Jordan, opposite to Jericho.

A-BI'A, the same as A-bi'-jah, a descendant of Eleazar, son of Aaron, and head of the eighth of the twenty-four companies into which the Jewish priests were divided.

A-BI'A-THAR, the tenth high priest among the Jews, and fourth in descent from Eli, 2 Sam. viii, 17.

A'BIB, the name of the first Hebrew sacred month, Exod. xiii, 4. This month was afterward called Ni'san; it contained thirty days, and answered to part of our March and April. Abib signifies green ears of corn, or fresh fruits. It was so named because corn, particularly barley, was in ear at that time.

A-BI'HU, the son of Aaron, the high priest, was consumed, together with his brother Nadab, by fire sent from God, because he had offered incense with strange fire, instead of taking it from the altar, Lev. x, 1, 2. This calamity happened A. M. 2514; within eight days after the consecration of Aaron and his sons.

AB-I-LE'NE, a small province in Cœlo Syria, between Lebanon and Antilibanus.

A-BIM'E-LECH. This seems to have been the title of the kings of Philistia, as Cæsar was of the Roman emperors, and Pharaoh of the sovereigns of Egypt. It was the name also of one of the sons of Gideon, who became a judge of Israel, Judges ix; and of a Jewish high priest, 1 Sam. xxi, 1.

A-BI'RAM, the eldest son of Hiel, the Bethelite.

2. ABIRAM, the son of Eliab, of the tribe of Reuben, was one of those who conspired with Korah and Dathan against Moses in the wilderness.

AB'I-SHAG, a young woman, a native of Shunam, in the tribe of Issachar.

A-BISH'A-I, the son of Zeruiah, David's sister.

AB'NER was the uncle of King Saul, and the general of his army.

A-BOM-IN-A'TION. This word is applied to *idolatry* and *idols*, not only because the worship of idols is in itself an abominable thing, but likewise because the ceremonies of idolaters were almost always of an infamous and licentious nature. The "abomination of desolation," Matt. xxiv, 15, 16; Mark xiii, 14; without doubt, signifies the *ensigns of the Roman armies* under the command of Titus, during the last siege of Jerusalem. The images of their gods and emperors were delineated on these ensigns; and the ensigns themselves, especially the eagles, which were carried at the heads of the legions, were objects of worship; and, according to the usual style of Scripture, they were therefore an abomination.

In general, whatever is morally or ceremonially impure, or leads to sin, is designated an *abomination* to God. Thus lying lips are said to be an *abomination* to the Lord. Every thing in doctrine or practice which tended to corrupt the simplicity of the Gospel is also in Scripture called abominable; hence Babylon is represented, Rev. xvii, 4, as holding in her hand a cup "full of abominations." In this view, to "work abomination," is to introduce idolatry, or any other great corruption, into the Church and worship of God, 1 Kings xi, 7.

A'BRAM, and A'BRAHAM, *father of a great multitude*, the son of Terah, born at Ur, a city of Chaldea.

A. M. 2006, only two years after the death of Noah.

The wide and deep impression made by the character of Abraham upon the ancient world is proved by the reverence which people of almost all nations and countries have paid to him, and the manner in which the events of his life have been interwoven in their mythology, and their religious traditions. His history is given in the book of Genesis, and is one of deep interest.

AB'SA-LOM, the son of David by Ma'a-chah, daughter of the king of Geshur; distinguished for his fine person, his vices, and his unnatural rebellion.

AC'CAD, one of the four cities built by Nimrod, the founder of the As-syr'i-an empire. (See *Nimrod.*) Gen. x, 10. Thus it appears that Accad was contemporary with Babylon, and was one of the first four great cities of the world.

AC-CEPT', to take pleasure in, either in whole or in part. The phrase, *to accept the person of any one*, is a Hebrew idiom, and signifies, *to regard any one with favour or partiality.*

AC-CESS', free admission, open entrance. Our access to God is by Jesus Christ, the way, the truth, and the life, Rom. v, 2; Eph. ii, 18. Under the law, the high priest alone had access into the holiest of all; but when the veil of the temple was rent in twain, at the death of Christ, it was declared that a new and living way of access was laid open through the veil, that is to say, his flesh. By his death, also, the middle wall of partition was broken down, and Jew and Gentile had both free access to God; whereas before, the Gentiles had no nearer access in the temple worship than to the gate of the court of Israel. Thus the saving grace and lofty privileges of the Gospel are equally bestowed upon true believers of all nations.

AC'CHO, a seaport of Palestine, thirty miles south of Tyre, Acts xxi, 7; afterward called Ptol-e-ma'is, and now Akka by the Arabs, and Acre by the Turks. It was given to the tribe of Asher, Judges i, 31.

AC-CURS'ED, denotes the cutting off or separating any one from the communion of the Church, the number of the living, or the privileges of society; and also the devoting an animal, city, or other thing to destruction. *A-nath'e-ma* was a species of *excommunication* among the Jews, and was often practised after they had lost the power of life and death, against those persons who, according to the Mosaic law, ought to have been executed. *Mar-a-na'tha,* a Syriac word, signifying *the Lord cometh,* was added to the sentence to express their persuasion that the Lord God would come to ake vengeance upon that guilt which they, circumstanced as they were, had not the power to punish, 1 Cor. xvi, 22.

According to the idiom of the Hebrew language, *accursed* and *crucified* were synonymous terms. By the Jews every one who died upon a tree was reckoned *accursed*, Deut. xxi, 23.

A-CEL'DA-MA, (*A-sel'-da-ma*,) a piece of ground without the south wall of Jerusalem, on the other side of the brook Silo'am. It was called the Potter's Field, because an earth or clay was dug in it, of which pottery was made. It was likewise called the Fuller's Field, because cloth was dried in it. But it having been afterward bought with the money by which the high priest and rulers of the Jews purchased the blood of Jesus, it was called "Aceldama," or the *Field of Blood.*

A-CHA'I-A. This name is used to denote the whole of Greece, as it existed as a Roman province; or A-cha'-i-a Proper, a district in the northern part of the Pel-o-pon-ne'-sus, on the bay of Cor'inth, and in which the city of that name stood. It appears to have been used in the former sense in 2 Cor. xi, 10; and in the latter, in Acts xix, 21.

ACHAICUS, (*A-kay'-e-kus*,) a native of A-cha'i-a, and disciple of St. Paul.

A'CHAN, the son of Car-mi, of the tribe of Judah, who having taken a part of the spoils of Jericho, against the injunction of God, who had *accursed* or devoted the whole city, was, upon being taken by lot, doomed to be stoned to death. The whole history is recorded, Joshua vii.

A'CHISH, king of Gath, to whom David withdrew from the dominions of Saul.

ACH'ME-THA. The same with *Ec-bat'a-na*, the royal city, Ezra vi, 2.

A'CHOR, *troubling*, a valley between Jericho and A'i. So called from the trouble brought upon the Israelites by the sin of Achan.

ACH'ZIB, a city on the coast of the Mediterranean, in the tribe of Ash'er, and one of the cities out of which that tribe did not expel the inhabitants, Judges i, 31. It is situated about ten miles north of Ptol-e-ma'is.

ACTS OF THE APOSTLES. This book, in the very beginning, professes itself to be a continuation of the Gospel of St. Luke; and its style bespeaks it to be written by the same person.

This is the only inspired work which gives us any historical account of the progress of Christianity after our Saviour's ascension. It comprehends a period of about thirty years, but it by no means contains a general history of the Church during that time. The latter part of the book is confined to the history of St. Paul, of whom St. Luke was the constant companion for several years.

As this account of St. Paul is not continued beyond his two years' imprisonment at Rome, it is probable that this book was written soon after his release, which happened in the year 63; we may therefore consider the Acts of the Apostles as written about the year 64.

AD'AM. The manner in which the creation of Adam is narrated indicates something peculiar and eminent in the being to be formed, and which serves to impress us with a sense of the greatness of the work. Every thing as to man's creation is given in a solemn and deliberative form, and contains also an intimation of a trinity of persons in the Godhead, all equally possessed of *creative* power, and therefore *Divine*, to each of whom man was to stand in relations the most sacred and intimate: —" And God said, Let us make man in *our* image, after our likeness; and let them have dominion," &c.

2. It may be next inquired in what that image of God, in which man was made, consists.

It is manifest from the history of Moses, that human nature has two essential constituent parts, the BODY formed out of pre-existing matter, the earth; and a LIVING SOUL, breathed into the body by an *inspiration* from God.

The "image" or likeness of God in which man was made has, by some, been assigned to the body; by others, to the soul. It has, also, been placed in the circumstance of his having "*dominion*" over the other creatures. As to the body, it is not necessary to prove that in no sense can it bear the image of God; that is, be "*like*" God.

Equally unfounded is the notion that the image of God in man consisted in the "dominion" which was granted to him over this lower world.

When God is called "the Father of spirits," a likeness is suggested between man and God in the *spirituality* of their nature. In *spirituality*, and, consequently, immateriality, this image of God in man, in the first instance, consists.

The sentiment expressed in Wisdom ii, 23, is an evidence that, in the opinion of the ancient Jews, the image of God in man comprised *immortality* also.

To these we are to add the *intellectual powers*, and we have what divines, in perfect accordance with the Scriptures, have called "the NATURAL image of God in his creatures," which is essential and ineffaceable. Man was made capable of *knowledge*, and he was endowed with liberty of *will*.

This natural image of God was the foundation of that MORAL image by which also man was distinguished. Unless he had been a spiritual, knowing, and willing being, he would have been wholly incapable of *moral* qualities. That he had such qualities eminently, and that in them consisted the image of God, as well as in the natural attributes just stated, we have also the express testimony of Scripture, Eccl. vii, 29; Col. iii, 10; Eph. iv, 24.

3. On the intellectual and moral endowments of Adam as to *capacity*, his intellect must have been vigorous beyond that of any of his fallen descendants; which itself gives us very high views of the strength of his understanding, although we should allow him to have been created "lower than the angels."

On the degree of moral excellence also in the first man, if we attend to the passages of Holy Writ above quoted, we shall be able to ascertain, if not the exact degree of his moral endowments, yet that there is a certain standard below which they cannot be placed. Generally, he was made in the *image* of God, which, we have already proved, is to be understood *morally* as well as *naturally*. Man, therefore, in his original state was *sinless;* there was no obliquity in his moral principles, his mind, or affections; none in his conduct. He was perfectly sincere and exactly just, rendering from the heart all that was due to God and to the creature. Tried by the exactest *plum-*

met, he was *upright;* by the most perfect *rule,* he was *straight.*

4. The salvation of Adam has been disputed; for what reason does not appear, except that the silence of Scripture, as to his after life, has given bold men occasion to obtrude their speculations upon a subject which called for no such expression of opinion. As nothing to the contrary appears, the charitable inference is, that as he was the first to receive the promise of redemption, so he was the first to prove its virtue. It is another presumption, that as Adam and Eve were clothed with skins of beasts, which could not have been slain for food, these were the skins of their sacrifices; and as the offering of animal sacrifice was an expression of faith in the appointed propitiation, to that refuge we may conclude they resorted, and through its merits were accepted.

5. That Adam was a type of Christ, is plainly affirmed by St. Paul, who calls him "The figure of him who was to come." Adam and Christ were each a public person, a *federal head* to the whole race of mankind; but the one was the fountain of sin and death, the other of righteousness and life.

AD'A-MANT, a stone of impenetrable hardness.

A'DAR, the twelfth month of the ecclesiastical, and the sixth of the civil year among the Hebrews. It contains but twenty-nine days, and answers to our February, and sometimes enters into March, according to the course of the moon, by which they regulated their seasons.

AD'DER, a venomous serpent, more usually called the viper. *See viper.*

In Psalm lviii, 5, reference is made to the effect of musical sounds upon serpents. That they might be rendered tame and harmless by certain charms, or soft and sweet sounds, and trained to delight in music, was an opinion which prevailed very early and universally.

But on some serpents these charms seem to have no power; and it appears from Scripture, that the adder sometimes takes precautions to prevent the fascination which he sees preparing for him: "for the deaf adder shutteth her ear, and will not hear the voice of the most skilful charmer." The threatening of the Prophet Jeremiah proceeds upon the same fact: "I will send serpents" (cockatrices) "among you, which will not be charmed, and they shall bite you." In these quotations, the sacred writers, while they take it for granted that many serpents are disarmed by charming, plainly admit that the powers of the charmer are in vain exerted upon others.

To AD-JURE', to bind by oath, as under the penalty of a fearful curse, Joshua vi, 26; Mark v, 7. 2. To charge solemnly, as by the authority, and under pain, of the displeasure of God, Matt. xxvi, 63; Acts xix, 13.

AD'MA, one of the five cities which were destroyed by fire from heaven, and buried under the waters of the Dead Sea, Gen. xiv, 2; Deut. xxix, 23.

AD'-O-NI-BE'-ZEK, i. e. *the lord of Bezek*, king of the city Bezek, in Canaan, seventeen miles north-east from Napolose. He was a powerful and cruel prince, who, having at various times taken seventy kings, ordered their thumbs and great toes to be cut off, and caused them, like dogs, to feed on the crumbs that fell from his table. After Joshua's death the tribes of Judah and Simeon marched against Adoni-Bezek, vanquished him; and, having taken him prisoner, cut off his thumbs and great toes. Adoni-Bezek acknowledged the retributive justice of this punishment from God. He was carried to Jerusalem, where he died, A. M. 2570, Judges i, 4–7.

A-DOP'TION. An act by which one takes another into his family, owns him for his son, and appoints him his heir.

2. Adoption, in a theological sense, is that act of God's free grace, by which, upon our being justified by faith in Christ, we are received into the family of God, and entitled to the inheritance of

heaven. This appears not so much a distinct act of God, as involved in, and necessarily flowing from, our justification; so that at least the one always implies the other. The apostles in using the term appear to have had before them the simple view, that our sins had deprived us of our sonship, the favour of God, and the right to the inheritance of eternal life; but that, upon our return to God, and reconciliation with him, our forfeited privileges were not only restored, but greatly heightened through the paternal kindness of God.

3. To this state belong, freedom from a servile spirit, for we are not servants but sons; the special love and care of God our heavenly Father; a filial confidence in him; free access to him at all times and in all circumstances; a title to the heavenly inheritance; and the Spirit of adoption, or the witness of the Holy Spirit to our adoption, which is the foundation of all the comfort we can derive from those privileges, as it is the only means by which we can know that they are ours.

4. The last mentioned great privilege of adoption merits special attention. It consists in the inward witness or testimony of the Holy Spirit to the sonship of believers, from which flows a comfortable persuasion or conviction of our present acceptance with God, and the

hope of our future and eternal glory. This is taught in several passages of Scripture: Rom. viii, 15, 16; Gal. iv, 4–6. To these texts are to be added all those passages, so numerous in the New Testament, which express the confidence and the joy of Christians; their friendship with God; their confident access to him as their God; their entire union and delightful intercourse with him in spirit.

A-DRAM'ME-LECH, the son of Sen-nach'e-rib, king of Assyria.

Also one of the gods adored by the inhabitants of Sephar-va'im, who were settled in the country of Sa-mar'i-a, in the room of the Israelites, who were carried beyond the Euphrates.

AD-RA-MYT'TI-UM, a city in Lesser Asia, on the west coast of Mys'i-a, over against the isle of Lesbos.

A'DRI-A. This name is now confined to the Gulf of Venice. But in St. Paul's time it was extended to all that portion of the Mediterranean between Crete and Sicily.

A-DUL'LAM, a city in the tribe of Judah, to the west of Hebron, whose king was slain by Joshua, Josh. xii, 15.

A-DUL'TER-Y, the violation of the marriage bed. The law of Moses punished with death both the man and the woman who were guilty of this crime, Lev. xx, 10.

If a woman was betrothed to a man, and was guilty of this infamous crime before the marriage was completed, she was, in this case, along with her paramour, to be stoned, Deut. xxii, 22–24.

This procedure had the effect of keeping in mind, among the Jews, God's high displeasure against this violation of his law; and the Christian will always remember the solemn denunciations of the New Testament against a crime so aggravated, whether considered in its effects upon the domestic relations, upon the moral character of the guilty parties, or upon society at large,— "Whoremongers and adulterers God will judge."

In the prophetic scriptures it is often metaphorically taken, and signifies idolatry, and apostasy from God, by which men basely defile themselves, and wickedly violate their covenant relation to God, Hos. ii, 2; Ezek. xvi.

AD'VO-CATE, *a patron*, one who pleads the cause of any one before another. In this sense the term is applied to Christ our intercessor, 1 John ii, 1.

AG'A-BUS, a prophet, and, as the Greeks say, one of the seventy disciples of our Saviour.

A'GAG. This seems to have been a common name of the princes of Am'a-lek, one of whom was very powerful as early as the time of Moses, Num. xxiv, 7.

A'GAR, Mount Si'nai, so called, Gal. iv, 24, 25.

AG'ATE. A precious stone, a variety of the flint and semipellucid. Its variegations are without end, and sometimes most beautifully disposed, representing plants, trees, rivers, clouds, &c.

AGE, in the most general sense of the term, denotes the duration of any substance, animate or inanimate; and is applied either to the whole period of its existence, or to that portion of it which precedes the time to which the description of it refers. In this sense it is used to signify either the whole natural duration of the LIFE of man, or any interval of it that has elapsed before the period of which we speak. When age is understood of a certain portion of the life of man, its whole duration is divided into four different ages, viz., infancy, youth, manhood, and old age: the first extending to the fourteenth year; the second, denominated youth, adolescence, or the age of puberty, commencing at fourteen, and terminating at about twenty-five; manhood, or the virile age, concluding at fifty; and the last ending at the close of life.

In *chronology* is used for a *century*, or a period of one hundred years; and is sometimes used among the ancient poets in the same sense as *generation*, or a period of thirty years.

A-GRIP'PA, surnamed

Herod, the son of Ar-is-to-bu'lus and Berenice and grandson of Herod the Great, was born three years before the birth of our Saviour, and seven years before the vulgar æra. After the death of his father Aristobulus, Jo-se'phus informs us that He-rod, his grandfather, took care of his education, and sent him to Rome to make his court to Ti-be'rius. Soon after this, Ti-be'rius died; and Ca-lig'u-la, succeeding him, heaped many favours and much wealth upon Agrip-pa, set a royal diadem on his head, and gave him the te-trarchy which Philip, the son of Herod the Great, had possessed, that is, Batanæa and Trach-o-ni'tis. To this he added that of Ly-sa'ni-as; and Agrippa returned very soon into Judea, to take possession of his new kingdom; to which was afterward added, A. D. 41, by Claudius, all Judea and the kingdom of Chalcis, which had been possessed by Herod his brother. Thus Agrippa became of a sudden one of the greatest princes of the east, and was possessed of as much, if not more territory, than had been held by Herod the Great, his grandfather. He returned to Judea, and governed it to the great satisfaction of the Jews. But the desire of pleasing them, and a mistaken zeal for their religion, induced him to put to death the Apostle James, and to cast Peter into prison with the same design;

and, but for a miraculous interposition, which, however, produced no effect upon the mind of the tyrant, his hands would have been imbrued in the blood of two apostles, the memory whereof is preserved in Scripture. At Cæs-a-re'a the inhabitants of Tyre and Sidon waited on him to sue for peace. Agrippa, being come early in the morning into the theatre, with a design to give them audience, seated himself on his throne, dressed in a robe of silver tissue, worked in the most admirable manner. The rising sun darted his golden beams thereon, and gave it such a lustre as dazzled the eyes of the spectators; and when the king began his speech to the Tyrians and Sidonians, the parasites around him began to say, it was "the voice of a god and not of a man." Instead of rejecting these impious flatteries, Agrippa received them with an air of complacency; and the angel of the Lord smote him because he did not give God the glory. Being therefore carried home to his palace, he died at the end of five days, racked with tormenting pains in his bowels, and devoured with worms. Such was the death of Herod Agrippa, A. D. 44, after a reign of seven years. He left a son of the same name, and three daughters—Ber-ni'ce, who was married to her uncle Herod, her father's brother.

A-GRIP'PA, son of the

former Agrippa. Claudius gave him the provinces of Gaulonitis, Trach-o-ni'tis, Batanæa, Paneas, and Ab-i-le'ne, which formerly had been in the possession of Lysanias. After the death of Claudius, Nero, who had a great affection for Agrippa, to his other dominions added Julias in Peræ'a, and that part of Galilee to which Tari-chæa and Tiberias belonged. Festus, governor of Judea, coming to his government, A. D. 60, King Agrippa and Berni'ce, his sister, went as far as Cæsarea to salute him; and as they continued there for some time, Festus talked with the king concerning the affair of St. Paul, who had been seized in the temple about two years before, and within a few days previous to his visit had appealed to the emperor. Agrippa wishing to hear Paul, that apostle delivered that noble address in his presence which is recorded, Acts xxvi.

A'GUR. The thirtieth chapter of Proverbs begins with this title: "The words of Agur, the son of Ja'keh;" and the thirty-first, with "the words of King Lemuel;" with respect to which some conjecture that Solomon describes himself under these appellations; but it seems most reasonable to consider them as denoting real persons—some inspired Jewish writers.

A'HAB, the son and successor of Omri. He began his reign over Israel, B. C. 914, and reigned twenty-two years.

2. AHAB and Zedekiah were two false prophets, who, about B. C. 594, seduced the Jewish captives at Babylon with hopes of a speedy deliverance, and stirred them up against Jeremiah, Jer. xxix, 21, 22.

A-HAS-U-E'RUS was the king of Persia. The Ahasuerus of the book of Esther is supposed to be Xerxes of profane history, who succeeded his father Darius about B. C. 485, and was succeeded by his son Artaxerxes Longim'a-nus, about B. C. 464, and is chiefly known in history by the vast preparations which he made for the invasion of Greece. Ahasuerus is also a name given in Scripture, Ezra iv, 6, to Cam-by'-ses, the son of Cyrus; and to As-ty'a-ges, king of the Medes, Dan. ix, 1.

A-HA'VA. The name of a river of Babylonia, or rather of Assyria, Ezra viii, 15.

A'HAZ succeeded his father Jotham, as king of Israel at the age of twenty years, reigned till the year before Christ, 726, and addicted himself to the practice of idolatry.

A-HITH'O-PHEL, a native of Giloh, who, after having been David's counsellor, his most intimate and valued friend, joined in the rebellion of Absalom, and assisted him with his advice, B. C. 1023 2 Sam. xv, xvii.

A-HOL'I-BAH. This and Aholah are two feigned names made use of by Ezekiel, xxiii, 4, to denote the two kingdoms of Judah and Samaria. Aholah and A-hol'i-bah are represented as two sisters, of Egyptian extraction. Aholah stands for Samaria, and Aholibah for Jerusalem.

A'I, a town of Palestine, situate west of Bethel, and at a small distance north-west of Jericho.

AIR, that thin, fluid, elastic, compressible body, called the atmosphere, which surrounds the earth to a considerable height. In Scripture it is sometimes called *heaven*; as, "the birds of heaven." To "beat the air," to "speak in the air," 1 Cor. ix, 26, signify to fatigue ourselves in vain, and to speak to no purpose.

A'JA-LON, (*Ad'ja-lon*,) a city of the Canaanites; the valley adjoining to which is memorable in sacred history from the miracle of Joshua, Josh. x, 12, 13.

AL'A-BAS-TER, the name of a genus of fossils nearly allied to marble. It is a bright, elegant stone, sometimes of a snowy whiteness. It may be cut freely, and is capable of a fine polish; and, being of a soft nature, it is wrought into any form or figure with ease. Vases or cruises were anciently made of it, wherein to preserve odoriferous liquors and ointments.

AL-BETT. An old word, for although, notwithstanding.

AL-EX-AN'DRI-A, a famous city of Egypt, and, during the reign of the Ptolemies, the regal capital of that kingdom. It was founded by Alexander the Great, who drew the plan of the city himself, and peopled it with colonies of Greeks and Jews.

Alexandria owed much of its celebrity as well as its population to the Ptolemies. Ptolemy Soter, one of Alexander's captains, who, after the death of this monarch, was first governor of Egypt, and afterward assumed the title of king, made this city the place of his residence, about B. C. 304. This prince founded an academy, called the Muse'um, in which a society of learned men devoted themselves to philosophical studies, and the improvement of all the other sciences; and he also gave them a library, which was prodigiously increased by his successors. He likewise induced the merchants of Syria and Greece to reside in this city, and to make it a principal mart of their commerce. His son and successor, Ptolemy Philadelphus, pursued the designs of his father.

In the hands of the Romans, the successors of the Macedonians in the government of Egypt, the trade of Alexandria continued to flourish, until luxury and licentiousness paved the way, as in every similar instance, for its overthrow.

Alexandria, together with

the rest of Egypt, passed from the dominion of the Romans to that of the Sar'a-cens. With this event, the sun of Alexandria may be said to have set: the blighting hand of Is'lam-ism was laid on it; and although the genius and the resources of such a city could not be immediately destroyed, it continued to languish until the passage by the Cape of Good Hope, in the fifteenth century, gave a new channel to the trade which for so many centuries had been its support; and at this day, Alexan'dri-a, like most eastern cities, presents a mixed spectacle of ruins and wretchedness,—of fallen greatness and enslaved human beings.

It was in a ship belonging to the port of Alexandria, that St. Paul sailed from My'ra, a city of Lyc'i-a, on his way to Rome, Acts xxvii, 5, 6. Alexandria was also the native place of Apollos.

A'LI-EN. Foreigner, one belonging to another country.

AL'LE-GO-RY, a figure in rhetoric, whereby we make use of terms which, in their proper signification, mean something else than what they are brought to denote; or it is a figure whereby we say one thing, expecting it shall be understood of another, to which it alludes; or which, under the literal sense of the words, conceals a foreign or distant meaning. An allegory is, properly, a continued metaphor, or a series of several metaphors in one or more sentences. Such is that beautiful allegory in Psalm lxxx; in which the people of Israel are represented under the image of a vine, and the figure is supported throughout with great correctness, and beauty. Whereas, if, instead of describing the vine as wasted by the boar from the wood, and devoured by the wild beasts of the field, the psalmist had said, it was afflicted by heathens, or overcome by enemies, which is the real meaning, the figurative and the literal meaning would have been blended, and the allegory ruined.

AL-LE-LU'IA, (*Al-le-lu'-yah*,) *praise the Lord;* or, *praise to the Lord.* This word occurs at the beginning or at the end of many psalms. Alleluia was sung on solemn days of rejoicing. This expression of joy and praise was transferred from the synagogue to the church.

AL-MIGHT'Y, an attribute of the Deity, Gen. xvii, 1. Of the omnipotence of God, we have a most ample revelation in the Scriptures, expressed in the most sublime language. From the annunciation by Moses of a Divine existence who was "in the beginning," before all things, the very first step is to the display of his almighty power in the creation out of nothing, and the immediate arrangement in order and perfection, of the "*heaven and the earth;*"

by which is meant, not this globe only with its atmosphere, or even with its own celestial system, but the universe itself; for " *he made the stars also.*" We are thus at once placed in the presence of an agent of unbounded power; for we must all feel that a being which could create such a world as this, must, beyond all comparison, possess a power greater than any which we experience in ourselves, than any which we observe in other visible agents, and to which we are not authorized by our observation or knowledge to assign any limits of space or duration.

One limitation of the Divine power, it is true, we can conceive, but it detracts nothing from its perfection. Where things in themselves imply a contradiction, they cannot be done by God, because contradictions are impossible in their own nature. In like manner, God cannot do any thing that is repugnant to his other perfections: he cannot lie, nor deceive, nor deny himself; for this would be injurious to his truth. He cannot love sin, nor punish innocence; for this would destroy his holiness and goodness: and therefore to ascribe a power to him that is inconsistent with the rectitude of his nature, is not to magnify but debase him; for all unrighteousness is weakness, a defection from right reason, a deviation from the perfect rule of action, and arises from a want of goodness and power. In a word, since all the attributes of God are essentially the same, a power in him which tends to destroy any other attribute of the Divine nature, must be a power destructive of itself. Well, therefore, may we conclude him absolutely omnipotent, who, by being able to effect all things consistent with his perfections, showeth infinite ability. and, by not being able to do any thing repugnant to the same perfections, demonstrates himself subject to no infirmity.

AL'MOND TREE. A tree resembling the peach tree in its leaves and blossoms, but the fruit is longer and more compressed, the outer green coat is thinner and drier when ripe, and the shell of the stone is not so rugged. This stone, or nut, contains a kernel, which is the only esculent part. The whole arrives at maturity in September, when the outer tough cover splits open and discharges the nut.

The hoary head is beautifully compared by Solomon to the almond tree, covered in the earliest days of spring with its snow-white flowers, before a single leaf has budded: " The almond tree shall flourish, and the grasshopper shall be a burden, and desire shall fail," Eccl. xii, 5. Man has existed in this world but a few days, when old age begins to appear, sheds its snows upon his head, prematurely nips his hopes, darkens his earthly prospects, and hurries him into the grave.

ALMS. Any thing given to relieve the afflicted and destitute.

AL'MUG TREE, a certain kind of wood.

A'LOE, (*Alo*,) commonly called the aloe-wood, an East Indian tree that grows about 8 or 10 feet high. It is highly odoriferous, and, in connection with other aromatics, was used by the ancients to preserve dead bodies from putrefaction.

AL'PHA, the first letter of the Greek alphabet; Omega being the last letter. Hence Alpha and O-me'ga is a title which Christ appropriates to himself, Rev. i, 8; xxi, 6; xxii, 13; as signifying the beginning and the end, the first and the last, and thus properly denoting his perfection and eternity.

AL-PHE'US, father of James the Less, Matt. x, 3; Luke vi, 15. Alpheus was the husband of Mary, believed to have been sister to the mother of Christ; for which reason James is called the Lord's brother; but the term brother is too general in its application to fix their relation, though the fact is probable.

2. ALPHEUS, father of Levi, or Matthew, whom Jesus took to be an apostle and evangelist, Mark ii, 14.

AL'TAR. Sacrifices are nearly as ancient as worship, and altars are of almost equal antiquity. The first altars which God commanded Moses to raise were of earth or rough stones; and it was declared that if iron were used in constructing them, they would become impure, Exod. xx, 24, 25. The altar which Solomon erected in the temple was of brass, but filled, it is believed, with rough stones, 2 Chron. iv, 1–3. It was twenty cubits long, twenty wide, and ten high. That built at Jerusalem, by Zerub'ba-bel, after the return from Babylon, was of rough stones; as was that of Maccabeus. Josephus says that the altar which in his time was in the temple was of rough stones, fifteen cubits high, forty long, and forty wide.

The principal altars among the Jews were those of incense, of burnt offering, and the altar or table for the show bread. The altar of incense was a small table of shittim wood covered with plates of gold. It was a cubit long, a cubit broad, and two cubits high. At the four corners were four horns. The priest, whose turn it was to officiate, burnt incense on this altar, at the time of the morning sacrifice. He did the same also in the evening. At the same time the people prayed in silence, and their prayers were offered up by the priests. The altar of burnt offering was of shittim wood also, and carried upon the shoulders of the priests,

Covel's Dic.   p. 21.

ALTAR OF INCENSE,

by staves of the same wood, overlaid with brass. In Moses' days it was five cubits square, and three high: but it was greatly enlarged in the days of Solomon, being twenty cubits square, and ten in height. It was covered with brass, and had a horn at each corner to which the sacrifice was tied. This altar was placed in the open air, that the smoke might not sully the inside of the tabernacle or temple. On this altar the holy fire was renewed from time to time, and kept constantly burning. Hereon, likewise, the sacrifices of lambs and bullocks were burnt, especially a lamb every morning at the third hour, or nine of the clock, and a lamb every afternoon at three, Exod. xx, 24, 25; xxvii, 1, 2, 4; xxxviii, 1. The altar of burnt offering had the privilege of being a sanctuary or place of refuge.

Sacrifices, according to the laws of Moses, could not be offered except by the priests; and at any other place than on the altar of the tabernacle or the temple. Furthermore, they were not to be offered to idols, nor with any superstitious rites. See Lev. xvii, 1–7; Deut. xii, 15, 16.

AM'A-LEK-ITES, a people whose country adjoined the southern border of the land of Canaan, in the northwestern part of Arabia Petræa.

AM-BAS'SA-DOR, a mes- se- _er_ sent by a sovereign, to

transact affairs of great moment. Ministers of the Gospel are called *ambassadors*, because, in the name of Jesus Christ, the King of kings, they declare his will to men, and propose the terms of their reconciliation to God, 2 Cor. v, 20; Eph. vi, 20.

AM'BER, Ezek. i, 4, 27; viii, 2; a hard, inflammable bitumen, chiefly found in the mines of Prussia. When rubbed it is highly endowed with that remarkable property called *electricity;* a word which the moderns have formed from its Greek name, "*electron.*" But the ancients had also a mixed metal of fine copper and silver, resembling the amber in colour, and called by the same name.

A-MEN', in Hebrew, signifies *true, faithful, certain.* It is also understood as expressing a wish, "Amen! so be it!" or an affirmation, "Amen, yes, I believe it," Num. v, 22. At the conclusion of the public prayers, the people anciently answered with a loud voice, "Amen."

AMEN is a title of our Lord. "The Amen, the true and faithful witness," Rev. i, 14.

AM'E-THYST, (*Am'me-thist.*) A transparent gem of a colour which seems composed of a strong blue and deep red; and, according as either prevails, affords different tinges of purple, sometimes approaching to violet, and sometimes even fading to a rose colour. The oriental is the hardest, scarcest, and most valuable. It was the ninth stone in the pectoral of the high priest, and is mentioned as the twelfth, in the foundations of the New Jerusalem.

A-MIN'A-DAB, a Levite, with whom the ark was deposited after it was brought back from the land of the Philistines. Also, some skilful charioteer who was celebrated for his swift driving, Cant. vi, 12.

AM'MON, or BEN-AM'-MI, the son of Lot, by his youngest daughter, Gen. xix, 38. He was the father of the Ammonites, and dwelt on the east side of the Dead Sea, in the mountains of Gilead.

AM'MON-ITES, the descendants of Ammon, the son of Lot. They took possession of the country called by their name, after having driven out the Zamzummins, who were its ancient inhabitants. The precise period at which this expulsion took place is not ascertained. The Ammonites had kings, and were uncircumcised, Jer. ix, 25, 26, and seem to have been principally devoted to husbandry. They, as well as the Moabites, were among the nations whose peace or prosperity the Israelites were forbidden to disturb, Deut. ii, 19, &c. However, neither the one nor the other were to be admitted into the congregation to the tenth generation, because they did not come out to relieve them in the wilderness, and were implicated in hiring Ba'laam to curse them. Their chief and peculiar deity is, in Scripture, called Moloch.

AM'O-RITES, the descendants of the fourth son of Canaan, (Gen. x, 16,) whose first possessions were in the mountains of Judea, among the other families of Canaan: but afterward they passed the Jordan, and extended their conquests over the finest provinces of Moab and Ammon; seizing and maintaining possession of that extensive and almost insulated portion of country included between the rivers Jordan, Jabbok, and Arnon.

A'MOS, the fourth of the minor prophets, who in his youth had been a herdsman in Tekoa, a small town about twelve miles south-east of Jerusalem. He was sent to the people of Samaria, to bring them back to God by repentance, and reformation of manners. Amos was called to the prophetic office in the time of Uzziah, king of Judah, and Jeroboam, the son of Joash, king of Israel, B. C. 785. The whole book of Amos is animated with a fine and masculine eloquence.

A'NAK, AN'A-KIM, famous giants in Palestine, whose descendants were terrible for their fierceness and stature.

A-NATH'E-MA, signifies something set apart, separated, or devoted, or the formula by which this is effected. To anathematize is generally understood to denote the cutting off or separating any one from the communion of the faithful, the number of the living, or the privileges of society; or the devoting of an animal, city, or other thing to destruction. See ACCURSED.

A-NATH'E-MA MAR-A-NA-THA. "If any man love not the Lord Jesus Christ, let him be Anathema, Maranatha," 1 Cor. xvi. 22. Why these two words, one Greek and the other Syriac, were not translated, is not obvious. They are the words with which the Jews began their greater excommunication, whereby they not only excluded sinners from their society, but delivered them up to the Divine anathema, that is, to misery in this life, and perdition in the life to come. "Let him be Anathema," is "Let him be accursed." Maranatha signifies, "The Lord cometh," or "will come;" that is, to take vengeance. See ACCURSED.

AN'DREW, an apostle of Jesus Christ, a native of Beth-sai'da, and the brother of Peter. He was at first a disciple of John the Baptist, whom he left to follow our Saviour, after the testimony of John, John i. 29, and was the first disciple received by our Saviour. Andrew then introduced his brother Simon, and they went with him to the marriage in Cana, but afterward returned to their ordinary occupation, not expecting, perhaps, to be farther employed in his service. However, some months after, Jesus meeting them, while fishing together, called them to a regular attendance upon him, and promised to make them fishers of men, Matt. iv. 19.

AN'GEL, an intelligent spirit, the first in rank and dignity among created beings. The word *angel* is not properly a denomination of nature, but of *office*; signifying a *messenger*, a person employed to carry one's orders, or declare his will. Thus it is St. Paul represents angels, Heb. i, 14, where he calls them "ministering spirits." Some of these are spoken of in Scripture in such a manner as plainly to signify that they are real beings, of a spiritual nature, of high power, perfection, dignity, and happiness. Others of them are distinguished as not having kept their first station, Jude 6. These are represented as evil spirits, enemies of God, and intent on mischief. The devil, as the head of them, and they as his angels, are represented as the rulers of the darkness of this world.

Following the Scripture account, we shall find mention made of different orders of these superior beings; for such a distinction of orders seems intimated in the names given to different classes. Thus we have *thrones, dominions, principalities,* or prince doms, *powers, authorities, living ones, cherubim and seraphim.* We learn also from Scripture, that they dwell in the immediate presence of God; that they "excel in strength;" that they are immortal; and that they are the agents through which God very often accomplishes his special purposes of judgment and mercy. Nothing is more frequent in Scripture than the missions and appearances of good and bad angels, whom God employed to declare his will; to correct, teach, reprove and comfort. God gave the law to Moses, and appeared to the old patriarchs, by the mediation of angels, who represented him, and spoke in his name, Acts vii, 30, 35; Gal. iii, 19; Heb. xiii, 2.

Some think that angels existed long before the formation of our solar system; and Scripture seems to favour this opinion, Job xxxviii, 4, 7, where God says, "Where wast thou when I laid the foundations of the earth?— and all the sons of God shouted for joy."

As to the doctrine of guarding angels presiding over the affairs of empires, nations, provinces, and particular persons, though received by the later Jews, it appears to be wholly pagan in its origin, and to have no countenance in the Scriptures. The passages in Daniel brought to favour this notion are. capable of a much better explana-

tion; and when our Lord declares that the "*angels*" of little children "do always behold the face of God," he either speaks of children as being the objects of the general ministry of angels, or, still more probably, by *angels* he there means the disembodied spirits of children; for that the Jews called disembodied spirits by the name of angels, appears from Acts xii, 15.

The exact number of angels is nowhere mentioned in Scriptuie; but it is always represented as very great, Daniel vii, 10; Matt. xxvi, 53; Psa. lxviii, 17. These are all intended not to express any exact number, but indefinitely a very large one.

Dr. Prideaux observes, that the minister of the synagogue, who officiated in offering the public prayers, being the mouth of the congregation, delegated by them as their representative, messenger, or angel, to address God · in prayer for them, was called the *angel of the Church*; and that from hence the chief ministers of the seven Churches of Asia are in the Revelation, by a name borrowed from the synagogue, called angels of those Churches.

THE ANGEL OF THE LORD, or, *the Angel Jehovah*, a title given to Christ. in his different appearances to the patriarchs and others in the Old Testament.

The collation of a few passages, or of the different parts

of the same passages of Scripture, will show that Jehovah, and "the Angel of the Lord," when used in this eminent sense, are the same person. Jacob says of Bethel, where he had exclaimed, "Surely *Jehovah* is in this place;" "The *Angel* of God appeared to me in a dream, saying, I am the God of Bethel." Upon his deathbed he gives the names of *God* and *Angel* to this same person: "The *God* which fed me all my life long unto this day, the *Angel* which redeemed me from all evil, bless the lads." So in Hosea xii, 4, 5, it is said, "By his strength he had power with *God;* yea, he had power over the *Angel*, and prevailed." "We found him in Bethel, and there he spake with us, even the *Lord God of hosts;* the Lord is his memorial." Here the same person has the names, *God, Angel,* and *Lord God of hosts.* "The *Angel of the Lord* called to Abraham a second time from heaven, and said, By *myself* have I sworn, saith the Lord, (JEHOVAH,) that, since thou hast done this thing, in blessing will I bless thee." The *Angel of the Lord* appeared to Moses in a flame of fire; but this same Angel "called to him out of the bush, and said, I am the God of thy fathers, the God of Abraham, the God of Isaac, and the God of Jacob; and Moses hid his face, for he was afraid to look upon God."

The Jews held this Word, or Angel of the Lord, to be the future Messiah, as appears from the writings of their older rabbins.

ANG'ER, a resentful emotion of the mind, arising upon the receipt, or supposed receipt, of an affront or injury; and also simple feeling of strong displacency at that which is in itself evil, or base, or injurious to others. In the latter sense it is not only innocent but commendable. Strong displeasure against evil doers, provided it be free from hatred and malice, and interferes not with a just placableness, is also blameless, Eph. iv, 26. When it is vindictive against the person of our neighbour, or against the innocent creatures of God, it is wicked, Matt. v, 22. When anger, hatred, wrath, and fury, are ascribed to God, they denote no tumultuous passion, but merely his holy and just displeasure with sin and sinners, and the evidence of it in his terrible threatenings, or righteous judgments, Psa. vi, 1, and vii, 11.

ANI-MAL, is an organized and living body, endowed with sensation. The Hebrews distinguished animals into pure and impure, clean and unclean; or those which might be eaten and offered, and those whose use was prohibited. The sacrifices which they offered were of the beeve and of the sheep kind.

Beside these, many others might be eaten, wild or tame;

as the stag, the roebuck, and in general all that have cloven feet, and that chew the cud, Lev. xi, 2, 3, &c. All that have not cloven hoofs, and do not chew the cud, were esteemed impure, and could neither be offered nor eaten. The fat of all sorts of animals sacrificed was forbidden to be eaten. The blood of all kinds of animals, and in all cases, was prohibited on pain of death, Lev. iii, 17; vii, 23–27. Neither did the Israelites eat animals which had been taken and touched by a devouring or impure beast, as a dog, a wolf, a boar, &c., Exod. xxii, 3; nor of any animal that died of itself. Whoever touched its carcass was impure until the evening; and till that time, and before he had washed his clothes, he did not return to the company of other Jews, Lev. xi, 39, 40; xvii, 15; xxii, 8. Fish that had neither fins nor scales were unclean, Lev. xi, 20. Birds which walk on the ground with four feet, as bats, and flies that have many feet, were impure. The law, however, excepts locusts, which have their hind feet higher than those before, and rather leap than walk. These were clean, and might be eaten, Lev. xi, 21, 22, as they still are in Palestine.

AN'ISE, an annual plant, well known, the seeds of which have an aromatic smell, a pleasant warm taste, and a carminative quality.

AN'NA, the daughter of Pha-nu'el, a prophetess and widow, of the tribe of Asher, Luke ii, 36, 37. She was married early, and had lived only seven years with her husband. Being then disengaged from the ties of marriage, she thought only of pleasing the Lord; and continued without ceasing in the temple, serving God night and day, with fasting and prayer, as the evangelist expresses it; which "is to be understood no otherwise than that she constantly attended the morning and evening sacrifice at the temple; and then with great devotion offered up her prayers to God; the time of morning and evening sacrifice being the most solemn time of prayer among the Jews, and the temple the most solemn place for this devotion."

AN'NAS was the son of Seth, and high priest of the Jews. He succeeded Jo-a'-zar, the son of Simon, enjoyed the high priesthood eleven years, and was succeeded by Ishmael, the son of Pha'bi. After he was deposed, he still preserved the title of high priest, and had a great share in the management of public affairs. He is called high priest in conjunction with Cai'a-phas, when John the Baptist entered upon the exercise of his mission.

A-NOINT', to pour oil upon, Gen. xxviii, 18; xxxi, 13. Under the law persons and things set apart for sacred purposes were anointed with the holy oil; which appears to have been a typical representation of the communication of the Holy Ghost to Christ and to his Church. See Exod. xxviii, xxix. Hence the Holy Spirit is called an *unction* or *anointing*, 1 John ii, 20, 27; and our Lord is called the "Mes-si'-ah," or "Anointed One," to denote his being called to the offices of mediator, prophet, priest, and king, to all of which he was consecrated by the anointing of the Holy Ghost, Matt. iii, 16, 17.

ANON, a word in use when our translation of the Bible was made, and signifies *quickly, immediately.*

ANSWER, (*an'ser.*) Beside the common usage of this word in the sense of a reply, it has other significations. Moses, having composed a thanksgiving, after the passage of the Red Sea, Mir'i-am, it is said, *answered,* "Sing ye to the Lord," &c.,—meaning that Moses, with the men on one side, and Mir'i-am, with the women, on the other side, sung the same song, as it were, in two chorusses, or divisions; of which one *answered* the other, Num. xxi, 17, "Then Israel sung this song, Spring up, O well, *answer* unto it;" that is, sing responsively, one side (or choir) singing first, and then the other. Exod. 15, 21.

To answer is also used in Scripture for the commencement of a discourse, when no reply to any question or objection is intended. This mode of speaking is often used by the evangelists, "And Jesus *answered* and said." It is a Hebrew idiom.

ANT, a little insect, famous from all antiquity for its social habits, its economy, unwearied industry, and prudent foresight. It has afforded a pattern of commendable frugality to the profuse, and of unceasing diligence to the slothful. Solomon calls the ants "exceeding wise; for though a race not strong, yet they prepare their meat in the summer." He therefore sends the sluggard to these little creatures to learn wisdom, foresight, care, and diligence.

AN'TI-CHRIST, compounded of *Anti*, against, and *Christ*, may either signify one who assumes the place and office of Christ, or one who maintains a direct enmity and opposition to him. The anti-christ mentioned by the Apostle John, 1st epistle ii, 18, and more particularly described in the book of Revelation, seems evidently to be the same with the *man of sin*, &c., characterized by St. Paul, Thess. ii; and the whole description literally applies to the papal power.

AN'TI-OCH, 1, a city of Upper Syria, on the river Orontes, about twenty miles from the place where it discharges itself into the Mediterranean. It was built by Se-leu'cus Ni-ca'nor, about three hundred years before

Christ; and became the seat of empire of the Syrian kings of the Mac-e-do'ni-an race and afterward of the Roman governors of the eastern provinces; being very centrally and commodiously situated midway between Constantino'ple and Al-ex-an'dri-a, about seven hundred miles from each, in 37° 17′ north latitude, and 36° 45′ east longitude. No city, perhaps, Jerusalem excepted, has experienced more frequent revolutions, or suffered more numerous and dire calamities, than An'ti-och; as, beside the common plagues of eastern cities, pestilence, famine, fire, and sword, it has several times been entirely overthrown by earthquakes.

Antioch was the birthplace of St. Luke and The-oph'i-lus, and the see of the martyr Ig-na'ti-us. In this city the followers of Christ had first the name of Christians given them.

2. Beside the Syr'ian capital, there was another Antioch, visited by St. Paul when in Asia, and called, for the sake of distinction, *Antioch of Pi-si'di-a*, as belonging to that province, of which it was the capital. Here Paul and Barnabas preached; but the Jews, jealous, as usual, of the reception of the Gospel by the Gentiles, raised a sedition against them, and obliged them to leave the city, Acts xiii, 14, to the end.

AN'TI-PAS, the faithful martyr or witness mentioned in the book of Revelation, ii, 13.

AN-TIP'A-TRIS, a town in Palestine, situated in a pleasant valley, near the mountains, in the way from Jerusalem to Cæs-a-re'a. Jose'phus places it at about the distance of seventeen miles from Jop'pa. To this place St. Paul was brought in his way to the governor of Judea at Cæs-a-re'a, Acts xxiii, 31.

APE. We now distinguish this tribe of creatures into, 1. *Monkeys*, those with long tails; 2. *Apes*, those with short tails. 3. *Baboons* those without tails. The ancient Egyptians are said to have worshipped apes; it is certain that they are still adored in many places in India.

A-PHAR'SA-CHITES, a people sent by the kings of As-syr'i-a to inhabit the country of Sa-mar'i-a, in the room of those Israelites who had been removed beyond the Eu-phra'tes, Ezra v, 6. They, with the other Sa-mar'i-tans, opposed the rebuilding of the walls of Jerusalem, Ezra iv, 9.

A-POC'RY-PHA, books *not* admitted into the sacred canon, being either spurious, or at least not acknowledged to be Divine.

They possess no authority whatever, either external or internal, to procure their admission into the sacred canon. None of them are extant in Hebrew; all of them are in the Greek language, except the fourth book of Es'dras, which is only extant in Latin. They were written for the most part by Al-ex-an'dri-an Jews, subsequently to the cessation of the prophetic spirit, though before the promulgation of the Gospel. Not one of the writers in direct terms advances a claim to inspiration; nor were they ever received into the sacred canon by the Jewish Church, and therefore they were not sanctioned by our Saviour. No part of the apocrypha is quoted or even alluded to by him, or by any of his apostles; and both Phi'lo and Jose'phus, who flourished in the first century of the Christian era, are totally silent concerning them.

A-POL'LOS was a Jew of Al-ex-an'dri-a, who came to Ephesus in the year of our Lord 54, during the absence of St. Paul, who had gone to Jerusalem, Acts xviii, 24. He was an eloquent man, and mighty in the Scriptures; but he knew only the baptism of John, and was not fully informed of the higher branches of Gospel doctrine. However, he acknowledged that Jesus Christ was the Messiah, and declared himself openly as his disciple. At Ephesus, therefore, he began to speak boldly in the synagogue, and demonstrated by the Scriptures that Jesus was the Christ. Aq'ui-la and Priscilla, having heard him there, took him with them, and instructed him more fully in the ways of God. Some time after, he

was inclined to go into A-cha'i-a, and the brethren wrote to the disciples there, desiring them to receive him. He was very useful at Corinth, where he watered what St. Paul had planted, 1 Cor. iii, 6.

A-POL'LYON, (A-pol'-yon.) See ABAD'DON.

A-POS'TLE, (a-pos'-el,) a messenger of Christ, one of the twelve disciples commissioned by him to preach his Gospel, and propagate it to all parts of the earth. They were limited to the number twelve, in allusion to the twelve tribes of Israel. See Matt. xix, 28; Luke xxii, 30; Rev. xxi, 12-14; and compare Exod. xxiv, 4; Deut. i, 23; and Josh. iv, 2, 3. Accordingly care was taken, on the death of Judas, to choose another, to make up the number, Acts i, 21, 22, 26. Of the first selection and commission of the twelve apostles, we have an account, Luke vi, 13, &c.; Matt. x, 1, &c. Of these, Simon, Andrew, James the Greater, and John, were fishermen; Matthew, and James the son of Alphe'us, were publicans; and the other six were probably fishermen, though their occupation is not distinctly specified. The place of Judas the traitor was supplied by Matthias; and about the year 37, Saul, a furious opposer of Christianity, was converted, and numbered among the apostles.

St. Paul is frequently called the apostle, by way of eminence; and the *apostle of the Gentiles*, because his ministry was chiefly employed for the conversion of the Gentiles, as that of St. Peter was for the Jews, who is therefore styled the *apostle of the circumcision.*

The apostles having continued at Jerusalem twelve years after the ascension of Christ, as tradition reports, according to his command, determined to disperse themselves in different parts of the world.

It appears that all of the apostles did not die by martyrdom. Heraclion, cited by Cle'mens Alexandri'nus, reckons among the apostles who did not suffer martyrdom, Matthew, Thomas, Philip, and Levi, probably meaning Leb-be'us.

To the apostles belonged the peculiar and exclusive prerogative of writing doctrinal and preceptive books of authority in the Christian Church; and it sufficiently appears that no epistles or other doctrinal writings of any person who was of a rank below that of an apostle, were received by Christians as a part of their rule of faith. With respect to the writings of Mark and Luke, they are reckoned historical, not doctrinal or dogmatical; and Augustine says that Mark and Luke wrote at a time when their writings might be approved, not only by the Church, but by apostles still living.

AP'PI-I FO'RUM, a place about fifty miles from Rome, near the modern town of Piperno, on the road to Naples. It probably had its name from the statue of Ap'pi-us Claudius, a Roman consul, who paved the famous way from Rome to Cap'u-a, and whose statue was set up here. To this place some Christians from Rome came to meet St. Paul, Acts xxviii, 15.

APPLE-TREE. Although apple trees are not very common in Palestine, and their comparative rarity would naturally give them some value; Mr. Parkhurst says it most probably means the citron tree, a species of lemon, known to the Jews several generations before our Saviour.

AQ'UI-LA. This person was a native of Pontus in Asia Minor, and was converted by St. Paul, together with his wife Priscilla, to the Christian religion. As Aquila was by trade a tentmaker, Acts xviii, 2, 3, as St. Paul was, the apostle lodged and wrought with him at Corinth.

AR, the capital city of the Moabites, situated in the hills on the south of the river Arnon.

AR-A'BI-A, a vast country of Asia, extending 1500 miles from north to south, and 1200 from east to west; containing a surface equal to four times that of France. This is one of the most interesting countries on the face of the earth. It has, in agreement with prophecy, never been subdued; and its inhabitants, at once pastoral, commercial, and warlike, are the same wild, wandering people as the immediate descendants of their great ancestor Ishmael are represented to have been.

Arabia, it is well known, is divided by geographers into three separate regions, called Arabia Pe-træ'a, Arabia Deserta, and Arabia Felix.

The first, or Arabia Petræa, is the north western division, and is bounded on the north by Palestine and the Dead Sea, on the east by Arabia Deserta, on the south by Arabia Felix, and on the west by the western branch of the Red Sea and the Isthmus of Suez. The greater part of this division was more exclusively the possession of the Midianites, or land of Midian.

The second region, or Arabia Deserta, is bounded on the north and north-east by the Euphrates, on the east by a ridge of mountains which separates it from Chaldea, on the south by Arabia Felix, and on the west by Syria, Judea, and Arabia Petræa. This was more particularly the country, first of the Cushites, and afterward of the Ishmaelites; as it is still of their descendants, the modern Bedouins, who maintain the same predatory and wandering habits. It consists almost entirely of one vast and lonesome wilderness, a boundless level of sand, whose dry and burning surface denies existence to all but the Arab and his camel.

The third region, or Arabia Felix, so denominated from the happier condition of its soil and climate, occupies the southern part of the Arabian peninsula. It is bounded on the north by the two other divisions of the country; on the south and south-east by the Indian Ocean; on the east by part of the same ocean and the Persian Gulf; and on the west by the Red Sea.

St. Paul first preached the Gospel in Arabia, Gal. i, 17; the northern part of Arabia Deserta, no doubt, which lay near Damascus. Christian Churches were subsequently founded, and many of their tribes embraced Christianity prior to the fifth century; most of which appear to have been tinctured with the Nestorian heresy.

A'RAM, the fifth son of Shem, Gen. x, 22. He was the father of the Syrians, who from him were called Aramæ'ans, or Aramites.

AR'A-RAT. This name occurs but twice in the Bible, Gen. viii, 4; Jer. li, 27, and in both places signifies a region of country which is situated nearly in the centre of Armenia. The tradition that the ark of Noah, after the deluge, lodged on a mountain in this region, which is still called "*Mount Ararat*," is confirmed by the most weighty testimony of antiquity, and is one of the oldest that has come down to our time. This mountain, consisting of two peaks, rises in the midst of a vast plain not far from Erivan, the capital of Armenia, and elevates its highest, covered with perpetual snow and ice, 16,000 feet above the level of the sea.

This place had never been trodden by the foot of man, since the day of Noah, till the 27th of September, 1829, Professor Parrot, by dint of the most determined perseverance reached the spot.

ARCH-AN'GEL, (*ark-a'ngel*,) according' to some, means an angel occupying the highest rank in the celestial order or hierarchy; but others reckon it a title only applicable to our Saviour; Jude 9; Dan. xii, 1; 1 Thess. iv, 16.

AR-CHE-LA'US, son of Herod the Great, and Maltace, his fifth wife. Herod having put to death his sons Alexander, Ar-is-to-bu'lus, and An-tip'a-ter, and expunged out of his will Herod Antipas, whom he had declared king, he substituted Archelaus, and gave Antipas the title of tetrarch only. After the death of Herod, Archelaus ordered that king's will to be read, wherein he, Archelaus, was declared king, on condition that Augustus consented. Hereupon the assembly cried "Long live King Archelaus!" He then gave a splendid entertainment to the people, went to the temple, harangued the multitude, promised them

good treatment, and declared he would not assume the title of king till the emperor had confirmed it, A. M. 4001; B. C. 3. After this he embarked at Cæsarea for Rome, to procure from Augustus the confirmation of Herod's will. Antipas, his brother, went to Rome likewise, to dispute his title, pretending that Herod's first will should be preferred to his last, which he alleged to have been made by him when his understanding was not sound.

The two brothers, Archelaus and Antipas, procured able orators to display their pretensions before the emporor; and when they had done speaking, Archelaus threw himself at Augustus's feet. Augustus gently raised him, said he would do nothing contrary to Herod's intention or his interest, but he refused to decide the affair at that time. Sometime afterward, he sent for Archela'us, gave him the title not of king, but of ethnarch, promising him the crown likewise, if his good conduct deserved it; but he governed Judea with so much violence, that, after seven years, the chiefs of the Samaritans and Jews accused him before Augustus, who ordered Archelaus to Rome, to give an account of his conduct. On his arrival at Rome, the emperor called for his accusers, and permitted him to defend himself; which he did so insufficiently, that Augustus banished him to Vienne, in Gaul, where he continued in exile to the end of his life.

ARC-TU'RUS, supposed to be the constellation called *the great bear*, which is near the north pole. The "*sons of Arcturus*" may mean the neighbouring stars. Job xxxviii, 32.

A-RE-OP'A-GUS, the high court at Athens, famed for the justice of its decisions; and so called, because it sat on a hill of the same name, or in the suburbs of the city, dedicated to Mars, the god of war, as the city was to Minerva, his sister. St. Paul, Acts xvii, 19, &c., having preached at Athens, was carried before the A-re-op'a-gites, as "a setter-forth of strange gods." On this occasion he delivered that fine sermon which is in substance recorded in Acts xvii. Di-o-nys'i-us, one of the judges, was converted; and the apostle was dismissed without any farther trouble.

A-RE'TAS the proper name of several kings of Arabia Pe-træ'a. In A. D. 39, one of these kings seems to have got possession of Damascus, and, at the instigation of the Jews, attempted to put Paul in prison. 2 Cor. xi. 32, 33.

AR'GOB, a canton lying beyond Jordan, in the half tribe of Manasseh, and in the country of Bashan, one of the most fruitful on the other side of Jordan, Deut. iii, 4-14; 1 Kings iv, 13. But Argob was more peculiarly the name of the capital city of the region of Argob, which Eu-se'bi-us says was fifteen miles west of Gerara.

A-RI'EL. This word signifies *a lion of God*, that is, a strong lion, a hero. It is applied to Jerusalem as a heroic or invincible city.

AR-I-MA-THE'A, or RA'-MAH, a pleasant town, beautifully situated on the borders of a fertile and extensive plain, abounding in gardens, vineyards, olive and date trees. It stands about thirty miles north-west of Jerusalem, on the high road to Jaffa. At 'this Ramah, which was likewise called Ra-math-a'im Zophim, as lying in the district of Zuph, or Zoph, Samuel was born, 1 Sam. i. This was likewise the native place of Joseph, called Joseph of Arimathea, who begged and obtained the body of Jesus from Pilate, Matt. xxvi, 57. There was another Ramah, about six miles north of Jerusalem. This is the Ramah, supposed to be alluded to in the lamentation of Rachel for her children.

AR-IS-TAR'CHUS, a Macedonian, and a native of Thessalonica.

ARK, denotes a kind of floating vessel built by Noah. for the preservation of himself and family, with several species of animals, during the deluge. Although the ark answered, in some respects, the purpose of a ship, it is not so certain that it was of the same form and shape. It appears to have had neither helm, nor mast, nor oars; but was merely a bulky capacious vessel, light enough to be raised aloft with all its contents by the gradual rise of the deluge. Its shape, therefore, was of little importance; more especially as it seems to have been the purpose of Providence, in this whole transaction, to signify to those who were saved, as well as to their latest posterity, that their preservation was not in any degree effected by human contrivance. The ark in which Moses was exposed bears the same name; and some have thought that both were of the same materials.

Dr. Hales proves the ark to have been of the (burden of forty-two thousand four hundred and thirteen tons; and asks, " Can we doubt of its being sufficient to contain eight persons, and about two hundred or two hundred and fifty pair of four-footed animals, (a number to which, according to M. Buffon, all the various distinct species may be reduced,) together with all the subsistence necessary for a twelvemonth, with the fowls of the air, and such reptiles and insects as cannot live under water?" All these various animals were controlled by the power of God, whose special agency is supposed in the whole transaction, and "the lion was made to lie down with the kid."

ARK OF THE COVE-NANT, a small chest or coffer, three feet nine inches in length, two feet three inches in breadth, and two feet three inches in height; in which were contained the golden pot that had manna, Aaron's rod, and the tables of the covenant, Num. xvii, 10; Heb. ix, 4. This coffer was made of shittim wood, and was covered with a lid, called the *mercy seat*, Exod. xxv, 17–22, &c., which was of solid gold, at the two ends whereof were two figures called *cherubim*, looking toward each other, with expanded wings, which, embracing the whole circumference of the mercy seat, met in the middle. Over this it was that the Shechi'nah, or visible display of the Divine presence in a luminous cloud rested, both in the tabernacle and in the temple, Lev. xvi, 2; and from hence the Divine oracles were given forth by an audible voice, as often as God was consulted in behalf of his people. On the two sides of the ark there were four rings of gold, two on each side, through which staves, overlaid with gold, were put, by means whereof they carried it as they marched through the wilderness, &c., on the shoulders of the Levites, Exod. xxv, 13, 14; xxvii, 5. After the passage of the Jordan, the ark continued for some time at Gilgal, from whence it was removed to Shiloh. From this place the Israelites carried it to their camp, where, in an engagement with the Philistines, it fell into their hands. The Philistines carried it in triumph to one of their principal cities, named Ashdod, and placed it in the temple of Dagon, whose image fell to the ground and was broken. They afterward returned the ark with various presents; and it was lodged at Kirjath-Jearim, and afterward at Nob. David conveyed ● to the house of Obededom, and from thence to his palace at Zion; and lastly, Solomon brought it into the temple which he had built at Jerusalem. It remained in the temple till the times of the last kings of Judah, who gave themselves up to idolatry. The priests, being unable to bear this profanation, took the ark and carried it from place to place, to preserve it from the hands of those impious princes. Josiah commanded them to bring it back to the sanctuary, and it was accordingly replaced, 2 Chron. xxxv, 3. What became of the ark at the destruction of the temple by Nebuchadnezzar, is a dispute among the rabbins: it is probable that it was destroyed with the temple.

The ark was called the *ark of the covenant*, because it was a symbol of the covenant between God and his people. It was also named the *ark of the testimony*, because the two tables which were deposited in it were witnesses against every transgression.

ARM. As it is by this member of the body that we chiefly exert our strength, it is therefore used in Scripture for an emblem of power, Deut. v, 15; 1 Sam. ii, 31.

AR-MA-GED'DON, a place spoken of, Revelation xvi, 16, which literally signifies "the mountain of Mageddon," or "Megiddo," a city situated in the great plain at the foot of Mount Carmel, Rev. xvi, 13, 14; where the word Armageddon, according to Mr. Pool, does not signify any particular place, but is used in allusion to Megiddo, mentioned Judges v, 19, where Barak overcame Sisera with his great army, and where Josiah was slain, 2 Kings xxiii, 30. If so, the term must have been a proverbial one for a place of destruction and mourning.

AR-ME'NIA, a considerable province of Asia, north of Mesopotamia. Care must be taken to distinguish it from Aramæa, which is Syria.

ARMOUR. The Hebrews do not appear to have any peculiar military habit. They used the same arms as the neighbouring nations, and these were made either of iron or of copper, principally of the latter metal. Of the defensive arms of the Hebrews, the following were the most remarkable; namely,

1. The helmet, for covering and defending the head.

2. The breastplate was another piece of defensive armour. Goliath, and the soldiers of Antiochus, 1 Sam. xvii, 5; 1 Mac. vi, 35, were

accoutred with this defence; which in our authorized translation, is variously rendered *habergeon, coat of mail,* and *brigandine,* 1 Sam. xvii, 38; 2 Chron. xxvi, 14; Isa. lix, 17; Jer. xlvi, 4. Between the joints of this *harness,* as it is termed in' 1 Kings xxii, 4, the profligate Ahab was mortally wounded by an arrow, shot at a venture.

3. The shield defended the whole body during the battle. It was of various forms, and made of wood covered with tough hides, or of brass, and sometimes was overlaid with gold, 1 Kings x. 16, 17; xiv, 26, 27.

The loss of the shield in fight was excessively resented by the Jewish warriors, as well as lamented by them; for it was a signal aggravation of the public mourning that "the shield of the mighty was vilely cast away," 2 Sam. i, 21.

4. Another defensive provision in war was the military girdle, which was for a double purpose: first, in order to hold the sword, which hung, as it does this day, at the soldier's girdle or belt, 1 Sam. xvii, 39; secondly, it was necessary to gird the clothes and the armour together. *To gird* and *to arm* are synonymous words in Scripture; and hence comes the expression of "girding to the battle," 1 Kings xx, 11; 2 Samuel xxii, 40; 1 Samuel xviii, 4.

5. Boots or greaves were part of the ancient defensive harness.

The offensive weapons were of two sorts; namely, such as were employed when they came to a close engagement, and those with which they annoyed the enemy at a distance. Of the former description were the sword and the battle axe.

1. The sword is the most ancient weapon of offence mentioned in the Bible. It was worn on the thigh, Psalm xlv, 4; Exod. xxxii, 27.

2. Of the battle axe we have no description in the sacred volume.

3. The spear and javelin were of different kinds, according to their length or make. Some of them might be thrown or darted, 1 Sam. xviii, 11; others were a kind of long swords, Num. xxv, 8; and it appears from 2 Sam. ii, 23, that some of them were pointed at both ends. When armies were encamped, the spear of the general or commander-in-chief was stuck into the ground at his head.

4. Slings are enumerated among the military stores collected by Uzziah, 2 Chron. xxvi, 14. In the use of the sling David eminently excelled, and he slew Goliath with a stone from one. The Benjamites were celebrated in battle because they had attained to great skill and accuracy in handling this weapon; "they could sling stones to a hair's breadth, and not miss," Judges xx, 16.

5. Bows and arrows are of great antiquity, Gen. xxi, 22.

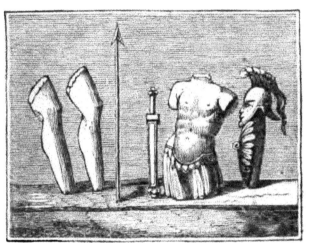

Corel's Dic.

ANCIENT ARMOUR.

p. 30

This weapon was thought so necessary in war, that it is there called, "the bow of war," or the "battle bow," Zech. ix, 10; x, 4.

Before battle the various kinds of arms were put into the best order; the shields were anointed, and the soldiers refreshed themselves by taking food, lest they should become weary and faint under the pressure of their labours, Jer. xlvi, 3, 4; Isa. xxi, 5.

AR'NON, a river or brook. Its spring head is in the mountains of Gilead, or of the Moabites, and it discharges itself into the Dead Sea.

AR'ROW, a sharp, slender, barbed weapon, shot from a bow, 1 Sam. xx, 36. The word is often taken figuratively for lightning and other meteors. In Psalm xci, 5, it is used, no doubt, for *danger* in general; *terror* by night and *arrows* by day include all species of calamity—the *arrows* of God's judgments.

AR-TA-XERX'ES, a name or title, common to several kings of Persia, Ezra iv, 7.

AR-TA-XERX'ES LON-GIM'-A-NUS was the son of Xerx'-es, and grandson of Darius Hystas'pes, and reigned in Persia from the year 469 to 421 B. C. He permitted Ezra, with all those inclined to follow him, to return into Judea, in the year B. C. 463, Ezra vii, viii. Afterward Nehemiah also obtained leave to return, and to build the walls and gates of Jerusalem, in the year B. C. 450,

From this year chronologers reckon the beginning of Daniel's seventy weeks, Daniel xi, 29. These are weeks of years, and make four hundred and ninety years. Dr. Prideaux, who discourses with great learning on this prophecy, maintains that the decree mentioned in it for the rebuilding of Jerusalem cannot be understood of that granted to Nehemiah, but of that granted to Ezra. From that time to the death of Christ are exactly four hundred and ninety years, to a month: for in the month of Nisan the decree was granted to Ezra; and in the middle of the same month Nisan, Christ suffered, just four hundred and ninety years afterward.

AR'TE-MAS, St. Paul's disciple, who was sent by that apostle into Crete, in the room of Titus, chap. iii, 12, while he continued with St. Paul at Ni-cop'o-lis, where he passed the winter.

ARTS. "Curious arts" are magical arts, which were so famous in Ephesus that their books bore a great price.

A'SA, the son and successor of Abijam, king of Judah, began to reign in the year before Christ 955.

The Scripture reproaches Asa with not destroying the high places, which, perhaps, he thought it politic to tolerate, to avoid the greater evil of idolatry.

AS'A-HEL, the son of Zeruiah, and brother of Joab.

A'SAPH, a celebrated musician in the time of David, was the son of Bar-a-chi'as, of the tribe of Levi. Asaph, and also his descendants, presided over the musical band in the service of the temple. Several of the psalms have the name of Asaph prefixed; but it is not certain whether the words or the music were composed by him. With regard to some of them, which were written during the Babylonish captivity, they cannot in any respect be ascribed to him. Perhaps they were written or set to music by his descendants, who bore his name, or by some of that class of musicians of which the family of Asaph was the head, 1 Chron. vi, 39; 2 Chron. xxix, 30; xxxv, 15; Neh. xii, 46.

ASCENSION OF CHRIST, his visible elevation to heaven. The evidences of this fact were numerous. The disciples saw him ascend, Acts i, 9, 10. Two angels testified that he did ascend, Acts i, 11 Stephen, Paul, and John saw him in his ascended state, Acts vii, 55, 56; ix; Rev. i. The ascension was demonstrated by the descent of the Holy Ghost, John xvi, 7, 14; Acts ii, 33; and the terrible overthrow and dispersion of the Jewish nation is still a standing proof of it, John viii, 21; Matt. xxvi, 64. The time of Christ's ascension was forty days after his resurrection. As to the manner of his ascension, it was from Mount Olivet to heaven, not in appearance only, but in reality, and that visibly and locally.

ASH'DOD, or Azotus, a city which was assigned by Joshua to the tribe of Judah, but was possessed a long time by the Philistines, and rendered famous for the temple of their god Dagon, Joshua xv, 47. It lies upon the Mediterranean Sea, about nine or ten miles north of Gaza. Here the ark of Jehovah triumphed over the Philistine idol Dagon, 1 Sam. v, 2.

ASH'ER, tribe of. The province allotted to this tribe was a maritime one, stretching along the coast from Sidon on the north to Mount Carmel on the south. Asher was the most northerly of the tribes; and had that of Naphtali on the west, and Zebulun on the south.

ASHES. Several religious ceremonies, and some symbolical ones, anciently depended upon the use of ashes. To repent in sackcloth and ashes, or, as an external sign of self-affliction for sin, or of suffering under some misfortune, to sit in ashes are expressions common in Scripture.

ASH'KE-NAZ, one of the sons of Gomer, and grandson of Japheth, who gave his name to the country first peopled by him in the north and north-western part of Asia Mi'nor, answering to Bithynia.

ASH'TA-ROTH, or AS-TAR'TE, a goddess of the Zi

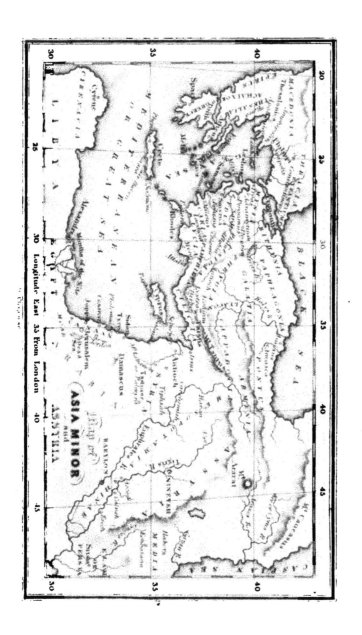

donians : she was goddess of woods, and groves were her temples. In groves consecrated to her such lasciviousness was committed as rendered her worship infamous, She was also called the queen of heaven ; and sometimes her worship is said to be that of "the host of heaven."

Solomon, seduced by his foreign wives, introduced the worship of Ashtaroth into Israel; but Jezebel, daughter of the king of Tyre, and wife to Ahab, principally established her worship. She caused altars to be erected to this idol in every part of Israel ; and at one time four hundred priests attended the worship of Ashtaroth, 1 Kings xviii, 19.

ASH'UR, the son of Shem, who gave his name to Assyr'i-a.

A'SI-A, one of the four grand divisions of the earth. It is also used in a more restricted sense for Asia Minor, Anatolia, or Nato'lia. In the New Testament it always signifies the Roman Proconsular Asia, i. e., the whole western coast, of which *Ephesus* was the capital, and in which the seven churches were situated.

AS'KE-LON, a city in the land of the Philistines, situated between Azoth and Gaza, upon the coast of the Mediterranean Sea, about sixty-five miles from Jerusalem.

AS-NAP'PER, the king of Assyria, who sent the Cutheans into the country belonging to the ten tribes, Ezra iv, 10.

ASP. A small poisonous serpent of Egypt and Libya, whose bite occasions inevitable death, but without pain. To tread upon the asp is attended with extreme danger; therefore, to express in the strongest manner the safety which the godly man enjoys under the protection of his heavenly Father, it is promised, that he shall tread with impunity upon these venomous creatures. No person, of his own accord, approaches the hole of these deadly reptiles ; for he who gives them the smallest disturbance is in extreme danger of paying the forfeit of his rashness with his life.

ASS. The prevailing colour of this animal in the east is reddish. In his natural state he is fleet, fierce, formidable, and intractable ; but when domesticated, the most gentle of all animals, and assumes a patience and submission even more humble than his situation. Le Clerc observes, that the Israelites, not being allowed to keep horses, the ass was not only made a beast of burden, but used on journeys; and that even the most honourable of the nation were wont to be mounted on asses, which in the eastern countries were much larger and more beautiful than they are with us.

The *wild ass* is taller and a much more dignified animal than the common or domestic ass; its legs are more elegantly shaped; and it bears its head higher. It is peculiarly distinguished by a dusky woolly mane, long erect ears, and a forehead highly arched. The colour of the hair, in general, is of a silvery white. These animals associate in herds, under a leader, and are very shy. They inhabit the mountainous regions and desert parts of Tartary, Persia, &c. Anciently they were likewise found in Lycaonia, Phrygia, Mesopotamia, and Arabia Deserta. They are remarkably wild; and Job, xxxix, 5–8, describes the liberty they enjoy, the place of their retreat, their manners, and wild, impetuous, and untamable spirit.

AS-SUR'ANCE is the firm persuasion we have of the certainty of a thing; "the full assurance of understanding," Col. ii, 2, is a well grounded knowledge of Divine things. "The full assurance of faith," Heb. x, 22, is a full persuasion that God will accept of us for the sake of his Son. And "the full assurance of hope," Heb. vi, 11, is a firm expectation that God will grant us the complete enjoyment of what he has promised.

We must certainly conclude that such an assurance is attainable, and what every Christian ought to aim at. This, however, does not exclude occasional doubt and weakness of faith from the earlier stages of his experience.

AS-SYR'I-A, the most ancient empire of Asia, founded by Nimrod. In Gen. x, 11, the passage should be read as it is in the margin of our English Bibles, "Out of that land he went forth into Ashur, and built Nineveh," that is, Nimrod went forth.

Great obscurity rests on this portion of ancient history.

The word is employed in the Old Testament in three different significations.

1. The ancient kingdom of Assyria, which lay east of the Tigris, between Armenia, Susiana, and Media.

It is the region which mostly comprises the modern Kurdistan and the pashalik of Mosul.

2. *The ancient* kingdom, including Babylonia and Mesopotamia.

3. After the overthrow of the Assyrian state the name continued to be applied to those countries which had been formerly under its dominion.

1. To Babylonia, where Nebuchadnezzar is called king of Assyria.

2. To Persia, where Darius is so called.

Of the government, laws, religion, learning, customs, &c. of the ancient Assyrians, nothing absolutely certain is recorded. Their kingdom was at first small, and subsisted for several ages under hereditary chiefs; and their government was simple. Afterward, when they rose to the sublimity of empire, their government seems to have been despotic, and the empire hereditary. Their laws were probably few, and depended upon the mere will of the prince. The Assyrians have been competitors with the Egyptians for the honour of having invented alphabetic writing. It appears from the few remains now extant of the writing of these ancient nations, that their letters had a great affinity with each other. They much resembled one another in shape, and they ranged them in the same manner, from right to left.

AS-TROL'O-GER, one who foretells future events, from the aspects, positions, and influences of the heavenly bodies. This art, which owed its origin to the practice of knavery on credulity, is now universally exploded by the intelligent part of mankind: it denies God and his providence, and is therefore condemned in the Scriptures, and ranked with practices the most offensive and provoking to the Divine Majesty.

A-SUP'PIM signifies *gatherings*, and is the name of the treasury of the temple of Jerusalem, 1 Chron. xxvi. 15.

ATH-A-LI'AH, daughter of Ahab, king of Israel, and granddaughter of Omri, and wife of Joram, king of Judah. She was extremely wicked herself, and seduced her husband and son to follow the idolatrous courses of her father, 2 Kings viii. 18–26.

ATH'ENS, a celebrated city and commonwealth of Greece, distinguished by the military talents, learning, eloquence, and politeness of its inhabitants; where Socrates, Plato, Pytha'goras, and the most illustrious philosophers of antiquity lived and taught. When Paul visited this place in A. D. 52, he found it plunged in idolatry; occupied in hearing and reporting news; curious to know every thing; and divided in opinion concerning religion and happiness.

A-TONE'MENT, the satisfaction offered to Divine justice by the death of Christ for the sins of mankind, by virtue of which all true penitents who believe in Christ are personally reconciled to God, are freed from the penalty of their sins, and entitled to eternal life. The atonement for sin made by the death of Christ is represented in the Christian system as the means by which mankind may be delivered from the awful catastrophe of eternal death; from judicial inflictions of the displeasure of a Governor whose authority has been contemned, and whose will has been resisted, which shall know no mitigation in their degree, nor bound to their duration. This end it professes to accomplish by means which, with respect to the Supreme Governor himself, preserve his character from mistake, and maintain the authority of his government; and with respect to man, give him the strongest possible reason for hope, and render more favourable the condition of his earthly probation.

How sin may be forgiven without leading to such misconceptions of the Divine character as would encourage disobedience, and thereby weaken the influence of the Divine government, must be considered as a problem of very difficult solution. The only answer is found in the Holy Scriptures. They alone show, and, indeed, they alone profess to show, how God may be "just," and yet the "justifier" of the ungodly. Other schemes show how he may be merciful; but the difficulty does not lie there. The Gospel meets it, by declaring "the righteousness of God," at the same time that it proclaims his mercy. The voluntary sufferings of the Divine Son of God "for us," that is, in our room and stead, magnify the justice of God; display his hatred to sin; proclaim "the exceeding sinfulness" of transgression, by the deep and painful manner in which they were inflicted upon the Substitute; warn the persevering offender of the terribleness as well as the certainty of his punishment; and open the gates of salvation to every penitent. It is a part of the same Divine plan also to engage the influence of the Holy Spirit to awaken penitence in man, and to lead the wanderer back to himself; to renew our fallen nature in righteousness at the moment we are justified through faith, and to place us in circumstances in which we may henceforth "walk not after the flesh, but after the Spirit." All the ends of government are here answered—no license is given to offence,—the moral law is unrepealed,—a day of judgment is still appointed,—future and eternal punishments still display their awful sanctions,—a new and singular display of the awful purity of the Divine character is afforded,—yet pardon is offered to all who seek it; and the whole world may be saved.

The passages that follow plainly and distinctly declare the atoning efficacy of Christ's death: "Now once in the end of the world hath he appeared to put away sin by the sacrifice of himself." "Christ was once offered to bear the sins of many; and unto them that look for him shall he appear the second time without sin unto salvation," Heb. ix, 26, 28. "This man, after he had offered one sacrifice for sin, for ever sat down on the right hand of God; for by one offering he hath perfected for ever them that are sanctified," Heb. x, 12. It is observable that nothing similar is said of the death of any other person, and that no such efficacy is imputed to any other martyrdom. "While we were yet sinners Christ died for us;

much more then, being now justified by his blood, we shall be saved from wrath through him : for if, when we were enemies, we were reconciled to God by the death of his Son, much more, being reconciled, we shall be saved by his life," Rom. v, 8–10. The words, "reconciled to God by the death of his Son," show that his death had an efficacy in our reconciliation ; but reconciliation is only preparatory to salvation. "He has reconciled us to his Father in his cross, and in the body of his flesh through death," Col. i, 20, 22. What is said of reconciliation in these texts, is in some others spoken of sanctification—which is also preparatory to salvation. "We are sanctified"—how ? "By the offering of the body of Christ once for all," Heb. x. 10. In the same epistle the blood of Jesus is called "the blood of the covenant by which we are sanctified." In these and many other passages that occur in different parts of the New Testament, it is therefore asserted that the death of Christ had an efficacy in the procuring of human salvation. Such expressions are used concerning no other person, and the death of no other person ; and it is therefore evident, that Christ's death included something more than a confirmation of his preaching; something more than a pattern of a holy and patient martyrdom ; something more

than a necessary antecedent to his resurrection, by which he gave a grand and clear proof of our resurrection from the dead. Christ's death was all these, but it was something more. It was an atonement for the sins of mankind ; and in this way only it became the accomplishment of our eternal redemption.

AU-GUS'TUS, emperor of Rome, and successor of Julius Cæsar. The battle of Actium, which he fought with Mark Antony, and which made him master of the empire, happened fifteen years before the birth of Christ. This is the emperor who appointed the enrolment mentioned Luke ii, 1. He had the honour also to shut the temple of Janus, in token of universal peace, at the time when the Prince of peace was born ; this was remarkable, as the temple was shut but few times. He died A. D. 14 ; the name, which signifies august, venerable, was also retained by his successors.

A'VEN, a city of Egypt.

A-VENG'ER OF BLOOD. He who prosecuted the manslayer under the law was called the avenger of blood, and had a right to slay the person, if he found him without a city of refuge.

A'VIM, a people descended from Hevus, the son of Canaan. They dwelt at first in the country which was afterward possessed by the Caphtorims, or Philistines.

AXE, a well known instrument of iron, used for cutting; and often metaphorically employed in Scripture, for a person or power, who, as a cutting instrument in the hand of God, is employed to lop off branches and boughs, and sometimes to cut down the tree itself. "The axe is laid to the root of the trees," Matt, iii. 10; irresistible punishment, destruction is near. We risk little in referring this (ultimately) to the Roman power and armies; which, as an axe, most vehemently cut away the very existence of the Jewish polity and state.

AZO'TUS. This is the Greek name of the city which in Hebrew is called Ashdod. It was taken by Joshua, and being surrounded with a wall of great strength, it became a place of great importance, and one of the five governments of the Philistines. See Ashdod.

BA'AL, BEL, or BE'LUS, denoting *lord*, a divinity among several ancient nations; as the Canaanites, Phœ-nic'i-ans, Si-do'nians, Carthagi'-nians, Babylonians, Chalde'-ans, and As-syr'ians; and thus were introduced a variety of divinities, called *Baalim*, or *Baal*, with some epithet annexed to it, as *Baal Be'rith, Baal Gad, Baal Mo'-loch, Baal Peor, Baal Zebub,* &c.

The temples and altars of Baal were generally placed on eminences: they were places inclosed by walls, within which was maintained a perpetual fire; and some of them had statues or images. Baal had his prophets and his priests in great numbers; accordingly, we read of four hundred and fifty of them that were fed at the table of Jezebel only; and they conducted the worship of this deity, by offering sacrifices, by dancing around his altar with violent gesticulations and exclamations, by cutting their bodies with knives and lancets, and by raving and pretending to prophesy, as if they were possessed by some invisible power.

The Hebrews often imitated the idolatry of the Canaanites in adoring Baal. They offered human sacrifices to him in groves, upon high places, and upon the terraces of houses. All sorts of infamous and immodest actions were committed in the festivals of Baal and As-tar'te. See Jer. xxxii, 35; 2 Kings xvii, 16. This false deity is frequently mentioned in Scripture in the plural number, *Baalim,* which may intimate that the name *Baal* was given to several different deities.

BA'AL BE'RITH, the god of the Shechemites, Judges viii, 33; ix, 4, 46.

BA'AL PE'OR was probably the temple of the idol Baal, belonging to the Moabites, on Mount Ab'a-rim, which the Israelites worshipped when encamped at Shittim. Baal was in an eminent degree the god of impurity. Hosea, speaking of the worship of this idol, emphatically calls it "that shame," Hos. ix, 10. Yet in the rites of this deity the Moabite and Midianite women seduced the Israelites to join.

BA'AL ZE'BUB, the same as BE-EL'ZE-BUB, or BEL'ZE-BUB.

BA'AL ZE'PHON, or *the god of the watch tower,* was probably the temple of some idol. It was situated on a cape or promontory on the eastern side of the western or Heroopolitan branch of the Red Sea, near its northern extremity, over against Pi-hahi'roth, or the opening in the mountains which led from the desert, on the side of Egypt, to the Red Sea.

BA'A-SHA, the son of Ahijah, commander-in-chief of the armies belonging to Nadab, the son of Jerobo'am, king of Israel.

BAB'BLER, an idle talker.

BA'BEL, the tower and city founded by the descendants of Noah in the plain of Shi'nar. The different tribes descended from Noah were here collected, and from this point were dispersed, through the confusion of their language.

All the descendants of Noah remained in Armenia during the lifetime of the four royal patriarchs, or till about the beginning of the sixth century after the flood; when, gradually falling off from the pure worship of God, seduced by the schemes of the ambitious Nimrod, and actuated by a desire for a more fertile country, they migrated in a body southward, till they reached the plains of Shi'nar, probably about sixty years after the death of Shem. Here, under the command of their new leader, and with the express view to counteract the designs of the Almighty in their dispersion into different countries, they began to build the city and tower, and set up a banner which should serve as a mark of national union, and concentrate them in one empire, when they were defeated and dispersed by the miraculous confusion of tongues. The tower of Belus in Babylon was probably either the original tower of Babel repaired, or it was constructed upon its massive foundations. The remains of this tower are still to be seen.

BAB'Y-LON, 2 Kings xxiv 1. The capital of Chal-de'a, built by Nimrod, Gen. x, 10. (See Assyria.) It was under Nebuchadnezzar that Babylon is supposed to have acquired that extent and magnificence, and that those stupendous works were completed, which rendered it the wonder of the world; and accordingly this prince arrogated to himself the whole glory of its erection; and in the pride of his heart exclaimed, "Is not this great Babylon that I have built?" The city at this period stood on both sides of the river, which intersected it in the middle. It was, according to the least computation, that of Di-o-do'-rus Sic'u-lus, forty-five miles in circumference; and according to He-rod'o-tus, sixty miles. Its shape was that of a square, traversed each way by twenty-five principal streets; which of course intersected each other, dividing the city into six hundred and twenty-six squares. These streets were terminated at each end by gates of brass, of prodigious size and strength, with a smaller one opening toward the river. The walls, from the most moderate accounts, were seventy-five feet in height, and thirty-two in breadth; while Herod'otus makes them three hundred in height and seventy-five in breadth: which last measurement, incredible as it may seem, is worthy of credit, as Herod'otus is much the oldest author who describes them, and who gives their original height; whereas those who follow him in their accounts of these stupendous walls describe them as they were after they had been taken down to the less elevation by Darius Hys-tas'pes. They were built of brick cemented with bitumen instead of mortar; and were encompassed by a broad and deep ditch, lined with the same materials, as were also the banks of the river in its course through the city; the inhabitants descending to the water by steps through the smaller brazen gates before mentioned. The houses were three or four stories high, separated from each other by small courts or gardens, with open spaces or even fields interspersed over the immense area enclosed within the walls. Over the river was a bridge, connecting the two halves of the city, the river running nearly north and south. The bridge was five furlongs in length, and thirty feet in breadth, and had a palace at each end, with, it is said, a subterraneous passage beneath the river, from one to the other; the work of Semiramis. Within the city was the temple of Belus, or Jupiter, which Herod'otus describes as a square of two stadia, or a quarter of a mile; in the midst of which arose the celebrated tower, to an elevation of one stadium, or six hundred and sixty feet; and the same measure at its base; the whole being divided into eight separate towers, one above another, of decreasing dimensions to the summit; where stood a chapel, containing a couch, table, and other things, of gold. Here the principal devotions were performed; and over this, on the highest platform of all, was the observatory, by the help of which the Babylonians arrived to such perfection in astronomy, that Cal-is'the-nes the philosopher, who accompanied Alexander to Babylon, found astronomical observations, which reach as high as the 115th year after the flood. On each side of the river, according to Diodorus, adjoining to the bridge, was a palace; that on the western bank being by much the larger. This palace was eight miles in circumference, and strongly fortified with three walls, one within another. Within it were the celebrated hanging gardens, enclosed in a square of four hundred feet. These gardens were raised on terraces, supported by arches, or rather by piers, laid over with broad flat stones; the arch appearing to be unknown to the Babylonians: which courses of piers rose one above another till they reached the level of the top of the city walls. On each terrace or platform a deep layer of mould was laid, in which flowers, shrubs, and trees were planted, some of which are said to have reached the height of fifty feet. On the highest level was a reservoir, with an engine to draw water up from the river, by which the whole was watered. This novel and astonishing structure, the work of a monarch who knew not how to create food for his own pampered fancy, or labour for his debased subjects or unhappy captives, was undertaken to please his wife Amyitis; that she might see an imitation of the hills and woods of her native country, Media.

Yet, while in the plenitude of her power, and, according to the most accurate chronologers, one hundred and sixty years before the foot of an enemy had entered it, the voice of prophecy pronounced the doom of the unconquered Babylon. A succession of ages brought it gradually to the dust; and the gradation of its fall is marked till it sinks at last into utter desolation. At a time when nothing but magnificence was around this city, emphatically called the great, fallen Babylon was delineated by the pencil of inspiration exactly as every traveller now describes its ruins.

BA'CA, *tears or weeping.* "The valley of Baca," Psa. lxxxiv, 6, is a *rough, barren, desolate* valley, such as could not be passed without *labour* and *tears.* This valley is here taken figuratively, referring to those who are travelling in the ways mentioned, ver. 5, i. e., the ways which lead to Jerusalem, where the temple is, and where the pleasure of worship can be enjoyed. Such is the object of their journey, and of their hopes, that no misfortune by the way, no passing through the *valley of Baca,* will render them unhappy; be their troubles and wants ever so many, God will relieve the one and provide for the other. They shall find this dry, unfruitful valley full of springs, and clothed with verdure by timely rains. This is a delightful image of the kindness vouchsafed to those "in whose hearts the ways of Zion are."

BACK-BITE, to speak evil of an absent person. Paul classes this sin with several others of a heinous nature, Rom. i, 30.

BACK-SLID'ING, a falling off, or defection in matters of religion; an apostacy. This may be either partial or complete: partial, when it is in the heart, as Prov. xiv, 14; complete, as that described in Heb. vi, 4, &c.; x, 6, &c. It is important in interpreting these passages to keep it steadfastly in mind that the apostacy they speak of is not only *moral* but *doctrinal*.

BADG'ER is a small inoffensive animal, of the bear genus, an inhabitant of cold countries, and remains torpid during the winter. It is therefore not found in Arabia; nor is there any thing in its skin peculiarly proper either for covering the tabernacle or making shoes. Bochart thinks that not an *animal*, but a *colour*, was intended, Exodus xxv, 5; so that the covering of the tabernacle was to be azure, or sky-blue.

BA'LAAM, (*Ba'lam*,) a prophet of the city of Pethor, or Bosor, upon the Eu-phra'-tes, whose intercourse with Ba'lak, king of the Moabites, who sent for him to curse the Israelites, is recorded at large by Moses, Num. xxii–xxiv. It cannot be denied that the Scripture expressly calls him a prophet, 2 Pet. ii, 15; and therefore those are probably right who think that he had once been a good man and a true prophet, till, loving the wages of unrighteousness, and prostituting the honour of his office to covetousness, he apostatized from God, and, betaking himself to idolatrous practices, fell under the delusion of the devil, of whom he learned all his magical enchantments; though at this juncture, when the preservation of his people was concerned, it might be consistent with God's wisdom to appear to him and overrule his mind by the impulse of real revelations.

BAL-ANCE, in Scripture an instrument much of the same nature probably as the Roman steelyard, where the weight is hung at one end of the beam, and the article to be weighed at the other end. Balances, in the plural, generally appear to mean scales— a pair of scales.

BALD'NESS is a natural effect of old age, in which period of life the hair of the head, wanting nourishment, falls off, and leaves the head naked. Artificial baldness was used as a token of mourning: it is threatened to the voluptuous daughters of Israel, instead of well set hair, Isa. iii, 24. See Mic. i, 16; and instances of it occur, Isa. xv, 2; Jer. xlvii, 5. See Ezek. vii, 18; Amos viii, 10.

BALM, or balsam, is a common name for many of those oily resinous substances which flow spontaneously or by incision, from certain trees or plants, and are of considerable use in medicine and surgery.

The "balm of Gilead," mentioned in the Scriptures, is the juice of the balsam tree, which is an evergreen, growing spontaneously, about fourteen feet high, in Azab, its native country, in Gilead, and on the coast of Babel-mandel. After the tree blossoms it yields a yellow, fine scented seed, enclosed in a reddish-black, pulpy nut, which contains a yellowish liquor, like honey: they are bitter, and a little tart upon the tongue, of the same shape and size of the fruit of the turpentine tree.

The great value set upon this drug in the east, is traced to the earliest ages. Arabian merchants, trafficking with the commodities of their own country into Egypt, brought with them balm as a part of their cargo, Gen. xxxvii, 25.

The best was that which flowed spontaneously, or by means of incision, from the trunk or branches of the tree, in summer.

BAN'NER, an ensign, or standard, used by armies or caravans on their journeys in the eastern countries.

BAN'QUET, a splendid feast, or a rich entertainment of meat and drink.

BAP'TISM, from the Greek word *baptizo*, is a rite or ceremony by which persons are initiated into the profession of the Christian religion; or by which a person assumes the profession of Christianity. It was by this mode that those who believed the Gospel were to be separated from unbelievers, and joined to the visible Christian Church. The rite was probably intended to represent the washing away, or renouncing, the impurities of some former state, viz. the sins that had been committed, and the vicious habits that had been contracted; and to this purpose it may be observed, that the profession of repentance always accompanied, or was understood to accompany, the profession of faith in Christ. That our Lord instituted such an ordinance as baptism is plain from the commission given to the apostles after his resurrection, and recorded in Matt. xxviii, 19, 20. To this rite there is also an allusion in Mark xvi, 16; John iii, 5; Acts ii, 41; viii, 12, 36–38; xxii, 16. The design of this institution, which was to express faith in Christ on the part of those who were baptized, and to declare their resolution of openly professing his religion, and cultivating real and universal holiness, appears from Rom. vi, 3, 4; 1 Pet. iii, 21; Ephes. v, 26; and Titus iii, 5. We find no account of baptism as a distinct religious rite before the mission of John, the forerunner of Christ, who was called the "Baptist," on account of his being commanded by God to baptize with water all who should hearken to his invitation to repent. Washing, however, accompanied many of the Jewish rites, and, indeed, was required after contracting any kind of uncleanness. Also, soon after the time of our Saviour, we find it to have been the custom of the Jews solemnly to baptize, as well as to circumcise, all their proselytes. As their writers treat largely of the reasons for this rite, and give no hint of its being a novel institution, it is probable that this had always been the custom antecedent to the time of Moses, whose account of the rite of circumcision, and of the manner of performing it, is by no means circumstantial. Or, baptism, after circumcision, might have come into use gradually from the natural propriety of the thing, and its easy conformity to other Jewish customs. For if no Jew could approach the tabernacle or temple, after the most trifling uncleanness, without washing, much less would it be thought proper to admit a proselyte from a state so impure and unclean as heathenism was conceived to be, without the same mode of purification. There is also a strong intimation, even in the Gospel itself, of such a known practice among the Jews in the time of John the Baptist, John i, 25.

2. The word *baptism* is frequently taken for *sufferings*, Mark x, 38; Luke xii, 50; Matt. xx, 22, 23.

3. As to the subjects of baptism, the Pædobaptists believe that qualified adults, who have not been baptized before, are certainly proper subjects; but then they think, also, that infants ought not to be excluded. They believe that, as the Abrahamic and Christian covenants are the same, Gen. xvii, 7; Heb. viii, 12; that as children were admitted under the former; and that as baptism is now a sign, seal, or confirmation of this covenant, infants have as great a right to it as the children of the Israelites had to the seal of circumcision under the laws, Acts ii, 39; Rom. iv, 11. Farther, if children are not to be baptized because there is no positive command for it, for the same reason they say that women should not come to the Lord's Supper; nor ought we to keep holy the first day of the week; neither of these being expressly commanded. If baptizing infants had been a human invention, they also ask, how such a practice could have been so universal in the first three hundred years of the Church, and yet no record have remained when it was introduced, nor any dispute or controversy about it have taken place? Some reduce the matter to a narrower compass; urging, (1.) That God constituted in his Church the membership of infants, and admitted them to that privilege by a religious ordinance, Gen. xvii; Gal. iii, 14, 17.

(2.) That this right of infants to Church membership was never taken away: and this being the case, they argue that infants must be received, because God has appointed it; and, since they must be received, it must be either with baptism or without it; but none must be received without baptism; therefore infants must of necessity be baptized. Hence it is clear that under the Gospel, infants are still continued exactly in the same relation to God and his Church in which they were originally placed under former dispensations. That infants are to be received into the Church, and as such baptized, is also inferred from the following passages of Scripture:—Gen. xvii; Isa. xliv, 3; Matt. xix, 13; Luke ix, 47, 48; Acts ii, 38, 39; Rom. xi, 17, 21; 1 Cor. vii, 14.

Finally, it is generally acknowledged that if infants die, (and a great part of the human race die in their infancy,) they are saved. If this be the case, then why refuse them the sign of union with Christ, if they be capable of enjoying the thing signified?

4. As to the mode, the Pædobaptists deny that the term *baptize* is invariably used in the New Testament to express plunging. It is denied that dipping is its only meaning; that Christ absolutely enjoined immersion; and that it is his positive will, that no other mode should be used.

As the word *baptize* is used to express the various ablutions among the Jews, such as sprinkling, pouring, &c., Heb. ix, 10, for the custom of washing before meals, and the washing of household furniture, pots, &c., it is evident from hence that it does not express the manner of doing a thing, whether by immersion or effusion, but only the thing done; that is, washing, or the application of water in some form or other. It nowhere signifies *to dip*, but in denoting a mode of, and in order to, washing or cleansing; and the mode or use is only the ceremonial part of a positive institute; just as in the Lord's Supper, the time of day, the number and posture of the communicants, the quantity and quality of bread and wine, are circumstances not accounted essential by any part of Christians. If in baptism there be an expressive emblem of the descending influence of the Spirit, pouring must be the mode of administration; for that is the scriptural term most commonly and properly used for the communication of Divine influences, Matt. iii, 11; Mark i, 8, 10; Luke iii, 16–22; John i, 33; Acts i, 5; ii, 38, 39; viii, 12, 17; xi, 15, 16. The term *sprinkling*, also, is made use of in reference to the act of purification, Isa. lii, 15; Ezek. xxxvi, 25; Heb. ix, 13, 14; and therefore cannot be inapplicable to baptismal purification.

Jesus, it is said, came up *out of* the water; but this is no proof that he was immersed, as the Greek term *apo*, often signifies *from:* for instance, " Who hath warned you to flee *from*," not *out of*, " the wrath to come ?" with many others that might be mentioned. Again: it is urged that Philip and the eunuch went down both into the water. To this it is answered, that here also is no proof of immersion : for, if the expression of their going down *into* the water necessarily includes dipping, then Philip was dipped, as well as the eunuch. The preposition *eis*, translated *into*, often signifies no more than *to*, or *unto:* see Matt. xv, 24 ; Rom. x. 10 ; Acts xxviii, 14 ; Matt. iii, 11 ; xvii, 27 : so that from none of these circumstances can it be proved that there was one person of all the baptized, who went into the water ankle deep. As to the apostle's expression, "buried with him in baptism," that has no force in the argument for immersion, since it does not allude to a custom of dipping, any more than our baptismal crucifixion and death has any such reference. It is not the sign, but the thing signified, that is here alluded to. As Christ was buried, and rose again to a heavenly life, so we by baptism signify that we are separated from sin, that we may live a new life of faith and love.

To conclude : it is urged against the mode of immersion, that, as it carries with it too much of the appearance of a burthensome rite for the Gospel dispensation; as it is too indecent for so solemn an ordinance ; as it has a tendency to agitate the spirits, often rendering the subject unfit for the exercise of proper thoughts and affections, and indeed utterly incapable of them : as in many cases the immersion of the body would in all probability be instant death ; as in other situations it would be impracticable, for want of water ; it cannot be considered as necessary to the ordinance of baptism; and there is the strongest improbability that it was ever practised in the times of the New Testament, or in the earliest periods of the Christian Church.

BAR signifies *son:* Barjona, i. e. son of Jonah ; a name by which our Saviour sometimes calls Peter.

BAR-A-CHI'AS, the father of Zachari'as, mentioned Matt. xxiii, 35, as slain between the temple and the altar. See ZACHARIAH.

BA'RAK, son of Abinoam, chosen by God to deliver the Hebrews from that bondage under which they were held by Ja'bin, king of the Canaanites, Judges iv, 4, 5, &c.

BAR-BA'RI-AN signifies *a stranger* or *foreigner ;* one who does not speak our native language, or one in a rude and uncivilized state.

BAR-JE'SUS was a Jewish magician in the island of Crete, Acts xiii, 6. St. Luke calls him El'y-mas.

BAR'LEY, a well known kind of grain. Pliny, on the testimony of Me-nan'der, says that barley was the most ancient aliment of mankind. In Palestine the barley was sown about October, and reaped in the end of March, just after the passover. In Egypt the barley harvest was later; for when the hail fell there, Exodus ix, 81, a few days before the passover, the flax and barley were bruised and destroyed. The Hebrews frequently used barley bread, as we find by several passages of Scripture.

BAR'NA-BAS, a disciple of Jesus Christ, and companion of St. Paul in his labours. He was a Levite, born in the isle of Cyprus. His proper name was Joses, to which the apostles added Barnabas, signifying *the son of consolation.* He is generally considered one of the seventy disciples chosen by our Saviour. He was brought up, with Paul, at the feet of Gamaliel. When that apostle came to Jerusalem, three years after his conversion, Barnabas introduced him to the other apostles, Acts ix, 26, 27, about A. D. 37.

BAR'SA-BAS. Joseph Barsabas, surnamed Justus, was one of the first disciples of Jesus Christ, and probably one of the seventy, Acts i, 21. Bar'sa-bas was nominated along with Matthias; but the lot fell on Matthias, who was therefore numbered with the eleven apostles.

2. BARSABAS was also the surname of Judas, one of the principal disciples, mentioned, Acts xv, 22, &c.

BAR-THOL'O-MEW, one of the twelve apostles, Matt. x, 3, is supposed to be the same, person who is called Nathanael, one of the first of Christ's disciples.

BA'RUCH, the son of Neriah, and grandson of Maaseiah, was of illustrious birth, and of the tribe of Judah. He had a brother of the name of Seraiah, who occupied an important station in the court of King Zed-e-ki'ah; but he himself adhered to the person of the prophet Jeremiah, and was his most steady friend, though his attachment to him drew on himself several persecutions and much ill treatment. He appears to have acted as his secretary during a great part of his life, and never left him till they were parted by death.

BA'SHAN, called by the Greeks *Batanæ'a,* one of the most fertile districts of Canaan, which was bounded on the north by the land of Geshur, on the east by the mountains of Gilead, on the south by the brook Jabbok, and on the west by the river Jordan. The whole kingdom took its name from the hill of Ba'shan, which is situated in the middle of it. It had no less than sixty walled towns in it, beside villages. It afforded an excellent breed of cattle, and stately oaks, and was, in short, a plentiful and populous country.

BASTARD, one born out of wedlock. A bastard among the Greeks was despised, and exposed to public scorn, on account of his spurious origin. The Jewish father bestowed as little attention on the education of such children as the Greek: he seems to have resigned them, in a great measure, to their own inclinations; he neither checked their passions, nor corrected their faults, nor stored their minds with useful knowledge. This is evidently implied in Heb. xii, 7, 8.

BAT, an unclean animal, having the body of a mouse, and wings not covered with feathers, but of a leathery membrane, expansible for the purpose of flying. They bring forth their young alive, in the tops of houses, and suckle them like four-footed beasts. Some of the bats of Africa have long tails, like mice, which extend beyond their wings. They never become tame, but feed on flies, insects, and fat things, such as candles: they fly about at night when the weather is fine and warm. Extremely well described in Deut. xiv, 19. It has feet or claws growing out of its pinions, and contradicts the general order of nature, by creeping with the instruments of its flight.

BATH, a measure of capacity for things liquid, being the same with the ephah, Ezek. xlv, 11, and containing ten homers, or seven gallons and four pints.

BATTLE-MENT, a wall round the top of flat-roofed houses; as were those of the Jews, and other eastern people. (See *Houses*.)

BAY-TREE, the common *laurel*, mentioned only in Psalm xxxvii, 35, 36: some say that the original means only *a native tree*, a tree growing in its native soil, not having suffered by transplantation. Such a tree spreads itself luxuriantly.

BDELL'IUM, (*del'yum*,) a gum used as incense for burning, and of an aromatic smell. —*Stuart*.

BEAM, the cylindrical piece of wood belonging to a weaver's loom, on which the web is gradually rolled as it is woven; also, gross, palpable faults.

BEAR. Bears were common in Palestine. Their strength, rapacity, and fierceness, furnish many expressive metaphors to the Hebrew poets. David had to defend his flock against bears as well as lions, 1 Sam. xvii, 34.

BEARD. Nothing has been more fluctuating in the different ages of the world and countries, than the fashion of wearing the beard. Some have cultivated one part and some another; some have endeavoured to extirpate it entirely, while others have almost idolized it; the revolutions of countries have scarcely been more famous than the revolutions of beards. It is a great mark of infamy among the Arabs to cut off the beard. Many people would prefer death to this kind of treatment: hence we may easily learn the magnitude of the offence of the Am'mon-ites, in their treatment of David's ambassadors, 2 Sam. x, 4, 5. 1 Chron. xix, 5, and also the force of the emblem used, Ezek. v, 1-5.

BEASTS. When this word is used in opposition to man, as Psalm xxxvi, 5, any brute creature is signified; when to creeping things, as Lev. xi, 2, 7, xxix, 30, four-footed animals, from the size of the hare and upward, are intended; and when to wild creatures, as Gen. i, 25, cattle, or tame animals, are spoken of. St. Paul, 1 Cor. xv, 32, speaks of fighting with beasts, &c: by which he means that he had to contend at Ephesus with the fierce uproar of Demetrius and his associates. Wild beasts are used in Scripture as emblems of tyrannical and persecuting powers. The most illustrious conquerors of antiquity also have not a more honourable emblem.

BED. Mattresses, or thick cotton quilts folded, were used for sleeping upon. These were laid upon the divan, a part of the room elevated above the rest, covered with a carpet in winter, and a fine mat in summer. The people of the East do not keep their beds made; the mat-

tresses are rolled up, carried away, and placed in a cupboard till they are wanted at night. And hence the propriety of our Lord's address to the paralytic, "Arise, take up thy bed," or mattress, "and walk," Matt. ix, 6.

BE-EL'ZE-BUB, Matt. x, 25, (Fly-god.) The country of the Philistines being greatly infested, during the rainy season, with flies, gnats, &c. they paid their devotions to the god of flies, in order that he might protect them from this evil. The temple and worship of this false god appear to have been in great repute at the time of Elijah. The designation of this chief idol of the heathen world, as the "the prince of the devils," was very natural, since the Jews were taught in their own Scriptures to consider all idols of the heathens "devils."

BE-ER'SHE-BA, the well of the oath; so named from a well which Abraham dug in this place, and the covenant which he here made with A-bim'e-lech, king of Gerar, Gen. xx, 31. It was situated twenty miles south of Hebron, in the extreme south of the land of Israel, as Dan was on the north. The two places are frequently thus mentioned in Scripture, as "from Dan to Beersheba," to denote the whole length of the country, about one hundred and fifty miles.

BEE, a well known, small, industrious insect; whose

form, propagation, economy, and singular instinct and ingenuity, have attracted the attention of the most inquisitive and laborious inquirers into nature. Bees were very numerous in the east. Canaan was celebrated as "a land flowing with milk and honey." The wild bees formed their comb in the crevices of the rocks, and in the hollows of decayed trees.

BEE'TLE. It occurs only Lev. xi, 22. A species of locust is thought to be there spoken of. See LOCUST.

BE'HE-MOTH. This animal is now generally supposed to be the hippopot'a-mus, or river horse, an animal altogether uncouth in its appearance, its body being extremely large, and the head enormously large in proportion; and the legs as disproportionately short. The length of the male has been known to be seventeen feet; height seven feet, and the circumference fifteen. The general colour of the animal is brownish, and the armament of teeth in its mouth is truly formidable. It is found in the lakes and rivers of Africa, feeds chiefly on vegetables, and is never offensive unless provoked or wounded.

BEL, or BE'LUS, a name by which many heathens, and particularly the Babylonians, called their chief idol. Bel had a temple erected to him in the city of Babylon, on the very uppermost range of the famous tower of Babel, wherein were many statues of this pretended deity; and one, among the rest, of massy gold, forty feet high. See BABEL.

BE'LI-AL, strictly means *worthlessness, wickedness.* A man or son of Belial is a *wicked, worthless man.* It was given to the inhabitants of Gibeah, who abused the Levite's wife, Judges xix, 22; and to Hophni and Phin'ehas, the wicked and profane sons of Eli, 1 Sam: ii, 12. In later times the name denoted Satan. "What concord hath Christ with Belial?" 2 Cor. vi, 15; for Satan is the author of evil, and eminently, "the Evil One."

BE'LIEVE means to *credit* the truths of the Gospel, and *trust* in the merit of Christ for pardon and acceptance. (See *Faith.*)

BELLS. Moses ordered that the lower part of the blue robe, which the high priest wore in religious ceremonies, should be adorned with pomegranates and bells, intermixed alternately, at equal distances. The pomegranates were of wool, and in colour blue, purple, and crimson; the bells were of gold. Moses adds, "And it shall be upon Aaron to minister; and his sound shall be heard when he goeth in unto the holy place before the Lord, and when he cometh out; that he die not." Their sound intimated when he was about to enter the sanctuary, and served to keep up the attention of the people.

A reverential respect for the Divine Inhabitant was also indicated. Bells were a part of the martial furniture of horses employed in war.

BELLY is used in Scripture for gluttony, Titus i, 12; Philip. iii, 16; Rom. xvi, 18. For the heart, or the secrets of the mind, Prov. xx, 27, 30; xxii, 18. "The belly of hell" signifies the grave, or some imminent danger, or deep distress, Jonah ii, 2; Ecclus. ii, 5.

BEL-SHAZ'ZAR, the last king of Babylon, and, according to Hales and others, the grandson of Neb-u-chad-nez'-zar, Dan. v, 18. The only circumstances of his reign recorded, are the visions of the Prophet Daniel, and his sacrilegious feast and violent death, Dan. v, 1–30. See BABYLON.

BEN'JA-MIN, the youngest son of Jacob and Rachel, who was born, A. M. 2272, not far from Bethlehem, whom, with her last breath, his mother named Be-no'ni, that is, "the son of my sorrow;" but soon afterward Jacob changed his name, and called him Benjamin, that is, "the son of my right hand."

BE-RE'A, a city of Macedonia.

BER-NI'CE, the daughter of Agrippa, surnamed the Great, king of the Jews, and sister to young Agrippa, also king of the Jews. This lady was first betrothed to Mark, the son of Alexander Ly-sym'a chus, Al'ba-rach, of Al-ex-an'dria; afterward she married Herod, king of Chalcis, her own uncle by the father's side. After the death of Herod, which happened A. D. 48, she was married to Pol'e-mon, king of Pontus, but did not long continue with him. She returned to her brother A-grip'pa, and with him heard the discourse which Paul delivered before Festus, Acts xxv.

BER'YL, a pellucid gem of a bluish green colour, found in the East Indies, Peru, Sibe'ria, and Tartary. It has a brilliant appearance, and is generally transparent. The tenth stone belonging to the high priest's breastplate. See *Precious Stones.*

BETH, in Hebrew, signifies *house;* and is prefixed to very many proper names and other words, thus forming with them the name of a place; as Beth-el, "*house of God;*" Beth-lehem, "*house of bread,*" &c.

BETH-AB'A-RA, signifies in the Hebrew a place of passage, because of its ford over the river Jordan, on the east bank of which river it stood over against Jericho, Joshua ii, 7; iii, 15, 16.

BETH'A-NY, a considerable place, situated on the ascent of the mount of Olives, about two miles east from Jerusalem.

BETH-A'VEN, a city of the tribe of Benjamin, eastward of Bethel. There was also a desert of the same name.

BETH'EL, a city which lay to the west of Ai, about twelve miles to the north of Jerusalem, in the confines of the tribe of Ephraim and Benjamin. Here Jacob slept and had his vision. The name of this city had formerly been Luz, which signifies *an almond*, and was probably so called from the number of almond trees which grew in those parts. BETHEL was also called Beth-a'ven, by the prophets; which signifies *"house of vanity,"* in derision of the worship of the golden calves established there.

BETH-ES'DA. This word signifies *the house of mercy*, and was the name of a pool, or public bath at Jerusalem, which had five porticoes, piazzas, or covered walks around it. This bath was called Bethesda, from the great goodness of God manifested to his people, in bestowing healing virtues upon its waters, John v, 2–4. There appears a mercy and a wisdom in this miracle which must strike every one who attentively considers the account, unless he be a determined unbeliever in miraculous interposition. For, 1. The miracle occurred from time to time, that is, occasionally, perhaps frequently. 2. Though but one at a time was healed, yet, as this might often occur, a singularly gracious provision was made for the relief of the sick inhabitants of Jerusalem in desperate cases. 3. The angel probably acted invisibly, but the commotion in the waters was so strong and peculiar as to mark a supernatural agent. 4. There is great probability in what Doddridge, following Tertullian, supposes, that the waters obtained their healing property not long before the ministry of Christ, and lost it after his rejection and crucifixion by the Jews. In this case a connection was established between the healing virtue of the pool and the presence of Christ on earth, indicating HIM to be the source of this benefit, and the true agent in conferring it; and thus it became, afterward at least, a confirmation of his mission.

BETH-HO'RON stood on the confines of Ephraim and Benjamin, which is supposed to be Bethoor, an Arab village about twelve miles from Jerusalem.

BETH'LE-HEM, a city in the tribe of Judah, about six miles south from Jerusalem, Judges xvii, 7; and likewise called Eph'rath, Gen. xlviii, 7; or Eph'ra-tah, Micah v, 2; and the inhabitants of it Eph'rath-ites, Ruth i, 2; 1 Sam. xvii, 12. Here David was born, and spent his early years as a shepherd. And here also the scene of the beautiful narrative of Ruth is supposed to be laid. But its highest honour is, that here our Divine Lord condescended to be born of woman.

BETH'PHA-GE, (*Beth'-fa-je*,) so called from its producing figs, a small village situated in Mount Olivet, and, as it seems, somewhat nearer Jerusalem than Beth'a-ny. The distance between Beth'-phage and Jerusalem is about fifteen furlongs.

BETH'SA'I-DA, (or *Beth-sai'da*,) a city whose name in Hebrew imports a place of fishing or of hunting, and for both of these exercises it was well situated. As it belonged to the tribe of Naph'ta-li, it was in a country remarkable for plenty of deer; and as it lay on the north end of the lake Gen-nes'a-reth, just where the river Jordan runs into it, became the residence of fishermen. Three of the apostles, Philip, Andrew, and Peter, were born in this city. It is not mentioned in the Old Testament, though it frequently occurs in the New; the reason is, that it was but a village, as Josephus tells us, till Philip the tetrarch enlarged it, making it a magnificent city, and gave it the name of Ju'li-us, out of respect to Ju'li-a, the daughter of Au-gus'tus Cæsar.

BETH'SHAN, a city belonging to the half tribe of Ma-nas'seh, on the west of Jordan, and not far from the river. It is said to be seventy-five miles from Jerusalem, 2 Macc. xii, 29.

BE-THU'EL, the son of Nahor and Milcah. He was Abraham's nephew, and father to Laban and Re-bek'ah, the wife of Isaac, Gen. xxii. 20, 23.

BE-TROTH', to contract any one in order to a future marriage. The word imports as much as giving one's *troth*; that is, true *faith* or *promise*. Among the ancient Jews, the betrothing was performed either by a writing, or by a piece of silver given to the bride. After the marriage was contracted, the young people had the liberty of seeing each other, which was not allowed them before. If, after the betrothment, the bride should trespass against that fidelity she owed to her bridegroom, she was treated as an adulteress. See MARRIAGE.

BE-WRAY', an old word, signifying to betray, to show or make visible.

BE'ZER, or Boz'ra, or Bos'tra, a city beyond Jordan, given by Moses to Reuben: this town was designed by Joshua to be a city of refuge; it was given to the Levites of Ger'shom's family, Deut. iv, 43. When Scripture mentions Bezer, it adds, " in the wilderness," because it lay in Arabia Deserta, and the eastern part of Edom, encompassed with deserts.

BIER, the funeral couch in which the dead, without coffins, were carried forth.

BIL'DAD, the Shu'hite, one of Job's friends, thought by some to have descended from Shu'ah, the son of Abraham by Ke-tu'rah, Job ii, 11.

BIND and *Loose*, a usual phrase for declaring what was lawful or unlawful; that which was *binding* upon men's conscience, and that from the obligation of which they were *loosed* or freed.

Under these terms our Lord gave his disciples authority, through the guidance of his own teaching, and the inspiration of the Holy Spirit, to declare the laws of the Gospel dispensation. And he promises that these laws shall be *confirmed* in heaven, as his own law, and the rule of moral government. They were thus made the infallible teachers of the whole truth of his religion.

No man, therefore, or body of men, can have power to bind or loose in the Church, but he who is inspired to know what the laws of the Divine government are; for nothing which is declared on earth can hold good in heaven, as determining what is pleasing or displeasing to God, but what is in fact a revelation of God's own will, which is the law of his creatures.

The apostles only had that revelation, and they only, therefore, had the power to declare what was lawful or the contrary, " to bind and to loose." See *Keys*.

BIRD, a common name for all birds, but is sometimes used for the sparrow in particular.

Birds are distinguished by the Jewish legislator into clean and unclean. Such as fed upon grain and seeds were allowed for food, and such as devoured flesh and carrion were prohibited.

Moses, to inspire the Israelites with sentiments of tenderness toward the brute creation, commands them, if they find a bird's nest, not to take the dam with the young, but to suffer the old one to fly away, and to take the young only, Deut. xxii, 6. This is one of those merciful institutions in the law of Moses which respect the animal creation, and tended to humanize the heart of that people, to excite in them a sense of the Divine providence extending itself to all creatures, and to teach them to exercise their dominion over them with gentleness. Besides, the young never knew the sweets of liberty; the dam did: they might be taken and used for any lawful purpose; but the dam must not be brought into a state of captivity.

BIRTH'RIGHT, the right of the first-born son. The birthright had many privileges annexed to it. The first born was consecrated to the Lord, Exod. xxii, 29; had a double portion of the estate allotted him, Deut. xxi, 17; had a dignity and authority over his brethren, Gen. xlix, 3; succeeded in the government of the family or kingdom, 2 Chron. xxi, 3; and, as some with good reason suppose, in ancient times to the priesthood or chief government in ecclesiastical matters.

BISHOP signified *an overseer*, or one who has the inspection and direction of any thing. The most common acceptation of the word *bishop* is that in Acts xx, 28, and in St. Paul's Epistles, Philip. i, 1, where it signifies the pastor of a Church. The word, as used by the apostolic writers, when referring to the pastors of Christian Churches, is evidently of the same import as *presbyter* or *elder ;* for the terms, as they occur in the New Testament, appear to be synonymous, and are used indifferently. In Titus i, 5, it is said, " For this cause left 1 thee in Crete, that thou shouldest set in order the things that are wanting, and ordain elders in every city ;" and then it follows in verse 7, " For a bishop must be blameless."

BI-THYN'I-A, a country of Asia Mi'nor, stretching along the shore of the Black Sea, from Mys'i-a to Paph-la-go'ni-a ; having Phryg'i-a and Gala'tia on the south. St. Peter addressed his first Epistle to the Hebrew Christians who were scattered through this and the neighbouring countries.

BITTER, denoting vexation, anger, fury.. Sometimes bitterness of soul signifies only grief, 1 Sam. i, 10 ; 2 Kings iv, 27. " Bitter envying," James iii, 14, denotes mortal and permanent hatred. King Hezekiah in his hymn says, Isaiah xxxviii, 17, that " in the midst of his peace, he was attacked with *great bitterness,*" i. e., a very dangerous disease.

BITTERN, a fowl about the size of the heron, and of the same species.

BLACK denotes great distress and consternation, Joel ii, 6; men in fear *turn pale,* but in despair the whiteness of a sudden fright turns into blackness.

BLAS'PHE-MY properly denotes *calumny, detraction, reproachful* or *abusive language,* against whomsoever it be vented. To blaspheme God is to revile him, by denying or ridiculing his perfections, word, or ordinances, and by ascribing to him any thing base or sinful, 2 Sam. xii, 14 ; Tit. ii, 5 ; Revelation xiii, 6.

" Blasphemy against the Holy Spirit," Matt. xii, 31, 32; Mark iii, 28, 29; Luke xii, 10, is imputing the miracles wrought by the power of the Holy Ghost to the power of the devil. The Pharisees were the persons charged with the crime : the sin itself manifestly consisted in ascribing what was done by the finger of God to the agency of the devil ; and the reason, therefore, why our Lord pronounced it unpardonable, is plain ; because, by withstanding the evidence of miracles, they resisted the strongest means of conviction, and that wilfully and malignantly ; and, giving way to their passions, opprobriously treated that Holy Spirit whom they ought to have adored. From all which it will probably follow that no person can now be guilty of the blasphemy against the Holy Ghost, in the sense in which our Saviour originally intended it; but there may be sins which bear a very near resemblance to it. This appears from the case of the apostates mentioned in the Epistle to the Hebrews. It may be laid down as certain, for the relief of those who may be tempted to think that they have committed the unpardonable sin, that their horror of it, and the trouble which the very apprehension causes them, are the sure proofs that they are mistaken.

BLEMISH, whatever renders a person or thing imperfect or uncomely. The Jewish law required the priests to be free from blemishes of person, Lev. xxi, 17–23; xxii, 20–24. Scandalous professors are blemishes to the Church of God, 2 Peter ii, 13; Jude 12, and therefore ought to be put away from it, in the exercise of a godly discipline.

BLESS, BLESSING. There are three points of view in which the acts of blessing may be considered. The first is, when men are said to bless God, as in Psalm ciii, 1, 2, they only ascribe to him that praise, and dominion, and honour, and glory, and blessing, which it is equally the duty and joy of his creatures to render. But when God is said to bless his people, Gen. i, 22; Eph. i, 3; the meaning is, that he confers benefits upon them, either temporal or spiritual, and so communicates to them some portion of that blessedness which, in infinite fulness, dwells in himself, James i, 17; Psalm civ, 24, 28; Luke xi, 9–13. In the third place men are said to bless their fellow creatures. From the time that God entered into covenant with Abraham, and promised extraordinary blessings to his posterity, it appears to have been customary for the father of each family, in the direct line, or line of promise, previous to his death, to call his children around him, and to inform them, according to the knowledge which it pleased God then to give him, how, and in what manner the Divine blessing conferred upon Abraham was to descend among them. Upon these occasions the patriarchs enjoyed a Divine illumination; and under its influence their benediction was deemed a prophetic oracle, foretelling events with the utmost certainty, and extending to the remotest period of time. Thus Jacob blessed his sons, Gen. xlix; and Moses instructed Aaron, and his descendants, to bless the congregation. "In this wise shall ye bless the children of Israel, saying unto them, The Lord bless thee, and keep thee; the Lord make his face to shine upon thee; the Lord lift up his countenance upon thee, and give thee peace," Num. iv, 23.

BLINDNESS is often used in Scripture to express ignorance or want of discernment in divine things, as well as the being destitute of natural sight. See Isa. xlii, 18, 19; vi, 10; Matt. xv, 14. "Blindness of heart" is the want of understanding arising from the influence of vicious passions.

BLOOD is used, 1, for the fluid which circulates in the veins of men, and other animals. 2. Bloodshed, murder, blood guiltiness, cruelty. 3. For any thing which appears like blood, as the juice of the grape. "The moon shall be changed into blood," appear red like blood, as it does, in some degree, during a total eclipse. 4. For the sacrificial death of Christ. "We are justified by his blood," &c.; "We have redemption through his blood," &c. The *eating of blood* was forbidden to Noah and his descendants, and the Israelites; the restraint was also enjoined, under the new covenant, upon believing Gentiles, as "a burden, which it seemed necessary to the Holy Spirit to impose upon them." This emphatic prohibition was made, no doubt, for two reasons :—

1. To prevent cruelty and murder. This is plainly intimated, Gen. ix, 4–6.

2. To be a constant memorial to men, that their lives were forfeited to Divine justice, and that without *shedding the blood of the great Sacrifice there was no remission.* See Lev. xvii, 10–14.

BO-A-NER'GES. When our Saviour named the sons of Zebedee Boanerges, he perhaps had an eye to that prophecy of Haggai, "Yet once, and I will shake the heavens and the earth," ii, 6; which is by the apostle to the Hebrews, xii, 26, applied to the great alteration made in the economy of the Jews by the publication of the Gospel. The name Boanerges, therefore, given to James and John, imports that they should be eminent instruments in accomplishing the wondrous change, and should, like an earthquake or thunder, mightily bear down all opposition, by their inspired preaching and miraculous powers. That it does not relate to their *mode* of preaching is certain; for that clearly appears to have been calmly argumentative, and sweetly persuasive —the very reverse of what is usually called a thundering ministry.

BOAR. The wild boar is considered as the parent stock of our domestic hog. He is smaller, but at the same time stronger and more undaunted than the hog. In his own defence, he will turn on men or dogs; and scarcely shuns any denizen of the forest, in the haunts where he ranges. His colour is always an iron gray, inclining to black. His snout is longer than that of the common breed, and his ears are comparatively short. His tusks are very formidable, and all his habits are fierce and savage. The destructive ravages of these animals are mentioned in Psalm lxxx, 14. Dr. Pococke observed very large herds of wild boars on the side of Jordan, where it flows out of the sea of Tiberias; and saw several of them on the other side lying among the reeds by the sea.

BOCHIM, the place of weepings, where the Hebrews celebrated their solemn feasts. Here the angel of the covenant appeared to them, and denounced the sinfulness of their idolatry, which caused bitter *weeping* among the people; whence the place had its name, Judg. ii, 5.

BODY, the animal frame of man, as distinguished from his spiritual nature. The body of any thing, in the style of the Hebrews, is the very reality of the thing. The "body of day," "the body of purity," "the body of death," "the body of sin," signify broad day, innocence itself, &c. "The body of death" signifies either our mortal body, or the body which violently engages us in sin by concupiscence, and which domineers in our members. An assembly or community is called a body, 1 Cor. x, 17.

BONDS were of two kinds, public and private; the former were employed to secure a prisoner in the public jail, after confession or conviction; the latter when he was delivered to a magistrate, or oven to private persons, to be kept at their houses till he should be tried. The Apostle Paul was subjected to private bonds by Felix, the Roman governor, who "commanded a centurion to keep him, and to let him have liberty, and that he should forbid none of his acquaintance to minister, or come unto him," Acts xxiv, 23.— And after he was carried prisoner to Rome, he "dwelt two whole years in his own hired house, and received all that came in unto him," xxviii, 30.

BONNET was a covering for the head, worn by the Jewish priests.

BOOK, a writing composed on some point of knowledge by a person intelligent therein, for the instruction or amusement of the reader.

2. Several sorts of materials were formerly used in making books: stone and wood were the first materials employed to engrave such things upon as men were desirous of having transmitted to posterity. The laws of Jehovah were written on tables of stone, and those of Solon on wooden planks. Tables of wood and ivory were common among the ancients: those of wood were very frequently covered with wax, that persons might write on them with more ease, or blot out what they had written. And the instrument used to write with was a piece of iron called a *style*; and hence

the word "style" came to be taken for the composition of the writing. The leaves of the palm tree were afterward used instead of wooden planks, and the finest and thinnest part of the bark of such trees as the lime, ash, maple, and elm; and especially the Egyptian *papyrus*. Hence came the word *liber*, (a book,) which signifies the inner bark of the trees. And as these barks were rolled up in order to be removed with greater ease, each roll was called *volumen*, a volume; a name afterward given to the like rolls of paper or parchment. From the Egyptian papyrus the word *paper* is derived. After this, leather was introduced, especially the skins of goats and sheep. For the king of Per'ga-mus, in collecting his library, was led to the invention of parchment made of those skins. The ancients likewise wrote upon linen.

3. If the ancient books were large, they were formed of a number of skins, of a number of pieces of linen and cotton cloth, or of pa-py'rus, or parchment, connected together. The leaves were rarely written over on both sides, Ezek. ii, 9; Zech. v, 1. Books, when written upon very flexible materials, were rolled around a stick; and if they were very long, around two, from the two extremities. The reader unrolled the book to the place which he wanted, and rolled it up again when he had read it, Luke iv, 17–20; whence the name *a volume*, or thing rolled up. The leaves thus rolled around the stick, which has been mentioned, and bound with a string, could be easily sealed, Isa. xxix, 11; Dan. xii, 4; Rev. v, 1; vi, 7. Those books which were inscribed on tablets of wood, lead, brass, or ivory, were connected together by rings at the back, through which a rod was passed to carry them by.

Books, *Writers of.* The ancients seldom wrote their treatises with their own hand, but dictated them to their freedmen and slaves. A great part of the books of the New Testament was dictated after this custom. St. Paul noted it as a particular circumstance in the Epistle to the Galatians, that he had written it with his own hand, Gal. vi, 11. But he affixed the salutation with his own hand, 2 Thess. iii, 17; 1 Cor. xvi, 21; Col. iv, 18. The a-man-u-en'sis who wrote the Epistle to the Romans, has mentioned himself near the conclusion, Rom. xvi, 22.

Book of Life, or Book of the Living, or Book of the Lord, Psa. lxix, 28. Some have thought it very probable that these descriptive phrases, which are frequent in Scripture, are taken from the custom, observed generally in the courts of princes, of keeping a list of persons who are in their service, of the provinces which they govern, of the officers of their armies, of the number of their troops, and sometimes even of the names of their soldiers. Thus, when it is said that any one is written in the book of life, it means that he particularly belongs to God, and is enrolled among the number of his friends and servants : and to be "blotted out of the book of life," is to be erased from the list of God's friends and servants, as those who are guilty of treachery are struck off the roll of officers belonging to a prince. The most satisfactory explanation of these phrases is, however, that which refers them to the genealogical lists of the Jews, or to the registers kept of the living, from which the names of all the dead were blotted out.

BOOK OF JUDGMENT. Daniel, speaking of God's judgment, says, "The judgment was set, and the books were opened," Dan. vii, 10. This is an allusion to what was practised when a prince called his servants to account. The accounts are produced and examined. It is possible he might allude, also, to a custom of the Persians, among whom it was a constant practice every day to write down the services rendered to the king, and the rewards given to those who had performed them. Of this we see an instance in the history of A-has-u-e'rus and Mor'de-cai, Esth. iv, 12, 34. When, therefore,

the king sits in judgment, the books are opened : he obliges all his servants to reckon with him : he punishes those who have failed in their duty : he compels those to pay who are indebted to him; and he rewards those who have done him services. A similar proceeding will take place at the day of God's final judgment.

SEALED BOOK, mentioned Isa. xxix, 11, and the book sealed with seven seals, in Revelation v, 1–3, are the prophecies of Isaiah and of John, which were written in a book, or roll, after the manner of the ancients, and were sealed, which figure truly signifies that they were mysterious : they had respect to times remote, and to future events; so that a complete knowledge of their meaning could not be obtained till after what was foretold should happen, and the seals, as it were, taken off.

BOOTH, a tent made of poles, and used as a temporary residence.

BOOTY, spoils taken in war, Num. xxxi, 27–32.

BOSOM, the front of the upper part of the body ; the breast. The orientals generally wore long, wide, and loose garments ; and when about to carry any thing away that their hands would not contain, they used for the purpose a fold in the bosom of their robe. To this custom our Lord alludes ;--"Good measure shall men give into your bosoms," Luke vi, 38. Favourites commonly lay in the " bosom of their friends ;" that is, they were placed next below them, John xiii, 23. Hence, to have one in "our bosom" implies kindness, secrecy, intimacy, Gen. xvi, 5; 2 Sam. xii, 8. Christ is in the bosom of the Father; that is, possesses the closest inti-macy, and most perfect knowledge of the Father, John i, 18. Our Saviour is said to carry his lambs in his bosom, which beautifully represents his tender care and watchfulness over them, Isa. xi, 11. See EATING.

BOS'SES, the thickest and strongest parts of a buckler, Job xv, 20.

THE EASTERN BOTTLE.

BOT'TLE. The eastern bottle is made of a goat or kid skin, stripped off without opening the belly: the apertures, made by cutting off the tail and legs, are sewed up, and when filled, it is tied about the neck. On receiving the liquor poured into it, a skin bottle must be greatly swelled and distended; and it must be swelled still farther by the fermentation of the liquor within it, as that advances to ripeness. In this state, if no vent be given to the liquor, it may overpower the strength of the bottle, or it may penetrate by some secret crevice or weaker part. Hence arises the propriety of putting new wine into new bottles, which, being strong, may resist the expansion, the internal pressure of their contents, and preserve the wine in due maturity; while old bottles may, without danger, contain old wine, whose fermentation is already past, Matt. ix, 17; Luke v, 38. Such bottles or vessels of skin are almost universally employed at the present day in travelling in the east.

BOUNDS, *limits.* "Thou hast appointed his bounds," Job, xiv, 5. We are not to understand the *bounds* applying to individuals, but to the race in general. The general term of human life is fixed by God himself: in vain are all attempts to prolong it beyond this term; yet man may so live as never to reach them; for folly and wickedness abridge the term of human life, Psa. lv, 23.

BOW. The expression "to break the bow," so frequent in Scripture, signifies to destroy the power of a people, because the principal offensive weapon of armies was anciently the bow. "A deceitful bow" is one that, from some defect, either in bending or the string, carries the arrow wide of the mark, however well aimed. In 2 Sam. i, 18, we read, "Also he (David) bade them teach the children of Judah *the use of* THE BOW." Here the words "*the use of*," are not in the Hebrew. It should be "teach them the bow," i. e. *the song of* THE BOW, the lamentation over Saul and Jonathan which follows; and which is called, by way of distinction, THE BOW, from the mention of this weapon in verse 22. See ARMOUR.

BOWELS. According to the Jews, the bowels are the seat of mercy, tenderness, and compassion. Joseph's bowels were moved at the sight of his brother Benjamin; that is, he felt himself softened and affected.

BOX TREE, a species of tree, an evergreen.

BRACE'LET, an ornamental chain or clasp, made of various metals, to wear about one's wrist or leg, commonly worn by the oriental princes, as a badge of power and authority. This was probably the reason that the Amalekite brought the bracelet which he found on Saul's arm, along with his crown, to David, 2 Sam. i, 10. It was a royal ornament, and belonged to the regalia of the kingdom. The bracelet was worn both by men and women of different ranks.

BRAMBLE, the raspberry or blackberry bush, or any other prickly shrub. In the Old Testament, the *buckthorn.*

BRANCH, a title of Messiah, Isa. xi, 1. Christ is represented as a slender twig, shooting out from the trunk of an old tree lopped to the very root and decayed, and becoming itself a mighty tree: reference is made, 1. To the kingly dignity of Christ, springing up from the decayed house of David. 2. To the exaltation which was to succeed his humbled condition on earth, and to the glory and vigour of his mediatorial reign.

Covel's Dic.   p. 74.

HIGH PRIEST AND BREASTPLATE.

BRASS. The word *brass* occurs very often in the Bible; but that is a mixed metal, an alloy of copper and zinc, for the making of which we are indebted to the Germans of the thirteenth century. That the ancients knew not the art of making it, is almost certain. None of their writings even hint at the process. There can be no doubt that copper is intended. This is spoken of as known prior to the flood.

BREAD, a term which in Scripture is used, as by us, frequently for food in general; but is also often found in its proper sense. Sparing in the use of flesh, like all the nations of the east, the chosen people usually satisfied their hunger with bread, and quenched their thirst in the running stream. Their bread was generally made of wheat or barley, or lentiles and beans. Bread of wheat flour, as being the most excellent, was preferred; barley bread was used only in times of scarcity and distress.

2. SHEW BREAD was bread offered every Sabbath day upon the golden table in the holy place, Exod. xxv, 30. The Hebrews affirm that these loaves were square, and had four sides, and were covered with leaves of gold. They were twelve in number, according to the number of the twelve tribes, in whose names they were offered. Every loaf was composed of two assarons of flour, which make about five pints and one tenth. These loaves were unleavened. They were presented hot every Sabbath day, the old ones being taken away and eaten by the priests only. This offering was accompanied with salt and frankincense. The twelve loaves, because they stood before the Lord, were called the bread of faces, or of the presence ; and are therefore denominated in our English translation *the shew bread.*

Since part of the frankincense put upon the bread was to be burned on the altar for a memorial, even an offering made by fire unto the Lord ; and since Aaron and his sons were to eat it in the holy place, Lev. xxiv, 5–9, it is probable that this bread typified Christ, first presented as a sacrifice to Jehovah, and then becoming spiritual food to such as in and through him are spiritual priests to God, even his Father, Rev. i, 6; v, 10; xx, 6; 1 Peter ii, 5. It appears from some places in Scripture, (see Exodus xxix, 32, and Numbers vi, 15,) that there was always near the altar a basket full of bread, in order to be offered together with the ordinary sacrifices.

BREAST'PLATE, one part of the priestly vestments, belonging to the Jewish high priests. It was about ten inches square, Exod. xxviii, 13–31; and consisted of a folded piece of the same rich embroidered stuff of which the ephod was made. It was worn on the breast of the high priest, and was set with twelve precious stones, on each of which was engraven the name of one of the tribes. They were set in four rows, three in each row, and were divided from each other by the little golden squares or partitions in which they were set.

This breastplate was fastened at the four corners, those on the top to each shoulder, by a golden hook or ring at the end of a wreathen chain; and those below to the girdle of the ephod, by two strings or ribands, which had likewise two rings or hooks. This ornament was never to be separated from the priestly garment; and it was called the *memorial*, because it was a sign whereby the children of Israel might know that they were presented to God, and that they were had in remembrance by him. It was also called the *breastplate of judgment*, because it contained the divine oracle. See URIM and THUMMIM.

2. BREASTPLATE, a piece of defensive armour to protect the heart. Righteousness, like a breastplate, renders the whole conduct unassailable to any accusation, Eph. vi, 14.

BRIDE, a new married female. The new married woman was considered among the Jews to be a bride for 30 days. It signifies spiritually the *Church of Christ*, Rev. xxi, 9, while the faithful are in this mortal state.

It was the custom among the ancient Greeks, and the nations around them, to conduct the new married couple with torches and lamps to their dwelling. A Jewish marriage seems to have been conducted in much the same way. See Psalm xlv, 12, &c. In the parable of the ten virgins, the same circumstances are introduced. "While the bridegroom tarried," leading the procession through the streets of the city, the women and domestics that were appointed to await his arrival at home, "all slumbered and slept. And at midnight there was a cry made, Behold, the bridegroom cometh! Go ye out to meet him. Then all those virgins arose and trimmed their lamps. And the foolish said unto the wise, Give us of your oil; for our lamps are gone out," Matt. xxv, 6.

Those that were invited to the marriage were expected to appear in their best and gayest attire. If the bridegroom was in circumstances to afford it, wedding garments were prepared for all the guests, which were hung up in the antechamber for them to put on over the rest of their clothes as they entered the apartments where the marriage feast was prepared. To refuse, or even to neglect putting on the wedding garment, was reckoned an insult to the bridegroom; aggravated by the circumstance that it was provided by himself for the very purpose of being worn on that occasion, and was hung up in the way to the inner apartment. This accounts for the severity of the sentence pronounced by the king who came in to see the guests, and found among them one who had neglected to put it on: "And he said unto him, Friend, how camest thou in hither, not having a wedding garment? And he was speechless," Matt. xxii, 11, because it was provided at the expense of the entertainer, and placed full in his view. "Then said the king to the servants, Bind him hand and foot, and take him away, and cast him into outer darkness; there shall be weeping and gnashing of teeth."

BRIER. See THORN.

BRIGANDINE, an ancient kind of mail, or steel net work, worn in battle to secure soldiers from sword cuts.

BRIMSTONE, Gen. xix, 24, a well known substance, extremely inflammable. Fire and brimstone are represented in many passages of Scripture as the elements by which God punishes the wicked; both in this life and another. There is in this a manifest allusion to the overthrow of the cities of the plain by showers of ignited sulphur, to which the physical appearances of the country bear witness to this day. The soil is bituminous, and might be raised by eruptions into the air, and then inflamed and return in horrid showers of overwhelming fire. This awful catastrophe, therefore, stands as a type of the final and eternal punishment of the wicked in another world.

BROOK is distinguished from a river by its flowing only at particular times; for example, after great rains, or the melting of the snow; whereas a river flows constantly at all seasons. However, this distinction is not always observed in the Scripture; and one is not unfrequently taken for the other—the great rivers, such as the Euphrates, the Nile, the Jordan, and others, being called brooks. Thus the Euphrates, Isaiah xv, 7, is called the brook of willows. To deal deceitfully "as a brook," and to "pass away as the stream thereof," is to deceive our friend when he most needs and expects our help and comfort, Job vi, 15; because brooks, being temporary streams, are dried up in the heats of summer, when the traveller most needs a supply of water on his journey.

BROTHER. 1. A brother by the same mother, Matt. iv, 21; xx, 20. 2. A brother, though not by the same mother, Matt. i, 2. 3. A near kinsman, a cousin, Matt. xiii, 55; Mark vi, 3. Observe, that in Matt. xiii, 55, James, and Joses, and Judas, are called the *brethren* of Christ, but were most probably only his cousins by his mother's side; for James and Joses were the sons of Mary, Matt. xxvii, 56; and James and Judas, the sons of Alpheus, Luke vi, 15, 16; which Alpheus is therefore probably the same with Cleopas, the husband of Mary, sister to our Lord's mother, John xix, 25.

BUCK'LER. A defensive piece of armour, of the nature of a shield; and is spoken figuratively of God, and of his truth.

BUILD. Beside the proper and literal signification of this word, it is used with reference to children and a numerous posterity, Job xxii, 23. Building up families, cities, and nations, denotes increasing their number, honour, and power, 1 Chron. xvii, 10.

BUL, the eighth month of the ecclesiastical year of the Jews, and the second month of the civil year. It answers to October, and consists of twenty-nine days. We find the name of this month mentioned in Scripture but once, 1 Kings vi, 38.

BULL, the male of the beeve kind; and it is to be recollected that the Hebrews never castrated animals. This animal was reputed by the Hebrews to be clean, and was generally made use of by them for sacrifices. The Egyptians had a particular veneration for it, and paid divine honors to it; and the Jews imitated them in the worship of the golden calves or bulls, in the wilderness, and in the kingdom of Israel. The wild bull is found in the Syrian and Arabian deserts. Bulls, in a figurative and allegorical sense, are taken for powerful, fierce, and insolent enemies, Psalms xxii, 12; lxviii, 30.

BULRUSH. A plant growing on the banks of the Nile, and in marshy grounds. The stalk rises to the height of six or seven cubits, besides two under water. This stalk is triangular, and terminates in a crown of small filaments resembling hair. This reed, the *Cyperus pa-py'rus* of Linnæus, commonly called "the Egyptian reed," was of the greatest use to the inhabitants of the country where it grew; the pith contained in the stock served them for food, and the woody part for building vessels. For this purpose they made it up, like rushes, into bundles; and, by tying these bundles together, gave their vessels the necessary shape and solidity. "The vessels of bulrushes," or papy'rus, "that are mentioned in sacred and profane history," says Dr. Shaw, "were no other than large fabrics of the same kind with that of Moses, Exod. ii, 3; which, from the late introduction of plank and stronger materials, are now laid aside." These vegetables require much water for their growth; when, therefore, the river on whose banks they grew was reduced, they perished sooner than other plants. This explains Job viii, 11. See RUSH.

BURDEN, a heavy load. The word is commonly used in the prophets for a *disastrous prophecy*. "*Burden of the day*," Matt. xx, 12, expresses the labour and toil, during many hours, especially the meridian heat.

BURI-AL, the interment of a deceased person; an office held so sacred, that they who neglected it have in all nations been held in abhorrence. As soon as the last breath had fled, the nearest relation, or the dearest friend, gave the lifeless body the parting kiss, the last farewell and sign of affection to the departed relative. This was a custom of immemorial antiquity; for the patriarch Jacob had no sooner yielded up his spirit, than his beloved Joseph, claiming for once the right of the first-born, "fell upon his face and kissed him." The parting kiss being given, the company rent their clothes, which was a custom of great antiquity, and the highest expression of grief in the primitive ages. After closing the eyes, the next care was to bind up the face, which it was no more lawful to behold. The next care of surviving friends was to wash the body, probably, that the ointments and perfumes with which it was to be wrapped up, might enter more easily into the pores when opened by warm water. Thus the body of Dorcas was washed, and laid in an upper room. After the body was washed, it was shrouded, and swathed with a linen cloth; and the head was bound about with a napkin. Such were the napkin and grave clothes in which the Saviour was buried.

2. The body was sometimes embalmed. They wrapped up the body with sweet spices and odours, without extracting the brain, or removing the bowels. This is the way in which it was proposed to embalm the lifeless body of our Saviour; which was prevented by his resurrection. The meaner sort of people seem to have been interred in their grave clothes without a coffin. In this manner was the sacred body of our Lord committed to the tomb. The body was sometimes placed upon a bier, which bore some resemblance to a coffin or bed, in order to be carried out to burial. Upon one of these was carried forth the widow's son of Nain, whom our compassionate Lord raised to life, and restored to his mother.

3. The Israelites committed the dead to their native dust; and from the Egyptians, probably, borrowed the practice of burning many spices at their funerals. "They buried Asa in his own sepulchres, which he made for himself in the city of David, and laid him in the bed which was filled with sweet odours, and divers kinds of spices, prepared by the apothecaries' art; and they made a very

great burning for him," 2 Chron. xvi, 14. Thus the Old Testament historian entirely justifies the account which the evangelist gives of the quantity of spices with which the sacred body of Christ was swathed. Why then should it be reckoned incredible, that Nicodemus brought of myrrh and aloes about a hundred pounds' weight, to embalm the body of Jesus?

4. The funeral procession was attended by professional mourners, eminently skilled in the art of lamentation, whom the friends and relations of the deceased hired, to assist them in expressing their sorrow. The children in the streets through which they passed often suspended their sports to imitate the sounds, and joined with equal sincerity in the lamentations, Matt. xi, 17. Music was afterward introduced to aid the voices of the mourners: the trumpet was used at the funerals of the great, and the small pipe or flute for those of meaner condition. Such were the minstrels whom our Lord found in the house of Jairus, making so great a noise round the bed on which the dead body of his daughter lay. The noise and tumult of these retained mourners, and the other attendants, appear to have begun immediately after the person expired. It is evident that this sort of mourning and lamentation was a kind of art among the Jews: "Wailing shall be in the streets; and they shall call such as are skilful of lamentation to wail," Amos v, 16. To the dreadful noise and tumult of the hired mourners, the following passage of Jeremiah indisputably refers, and shows the custom to be derived from a very remote antiquity: "Call for the mourning women, that they may come; and send for cunning women, that they may come, and let them make haste, and take up a wailing for us, that our eyes may run down with tears, and our eyelids gush out with waters," Jer. ix, 17. See *Sepulchres.*

BUSHEL is used in our English version to express a measure of capacity among tha Jews, containing about a peck, Matt. v, 15.

BUTTER is taken in Scripture, as it has been almost perpetually in the east, for cream or liquid butter. "He asked water, and she gave him milk; she brought forth butter in a lordly dish," Judges iv, 19; v, 25. The word which our translators rendered *butter,* properly signifies *cream;* which is undoubtedly the meaning of it in this passage: for Sisera complained of thirst, and asked a little water to quench it;—a purpose to which butter is but little adapted. Yet it is plain from Prov. xxx, 33, that churning butter was not unknown in Judea. Whether the milk was agitated in a skin, as is the custom at present among the Moors and Arabs, or otherwise, we know not. To *wash one's steps with butter* is to enjoy great and delightful prosperity, Job xxix, 6. In Isaiah vii, 15, butter and honey are mentioned as food which, in Egypt and other places in the East, is in use to this day. The butter and honey are mixed, and the bread is then dipped in it.

CAB, a Hebrew measure, containing three pints and one-third.

CA'BUL, the name which Hiram, king of Tyre, gave to the twenty cities in the land of Galilee, of which Solomon made him a present, in acknowledgment for his great services in building the temple, 1 Kings ix, 13.

CÆ'-SAR, a title borne by all the Roman emperors. In Scripture, the reigning emperor is generally mentioned by the name of Cæsar, without expressing any other distinction. The Cæsars mentioned in the New Testament are, Augustus, (Luke ii, 1;) Tiberius, (Luke iii, 1;) Claudius, (Acts xi, 28;) Nero, (Acts xxv, 8;) but Ca-lig'u-la, who succeeded Tiberius, is not mentioned.

CÆS-A-RE'A, a city and port of Palestine, 62 miles northwest of Jerusalem, built by Herod the Great, and thus called in honour of Augustus Cæsar. It was on the site of the tower of *Strato.* This city is often mentioned in the New Testament. When Judea was reduced to the state of a

Roman province, Cæsarea became the stated residence of the proconsul, which accounts for the circumstance of Paul being carried thither from Jerusalem, to defend himself. It is now deserted and desolate.

CÆS-A-RE'A PHIL-IP'PI was first called Laish or Le'shem, Judges xviii, 7. After it was subdued by the Danites, it received the name of Dan. Philip, the youngest son of Herod the Great, made it the capital of his tetrarchy, enlarged and embellished it, and gave it the name of Cæsare'a Philippi. It was situated at the foot of Mount Hermon, near the head of the Jordan; and was about fifty miles from Damascus, and thirty from Tyre. Our Saviour visited and taught in this place, and healed one who was possessed of an evil spirit: here also he gave the memorable rebuke to Peter. Mark viii.

CAI'A-PHAS, (Ca-e'-a-phas,) high priest of the Jews, succeeded Simon, son of Camith; and after possessing this dignity nine years, from A. D. 25 to 34, he was succeeded by Jonathan, son of Ananas, or Annas. He married a daughter of Annas, who also is called high priest in the gospel, because he had long enjoyed that dignity. When the priests deliberated on the seizure and death of Jesus Christ, Caiaphas declared that there was no room for debate on that matter,

6

John xi, 49, 50. When Judas had betrayed Jesus, he was first taken before Annas, who sent him to his son-in-law, Caiaphas, who possibly lived in the same house, John xviii, 24.

Two years after this, Vitellus, governor of Syria, coming to Jerusalem at the passover, deposed the high priest Caiaphas. From this it appears that Caiaphas had fallen under popular odium, for his deposition was to gratify the people.

CAIN, the eldest son of Adam and Eve. He was the first man who had been a child, and the first man born of woman. The face of the earth from which Cain was driven, means, probably, from his own native district, and from the presence of his kindred.

CAKE, a composition of flour, butter, or other ingredients, baked in a small mass; and among the ancients under the ashes.

CALAMUS, an aromatic reed, growing in most places in Egypt, in Judea near lake Ge-nes'a-reth, and in several parts of Syria. It grows to about two feet in height; bearing from the root a knotted stalk, quite round, containing in its cavity a soft white pith. The whole is of an agreeable aromatic smell; and the plant is said to scent the air with a fragrance even while growing. When cut down, dried, and powdered, it makes an ingredient in the richest perfumes. It was used for this purpose by the Jews.

CALF, the young of the ox kind. There is frequent mention in Scripture of calves, because they were made use of commonly in sacrifices. The "fatted calf" was stall-fed, with special reference to a particular festival or extraordinary sacrifice. The "calves of the lips," Hosea xiv, 2, signify the sacrifices of praise which the captives of Babylon addressed to God. The "golden calf" was an idol set up and worshipped by the Israelites at the foot of Mount Sinai, in their passage through the wilderness to the land of Canaan. The image is supposed to have been like the Egyptian deity, *Apis*, which was an ox, an animal used in agriculture, and so a symbol of the god who presided over their fields, or of the productive power of the Deity. It is plain, from Aaron's proclaiming a fast to Jehovah, Exod. xxxii, 4, and from the worship of Jeroboam's calves being so expressly distinguished from that of Baal, 2 Kings x, 28-31, that both Aaron and Jeroboam meant the calves they formed and set up for worship to be *emblems* of Jehovah.

CALL, to name a person or thing, Acts xi, 26; Rom. vii, 3. *To be called*, according to the Hebrew manner of speaking, means that the person spoken of shall really be what he is called, and actually fulfil that title. Thus, Isa. ix, 6, He shall be truly the Wonderful, the mighty God, &c., Luke i, 35. To call any thing by its name is an act of authority: the father names his son: "God calleth the stars by their names," Psa. cxlvii, 4. 2. To cry to another for help; and hence, to pray: Gen. iv, 26, "Then began men to call on the name of the Lord;" the meaning of which seems to be, that they then first began to worship him in public assemblies. In both the Old and New Testament, to call upon the name of the Lord, imports invoking the true God in prayer. In this view the phrase is applied to the worship of Christ.

3. "To call" signifies to invite to the blessings of the Gospel, to offer salvation through Christ, either by God himself, or, under his appointment, by his servants. "Calling" has reference to those parables of our Lord in which the Gospel is represented under the figure of a royal feast, to which numerous guests are invited. Those who accept the invitation, and are received by the master of the feast, are denominated THE CALLED, or invited, by way of eminence, and thus, rather than from military levies, or any other custom, was the term brought into the common theological language of the early Church. The great invitation to the free partici-

pation of evangelical blessings was, under the authority and in the name of Christ, made by the apostles and first preachers to *all nations*, without distinction; and those who embraced it were eminently *the called of Christ Jesus*.

"Whom he did predestinate, them he also *called*; and whom he *called*, them he also justified; and whom he justified, them he also glorified," Rom. viii, 30. The context declares that those who are foreknown and predestinated to eternal glory are true believers, those who "love God," as stated in a subsequent verse; for of such only the apostle speaks; and when he adds, "Moreover, whom he did predestinate, them he also called; and whom he called, them he also justified; and whom he justified, them he also glorified;" he shows in particular how the Divine purpose to glorify believers is carried into effect through all its stages. The great instrument of bringing men to "love God" is the Gospel; they are, therefore, *called*, invited by it, to this state and benefit; the calling being obeyed, they are *justified*; and being justified, and continuing in that state of grace, they are *glorified*. Nothing, however, is here said to favour the conclusion, that many others who were *called* by the Gospel, but refused, might not have been justified and glorified as well as they; nothing to distinguish this calling into common and effectual : and the very guilt which those are everywhere represented as contracting who despised the Gospel calling, shows that they reject a grace which is sufficient, and sincerely intended, to save them.

CAL'NEH, a city in the land of Shi'nar, built by Nimrod, Gen. x, 10. It is believed to be the same with Calno, Isa. x, 9.

CALVARY, or, as it is called in Hebrew, *Golgotha*, " a skull," or "place of skulls," supposed to be thus denominated from the similitude it bore to the figure of a skull or man's head, or from its being a place of burial. It was a small eminence or hill to the northwest of Jerusalem, upon which our Lord was crucified. The ancient summit of Calvary has been much altered, by reducing its level in some parts, and raising it in others, in order to bring it within the area of a large and irregular building, called " The Church of the Holy Sepulchre," which now occupies its site.

CAMEL. This animal is very common in Arabia, Judea, and the neighbouring countries ; and is often mentioned in Scripture, and reckoned among the most valuable property, 1 Chron. v, 21 ; Job i, 3, &c. " No creature," says Volney, "seems so peculiarly fitted to the climate in which he exists as the camel. Designing this animal to dwell in a country where

he can find little nourishment, nature has been sparing of her materials in the whole of his formation. So great is the importance of the camel to the desert, that, were it deprived of that useful animal, it must infallibly lose every inhabitant." The chief use of the camel has always been as a beast of burden, and for performing journeys across the deserts. They have sometimes been used in war, to carry the baggage of an oriental army, and mingle in the tumult of the battle, 1 Sam. xxx, 17. Matt. xix, 24 contains a proverb which, among the Jews, signified a thing impossible.

CA-ME'LE-ON a kind of lizard usually of a greenish-yellow colour; capable of making a number of variations in its appearance.

CAMEL'S HAIR, an article of clothing. There is a coarse cloth made of camel's hair in the east, which is used for manufacturing the coats of shepherds and camel drivers, and also for the covering of tents. It was doubtless this coarse kind which was used by John.

CAMP, the disposition of an army for the purpose of rest, 1 Sam. iv, 7. Nothing could be more exactly regulated than the camp of the Hebrews in the desert. The tents were so arranged as to enclose the tabernacle in the form of a square, and each under one general standard. There were forty-one en-

campments, from their first in tho month of March, at Ram'e-scs, in the land of Goshen, in Egypt, and in the wilderness, until they reached the land of Canaan. They are enumerated in Num. xxxiii.

n the second year after their exodus from Egypt they were numbered, and, upon an exact poll, the number of their males amounted to 603,550, from twenty years old and upward, Num. i, ii. This vast mass of people, encamped in beautiful order, must have presented a most imposing spectacle.

CAM'PHIRE, or gum camphor, a substance, used as a medicine, obtained from a tree of the laurel species growing in Japan. But the camphire mentioned Cant. i, 14, and iv, 13, is an odoriferous shrub, common in the Isle of Cyprus, where it is called *Henna*. This is one of the plants which is most grateful to the eye and the smell. The deep colour of its bark, the light green of its foliage, the softened mixture of white and yellow with which the flowers, collected into long clusters like the lilac, are coloured; the red tint of the ramifications which support them, form an agreeable combination. The flowers, whose shades are so delicate, diffuse around the sweetest odours, and embalm the gardens and apartments which they embellish. The women take pleasure in decking themselves with them.

CA'NA, a town of Galilee, in the tribe of Zebulun, not far from Nazareth.

CA'NAAN, (*Ca'nan*,) the son of Ham. The Hebrews believe that Canaan, having first discovered Noah's nakedness, told his father Ham; and that Noah, when he awoke, having understood what had passed, cursed Canaan, the first author of the offence. Others are of opinion that Ham was punished in his son Canaan, Gen. ix, 25.

The posterity of Canaan was numerous. His eldest son, Si'don, founded the city of Sidon, and was father of the Sidonians and Phenicians. Canaan had ten other sons, who were fathers of as many tribes, dwelling in Palestine and Syria: namely, the Hittites, the Jebusites, the Amorites, the Gir'gasites, the Hivites, the Arkites, the Sinites, the Arvadites, the Zemarites, and the Hemathites. It is believed that Canaan lived and died in Palestine, which from him was called the land of Canaan.

CANAAN, LAND OF. In the map it presents the appearance of a narrow slip of country, extending along the eastern coast of the Mediterranean; from which, to the river Jordan, the utmost width does not exceed fifty miles. This river was the eastern boundary of the land of Canaan, or Palestine, properly so called, which derived its name from the Philistines or Palestines originally inhabiting the coast. To three of the twelve tribes, however, Reuben, Gad, and Ma-nas'-seh, portions of territory were assigned on the eastern side of the river, which were afterward extended by the subjugation of the neighbouring nations. The territory of Tyre and Sidon was its ancient border on the northwest; the range of the Libanus and Antilibanus forms a natural boundary on the north and northeast; while in the south it is pressed upon by the Syr'i-an and Arabian deserts. Within this circumscribed district, such were the physical advantages of the soil and climate, there existed, in the happiest periods of the Jewish nation, an immense population. The kingdom of David and Solomon, however, extended far beyond these narrow limits.

Damascus revolted during the reign of Solomon, and shook off the Jewish yoke. At his death ten of the tribes revolted under Jeroboam, and the country became divided into the two rival kingdoms of Judah and Israel, having for their capitals Jerusalem and Samaria.

2. At the time of the Christian era, Palestine was divided. into five provinces: Jude'a, Sa-mar'ia, Galilee, Pere'a, and Id-u-me'a. On the death of Herod, Archela'us, his eldest son, succeeded to the government of Judea, Samaria, and Idumea, with the title of tetrarch; Galilee being assigned to Herod Antipas, and Perea, or the country beyond Jordan, to the third brother, Philip. But in less than ten years the dominions of Archelaus became annexed, on his disgrace, to the Roman province of Syria: and Judea was thenceforth governed by Roman procurators.

3. A few additional remarks upon the topography and climate will tend to elucidate the force of many of those parts of Scripture which contain allusions to these topics. The hills of Judea frequently rise into mountains, the most considerable of which are those of Lebanon and Hermon, on the north; those which surround the Sea of Galilee, and the Dead Sea, also retain a respectable elevation. The other mountains of note are Carmel, Tabor, E'bal, and Ger'i-zim, and the mountains of Gilboa, Gilead, and Ab'a-rim; with the summits of the latter, Nebo and Pisgah: a description of which will be found under their respective heads. Many of the hills and rocks abound in caverns, the refuge of the distressed or the resorts of robbers.

4. From the paucity of rain which falls in Judea, and the heat and dryness of the atmosphere for the greater part of the year, it possesses but few rivers; and as these have all their rise within 'ts boun-

daries, their course is short, and their size inconsiderable : the principal is the Jordan, which runs about a hundred and thirty miles. The other remarkable streams are the Arnon, the Jabbok, the Ki'-shon, the Ke'dron, the Be'sor, the So'rek, and the stream called the River of Egypt. These, also, will be found described under their respective heads. This country was once adorned with woods and forests; as we read of the forest of cedars in Lebanon, the forest of oaks in Bashan, the forest or wood of Ephraim, and the forest of Ha'reth in the tribe of Judah. Of these, the woods of Bashan alone remain ; the rest have been swept away by the ravages of 'time and of armies, and by the gradual consumption of the inhabitants, whose indolence and ignorance have prevented their planting others.

5. The climate of Judea, from the southern latitude of the country, is necessarily warm. The cold of winter is, indeed, sometimes greater than in European climates situated some degrees farther to the north; but it is of short duration, and the general character of the climate is that of heat. Both heat and cold are, however, tempered by the nature of the surface ; the winter being scarcely felt in the valleys, while in the summer the heat is almost insupportable ; and, on the contrary, in the more elevated parts, during the winter months, or rather weeks, frosts frequently occur, and snow sometimes falls, while the air in summer is comparatively cool and refreshing. Many winters pass without either snow or frost ; and in the coldest weather which ever occurs, the sun in the middle of the day is generally warm, and often hot; so that the pain of cold is in reality but little felt.

6. Rain only falls during the autumn, winter, and spring, when it sometimes descends with great violence : the greatest quantity, and that which properly constitutes the rainy season, happening between the autumnal equinox, or somewhat later, and the beginning of December; during which period heavy clouds often obscure the sky, and several days of violent rain sometimes succeed each other with winds. This is what in Scripture is termed the early or the former rain. Showers continue to fall at uncertain intervals with some cloudy but more fair weather, till toward the vernal equinox, when they become again more frequent and copious till the middle of April. These are the latter rains, Joel ii, 23.

Hail frequently falls in the winter and spring in very heavy storms, and with hail-stones of an enormous size. Dr. Russel says that he has seen some at Aleppo which measured two inches in dia meter; but sometimes they are found to consist of irregularly shaped pieces, weighing near three ounces. The copious dew forms another peculiarity of this climate, frequently alluded to in Scripture: so copious, indeed, is it sometimes, as to resemble small rain, and to supply the wants of superficial vegetation. Mr. Maundrell, when travelling near Mount Hermon, says, "We were instructed by experience what the psalmist means by 'the dew of Hermon,' Psa. cxxxiii, 3; our tents being as wet with it as if it had rained all night."

CA'-NAAN-ITES, the posterity of Canaan by his eleven sons, who are suppposed to have settled in the land of Canaan, soon after the dispersion of Babel. Five of these are known to have dwelt in the land of Canaan; viz., Heth, Je'bus, He'mor or A'mor, Gir'ga-shi, and Hevi or Hivi; and these, together with their father Canaan, became the heads of so many nations.

When the measure of the idolatries and abominations of the Canaanites was filled up, God delivered their country into the hands of the Israelites, who conquered it under Joshua. However, they resisted with obstinate valour, and kept Joshua employed six years from the time of his passing the river Jordan, and entering Canaan, in the year B. C. 1451, to the year B. C. 1445, the sabbatical year beginning from the autumnal equinox; when he made a division of the land among the tribes of Israel, and rested from his conquests.

The Canaanites were destroyed for their wickedness. This is plain from Lev. xviii, 24, &c. Now the facts disclosed in this passage sufficiently testify that the Canaanites were a wicked people; that detestable practices were general among them, and even habitual; that it was for these enormities the nations of Canaan were destroyed. It was not, as some have imagined, to make way for the Israelites; nor was it simply to make away with their idolatry; but it was because of the abominable crimes which usually accompanied the latter.

Another reason which made this destruction both more necessary, and more general, than it would have otherwise been, was the consideration, that if any of the old inhabitants were left, they would prove a snare to those who succeeded them in the country; would draw and seduce them by degrees into the vices and corruptions which prevailed among themselves. Vices of all kinds, but vices more particularly of the licentious kind, are astonishingly infectious. A little leaven leaveneth the whole lump. A small number of persons addicted to them, and allowed to practise them with impunity or encouragement, will spread them throughout the whole mass. This reason is formally and expressly assigned, not simply for the punishment, but for the extent to which it was carried; namely, extermination: "Thou shalt utterly destroy them, that. they teach you not to do after all their abominations, which they have done unto their gods."

CANDACE, the name of an Ethiopian queen. Candace was the common name of the queens of that country.

CANKER WORM, a worm destructive to trees or plants The insect signified by the Hebrew is not known; perhaps a species of beetle.

CA-PERN'A-UM stood on the coast of the Sea of Galilee, in the borders of Zebulun and Naph'talim, Matt. iv, 15, and consequently toward the upper part of it. As it was a convenient port from Galilee to any place on the other side of the sea, this might be our Lord's inducement to make it the place of his most constant residence.

CAP-PA-DO'CI-A, a region of Asia south of Pontus.

CAPTIVITY, the abridgment of one's liberty by the rights of war. God generally punished the sins of the Jews by captivities; the most remarkable are the As-syr'i-an and Babylonish captivities. In the year B C. 717, Shalman-e'ser took and destroyed Samaria, after a siege of three years, and transplanted the tribes that had been spared by Tiglath-pileser, to provinces beyond the Euphrates. 2 Kings xviii, 10, 11. It is generally believed there was no return of the ten tribes from this captivity. But when we examine carefully the writings of the prophets, we find a return of at least a great part of Israel from the captivity clearly pointed out, Amos ix, 14; Obad. x, 18, 19; Isa. xi, 12, 13.

The captivities of Judah are generally reckoned four: the first, B. C. 602, under King Jehoiakim, when Daniel and others were carried to Babylon; and the last in the year B. C. 584, under Zedekiah, from which period begins the captivity of seventy years, foretold by the Prophet Jeremiah. Dr. Hales computes that the first of these captivities, which he thinks formed the commencement of the Babylonish captivity, took place in the year before Christ 605. The Jews were removed to Babylon by Nebuchadnezzar. Cyrus, in the year B. C. 543, and in the first year of his reign at Babylon, permitted the Jews to return to their own country, Ezra i, 1. However, they did not obtain leave to rebuild the temple; and the completion of those prophecies which foretold the termination of their captivity, after seventy years, was not till the year B. C. 514.

CARBUNCLE, the name of a precious stone of a *deep red colour :* but the stone signified by the Hebrew is not known. See *Precious Stones.*

CARMEL, a celebrated range of hills running northwest from the plain of Esdraelon,and ending in the promontory which forms the Bay of Acre. The foot of the northern part approaches the water, so that seen from the hills northeast from Acre, Carmel appears as if "dipping his feet in the western sea."

This mountain, according to travellers, well deserves its Hebrew name, which signifies *" an orchard or garden of trees."*

The most beautiful mountain in Palestine, of great length, and in many parts covered with wild odoriferous plants and flowers. Isaiah speaks of the *"excellency of Carmel."*

From the graceful form and verdant beauty of its summit, the head of the bride (Song vii, 5) is compared to Carmel. It is said that this mountain contains more than a thousand caves; that many, fleeing from punishment, might "hide themselves in the top of Carmel," Amos ix, 3. These, in very ancient times, were the resort and dwelling of prophets, and other religious persons :— hence Elijah and Elisha often resorted thither. This is also the name of a city of Judah, ten miles east of He-

bron, on a mountain of the same name.

CARNAL, fleshly, sensual. Wicked or unconverted men are represented as under the domination of a "carnal mind, which is enmity against God," and which must issue in death, Rom. viii, 6, 7. Worldly enjoyments are *carnal,* because they only minister to the wants and desires of the *animal* part of man, Romans xv, 27; 1 Cor. ix, 11. The ceremonial parts of the Mosaic dispensation were *carnal;* they related immediately to the *bodies* of men and beasts, Heb. vii, 16; ix, 10. The weapons of a Christian's warfare are not *carnal;* they are not of human origin, nor are they directed by human wisdom, 2 Cor. x, 4.

CART, a machine used in Palestine to force the corn out of the ear, and bruise the straw, Isaiah xxviii, 27, 28. The wheels of these carts were low, broad, and shod with iron, and were drawn over the sheaves spread on the floor, by means of oxen.

CASSIA, (*cash'ia,*) a species of *launus,* the bark of which usually passes under the name of *Cinnamon.*

CAS'TOR and POL'LUX. It is said that the vessel which carried Paul to Rome had the *sign* of Castor and Pollux, Acts xxviii, 11. Castor and Pollux were sea gods, and invoked by sailors. It is to be observed that St. Luke does not mention the name, but the *sign*, of the ship. By the word *sign*, the sacred writer meant the image of the deity to whom the vessel was in some sort consecrated, carried upon its *bow*, which served to distinguish it from all others.

CATH'O-LIC denotes what is general or universal.

Epistles are called catholic because directed to Christian converts generally, and not to any particular Church.

CAUSEWAY, a way raised above the natural level, serving as a dry passage over wet ground.

CAVES, or CAVERNS. The country of Judea, being mountainous and rocky, is in many parts full of caverns, to which allusions frequently occur in the Old Testament. At Engedi, in particular, there was a cave so large that David, with six hundred men, hid themselves in the sides of it, and Saul entered the mouth of the cave without perceiving that any one was there, 1 Sam. xxiv.

CE'DAR, a large and noble evergreen tree. Its lofty height, and its far extended branches, afford a spacious shade, Ezek. xxxi, 3, 6, 8. The wood is very valuable; of a reddish colour, of an aromatic smell, and reputed incorruptible. This is owing to its bitter taste, which the worms cannot endure, and to its resin, which preserves it from the injuries of the weather. The ark of the covenant, and much of the Temple of Solomon, and that of Di-a'na at Ephesus, were built of cedar. The tree is much celebrated in Scripture. It is called, "the glory of Lebanon," Isa. lx, 13. On that mountain it must in former times have flourished in great abundance. There are some cedars still growing there. The American missionaries, Fisk and King, state, that the handsomest and tallest are those of two or three feet in diameter, the body straight, the branches almost horizontal, forming a beautiful cone, and about ninety feet in height. The tree bears a small cone like that of the pine.

CE'DRON, See KED'RON.

CEN-CHRE'A, (*Sen-kre'a*,) a port of Corinth, whence Paul sailed for Ephesus, Acts xviii, 18. It was situated on the eastern side of the isthmus, about nine miles from the city. The other port, on the western side of the isthmus, was Let chœ'um.

CEN'SER, a fire pan in which fire and incense were carried in certain parts of the Hebrew worship.

CEN-TU'RI-ON, an officer in the Roman army, who, as the term indicates, had the command of a hundred men, usually stationed in the towns of the Roman provinces to preserve order.

CE'PHAS, a *rock*. See PETER.

CHAFF, the refuse of winnowed corn. The ungod

ly are represented as the chaff, a simile most forcible and appropriate. Whatever defence they may afford to the saints, who are the wheat, they are in themselves worthless and inconsistent, easily driven about with false doctrines, and will ultimately be driven away by the blast of God's wrath, Psalm i, 4; Matt. iii, 12, &c., False doctrines are called *chaff;* they are unproductive, and cannot abide the trial of the word and Spirit of God, Jer. xxiii, 28.

CHAL'CE-DO-NY, a precious stone, in colour like a car'buncle.

CHAL-DE'A, or Babylonia, the country lying on both sides of the Euphrates, of which Babylon was the capital; and extending southward to the Persian Gulf, and northward into Mes-o-po-ta'-mi-a, at least as far as Ur, which is called Ur of the Chaldees. This country had also the name of Shi'nar. See BABYLON.

CHAL-DE'ANS. This word is taken, 1. For the people of Chal-de'a and the subjects of that empire generally. 2. For philosophers, naturalists, or soothsayers; whose principal employment was the study of mathematics and astrology; by which they pretended to foreknow the destiny of men born under certain constellations.

CHAMBER. See UPPER ROOM.

CHAMBERLAIN, a stew-ard or treasurer, one that manages the affairs of another.

CHAMOIS, (*Shamme,*) an animal of the goat kind.

CHANT, to repeat words in a kind of singing tone of voice, Amos vi, 6. To sing in concert.

CHARGER, a large dish, a salver or waiter.

CHAPITER, an ornamental finish to the top of a pillar.

CHARIOTS of war. The Scripture speaks of two sorts of these chariots, one for princes and generals to ride in, the other used to break the enemies' battalions, by letting them loose armed with iron, which made dreadful havoc among the troops. The most ancient chariots of which we have any notice are Pharaoh's, which were overwhelmed in the Red Sea, Exodus xiv, 7. As Judea was a very mountainous country, chariots could be of no great use there, except in the plains; and the Hebrews often evaded them by fighting on the mountains. The kings of the Hebrews, when they went to war were themselves generally mounted in chariots, from which they fought and issued their orders; and there was always a second chariot empty, which followed each of them, that if the first was broken he might ascend the other, 2 Chron, xxxv, 24.

CHARITY, considered as a Christian grace, ought in our translation, in order to avoid mistake, to have been translated *love.* It is the love of God, and the love of our neighbour flowing from the love of God; and is described with wonderful copiousness, felicity, and even grandeur, by St. Paul, 1 Cor. xiii; a portion of Scripture which, as it shows the habitual temper of a true Christian, cannot be too frequently referred to for self-examination, and ought to be constantly present to us as our rule. 2. In the popular sense, charity is alms-giving; a duty of practical Christianity which is solemnly enjoined, and to which special promises are annexed.

CHARMER, one who, by incantation, subdues and controls some opposing enemy or influence.

CHE'BAR, a river of Chaldea, which runs through Mesopota'mia, to the south-west, and falls into the Euphrates.

CHE'DOR-LA-O'MER, a king of the Elamites, who were either Persians, or people bordering upon the Persians, Gen. xiv.

CHEM'A-RIM. By this word the best commentators understand the *priests of false gods*, and in particular the worshippers of fire.

CHE'MOSH, an idol of the Moabites, Num. xxi, 29.

CHER'ETH-IM, or Cher'-eth-ites, are denominations for the Philistines. It may be inferred that guards were called Cherethites, because they went with David into Philistia, where they continued with him all the time he was under the protection of A'chish. It is not uncommon for soldiers to derive their names, not from the place of their nativity, but of their residence.

CHER'UB, plural cherubim. It appears from Gen. iii, 24, that this is a name given to angels; but whether it is the name of a distinct class of celestials, or designates the same order as the seraphim, we have no means of determining. But the term *cherubim* generally signifies those figures which Moses was commanded to make and place at each end of the mercy seat, and which covered the ark with expanded wings in the most holy place of the Jewish tabernacle and temple. See Exodus xxv, 18, 19. The original meaning of the term, and the shape or form of these, any farther than that they were "winged creatures," is not certainly known. The opinion of most critics, taken, it seems, from Ezek. i, 9, 10, is, that they were figures composed of parts of various creatures; as a man, a lion, an ox, an eagle. But certainly we have no decided proof that the figures placed in the holy of holies, in the tabernacle, were of the same form with those described by Ezekiel.

The cherubim of the sanctuary were two in number; one at each end of the mercy seat; which, with the ark, was placed exactly in the middle, between the north and south sides of the tabernacle

It was here that atonement was made, Lev. xvi, 14; the glory of God appeared, and from hence he gave forth his oracles; whence the whole holy place was called *the oracle*. These cherubim, it must be observed, had feet whereon they stood, 2 Chron. iii, 13; and their feet were joined, in one continued beaten work, to the ends of the mercy seat, so that they were wholly over or above it. Those in the tabernacle were of beaten gold, being but of small dimensions, Exod. xxv, 18; but those in the temple of Solomon were made of the wood of the olive tree, overlaid with gold; for they were very large, extending their wings to the whole breadth of the oracle, which was twenty cubits, 1 Kings vi, 23–28; 2 Chron. iii, 10–13. They are called "cherubim of glory," because they had the glory of God, or the glorious symbol of his presence, "the Shechinah," resting between them. *As this glory abode in the inward tabernacle, and as the figures of the cherubim represented the angels who surround the manifestation of the Divine presence in the world above, that tabernacle was rendered a fit image of the court of heaven, in which light it is considered everywhere in the Epistle to the Hebrews. See chapters iv, 14; viii, 1; ix, 8, 9, 23, 24; xii, 22, 23.

CHIEF CAPTAIN, a Roman officer, and commander of a thousand men; a colonel.

CHILD. See Son.

CHIOS, now called Scio, an island of Greece, famous for the massacre of a great number of its inhabitants in the late revolution, by the Turks.

CHIS'LEU, the third month of the Jewish civil year, and the ninth of their sacred, answering to our November and December, Neh. i, 1. It contains thirty days.

CHITTIM, is the island of *Cyprus*, so called from the Phenician colony *Citium*, in the southern part of this island; but the name *Chittim* was at a later period employed also in a wider sense, to designate other *islands* and *countries* adjacent to the coasts of the Mediterranean.

CHIUN, (*ky'un*,) the name of a god worshipped by the Israelites in the desert. Some suppose it to be Sa'turn.

CHO-RA'ZIN, a town in Galilee, near to Cap-er'na-um, not far distant from Beth-sai'-da, and consequently on the western shore of the Sea of Galilee.

CHRIST, an appellation synonymous with Messiah, which signifies *anointed*. The names of Messiah and Christ were originally derived from the ceremony of anointing, by which the kings and the high priests of God's people, and sometimes the prophets, 1 Kings xix, 16, were consecrated and admitted to the exercise of their functions; for all these functions were accounted holy among the Israelites. But the most eminent application of the word is to that illustrious personage, typified and predicted from the beginning, who is described by the prophets under the character of God's Anointed, the Messiah, or the Christ.

CHRISTIAN, a follower of the religion of Christ. It is probable that the name of Christian, like that of Nazarenes and Galileans, was given to the disciples of our Lord in reproach or contempt. Some have indeed thought that this name was given by the disciples to themselves; others, that it was imposed on them by Divine authority; in either of which cases surely we should have met with it in the subsequent history of the Acts, and in the apostolic epistles, all of which were written some years after; whereas it is found but in two more places in the New Testament, Acts xxvi, 28, where a Jew is the speaker, and in 1 Pet. iv, 16, where reference appears to be made to the name as imposed upon them by their enemies. They were denominated Christians, A. D. 42 or 43; and though the name was first given reproachfully, they gloried in it, as expressing their adherence to Christ, and they soon generally assumed it.

CHRONICLES, Books of. This name is given to two historical books of Scripture, They were compiled, and probably by Ezra, from the ancient chronicles of the kings of Judah and Israel, and they may be considered as a kind of supplement to the preceding books of Scripture. The first book of Chronicles contains a great variety of genealogical tables, the death of Saul, and a history of the reign of David. The second book of Chronicles contains a brief sketch of the Jewish history, from the accession of Solomon to the return from the Babylonian captivity, being a period of four hundred and eighty years; and in both these books we find many particulars not noticed in the other historical books of Scripture.

CHRYS'O-LITE, a precious stone of a golden colour, with a mixture of green, which displays a fine lustre. It is transparent, and supposed to be a species of the topaz.

CHRYS'O-PRA-SUS, a precious stone. Its colour was green, inclining to gold, as its name imports.

CHUB probably signifies the *Cubians*.

CHURCH, the collective body of Christians, or all those over the face of the earth who profess to believe in Christ, and acknowledge him to be the Saviour of mankind; this is called the visible Church. But by the word *Church*, we are more strictly to understand the whole body of God's true people, in every period of time: this is the invisible or spiritual Church. The people of God on earth are called the church militant, and those in heaven the Church triumphant. It is common with divines to speak of the Jewish and the Christian Churches, as though they were two distinct and totally different things. The Christian Church is not another Church, but the very same that was before the coming of Christ, having the same faith with it, and interested in the same covenant. Great alterations indeed were made in the outward state and condition of the Church, by the coming of the Messiah. The ordinances of worship suited to that state of things then expired, and came to an end. New ordinances of worship were appointed, suitable to the new light and grace which were then bestowed upon the Church. The Gentiles came into the faith of Abraham along with the Jews, being made joint partakers with them in his blessing. But none of these things, nor the whole collectively, did make such an alteration in the Church, but that it was still one and the same. The olive tree was still the same, only some branches were broken off, and others grafted into it. The Jews fell, and the Gentiles came in their room.

2. By the Church we sometimes understand an assembly of Christians united together, and meeting in one place, for the solemn worship of God.

3. Church members are those who compose or belong to the visible Church. As to the real Church, the true members of it are such as come out from the world, 2 Cor. vi, 17; who are born again, 1 Peter i, 23; or made new creatures, 2 Cor. v, 17; whose faith works by love to God and all mankind, Gal. v, 6; James ii, 14, 26; who walk in all the ordinances of the Lord blameless. None but such are members of the true Church.

4. Church fellowship is the communion that the members enjoy one with another. The ends of Church fellowship are the maintenance of a system of sound doctrine; the support of the ordinances of worship in their purity; the impartial exercise of Church government; the promotion of holiness in all manner of conversation. The more particular duties are earnest study to keep peace and unity; bearing of one another's burdens, Gal. vi, 1, 2; earnest endeavours to prevent each other's stumbling, 1 Cor. x, 23–33; Heb. x, 24–27; Rom. xiv, 13; steadfast continuance in the faith and worship of the Gospel, Acts ii, 42; praying for and sympathizing with each other, 1 Sam. xii, 23; Eph. vi, 18. The advantages are peculiar incitement to holiness; the right to some promises applicable to none but those who attend the ordinances of God, and hold communion with the saints, Psalm xcii, 13; cxxxii, 13, 16; xxxvi, 8; Jer. xxxi,

12; the being placed under the watchful eye of pastors, Heb. xiii, 7; that they may restore each other if they fall, Gal. vi, 1; and the more effectually promote the cause of true religion.

CIL-IC I-A, (*Sil-ish'e-a*,) a country in the southeast of Asia Mi'nor, and lying on the northern coast, at the east end of the Mediterranean Sea. The capital city thereof was Tarsus, the native city of St. Paul, Acts xxi, 39.

CINNAMON, a well known bark, of a dark red colour, of a poignant taste, aromatic, and very agreeable. The finest comes from a tree growing in Ceylon. It is mentioned among the materials in the composition of the holy anointing oil.

CIN'NER-OTH, or CIN'-NER-ETH, a city on the northwest side of the sea of Galilee; which, from it, is frequently called in the Old Testament the sea of Cinneroth-

CIR-CUM-CIS ION, a Latin term, signifying to cut round," because the Jews, in circumcising their children, cut off, after this manner, the skin which forms the prepuce. God enjoined Abraham to use circumcision, as a sign of his covenant, Gen. xvii, 10, and repeated the precept to Moses. The Jews have always been very exact in observing this ceremony, and it appears that they did not neglect it when in Egypt. By the term St. Paul frequently means the *Jews*.

CIRCUMCISION, *Covenant of*. That the covenant with Abraham, of which circumcision was made the sign and seal, Gen. xvii, 7–14, was the general covenant of grace, and not wholly, or even chiefly, a political and national covenant, may be satisfactorily established. And as this rite was enjoined upon Abraham's posterity, so that every "uncircumcised man-child whose flesh of his foreskin was not circumcised on the eighth day," was to be "cut off from his people," by the special judgment of God, and that because "he had broken God's *covenant*," Gen. xvii, 14; it therefore follows that this rite was a constant publication of God's covenant of grace among the descendants of Abraham, and its re petition a continual confirmation of that covenant, on the part of God, to all practising it in that faith of which it was the ostensible expression.

CIRCUMSPECT. Cautious, seriously attentive to every part of the revealed will of God, and very careful not to cast stumbling blocks in the way of others, Exod. xxiii, 13; Eph. v, 15.

CIS'LEU, the ninth month of the ecclesiastical, and the third of the civil year, among the Hebrews. It answers nearly to our November.

CISTERN, a reservoir, chiefly for rain water. Numbers of these are still to be seen in Palestine, some of which are one hundred and fifty paces long, and sixty broad. The reason of their being so large was, that their cities were many of them built in elevated situations; and the rain falling only twice in the year, namely, spring and autumn, it became necessary for them to collect a quantity of water, as well for the cattle as for the people. A broken cistern would, of course, be a great calamity to a family, or in some cases even to a town; and with reference to this we may see the force of the reproof, Jer. ii, 13.

CITIES. By referring to some peculiarities in the building, fortifying, &c., of eastern cities, we shall the better understand several allusions and expressions of the Old Testament. It is evident that the walls of fortified cities were sometimes partly constructed of combustible materials. One method of securing the gates of fortified places, among the ancients, was to cover them with thick plates of iron; a custom which is still used in the east; and seems to be of great antiquity, Acts xii, 10. Some of their gates are plated over with brass, Psa. cvii, 16; Isa. xlv, 2. But, conscious that all these precautions were insufficient for their security, the orientals employed watchmen to patrol the city during the night, to suppress any disorders in the streets, or to guard the walls

against the attempts of a foreign enemy, Song v, 7. This custom may be traced to a very remote antiquity, Ezek. xxxiii, 2. They were also charged, as with us, to announce the progress of the night to the slumbering city, Isa. xxi, 11.

CITIES OF REFUGE. See REFUGE.

CLAU'DA, a small island toward the southwest of Crete.

CLAU'DI-US, a Roman emperor; he succeeded Ca'i-us Ca-lig'u-la, A. D. 41, and reigned thirteen years, eight months, and nineteen days, dying A. D. 54. King Agrippa was the principal means of persuading Claudius to accept the empire, which was tendered him by the soldiers. As an acknowledgment for this service, he gave Agrippa all Judea, and the kingdom of Chalcis to his brother Herod. King Agrippa dying A. D. 44, the emperor again reduced Judea into a province, and sent Cuspius Fadus to be governor. About the same time the famine happened which is mentioned Acts xi, 28–30, and was foretold by the Prophet Ag'a-bus. Claudius, in the ninth year of his reign, published an edict for expelling all Jews out of Rome, Acts xviii, 2. It is very probable that the Christians, who were at that time confounded with the Jews, were banished likewise.

2. CLAUDIUS FELIX, successor of Cumanus in the

government of Judea. Felix found means to solicit and engage Drusilla, sister of Agrippa the Younger, to leave her husband Azizus, king of the Emessenians, and to marry him, A. D. 53. St. Paul, being brought to Ces-a-re′a, where Felix usually resided, was well treated by this governor, who permitted his friends to see him, and render him services, hoping the apostle would procure his redemption by a sum of money. He, however, neither condemned Paul, nor set him at liberty, when the Jews accused him ; but adjourned the determination of this affair till the arrival of Lys′i-as, who commanded the troops at Jerusalem, where he had taken Paul into custody, and who was expected at Cesarea, Acts, xxiii, 26, 27, &c. ; xxiv, 1-3, &c.

While the apostle was thus detained, Felix, with his wife Drusilla, who was a Jewess, sent for him, and desired him to explain the religion of Jesus Christ. The apostle spoke with his usual boldness, and discoursed to them on justice, temperance, and the last judgment. Felix trembled before this powerful exhibition of truths so arousing to his conscience ; but he remanded St. Paul to his confinement. He farther detained him two years at Cesarea, in compliance with the wishes of the Jews, and in order to do something to propitiate them, because they were extremely dissatisfied with his government. He was recalled to Rome, A. D. 60, and was succeeded in the government of Judea by Por′tius Festus.

CLEMENT, mentioned in Phil. iv, 3 ; supposed to be the same with *Clemens Romanus*, famous in church history as the chief uninspired writer of the first century.

CLE′O-PAS, according to Eu-se′bi-us and Ep-i-pha′ni-us, was brother of Joseph, both being sons of Jacob. He was the father of Simeon, of James the Less, of Jude, and Joseph or Joses. Cleopas married Mary, sister to the blessed virgin. He was, therefore, uncle to Jesus Christ, and his sons were first cousins to him. Cleopas, his wife, and sons were disciples of Christ. Having beheld our Saviour expire upon the cross, he, like the other disciples, appears to have lost all hopes of seeing the kingdom of God established by him on earth. The third day after our Saviour's death, on the day of his resurrection, Cleopas, with another disciple, departed from Jerusalem to Em-ma′us ; and in the way discoursed on what had lately happened. Our Saviour joined them, appearing as a traveller ; and, taking up their discourse, he reasoned with them, convincing them out of the Scriptures that it was necessary the Messiah should suffer death, previously to his being glorified. No other actions of Cleopas are known.

CLOSET, a chamber, or any place of privacy or retirement.

CLOUD, a collection of vapours suspended in the atmosphere. When the Israelites had left Egypt, God gave them a pillar of cloud to direct their march, as the generality of commentators are of opinion, to the passage of Jordan, Ex. xiii, 21, 22. It was clear and bright during night, in order to afford them light; but in the day it was thick and gloomy, to defend them from the excessive heats of the deserts. "The angel of God which went before the camp of Israel, removed and went behind them; and the pillar of the cloud went from before their face, and stood behind them," Exod. xiv, 19. Here we may observe that the angel and the cloud made the same motion, as it would seem, in company. The cloud by its motions gave the signal to the Israelites to encamp or to decamp. Where, therefore, it stayed, the people stayed till it rose again; then they broke up their camp, and followed it till it stopped. It was called a pillar, by reason of its form, which was high and elevated. It is common in Scripture, when mentioning God's appearing, to represent him as encompassed with clouds, which serve as a chariot, and contribute to veil his dreadful majesty, Job xxii, 14; Matt. xvii, 5; Psa. xviii, 11, 12.

CNIDUS, (Ny'dus,) a city standing on a promontory of the same name, in that part of the province of Ca'ri-a which was called Doris, a little northwest from Rhodes.

COCK. This well known bird generally crows three times in the night: at midnight, two hours before day, and at daybreak. The second; being more noticeable than the first, was often so called by way of eminence. St. Mark refers to this as the *second* crowing of the cock, and therefore says, "Before the cock crow *twice*." The other evangelists, referring only to that which was popularly observed and spoken of as the cock-crowing, take no notice of the former period, and speak as if the latter were the only time of cockcrow; and thus the apparent discrepancy is reconciled.

COCK'A-TRICE, a venomous serpent, but of what particular species is unknown. It seems to have been one of the most poisonous kind, which lurked in holes of the earth, and whose eggs were rank poison.

CO-LOS'SE, a city of Phryg'i-a, which stood on the river Ly-ce'us, at an equal distance between Laodicea and Hi-e-rap'o-lis. Dr. Lardner says, "It appears to me very probable that the church at Colosse had been planted by the Apostle Paul, and that the Christians there were his friends, disciples, and converts." The Epistle to the

Colossians, which was written about A. D. 62, greatly resembles that to the Ephesians, both in sentiment and expression.

COL'OURS. *White* was esteemed the most appropriate colour for cotton cloth, and *purple* for others. Kings and princes were clothed with *purple*, Luke xvi, 19. *Scarlet*, first mentioned in Gen. xxxviii, 28, and frequently afterward, was very much admired. The dark *blue* (Ezek. xxiii, 6) was highly esteemed among the Assyrians. The *black* is said to have been used on occasions of mourning, and sometimes for common wear. See Raiment.

COMFORTER, one of the titles by which the Holy Spirit is designated in the New Testament, John xiv, 16, 26; xv, 26. The name has, no doubt, a reference to his peculiar office in the economy of redemption; namely, that of imparting consolation to the hearts of Christ's disciples, which he effects by "taking of the things that are Christ's," and explaining them; or, in other words, by illuminating their mind as to the meaning of the Scriptures, assuring them of the Saviour's love, bringing to their recollection his consolatory sayings, and filling their souls with peace and joy in believing them.

COMMON, profane, ceremonially unclean.

COMMUNION, fellow-ship, concord, agreement, 1 Cor. x, 16; 2 Cor. vi, 14; 1 John i, 3.

COM'PASS. The expression "*fetched a compass*," signifies, coasted around the island. To *compass sea and land* is a proverbial expression, used to denote the most strenuous exertions to accomplish an object.

CONCISION, *the cutting*. Circumcision being now ceased, the apostle will not call the Jews *the circumcision*, but coins a term on purpose, taken from a Greek word which signifies *a cut*, and alludes to such *cutting* as God had forbidden, Lev. xxi, 5.

CON'CU-BINE. This term, in western authors, commonly signifies a woman, who, without being married to a man, yet lives with him as his wife; but, in the sacred writers, the word concubine is understood in another sense; meaning a lawful wife, but one not wedded with all the ceremonies and solemnities of matrimony; a wife of the second rank, inferior to the first wife, or mistress of the house. Children of concubines did not inherit their father's fortune; but he might provide for, and make presents to them. Since the abrogation of polygamy by Jesus Christ, and the restoration of marriage to its primitive institution, concubinage is ranked with adultery or fornication.

CON-CU'PIS-CENCE is taken for unlawful or sinful

desire; particularly for carnal inclinations. Bad desires, as well as bad actions, are forbidden; and the first care of such as would please God, is to restrain them.

CONDEMNATION, the act of passing sentence against a person, by which he is doomed to punishment. The punishment itself.

CO'NEY, called in Hebrew *Shaphan.* It is an unclean animal; described as chewing the cud, Lev. xi, 5; as inhabiting mountains and rocks, Psa. civ, 18; and as gregarious and sagacious, Prov. xxx, 26; hence it is not the *coney,* an old name for the rabbit, which burrows most generally in the sand. But Mr. Bruce proves that the *ashkoko* is intended, a harmless animal, of nearly the same size and quality as the rabbit, but of a browner colour, smaller eyes, and a more pointed head. Its feet are round and very fleshy, notwithstanding which, however, it builds its house in the rocks. "He is above all other animals so much attached to the rocks, that I never once," says Mr. Bruce, "saw him on the ground, or from among large stones in the mouth of caves, where is his constant residence. He lives in families or flocks. He is in Judea, Palestine, and Arabia; and, consequently, must have been familiar to Solomon."

CONFESS. To confess is to acknowledge our sins to God, who can pardon or punish

us, or to our neighbour whom we have wronged, or to some pious friend who can give us instruction and comfort, Jas. v, 16; Psa. xxxii, 5. "*To confess Christ,*" is openly to acknowledge our faith in him, and publicly to observe the rules of his religion. The original word signifies, "to use the same language, or words, as another;" hence, by implication, to profess the same things as another, to admit what another professes. He, therefore, who publicly confesses Jesus to be what he professes to be, that is, the Christ, and acts suitably to that belief, him will Christ publicly confess to be what he himself professes to be—that is, a true disciple of Christ.

CONSCIENCE is that faculty within us, which decides on the merit or demerit of our own actions. A conscience well informed, and possessed of sensibility, is the best security for virtue, and the most awful avenger of wicked deeds; an ill-informed conscience is the most powerful instrument of mischief.

The rule of conscience is the will of God, so far as it is made known to us, either by the light of nature, or by that of revelation. With respect to the knowledge of this rule, conscience is said to be rightly informed, or mistaken; firm, or wavering, or scrupulous, &c. With respect to the conformity of our actions to this rule when known, conscience is said to be good or evil. In a moral view, it is of the greatest importance that the understanding be well informed, in order to render the judgment or verdict of conscience a safe directory of conduct, and a proper source of satisfaction.

CONSTELLATION, a cluster of stars. About 3,000 visible stars are classed into fifty-nine constellations, twelve of which are in the Zodiac, or middle region of the firmament, twenty-three in the north part, and twenty-four in the south.

CONTEMN, to despise, to neglect as unworthy of regard.

CONVERSATION. The English word conversation has now a more restricted sense than formerly; and it is to be noted that in several passages of our translation of the Bible it is used to comprehend *our whole conduct*.

CONVERT, to change from one state or character to another. Conversion, considered theologically, consists in a renovation of the heart and life, or a being turned from sin and the power of Satan unto God, Acts xxvi, 18; and is produced by the influence of Divine grace upon the soul. But this is not the only Scriptural import of the term; for the first *turning* of the whole heart to God in penitence and prayer is generally termed conversion.

CONVOCATION, an as-sembly met for the solemn worship of God.

COOS, a small island in the Mediterranean Sea, near the southwest point of Asia Minor, now called *Stancore*.

COPPER, one of the most ductile and malleable of metals, except gold, silver, and platina. Anciently, copper was employed for all the purposes for which we now use iron. Arms, and tools for husbandry and the mechanic arts, were all of this metal for many ages.

COR, a Hebrew measure, which holds about six bushels, some say more.

COR'AL, a hard, cretaceous, marine production, resembling in figure the stem of a plant, divided into branches. It is of different colours, black, white, and red. The latter is the sort emphatically called coral, as being the most valuable, and usually made into ornaments.

COR'BAN. It denotes a *gift*, a *present* made to God, or to his temple. The Jews sometimes swore by corban, or by gifts offered to God, Matt. xxiii, 18. Jesus Christ reproaches the Jews with cruelty toward their parents, in making a *corban* of what should have been appropriated to their use. For when a child was asked to relieve the wants of his father or mother, he would often say, "*It is a gift*," *corban*, "by whatsoever thou mightest be profited by me;" that is, I have devoted *that* to God which you ask of me ; and it is no longer *mine* to give, Mark vii, 11. Thus they violated a precept of the moral law, through a superstitious devotion to Pharisaic observances.

CO-RI-AN'DER, a strongly aromatic plant. It bears a small round seed, of a very agreeable smell and taste. The manna might be compared to the coriander seed in respect to its form or shape, as it was to bdellium in its colour.

COR'INTH, a celebrated city, the capital of A-cha'i-a, situated on the isthmus which separates the Pel-o-pon-ne'-sus from Attica. This city was one of the best peopled and most wealthy of Greece. Its situation between two seas drew thither the trade of both the east and west. Its riches produced pride, ostentation, effeminacy, and all vices, the consequences of abundance. For its insolence to the Roman legates, it was destroyed by L. Mum'-mi-us. In the burning of it, so many statues of different metals were melted together, that they produced the famous Corinthian brass. It was afterward restored to its former splendour by Julius Cæsar.

Christianity was first planted at Corinth by St. Paul, who resided here eighteen months, between the years 51 and 53 ; during which time he enjoyed the friendship of Aquila and his wife Priscilla, two Jewish Christians, who had been expelled from Itily, with other Jews, by an edict of Claudius.

The Church consisted both of Jews and of Gentiles.

CO-RINTH'I-ANS, *Epistles to.* St. Paul wrote his First Epistle to the Corinthians from Ephesus, in the beginning of A. D. 56. In this epistle he reproves some who disturbed the peace of the Church, complains of some disorders in their assemblies, of law suits among them, and of a Christian who had committed incest with his mother-in-law, the wife of his father, and had not been separated from the Church. This letter produced in the Corinthians great grief, vigilance against the vices reproved, and a very beneficial dread of God's anger. They repaired the scandal, and expressed abundant zeal against the crime committed, 2 Cor. vii, 9–11.

Paul, having understood the good effects of his first letter among the Corinthians, wrote a second to them, A. D. 57, from Macedonia, and probably from Philippi. He expresses his satisfaction at their conduct, justifies himself, and comforts them. He glories in his suffering, and exhorts them to liberality.

COR'MO-RANT, a large sea bird. It has a most voracious appetite, and lives chiefly upon fish, which it devours with unceasing gluttony. It darts down very rapidly upon its prey.

CORN, the generic name for grain in the Old Testament writings. It is evident from Ruth ii, 14; 2 Sam. xvii, 28, 29, &c., that parched corn [i. e., grain] constituted part of the ordinary food of the Israelites, as it still does of the Arabs resident in Syria.

CORNELIUS, a Roman centurion, belonging to the legion surnamed Italian.

CORNER. Amos iii, 12. Sitting in the corner is a stately attitude. The place of honour is the corner of the room, and there the master of the house sits and receives his visitants. Corner is taken likewise for the side or extremity of any thing, Prov. xxi, 9; Lev. xix, 27. Zechariah, speaking of Judah after the return from captivity, says, "Out of him came forth the *corner*," x, 4; i. e., the corner stone, the ornament and completion of the building. This tribe shall afford corners, i. e., chiefs or heads.

CORNER STONE. Our Lord is compared in the New Testament to a *corner stone*, in three different points of view. 1. As this stone lies at the foundation, and serves to give support and strength to the building. 2. As the corner stone occupies an important and conspicuous place, Jesus is compared to it, 1 Peter ii, 6; because God has made him distinguished, and has advanced him to a dignity and conspicuousness above all others. 3. Since men often stumble against a projecting corner stone, Christ is therefore so called, because his Gospel will be the cause of aggravated condemnation to those who reject it.

COTTAGE, a mean hut or house for shepherds or poor people, Zeph. ii, 6.

COUCH, a mean bed, or small mattress, capable of holding one person.

COUNCIL is occasionally taken for any kind of assembly; sometimes for that of the *sanhedrim*, the supreme council of the Jewish nation, in which were despatched all the great affairs both of religion and policy. It consisted of chief priests, elders, and scribes, amounting to seventy-two. Whatever might have been the origin of the sanhedrim, it subsisted in the time of our Saviour, since it is spoken of in the Gospel, Matt. v, 21; Mark xiii, 9; xiv, 55; xv, 1; Matt. xxvii, 1; and since Jesus Christ himself was arraigned and condemned by it.

COUNSEL, beside the common signification as denoting the consultations of men, it is used in Scripture for the purpose of God, the orders of his providence, and his gracious designs, Luke vii, 30.

COURT, an enclosed space near a house. That which was around the tabernacle was formed of pillars, and veils hung by cords. The method of building houses in the form of a hollow square made the court on the inside.

COV'E-NANT. A covenant implies two parties, and mutual stipulations. The new covenant must derive its name from something in the nature of the stipulations between the parties different from that which existed before; so that we cannot understand the propriety of the name, *new*, without looking back to what is called the *old*, or *first*. On examining the passages in Gal. iii, in 2 Cor. iii, and in Heb. viii-x, where the *old* and the *new* covenant are contrasted, it will be found that the *old* covenant means the *dispensation given by Moses* to the children of Israel; and the *new* covenant the *dispensation of the Gospel published by Jesus Christ*; and that the object of the apostle is to illustrate the superior excellence of the latter dispensation.

No sooner had Adam broken the covenant of works, than a promise of a final deliverance from the evils incurred by the breach of it was given. This promise was the foundation of that transaction which almighty God, in treating with Abraham, condescends to call "my covenant with thee," and which, upon this authority, has received in theology the name of the Abrahamic covenant. Upon the one part, Abraham, whose faith was counted to him for righteousness, received this charge from God, "Walk before me, and be thou perfect;" upon the other part, the God whom he believed, and whose voice he obeyed, besides promising other blessings to him and his seed, uttered these significant words, "In thy seed shall all the families of the earth be blessed." In this transaction, then, there was the essence of a covenant; for there were mutual stipulations between two parties; and there was superadded, as a seal of the covenant, the rite of circumcision, which, being prescribed by God, was a confirmation of his promise to all who complied with it; and being submitted to by Abraham, was, on his part, an acceptance of the covenant.

There are only two covenants, essentially different, and opposite to one another: the covenant of works, made with the first man, having for its terms, "Do this and live;" and the covenant of grace, which was the substance of the Abrahamic covenant, and which entered into the constitution of the Sinaitic covenant, but which is more clearly revealed, and more extensively published in the Gospel. This last covenant, which the Scriptures call *new*, has received, in the language of theology, the name of the covenant of grace, for the two following obvious reasons: because, after man had broken the covenant of works, it was pure grace or favour in the Almighty to enter into a new covenant with him:

and because, by the covenant, there is conveyed that grace which enables man to comply with the terms of it. It could not be a covenant unless there were terms,—something required, as well as something promised or given,—duties to be performed, as well as blessings to be received, Heb. viii, 10. But although there are mutual stipulations, the covenant retains its character of a covenant of grace, and must be regarded as having its source purely in the grace of God. For the very circumstances which rendered the new covenant necessary take away the possibility of there being any merit upon our part: the faith by which the covenant is accepted is the gift of God; and all the good works by which Christians continue to keep the covenant originate in that change of character which is the fruit of the operation of his Spirit.

Covenants were anciently confirmed by eating and drinking together; and chiefly by feasting on a sacrifice. In this manner Abimelech, the Philistine, confirmed the covenant with Isaac, and Jacob with his father Laban, Gen. xxvi, 26–31; xxxi, 44–46, 54. Sometimes they divided the parts of the victim, and passed between them, by which act the parties signified their resolution of fulfilling all the terms of the engagement, on pain of being divid-ed or cut asunder as the sacrifice had been, if they should violate the covenant, Gen. xv, 9, 10, 17, 18; Jer. xxxiv, 18. When the law of Moses was established, the people feasted in their peace-offerings on a part of the sacrifice, in token of their reconciliation with God, Deut. xii, 6, 7. See CIRCUMCISION.

COVER, a figurative expression, applied to the remission of sins. *To cover*, or *conceal*, is to remove from sight or notice; and sins which are left out of sight and out of notice, of course, are sins which are not punished, and, therefore, pardoned. Compare the expressions in Isa. xxxviii, 17; Mic. vii, 19; Job xiv, 17.

COVET. This word is sometimes used in a good sense, as, " *To covet the best gift*," 1 Cor. xii, 31; but generally in a bad sense, to denote an inordinate desire of earthly things, especially of that which belongs to another. Covetousness is declared by the apostle to be *idolatry*, Col. iii, 5.

CRANE, a tall and long necked fowl, which, according to Isidore, takes its name from its voice, which we imitate in mentioning it. The Prophet Jeremiah mentions this bird knowing the seasons by an instinctive and invariable observation of their appointed times, as a circumstance of reproach to the chosen people of God, who, although taught by reason and religion, "know not the judgment of the Lord," Jer. viii, 7.

CREATION signifies the bringing into being something which did not exist before. The term is, therefore, most generally applied to the original production of the materials whereof the visible world is composed. It is also used in a secondary or subordinate sense, to denote those subsequent operations of the Deity upon the matter so produced, by which the whole system of nature, and all the primitive *genera* of things, received their forms, qualities, and laws. First of all, the materials of which the future universe was to be composed were created. These were jumbled together in one indigested mass, which the ancients called *chaos*, and which they conceived to be eternal; but which Moses affirms to have been created by the power of God. The materials of the chaos were either held in solution by the waters, or floated in them, or were sunk under them; and they were reduced into form by the Spirit of God moving upon the face of the waters. Light was the first distinct object of creation; fishes were the first living things; man was last in the order of creation.

The account given by Moses is distinguished by its simplicity.

CRETE, a large island, now called Candia, in the Mediterranean. The Cretans affected the utmost antiquity as a nation; and, being surrounded by the sea, were excellent sailors, and their vessels visited all coasts. Their glory was MINOS, the legislator, the first, it is said, who reduced a wild people to regularity of life. But their character for lying had passed into a common proverb, hence that detestable description which Paul has given of them, (Tit. i, 12,) that they were "*always liars.*"

CROSS, an ancient instrument of capital punishment. Death by the cross was the punishment inflicted by the Romans on servants who had perpetrated crimes, on robbers, assassins, and rebels; among which last Jesus was reckoned, on the ground of his making himself king or Messiah, Luke xxiii, 1–5, 13–15. The cross consisted of a piece of wood erected perpendicularly, which rarely exceeded ten feet in height, and intersected by another at right angles near the top, so as to resemble the letter T. Our Saviour says that *whosoever will be his disciple must take up his cross and follow him*, Matt. xvi, 24; by which is meant, that his disciples must *patiently submit to every kind of suffering*, and even to *die an ignominious and cruel death*, like Christ himself, when called to it. The cross stands for *death*, in its most frightful forms, but comprehends all other sufferings to be endured for the truth; but it is ridiculous to apply this phrase, as is often done, to express submission to some little mortification of our will, or to some duty not quite agreeable to our views and feelings. The cross is also often put for the whole of Christ's sufferings, Eph. ii, 16; Heb. xii, 2; and for the doctrine of his atonement, Gal. vi, 14.

CROWN is a term properly taken for a *cap of state*, worn on the heads of sovereign princes, as a mark of regal dignity. In Scripture there is · frequent mention made of crowns; and the use of them seems to have been very common among the Hebrews. The high priest wore a crown, which was girt about his mitre, or the lower part of his bonnet, and was tied about his head, Exod. xxviii, 36; xxix, 6. New-married persons of both sexes wore crowns upon their wedding day, Cant. iii, 11; and, alluding to this custom, it is said that when God entered into covenant with the Jewish nation he put a beautiful crown upon their head, Ezek. xvi, 12.

The crown of a king was generally a white fillet bound about his forehead, the extremities whereof, being tied behind the head, fell back on the neck. Sometimes they were made of gold tissue, adorned with jewels. That of the Jewish high priest, which is the most ancient of which we have any description, was a fillet of gold placed upon his forehead, and tied with a riband, of a hyacinth colour, or azure blue. Crowns were bestowed upon kings and princes, as the principal marks of their dignity. David took the crown of the king of the Ammonites from off his head. The crown weighed a talent of gold, and was moreover enriched with jewels, 2 Sam. xii, 30; 1 Chron. xx, 2. The elders, in Rev. iv, 10, are said to "cast their crowns before the throne." The allusion is here to the tributary kings dependent upon the Roman emperors.

Pilate's guard platted a crown of thorns, and placed it on the head of Jesus Christ, Matt. xxvii, 29, with an intention to insult him, under the character of the king of the Jews. In a figurative sense, a crown signifies honour, splendour, or dignity, Lam. v, 16; Phil. iv, 1; and is also used for reward, because conquerors in the Grecian games were crowned, 1 Cor. ix, 25.

CRUCIFIXION, a mode of punishment among the Romans. The person who was crucified was deprived of all his clothes, excepting something around the loins. In this state he was sometimes beaten with rods, but more generally with whips; and to such a degree of severity that numbers died under it. He was then obliged to carry the cross himself to the place of punishment, which was commonly a hill, near the public way, and out of the city. The common way of crucifying was by fastening the criminal with nails, one at each hand, and one at each foot, or one at both his feet. Sometimes they were bound with cords, which, though it seems gentler, because it occasions less pain, was really more cruel, because the sufferer was hereby made to languish longer. Sometimes they used both nails and cords for fastenings; and when this was the case, there was no difficulty in lifting up the person, together with the cross, he being sufficiently supported by the cords. Those who were fastened to the cross lived in that condition from three to nine days; during that time they were watched by a guard. Hence Pilate was astonished at our Saviour's dying so soon, because, naturally, he must have lived longer, Mark xv, 44. The corpse was not buried, except by express permission, which was granted only to a few. An exception, however, to this general practice, was made by the Romans in favour of the Jews, on account of their law, (Deut. xxi, 22, 23,) which forbade the bodies to hang after sunset. And, to hasten the extinction of life, their bones were broken upon the cross with a mallet.

The Jews, under the jurisdiction of the Romans, were accustomed to give the criminal, before the commencement of his suffering, a medicated drink of wine and myrrh, Prov. xxxi, 6. The object was to produce intoxication, and thereby render the pains of the crucifixion less sensible to the sufferer. This was refused by the Saviour, for the obvious reason that he chose to die with the faculties of the mind undisturbed and unclouded, Matt. xxvii, 34; Mark xv, 23. This sort of drink, which was probably offered out of kindness, was different from the vinegar which was subsequently offered by the Roman soldiers. The latter, mixed with water, was a common drink for the soldiers in the Roman army. See John xix, 29. An inscription, representing the cause of the punishment, was ordinarily written on a piece at the top of the cross.

CRUSE, a small vessel for holding water and other liquids, 1 Sam. xxvi, 11.

CRYS'TAL. This term primarily denotes *ice*, and it is given to a perfectly transparent gem, like *glass*, from its resemblance to ice.

CU'BIT, a measure used among the ancients. A cubit originally was the distance from the elbow to the extremity of the middle finger: this is the fourth part of a well proportioned man's stature. The common cubit is eighteen inches. The opinion, however, is very probable, that the cubit varied in different districts and cities, and at different times, &c.

CU'CUM-BER, the fruit of a plant very common in our gardens. They are very plentiful in the east, especially in Egypt, and much superior to ours; more agreeable to the taste, and easier of digestion.

CUD, that portion of food which ruminating animals bring from the first stomach and chew at one time.

CUM'MIN. This is an umbelliferous plant, in appearance resembling fennel, but smaller. Its seeds have a warm and bitter taste, accompanied with an aromatic flavour, not of the most agreeable kind. An essential oil is obtained from them by distillation. The Jews sowed it in their fields, and when ripe threshed out the seed with a rod, Isaiah xxviii, 25, 27.

CUP. This word is taken in a twofold sense; proper and figurative. In a proper sense, it signifies a vessel, such as people drink out of at meals, Gen. xl, 13. It was anciently the custom, at great entertainments, for the governor of the feast to appoint to each of his guests the kind and proportion of wine which they were to drink, and what he had thus appointed them it was deemed a breach of good manners either to refuse or not to drink up; hence a man's cup, both in sacred and profane authors, came to signify the *portion*, whether of good or evil, *which happens to him*

in this world. Thus, to drink " *the cup of trembling*," or of " *the fury of the Lord*," is to be afflicted with sore and terrible judgments, Isaiah li, 17; Jer. xxv, 15–29; Psa. lxxv, 8.

CUP OF BLESSING, 1 Cor. x, 16, is that which was blessed in entertainments of ceremony, or solemn services; or, rather, a cup over which God was blessed for having furnished its contents; that is, for giving to men the fruit of the vine. Our Saviour, in the last supper, blessed the cup, and gave it to each of his apostles to drink, Luke xxii, 20.

CUP OF SALVATION, Psa. cxvi, 13, a phrase of nearly the same import as the former, a cup of thanksgiving, of blessing the Lord for his saving mercies.

CURSE. To curse signifies to imprecate, to call for mischief upon, or wish evil to any one. The curses mentioned Gen. ix, 25, and elsewhere, were ordained by God himself, and pronounced by men under the influence of his Spirit; or they were predictions of certain evils which would happen to individuals, or to a people, uttered in the form of imprecations. They were not the effects of passion, impatience, or revenge; and, therefore, were not things condemned by God in his law, like the cursing mentioned Exod. xxi, 17.

CUSH, and CUSHAN, *Ethiopia*, the countries peopled by the descendants of Cush, the eldest son of

Ham, whose first plantations were on the gulf of Persia, and from whence they spread over India and great part of Arabia; particularly on the coast of the Red Sea; invaded Egypt, under the name of shepherd kings; and thence passed into Central Africa, and first peopled the countries to the south of Egypt. See ETHIOPIA.

CUTTINGS *in the flesh.* It may be taken as an instance of earnest entreaty, of conjuration, by the most powerful marks of affection; q. d., " Dost thou not see, O Baal! with what passion we adore thee? How we give most decisive tokens of our affection? We shrink at no pain, we decline no disfigurement, to demonstrate our love for thee; and yet thou answerest not! By every token of our regard, answer us! By the freely flowing blood we shed for thee, answer us!" &c. They certainly demonstrated their attachment to Baal; but Baal did not testify his reciprocal attachment to them, in proof of his divinity; which was the point in dispute between them and Elijah.

CYMBAL, a musical instrument, consisting of two broad plates of brass, of a convex form, which, being struck together, produce a shrill, piercing sound.

CYPRESS, a large evergreen tree. The wood is fragrant, compact, heavy, and almost incorruptible. The chests which contain the Egyptian mummies are of cypress. The gates of St. Peter's church at Rome, which had lasted from the time of Constantine to that of Pope Eugene IV., 1100 years, were of cypress, and had at that time suffered no decay.

CYPRUS, a large island in the Mediterranean, situated between Ci-lic'i-a and Syria. Its inhabitants were plunged in all manner of luxury and debauchery. Their principal deity was Venus. The apostles, Paul and Barnabas, landed in the island A. D. 44, Acts xiii, 4.

CY-RE'NE was a city of Lyb'i-a in Africa. This city was once so powerful as to contend with Carthage for pre-eminence. It is mentioned as the birthplace of Simon, whom the Jews compelled to bear our Saviour's cross, Luke xxiii, 26. At Cyrene resided many Jews, a great part of whom embraced the Christian religion; but others opposed it with much obstinacy. Among the most inveterate enemies of Christianity, Luke reckons those of this province, who had a synagogue at Jerusalem, and excited the people against St. Stephen, Acts xi, 20.

CY-RE'NI-US, governor of Syria, Luke ii, 1, 2.

CY'RUS, son of Cam-by-ses, the Persian, and of Mandane, daughter of As-ty'a-ges, king of the Medes. At the age of thirty, Cyrus was made general of the Persian troops, and sent, at the head of thirty thousand men, to assist his uncle, Cy-ax'a-res, whom the Babylonians were preparing to attack. Cyaxares and Cyrus gave them battle and dispersed them. After this, Cyrus carried the war into the countries beyond the river Ha'lys; subdued Cappadocia; marched against Crœsus, king of Lydia, defeated him, and took Sardis, his capital. Having reduced almost all Asia, Cyrus repassed the Euphrates, and turned his arms against the Assyrians: having defeated them, he laid siege to Babylon, which he took on a festival day, after having diverted the course of the river which ran through it. On his return to Persia, he married his cousin, the daughter and heiress of Cyaxares; after which he engaged in several wars, and subdued all the nations between Syria and the Red Sea. He died at the age of seventy, after a reign of thirty years. Authors differ much concerning the manner of his death.

2. We learn few particulars respecting Cyrus from Scripture; but they are more certain than those derived from other sources. Daniel, in the remarkable vision in which God showed him the ruin of several great empires which preceded the birth of the Messiah, represents Cyrus as "a ram which had two horns, both high, but one rose higher than the other, and the higher came up last. This ram pushed

westward, and northward, and southward, so that no beasts might stand before him, neither was there any that could deliver out of his hand; but he did according to his will, and became great," Dan. viii, 3, 4, 20. The two horns signify the two empires which Cyrus united in his person, that of the Medes and that of the Persians. In another place, Daniel compares Cyrus to a bear with three ribs in its mouth, to which it was said, "Arise, devour much flesh." Cyrus succeeded Cambyses in the kingdom of Persia, and Da-ri'us the Mede also in the kingdom of the Medes, and the empire of Babylon. He was monarch, as he speaks, "of all the earth," Ezra i, 1, 2; 2 Chron. xxxvi, 22, 23; when he permitted the Jews to return to their own country, B. C. 538. He had always a particular regard for Daniel, and continued him in his great employments.

3. The prophets foretold the exploits of Cyrus. Isaiah xliv, 28, particularly declares his name, above a century before he was born. The peculiar designation by name which Cyrus received, must be regarded as one of the most remarkable circumstances in the prophetic writings.

4. Pliny notices the tomb of Cyrus at Passagardæ, in Persia. Alexander the Great opened the tomb, and found, not the treasures he expected, but a rotten shield, two

8

Scythian bows, and a Persian cimeter. Cyrus, in his last instructions to his children, desired that "his body, when he died, might not be deposited in gold or silver, nor in any other sumptuous monument, but committed, as soon as possible, to the ground."

DAGON, a god of the Philistines. The name is derived from the Hebrew, *dag, fish,* and signifies *a large fish.* Scripture shows clearly that the statue of Dagon was human, at least the upper part of it, 1 Sam. v, 4, 5.

DAILY BREAD signifies *that which is sufficient,* or *just enough for the day.* The petition accords with various passages. Solomon prays, (Prov. xxx, 8,) "*Feed me with food convenient for me.*" James has the expression, "*Things which are needful to the body,*" James ii, 16.

DAL-MA-NU'THA, Mark viii, 10, but St. Matthew calls it Magdala, Matt. xv, 39. It seems that Dalmanutha was near to Magdala, on the western side of the lake.

DAL-MA'TIA, (*Dal-ma'-she-a,*) a part of old Illyria, lying along the gulf of Venice. Titus preached here, 2 Tim. iv, 10.

DA-MAS'CUS, a celebrated city of Asia, and anciently the capital of Syria, may be accounted one of the most venerable places in the world for its antiquity. It is known to have existed in the time of Abraham, Gen. xv, 2. It was the residence of the Syrian kings, during the space of three centuries; and experienced a number of vicissitudes in every period of its history. Its sovereign, Hadad, whom Josephus calls the first of its kings, was conquered by David, king of Israel. In the reign of Ahaz, it was taken by Tig'lath Pil-e'ser, who slew its last king, Rezin, and added its provinces to the Assyrian empire. It was taken and plundered, also, by Sen-nach'e-rib, Neb-u-chad-nez-zar, the generals of Alexander the Great, Judas Mac-ca-be'us, and at length by the Romans in the war conducted by Pompey against Ti-gra'nes, in the year before Christ 65. During the time of the emperors, it was one of their principal arsenals in Asia, and is celebrated by the Emperor Julian as, even in his day, "the eye of the whole east." About the year 634, it was taken by the Saracen princes, who made it the place of their residence, till Bagdad was prepared for their reception; and, after suffering a variety of revolutions, it was taken and destroyed by Tamerlane, A. D. 1400.

DAMN, and DAMNA-TION, are words synonymous with *condemn* and *condemnation,* Matt. xxiii, 14. Generally speaking, these words are taken to denote the final and eternal punishment of the ungodly. These terms, however, sometimes occur in the New Testament in what may be termed a less strict, or secondary sense. Thus, "He that doubteth," namely, the lawfulness of what he is doing, "is *damned* if he eat," Rom. xiv, 23; the meaning is, he is worthy of condemnation.

DAN, the fifth son of Jacob. The city of Dan was situated at the northern extremity of the land of Israel: hence the phrase "from Dan to Be-er'-she-ba," denoting the whole length of the land of Canaan, 2 Sam. xxiv, 7, a hundred and fifty miles.

DANCING. It is still the custom in the east to testify their respect for persons of distinction by music and dancing. In the oriental dances, in which the women engage by themselves, the lady of highest rank in the company takes the lead, and is followed by her companions, who imitate her steps, and if she sings, make up the chorus. This statement may enable us to form a correct idea of the dance which the women of Israel performed under the direction of Miriam, on the banks of the Red Sea.

DAN'IEL was a descendant of the kings of Judah, and is said to have been born at Upper Beth-o'ron, in the territory of Ephraim. He was carried away captive to Babylon when he was about eighteen or twenty years of age, in the year 606 before the Christian era. He was placed in the court of Neb-u-chad-nez'zar, and was afterward raised to situations of great rank and power, both in the empire of Babylon and of Persia. He lived to the end of the captivity, but being then nearly ninety years old, it is most probable that he did not return to Judea. It is generally believed that he died at Susa, soon after his last vision, which is dated in the third year of the reign of Cyrus. Daniel seems to have been the only prophet who enjoyed a great share of worldly prosperity; but amid the corruptions of a licentious court he preserved his virtue and integrity inviolate, and no danger or temptation could divert him from the worship of the true God. The book of Daniel is a mixture of history and of prophecy: part of it is written in the Chaldaic language, namely, from the fourth verse of the second chapter to the end of the seventh chapter; these chapters relate chiefly to the affairs of Babylon, and it is probable that some passages were taken from the public registers. This book abounds with the most exalted sentiments of piety and devout gratitude, its style is clear, simple, and concise; and many of its prophecies are delivered in terms so plain and circumstantial, that some unbelievers have asserted, in opposition to the strongest evidence, that they were written after the events which they describe had taken place.

DA-RI'US was the name of several princes in history.

DARIUS the Mede, spoken of in Daniel ix, 1; xi, 1, &c., who succeeded Bel-shaz'zar, B. C. 551, Dan. v, 31, is supposed to be the same as Cyaxares, the son of As-ty'a-ges, king of the Medes, and brother to Mandane, the mother of Cyrus. See MEDE.

DARKNESS, the absence of light. "Darkness was upon the face of the deep," Gen. i, 2; that is, the chaos was immersed in thick darkness, because light was withheld from it. The most terrible darkness was that brought on Egypt as a plague; it was so thick as to be, as it were, palpable; so horrible, that no one durst stir out of his place; and so lasting that it endured three days and three nights, Exodus x, 21, 22. The darkness at our Saviour's death began at the sixth hour, or noon, and ended at the ninth hour, or three o'clock in the afternoon. Thus it lasted almost the whole time he was on the cross; compare Matt. xxvii, 45, with John xix, 14, and Mark xv, 25. Or'i-gen says it was caused by a thick mist, which precluded the sight of the sun. That it was preternatural is certain, for, the moon being at full, a natural eclipse of the sun was impossible. Darkness is sometimes used metaphorically for death. "The land of darkness" is the grave, Job x, 22; Psalm cvii, 10. It is also used to denote misfortunes and calamities. "A day of darkness" is a day of affliction, Esther xi, 8. "Let that day be darkness; let darkness stain it,"—let it be reckoned among the unfortunate days, Job iii, 4, 5. The expressions, "I will cover the heavens with darkness;" "The sun shall be turned into darkness, and the moon into blood," &c., signify very great political calamities—involving the overthrow of kings, princes, and nobles, represented by the luminaries of heaven. In a moral sense, darkness denotes ignorance and vice; hence "the children of light," in opposition to "the children of darkness," are the righteous distinguished from the wicked.

DATE, the fruit of the palm tree, of a sweet and agreeable taste.

DAUGHTER. The state of daughters, that is, young women, in the east, their employments, duties, &c., may be gathered from various parts of Scripture; and seem to have borne but little resemblance to the state of young women of respectable parentage among ourselves. Rebekah drew and fetched water; Rachel kept sheep, as did the daughters of Jethro, though they superintended and performed domestic services for the family; Tamar, though a king's daughter, baked bread; and the same of others.

DA'VID, the celebrated king of Israel, was the youngest son of Jesse, of the tribe of Judah, and was born 1085 years before Christ.

When David is called "the man after God's own heart," his general character, and not every particular of it, is to be understood as approved by God; and especially his faithful and undeviating adherence to the true religion, from which he never deviated into any act of idolatry. His inspired Psalms not only place him among the most eminent prophets; but have rendered him the leader of the devotions of good men, in all ages. The hymns of David excel no less in sublimity and tenderness of expression than in loftiness and purity of religious sentiment. In comparison with them the sacred poetry of all other nations sinks into mediocrity. The songs which cheered the solitude of the desert caves of Engedi have been repeated for ages in almost every part of the habitable world, in the remotest islands of the ocean, among the forests of America, or the sands of Africa.

DAY. The Hebrews, in conformity with the Mosaic law, reckoned the day from evening to evening, Lev. xxiii, 32. The natural day, that is, the portion of time from sunrise to sunset, was divided by the Hebrews, as it is now by the Arabians, into six unequal parts. These divisions were as follows:—1. the break of day, Mark xvi, 2; John xx, 1. 2. The morning or sunrise.

3. The heat of the day. This began about nine o'clock, Gen. xviii, 1; 1 Sam. xi, 11. 4. Midday. 5. The cool of the day; literally, the wind of the day. This expression is grounded on the fact that a wind commences blowing regularly a few hours before sunset, and continues till evening, Gen. iii, 8. 6. The evening.

There is another day, which may be termed *prophetic*, where a day is put for *a year*, (See Ezek. iv, 5, 6,) of which there is an example in the explanation given of Daniel's *seventy weeks*, a week is seven years. *To-day* signifies any definite time, as we say, "*The people of the present day*."

DAYSPRING, the dawn, first appearance of the light, the springing of the day.

DEACON denotes a *servant* who attends his master, waits on him at table, and is always near his person to obey his orders. But a deacon, in the primitive Church, means one who collects and distributes alms to the poor. Their office consisted in a general inquiry into the situation and wants of the poor, in taking care of the sick, and in administering all proper relief. The appointment of deacons is distinctly recorded, Acts vi, 1–16.

The qualifications of deacons are stated by the Apostle Paul, 1 Tim. iii, 8–12. There were also in the primitive Churches females invested with this office, who were termed deaconesses. Of this number was Phœbe, a member of the Church of Cenchrea, mentioned by St. Paul, Rom. xvi, 1. "They served the Church," says Calmet, "in those offices which the deacons could not themselves exercise, visiting those of their own sex in sickness, or when imprisoned for the faith. They were persons of advanced age, when chosen; and appointed to the office by imposition of hands." It is probably of these deaconesses that the apostle speaks, where he describes the ministering widows, 1 Tim. v, 5–10.

DEAD. 1. Destitute of natural life, Matt. xxii, 32; Job xxvi, 5: "*For this cause was the Gospel preached to them that are dead,*" 1 Peter iv, 6; i. e. formerly preached to them that are *now* dead; see Ruth i, 8. 2. Without spiritual life, dead in sin, Matt. viii, 22. Let the dead in sin bury those who are naturally dead; see Rev. iii, 1; Eph. ii, 1; 1 Tim. v, 6. 3. Mortal, devoted, or exposed to death, Rom. viii, 10; Gen. xx, 3. 7.

Dead faith, James ii, 17, is a mere assent to truth, which does not produce good works. *Dead works,* Heb. ix, 14, are works which spring from spiritual death in the soul. *Dead to the law,* Gal. ii, 19, is having no hope of justification from it. Saints are dead to sin, Rom. vi, 2, when they have nothing to do with it.

DEATH is taken in Scripture, (1.) for the separation of body and soul, the *first death,* Gen. xxv, 11. (2.) For alienation from God and exposure to his wrath, 1 John iii, 14, &c. (3.) For the *second death,* that of eternal damnation. (4.) For any great calamity, danger, or imminent risk of death, as persecution, 2 Cor. i, 10.

DE'BO-RAH, a prophetess, wife of Lap'i-doth, judged the Israelites, and dwelt under a palm tree between Ramah and Bethel, Judges iv, 4, 5.

DEBTOR, DEBT, an *obligation* which must be discharged by the party bound to do so. This may be either special or general: special obligations or debts are where the party has contracted to do something in return for a service received; general obligations are those to which a man is bound by his relative situation: "Whosoever shall swear by the gold of the temple—by the gift on the altar—is a debtor," Matt. xxiii, 16, is bound by his oath; is obliged to fulfil his vow. "I am debtor to the Greeks and the barbarians," Rom. i, 14, under obligations to persons of all nations and characters. Gal. v, 3, "a debtor"—*is bound* "to do the whole law." *Debts* signify *sins,* Matt. vi, 12, a manner of speaking common among the Jews. In this view a *debtor* is one who has failed in duty to us, or one who has injured us.

DE-CAP'O-LIS, a part of Syria lying on the east of the Sea of Galilee, and so named from its ten cities.

DEDAN, the name of a people and country in Arabia.

DEDICATION, a religious ceremony by which any thing is declared to be consecrated to the worship of God.

" *The feast of dedication,*" John x, 22, was instituted by Judas Maccabeus, 1 Mac. iv, 59, when he purged and dedicated the altar and the temple after they had been polluted.

DEEP. (1.) Hell, the place of punishment, the bottomless pit, which the devils evidently dreaded, Luke viii, 31. (2.) The common receptacle of the dead; the grave, the deep earth, under which the body being deposited, the state of the soul corresponding thereto; still more unseen, still deeper, still farther distant from human inspection, is that remote country, that "bourne from whence no traveller returns," Rom. x, 7. (3.) The deepest parts of the sea, Psa. cvii, 26. (4.) The chaos, which, in the beginning of the world, was unformed and vacant, Gen. i, 2.

DE GREES', a name given to fifteen psalms, from the cxx; the reason for it is unknown.

DENY signifies to *renounce* and *disregard.* For the disciple to "*deny himself,*" is to disregard all personal considerations of ease, honour,

liberty, and life when they come in competition with his allegiance to Christ.

DEPUTY, one who acts for another, a governor of a Roman province.

DESERT means an uncultivated place, particularly if mountainous. Some deserts were entirely dry and barren; others were beautiful, and had good pastures. Scripture speaks of the beauties of the desert, Psalm lxv, 12, 13. Scripture names several deserts in the Holy Land; and there was scarcely a town without one belonging to it, i, e., uncultivated places for woods and pasture. The desert, through which the Israelites passed before they came to Moab, lies between the Jordan or the mountains of Gilead and the river Euphrates, Exod. xxiii, 31. God promised the children of Israel all the land between the desert and the river; that is, all the country from the mountains of Gilead to the Euphrates. The wilderness, where John the Baptist preached, began near Jericho, and extended to the mountains of Edom, Matt. iii, 1.

DEVIL, a fallen angel and chief of those who were expelled from heaven for rebellion against God. The word signifies " *a false accuser or a slanderer,*" because he slandered God in paradise, as averse to man's knowledge and happiness, and still he slanders him by false suggestions. "He is the accuser of our brethren which accused them before our God day and night," Rev. xii, 10.

The word in the plural, *devils*, is an improper translation; it should have been *demons or evil angels.*

There is a numerous band of these fallen spirits, Mark v, 9, and the devil appears to have them under his control. They are all "*reserved unto the judgment of the great day,*" and for the "*fire prepared for the devil and his angels.*"

DEU-TER-ON′O-MY, *the second law*; the last book of the Pentateuch or five books of Moses. As its name imports, it contains a repetition of the civil and moral law, which was a second time delivered by Moses, with some additions and explanations, as well to impress more forcibly upon the Israelites in general, as in particular for the benefit of those who, being born in the wilderness, were not present at the first promulgation of the law. It contains also a recapitulation of the several events which had befallen the Israelites since their departure from Egypt, with severe reproaches for their past misconduct, and earnest exhortations to future obedience. The Messiah is explicitly foretold in this book. The book of Deuteronomy finishes with an account of the death of Moses, which is supposed to have been added by his successor, Joshua.

DEW. Dews in Palestine are very plentiful, like a small shower of rain every morning. In those warm countries where it seldom rains, the night dews supply the want of showers. Isaiah speaks of rain as if it were a dew, Isa. xviii, 4. Some of the most beautiful and illustrative of the images of the Hebrew poets are taken from the dews of their country. The reviving influence of the gospel, the copiousness of its blessings, and the multitude of its converts, are thus set forth.

DIADEM. See CROWN.

DIAL, an instrument for the measuring of time by the shadow of the sun. Dials are not mentioned before the days of Ahaz, nor hours till the time of Daniel's captivity in Babylon. Dan. iv, 19.

DI′A-MOND, a precious stone, remarkable for its hardness, as it scratches all other minerals; considered, from remote antiquity, the most valuable, or properly, the most costly substance in nature; because of its rarity, hardness, and brilliancy. When pure it is clear and transparent, but sometimes it is *coloured*. See *Precious Stones.*

DI-A′NA, a celebrated goddess of the heathens, who was honoured principally at Ephesus, Acts xix, where she had a famous temple adorned with one hundred and twenty-seven columns of Parian marble, each of a single shaft, and sixty feet high, and which formed one of the seven wonders of the world. This temple could hold twenty thousand people, and was seven times set on fire. One of the principal conflagrations happened on the very day that Socrates was poisoned, (four hundred years before Christ,) the other on the same night in which Alexander was born.

A person by the name of *Erostratus* set it on fire, according to his own confession, that his name might go down to posterity. The remains of this temple are still to be seen.

DID'Y-MUS, *a twin*. This is the signification of the Hebrew or Syriac word Thomas.

DI-O-NYS'I-US, (*Dy-o-nish'e-us*,) the A-re-op'a-gite, a convert of St. Paul, Acts xvii, 34. Chrys'os-tom declares Di-o-nys'i-us to have been a citizen of Athens; which is credible, because the judges of the Areopagus generally were so.

DIS-CI'PLE. The proper signification of this word is a *learner*; but it signifies in the New Testament, a believer, a Christian, a follower of Jesus Christ. Disciple is often used instead of apostle in the Gospels; but subsequently apostles were distinguished from disciples.

DISPENSA'TION, a stewardship or commission to dispense the gospel, 1 Cor. ix, 17; Eph. iii, 2.

DIV-I-NA'TION, a conjecture formed concerning future events from things which are supposed to presage them. The eastern people were always fond of divination, magic, the curious art of interpreting dreams, and of obtaining a knowledge of future events. When Moses published the law, this disposition had long been common in Egypt and the neighbouring countries. To prevent the Israelites from consulting diviners, fortune tellers, interpreters of dreams, &c., he enacted very severe penalties. Deut. xviii, 10. The writings of the prophets are full of invectives against the Israelites who consulted diviners; and against false prophets who by such means seduced the people.

DI-VORCE'. A dissolution of the bonds of matrimony. Moses did not encourage divorces, nor did he prohibit them strictly within the rule of the original law, because of the hardness of their hearts; meaning probably in compassion to the oppressed condition of the women themselves, put under the tyranny of a rigid race of men. In all such cases he commanded that a bill of divorce should be given, Deut. xxiv, 1–4, in order that there might be time for reflection, and that the separation should not be made on the impulse of passion. Our Lord allows the bill of divorce, but restrains it absolutely to cases which directly and essentially violate the marriage covenant. This covenant no man is at liberty to break, and no legislature or state has the power to modify or alter. The bond is absolutely indissoluble in every case, except in the single case of adultery, which the great Lawgiver himself has excepted.

DOCTORS, or TEACHERS, of the law, a class of men in great repute among the Jews. They had studied the law of Moses in its various branches, and the numerous interpretations which had been grafted upon it in later times ; and, on various occasions, they gave their opinion on cases referred to them for advice. Doctors of the law were chiefly of the sect of the Pharisees ; but they are sometimes distinguished from that sect, Luke v, 17.

DOCTRINE. Whatever is taught as true by an instructer, knowledge, the truths of the gospel in general, divine injunctions. "*Teaching for doctrines the commandments of men.*" Matt. xv, 9.

DOG, a well known animal. By the law of Moses, the dog was declared unclean, and was held in great contempt among the Jews, 1 Sam, xvii, 43 ; xxiv, 14 ; 2 Sam. ix, 8 ; 2 Kings viii, 13. Yet they had them in considerable numbers in their cities. They were not, however, shut up in their houses or courts, but forced to seek their food where they could find it. The psalmist compares violent men to dogs, who go about the city in the night, prowl about for their food, and growl, and become clamorous if they be not satisfied, Psa. lix, 6, 14, 15. The irritable disposition of the dog is the foundation of that saying, "He that passeth by, and meddleth with strife belonging not to him, is like one that taketh a dog by the ears," Prov. xxvi, 17 ; that is, he wantonly exposes himself to danger.

In Matt. vii, 6, we have this direction of our Saviour : "Give not that which is holy unto the dogs, neither cast ye your pearls before swine, lest they," the swine, "trample them under their feet, and," the dogs, "turn again and tear you." It was customary with the people of that age to denote certain classes of men by animals supposed to resemble them among the brutes. Our Saviour was naturally led to adopt the same concise and energetic method. By *dogs*, which were held in great detestation by the Jews, he intends *men of odious character* and *violent temper ;* by *swine*, the usual emblem of moral filth, he means the sensual and profligate ; and the purport of his admonition is, that as it is a maxim with the priests not to give any part of the sacrifices to dogs, so it should be a maxim with you not to impart the holy instruction with which you are favoured, to those who are likely to blaspheme and to be only excited by it to rage and persecution. It is, however, a maxim of *prudence*, not of *cowardice*; and is to be taken along with other precepts of our Lord, which enjoin the publication of truth, at the expense of ease and even life.

DOORS. 1. *To be at the doors*, is a proverbial expression for *being near at hand*, Matt. xxiv, 33; James v, 9; 2. It is applied figuratively to Christ, who is the *door*, by which we must enter into his Church, and into eternal life, John x, 9; to an *opportunity* of receiving the Gospel, or of preaching it, Rev. iii, 8.

DOTHAN, a town about twelve miles north of Sama'ria.

DOUBLE has many significations in Scripture. "A double garment" may mean a lined habit, such as the high priest's pectoral. *Double* heart, *double* tongue, *double* mind, are opposed to a simple, honest, sincere heart, tongue, mind, &c. For the right understanding of Isaiah xl, 2, "She hath received of the Lord's hand *double* for all her sins," read. that which is *adequate*, all things considered, as a dispensation of punishment. This passage does not mean twice as much as had been deserved, double what was just, but the *fair, commensurate, adequate retribution.*

DOVE, a beautiful bird, very numerous in the east. In its wild state it is called a *pigeon*, and builds its nest in holes and clefts of rocks, or excavated trees.

Doves easily become familiar with men, and build in structures erected for their accommodation, called "*dove cotes.*" They are classed by Moses among the clean birds, and were always held in the highest estimation among the eastern nations. In the Scripture, the dove is mentioned as the symbol of simplicity, innocence, gentleness, and fidelity, Matt. x, 16. Noah probably sent a dove out of the ark because it was a tame bird, and averse to carrion.

DOWRY, the portion of money or goods which is given with a wife. But, in the Scriptures, it is that sum of money or goods which a bridegroom offers to the father, as a token of honour, to engage his favourable interest, before he can expect to receive his daughter in marriage.

DRACHM, a Persian coin; probably a golden daric, worth about twenty shillings.

DRAGON, a large kind of venomous serpent, unknown to modern naturalists. But some suppose it to be the *crocodile*, or some *sea monster*; others, some species of enormous land serpent, perhaps the *boa constrictor*, the largest known. It is often used for the devil, who is called the "*old serpent,*" Rev. xx, 2.

DREAMS, the thoughts of a person in sleep, which, not being under the command of reason, are wild and irregular. The prophetic dreams of the Scripture were not, however, common dreams, but impressions made on the mind by Divine agency, and probably accompanied with an internal evidence which distinguished them from the ordinary rovings of the mind in sleep, and afforded sufficient conviction of their supernatural character. This powerful means of working on the mind of man, though, by abuse, it has become, and still continues, a fruitful source of superstition, may, nevertheless, occasionally be employed to warn the wicked and direct the good.

DROMEDARY, a species of camel, called also the *Arabian camel*, which differs from the *Bractrian* only by its being somewhat less, with one bunch on its back, while the other has two. It is remarkable for its prodigious swiftness, going as far in one day as that will in three; for this reason it is used to carry messengers where haste is required. It also endures the heat better, crossing immense deserts, where no water is found, and not even moistened by the dew of heaven. It is endued with the wonderful power, at one watering place, to lay in a store, which supplies him for many days to come.

DRUNK, overpowered by spirituous liquor. Drenched with some moisture. "I will make my arrows *drunk* with blood," Deut. xxxii, 42. Persons under the influence of superstition and idolatry, in which they make no use of their natural reason, are said to be *drunk*. "To add *drunkenness* to thirst," Deut. xxix, 19, is to add one sin to another, i. e. not only to pine in secret after idol worship, but openly practise it.

DULCIMER, an instrument of music, of a triangular form, strung with about fifty wires, and struck with an iron key, while laying on a table before the performer.

DUMAH, a tribe and country of the Ishmaelites, situated on the confines of the Arabian and Syrian deserts, with a fortress, Isa. xxi, 11.

DUNG. The prophet was commanded to *bake his bread* by a fire made of this material. This was designed to show the extreme degree of wretchedness to which they should be exposed, and want of fuel, during the siege of Jerusalem, Ezek. iv.

DURA, a great plain, near Babylon.

DUST, fine dry particles of earth, unorganized earthly matter. "*Dust thou art.*" The grave, Job vii, 21. A low condition. "*God raiseth the poor out of the dust,*" 1 Sam. ii, 8. A great multitude. "Who can count the *dust* of Jacob," Num. xxiii, 10. In affliction, the Hebrews put dust on their heads, or sat down in it. The Jews thought the dust of heathen lands polluted, and were careful to free themselves from it; hence our Saviour commanded his apostles to "*shake off the dust of their feet,*" that by this significant act they might declare the house or city which rejected them, as worthy only to be ranked with the polluted city of the heathen.

EAGLE. The eagle has always been considered as the king of birds, on account of its great strength, rapidity, and elevation of flight, natural ferocity, and the terror it inspires into its fellows of the air. Its voracity is so great, that a large extent of territory is requisite for the supply of proper sustenance; and Providence has therefore constituted it a solitary animal. Two pairs of eagles are never found in the same neighbourhood, though the genus is dispersed through every quarter of the world. Its sight is quick, strong, and piercing to a proverb, Job xxxix, 27.

The flight of this bird is as sublime as it is rapid and impetuous. None of the feathered race soar so high. In his daring excursions he is said to leave the clouds of heaven, and regions of thunder, and lightning, and tempest, far beneath him, and to approach the very limits of ether. There is an allusion to this lofty soaring in Jer. xlix, 16. The eagle lives and retains its vigour to a great age; and, after shedding its feathers, renews its vigour so surprisingly, as to be said, hyperbolically, to become young again, Psa. ciii, 5, and Isa. xl, 31.

EAR, the organ of hearing; it denotes, also, the *ear of the mind.* That faculty of the mind by which we *consider* and *distinguish*, of which the bodily *ear* is a very proper and instructive emblem. People who have "*heavy ears*" are those who *disregard* the admonitions of the prophets, who are said in the Scripture "*to do*" what they only *foretel,* Isa. vi, 10.

EARING, an old English word for *ploughing.* "*Earing time,*" Ex. xxxiv, 21, means the time of ploughing or planting. We ought to make great allowances for changes in our language since the time of our translators, and not blame them for the use of words *now* become obsolete; but which, in their day, well expressed their meaning.

EARNEST, *first fruits,* that which gives promise of something to come, but used in the New Testament in a figurative sense, and spoken of the Holy Spirit which God hath given to believers in this present life, to *assure* them of their future and eternal inheritance, 2 Cor. i, 22.

EARTH. Beside the usual senses in which the word is taken, it often means the *land of Canaan,* which was promised to the Jews, and which represented to the mind of spiritual Israel the great inheritance of heaven, Psa. xxxvii, 11. "The meek shall inherit the *earth*," which, taken figuratively, denotes *heaven.*

EARTHQUAKE. a terrible shaking of the earth. The agents concerned in the production of earthquakes and volcanoes, are immense quantities of *gas* and *steam*, generated by the decomposition of substances in the bowels of the earth. The position of volcanoes. always near the sea, the agitation of the sea during an eruption, the large quantities of boiling water frequently ejected. and the saline matter in the ejected substances, render it very clear that the sea supplies the water by subterranean communication. The Scripture speaks of several earthquakes, Amos 1, 1; Zech. xiv, 5. A very memorable earthquake is that which happened at our Saviour's death, Matt. xxvii, 51. It must have been terrible, since the centurion and those with him were so affected by it, as to acknowledge the innocence of our Saviour, Luke xxiii, 47. The effects of God's power, wrath, and vengeance, are compared to earthquakes, Psa. xviii, 7. An earthquake signifies also, in prophetic language, the dissolution of governments and the overthrow of states.

EAST, one of the four cardinal points of the world; namely, that particular point of the horizon in which the sun is seen to rise. The Hebrews express the east, west, north, and south, by words which signify before, behind, left, and right, according to the situation of a man who has his face turned toward the east. By the east, they frequently describe. not only Arabia Deserta, and the lands of Moab and Ammon. which lay to the east of Palestine, but also Assyria, Mesopotamia, Babylonia, and Chaldea, though they are situated rather to the north than to the east of Judea.

EASTER (*Ee's-ter,*) the day on which the Christian Church commemorates our Saviour's resurrection. In Acts xii, 4, the word should be rendered *passover*, which is a feast of the Jews well known. .

EATING. The ancient Hebrews did not eat indifferently with all persons. In Joseph's day they neither ate with the Egyptians, nor the Egyptians with them, Gen. xliii, 32; nor, in our Saviour's time, with the Samaritans, John iv, 9. The Jews were provoked at Christ's eating with publicans and sinners, Matt. ix, 11. As there were several sorts of meats, the use of which was prohibited, they could not conveniently eat with those who partook of them, fearing to receive pollution by touching such food, or if by accident any particle of it should fall on them. The ancient Hebrews, at their meals, had each his

ANCIENT MODE OF EATING.

separate table, Gen. xliii, 32, &c. Elkanah, Samuel's father, who had two wives, distributed their portions to them separately, 1 Sam. i, 4, 5.

The custom of reclining at tables was introduced from the nations of the east, and particularly from Persia, where it seems to have been adopted at a very remote period. The Old Testament Scriptures allude to both customs; but they furnish undeniable proofs of the antiquity of sitting. It was not till after the lapse of many ages, and when degenerate man had lost much of the firmness of his primitive character, that he began to recline.

The tables were constructed of three different parts or separate tables, making but one in the whole. One was placed at the upper end crossways, and the two others joined to its ends, one on each side, so as to leave an open space between, by which the attendants could readily wait at all the three. Around these tables were placed beds or couches, one to each table. At the end of each was a footstool, for the convenience of mounting up to it. These beds were formed of mattresses, and supported on frames of wood, often highly ornamented; the mattresses were covered with cloth or tapestry, according to the quality of the entertainer. The guests lay on these couches, each having a pillow at his left side, on which he supported his

elbow;—a knife and fork was not then in use, the food was conveyed to the mouth by the right hand;—and he that sat next him, on the right side, was said to lie in his bosom. Accordingly, the expression of Lazarus lying in Abraham's bosom, implies, that he was in the highest place of honour and happiness.

Partaking of the benefits of Christ's passion by faith is called eating, because this is the support of our spiritual life, John vi, 53, 56. Hosea reproaches the priests of his time with eating the sins of the people, Hosea iv, 8; that is, feasting on their sin offerings, rather than reforming their manners. John the Baptist is said to have come "neither eating nor drinking," that is, as other men did; for he lived in the wilderness, on locusts, wild honey, and water, Matt. iii, 4. This is expressed in Luke vii, 33, by his neither eating "bread," nor drinking "wine." On the other hand, the Son of man is said, in Matt. xi, 19, to have come "eating and drinking;" that is, as others did; and that too with all sorts of persons, Pharisees, publicans, and sinners.

E'BAL, a celebrated mountain, or rock, in the tribe of Ephraim, near Shechem, over against Mount Gerizim. These two mountains are separated by a deep valley, about two hundred paces wide, in which stood the town of Shechem. The two mountains are much alike in magnitude and form, being of a semicircular figure, about a mile and a half in length, not exceeding eight hundred feet in altitude, and, on the sides nearest Shechem, nearly perpendicular. One of them is barren; the other, covered with a beautiful verdure.

EB-EN-E'ZER, *the stone of help:* a witness stone erected by Samuel, 1 Sam.vii. Perhaps a *pillar* is meant by the word stone.

EBONY, a species of hard, heavy, and durable wood, said to be brought from Madagascar, which admits of a fine polish. The best is a jet black; some is red and some is green.

EC-CLE-SI-AS'TES, a canonical book of the Old Testament, of which Solomon was the author, as appears from the first sentence. The design of this book is to show the vanity of all sublunary things; and, from a review of the whole, the author draws this pertinent conclusion, " Fear God, and keep his commandments, for this is the whole of man;"—his whole wisdom, interest, and happiness, as well as his whole duty.

EDEN, *delight, pleasure,* a pleasant region in Asia, the situation of which is described Gen. ii, 10–14; and in which was placed the garden of our first parents during their state of innocence. The name has been given to several other places which, from their situation, were pleasant or delightful, Joel ii, 3.

EDOM, the posterity of Esau, and likewise their country, Idumea. This country was the mountainous tract between the Dead Sea and the Elanitic or eastern gulf of the Red Sea, and called also Mount *Seir*.

EDIFY, *to build;* hence we call a building an *edifice*. In a spiritual sense, it signifies to instruct, improve, and comfort the mind; and a Christian is edified when he is encouraged and animated in the ways and works of the Lord.

The means to promote our own edification are, prayer, self-examination, reading the Scriptures, bearing the Gospel, and attendance on all appointed ordinances.

EGYPT. A celebrated country of Africa, bounded on the east by Arabia, on the south by Nubia, on the west by the deserts of Africa, and on the north by the Mediterranean Sea.

Through a valley formed by ranges of mountains on the east and west, the river Nile pours its waters. At the place where this valley terminates, eight miles below Cairo, and about forty or fifty miles from the sea coast, the river divides itself into several streams, forming a triangle, the base of which is the seacoast, resembling the Greek letter Δ. Hence this part of Egypt received and still retains the name of the

Delta. Every year, in the months of August and September, it overflows its banks, inundates the adjacent country, fertilizes it by a deposition of black mud, and empties at last into the Mediterranean. Egypt is then, from one end of the country to the other, nothing but a beautiful garden, a verdant meadow, a field sown with flowers, or a waving ocean of grain in the ear. This fertility, as is well known, depends upon the annual and regular inundation of the Nile. The height to which the Nile rises at these times is from eighteen to twenty-four feet.

The sky is constantly a pure unclouded arch, of a colour and light more white than azure. The atmosphere has a splendour which the eye can scarcely bear; and a burning sun, whose glow is tempered by no shade, scorches through the whole day these vast and unprotected plains. It is almost a peculiar trait in the Egyptian landscape, that although not without trees, it is yet almost without shade. The only tree is the date tree, which is frequent; but with its tall, slender stem, and bunch of foliage on the top, this tree does very little to keep off the light, and casts upon the earth only a pale and uncertain shade. Egypt, accordingly, has a very hot climate. The early history of ancient Egypt is involved in great obscurity. From ancient histories and from modern discoveries in the hieroglyphics, writers have been led to divide the history of the Egyptian empire into five periods.

1. The first begins with the establishment of their government, and comprehends the time during which all religious and political authority was in the hands of the priesthood, who laid the first foundation of the future power of Egypt. It continued to Menes, B. C. about 1700.

2. The second period begins at the abolition of this primitive government, and the first establishment of the monarchical government of Menes. From this time commences what is generally called the "*Pharaonic age,*" and ends at the irruption of Cambyses, B. C. about 525.

This is the most brilliant period of Egyptian history; during which Egypt was covered with those magnificent works which still command our admiration and excite our astonishment; and by the wisdom of its institutions and laws, and by the *learning* of its priests, was rendered the most rich, populous, and enlightened country in the world.

3. The third epoch includes the period of the Persian dominion, about two hundred years.

4. The fourth covers the reigns of the *Ptolemies.*

5. The fifth begins when Egypt became a Roman province, B. C. 30, and continues

to the middle of the fourth century.

The religion of Egypt consisted in the worship of the heavenly bodies and the powers of nature; the priests cultivated at the same time astronomy and astrology, and to these belong probably the wise men, sorcerers, and magicians, mentioned, Ex. vii, 11–22.

But the Egyptian religion had this peculiarity, that it adopted living *animals* as symbols of the real objects of worship.

The Egyptians not only esteemed many species of animals as sacred, which might not be killed without punishment of death, but individual animals were kept in temples and worshipped with sacrifices, as gods. It was in consequence of this, that the destruction of the first-born in Egypt was made to extend also to the *beasts*.

The ancient Egyptians spoke the *Coptic language*, which differed from that of the Hebrews, Gen. xlii, 23. This is now abundantly confirmed by inscriptions found in Egypt on monuments of various kinds, some of which are coeval with the Pharaohs and even antecedent to the time of Joseph.

The most extraordinary monuments of their power and industry were the pyramids, which still subsist, to excite the wonder and admiration of the world. The largest is near Cairo. It is five hundred feet high, and covers more than eleven acres of ground. *When*, by *whom*, and *for what purpose*, erected, is entirely unknown.

ELAM, a province of Persia, in which was the capital Susa, Dan. viii, 2; in the earlier writers it includes, perhaps, the whole of Persia. See Gen. x, 22, where the origin of the Elamites is deduced from Shem.

ELATH or ELOTH, a city at the northern extremity of the eastern branch of the Red Sea, called by Josephus *Elana*, whence the name of the *Elanitic Gulf*. 1 Kings ix, 26.

ELDER, *a person advanced in life*, and who, on account of his age, experience, and wisdom, is selected for office. Thus the *heads of the tribes of Israel*, who had a government and authority over their own families and the people, were called *elders*. Thus also the ordinary *pastors* and *teachers* of the Christian Church are called *elders* or *presbyters*, and are the same as *bishops* or *overseers*. Tit. i, 5, 6, 7; Acts xx, 17–28.

E-LE-A'ZAR, the third son of Aaron, and his successor in the dignity of high priest, Exod. vi, 23. He entered into the land of Canaan with Joshua, and is supposed to have lived there upward of twenty years. The high priesthood continued in his family till the time of Eli. He was buried in a hill that belonged to the son of

Phinehas, Josh. xxiv. There are several others of this name in Scripture.

E-LEC'TION. Of a Divine election, a choosing and separating from others, we have three kinds mentioned in the Scriptures. The first is the election of *individuals* to perform some particular and special service. Cyrus was "elected" to rebuild the temple; the twelve apostles were "chosen," elected, to their office by Christ; St. Paul was a "chosen," or elected "vessel," to be the apostle of the Gentiles. The second kind of election which we find in Scripture is the election of *nations*, or *bodies of people*, to eminent religious privileges, and in order to accomplish, by their superior illumination, the merciful purposes of God, in benefiting other nations or bodies of people. Thus the descendants of Abraham, the Jews, were *chosen* to receive special revelations of truth; and to be "the people of God," that is, his visible Church, publicly to observe and uphold his worship. "The Lord thy God hath *chosen* thee to be a peculiar people unto himself, above all people that are upon the face of the earth." "The Lord had a delight in thy fathers to love them, and he *chose* their seed after them, even you, above all people." It was especially on account of the application of the terms *elect, chosen*, and *peculiar*, to the Jewish people, that they were so familiarly used by the apostles in their epistles addressed to the believing Jews and Gentiles, then constituting the Church of Christ in various places.

The *third* kind of election is personal election; or the election of individuals to be the children of God, and the heirs of eternal life. This is not a choosing to particular offices and service, which is the first kind of election we have mentioned; nor is it that collective election to religious privileges and a visible Church state, of which we have spoken. The individuals properly called "the elect," are they who have been made partakers of the grace and saving efficacy of the Gospel. "Many," says our Lord, "are *called*, but few *chosen*." What true personal election is, we shall find explained in two clear passages of Scripture. It is explained by our Lord, where he says to his disciples, "I have chosen you out of the world:" and by St. Peter, when he addresses his First Epistle to the "elect according to the foreknowledge of God the Father, through sanctification of the Spirit, unto obedience and sprinkling of the blood of Jesus." To be elected, therefore, is to be separated from "the world," and to be sanctified by the Spirit, and by the blood of Christ. It follows, then, not only that election is an act of God done in *time*, but also that it is subsequent to the administration of the means of salvation. The "calling" goes before the "election;" the publication of the doctrine of "the Spirit," and the atonement, called by Peter "the sprinkling of the blood of Christ," before the "sanctification" through which they become "the elect" of God. In a word, "the elect" are the body of true believers; and *personal* election into the family of God is through *personal* faith. All who truly believe are elected; and all to whom the Gospel is sent have, through the grace that accompanies it, the power to believe placed within their reach; and all such might, therefore, attain to the grace of personal election.

ELEMENTS are the first principles of any thing. St. Paul calls the *ceremonial ordinances* of the Mosaic law "*worldly elements*," Gal. iv, 3; "weak and beggarly elements," ver. 9. *Elements*, as containing the rudiments of the knowledge of Christ, to which knowledge the law, as a pedagogue, Gal. iii, 24, was intended, by means of those ordinances, to bring the Jews; *worldly*, as consisting in outward worldly institutions, Heb. ix, 1; *weak* and *beggarly*, when considered in themselves, and set up in opposition to the great realities to which they were designed to lead. But, in Col. ii, 8, the elements or rudiments of the world are so closely connected with philosophy and vain deceit, or *an empty* and *deceitful philosophy*, that they must be understood there to include the dogmas of pagan philosophy; to which, no doubt, many of the Colossians were in their unconverted state attached, and of which the Judaizing teachers, who also were probably themselves infected with them, took advantage to withdraw the Colossian converts from the purity of the Gospel, and from Christ their living head.

E'LI, a high priest of the Hebrews, of the race of Ith'amar, who succeeded Abdon, and governed the Hebrews, both as priest and judge, during forty years. Eli appears to have been a pious, but indolent man, blinded by paternal affection, who suffered his sons to gain the ascendency over him; and for want either of personal courage, or zeal for the glory of God sufficient to restrain their licentious conduct, he permitted them to go on to their own and his ruin. A striking lesson to parents! God admonished him by Samuel, then a child; and Eli received those awful admonitions with a mind fully resigned to the Divine will. "It is the Lord," said he, "let him do what seemeth him good." God deferred the execution of his vengeance many years. 1 Sam. iv, 12–18.

ELIAS. See ELIJAH.

EL-I-E'ZER, a native of Damascus, and the steward

of Abraham's house. It seems that Abraham, before the birth of Isaac, intended to make him his heir:—" One born in my house," a domestic slave, " is mine heir," Gen. xv, 1-3. He was afterward sent into Mes-o-po-ta'mi-a, to procure a wife for Isaac, Gen. xxiv, 2, 3, &c.; which business he accomplished with fidelity and expedition.

ELI'HU. one of Job's friends. a descendânt of Na-hor. See JOB.

ELI'JAH, or ELI'AS, a celebrated prophet, the leader of the prophets in the kingdom of Israel during the reign of Ahab; distinguished by many miracles, and by being received up into heaven, 2 Kings ii, 11. He was raised up by God, to be set like a wall of brass, in opposition to idolatry, and particularly to the worship of Baal, which Jezebel and Ahab supported in Israel.

Elijah was one of the most eminent of that illustrious and singular race of men, *the Jewish prophets*. Every part of his character is marked by a moral grandeur, which is heightened by the obscurity thrown around his connections and his private history. He often wears the air of a supernatural messenger suddenly issuing from another world, to declare the commands of Heaven, and to awe the proudest mortals by the menace of fearful judgments. His boldness in reproof; his lofty zeal for the honour of God; his superiority to softness, ease, and suffering, are the characters of a man filled with the Holy Spirit; and he was admitted to great intimacy with God, and enabled to work miracles of a very extraordinary and unequivocal character. In the sternness and power of his reproofs he was a striking type of John the Baptist, and the latter is therefore prophesied of under his name, Malachi iv, 5, 6. Our Saviour also declares that Elijah had already come in spirit, in the person of John the Baptist. At the transfiguration of our Saviour, Elijah and Moses both appeared and conversed with him respecting his future passion, Matt. xvii, 3, 4.

ELIM, the six encampments of the Israelites, on the northern skirts of the desert of Sin; supposed to be the valley of *Ghirondel*, about six miles from *Tor*, where only nine wells, mentioned by Moses, Exod. xv, 37, are found, the other three being filled up by drifts of sand.

ELISEUS, (*El-e-seius*,) the same as ELISHA, in the English translation of the New Testament.

ELI'SHA, a celebrated prophet, the disciple as well as the companion and successor of Elijah, and distinguished by many miracles. He flourished in the kingdom of the ten tribes, B. C. 892, 1 Kings xix, 16, &c.

E'LUL, the sixth month of the Hebrew ecclesiastical

year, and the twelfth of the civil year, answering to our August and part of September, containing 29 days.

EL'Y-MAS,(*El'e-mas.*)See BAR-JESUS.

EM-BALM'ING, the art of preserving dead bodies from putrefaction. It was much practised by the Egyptians of ancient times, and from them seems to have been borrowed by the Hebrews. It consisted in opening the body, taking out the intestines, and filling the place with odoriferous drugs and spices of a desiccative quality. The Scripture mentions the embalming of Joseph, King Asa, and our Saviour. See BURIAL.

EM'E-RALD is one of the most beautiful of all the gems, and is of a bright green colour, without the admixture of any other. Besides, these stones seem larger at a distance, by tinging the circumambient air. Their lustre is not changed by the sun, by the shade, nor by the light of lamps; but they have always a sensible moderate brilliancy. The true oriental emerald is very scarce, and is only found at present in the kingdom of Cambay.

EM'E-RODS, the disease of the Philistines; supposed to be painful swellings in the hemorrhoidal vessels, *the piles.*

E'MIMS, ancient inhabitants of the land of Canaan, beyond Jordan, who were defeated by Che'dor-la-o'mer and his allies, Gen. xiv, 5.

The Emims were a warlike people, of a gigantic stature.

EMMANUEL, *God with us,* a Hebrew phrase, from Isaiah vii, 14, similar to other expressions in the New Testament. *The word was God—was made flesh—God was manifested in the flesh.* So we are to understand, *God with us* is *God incarnated—God in human nature.*

EM-MA'US, a village about eight miles northwest of Jerusalem, celebrated for our Lord's conversation with two disciples who went thither on the day of his resurrection, Luke xxiv, 13.

EMULATION, a generous ardour, kindled by the praiseworthy example of others, which impels us to imitate, to rival, and, if possible, to excel them. This passion involves in it esteem of the person whom we emulate, and a desire of resemblance, together with a joy springing from hope of success.

EN-EG-LA'IM, a place at the head of the Dead Sea, where the Jordan enters it.

EN'DOR, a city in the tribe of Manasseh, where the witch resided whom Saul consulted a little before the battle of Gilboa, 1 Sam. xxviii, 13. That the real Samuel appeared is plain, both from the affright of the woman herself, and from the fulfilment of his prophecy. It was an instance of God's overruling the wickedness of men, to manifest his own supremacy and justice.

EN'GE-DI abounded with

cyprus vines, and trees that produced balm. Solomon speaks of the "vineyards of Engedi," Cant. i, 14. This city, according to Josephus, stood near the lake of Sodom, about thirty-seven miles from Jerusalem, not far from the mouth of the river Jordan. It was in the cave of Engedi that David had it in his power to kill Saul.

ENOCH, the father of Methuselah, translated to heaven on account of his piety, Gen. v, 18-24.

He was born A. M. 622. The encomium of Enoch is, that he "*walked with God.*" While mankind were living in open rebellion against Heaven, and provoking the Divine vengeance daily by their ungodly deeds, he obtained the exalted testimony, "that he pleased God." This he did, not only by the exemplary tenor of his life, and by the attention which he paid to the outward duties of religion, but by the soundness of his faith, and the purity of his heart and life, Heb. xi, 5, 6. Enoch is said, by another evangelical writer, to have spoken of the coming of Christ to judgment unto the antediluvian sinners, Jude xiv, 15. This prophecy is a clear, and it is also an awful description of the day of judgment. In the departure of Enoch from this world of sin and sorrow, the Almighty altered the ordinary course of things, and gave him a dismissal as glorious to himself as it was instructive to mankind. To convince them how acceptable holiness is to him, and to show that he had prepared for those that love him a heavenly inheritance, he caused Enoch to be taken from the earth without passing through death.

ENON, a place eight miles south of Scythop'olis, between Salim and Jordan. And because there were "*many waters,*" (*the words in the original are plural,*) John went there to baptize, that the wants of the multitudes who attended to his preaching might be supplied.

ENSIGN, a military token or signal to be followed—a standard. The ancient Jewish ensign was a long pole, at the end of which was a kind of chafing dish, made of iron bars, which held a fire, the light, shape, &c., of which, denoted the party to which it belonged. Christ is called an ensign, Isa. xi, 10, because he will *draw all men to him,* as men follow an ensign.

ENVY, a malignant disposition, or state of mind, which grudges at the welfare of others, and would willingly deprive them of their advantages.

EP'A-PHRAS. It is not improbable that Epaphras is the same person with E-paphro-di'tus, the former name being merely contracted from the latter.

E-PAPH-RO-DI'TUS, one who was sent by the Philippians to carry money to Paul, then in bonds, A. D. 61, and to do him service; who executed his mission with much zeal, and brought upon himself a dangerous illness.

E'PHAH, a region and tribe of the Midianites, Gen. xxv, 4; on the eastern shore of the Dead Sea. 2. A dry measure, containing a little more than a bushel English, and of the same capacity with the *bath* in liquids, Zech. v; 6.

EPH'E-SUS, a much celebrated city of Ionia, in Asia Minor, situated upon the river Ca-ys'ter, and on the side of a hill. It was the metropolis of Asia Minor, and formerly in great renown among the heathen authors on account of its famous temple of Diana. 2. The Apostle Paul first visited this city A. D. 54; but being then on his way to Jerusalem, he abode there only a few weeks, Acts xviii, 19–21: but he promised to return, which he did a few months afterward, and continued there three years, Acts xix, 10; xx, 31. While the apostle abode in Ephesus and its neighbourhood, he gathered a numerous Christian Church, to which, at a subsequent period, he wrote that epistle which forms so important a part of the apostolic writings. He was then a prisoner at Rome, and the year in which he wrote it must have been 60 or 61 of the Christian era. It appears to have been transmitted to them by the hands of Tychisus, one of his companions in travel, Eph. vi, 21. The critics have remarked, that the style of the Epistle to the Ephesians is exceedingly elevated; and that it corresponds to the state of the apostle's mind at the time of writing it. The epistle, says Macknight, is written as it were in a rapture. Grotius remarks that it expresses the sublime matters contained in it, in terms more sublime than are to be found in any human language; to which Macknight subjoins this singular but striking observation, that no real Christian can read the doctrinal part of the Epistle to the Ephesians, without being impressed and roused by it, as by the sound of a trumpet.

3. Ephesus was one of the seven Churches to which special messages were addressed in the book of Revelation, Rev. ii, 5. The contrast which its present state presents to its former glory, is a striking fulfilment of this prophecy. A few heaps of ruins, and some miserable mud cottages, occasionally tenanted by Turks, without one Christian residing there, are all the remains of ancient Ephesus. St. John passed the latter part of his life in Asia Mi'nor, and principally at Eph'e-sus, where he died.

EPH'OD, an ornamental part of the dress of the Jewish priests; a kind of short cloak without sleeves, worn above the tunic and robe, and open below the arms on each side, consisting of two parts, one of which was suspended over the back, and the other over the fore part of the body; both pieces being united by a clasp on the shoulder.

There were two kinds of ephod: one was made plain; and that which was intended for the high priest was *embroidered*, and is described in Ex. xxviii, 6-14. On that part of the ephod which covered the shoulders were two large precious stones, on which were engraven the names of the twelve tribes of Israel—six on each stone. These stones were different from those on the breastplate. The breastplate was confined to the ephod by means of ribands of dark blue. To the ephod belonged a curious girdle of the same rich fabric; that is, woven with the ephod. See BREASTPLATE.

E'PHRA-IM, the youngest son of Joseph, and founder of the tribe of Ephraim, the territory of which lay almost in the middle of the Holy Land, Josh. xvi, 5. In this tract was *Mount 'Ephraim.* The *forest of Ephraim* is to be sought beyond the Jordan, (compare 2 Sam. xvii, 24, with chap. xviii, 6,) probably so called from the slaughter of the Ephraimites, Jud. xii. The kingdom of the ten tribes, or Samaria, was called *Ephraim,* because that tribe was the most important, and also because the family of Jeroboam, the first king, was of that tribe, 1 Kings xi, 26. There was also a city in this tribe, near the river Jordan, by the name of Ephraim, John xi, liv.

EPH'RATA, the same as Bethlehem.

EP-I-CU'RE-ANS, a sect of philosophers, in Greece and Rome, the disciples of Epicurus, who flourished about 300 years B. C. They believed that the world was formed, not by God, nor with design, but by the fortuitous concourse of atoms. They denied that God governs the world, or in the least condescends to interfere with creatures below. They held that sensual pleasure was man's chief good, and that the soul died with the body.

EPISTLES, *letters* written by the apostles, or first preachers of Christianity, to particular Churches or persons, on particular occasions or subjects. The Apostle Paul, who was more accustomed to dictate his epistles than to write them himself, was the author of fourteen; James and Jude each of one; Peter of two; John of three.

E'SAR-HAD'DON, a king of Assyria, the son and successor of Sen-nach'e-rib, 2 Kings xix, 37. Before his father's death, he had been made viceroy over the province of Babylonia, with regal honours. He died B. C. 664.

E'SAU, son of Isaac, and twin brother of Jacob. Born B. C. 1836. The time of his death is not mentioned; but Bishop Cumberland thinks it probable that he died about the same time with his brother Jacob, at the age of about one hundred and forty-seven years.

The conduct of Esau in selling his birthright was both wanton and profane. It was wanton, because he, though faint, could be in no danger of not obtaining a supply of food in his father's house; and was therefore wholly influenced by his appetite, excited by the delicacy of Jacob's pottage. It was profane, because the blessings of the birthright were spiritual as well as civil. The Church of God was to be established in the line of the first-born; and in that line the Messiah was to appear. These high privileges were despised by Esau, who is therefore made by St. Paul a type of all apostates from Christ, who, like him, profanely despise their birthright as the sons of God. See BIRTHRIGHT.

ESH'COL, a valley abounding in vines, in the south part of Palestine. Num. xiii, 23.

ESPOUSE, to promise or engage in marriage by contract in writing or by some pledge. And this contract was made in presence of witnesses, between the father and brothers of the bride, and the father of the bridegroom.

Espousals in the east are frequently made years before the parties are married, and sometimes also in very early youth.

ESTHER, a Jewish virgin, remarkable for her accomplishments, formerly called *Hadassa*, Esth. ii, 7, who became the wife of Xerxes and *queen* of Persia. There is a good degree of probability that Ahasuerus was no other than Xerxes of profane history, who succeeded his father, Darius, B. C. about 485, and is chiefly known by the vast preparations which he made for the invasion of Greece, against which he marched at the head of an army, some say, of five millions of men.

The book of Esther has always been esteemed canonical both by Jews and Christians, and the author is supposed to be *Mordecai*. Esth. ix, 20–32, favours this opinion.

ETHAM, the second station of the Israelites coming out of Egypt. Mr. Stuart thinks it the same encamping place which is now called *Adjerout*, northwest from Suez about twelve miles, where fresh water is found, and the only watering place in this quarter.

E'THAN, the Ezrahite, son of one of the wisest men of his time, Solomon excepted, 1 Kings iv, 31. He was a principal master of the temple music, 1 Chron. xv, 17.

E-THAN'IM, one of the Hebrew months. After the Jews returned from the captivity, the month was called Tisri, which answers to our September.

E-THI-O'PIA, the region on both sides of the Red Sea,

inhabited by people of colour. That is, the Ethiopia in Africa which lies south of Egypt on the Nile; and the southern part of Arabia, connected with the former place as the language shows. Moses married one of the natives of this place, during the march of the Israelites through the Arabian desert. Num. xii, 1. It also includes all the country east of the Tigris, from the Caspian Sea down to the Persian Gulf. This is the country referred to by Moses, Gen. ii, 13. See CUSH.

EU'NICE, the mother of Timothy, a Jewess by birth, but married to a Greek, Timothy's father, 2 Tim. i, 5. When Paul came to Lystra, he found there Eunice and Timothy, already far advanced in grace and virtue.

EU'NUCH. The word signifies *a keeper of the bed.* In the courts of eastern kings, the care of the beds and apartments is generally committed to eunuchs; they have the charge chiefly of the princesses, who live secluded. But in Scripture this word often denotes an officer belonging to a prince, attending his court, and employed in the interior of his palace, as a *name of office and dignity.* Our Saviour speaks of men who "*made themselves eunuchs for the kingdom of heaven's sake,*" Matt. xix, 12; that is, who in times of great persecution and danger chose to remain unmarried, in order to give up themselves uninterruptedly to establish and extend the Gospel.

EU-PHRA'TES, a river of Asiatic Turkey, which rises from the mountains of Armenia; and, chiefly pursuing a southwest direction to Semisat, it would there fall into the Mediterranean, if not prevented by a high range of mountains. At Semisat, the ancient Samosata, this noble river assumes a southerly direction, then runs an extensive course to the southeast, and after receiving the Tigris, falls by two or three mouths into the gulf of Persia, about fifty miles southeast of Bassora; north latitude 29° 50'; east longitude 66° 55'. The comparative course of the Euphrates may be estimated at about one thousand four hundred miles. This river is navigable for a considerable distance from the sea. The Euphrates and Tigris, the most considerable as well as the most renowned rivers of western Asia, are remarkable for their rising within a few miles of each other, running the same course, never being more than one hundred and fifty miles asunder, and sometimes, before their final junction, approaching within fifteen miles of each other, as in the latitude of Bagdad. The space included between the two is the ancient country of Mes-o-po-ta'mi-a. The Scripture calls it "the great river," and assigns it for the eastern boundary of that land which God promised to the Israelites, Deut. i, 7 ; Joshua i, 4.

EU-ROC'LY-DON, the Greek name for the *northeast wind*, very dangerous in the eastern part of the Mediterranean Sea, of the nature of the whirlwind, which falls of a sudden upon ships, Acts xxvii, 14. The same wind is now called a *Levanter*.

E-VAN'GEL-ISTS, *messengers of good tidings, preachers of the Gospel*, not located in any place, but travelling as missionaries to preach the Gospel, and found churches. 2 Tim. iv, 5. They were assistants to the apostles ; or, as they might be termed, *vice apostles*, who acted under their authority and direction. As they were directed to ordain pastors or bishops in the churches, but had no authority to ordain successors in their particular office, they must be considered as but temporary officers, like the apostles and prophets. The term evangelist is at present confined to the writers of the four gospels.

EVE, the first woman. She was called *Eve*, Gen. iii, 20, a word that signifies *life*, because she was to be the mother of all that live. Our translators, therefore, might have called her *Life*. See ADAM.

EVENING, the ending of the day, when it begins to grow dark, or at least when the sun is considerably declined, Neh. xiii, 19.

EVEN-TIDE, the time of evening. *A word nearly obsolete.*

EVERLASTING, *lasting or enduring for ever.* The word occurs as an *attribute* of God, Gen. xxi, 33, and therefore can mean no *limited time*, because nothing of this kind can be attributed to God. It is the same word which is translated *eternal*.

It is that duration which is *always existing ;* still running ON, but never running OUT ; an interminable and immeasurable duration.

EVIL is distinguished into natural and moral. Natural evil is whatever destroys or any way disturbs the perfection of natural beings, such as blindness, diseases, death, &c. Moral evil is the disagreement between the actions of a moral agent, and the rule of those actions, whatever it be. Applied to choice, or acting contrary to the moral or revealed laws of the Deity, it is termed *wickedness*, or *sin.* Applied to an act contrary to a mere rule of fitness, it is called a *fault.*

EXODUS, (*a departure,*) the name of the second book of Moses, and is so called in the Greek version because it relates to the departure of the Israelites out of Egypt. It comprehends the history of about 145 years ; and the principal events contained in it are, the bondage of the Israelites in Egypt, and their miraculous deliverance by the hand of Moses ; their entrance into the wilderness of Sinai; the promulgation of the law, and the building of the tabernacle.

EX'ORCISTS, those who, by certain arts or charms, supposed to be derived from Solomon, pretended to cast out devils.

EYE, the organ of sight. *Between the eyes* is upon the forehead, the front part of the head, Deut. vi, 8. To *set the eyes upon* any one is mostly in the sense of *kindness*, to look with favour; on the contrary, to set the *face*, everywhere implies *unkindness: love* is seen in the *eyes*, anger in the whole face. "*The Lord's eyes are over the righteous*," 1 Pet. iii, 12. Since many affections of the mind, as *envy, pride, pity, desire*, are manifested through the eyes, so Hebrew writers often attribute those things to the eyes which strictly belong to the *persons themselves*, e. g., "*Thine eye is evil against thy poor brother*," Deut. xv, 9, i. e., to *envy* him, Deut. vii, 16; Ezek. v, 11, the ideas of *pity* and *sparing* are attributed to the *eyes* rather than to the person himself. So *weakness* and *strength* are attributed to the hands. See Isa. xxxv, 3.

Eyes are often taken for the understanding, or eyes of the mind, Gen. iii, 7; Deut. xvi, 19.

Eye service is service rendered only while under inspection, Eph. vi, 6.

"*If thine eye be single*," Matt. vi, 22, i. e., *sound*, vision perfect. "*But if thine eye be evil*," i. e., diseased, overgrown with a film or speck.

Deprivation of sight was a very common punishment in the east. The objects of this barbarity were usually persons who aspired to the throne, or who were considered likely to make such an attempt. It was also inflicted on chieftains, whom it was desirable to deprive of power without putting them to death, Jer. lii, 11. Females, in conformity to a custom which prevailed in the earliest ages, used to paint their eyes, Ezek. xxiii, 40.

E-ZE'KI-EL, like his contemporary Jeremiah, was of the sacerdotal race. He was carried away captive to Babylon with Je-hoi'a-chim, king of Judah, 598 B. C., and was placed with many others of his countrymen upon the river Chebar, in Mes-o-po-ta'mi-a, where he was favoured with the Divine revelations contained in his book. He began to prophesy in the fifth year of his captivity, and is supposed to have prophesied about twenty years. The boldness with which he censured the idolatry and wickedness of his countrymen, is said to have cost him his life, but his memory was greatly revered, not only by the Jews, but also by the Medes and Persians. The style of this prophet is characterized by Bishop Lowth as bold, vehement, and tragical; as often

worked up to a kind of tremendous dignity. He is highly parabolical, and abounds
in figures and metaphorical
expressions. He displays a
rough but majestic dignity;
an unpolished though noble
simplicity; inferior perhaps
in originality and elegance to
others of the prophets, but
unequalled in that force and
grandeur for which he is particularly celebrated.

EZION-GE'BER, a sea-
port of Arabia on the Elanitic,
i. e., the eastern gulf of the
Red Sea; and close by the
city of Elath, Deut. ii, 8,
from whence the fleet of Solomon sailed to Ophir.

EZRA, a famous Jewish
high priest and *scribe*, who, in
the seventh year of Artaxerxes Longimanus, 458 B. C.,
led up a colony of Jews from
Babylon to Jerusalem. He
succeeded Zerub'babel in the
government of Judea; was
also a great reformer, and
the author of the book which
bears his name. This book
begins with the repetition of
the last two verses of the second book of Chronicles, and
carries the Jewish history
through a period of seventy-
nine years, commencing from
the edict of Cyrus. The first
six chapters contain an account of the return of the
Jews under Zerubbabel, after the captivity of seventy
years; of their re-establishment in Judea; and of the
building and dedication of
the temple at Jerusalem. In
the last four chapters, Ezra
relates his own appointment
to the government of Judea
by Artaxerxes Lon-gim'a-nus,
his journey thither from Babylon, the disobedience of
the Jews, and the reform
which he immediately effected among them. Till the arrival of Nehemiah, Ezra had
the principal authority in
Jerusalem.

Ezra was the restorer and
publisher of the Holy Scriptures, after the return of the
Jews from the Babylonian
captivity. 1. He corrected
the errors which had crept
into the existing copies of
the sacred writings by the
negligence or mistake of
transcribers. 2. He collected all the books of which the
Holy Scriptures then consisted, disposed them in their
proper order, and settled the
canon of Scripture for his
time. 3. He added throughout the books of his edition
what appeared necessary for
illustrating, connecting, or
completing them; and of this
we have an instance in the
account of the death and
burial of Moses, in the last
chapter of Deuteronomy. In
this work he was assisted by
the same Spirit by which they
were at first written. 4. He
changed the ancient names
of several places become obsolete, and substituted for
them new names, by which
they were at that time called.
5. He wrote out the whole
in the Chaldee character;
that language having grown
into use after the Babylonish

captivity. The Jews have an extraordinary esteem for Ezra, and say that if the law had not been given by Moses, Ezra deserved to have been the legislator of the Hebrews.

FABLE, *a story destitute of truth*. St. Paul exhorts Timothy and Titus to shun profane and Jewish fables, 1 Tim. iv, 7; Tit. i, 14; as having a tendency to seduce men from the truth. The most of modern commentators interpret them of the vain traditions of the Jews; especially concerning meats, and other things, to be abstained from as unclean, which our Lord also styles "the doctrines of men," Matt. xv, 9. In another sense, the word is taken to signify an instructive tale, intended to convey truth under the concealment of fiction; as Jotham's fable of the trees, Judg. ix, 7-15, no doubt by far the oldest fable extant.

FACE. Moses begs of God to show him his *face*, Ex. xxxiii; he replies, "*I will make all my goodness pass before thee*," and I will proclaim my name; "*but my face thou canst not see; for there shall no man see it and live!*" And the persuasion was very prevalent in the world, that no man could support the sight of Deity; yet we read that God talked with the Hebrews "*face to face out of the midst of the fire*," Deut. v, 4. These places are to be understood simply, that God so manifested himself to the Israelites, that he made them hear his voice as distinctly as if he had appeared to them face to face; but not that they actually saw more than the *cloud of glory* which marked his presence. The *face* of God denotes sometimes his *anger* · "The face of the Lord is against them that do evil," Psalm xxxiv, 16.

FAIR-HAVEN, probably an open kind of harbour, not so much a port as a *bay*, on the southeast part of Crete.

FAITH, in Scripture, is presented to us under two leading views; the first is that of *assent* or *persuasion*; the second, that of *confidence* or *reliance*. The former may be separated from the latter, but the latter cannot exist without the former. Faith, in the sense of an intellectual assent to truth, is, by St. James, allowed to devils. A dead, inoperative faith is also supposed, or declared, to be possessed by wicked men, professing Christianity; for our Lord represents persons coming to him at the last day, saying, "Lord, have we not prophesied in thy name?" &c., to whom he will say, "Depart from me, I never knew you." And yet the charge in this place does not lie against the sincerity of their belief, but against their conduct as "workers of iniquity." As this distinction is taught in Scripture, so it is also observed in experience: assent to the truths of revealed religion may result from examination and conviction, while yet the spirit and conduct may remain unrenewed and sinful.

2. The 'faith which is required of us as a condition of salvation always includes *confidence* or *reliance*, as well as *assent* or *persuasion*. That faith by which "the elders obtained a good report" was of this character; it united *assent* to the truth of God's revelations with a noble *confidence* in his promise. "Our fathers *trusted* in thee, and were not confounded."

3. That faith in Christ which in the New Testament is connected with salvation, is clearly of this nature; that is, it combines *assent* with *reliance*, *belief* with *trust*. "Whatsoever ye ask the Father in my name," that is, in dependance upon my interest and merits, "he shall give it you." Christ was preached both to Jews and Gentiles as the object of their trust, because he was preached as the only true sacrifice for sin; and they were required to renounce their dependance upon their own accustomed sacrifices, and to transfer that dependance to his death and mediation,—and "in his name shall the Gentiles *trust*."

4. To the most unlettered Christian this then will be very obvious, that true and saving faith in Christ consists both of *assent* and *trust*; but this is not a blind and superstitious trust in the sacrifice of Christ, like that of the heathen in their sacrifices; nor the presumptuous trust of wicked and impenitent men, who depend on Christ to save them in their sins; but such a trust as is exercised according to the authority and direction of the word of God; so that *to know* the Gospel in its leading principles, and to have a cordial *belief* in it, is necessary to that more specific act of faith which is called *reliance*, or in systematic language, *fiducial assent*. The Gospel, as the scheme of man's salvation, declares that he is under the law; that this law of God has been violated by all; and that every man is under sentence of death. Serious consideration of our ways, confession of the fact, and sorrowful conviction of the evil and danger of sin, will, under the influence of Divine grace, follow the cordial belief of the testimony of God; and we shall then turn to God with contrite hearts, and earnest prayers and supplications for his mercy. This is called "repentance toward God;" and repentance being the first subject of evangelical preaching, and then the injunction to believe the Gospel, it is plain that Christ only is *immediately* held out, in this Divine plan of our redemption, as the object of trust in order to forgiveness to persons in this state of penitence, and under this sense of danger. The degree

of sorrow for sin, and alarm upon this discovery of our danger as sinners, is nowhere fixed to a precise standard in Scripture; only it is supposed everywhere, that it is such as to lead men to inquire earnestly, " What shall I do to be saved?" and with earnest seriousness to use all the appointed means of grace, as those who feel that their salvation is at issue, that they are in a lost condition, and must be pardoned or perish. To all such persons, Christ, as the only atonement for sin, is exhibited as the object of their trust, with the promise of God, "that whosoever believeth in him shall not perish, but have everlasting life." Nothing is required of such but this actual trust in, and personal apprehension or taking hold of, the merits of Christ's death as a sacrifice for sin; and upon their thus believing they are justified, their "faith is counted for righteousness," or, in other words, they are forgiven.

5. This is that qualifying condition to which the promise of God annexes justification; that without which justification would not take place; and in this sense it is that we are justified by faith; not by the merit of faith, but by faith instrumentally as this condition: for its connection with the benefit arises from the merits of Christ and the promise of God; so that the indissoluble connection of faith and justification is from God's institution, whereby he hath bound himself to give the benefit upon performance of the condition. It acknowledges on earth, as it will be perpetually acknowledged in heaven, that the whole salvation of sinful man, from the beginning to the last degree, whereof there shall be no end, is from God's freest love, Christ's merit and intercession, his own gracious promise, and the power of his own Holy Spirit.

6. Faith, in Scripture, sometimes is taken for the truth and faithfulness of God, Rom. iii, 3; and it is also taken for the persuasion of the mind as to the lawfulness of things indifferent, Rom. xiv, 22, 23; and it is likewise put for the doctrine of the Gospel, which is the object of faith, Acts xxiv, 24; Phil. i, 27; Jude 3; for the belief and profession of the Gospel, Rom. i, 8, and for fidelity in the performance of promises.

FAMILIAR SPIRIT, the spirit of divination, pretending to reveal sacred things and foretel future events.

FAN, a winnowing *shovel* with which grain is thrown up against the wind in order to separate it from the chaff. This word is figuratively applied to the *word* and *power* of Christ, with which he will purge the Jewish Church, separating the wicked from the righteous, Matt. iii, 12.

FASTING, *abstinence from food;* this has been practised in all ages, and by all nations, in times of mourning, sorrow, and affliction. We see no example of fasting, properly so called, before Moses. Since the time of Moses, examples of fasting have been very common among the Jews. The Jews, in times of public calamity, appointed extraordinary fasts, and made even the children at the breast fast, Joel ii, 16. Moses fasted forty days upon Mount Horeb, Ex. xxiv, 18. Elijah passed as many days without eating, 1 Kings xix, 8. Our Saviour fasted forty days and forty nights in the wilderness, Matt. iv, 2. These fasts were miraculous, and out of the common rules of nature. Acts xxvii, 9, refers to the great annual public fast of the Jews, the great day of the atonement, which occurred in the month Tisri, corresponding to the new moon of October, and thus served to indicate the season of the year after which the navigation of the Mediterranean became dangerous.

As to the fasts observed by Christians, it does not appear by his own practice, or by his commands to his disciples, that our Lord instituted any particular fast. Fasting is recommended by our Saviour in his sermon on the mount; not as a stated, but as an occasional duty of Christians, for the purpose of humbling their minds under the afflicting hand of God; and he requires that this duty be performed in sincerity, and not for the sake of ostentation, Matt. vi, 16.

FAT, the best, the richest part of any thing, as the "*fat of the land,*" Gen. xlv, 18; its best fruits, richest productions. The "*fat,*" or "*kidney fat of wheat,*" i. e., the finest wheat, the finest flour, Deut. xxxii, 14.

Abounding in spiritual grace and comfort, Psa. xcii, 14; also, an abundance of good things. "*A fat heart,*" i. e., a heart covered with fat, and therefore *torpid, dull, unfeeling,* Psa. xvii, 10.

FATHER. Besides the common acceptation of the word, it often has a wider sense. It signifies, 1. A forefather, ancestor, 2 Kings xiv, 3. 2. A founder, author, i. e., the first ancestor of a tribe or nation. "*The father of all such as handle the harp and organ,*" Gen. iv, 21, i. e., the founder of the family of musicians, the master, or inventor, of the science of music. 3. The *maker* of any thing, a *creator.* "*Hath the rain a father?*" Job xxxviii, 28; in this sense, God is the father of men. Christians, by reason of adoption, have a new right to call God a father. See SON.

The above senses come from the notion of *source, origin;* others are drawn from the idea of *paternal love* and *care,* the honour due to a father.

4. A *nursing father, benefactor,* as doing good, and providing for others in the

manner of a father. "*I was a father to the poor*," Job xxix, 16. By the same metaphor, God is called the father of kings and others, 2 Sam. vii, 14.

5. A *master, teacher*, from the idea of paternal instruction, 1 Sam. x, 12; hence priests and prophets, as being teachers sent with Divine authority, are saluted with the title of father, out of respect and favour, even by kings, Judges xvii, 10. Thus the Pharisees designated themselves as eminent instructers, wishing the people to have that implicit faith in them, in religious matters, which young children are apt to have in their parents, Matt. xxiii, 9; in this sense call no man father.

6. In a similar sense, Joseph is called "*a father to Pharaoh*," i. e., his chief adviser and prime minister, Gen. xlv, 8.

7. A *spiritual father*: one who converts another to the Christian faith, and is thus the instrument of his spiritual *birth*, or of his becoming a child of God, 1 Cor. iv, 15.

8. A person respected for his *age* and *dignity*, Acts vii, 2.

9. It expresses *intimate relationship*, close alliance. "*I have said to corruption, Thou art my father*," Job xvii, 14.

FEAR, a painful apprehension of danger. It is sometimes used for the object of fear; as, "*the fear of Isaac*," that is, the God whom Isaac feared, Gen. xxxi, 42. God says that he will send his fear before his people, to terrify and destroy the inhabitants of Canaan. Fear is used, also, for reverence: "God is greatly to be *feared* in the assembly of his saints." This kind of fear, being compatible with confidence and love, is sometimes called *filial fear*.

The filial fear of God is a holy affection, or gracious habit, wrought in the soul by God, Jer. xxxii, 40, whereby it is inclined and enabled to obey all God's commandments, even the most difficult, Gen. xxii, 12; Eccl. xii. 13; and to hate and avoid evil, Nehem. v, 15; Prov. viii, 13. Slavish fear is the consequence of guilt; an alarm within that disturbs the rest of the sinner. Fear is put for the whole worship of God: "I will teach you the fear of the Lord," Psa. xxxiv, 11; i. e. I will teach you the true way of worshipping and serving God.

FEASTS. God appointed several festivals among the Jews. 1. To perpetuate the memory of great events. 2. To keep them under the influence of religion, and to convey spiritual instruction, and to keep alive the expectation of the Messiah, and his more perfect dispensation. 3. To secure to them certain times of rest and rejoicings. 4. To render them familiar with the law; for, in their religious assemblies, the law of God was read and explained. 5. To renew the acquaintance, correspondence, and friendship of their tribes and families, coming from the several towns in the country, and meeting three times a year in the holy city.

The first and most ancient festival, the *sabbath*, commemorated the creation, Gen. ii, 3. *The passover*, the depurture out of Egypt, and the favour which God showed his people in sparing their first-born, Ex. xii, 14, &c. The feast of *pentecost* was celebrated on the fiftieth day after the passover. The feast of *trumpets* was celebrated on the first day of the civil year. The feast of *atonement* was celebrated on the tenth day of Tisri, which was the first month of the civil year. It was instituted for a general expiation of sins, irreverences, and pollutions of all the Israelites, from the high priest to the lowest of the people, committed by them throughout the year, Lev. xxiii, 27, 28; Num. xxix, 7. The feast of tents, or tabernacles, was kept on the fifteenth of Tisri. The three great feasts of the year, the passover, pentecost, and that of the tabernacles, were designed to commemorate the wonderful kindness of God. The first continued only for *one* day, the second *seven*, and the last *eight;* but the first and last days only were properly considered festival days, in which no employment farther than was necessary to prepare food, was permitted. And all the males of the nation were obliged to visit the temple at these three feasts. But the law did not require them to continue there during the whole time, except in the feast of tabernacles, when it seems they were obliged to be present for the whole eight days.

Beside these feasts, we find the feast of lots, or *purim*. The feast of the dedication of the temple, or rather of the restoration of the temple, which had been profaned by Antiochus Epiphanes, 1 Mac. iv, 52, &c., was celebrated in winter, and is supposed to be the feast of dedication mentioned in John x, 22.

In the Christian Church, no festival appears to have been expressly instituted by Jesus Christ, or his apostles. Yet Christians have always celebrated the memory of his resurrection, and observe this feast on every Sunday, which was commonly called the Lord's day, Rev. i, 10. By inference we may conclude this festival to have been instituted by apostolic authority.

FEASTS OF CHARITY, Jude, ver. 12; feasts which were kept by primitive Christians, in each particular church, at the time of celebrating the Lord's Supper. These feasts were furnished by the common oblations of the faithful. Rich and poor were to partake of them with decency and sobriety. It would seem at Corinth, in the apostles' days, they were held before

Covel's Dic., p. 152.

THE FIG.

the Lord's Supper; for when the Corinthians are blamed for an unworthy receiving of that ordinance, it is partly charged upon this, that some of them had indulged to excess at the preceding love feast, 1 Cor. xi, 21.

FEET. By this word the Hebrews modestly expressed what decency forbade them to name, Isa. vii, 20. *At the feet of any one* is to be in his *steps*, or *following* after him, Jud. iv, 10; or on his *track*, Hab. iii, 5. "*To water by the foot*," Deut. xi, 10, i. e., to irrigate land by machines with a tread wheel for raising water, such as are still used in Egypt for watering gardens. *Sitting at the feet*, Luke vii, 35, is an allusion to the position of disciples, who were accustomed to sit before their master or teacher. Thus Paul was brought up at the *feet* of Gamaliel as his scholar, Acts xxii, 3.

To *put under one's feet*, Rom. xvi, 20; 1 Cor. xv, 25; is to make subject to any one, in allusion to the ancient manner of treading the foot upon the necks of vanquished enemies, Josn. x, 24.

The orientals used to wash the feet of strangers, because they commonly walked with their legs bare, and their feet defended only by sandals. So Abraham washed the feet of the three angels, Gen. xviii, 4; and our Saviour gave his last lesson of humility by washing his disciples' feet, John xiii, 5.

To the *feet*, as the instrument of walking, is sometimes ascribed that which strictly belongs to the person who walks, i. e., a part of the person is taken for the whole, Rom. x, 15; Acts v, 9.

FELIX, the eleventh Roman procurator of Judea, about A. D. 51–58. He was a freed man of the Emperor Claudius, and hence is called *Claudius*. He first married Drusilla, a granddaughter of Anthony, and afterward another Drusilla, the daughter of Herod Agrippa, by whom he had a son, who perished in an eruption of Mount Vesuvius. He was a man of the most infamous character, and a plague to all the provinces over which he presided. See CLAUDIUS.

FELLER, one that *hews* or *cuts* down.

FERRET, an animal of the weasel kind; but the original word is supposed by Gesenius to be a species of *lizard*.

FES'TUS. Portius Festus succeeded Felix in the government of Judea, A. D. 60, Acts xxiv, 27.

FIG TREE. This is not a shrub, as in our gardens, but a *tree*, not altogether erect, but tall and leafy. The leaves are hand-shaped, like those of the mulberry. It flourishes in warm climates, and a sandy soil; and was very common in Palestine. The fruit which it bears is produced from the trunk and large branches, and not from

FIG   154   FIN

small shoots, as in most other trees. These trees do not properly blossom: they send out their fruit, like so many little buttons, with their flowers, small and imperfect as they are, enclosed within them. (See the engraving.) "*To sit under the vine and fig tree*," is to live a quiet and happy life, 1 Kings iv, 25; Zech. iii, 10.

The account of our Saviour's denunciation against the barren fig tree, Mark xi, 13, has occasioned some of the boldest cavils of infidelity. The whole difficulty arises from his disappointment in not finding *fruit* on the tree, when it is expressly said that "*the time of figs was not yet.*" But the expression does not signify the time of the *coming forth* of figs, but the time of the *gathering* in of ripe figs, as is plain from the parallel expressions. Thus "*the time of the fruit*," Matt. xxi, 34, most plainly signifies the time of *gathering in* ripe fruits, since the servants were sent to receive those fruits for their master's use. St. Mark and St. Luke express the same by the word *time*, or *season*: "At the *season* he sent a servant," &c., that is, at the season or time of gathering in ripe fruit, Mark xii, 2; Luke xx, 10. Certainly fruit might be expected on a tree whose leaves were distinguished afar off, whose fruit, if it bore any, appeared before the leaves, and the time of the gathering of whose fruit

was not yet. St. Matthew informs us that the tree was "*in the way*," that is, in the common road, and therefore, probably, no particular person's property; but if it was, being barren, the timber might be as serviceable to the owner as before. In the blasting of this barren fig tree, the distant appearance of which was so fair and promising, he delivered one more awful lesson to a degenerate nation, of whose hypocritical exterior, and flattering but delusive pretensions, it was a just and striking emblem.

FIGURE, *a type*, an emblem of something to come; thus Moses was commanded to "*make the tabernacle according to the fashion*," or *type*, "*that he had seen*," Acts vii, 44. Some distinguish figures or types into real and personal, by the former intending the tabernacle, temple, and religious institutions; and under the latter what are called providential and personal types. But we should be careful not to regard every thing mentioned in the Old Testament as typical. That any *person* or *thing* under the Old Testament dispensation was designed to prefigure something under the New, can be known to us only by Divine revelation; and what is not designated by that authority, must not be regarded as typical.

FINGER. The finger of God signifies his power, his operation, Luke xi, 20. To put forth one's finger, is a bantering, insulting gesture, Isaiah lviii, 9.

FIRE is often made use of as a symbol of the Deity: "The Lord thy God is a consuming fire," Deut. iv, 24. The Holy Ghost is compared to that purifying element: "*He shall baptize you with the Holy Ghost and with fire.*" Matt. iii, 11. To verify this prediction, he sent the Holy Ghost, which descended upon his disciples, in the form of tongues, or like *flames of fire*, Acts ii, 3. It is the work of the Holy Spirit to *enlighten*, *purify*, and sanctify the soul; and to *inflame* it with love to God, and zeal for his glory.

The torments of hell are described by *fire*. Our Saviour makes use of this similitude to represent the punishment of the damned, Mark ix, 44. He likewise speaks frequently of the eternal fire prepared for the devil, his angels, and reprobates, Matt. xxv, 41. The sting and remorse of conscience is the worm that will never die; and the wrath of God upon their souls and bodies, the fire that shall never go out— a clear indication of the *perpetuity* of future punishment. The word of God is compared to fire: "*Is not my word like a fire?*" Jer. xxiii, 29. It is full of life and efficacy; like a fire it warms, melts, and heats; and is powerful to consume the dross, and burn up the chaff and stubble. Fire is likewise taken

for *persecution, dissension, and division.* "*I am come to send fire on earth,*" Luke xii, 49; as if it was said, Upon my coming and publishing the Gospel, there will follow, through the devil's malice and corruption of men, much persecution to the professors thereof, and manifold divisions in the world, whereby men will be tried, whether they will be faithful or not; hence the tongue, as kindling strife and discord, is a fire, Jas. iii, 6.

FIRKIN, a measure of capacity, being the *fourth* part of a barrel; the size of the measure in the Greek is supposed to be 8¼ gallons.

FIRMAMENT, the *expanse* of the heavens, which is *spread out. expanded*, and appears like an immense arch above the earth, splendid and transparent as *sapphire*, Ex. xxiv, 10. Daniel speaks of the *brightness* of the firmament, Dan. xii, 3. In this the stars are said to be fixed; and above this the Hebrews supposed a celestial ocean to exist, Gen. i, 7; Psa. cxlviii, 4. But this expansion is properly the *atmosphere*, which encompasses the globe on all sides.

FIRST. This word has two significations: first in *point* or *order* of time, and first in degree, i. e., the most eminent or most important thing in the writer's intention. "1 delivered unto you *first* of all," i. e., the principal thing, 1 Cor. xv, 3. The following contains both significations: "*Seek ye first the kingdom of God*," Matt. vi, 33. 1. Give it the *first place* in your desires and pursuits; and, 2. Give it the *preference* to all other things. Seek it with all the *diligence* that its importance demands.

FIRST-BORN, *the eldest son on the father's side.* The first-born was the object of special affection to his parents, and inherited peculiar rights and privileges. 1. He received a double portion of the estate. Jacob, in the case of Reuben, his first-born, bestowed his additional portion upon Joseph, by adopting his two sons, Gen. xlviii, 5–8; Deut. xxi, 17. This was done as a reprimand, and a punishment of his incestuous conduct, Gen. xxxv, 22: but Reuben, notwithstanding, was enrolled as the first-born in the genealogical registers, 1 Chron. v, 1. 2. He was the priest of the whole family. The honour of exercising the priesthood was transferred, by the command of God, communicated through Moses, from the tribe of Reuben, to whom it belonged by right of primogeniture, to that of Levi, Num. iii, 12, 13. 3. He enjoyed an authority over those who were younger, similar to that possessed by a father. It is very easy to see, in view of these facts, how the word "*first-born*" came to express sometimes a great, and sometimes the highest dignity.

2. The *first*, the chief of its kind, whatever is most distinguished. *The first-born of death*, Job xviii, 13, is the *chief among deadly diseases,* the most terrible disease. By the common Hebrew idiom, disease is aptly termed *the son of death,* as being its precursor and attendant; and the most fatal and terrible disease is here figuratively described as the *first-born* among many. *The first-born of the poor*, Isa. xiv, 30; the very poorest, the most wretched, the chief among the sons of the poor.

3. God ordained that all the Jewish first-born, both of men and beasts, for service, should be consecrated to him. The male children only were subject to this law. If a woman's first child were a girl, the father was not obliged to offer any thing for her, or for the children after her, though they were males.

FIRST FRUITS. *That which is first of its kind, or that which is first in order of time.*

FIRST FRUITS were presents made to God of part of the fruits of the harvest, to express the submission, dependance, and thankfulness of the offerers. They were offered at the temple, before the crop was touched; and when the harvest was over, before any private persons used their corn. The first of these first fruits, offered in the name of the nation, was a sheaf of barley, gathered on the fifteenth of Ni'san, in the evening, and threshed in a court of the temple. After it was well cleaned, about three pints of it were roasted and pounded in a mortar. Over this was thrown a portion of oil, and a handful of incense. Then the priest took this offering, waved it before the Lord toward the four parts of the world, threw a handful of it into the fire upon the altar, and kept the rest. After this, every one was at liberty to get in his harvest. Beside these first-fruits, every private person was obliged to bring his first-fruits to the temple. St. Paul says, Christians have the first-fruits of the Spirit, Rom. viii, 23; that is, the first gift of the Spirit, the earnest, the pledge of future and still higher blessings. Christ is called the first-fruits of them that slept; for as the first-fruits were earnests to the Jews of the succeeding harvest, so Christ is the first-fruits or the earnest of the general resurrection.

FIR TREE. The fir tree is an evergreen of beautiful appearance, whose dense foliage, and lofty height, afford a spacious shelter and shade. The trunk of the tree is very straight. The wood was anciently used for spears, musical instruments, furniture for houses, rafters in building, and for ships.

FISH. This appears to be the general name in Scripture of aquatic animals. We have few names in Scripture, if any, for particular kinds of fish. Moses says, Lev. xi,

9, all sorts of fish may be eaten, if they have scales and fins; all others are unclean. Some interpreters believe that the fish which swallowed Jonah was a whale, but others with more probability, suppose that it was *a shark.*

FITCHES, a kind of tare.

FLAG, a species of plant. It probably denotes the sedge, or long grass, which grows in the meadows of the Nile, and which is very grateful to cattle.

FLAGON, an earthen vessel, with a narrow mouth, used for holding and conveying liquor. Gesenius says the original word signifies *cakes,* such as were prepared from dried grapes or raisins. They are mentioned as delicacies with which the weary and languid are refreshed, 2 Sam. vi, 19; and were also offered to idols in sacrifice, Hos. iii, 1.

FLAX, a plant very common, and too well known to need a description. It is a vegetable upon which the industry of mankind has been exercised with the greatest success and utility. From time immemorial Egypt was celebrated for the production or manufacture of flax. Wrought into garments, it constituted the principal dress of the inhabitants, and the priests never put on any other kind of clothing. The fine linen of Egypt is celebrated in all ancient authors, and its superior excellence mentioned in the sacred Scriptures. "The smoking flax," Matt. xii, 20, signifies the *wick* of a lamp, after the flame is extinct, and is still smoking. This expresses the almost expiring state of the *light* of truth in the minds of the Jewish people, calling for immediate attention to excite the flickering, dying flame.

FLEA. David likens himself to this insect; importing that, while it would cost Saul much pains to catch him, he would obtain but very little advantage from it.

FLESH. This term signifies, 1. The *body*, i. e., the matter of which the body is formed. *There is one flesh of men*, 1 Cor. xv, 39. 2. By an easy figure of speech, it is applied to denote *human nature*, or *mankind* universally. " *The end of all flesh is come before me,*" Gen. vi, 13.

3. *Relatives*, kinsmen by natural descent, Rom. xi, 14.

4. Because the fleshy part of our nature is perceived by the eye, it is sometimes used to denote *that* in religion which is merely *outward* and *ceremonial*, Gal. iii, 3.

5. On account of the deep and universal corruption of human nature, which displays itself in a peculiar manner, producing an addictedness to the indulgence of bodily or *fleshy* appetites, the term *flesh* is frequently used to denote *moral corruption*, or human nature considered as corrupt, Gal. v, 19–24. *Flesh and blood* is a Hebrew term for *man*, Matt. xvi, 17. See BLOOD.

FLIES. The kinds of flies are exceedingly numerous; some with two and some with four wings. They abound in warm and moist regions, as in Egypt, Chaldea, Palestine, and in the middle regions of Africa; and during the rainy seasons are very troublesome.

M. Sonnini, speaking of Egypt, says, " Of insects there the most troublesome are the flies. Both man and beast are cruelly tormented with them." Hence different people had deities whose office it was to defend them against flies. Among these may be reckoned Baalzebub, the *fly god* of Ekron.

The engraving is a very accurate design given by Mr. Bruce of the Ethiopian fly, called *Zimb*. It is very little larger than a bee, of a thicker proportion, and its wings, which are pure gauze without colour or spot upon them, are placed separate like those of a fly. As soon as this plague appears, and their buzzing is heard, all the cattle forsake their food, and run wildly about the plain till they die, worn out with fatigue, fright and hunger. When they are once attacked, the body, head and legs break out into swellings which break and putrify, to the certain destruction of the creature. No remedy remains but to leave the black earth, where they live, and hasten to the sands, whither this cruel enemy never dares to pursue them.

Isaiah has given an account of this insect, and its opera

HORNET, OR AFRICAN ZIMB.

Covel's Dic·   p. 159.

THE CONEY, OR ASHKOKO.
(From the Pictoral Bible.)

tions, Isa. vii, 18, 19, which implies that the fly shall cut off from the cattle their usual retreat to the desert. Solomon speaks of *dead flies*, Eccl. x, 1, meaning *deadly venomous flies;* any such would spoil a pot of ointment; so a foolish act ruins the character of him who has the reputation of being wise and good.

FLOCK. See SHEPHERD.

FLOOD, any great inundation; but more particularly that universal inundation by which all the inhabitants of the globe were destroyed, except Noah and his family. This remarkable event happened A. M. 1656; B. C. 2348. Its magnitude and singularity could scarcely fail to make an indelible impression on the minds of the survivers, which would be communicated from them to their children, and would not be easily effaced from the traditions even of their latest posterity. What we might reasonably expect has, accordingly, been actually and completely realized. The evidence which has been brought from almost every quarter of the world to bear upon the reality of this event is of the most conclusive and irresistible kind; and every investigation which has been made concerning heathen rites and traditions has constantly added to its force, no less than to its extent; and the globe itself now exhibits striking proofs that an event like the one in question has happened.

FLOOR, *for threshing,* a circular space, thirty or forty paces in diameter, in an elevated part of a field, exposed to the wind, destitute of walls and covering, where the ground was levelled down for threshing grain: hence we read of the "*chaff driven with the whirlwind out of the floor,*" Hos. xiii, 3.

FOOT. See FEET.

FOOL, one *dull, stupid;* one void of discernment, Psa. xlix, 11; Pro. xviii, 13; also an *impious, ungodly man. The fool hath said in his heart, There is no God,* Psa. xiv, 1. See the language of Tamar to her brother, 2 Sam. xiii, 12, 13, *One of the fools of Israel,* i. e., a very wicked person, one guilty of a shameful deed, *a crime.* Whosoever, with a malicious intent, shall say to his brother, *Thou fool,* shall be in danger of eternal destruction, Matt. v, 22.

The foolishness of God, 1 Cor. i, 25, is the Gospel which *men count foolish.*

FOREKNOWLEDGE, an attribute of God. On this subject some suppose that though the knowledge of God be infinite as his power is infinite, there is no more reason to conclude that his knowledge should be always exerted to the full extent of its capacity than that his power should be employed to the extent of his omnipotence; and that if we suppose him to *choose* not to know some contingencies, the infiniteness of his knowledge is not thereby impugned. To this it may be answered, that the infinite power of God is in Scripture represented, as in the nature of things it must be, as an infinite capacity, and not as infinite in act; but that the knowledge of God is on the contrary never represented there to us as a capacity to acquire knowledge, but as actually comprehending all things that are, and all things that can be. 2. That the notion of God's choosing to know some things, and not to know others, supposes a reason why he refuses to know any class of things or events; which reason, it would seem, can only arise out of their nature and circumstances, and therefore supposes at least a partial knowledge of them, from which the reason for his not choosing to know them arises. The doctrine is therefore somewhat contradictory. But, 3. It is fatal to this opinion that it does not at all meet the difficulty arising out of the question of the consistency of divine prescience, and the free actions of men; since some contingent actions, for which men have been made accountable, we are sure have been foreknown by God, because by his Spirit in the prophets they were foretold; and if the freedom of man can in these cases be reconciled to the prescience of God, there is no greater difficulty in any other case which can possibly occur.

The great fallacy in the argument, that the certain prescience of a moral action destroys its contingent nature, lies in supposing that contingency and certainty are the opposites of each other. If, however, the term *contingent* has any definite meaning at all, as applied to the moral actions of men, it must mean their *freedom*, and stands opposed, not to certainty, but to *necessity*. A free action is a voluntary one; and an action which results from the choice of the agent is distinguished from a necessary one in this, that it might not have been, or have been otherwise, according to the self-determining power of the agent. Simple knowledge is, in no sense, a cause of action, nor can it be conceived to be causal, unconnected with exerted power: for mere knowledge, therefore, an action remains free or necessitated as the case may be. Free actions foreknown will not, therefore, cease to be contingent. But how stands the case as to their certainty? Precisely on the same ground. The certainty of a necessary action foreknown does not result from the knowledge of the action, but from the operation of the necessitating cause; and, in like manner, the certainty of a free action does not result from the knowledge of it, which is no cause at all, but from the voluntary cause; that is, the determination of the will. It alters not the case in the least, to say that the voluntary action might have been otherwise. Had it been otherwise, the knowledge of it would have been otherwise; but as the will, which gives birth to the action, is not dependant upon the previous knowledge of God, but the knowledge of the action upon foresight of the choice of the will, neither the will nor the act is controlled by the knowledge; and the action, though foreseen, is still free or contingent. The foreknowledge of God has then no influence upon either the freedom or the certainty of actions, for this plain reason, that it is knowledge, and not influence; and actions may be certainly foreknown without their being rendered necessary by that foreknowledge. But here it is said, "If an action be certainly foreknown, it *cannot* happen otherwise." This is not the true inference. It *will* not happen otherwise. The objection is, that it is not possible that the action should otherwise happen. But why not? What deprives it of that power? If a necessary action were in question, it could not otherwise happen than as the necessitating cause shall compel; but then that would arise from the necessitating cause solely, and not from the prescience of the action, which is not causal. But if the action be free, and it enter into the very nature of a voluntary action to be unconstrained, then it might have happened in a thousand other ways, or not have happened at all; the foreknowledge of it no more affects its nature in this case than in the other.

FORESKIN. This was held as something *unclean* and *profane*, Deut. x, 16. *Circumcise the foreskin of your hearts*, i. e., put away impurity from your hearts. *Circumcise yourselves to the Lord*, Jer. iv, 4. Put away impurity and consecrate yourselves to God. See CIRCUMCISION.

FORNICATION, whoredom, or the act of incontinency between single persons; for if either of the parties be married, the sin is adultery. But sometimes adultery and fornication are confounded, Matt. v, 32; 1 Cor. v, 1, 11. Used also for *idolatry*, and for all kinds of *infidelity* toward God.

FORNICATOR, one who indulges in gross and sensual pleasures, or who is of an abandoned character, Heb. xii, 16. So our Saviour often speaks of the Jews as a wicked and adulterous generation; not literally adulterous, but so in a figurative sense of the word, viz., sensual, vicious, abandoned, profligate.

TO FORSWEAR, is to swear falsely, to *act* or *omit* any thing contrary to a *promissory oath*, Matt. v, 33, for our Saviour speaks of such oaths as are to be performed.

FOUNTAIN, the source or spring-head of running waters. There were several celebrated fountains in Judea, such as that of En-rogel, of Gihon, of Siloam, of Nazareth, &c.; and allusions to them are often to be met with in both the Old and New Testaments. As fountains of water were so extremely valuable to the inhabitants of the eastern countries, it is easy to understand why the inspired writers so frequently allude to them, and thence deduce some of their most beautiful and striking similitudes, when they would set forth the choicest spiritual blessings. Thus Jeremiah calls the blessed God "*the fountain of living waters*," Jer. ii, 13. As those springs or fountains of water are the most valuable and highly prized which never intermit or cease to flow, but are always sending forth their streams; such is Jehovah to his people: he is a perennial source of felicity. Zechariah, pointing in his days to the atonement which was to be made in the fulness of time, by the shedding of the blood of Christ, describes it as a fountain that was to be opened, in which the inhabitants of Jerusalem might wash away all their impurities.

FOX, called in the Bible the *little fox*, Sol. Song ii, 15. This well known animal is the most *sagacious* and *crafty* of all the beasts of prey. It is a native of almost every part of the globe, and has been the destroyer of grapes from the earliest records. Some suppose that the Hebrews under the term included also the *jackal*, the wild dog, an animal resembling a dog and a fox. Thus jackals seem to be meant in Judges xv, 4, where it is said that "*Samson caught three hundred foxes*," since the fox is a solitary animal, and is with great difficulty taken alive, whereas jackals are gregarious and found in great numbers about Gaza. Jackals seem to be meant also in Psa. lxiii, 10, "*They shall fall by the sword, they shall be a portion for foxes*," inasmuch as foxes do not generally feed on *dead bodies*; but a dead body is a favourite repast for the *jackal*. Jesus calls Herod, the tetrarch of Galilee, a *fox*, Luke xiii, 32, thereby signifying his *craft* and the refinements of his policy.

FRANKINCENSE is a transparent and fragrant gum which distils from incisions in a tree growing in Arabia and around Mount Lebanon, and was used by the ancients as *incense*, Ex. xxx, 34.

In modern times it is classed among drugs, and is sometimes called *olibanum*, Matt ii, 11.

FRIEND is taken for one whom we love and esteem above others, to whom we impart our minds more familiarly than to others, and that from a confidence of his in-

Covel's Dic

JACKAL, OR FOX OF THE BIBLE.

P. 165.

tegrity and good will toward us: thus Jonathan and David were mutually friends. The title "the friend of God," is principally given to Abraham. This title was given him because God frequently appeared to him, conversed familiarly with him, and revealed his secrets to him, Gen. xviii, 17; also because he entered into a covenant of perpetual friendship both with him and his seed. Our Saviour calls his apostles "friends:" "But I have called you friends;" and he adds the reason of it, John xv, 15. As men communicate their counsels and their whole mind to their friends, especially in things which are of any concern, or may be of any advantage for them to know and understand, so I have revealed to you whatever is necessary for your instruction, office, comfort, and salvation. And this title is not peculiar to the apostles, but is also common with all true believers. The friend of the bridegroom is the brideman; he who does the honours of the wedding, and leads his friend's spouse to the nuptial chamber. John the Baptist, with respect to Christ and his Church, was the friend of.the bridegroom; by his preaching he prepared the people of the Jews for Christ, John iii, 29. Friend is a word of ordinary salutation, whether to a friend or foe: he is called friend who had not on a wedding garment, Matt. xxii, 12. And our Saviour calls Judas the traitor, friend.

FOUNDATION sometimes means columns or pillars on which a building rests; and, metaphorically, *princes*, *nobles*, i. e., pillars of a state, Psa. xi, 3. When the *foundation*, i. e., the pillars, are overthrown; when the nobles, the firm supporters of what is right and good, have perished, &c. Foundations also signify the *ruins* of buildings destroyed to the foundations, so that those alone remain, Isa. lviii, 12.

FROG, a well known, harmless animal, that lives partly in the water and partly on the land. It exists in every part of the world, and is very tenacious of life. Reckoned unclean by the Hebrews.

FRONTLETS, *bands* or *fillets* worn on the forehead, especially the *prayer fillets* or *phylacteries* of the Jews; i. e., strips of parchment on which were written various sentences from the Mosaic law, and which the Jews were accustomed to bind around the forehead and the left wrist while they were at prayer.

FRUIT, produce both of trees and plants, and of the earth; often used figuratively for the result, consequences of an action or endeavour; the figure being often preserved. Isa. iii, 10: "They shall eat the *fruit* of their do ings," experience the consequences. "Earth is satisfied with the *fruit* of thy works,"

i. e., is watered with rain, which is the produce of the sky or clouds, Psa. civ, 13. "*Fruit* of the lips" signifies what the lips utter, as in the sacrifice of praise or thanksgiving, Heb. xiii, 15. "*Fruit* of the hands," Prov. xxxi, 16, gain, profits. "*Fruit* of the stout heart," Isa. x, 12, is boasting. "*Fruit* meet," i. e., works suitable or corresponding to repentance, Matt. iii, 8.

FUEL, Isa. ix, 19. The scarcity of fuel in some parts of the east obliges the inhabitants to collect for this purpose every kind of combustible matter that can be found, such as *thorns*, Psa. lviii, 9; the withered stalks of *herbs* and *flowers*; the tendrils of the vine; and even turf made of *dung* of the camel or the cow. See Ezek. iv, 15.

FULNESS. 1. *The contents*, that with which any thing is filled. "The *fulness* of the earth" is all that it contains, Psa. xxiv, 1.

2. *Full measure, abundance,* John i, 16. "The *fulness* of the Godhead," Col. ii, 9, is the plenitude of the divine perfections, or that perfection and government which are essential to the Godhead.

3. The *full number, complement*, multitude; so all the multitude of the Gentiles, Rom. xi, 25. So also the church is called the *fulness* of Christ, Eph. i, 23; because without the church, which is his body, Christ would not be complete.

4. The *full period*, the completion of time; the time foretold by the prophets, appointed by God, expected, and longed for by all the faithful.

FURLONG, a measure of distance, containing 660 feet, the eighth part of a mile. But *stadios*, translated furlong, is equivalent only to about 604½ feet, or 201½ yards English.

FURNACE, a fire-place for smelting metals. "The fining pot is for silver, the *furnace* for gold," Prov. xvii, 3. It signifies also a place of cruel bondage and oppression; such as Egypt was to the Israelites, who there met with much hardship, vigour, and severity, to try and purge them, Deut. iv, 20. The sharp and grievous afflictions and judgments wherewith God tries his people, Ezek. xxii, 18–22; also a place of torment, as the furnace of Nebuchadnezzar and *hell*, the place where the wicked shall be punished, Matt. xiii, 42.

FURY. See ANGER.

GAB'BA-THA, i. e., *an elevated place*, probably a *tribunal*. See John xix, 13, where it is called *a pavement*, properly a tesselated marble pavement, formed in little squares, common among the wealthy Romans at that time. This was the place whence Pilate pronounced sentence of death upon Jesus Christ. See PAVEMENT.

GABRIEL, *man of God;*

one of the principal angels of heaven, an archangel, Dan. ix, 21; Luke i, 19.

GAD'A-RA, a city east of the Jordan, which gave name to the country of the Gadarenes; situated on a steep rocky hill on the river Hieromax, or Yermuck, about five miles from its junction with the Jordan. The vicinity was likewise called the country of the Gergesenes. Thus the miracle of our Lord performed here is represented by St. Mark to have been done in the country of the Gadarenes, Mark v, 1; and by St. Matthew in that of the Gergesenes, Matt. viii, 28.

GAL-A'TIA, a province of Asia Minor, on the *Black Sea*. The *Gauls*, after the death of Alexander the Great, having conquered this country, called it *Galatia*, the ancient Greek name for *France*. St. Paul preached several times in these regions: first in A. D. 51, and established churches. It appears from the epistle which he subsequently wrote to them, that they received the Gospel with great joy, Gal. iv, 15. But some *Judaizing* teachers, (*teachers conforming to the doctrines and rites of the Jews,*) getting among them soon after, corrupted their minds from the simplicity of the Gospel; and, though mostly Gentiles, they were induced to mingle Jewish observances with their faith in Christ, to render it more available to their salvation.

This occasioned Paul's writing to them; and his object, throughout nearly the whole of his epistle, was to counteract the influence of their doctrine, especially as it respects the article of *justification*. The epistle was probably written about A. D. 51 or 52.

GAL'BA-NUM, a *gum* procured from a Syrian plant, of a strong, *fragrant smell*, and an acrid and bitterish taste. It was an ingredient in the holy incense of the Jews.

GALILEANS, *natives or inhabitants of Galilee*. They were brave and industrious; though the other Jews regarded them as stupid, unpolished, and seditious; and therefore proper objects of contempt, John i, 46, and vii, 52. They had a peculiar dialect, by which they were easily distinguished from the Jews of Jerusalem, Mark xiv, 70.

GALILEE, an extensive region of Palestine, which in the time of Christ included all the northern part of it, lying between the Jordan and the Mediterranean, and between Samaria and Phenicia. Before the exile, the name seems to have been applied only to a small *tract* bordering on the northern limits, 2 Kings xv, 29; and because many foreigners from the neighbouring countries were mixed with the population, it was called *Galilee of the Gentiles*, Matt. iv, 15.

In the time of Christ Galilee was divided into *Upper*

15

and *Lower*; the former lying north of the territory of Ze-bulon, and abounding in moun-tains; the latter being more level and fertile, and very populous. Lower Galilee is said to have contained four hundred and four towns and villages, of which Capernaum and Nazareth are the most frequently mentioned. This district was of all others most honoured by our Saviour's presence. The disciples, from being natives of this place, were called *men of Galilee*, Acts i, 11.

GALILEE, *sea of*, called also *Sea of Tiberias*, from a city on its western shore, John xxi, 1. It is about six-teen miles long and five broad, and is still celebrated for the purity and salubrity of its waters, and the abundance of its fish. Embosomed in lofty mountains, the scenery around it is the most romantic and picturesque in Palestine. It is subject to sudden, though not long-continued tempests. A strong current marks the passage of the Jordan through the middle of this lake.

GALL, something exces-sively *bitter*, and supposed to be poisonous, Sam. iii, 19. It is joined with wormwood; and, in the margin of our Bibles, explained to be "a very poisonous herb." "The *gall* of bitterness," Acts viii, 23, signifies *excessive wicked-ness*, as difficult to be cor-rected as to change gall into sweetness.

GAL'LI-O, the brother of Seneca the philosopher, and proconsul of A-cha'-ia. He was of a mild and agreeable temper; and, like his brother, he was put to death by order of Nero. The Jews were enraged at St. Paul for con-verting many Gentiles, and dragged him to the tribunal of Gallio, who, as proconsul, generally resided at Cor'inth, Acts xviii, 12, 13. They ac-cused him of teaching "men to worship God contrary to the law." St. Paul being about to speak, Gallio told the Jews that if the matter in question were a breach of justice, or an action of a cri-minal nature, he should think himself obliged to hear them; but, as the dispute was only concerning their law, he would not determine such differ-ences, nor judge them. Sos'-the-nes, the chief ruler of the synagogue, was beaten by the Greeks before Gallio's seat of justice; but this go-vernor did not *concern himself about it*. His abstaining from interfering in a religious con-troversy did credit to his prudence; nevertheless, his name has oddly passed into a reproachful proverb; and a man regardless of all piety is called a "*Gallio*," and is said, "*Gallio-like, to care for none of these things*." Little did this Roman suppose that his name would be so immortalized.

GAMALIEL, a celebrated Pharisee and doctor of the Jewish law, under whose tuition Paul was educated, Acts xxii, 3, distinguished for piety and Jewish learning; and for a long time president of the Sanhedrim. He gave the counsel contained in Acts v, 35–39. The assembly saw the wisdom of his counsel, and very prudently changed the sentence, upon which they were originally bent, against the aposties' lives, into that of corporeal punishment.

GAMMADIM. This word is not to be understood as the name of a people, but rather as *brave soldiers or warriors*, Ezek. xxvii, 11.

GARDENS, a place *surrounded and protected by a fence or wall*, where plants and trees were cultivated with greater care than in the open field. The gardens of primitive nations were commonly devoted to religious purposes. In these shady retreats were celebrated, for a long succession of ages, the rites of Pagan superstition, Isa. lxv, 3.

GARLAND, *an ornament of flowers, fruits, and leaves intermixed.* "Oxen and garlands," Acts xiv, 13, are victims adorned with fillets and garlands, as was customary in heathen sacrifices.

GARMENTS. This word includes the outward and inner garment, the *mantle* and the *tunic.* The mantle, or outward garment, seems to have been a large piece of woollen cloth, nearly square; and consequently loose and flowing, which was wrapped around the body, or fastened about the shoulders, and was used as a wrapper at night. This was often laid aside, Acts xxii, 20; Matt. xxi, 8. It does not appear that the Hebrews ever changed the fashion of their garments; but they dressed after the fashion of the country in which they dwelt. The practice of strewing the way with garments, branches, and flowers, to do honour to great men, and especially to princes, was common among many ancient nations. Plutarch mentions it as a circumstance of respect shown by the soldiers to Cato the younger, that they laid down their garments for him to tread upon. Herodian mentions the strewing of garlands and flowers when Commodus was joyfully received by the Romans. "A wedding *garment*," Matt. xxii, 11, 12, was a garment presented to guests in token of honour, according to oriental customs. (See Gen. xlv, 22.) As this garment constituted the meetness of a man to be received as a guest at a wedding feast, so the *wedding garment* in the parable, must represent all those qualities which constitute our meetness for heaven, which are comprised in that "holiness without which no man shall see the Lord." "Sheeps *clothing*," Matt. vii, 15, signifies to be clothed externally with the meekness and gentleness of sheep, in contrast to the spirit of wolves. See RAIMENT.

GATES, used for an entrance into a *camp, temple,* or *city;* hence for a city itself, Deut. xvii, 2; as the "king's *gate,*" Dan. ii, 49, i. e., of the royal palace, is put for the, palace itself. Hence also the *passes* into a country, where the enemy can have entrance, are called "*gates* of a land," Jer. xv, 7. At the gates of cities, i. e., *a broad open place at the gates,* public trials were held, Prov. xxxi, 23, and things exposed for sale. There the inhabitants came together either for business or to *sit* and converse together, Gen. xix, 1. Hence "in the *gate,*" means in judgment, before the tribunal, Job v, 4; Prov. xxii, 22. "Those who sit in the *gate,*" Psa. lxix, 12, are *idlers.*

"The *gates* of hell," Matt. xvi, 18, may mean hell itself, the powers of hell, Satan and his hosts, or simply *death.* The church shall be replenished from generation to generation by living members; so that death shall never annihilate it.

"*Gates* of righteousness," Psa. cxviii, 19, 20, are those of the temple, where the righteous pay their vows and praises to God; where none enter but purified Israelites— a nation of righteous men.

GATH, the fifth of the Philistine cities. It appears to have been the extreme boundary of the Philistine territory in one direction, as Ekron was on the other. Hence the expression, "from Ekron even unto *Gath,*" 1 Sam. vii, 14.

GAZA, one of the five cities of the Philistines, a royal city, Zech. ix, 5, situated on a hill near the Mediterranean, and southern border of Palestine, Gen. x, 19. It was assigned by Joshua to the tribe of Judah, who subdued it; but the possession of it was retained or soon recovered by the Philistines, Josh. xv, 47; Judg. i, 18. After having destroyed Tyre, Alexander the Great laid siege to Gaza also, which was then held by a Persian garrison, and took it after a siege of a year, and destroyed it. It was afterward rebuilt, and bestowed on Herod the Great, after whose death it was annexed to Syria.

GEBAL, *mountain,* a Phenician city, situated on a *hill,* and inhabited by seamen and builders, Ezek. xxvii, 9. Also the mountainous track, thirty or forty miles long, inhabited by the Edomites, extending from the Dead Sea southward to the wide valley, *El Goheyr,* which descends toward the west into the *El Ghor,* Psa. lxxxiii, 8.

GEN-E-AL'OGY signifies a *list of a person's ancestors.* The common Hebrew expression for it is, "the book of *generations.*" No nation was ever more careful to preserve their genealogies than the Jews. The sacred writings contain genealogies extended 3,500 years backward. The genealogy of our

Saviour is given by the evangelists from Adam to Joseph and Mary, through a space of 4,000 years and upward. Matthew gives it through Joseph his father, while Luke exhibits that of his mother Mary. The Jewish priests were obliged to produce an exact genealogy of their families before they were admitted to exercise their function. Wherever placed, the Jews were particularly careful not to marry below themselves; and to prevent this, they kept *tables of genealogy* in their several families, the originals of which were lodged at Jerusalem, to be occasionally consulted. These authentic monuments, during all their wars and persecutions, were taken great care of, and from time to time renewed. But since the last destruction of their city, and the dispersion of the people, their ancient genealogies are lost.

GENERATION. Besides the common acceptation of the word, as signifying *families, race, descent, lineage*, it is used for the *history* and *genealogy* of a person, Gen. v, 1. So Gen. ii, 4, the *history* of the creation. "The present *generation*"comprises all those who are now alive, Matt. xxiv, 34. Some now living shall witness the event now foretold, Isa. liii, 8, "Who shall declare his *generation?*" enumerate his *posterity?* He was cut off by an untimely death, yet his posterity, his followers, shall be *innumerable*. It signifies also a period of time from one descent to another, i. e., the average duration of human life, reckoned apparently by the ancient Hebrews at 100 years, by the Greeks, at three generations for every 100 years, i. e., 33⅓ years each. Hence, in the New Testament, signifies a less definite period for *an age, time*, or *period*.

GENESIS, the first book of Moses, so called from a Greek word which signifies *generation*, from its containing the history of the creation. It is the most ancient book in the world; and on account of the variety of its details, one of the most interesting. It comprises a period of about 2,369 years.

GENTILE. The word signifies *nations*, i. e., foreign nations, those who are not Israelites, and are ignorant of the true God. Since the promulgation of the Gospel, the true religion has been extended to all nations; God, who had promised by his prophets to call the Gentiles to the faith, having fulfilled his promise; so that the Christian church is composed principally of Gentile converts; the Jews being too proud of their privileges to acknowledge Jesus Christ as their Messiah and Redeemer.

GENNESARET, Matt. xiv, 34, a small region of Galilee on the western shore of the lake, described by Jose phus as about four miles in length, and three in breadth, and as distinguished for its fertility and beauty. It was so called from an ancient city, Josh. xix, 35, which also gave name to the adjacent lake, Num. xxxiv, 11.

GE'RAR, a royal city of the Philistines, situate not far from the angle where the south and west sides of Palestine meet.

GERGESENES, (*Ger-ge-seens,*) one of the ancient tribes of Canaan, destroyed by Joshua, who settled east of the sea of Galilee. See GAD'A-RA.

GER-I-ZIM, one of the mountains of Ephraim, situated over against Mount Ebal, between which lay the city of Shechem, Judges ix, 7. After the exile, a temple was built by the Samaritans on Mount Gerizim, as the seat of their national worship.

GETH-SEM'A-NE, the *oil press,* a small place or field, just out of Jerusalem, over the brook Cedron, and at the foot of the Mount of Olives. It is an even flat of ground, according to Maundrell, about fifty-seven yards square. To a garden belonging to this place our Saviour sometimes retired, Matt. xxvi, 36.

Fisk and King, American missionaries, were there in 1823. They tell us that the garden is about a stone's cast from the brook Cedron; that it now contains eight large and venerable looking olives, whose trunks show their great antiquity; the spot is sandy and barren, and appears like a forsaken place. A low broken wall surrounds it. Mr. King sat down beneath one of the trees, and read Isa. liii, and also the Gospel history of our Redeemer's sorrow during that memorable night in which he was betrayed; and the interest of the association was heightened by the passing through the place of a party of Bedouins, armed with spears and swords.

GHOST, a word signifying *spirit,* the *Holy Ghost,* the third person in the adorable Trinity.

GIANT, *a chief who beats and bears down other men.* Scripture speaks of giants before the flood: "*mighty men who were of old, men of renown,*" Gen. vi, 4. The Anakim, or the sons of Anak, were the most famous giants of Palestine. They dwelt at Hebron and thereabouts.

As to the existence of giants, several writers, both ancient and modern, have thought that the giants of Scripture were men famous for *violence* and *crime,* rather than for *strength* or *stature.* We may reasonably understand that the gigantic nations of Canaan were above the average size of other people, with instances among them of several families of gigantic stature. This is all that is necessary to suppose, in order to explain the

account of Moses. See RA-
PHAIM.

GIBEAH, a city of Benja-
min, the birthplace of Saul,
noted for the atrocious crime
committed by its inhabitants,
Judges xix. Like Bethel, it
seems to have been reckoned
among the ancient sanctuaries
of Palestine.

GIBEON, a large city of
the Hivites, Josh. x, 2, afterward belonging to Benja-
min. The inhabitants of this
place took advantage of the
oaths of Joshua, and of the
elders of Israel, procured by
an artful representation of
their belonging to a very remote country, Josh. ix. Joshua and the elders had not
the precaution to consult God
on this affair, but inconsider-
ately made a league with
these people. They soon discovered their mistake, and,
without revoking their promise of saving their lives,
they condemned them to labour in carrying wood and
water for the tabernacle; and
to other works, as slaves
and captives; in which state
of servitude they remained
till the entire dispersion of
the Jewish nation, 1451 B.C.

GIDEON, a celebrated
warrior and judge of Israel,
who delivered the nation from
the bondage of Midian, 1241
B. C., and continued his
government nine years. (See
Judg. vi, vii.)

GI'ER EAGLE, i. e., the
eagle vulture; gier being the
German name for a vulture.
It is a small species of vul-

ture, known in Arabia and
Egypt, and sometimes called
an eagle, it being of a doubtful kind between an eagle
and a vulture. It is a white
bird, feeding on dead bodies,
with a naked face and black
winged feathers, edged with
gray; and is still known by
the same Hebrew name.
These birds were anciently
held in great veneration in
Egypt, where many flocks of
them are observed at the present day in all the principal
towns; Deut. xiv, 17.

GIFT OF TONGUES, an
ability given to the apostles
and others, of readily and in-
telligibly speaking a variety
of languages which they had
never learned. This was a
glorious and decisive attesta-
tion to the Gospel, as well
as a suitable, and, indeed, in
their circumstances, a necessary qualification for the mission for which the apostles
and their coadjutors were
designed.

GIFTS. The practice of
making presents is very common in oriental countries.
The custom probably had its
origin among those men who
first sustained the office of
kings or rulers, and who, from
the novelty, and perhaps the
weakness attached to their
situation, chose, rather than
make the hazardous attempt
of exacting taxes, to content
themselves with receiving
those presents which might
be freely offered, 1 Sam. x,
27. Hence it passed into
a custom, that whoever ap

proached the king, should come with a gift. The custom of presenting gifts was subsequently extended to other great men; to men who were inferior to the king, but who were, nevertheless, men of influence and rank; it was also extended to those who were equals, when they were visited, Prov. xviii, 16. Gifts of this kind are not to be confounded with those which are called *bribes*, and which were presented to judges, not as a mark of esteem and honour, but for purposes of bribery and corruption. The former was considered an honour to the giver, but a gift of the latter kind has been justly reprobated in every age, Deut. xvi, 19; Psa. xxvi, 10; Isa. xxxiii, 15.

GI'HON, the name of one of the four rivers the source of which was in paradise, Gen. iii, 13. Reland, Calmet, &c., think that Gihon is the Araxes, which has its source, as well as the Tigris and Euphrates, in the mountains of Armenia, and, running with almost incredible rapidity, falls into the Caspian Sea. Gihon was also the name of a fountain to the west of Jerusalem, at which Solomon was anointed king by the high priest Zadok, and the prophet Nathan, 1 Kings i, 33.

GIL'BO-A, a mountain or mountainous track in the tribe of Issachar, where Saul was defeated and slain by the Philistines, 1 Sam. xxxi, 1.

This mountain is north of Bethshean, or Bethsan, which is about twenty-four miles south of Tiberias, between the valley of the Jordan and the great plain of Jez-re'el. It is said to be extremely dry and barren.

GILEAD, a district of Palestine, east of the Jordan, strictly comprehending the mountainous region south of the river Jabbok, extending to N. lat. 31½°, Gen. xxxi, 21–48, with a city of like name, Hos. vi, 8, apparently the same with *Ramoth Gilead*. The name *Gilead* was also employed in a wider sense, so as to include the whole mountainous track east of the Jordan, inhabited by the tribes of *Gad*, *Reuben*, and *Manasseh*, Num. xxxii, 26, 29, 39; Deut. iii, 12. Hence put for the territory of the tribes of *Gad* and *Reuben*, Psa. lx, 9; for the tribe of Gad, Judg. v, 16, 17. And it comprehends also Bashan, which extends from the Jabbok to Mount Hermon, the northern extremity of Palestine, Deut. xxxvi, 1, where it is said that God showed Moses from Mount Nebo *"all the land of Gilead unto Dan."*

Balm of Gilead is a balsam distilled from a tree or shrub growing in Gilead, and which was used for healing wounds; the exact species of the tree has never been fully ascertained. See BALM.

GIL'GAL, *rolling down or away*, a celebrated place,

situated between the Jordan and Jericho, where the Israelites encamped after the passage of that river, Josh. v, 9. In this place Samuel and Saul offered sacrifices. It was a station of justice; for Samuel in his circuit went yearly to Gilgal, 1 Sam. vii, 16; and consequently a place much resorted to by the Israelites.

GIRDLE, a sash or belt, common among the people of oriental countries; and, from the length and looseness of their garments, an indispensable article; but especially when engaged in running or fighting, or applying themselves to any kind of business. They were often made of precious stuffs, fabricated of linen, and of worsted, artfully woven into a variety of figures, and made to fold several times about the body. Scribes or writers suspended in them ink-horns, a custom as old as the Prophet Ezekiel, Ezek. ix, 2. Prophets and persons secluded from the world wore girdles of *skin* or *leather*, 2 Kings i, 8; Matt. iii, 4; and, in times of mourning, they used girdles of sackcloth, as marks of humiliation, Isa. xxii, 12.

To gird up the loins, is to bring the flowing robe within the girdle. The binding fast of the muscles, and girding the loins, increase one's strength and activity; hence *girding* is applied to warlike strength and fortitude, Psa.

xviii, 32–39. Hence also, "*Girding* up the loins of the mind," 1 Pet. i, 13, is to hold the mind in a state of constant preparation and activity.

The military girdle, or belt of the Hebrews, did not come over the shoulder as among us, but was worn upon the loins; whence the expression, *The sword girded upon the loins.*

GITTITH, an instrument of music; so called, either as being common among the Gittites, 2 Sam. xv, 18, or from GATH, a *wine press*, as if belonging to the wine press, and used to accompany the songs of the vintage. It occurs in the titles of some of the Psalms.

GLASS, an artificial substance, formed by melting silica or sand with potash. Doubtless its origin is unknown; but there is some reason to believe it was made by the Phenicians from the sand of the Belus, near Acra. About the commencement of the Christian era, drinking vessels were commonly made of *glass;* and glass bottles for holding wine and flowers were in common use. Glass sometimes means a *mirror*, and mirrors anciently were plates of polished mettle, "We see through a *glass* darkly," 1 Cor. xiii, 12, i. e. only a reflected image, obscurely, and not face to face, as we shall see hereafter. There seems to be no reference to glass in the original of the Old Testament, as the art of making it was not then known.

GLORIFY, to ascribe glory or honour to any one, to celebrate with praises; "That they may see your good works, and *glorify* your Father," Matt. v, 16.

2. To exalt in dignity, to render glorious. God is glorified when the divine character and attributes are rendered conspicuous and glorious, John xii, 28.

Christ and his followers are glorified when advanced to that state of bliss and glory which is the portion of those who dwell with God in heaven, John vii, 39; Rom. viii, 30.

GLORY. This word signifies, 1. That *honour* which is due to one, or which is rendered to one, i. e., *praise, applause.* "Nor of men sought we *glory*," 1 Thess. ii, 6.

2. That which excites admiration; to which honour, praise, or applause is given, as the regal splendour and majesty of kings, compare Mark x, 37, with Matt. xx, 21; "Solomon in all his *glory*," Matt. vi, 9; that is, his splendid apparel, and all the accompaniments of his royalty. So also that which reflects or exhibits this dignity is called *glory.* See 1 Cor. xi, 7, where St. Paul says, "That the man is the *glory* of God, and woman the *glory* of man."

3. The external appearance; as lustre, brightness, dazzling light; as of the sun, and of the face of Moses.

The glory of God is that *bright cloud* which surrounded the deity, and which declared his presence; and also the celestial splendour in which he sits enthroned, which constitutes the locality of the heavenly world. See 1 Tim. vi, 16.

4. Hence a glorified state, the exalted state of perfection and supreme happiness hereafter, Luke xxiv, 26.

5. The internal character which excites admiration; as *glorious moral attributes,* excellent perfection, the infinite majesty and holiness of God, Rom. i, 23.

GNAT, a small winged or flying insect, as found in acid wine. "Strain at a *gnat,* and swallow a camel," Matt. xxiii, 24. To strain *at* does not mean to make a violent effort to swallow, but to *filter* or *strain out;* and is spoken of those who are formal and diligent in the observance of lesser duties, but negligent of higher ones.

GOAT, a well-known animal, which was used under the law both for food and sacrifice. The kind most common in Palestine is not very unlike those in the United States. The colour is generally black. There is another species of goat called the *ibex,* the *wild* or mountain goat, Psa. civ, 18, larger than the tame, but resembling it much in the outer form. The horns are large, of an extraordinary size, weighing sometimes 16 or 18 pounds;

Covel's Dic.   p. 189.

IBEX, OR WILD GOAT.

and being of so singular a form, the animal is shown in the annexed engraving. Like other goats, it is peculiarly adapted for climbing, and delights in the most rugged and elevated mountains. It is indigenous to Arabia, and of amazing strength and agility. There is no crag so high or so steep, if it have protuberances enough to receive its feet, but this animal will mount it, 1 Sam. xxiv, 2. Mr. Burckhardt says, that the flesh is excellent, and has nearly the same flavour as that of deer. The Bedouins make water-bags, called in the Scriptures bottles, of their skins, and rings of their horns, which they wear on their thumbs. When they are found among the rocks, they usually elude the pursuit of the hunter, sometimes leaping twenty feet; but in the plains they are often taken.

GOATS' HAIR. Some species of goat have under a coat of long hair another of short wool, equal in fineness to the Cashmire. The shepherds carefully and frequently wash these goats in rivers; and in some parts of western Asia, the hair is manufactured into garments. See Exod. xxv, 4.

GOD. The one living and true God; the supreme Lord and Father of all; an unoriginated, eternal, immutable, and infinitely perfect being. By *immutable* is meant one who never changes the principles of his government.

1. The unity of the divine Being is a sublime and glorious truth, the corner-stone and basis of the ancient church; and the Gospel has revealed nothing to shake or remove this foundation. To us still there is but one God. But in the unity of this Godhead there are three persons of one substance, power, and eternity: "*The Father, the Son, and the Holy Ghost,*" Matt. xxviii, 19. This distinction in the Godhead was prior to all time, and absolutely eternal. The formula of baptism is a standing testimony to this doctrine, and to the offices of each person in the economy of redemption. The *name* is one, not *names.* The persons THREE, all of whom are manifestly represented as equal; because they are the common objects of trust, obedience, and worship; and they are the source of all blessing, 2 Cor. xiii, 14.

2. *To God* is said in Scripture to belong whatever is excellent, distinguished, pre-eminent in its kind, or which bears an august or divine appearance; since this was regarded by the ancients as especially proceeding from God, or created by him. Thus we read of the *hill of God,* Psa. lxviii, 15; *river of God,* Psa. lxv, 9; *the terror of God,* i. e., terror suddenly inspired by him, Gen. xxxv, 5. Lightning is *the fire of God;* the loftiest and most beautiful cedars are *trees of the Lord,* Psa. civ, 16.

3. *The god of any one*, is the god whom one makes the object of his worship, his protector. "They cried every one unto his *god*," Jonah i, 5. See GODS.

4. The practice of using the *name* of God on slight and trivial occasions, is not only in direct opposition to the third commandment, and to a variety of other passages which identify the character of God with his name, Isa. xxix, 23; Matt. vi, 9; but it is an infallible indication of irreverence toward the supreme Being. To connect the idea of God with what is most frivolous and ridiculous, is to treat him with contempt. With respect to the profane oaths and execrations which most of those who use the *name of God in vain* frequently utter, when they are transported with emotions of anger, their criminality is still greater as they approach the confines of blasphemy.

GODHEAD. The divine nature and perfection, divine greatness, power, and excellence. That which marks him as the supreme and eternal *One*.

GODLINESS, piety, resulting from the knowledge and love of God, and denoting the spontaneous feeling of the heart. In 1 Tim. iii, 16, it signifies *religion*, the Gospel scheme.

GODS. 1. Imaginary deities, as the "*gods* of the Egyptians," Exod. xii, 12;

"strange or foreign *gods*, Gen. xxxv, 2.

2. The expression is put for a godlike shape, apparition, spirit, "I saw *gods* ascending out of the earth," 1 Sam xxviii, 13.

3. An idol god, an image, *make us gods*, i. e., an *idol*, either a carved or a molten image. Moses says that the Israelites worshipped "*gods* whom they knew not, and whom he had not given unto them," Deut. xxix, 26, to whom they did not belong, which increased the ingratitude and crime of their rebellion. When judges and magistrates are called gods, Psa. lxxxii, 6, "I have said, Ye are *gods*," something is added which excludes them from a true divinity: as, that "*ye shall die like men*, or that they are the *rulers of the people*," Exod. xxii, 28. Moses was called *god* only in regard to Aaron and Pharaoh, to whom he was to speak God's message. The first idols, or false gods, that are said to have been adored are, the stars, sun, moon, &c. on account of the light, heat, and other benefits which we derive from them. (See IDOLATRY.) Afterward the earth came to be deified, for furnishing fruits necessary for the subsistence of men and animals: then fire and water became objects of divine worship, for their usefulness to human life. In process of time, and by degrees, gods became multiplied to infinity;

and there was scarce any thing but the weakness or caprice of some devotee or other elevated into the rank of deity: things useless, or even destructive, not excepted.

GOG. This name is applied in the Old Testament, Ezek. xxxviii, 39, to the king of a people called *Magog*, inhabiting regions far remote from Palestine. By Magog, the ancients would seem to have intended the northern nations of Europe and Asia generally, which they also called *Scythians*. In the New Testament, the name *Gog* is also apparently spoken of a similar remote people who will war against the Messiah, Rev. xx, 8. See MAGOG.

GOLD, a precious metal of a bright yellow colour, the most ductile and malleable of all, and the heaviest except pla-ti'na. It appears to have been known to the earliest races of men, and to have been esteemed as much by them as by the moderns. It is not found in the ore, but in the metallic state; either pure, or combined with other metals. It is sometimes found in mountains, but more frequently among sand in the beds of rivers. The principal supply is from South America, from the gold mines of Hungary, and from the Uralian mountains of Siberia, where separate masses in sand have been found, weighing 18 or 20 pounds. When pure, it is exceeding-

ly soft and flexible, and may be exposed for ages to air and moisture, or kept in a state of fusion in open vessels without change. (See *Dr. Turner's Chym.*) It was supposed to be imperishable in its nature, until recent experiments in chymistry discovered that when intensely ignited by means of electricity or the oxy-hydrogen blow-pipe, it burns with a greenish blue flame, and forms an oxide, which is dissipated in the form of a purplish powder. Gold coins contain about one-twelfth of copper, which gives to them a reddish tint. Gold is applied to any thing splendid or most valuable. *Golden oil*, Zech. iv, 12, means oil pure and bright as gold. Figuratively, it means those graces and blessings which constitute one rich toward God, Rev. iii, 18.

GOL-GO-THA, *a skull*, a small hill on the northwest of Jerusalem; so called either from its resembling a human skull, or because many skulls of those who had suffered crucifixion and other capital punishments were scattered there.

GOLIATH, a Philistine giant, slain by David in single combat; according to Calmet, he was ten feet and seven inches in height, 1 Sam. xvii, 4.

GOMER, a northern people sprung from Japheth, from whom the Armenians are said to have descended. They peopled a considerable part of Asia Minor, particularly the region of Phrygia; from these parts the descendants of Gomer emigrated till Germany, France, and Britain were peopled by them. They still continue marked, if not distinct, in the ancient Britons in Wales.

GO-MOR'RAH, one of the cities which formerly stood on the plain of Siddim, now covered by the Dead Sea. See Gen. xiii, 10; and chap. xix.

GO'PHER WOOD, *pitch trees*, resinous and durable wood; such as the pine, fir, cypress, cedar, and other trees of like kind, which are used in ship-building.

GOSHEN, a region where the Hebrews dwelt, 430 years from the time of Jacob until Moses, which in a good degree is now ascertained to be that part of Lower Egypt, whose western boundary was not far east from the Nile, and extending along its banks about eighty or ninety miles, and was about the same width, extending to Arabia. This was a wide range for pasturage; and although it has large tracts in it which are strictly *desert*, yet there are many parts of it, especially the valleys, which afford low bushes and sand-grass, such as the wandering tribes of the desert seek for the support of their flocks and herds; besides others which, being watered by the Nile, were exceeding fertile. It is now well ascertained that nearly all parts of the Isthmus of Suez abound in wadies, i. e., moderate ravines, or a kind of intervals of land in which water is easily obtained, and where, of course, vegetation may be made to abound in a manner that would astonish an inhabitant of a northern clime.

GOSPEL, a *history* of the life, actions, death, resurrection, ascension, and doctrine of Jesus Christ. The word is Saxon, and of the same import with the Greek *evangelion*, which signifies "glad tidings," or "good news;" the history of our Saviour being the best history ever published to mankind. This history is contained in the writings of Matthew, Mark, Luke, and John, who from thence are called *evangelists*. But we must remember that no one of them undertook to give an account of all the miracles which Christ performed, or of all the instructions which he delivered. They are written with different degrees of conciseness; but every one of them is sufficiently full to prove that Jesus was the promised *Messiah*, the *Saviour* of the world, who had been predicted by a long succession of prophets, and whose advent was expected at the time of his appearance, both by Jews and Gentiles.

2. That all the books which convey to us the history of events under the New Testament were written and imme-

diately published by persons cotemporary with the events, is most fully proved by the testimony of an unbroken series of authors, reaching from the days of the evangelists to the present times ; by the concurrent belief of Christians of all denominations ; and by the unreserved confession of avowed enemies to the Gospel.

3. The term *Gospel* is often used in Scripture to signify the whole *Christian doctrine* : hence, " *preaching the Gospel*" is declaring all the *truths*, *precepts*, *promises*, and *threatenings* of Christianity. This is termed " *the Gospel of the grace of God*," because it flows from God's free love and goodness, Acts xx, 24 ; and when truly and faithfully preached, is accompanied with the influences of the divine Spirit. It is called " *the Gospel of the kingdom*," because it treats of the kingdom of grace, and shows the way to the kingdom of glory. It is styled " *the Gospel of Christ*," because he is the author and great subject of it, Rom. i, 16 ; and " *the Gospel of peace and salvation*," because it publishes peace with God to the penitent and believing, gives to such peace of conscience and tranquillity of mind, and is the means of their salvation, present and eternal. As it displays the glory of God and of Christ, and insures to his true followers eternal glory, it is entitled " *the lorious Gospel*,"

and " *the everlasting Gospel*," because it commenced from the fall of man, is permanent throughout all time, and produces effects which are *everlasting.*

GOURD, Jonah iv, 6–10. Modern writers almost all agree that this plant is the *Palma Christi* or the *Rici'nus*, from which *castor oil* is extracted ; a tall biennial plant still cultivated in gardens, which attains in the east the character of a tree of an elegant appearance and rapid growth, with a soft and juicy stalk or trunk ; a slight injury of which causes the plant to wither and die. " The history in Jonah expressly says, *the Lord prepared* this plant : no doubt we may conceive of it as an extraordinary one of its kind, remarkably rapid in its growth, remarkably hard in its stem, remarkably vigorous in its branches, and remarkable for the extensive spread of its leaves and the deep gloom of their shadow ; and, after a certain duration, remarkable for a sudden withering, and a total uselessness to the impatient prophet."

GOURD, WILD, *wild cucumbers*, a plant which creeps on the earth, and produces leaves and branches similar to garden cucumbers. Its fruit is of the size and figure of an orange, of a light white substance, beneath the rind extremely bitter, and probably poisonous, 2 Kings iv, 39 ; it furnished a model for some of the carved work in Solomon's temple, 1 Kings vi, 18. The translation is *knops*.

GRACE. 1. The *favour* or good will of God and Christ, as exercised toward any of the human race.

2. The *blessings* which flow from God's favour, as manifested in the benefits of the Gospel, the pardon of sin, and admission into his kingdom.

3. *The Christian religion*, a gracious dispensation, a system of which grace is the prominent feature, Rom. vi, 14.

4. The favour or gift of the apostleship, Rom. i, 5; Eph. iii, 8.

5. It is taken for *beauty* or gracefulness of person and *agreeableness* of words, Prov. i, 19. Paul says, Col. iv, 6, "Let your speech be always with *grace*."

6. *Liberality*, "the grace of God bestowed on the churches of Macedonia," 2 Cor. viii, 1, means the charitable contribution given in the churches, excited by God's grace to them.

7. It is frequently used to signify the favour and kindness of man as well as of God. The phrase *grace unto you*, I take to include every Christian grace and virtue which the Spirit of God imparts to the followers of Christ.

GRAPE, the fruit of the vine, and among the valuable productions of Palestine. It would be easy to produce testimony that grapes in those regions grew to a prodigious size, Num. xiii, 23. One traveller says, "The grapes are as large as plumbs, and the bunches are surprising." The spies carrying the bunch of grapes on a staff between two men, was probably not rendered necessary by the size of the bunch or cluster, but to preserve it from being bruised, that the Israelites might have a fair specimen of the fruit. The grapes of Palestine are mostly red or black, whence originated the phrase *blood of the grape*, and were generally gathered in August; but grapes when not gathered, were sometimes found on vines until November or December. The Hebrews were required to leave gleanings for the poor, Lev. xix. The grapes were gathered and carried to the wine-press with great joy, Judg. ix, 27; Isa. xvi, 10. Sometimes the grapes were dried in the sun and preserved in masses, called raisins, 1 Sam. xxv, 18; from these dried grapes, when soaked in wine and pressed a second time, was manufactured *sweet wine*, which is also called *new wine*, Acts ii, 13.

Wild grapes, Isa. v, 2–4, are bad grapes, sour and worthless.

GRASS, a well known vegetable. Its feeble frame and transitory duration are mentioned in Scripture as emblematic of the frail condition and fleeting existence of man. See Psalm xc, 6, and particularly Isaiah xl, 6–8.

GRASSHOPPER, not the common grasshopper, but a voracious insect belonging to that genus; a species of locust, and a great scourge in oriental countries. The most particular description of this insect and of its destructive career mentioned in the Bible, is to be found in Joel ii, 2–10. This perhaps is one of the most striking and animated descriptions of any kind to be met with in the whole compass of prophecy. Solomon, describing the infelicities of old age, Eccl. xii, 5, says, "The *grasshopper* shall be a burden;" the lightest pressure shall be uncomfortable to the aged, as not being able to bear any weight.

GREAT SEA. That great mass of waters between Europe and Africa, which receives its name Mediterranean, *Midland*, from its position, and has its only communication with the ocean by the Straits of Gibraltar; it is about 2,000 miles long, and between 400 and 500 broad. It is called the utmost sea, Joel ii, 20; the hinder sea, Zech. xiv, 8; and was the western boundary of the promised land.

GREAVES, armour for the legs, a plate of brass or copper which covered the front of the leg from the knee to the instep, and buckled with a strap behind, 1 Sam. xvii, 6.

GREECE, or GRECIA, a country in the south-eastern part of Europe, surrounded by sea, except on the north, extending from the Adriatic on the west to Asia Minor on the east; and from Macedonia, which formed its northern boundary to the Mediterranean.

GREEK, the original language of all the books of the New Testament, with the exception of Matthew, which is reported to have been written in Hebrew, and a translation into Greek made by the apostle himself, or in his lifetime. They are not written, however, in the cultivated and polished style of learned and elegant authors, but rather in that which prevailed in daily use, and in the intercourse of common life. This may be observed by inspecting the received translation, which is pronounced by the best judges to be, though not unexceptionable, yet a faithful and truly excellent translation. The Greek language was used because it was best understood, being spoken and written, read and understood, throughout the Roman empire, and especially in Palestine.

GREEKS, inhabitants of Greece; but, in the widest sense, Greeks were all those who used the Greek language and customs, whether living in Greece or in other countries; and as this was then the prevailing language, the name *Greek* was often used to designate the *Gentiles*, i. e., all who were not Jews, Rom. i, 16; we read of *Greeks* going up to worship, and of *devout Greeks*. These were converts to Judaism, Greek proselytes.

GRECIANS. This word in the New Testament signifies those who were *Jews* by birth or by religion, whether converted to Christianity or not, who in all places spoke the Greek as their vernacular tongue, Acts vi, 1 ; ix, 29.

GRIND. "To *grind* the faces of the poor," Isa. iii, 15, is to oppress them with exactions, and by cruelty and oppression to make the poor look more thin and meagre than they did before. See MILL.

GRINDERS, in Solomon's allegory of old age, is supposed to signify the double teeth; so called from their grinding or masticating the food. "The sound of the *grinding* is low," Eccl. xii, 4; little noise is now made in eating, because the teeth have decayed.

GRIZZLED, *gray*; of a mixed colour, white and black; in the Bible it signifies *spotted*, sprinkled with spots, Gen. xxxi, 10.

GROSS, the same as *fat*.

HAB'AK-KUK, one of the minor prophets, concerning whom we have no certain information : he exercised the prophetic office, most probably, in the reign of Jehoiakim, and consequently was co-

temporary with Jeremiah. It is generally believed that he died in Judea about 612 B. C. The third chapter of his book is one of the most splendid portions of the prophetic writings.

HABER'GEON, (*ha-ber'-je-on,*) *a coat of mail*, Neh. iv, 16; an ancient piece of defensive armour, in the form of a coat, descending from the neck to the middle, and formed of small iron rings or meshes, linked into each other.

HA'DAD, king of Edom, and a name common to the kings of Syria.

HAGAR, *flight*, the handmaid of Sarah, of Egyptian birth, the mother of Ishmael ; so called, as having *fled* from her mistress, Gen. xxv, 12; and xxi, 14. In Gal. iv, 24, 25, Paul applies this name, by an allegorical interpretation, to the inferior condition of the Jews under the law, as compared with that of Christians under the Gospel.

HAGARENES, the same as *Hagarites ;* an Arabian people with which the tribes living beyond Jordan carried on war, Psa. lxxxiii, 6.

HAGGAI, the tenth in order of the minor prophets, but the first of the three who were commissioned to make known the divine will after the return from captivity. Nothing is certainly known concerning his tribe or birthplace. The Jews having for fourteen years discontinued the rebuilding of the temple, he was commissioned to encourage them in their work, about the year 520 B. C.

HAIL! a salutation, importing a wish for the welfare of the person addressed.

HAILSTONES are congealed drops of rain, formed into ice by the power of cold in the upper regions of the atmosphere.

HAIR. Our Maker has given a larger proportion of hair to the head of women than to that of men. The hair of the male rarely grows like that of the female unless art is used; and even then it bears but a small proportion to the former. Hence *nature* teaches that it is a shame to a man and the glory of a woman to have long hair, 1 Cor. xi, 14, 15. Black hair was thought to be the most beautiful, Song v. 11.

HAL-LE-LU'-JAH, (the last syllable pronounced *yah*,) a Hebrew word, signifying *praise the Lord.* This expression of joy and praise was transferred from the synagogue to the church, and is still occasionally used in devotion. See ALLELUIA.

To HAL'LOW. The English word is from the Saxon, and is properly *to make holy.* The name of God is hallowed when it is regarded and venerated as holy.

HAM, *warm, hot,* a son of Noah, whose posterity are described as occupying the southern regions of the known earth. It is believed that Ham had Africa for his inheritance, that he peopled it and dwelt in Egypt. Africa is called the "land of Ham," Gen. x.

HAMAN, a Persian nobleman, celebrated for his plots against the Jews, Esth. iii, 1.

HA'MATH, a large and important city of Syria, situated on the O-ron'-tes, near the northern boundary of the Holy Land.

HAND, metaphorically, *power, strength, might;* the hand being regarded as the seat of strength: hence human or divine *help.* And since the divine Spirit was communicated by the laying on of hands, it often signifies the *Spirit of God,* Jer. xv, 17. "I sit alone because of thy *hand,*" i. e., because of the divine Spirit which rests upon me, by which I am moved. *Hands* which hang down, enfeebled, hanging down from weariness and despondency, Heb. xii, 12, implying discouragement and faint-heartedness, compare 2 Sam. xvii, 2; so likewise one that hath a *short hand* is one without strength or power. A high hand is one lifted up, which indicates force and energy. The right hand signifies the south, since the Hebrew in speaking of the points of the compass always regarded himself as looking toward the east. Isaiah speaks of the *Philistines behind,* Isa. ix, 12, i. e., in the west. The ancients in taking an oath lifted up the hand, Deut. xxxii, 40: hence it signifies *to swear;* and this was done by the right hand. "They gave us the right *hand* of fellowship," Gal. ii, 9, in confirmation of a promise, agreement. *To sit or stand on the right hand of Christ or God* is to be next in rank or power; to have the highest seat of honour and distinction; to be at one's right *hand*, i. e., to be one's helper, protector, Acts ii, 25.

HAND-WRITING, a manuscript, something written by hand, as the Mosaic law, the letter in opposition to the spirit, Col. ii, 14, the literal or verbal meaning.

HANNAH, *favour*, the mother of Samuel; her history is recorded in 1 Sam. i.

HARAN, a city in the northern part of Mesopotamia, where Abraham for a time sojourned, and afterward celebrated for the defeat and death of Crassus, the Roman general.

To HARDEN, in a moral sense, *to make obstinate, perverse.* They are said to harden their hearts who, by sensual practices and irreligious principles, bring themselves into such a state of insensibility that neither the commands nor the threatenings of God make any impression on them.

And it is said also that God *hardened* Pharaoh's heart; not by an immediate and supernatural influence, because that would make God the author of men's sins; a blasphemy which the apostle James was at great pains to confute, James i, 13. But God hardened him *indirectly;* i. e., he withdrew his Spirit from him, and gave him up to a reprobate mind, for his unparalleled cruelty to Israel, Exod. i, 10–22; vii, 13. This is the sense in which God may harden all that imitate such obstinate unbelief: or he hardened him by his providence, which brought about events in view of which he hardened his own heart. By his long-suffering and delay of punishment, removing the plagues from Egypt, one after another, God hardened him, i. e., Pharaoh took an occasion from that respite to harden his heart; he made up his mind to persevere in his opposition to the departure of the Israelites. Hence by the permission of God in his providence, or his indirect agency, the stars are said in Deut. iv, 19, to be distributed among the nations as objects of their worship; while God has selected the people of Israel for his own. Compare 2 Sam. xxiv, 1, with 1 Chron. xxi, 1. "Whom he will he *hardeneth*," Rom. ix, 18. Some understand this passage to mean *to deal hardly with, to treat harshly,* and refer to Job xxxix, 16, where the seventy use the same word which occurs in the Greek of this passage, and most evidently in the same sense.

HARE, Lev. xi, 6. This animal resembles the rabbit, but is larger, and somewhat longer in proportion to its thickness.

HARLOT. This term,

though generally applied to an abandoned woman, is used figuratively, Isa. i, 21, the relation existing between God and the Israelitish people, being everywhere set forth by the prophets under the emblem of the conjugal union. See Hos. i, 2; Ezek. xvi, 22. The people in worshipping other gods are compared to a harlot or an adulteress.

HAR′O-SHETH, Judges iv, 2; a city supposed to be situated near Hazor, in the northern parts of Canaan, called Upper Galilee, or Galilee of the Gentiles.

HARP, a stringed instrument of music of great antiquity, whose tones are produced by the action of the thumb and fingers of both hands like the Theban harp. (See our engraving, *musical instruments*.) The form of the ancient harp is unknown. Gesenius supposes that it resembled the modern guitar. David danced when he used it, and played with the fingers, 1 Sam. xvi, 23. It was used as an accompaniment to the voice on joyful occasions, such as jubilees and festivals. Hence the sorrowing Jews during their captivity hung their harps upon the willows as useless.

HART, the stag, or male deer. Mr. Good observes that the hind and roe, the hart and the antelope, were held, and still continue to be, in the highest estimation in all the eastern countries, for the beauty of their eyes, the delicate elegance of their form, or their graceful agility of action. The names of these animals were perpetually applied, therefore, to persons, whether male or female, who were supposed to be possessed of any of their respective qualities. See HIND.

HARVEST is gathered in the southern parts of Palestine and in the plains about the middle of April; but in the northern and mountainous parts the first of May or later. The first handful of ripe barley was carried to the altar, and then the harvest commenced; the barley first, and then wheat and other grain. The time of harvest was a festival.

The reapers in Palestine and Syria make use of the sickle in cutting down their crops; and, according to the present custom in this country, "fill their hand" with the grain, and those who bind up the sheaves, "their bosom," Psa. cxxix, 7.

It appears from the beautiful history of Ruth, that, in Palestine, the women lent their assistance in cutting down and gathering in the harvest; for Boaz commands her to keep fast by his maidens. The women in Syria shared also in the labours of the harvest.

HATE. When the Hebrews compared a stronger affection with a weaker one, they called the first *love*, and the other *hatred*. Hence *hate* signifies *to love less, to slight*.

"He who spares the rod *hates* his son," i. e., has an improper affection toward him. See Luke xiv, 26. "Jacob have I loved, and Esau have I *hated*," Rom. ix, 3, i. e., on Jacob have I bestowed privileges and blessings such as are the proofs of affection. I have treated him 'as one treats a friend whom he loves; but from Esau have I withheld these privileges and blessings, and therefore treated him as one is wont to treat those whom he dislikes; compare Mal. i, 2, 3, from which the quotation here is made, and where the prophet adds to the last clause the following words: "*And laid his mountain and his heritage waste.*" That the whole refers to the bestowment of secular blessings, and the withholding of them, is clear, not only from this passage, but from comparing Gen. xxv, 23; xxvii, 27–29, 37–40.—*Stuart.*

HAURAN, a region beyond Jordan, eastward of Gau'lanites and Bashan, and westward of Trachoni'tis, extending from the Jabbok to the territory of Damascus, Ezek. xlvii, 16–18.

HAVILAH, probably *Colchis;* which was rich in gold, e. g., Jason went thither after the golden fleece, i. e., gold caught in fleeces, gold separated from the waters of the *Phasis* by means of them. Colchis, no doubt, like all the early countries 'of nomades and predatory hordes, was not a *definitely* bounded country. It lies at the east end of the Black Sea.—*Stuart.*

HAWK. As this is a bird of prey, cruel in its temper and gross in its manners, it was forbidden as food, and all others of its kind, in the Mosaic ritual. Most of the species of hawk, we are told, are birds of passage. The hawk is produced, in Job xxxix, 26, as a specimen of that wonderful instinct which teaches birds of passage to know their times and seasons, when to migrate out of one country into another for the benefit of food, or a warmer climate, or both. Her migration is not conducted by the wisdom and prudence of man, but by the superintending and upholding providence of the only wise God.

HAY, *mature grass cut and dried.* In the two places where his word occurs, Prov. xxvii, 25, and Isa. xv, 16, our translators have very improperly rendered it *hay.* It should be *grass;* for in those countries they made no hay; and, if they did, it appears from inspection that hay could hardly be the meaning of the word in either of those texts.

HAZAEL, one of the principal officers of Benhadad, who afterward was king of Syria.

HEAD is taken for the highest or chief of any thing, to which other things are subordinate, as the chief of a people or city or family, the the top of a mountain. It is used for what is first, foremost, i. e., the beginning, the first part, as four heads or beginning of streams, Gen. ii, 10, the four smaller streams into which a larger one divides itself. *Head of the way*, where ways branch off, crossway, Ezek. xvi. 25. Head is put emphatically for the whole person. " Your blood be upon your own *head*," Acts xviii, 6. The guilt of your destruction resteth upon yourselves. To heap coals on the *head*, is to overwhelm him with shame and remorse for his enmity toward thee. See Rom. xii, 20. " The stone which the builders rejected was made the *head* of the corner," Psa. cxviii, 22, it was the *first* in the angle, whether it were disposed at the *top* of that angle to adorn and crown it, or at the *bottom* to support it. This, in the New Testament, is applied to *Christ*, who is the strength and beauty of the church, and unites the several parts of it, namely, both Jews and Gentiles, together.

HEAR, HEARING. This word is used in several senses in Scripture. In its literal acceptation, it denotes the exercise of that bodily sense of which the ear is the organ; and as hearing is a sense by which the mind is excited to attention and obedience, so the ideas of attention and obedience are conveyed by the expression. God is said, speaking after the manner of men, to hear prayer, that is,

to attend to it, and comply with the requests it contains, Psa. cxvi, 1. On the contrary, God is said not to hear, that is, not to comply with, the requests of sinners, John ix, 31. Men are said to hear when they comply with the request of each other, or when they obey the commands of God; " He who is of God heareth," obeyeth, "God's words," John viii, 47.

HEART. By the heart, the Scriptures generally intend the innermost and the noblest powers of the mind, in opposition to external actions of the body. It denotes deliberate choice, understanding, and feeling, as distinguished from the semblance of devotion, consisting in a compliance with its visible forms and regulations. As the heart has usually (whether justly or not, it is not necessary to inquire) been looked upon as the seat of feeling, in like manner as the brain has been supposed to be the chief organ of thought, it has been by an easy metaphor employed to denote that faculty of the soul by which we perceive what appears desirable, and cleave to what affords us satisfaction, and taste the delight which certain objects are adapted to afford.—*Hall*. Hence *without heart*, is without understanding or prudence, Hosea vii, 11. A gross or fat *heart*, i. e., one covered with fat, is put for dulness of understanding, Isa. vi, 10. A *heart*

13

of stone is a hard, obdurate heart, or one of firm undaunted courage, Job xli, 24. Heart is used for the middle, midst, or inner part of a thing, Matt. xii, 40, "So shall the Son of man be in the *heart* of the earth." "The caul of the *heart*," Hosea xiii, 8, the pericardium, i. e., the part which surrounds and encloses the heart. "The prophets prophesy out of their own *heart*," Ezek. xiii, 2; that is, according to their own imagination, without any warrant from God.

The heart of man is naturally depraved and inclined to evil, Jer. xvii, 9. A divine power is requisite for its renovation, John iii, 1–11. When thus renewed, the effects will be seen in the temper, conversation, and conduct at large. Hardness of heart is obstinacy, perverseness.

HEATH, a shrub that grows in marshes. It is the opinion of Clarke, Parkhurst, and others, that the heath mentioned Jer. xvii, 6, and xlviii, 6, is a blasted tree, quite naked, or stripped of its foliage. If it be any particular tree, the *tamarisk* is as likely as any. "Like the *heath* in the desert;" i. e., like a blasted tree, without moisture, parched and withered.

HEATHEN. *The Gentile nations.* Applied to all who are not Israelites, who are ignorant of the true God, and idolatrous.

HEAVEN. 1. Properly the expanse of the sky, the firmament, the apparent concave hemisphere, which seems spread out like an arch above the earth; which was regarded by the Hebrews as solid, Gen. i, 8, 14; and poetically, as resting on columns, 2 Sam. xxii, 8; Job xxvi, 11. In this is represented as fixed, the sun, moon, and stars, called the *hosts of heaven.*

2. The lower heavens or regions below the firmament, as the air, atmosphere, where clouds and tempests are gathered, and lightning breaks forth; where the birds fly, hence called the birds of heaven, clouds of heaven, Matt. xxvi, 64.

3. The upper heaven beyond the visible firmament, the abode of God and his glory, Psa. ii, 4; of the Messiah, the angels, the glorified bodies of Enoch and Elijah, the spirits of the just after death, and generally of every thing which is said to be with God. "The third *heaven*," mentioned by St. Paul, 2 Cor. xii, 2, probably is an allusion to the three heavens as above specified. "The highest *heaven*," the abode of God, the spiritual paradise, Eph. iv, 10; Heb. iv, 14, and into which Christ ascended after his resurrection. "Heaven, and the heaven of heavens," Deut. x, 14, i. e., all the extent and regions of heaven, however vast and infinite. Heaven, as being the abode of God, is often put for *God himself*; as, "I have sinned

against *Heaven*," &c., Luke xx, 18.

HEAVY, grievous, burdensome, as crime or sin, Psa. xxxviii, 4, difficult, arduous ; Exod. xviii, 18, used of things not easily moved, as the eyes oppressed with sleep, also of the mind or heart, to be *dull, stupid, hardened.* "*Heavy* burdens," Matt. xxiii, 4, burdensome precepts, oppressive, hard to be borne.

HEBREW, *passer-over ;* an appellation first applied to Abraham, Gen. xiv, 13, by the Canaanites, and afterward to all his descendants ; because he was a stranger from beyond the Euphrates ; he was born in Mesopotamia, which he left to wander through the land of Canaan. This name, therefore, was current among foreign tribes and nations. They were also called Israelites, a name derived from the founder of the nation, and was in use among themselves. In the New Testament, Hebrews signifies *the Jews of Palestine,* who use the Hebrew language ; and to whom the language and country of their fathers peculiarly belong ;—the true seed of Abraham, in opposition to the *Grecians,* i. e., Jews born out of Palestine, and using chiefly the Greek language, Acts vi, 1.

Hebrew of the Hebrews, by way of emphasis, as *king of kings ;* a Hebrew of the most honourable kind, a pure Hebrew by descent and by language, 2 Cor. xi, 22. Such

were reckoned more honourable than the Jews who spoke the Greek tongue. See GRECIAN.

HEBREW, the language spoken by the Hebrews, in which the books of the Old Testament were written, and which bears marks of being the most ancient. It flourished in Palestine among the Phenicians and Hebrews until the Babylonish exile, soon after which it declined; for the Jews of Palestine lost, with their political independence, the independence also of their language ; and the Old Testament is the only specimen of the ancient language which now remains. The kindred languages are the Syriac, Chaldee, and Arabic ; the first two constitute what is sometimes called the *Aramæan.*

HEBREWS, *Epistle to the,* supposed to be written from Rome about the year 63.

There has been some little doubt concerning the persons to whom this epistle was addressed ; but by far the most general and most probable opinion is, that it was written to the Hebrews of Palestine who had been converted to the Gospel from Judaism. That it was written, notwithstanding its general title, to the Christians of one certain place or country, is evident from the following passages : "I beseech you the rather to do this, that I may be restored to you the sooner," Heb. xiii, 19. "Know ye that our brother Timothy is set at liberty, with whom, if he come shortly, I will see you," Heb. xiii, 23. And it appears from the following passage in the Acts, " When the number of the disciples was multiplied, there arose a murmuring of the Grecians against the Hebrews," Acts vi, 1, that certain persons were at this time known at Jerusalem by the name of Hebrews. They seem to have been native Jews, inhabitants of Judea, the language of which country was Hebrew, and therefore they were called Hebrews, in contradistinction to those Jews who, residing commonly in other countries, although they occasionally came to Jerusalem, used the Greek language, and were therefore called Grecians.

The general design of this epistle was to confirm the Jewish Christians in the faith and practice of the Gospel, which they might be in danger of deserting, either through the persuasion or persecution of the unbelieving Jews, who were very numerous and powerful in Judea.

HEBRON, an ancient city of the tribe of Judah, and which for a time was the royal residence of David, 2 Sam. ii, 1; v, 5; it was about twenty-seven miles south of Jerusalem, and was the birthplace of John the Baptist.

HEDGE, *a fence*, as enclosing any thing, e. g., a *thorn hedge* around a vineyard, besides which there was often a wall, Mark xii, 1.

" Highways and *hedges*," Luke xiv, 23, i. e., the narrow ways among the vineyards or hedges, designating sometimes *that* which encloses, and sometimes the *space* enclosed by *hedges*.

HELL. The word is from the Saxon, and answers exactly to the Greek word *Hades*, *a concealed* or *unseen place*. It designates, 1. *The abode* or *place of the dead*, the common receptacle of separate spirits, whether good or bad, without regard to their happiness or misery. See Matt. xvi, 18; Acts ii, 27; Rev. i, 18, and xx, 13, 14. 2. The place where the wicked are tormented—a hopeless separation from God and eternal happiness, Psa. ix, 17, 18; Luke xvi, 23; Matt. xxiii, 33. We have decisive evidence from Scripture that this punishment will be eternal, Mark iii, 29, and ix, 44; Rev. xiv, 11; Matt. xxv, 41. Hell is represented as a place of dismal darkness, not where sinners are purified, but where sinners are punished; where there is nothing but grief, despair, and gnashing of teeth. Those who fall into this *pit* shall never escape, but the *"smoke of their torment ascendeth up for ever and ever."* The same word expresses the duration of both the happiness of the righteous and the misery of the wicked, Matt. xxv, 46.

HELL, *Gates of*. See GATES.

HELMET, a kind of leather or metal cap for protect

ing the head of a warrior, and used figuratively for defence and protection, Eph. vi, 17. It was surmounted for ornament with a horsetail and a plume. See cut of *Ancient Armour*.

HEM signifies the *fringe* or *tassel* which was worn by the Israelites on the corners of their garments, Num. xv, 38, 39, probably to distinguish them from other nations. Our Lord conformed to the custom of his country in this respect. The Pharisees, for a show of piety, *enlarged these borders or fringes*, Matt xxiii, 5.

HEMLOCK, the *cicuta*, which grows on the borders of pools and streams, and whose leaves and root are poisonous, proving fatal to most animals which feed upon it, Hos. x, 4.

HEN, Matt. xxiii, 37; Luke xiii, 34. In these two passages the metaphor used is a very beautiful one. When the hen sees a bird of prey coming, she makes a noise to assemble her chickens, that she may cover them with her wings from the danger. The Roman eagle was about to fall upon the Jewish state; our Lord invited them to himself, in order to guard them from threatened calamities: they disregarded his invitations and warnings, and fell a prey to their adversaries. The affection of the hen to her brood is so strong as to nave become proverbial.

HERESY. Among the ancients, the word *heresy* appears to have had nothing of that odious signification which has been attached to it by ecclesiastical writers in later times. It simply means, wherever it occurs in the Scripture, *divisions* or *parties* in a religious community. "After the way which they call *heresy*," Acts xxiv, 14, a *sect* or *party*; for so the word signifies. Schism and heresy are nearly allied, 1 Cor. xi, 18, 19. An undue attachment to one part, and a consequent alienation of affection from another part of the Christian Church, comes under the denomination of *schism*. When this disposition has proceeded so far as to produce an actual party or faction among them, this effect is termed *heresy*. Paul enumerates among the works of the flesh "*heresies*," Gal. v, 20; such divisions in a religious community as alienate affection, and infuse animosity. "*Damnable heresies*," 2 Pet. ii, 1, are destructive divisions.

HERETIC, in the Scriptures, signifies a man that obstinately persists in contending about foolish questions, and thereby occasions strifes and parties in the Church. His punishment is fixed, Tit. iii, 10; reject him, avoid him; leave him to himself.

HERMON, a celebrated mountain in the Holy Land. It was in the northern boundary of the country lying around the sources of the

Jordan, and consisting of several summits or ridges. The dew forms on this mountain in the greatest abundance, Psa. cxxxiii, 3.

HEROD, name of four persons in the New Testament, Idumeans by descent, who were successively invested by the Romans with authority over the Jewish nation, in whole or in part. Their history is related chiefly by Josephus.

1. *Herod*, surnamed *the Great*. He was the son of Antipater, an Idumean, in high favour with Julius Cesar; at the age of fifteen was made procurator of Galilee, in which he was confirmed by Antony, with the title of tetrarch, about 41 B. C. Being driven out by the opposite faction, he fled to Rome; where, by the influence of Antony, he was declared king of Judea. He now collected an army, recovered Jerusalem, and extirpated the Maccabean family, 37 B. C. After the battle of Actium, he joined the party of Octavius, who confirmed him in his possessions. He now rebuilt and decorated the temple of Jerusalem, built and enlarged many cities, especially Cesarea, and erected theatres and gymnasia in both these places. He was notorious for his jealousy and cruelty, having put to death his own wife Mariamne, and her two sons Alexander and Aristobulus. He died A. D. 2, aged seventy years, after a reign of about forty years as king. It was near the close of his life that Jesus was born, and the massacre of infants took place in Bethlehem. At Herod's death half his kingdom, viz., Idumea, Judea, and Samaria, was given by Augustus to his son Archelaus, with the title of ethnarch; the remaining half being divided between two of his other sons, Herod Antipas and Philip, with the title of tetrarchs; the former having Galilee and Perea, and the latter Batanea, Trachonitis, and Auranitas, (now Haouran,) Luke iii, 1.

2. *Herod Antipas*, often called *Herod the tetrarch*, the son of Herod the Great by Malthace, and own brother to Archelaus. After his father's death, Augustus gave him Galilee and Perea, with the title of tetrarch, Luke iii, 1; whence also he is called by the very general title of king, Matt. xiv, 9. He first married a daughter of Aretas, whom he dismissed on becoming enamoured of Herodias. This latter, his own niece, and the wife of his brother, Philip Herod, he induced to leave her husband and live with him; and it was for his bold remonstrance on this occasion that John the Baptist was put to death through the arts of Herodias, Mark vi, 17–19. Herod went to Rome at the instigation of Herodias, to ask for the title and rank of king; but was there accused before Caligula, at the instance of Herod

Agrippa, her own brother, and banished with her to Lugdunum (Lyons) in Gaul, about A. D. 41, while his territories were given to Herod Agrippa.

3. *Herod Agrippa*, the elder, was the grandson of Herod the Great and Mariamne, and son of Aristobulus. See AGRIPPA.

4. *Herod Agrippa*, the younger, called in the New Testament only Agrippa; he was the son of the elder Agrippa. See AGRIPPA.

HERODIANS, a Jewish sect, probably *partisans of Herod*, (Antipas,) and therefore entertaining a partiality toward the Roman emperor, which the Pharisees did not. It is generally supposed that the great body of the Jews held that the law of Moses, Deut. xvii, 15, forbade their subjection to a foreign power; while Herod and his party (the Herodians) regarded that law as forbidding a voluntary subjection; but if they were reduced to subjection by force of arms, they considered it lawful to avow their allegiance and pay tribute; and they not only paid themselves, but urged others it, and to submit cheerfully to Rome. Hence the difficulty of the question proposed to Christ, Matt. xxii, 17. The Herodians also held that it was on the same principle lawful to comply with the customs, and adopt the rites, of the conquering nation. This is probably the leaven of *Herod*. They were probably, in general, of the sect of the Sadducees; compare Mark viii, 15 with Matt. xvi, 6.

HERODIAS, daughter of Aristobulus and Berenice, and granddaughter of Herod the Great. Her first husband was her uncle Philip; but he falling into disgrace, she left him, and married his brother Herod Antipas, tetrarch of Galilee. See PHILIP. For his boldness in censuring this incestuous marriage, John the Baptist lost his head.

HER'ON, a species of crane, of an irritable disposition.

HESH'BON was the ancient royal residence of the Amorites, Num. xxi, 26, celebrated for its *fish ponds*. Songs vii, 5. It was about fourteen miles east of Jordan, within the bounds of Reuben and Gad, Josh. xiii, 17.

HETH, the father of the Hittites, was the eldest son of Canaan, Gen. x, 15; and dwelt southward of the promised land, probably about Hebron.

HEZ-E-KI'AH, king of Judah, was born 728 B. C.

HIERAPOLIS, a city of Phrygia, celebrated for its warm baths, now called *Bambuk Kulase*, Col. iv, 13. It was situated near the junction of the rivers Clydus and Mander, not far from Colosse and Laodicea.

HIG-GA'ION (*Hig-ga'yon*) signifies meditation; perhaps meaning that we should me ditate on what has been said, Psa. ix, 16.

HIDDEKEL, the river *Tigris,* Gen. ii, 14; Dan. x, 4; a noble river, rising in the mountains of Armenia, and falling into the Persian Gulf.

HIGH PLACE, a general word, comprehending mountains and hills; hence a *strong hold, fortress,* situated on a height, Psa. xviii, 33. " He setteth me upon my *high places,*" i. e., he made me secure against my enemy. Whoever possess the *strong holds* of a country, i. e., its *heights,* has also secure possession of the whole land; hence the poetical phrase, "To tread upon the *high places,*" Deut. xxxiii, 29; sometimes spoken of God as Lord and governor of the world, Amos iv, 13. The Hebrews, like most other ancient nations, supposed that sacred rites performed on elevated places were peculiarly acceptable to the Deity; hence they were accustomed to offer sacrifices upon mountains and hills, both to idols and to God himself, 1 Kings iii, 4; and also to build chapels there, 2 Kings xvii, 29. And so tenacious of this ancient custom were the Jews, that even after the building of Solomon's temple, notwithstanding the express law in Deut. xii, they continued to erect such chapels on the mountains around Jerusalem, and to offer sacrifices in them. And those kings who in other respects strictly observed the law of Moses until Josiah, did not abolish these unlawful sacrifices among the people; nor themselves desist from them. Even Solomon himself sacrificed in chapels of this sort, 1 Kings iii, 3.

House of the high place means a *chapel* erected to God, or to idols upon a mountain or hill. Transferred also to any *chapel,* Jer. vii, 31.

HIGH PRIEST enjoyed peculiar dignities and influence. He only had the privilege of entering the holy of holies on the day of solemn expiation. The supreme administration of sacred things was confided to him; he was the final arbiter of all controversies: in later times, he presided over the sanhedrim, and held the next rank to the sovereign or prince. His authority, therefore, was very great at all times, especially when he united the dignities of priest and king in his own person. According to the law, the office was or ought to have been held for life, and retained

nay, even to individuals who were not of the sacerdotal race; and sometimes the office was made annual. The knowledge of this fact will explain the circumstance of several high priests being in existence at the same time, or rather of there being several pontifical men, (Annas and Caiaphas for instance,) who having once held the office for a short time, seem to have retained the dignity originally attached to the name.

The high priest, who was the chief man in Israel, and appeared before God in behalf of the people in their sacred services, and who was appointed for sacrifice, for blessing, and for intercession, was a type of Jesus Christ, that great high priest, who offered himself a sacrifice for sin, who blesseth his people, and who evermore liveth to make intercession for them.

HIGHWAY, a raised way for public use, used metaphorically for a walk or manner of life, Isa. xxxv, 8.

HIN, a liquid measure, as of oil, or of wine, containing *one gallon and two pints.*

HIND, the female of the red deer. It is a lovely creature, and of an elegant shape. It is noted for its swiftness and the sureness of its step as it jumps among the rocks. David and Hab'akkuk both allude to this character of the hind. "The Lord maketh my feet like *hinds'* feet, and causeth me to stand on the high places," Psa. xviii, 33; Hab. iii, 19.

HINNOM, *the valley of Hinnom,* Josh. xv, 8; the narrow valley skirting Jerusalem on the south, running westward from the valley of Jehoshaphat under Mount Zion, noted for the human sacrifices here offered to Moloch, Jer. vii, 31; this worship was broken up, and the place desecrated by Josiah, 2 Kings xxiii, 10-14; after which, it seems to have become the receptacle for all the filth of the city, as also for the carcasses of animals and the dead bodies of malefactors left unburied; to consume which, fires appear to have been from time to time kept up. It was also called Tophet, Jer. vii, 31.

HI'RAM, king of Tyre, mentioned by profane authors as distinguished for his magnificence, and for adorning the city of Tyre. Sometimes called *Hurom,* 2 Chron. ii, 2, also a Tyrian artificer, 2 Chron. iv, 11.

HIRELING, *one hired,* a *hired labourer.* "The days or years of a *hireling,*" Job xiv, 6, appear to signify an exact year or day, just as the hired servant does not continue his work beyond the stated hour.

HITTITES, the descendants of Heth, who dwelt in the vicinity of Hebron, Gen. xxiii, 7.

HIVITES, a people of Canaan, dwelling at the foot of Mount Hermon and Lebanon, but scattered also in other places, as at Shechem and Gibeon, Josh. xi, 3-19.

HOAR FROST, i. e., *white frost;* as the vapour in the atmosphere coming in contact with cold bodies, as a pitcher of water, the grass, or the cold earth, forms dew; so when this dew freezes as it forms, it constitutes the *hoar frost*, Job xxxviii, 29. The deposition of dew and of hoar frost is always most abundant under a clear, unclouded sky; because a covering of clouds serves as a mantle to the earth, and prevents the free escape of caloric. Hence the advantage of snow and artificial coverings in protecting plants.

HOLINESS, freedom from the defilement of guilt and sin; it comprehends also all those pious and virtuous dispositions which constitute a religious character. God is holy, for he abhors every kind of impurity. He is the avenger of right and justice, and the object of fear and reverence to men. The apostle exhorts us to be at great pains in attaining holiness for this most important of all considerations, that without it we cannot be admitted into heaven, Heb. xii, 14.

Places and *days* consecrated to God's service are called holy.

HOLLOW of the thigh, socket of the hip, by which the thigh is connected with the pelvis; the hip joint, Gen. xxxii, 25.—*Gesenius.*

HONOUR, a proper *tribute of respect, esteem*, a *mark* or *token of honour*, Acts xxviii, 10. "If any man serve me, him will my Father *honour*," John xii, 26; bestow on him special marks of honour and favour. The favour of God, and the distinctions which it may confer are *honour*, Rom. ii, 7. "*Honour* thy father and mother," Matt. xv, 4, i. e., not only show them respect, and cheerfully obey all their lawful commands, but also honour them with thy substance; if it be necessary, feed and clothe them, and supply all their wants with liberality and tender affection. The word is used in the same sense in Prov. iii, 9, "*Honour* the Lord with thy substance." The Hebrews used the word *double*, to express plenty of any thing. *Double honour* is a liberal maintenance, 1 Tim. v, 17.

HONEY. It is uncertain whether honey is merely collected by the bee from the nectaries of flowers, and then deposited in the hive unchanged, or whether the saccharine matter of the flower does not undergo some change in the body of the insect. Besides sugar, it contains mucilaginous, colouring, and odoriferous matter, and probably a vegetable acid.

Honey comb is the cells in which the honey is contained, and from which the purest honey distils. There is a sweet substance called honey or *honey dew*, which in Arabia and other regions of Asia is found upon the leaves of certain species of trees, becomes hard, and is then easily gathered. "*Honey* out of the rock," is honey from wild bees,

Psa. lxxxi, 16, which abounds in Palestine.

HOPE, *a confident expectation of future good.* " Jesus Christ is all our *hope*," 1 Tim. i, 1. Our *hope* in this life, and the next, arises from his merits, his promises, and his Spirit. . We are said to be " *saved by hope,*" by the hope, the expectation and desire of unseen things. And we read of the "*full assurance of hope,*" which may be taken synonymously with *cheerful and earnest expectation.* " The *hope* of Israel" was the end of the Babylonish captivity, the coming of the Messiah, and the happiness of heaven. " The prisoners of *hope*," Zech. ix, 12, are *the Israelites* who were in captivity, but cherishing a hope of deliverance.

HOR, Mount Hor, the burial place of Aaron, situated in the vicinity of *Petra*, on the east side of the Ghor, (see JORDAN,) at some distance up the Wady Mousa, and therefore in Mount Seir, nearly half way from Akaba to the Dead Sea. Even now it rears its bare and rugged summit above the lonely vale of Wady Mousa, and visible in every direction from a great distance around.

HOREB, *desert or waste,* the same as Sinai, perhaps a peak of the same mountain. This name was probably given to this mountain because it was a lofty eminence destitute of vegetation around its summit.

HORITES, *dwellers in* caves ; a people more ancient than the Edomites, Deut. ii, 12. This name is obviously taken from the habits of the people. The whole of the south part of Idumea, and especially Petra, the capital city is in a great measure composed of caves ; so that in fact the inhabitants were dwellers in caves.

HORN. Besides its ordinary meaning, as the horn of an animal, it signifies a *vessel* or *flask*, either made of horn, or a horn itself thus used, 1 Sam. xvi, 1-13. Metaphorically, horn is put as the symbol of *strength, might, power ;* the image being drawn from animals which push with their horns. Thus, " the *horn* of Moab is broken," Jer. xlviii, 25 ; hence used for kings and kingdoms, Dan. vii, 20-24. For God to exalt the horn of any one is to strengthen him, to increase his power and dignity, Psa. xcii, 11. " To lift up one's own *horn*," Psa. lxxv, 45, is to be *proud ;* spoken of those who place too much confidence in their own strength, and thus become overbearing. David calls God, Psa. xviii, 2, " the *horn* of salvation," i. e., the instrument, means of deliverance, a strong deliverer. "*Horns* of ivory," Ezek. xxvii, 15, i. e., elephants' teeth, so called because the ancients supposed them to be horns ; the word *horns* is used poetically for *rays* of light or splendour, Hab. iii, 4. So the Arabic poets compare the first rays of the rising sun to *horns.*

HORNET, an insect much larger and stronger than the wasp, whose sting gives severe pain, and in hot eastern countries is very venomous, and even deadly, Deut. vii, 20. How distressing and destructive a multitude of these fierce and severely stinging insects might be, any person may conjecture. No armour, no weapons could avail against them. A few thousands of them would be sufficient to overthrow the best-disciplined army, and put it into confusion and rout. From Joshua xxiv, 12, we find that two kings of the Amorites were actually driven out of the land by these hornets, so that the Israelites were not obliged to use either sword or bow in the conquest.

HORSE. Horses were very rare among the Hebrews in the early ages. The patriarchs had none ; and after the departure of the Israelites from Egypt, God expressly forbade their ruler to procure them, Deut. xvii, 16. In the time of the Judges we find horses and war chariots among the Canaanites, but still the Israelites had none; and hence they were generally too timid to venture down into the plains, confining their conquests to the mountainous parts of the country. Solomon was the first who established a cavalry force. Having married a daughter of Pharaoh, he procured a breed of horses from Egypt ; and so greatly did he multiply them, that he had four hundred stables, forty thousand stalls, and twelve thousand horsemen, 1 Kings iv, 26. It seems that the Egyptian horses were in high repute, and were much used in war. When the Israelites were disposed to place too implicit confidence in the assistance of cavalry, the prophet remonstrated in these terms : "The Egyptians are men, and not God ; and their horses are flesh, not spirit," Isa. xxxi, 3.

HORSE-LEECH, or *bloodsucker*, Prov. xxx, 15. A sort of worm that lives in water, of a black or brown colour, which fastens upon the flesh, and does not quit it till it is entirely full of blood. Solomon says, "The *horse-leech* hath two daughters, Give, give." This is so apt an emblem of an insatiable *rapacity* and *avarice*, that it has been generally used by different writers to express it. As the horse-leech had two daughters, cruelty and thirst of blood, which cannot be satisfied, so the oppressor of the poor has two dispositions, rapacity and avarice, which never say they have enough, but continually demand additional gratifications.

HO-SAN'NA, "Save, I beseech thee," or, "Give salvation ;" a word of joyful acclamation, Matt. xxi, 9–15.

HO-SE'A, son of Beeri, the first of the minor prophets. He is generally considered as a native and inhabitant of the kingdom of Israel, and is supposed to have begun to prophesy about 800 B. C. He exercised his office sixty years; but it is not known at what periods his different prophecies now remaining were delivered. The style of Hosea is peculiarly obscure; it is sententious, concise, and abrupt; the transitions of persons are sudden; and the connexive and adversative particles are frequently omitted; but we shall see abundant reason to admire the force and energy with which this prophet writes, and the boldness of the figures and similitudes which he uses.

2. HOSEA, or HOSHEA, son of Elah, was the *last king of Israel*. Sal-man-e′ser, king of Assyria, being informed that Hoshea meditated a revolt, and had concerted measures with So, king of Egypt, to shake off the Assyrian yoke, marched against him, and besieged Samaria. After a siege of three years, in the ninth year of Hoshea's reign, the city was taken, and was reduced to a heap of ruins, 717 B. C. The king of Assyria removed the Israelites of the ten tribes to countries beyond the Euphrates, and thus terminated the kingdom of the ten tribes.

HOST, *an army*, as going forth to war. The angels which stand around the throne of God. Frequently the sun, moon, and stars

The Lord of hosts, i. e., of the celestial armies; a very usual appellation for the most high God in the prophetical books, but does not occur in the pentateuch, nor in the book of Judges. The apostle speaks of *his host*, Rom. xvi, 23, i. e., *an entertainer*, one who had received him into his house, and had showed him hospitality.

To HOUGH,(*hok*,) *to hamstring*, i. e., to cut the sinews of the hind legs, by which the animal is rendered wholly useless and unable to stand; this was often, and is still done in war by the victors, when unable to carry off with them the horses captured, Josh. xi, 69.

HOUR, one of the twelve equal parts into which the natural day and also the night were divided. Hours were of course of different lengths at different seasons of the year. The mention of the *hour* first occurs in Dan. iii, 6. The hours of the day were counted from sunrise, and those of the night from sunset; hence the *sixth hour* was the middle of the day, and the *eleventh* was the hour before sunset. The hours of note, in the course of the day, were the third, sixth, and ninth, which were the hours of prayer, Dan. vi, 10; Acts iii, 1; x, 9. It is used figuratively for *a short time*, a brief interval, Dan. iv, 19; Rev. xvii, 12; sometimes it signifies *in the same moment*, instantly, Dan. v, 5.

HOUSE, *a place of resi-dence,* often built in the form of a hollow square, which is called the court. *The house of God* is the *tabernacle* or *temple,* where the presence of God was manifested, and where God was said to dwell, because there the symbol of the divine presence resided; but under the Gospel dispensation this appellation is given to the *church,* 1 Tim. iii, 15. By metonymy, a *household family,* those who live together in a house, as wife and children. It also signifies *posterity,* those who are descended from one head or ancestor, as *the house of David,* Luke i, 27; *a sepulchre,* the house of the dead, especially one costly, sumptuous, Isa. xiv, 18; called also the *long home,* Eccles. xii, 5.

Houses of clay, Job iv, 19, is a lively image of the frail and perishable nature of human bodies.

House top, Matt. xxiv, 17; the roofs of oriental houses are flat, covered with a composition of gravel, earth, &c., reduced to a solid substance by the application of blows, and surrounded by a wall or railing, breast-high, to prevent persons from falling, Deut. xxii, 8. Upon this surface grass and weeds frequently grew, Psa. cxxix, 6; and there the inhabitants spent much of their time to enjoy the open air, and often slept there. The walls of houses of the poorer classes are often built of clay or bricks burned in the sun, and of great thickness, which accounts for the expression of Job xxiv, 16.

HUMILITY, *lowliness, modesty* of mind and deportment, "*not to think of himself more highly than he ought to think, but to think soberly,*" Rom. xii, 3, i. e., to think modestly, prudently, in a rational way of himself, not being puffed up with his own attainments and gifts, having a knowledge of his unworthiness, and dependance upon God for every thing. It is the virtue of Christ and Christians, and stands opposed to pride and arrogance. It is a settled and permanent disposition of the mind, which shows itself in external actions, 1 Pet. v, 5.

To humble signifies often to afflict, to subdue, Isa. x, 33. To humble a virgin or woman, taken in war, signifies to pollute her honour, Deut. xxii, 24.

HUNTING. The earliest inhabitants of the world were compelled to hunt, in order to secure themselves from the attacks of wild beasts; and a great hunter was accounted a benefactor of mankind. "A mighty *hunter* before the Lord," Gen. x, 9, is one who is impetuous and successful; one whom God favours. Hunting required both speed and bravery. The implements employed were usually the same as those of war. Death is represented as a hunter armed with implements of destruction, Psa. xviii, 5; xci, 3; 1 Cor. xv. 55

HUSBANDRY. In the primitive ages of the world, agriculture, as well as the keeping of flocks, was a principal employment among men, Gen. ii, 15; iii, 17-19; iv, 2. It is an art which has ever been a prominent source, both of the necessaries and the conveniences of life. Those states and nations, especially Babylon and Egypt, which made the cultivation of the soil their chief business, arose in a short period to wealth and power. To these communities just mentioned, which excelled in this particular all the others of antiquity, may be added that of the Hebrews, who learned the value of the art while remaining in Egypt, and ever after that time were famous for their industry in the cultivation of the earth. Moses, following the example of the Egyptians, made agriculture the basis of the state. He accordingly apportioned to every citizen a certain quantity of land, and gave him the right of tilling it himself, and of transmitting it to his heirs.

HUSKS, the external covering of the fruits of certain plants, as of corn or beans. The lost son, oppressed by want, and pinched by hunger, desired to feed on the husks given to the swine, Luke xv, 16. The original word signifies *carob beans*, i. e., the fruit of the carob tree. "This tree is common in Syria and in the southern parts of Eu-rope. It produces long slender pods, shaped like a horn or sickle, containing a sweetish pulp, and several brown shining seeds, like beans. These pods are sometimes used as food by the lower classes in the east, and swine are commonly fed with them." —*Robinson.*

HYMN, a song, or ode, composed in honour of God. The Jewish hymns were accompanied with instruments of music, to assist the voices of the Levites and people. The word is used as synonymous with song, or psalm, which the Hebrews scarcely distinguish, having no particular term for a hymn, as distinct from a psalm. St. Paul requires Christians to edify one another with " psalms, and hymps, and spiritual songs." St. Matthew says, that Christ, having supped, *sung a hymn, and went out* He recited the hymns or psalms which the Jews were used to sing after the passover; that is, the Hallelujah Psalms.

HYPOCRITE, a word from the Greek, which signifies one who *feigns* to be what he is not; who puts on a *mask* or *character*, like *actors* in tragedies and comedies. It is generally applied to those who assume appearances of a virtue, without possessing it in reality. Our Saviour accused the Pharisees of hypocrisy. In the Old Testament, the Hebrew word which is rendered " hypocrite," "counterfeit," signifies also a profane wicked man, a man polluted, corrupted, a man of impiety, a deceiver.

HYS'SOP, a low plant or shrub, of a bitter taste, which grows out of the walls or rocks; and therefore a striking contrast to the tall and majestic cedar, 1 Kings iv, 33; found in great abundance around Mount Sinai; much used in the ritual purifications and sprinklings of the Hebrews; and, under this name, they appear to have comprised not only the common hyssop of the shops, but also other aromatic plants, especially mint, wild marjoram, and lavender.

ICONIUM, a large and populous city of Asia Minor, now called *Konieh*.

IDDO, a prophet of the kingdom of Judah, who wrote the history of Rehoboam and Abijah, 2 Chron. xii, 15.

IDLE, *not labouring, unemployed, inactive; idle words*, empty and vain words, i. e., void of truth, and to which the event does not correspond; the false, insincere language of a man who says one thing and means another.

IDOL, *an image;* it signifies an *idol god*, i. e., a heathen deity, or an *image,* a representation of one, any thing worshipped in room of the true God, 1 Cor. viii, 4.

An idol is nothing, i. e., has no existence as a God;

no share in the government of the world.

The pollutions of idols, Acts xv, 20, spoken of meat sacrificed to idols; see verse 29. The apostle here refers to the customs of heathen nations; among whom, after a sacrifice had been completed, and a portion of the victim given to the priest, the remaining part was either exposed by the owner for sale in the market, or became the occasion of a banquet, either in the temple or at his own house; and thus he became *polluted.*

IDOLATRY, *idol worship;* the worship and adoration of false gods, or the giving those honours to creatures or the works of man's hands which are only due to God. It is either external or internal. External is the paying homage to outward objects, either natural or artificial; and this is the common sense of the term. Internal is an inordinate love of the creatures, riches, honours, and the pleasures of this life Col. iii, 5; Phil. iii, 19. Soon after the flood, men fell into idolatry. A large portion of our race have ever practised this sin—dreadfully indicative of the corruption and degradation of human nature. Not only have the heavenly bodies and eminent benefactors of mankind been worshipped, but animals, plants, reptiles, and figures made by human hands. To these were paid not only reverence and devotion, but the most horrid rites. The most gross indecencies, the murder of children, suicide, torture, drunkenness, and every abomination have been considered proper acts of worship. In some countries, idolatry still retains these shocking characteristics.

The veneration which the Papists pay to the Virgin Mary, and other saints and angels, and to the bread in the sacrament, the cross, relics, and images, affords ground for the Protestants to charge them with being idolaters, though they deny that they are so. It is evident that they worship these persons and things, and that they justify the worship, but deny the idolatry of it, by distinguishing subordinate from supreme worship. This distinction is justly thought by Protestants to be futile and nugatory, and certainly has no support from Holy Writ.

Under the government of Samuel, Saul, and David, there was little or no idolatry in Israel. Solomon was the first Hebrew king who built temples and offered incense to strange gods. Jeroboam, who succeeded him in the greater part of his dominions, set up golden calves at Dan and Bethel. Under the reign of Ahab, this disorder was at its height, occasioned by Jezebel, the wife of Ahab, who did all she could to destroy the worship of the true God, by driving away and persecuting his prophets. God, therefore, incensed at the sins and idolatry of the ten tribes, abandoned those tribes to the kings of Assyria and Chaldea, who transplanted them beyond the Euphrates, from whence they never returned. The people of Judah were no less corrupted. The prophets give an awful description of their idolatrous practices. They were punished after the same manner, though not so severely, as the ten tribes; being led into captivity several times, from which at last they returned, and were settled in the land of Judea, after which we hear no more of their idolatry. They have been, indeed, ever since that period, distinguished for their zeal against it.

ID-U-ME'-A, *the land of Edom*, it being the softened Greek pronunciation for *Edom*. This country lay to the southeast of Palestine, along the great valley which extends from the Dead Sea to the Elanitic or Eastern Gulf of the Red Sea, called toward the north *El Ghor*, and toward the south *El Araba*, and chiefly on its eastern side, which is rough and mountainous. This valley is 110 miles long, and from eight to twelve broad. Here dwelt the descendants of Esau, who were conquered by David, 2 Sam. viii, 14; but were first completely subdued by John Hyr-ca'nus, about 125 B. C. During the Jewish exile, they had taken possession of Palestine as far north as *Hebron*. So in the

14

New Testament it includes this region also, Mark iii, 8. See SEIR.

ILLYRICUM, a country of Europe, on the eastern shore of the Adriatic Gulf, or Gulf of Venice, north of Epirus, and west of Macedonia. Dalmatia formed a part of it, Rom. xv, 19.

IMAGE, the representation or figure of any thing, as the head of a prince on a coin, Matt. xxii, 20; a likeness to any one, resemblance, similitude, as Christ is the image of the *invisible God*, he is a bright representation of all the perfections of the Deity, Col. i, 15, "Man was made in the *image* of God," possessing a *spiritual* and an *immortal* soul, endowed with knowledge and liberty, and also resembling God in his moral image, *righteousness, and true holiness.* See IDOLATRY.

IMMORTAL. That which will endure to all eternity, as having in itself no principle of alteration or corruption. God is absolutely immortal,—he cannot die. Angels are immortal; but God, who made them, can terminate their being. Man is immortal in part, that is, in his spirit; but his body dies. Inferior creatures are not immortal; they die wholly. Thus the principle of immortality is differently communicated, according to the will of Him who can render any creature immortal by prolonging its life; who can confer immortality on the body of man, together with his soul; and will do so at the resurrection. God only is absolutely perfect, and therefore absolutely immortal.

IMPUTE. We often mean by the word, to reckon to one what does not properly belong to him, or that which is not personally his own. But this is not the sense in which it is used in Scripture. It signifies to reckon to one *what actually does belong to him*, i. e., to treat him as actually possessing the thing or quality reckoned to him. "Abraham's faith was *imputed* to him for righteousness." He was treated on account of it as if he were righteous; God reckoned his faith as a righteous act. "*Counting for righteousness*," means *to accept and treat as righteous.* "To *impute* one's own iniquity to him," 2 Cor. v, 19, is to hold him accountable for it in respect to the demands of justice. "Happy the man to whom the Lord *imputeth* not iniquity," i. e., one who obtains forgiveness of his sins, and is accepted and treated as if he were righteous.

INCENSE, the odours of spices and gums burned in religious rites, or as an offering to some deity. That which is ordinarily so called is a precious and fragrant gum, issuing from the frankincense tree. The "*sweet incense*," mentioned Exod. xxx, 7, and elsewhere, was a compound of several drugs, agreeably to the direction in the 34th verse. To offer incense was an office peculiar to the priests. They went twice a day into the holy place; namely, morning and evening, to burn incense there. Upon the great day of expiation, the high priest took incense, or perfume, pounded and ready for being put into the censer, and threw it upon the fire the moment he went into the sanctuary. One reason of this was, that so the smoke which rose from the censer might prevent his looking with too much curiosity on the ark and mercy-seat. God threatened him with death upon failing to perform this ceremony, Lev. xvi, 13. Generally, incense is to be considered as an emblem of the *prayers of the saints*, and is so used by the sacred writers.

INCHANTMENTS. The law of God condemns *inchantments* and *inchanters*. It was common for magicians, sorcerers, and inchanters, to speak in a *low voice*, to *whisper*. They affected secrecy and mysterious ways, to conceal the vanity, folly, or infamy of their pernicious art. Their *pretended* magic often consisted in cunning tricks only, in sleight of hand, or some natural secrets, unknown to the ignorant. They affected obscurity and night, or would show their skill only before the uninformed, or mean persons, and feared nothing so much as serious examinations, broad day-light, and the inspection of the intelligent.

Respecting the inchantments practised by Pharaoh's magicians, (see Exod. viii, 18, 19,) in order to imitate the miracles which were wrought by Moses, they were mere *illusions*, whereby they imposed on the spectators.

INDIA, Esther i, 1, is thought to be the modern *Hindostan*, or that vast region of Asia which lies about the river *Indus*, from which it is supposed to have derived its name. This country was probably settled by the immediate descendants of Ham. The aboriginal inhabitants have lost very little of their primitive character, having but little resemblance either in their figure or manners to any of the surrounding nations.

INHERITANCE, a *patrimony*, an estate derived from an ancestor; *a portion, possession;* the territory assigned to each tribe in the promised land, and sometimes taken for the whole of Palestine. Hence figuratively it signifies admission to the kingdom of God and its attendant privileges, Acts xxvi, 32. "To *inherit* the earth," Matt. v, 3; *to possess the land*, i. e., primarily the land of Canaan, spoken of the quiet occupancy and abode of the Israelites in *Palestine* promised of old to Abraham, but understood in a spiritual sense of the highest prosperity and happiness of life, Psa. xxv, 13; xxxvii, 11-22, perhaps the *Messiah's kingdom.*

INK. The ink of the ancients was not so fluid as ours. The most simple method of preparation, and consequently the most ancient, was a mixture of charcoal, or soot and water, with the addition of a little gum. The custom of placing the inkhorn, a small portable case for pens and ink, by the side continues in the east to this day. Dr. Shaw informs us, that, among the Moors in Barbary, "the writers or secretaries suspend their inkhorns in their girdles ; a custom as old as the Prophet Ezekiel, ix, 2."

INN, *a lodging place*, either in the open air or under a roof ; a place where one puts up. The eastern inns generally are large square buildings near a fountain or well, in the centre of which is an era or open court, Jer. ix, 2. Most of the eastern cities contain one, at least, for the reception of strangers. Near them is generally a well, and a cistern for the cattle ; a brahmin, or fakeer, often resides there to furnish the pilgrim with food, and the few necessaries he may stand in need of. In the deserts of Persia and Arabia, these buildings are invaluable ; in those pathless plains, for many miles together, not a tree, a bush, nor even a blade of grass is to be seen ; all is one undulating mass of sand, like waves on the trackless ocean. In these ruthless wastes, where no rural village or cheerful hamlet, no inn or house of refreshment is to be found, how noble is the charity that rears the hospitable roof, that plants the shady grove, and conducts the refreshing moisture into reservoirs !

INSPIRATION, the imparting of such a degree of divine influence, as enabled the authors of the several books of Scripture to communicate religious knowledge to others without error or mistake. On this subject there are two opinions : 1. That every *thought* and *word* were suggested to them by the Spirit of God ; that they did nothing but write as the Spirit dictated. 2. That the Spirit of God inspired the *whole matter ;* but that they were left to express themselves in their own words and phrases, in which they give a faithful account of what the Spirit dictated to them, 2 Pet. i, 21. The sublime doctrines and precepts which the Scriptures contain ; the harmony and connection subsisting between their various parts ; their tendency to promote the happiness of mankind, as evinced by the blessed effects which are invariably produced by a cordial belief of the doctrines ; the *miracles* which they record, and the prophecies which have been fulfilled, and are daily fulfilling, show them to be divinely inspired, 2 Tim. iii, 16.

INTERCESSION, an address or application to one person in behalf of another. *To intercede*, conveys the general sense of aiding, assisting, managing one's concerns for his advantage. There is one Mediator, who is appointed by God to make an atonement for the sins of men by his death, and who in consequence of that atonement is authorized to intercede with God in behalf of sinners, and empowered to convey all his blessings to them. In this sense, there is but one " Mediator between God and man," and he is equally related to all. " Wherefore," says Macknight, " Christ's intercession for us is quite different from our intercession for one another. He intercedes, as having merited what he asks for us. Whereas we intercede for our brethren, merely as expressing our good will toward them. And because exercises of this kind have a great influence in cherishing benevolent dispositions in us, they are so acceptable to God, that, to encourage us to pray for one another, he hath promised to hear our prayers for others, when it is for his glory and their good."

IRON, a well known and very serviceable metal. The knowledge of working it is very ancient, as appears from Genesis iv, 22, where the word first occurs. We do not, however, find that Moses made use of iron in the fabric of the tabernacle in the wil-derness, or Solomon in any part of the temple at Jerusalem. Yet, from the manner in which the Jewish legislator speaks of iron, the metal, it appears, must have been in use in Egypt before his time, Deut. xxviii, 23–48; viii, 9; iv, 20.

ISAAC, the patriarch, son of Abraham and Sarah, born A. M. 2108. In Amos vii, 9–16, used poetically for the whole nation of Israel.

ISAIAH, the celebrated Hebrew prophet, who lived and had great influence under the reigns of Uzziah, Jotham, Ahaz, and Hezekiah, kings of Judah, who successively flourished between 806 and 694 B. C. He was contemporary with the prophets, Amos, Hosea, Joel, and Micah. Concerning the time or manner of his death nothing certain is known. Of all the prophets, none have so clearly predicted the circumstances relative to the advent, sufferings, atoning death, and resurrection of the Messiah, as Isaiah; who has from this circumstance been styled the evangelical prophet. His predictions yet unfulfilled of the ultimate triumph and extension of the Redeemer's kingdom, are unrivalled for the splendour of their imagery, and the beauty and sublimity of their language.

Bishop Lowth has selected the thirty-fourth and thirty-fifth chapters of this prophet, as a specimen of the poetic style in which Isaiah delivers his predictions, and has illustrated at some length the various beauties which eminently distinguish the simple, regular, and perfect poem contained in those chapters. But the grandest specimen of his poetry is presented in the fourteenth chapter, which is one of the most sublime odes occurring in the Bible, and contains the noblest personification to be found in the records of poetry. There is not a single instance in the whole compass of Greek and Roman poetry which, in every excellence of composition, can be said to equal or even to approach it.

IS-CART-OT, the surname of that disciple who betrayed our Saviour, Matt. x, 4.

ISH'BOSHETH, the son of Saul, who for two years after the death of his father and brothers reigned over eleven tribes in opposition to David, 2 Sam. ii, 4.

ISHMAELITES, Arabs descended from Ishmael, the son of Abraham and Hagar, and living a wandering life as nomades at the eastward of Judea and of Egypt, as far as the Persian Gulf and Assyria, i. e., Babylonia, Gen. xxv, 18, which same limits are elsewhere assigned to the Amalekites.

ISLANDS, ISLES. The Hebrew word which is more commonly . translated *isle*, means strictly *dry land*, habitable country, in opposition to water, or to seas and rivers, Gen. x, 5; Isa. xlii, 15, " I will make the rivers *dry land*," not *islands*, which would make no sense. Hence, as opposed to water in general, it means *lands adjacent to water*, either washed or surrounded by it ; i. e., *maritime country, coast, island.* The plural of this word, usually translated *islands*, was employed by the Hebrews to denote *distant regions beyond the sea*, whether coasts or islands, and especially the islands and maritime countries of the west, Isa. xxiv, 15.

ISRAEL, *a wrestler with God ;* a name given to Jacob after wrestling with the angel, Gen. xxxii, 24 ; but more frequently to his posterity, *the people of Israel.* Sometimes it is used emphatically for the *true* Israelites ; *an Israelite indeed*, John, i, 48, one who is distinguished for piety and virtue and worthy of the name, Isa. xlix, 3 ; Psa. lxxiii, 1. In the Old Testament, the kingdom of the ten tribes is called *Israel*, in opposition to that of Judah ; hence the descendants of David who reigned over Judah and Benjamin are called *the kings of Judah*, and those who reigned over the ten tribes *the kings of Israel ;* other names for the ten tribes were *Ephraim*, as the name of the most powerful tribe ; and *Samaria*, from the capital city, Hos. viii, 5, 6. But, in the New Testament, it is applied to all the descendants of Israel then remaining, and synonymous after the exile with *Jews*,

Matt. viii, 10, although chiefly consisting of the remains of Judah and Benjamin. Hence in the Chronicles, the name Israel is sometimes spoken of the kingdom of Judah, 2 Chron. xii, 1, and xv, 17.

IS'SA-CHAR, the fifth son of Jacob and Leah, Gen. xxx, 14–18. The tribe of Issachar nad its portion in one of the best parts of the land of Canaan, along the great plain or valley of Jezreel.

ITALY, a noted country, shaped like a boot, in the south of Europe.

ITURE'A, a region whose *exact* situation is doubtful, lying beyond Jordan, near the foot of Mount Hermon, and on the eastern shore of the sea of Galilee, Luke iii, 1. The Itureans were celebrated as skilful archers and daring robbers. Philip, one of the sons of Herod the Great, was tetrarch or governor of this country when John the Baptist commenced his ministry.

• IVORY, the substance of the tusk of the elephant. It is esteemed for its beautiful cream colour, the fineness of its grain, and the high polish it is capable of receiving. The use of ivory was well known in very early ages. We find it employed for arms, sceptres, and various other purposes; cabinets and wardrobes were ornamented with ivory, and it was therefore an article of commerce. It seems that Solomon had a throne decorated with ivory.

"*Ivory* houses," Amos iii, 15, were palaces with walls inlaid, or covered with ivory.

JAB'BOK, a small stream east of the Jordan, which takes its rise in the mountains of Gilead, and falls into the Jordan below the sea of Tiberias, Deut. ii, 37. Near this brook the angel wrestled with Jacob.

JA-BESH, or JABESH-GIL'E-AD, the name of a city in the half tribe of Manasseh, east of Jordan, at the foot of Mount Gilead.

JACINTH, or HYACINTH, a flower of a deep purple, or reddish *blue*; in the New Testament, a gem of like colour, related to the *Zircon* of mineralogists. See PRECIOUS STONES.

JACOB, the youngest of the twin sons of Isaac, called also *Israel*; the founder of the Israelitish nation. "Put for the land of *Jacob*," Gen. xlix, 7; also the posterity of Jacob, the Jewish people, Rom. xi, 26; rarely used for the kingdom of Ephraim or the ten tribes, Micah i, 5.

Jacob was of a meek and peaceable temper, and loved a quiet pastoral life; whereas Esau was of a fierce and turbulent nature, and was fond of hunting. Isaac had a particular fondness for Esau; but Rebekah was more attached to Jacob. As to the purchase of the birth-right, see ESAU.

Jacob appears to have been innocent so far as any guile

on his part or real necessity from hunger on the part of Esau is involved in the question; but his obtaining the ratification of this by the blessing of Isaac, though agreeable, indeed, to the purpose of God, that the elder should serve the younger, was blameable as to the means employed.

According to Dr. Hales, all the parties were more or less culpable; Isaac, for endeavouring to set aside the oracle which had been pronounced in favour of his younger son; but of which he might have an obscure conception; Esau, for wishing to deprive his brother of the blessing which he had himself relinquished; and Rebekah and Jacob, for securing it by fraudulent means, not trusting wholly in the Lord. But though the intention of Rebekah and Jacob might have been free from worldly or mercenary motives, they ought not to have done evil that good might come. And they were both severely punished in this life for their fraud, which destroyed the peace of the family, and planted a mortal enmity in the breast of Esau against his brother. "Is he not rightly named *Jacob?*" a *heel-catcher*, a *supplanter*; "for he hath supplanted me these two times: he took away my birthright, and lo, now he hath taken away my blessing. The days of mourning for my father are at hand; then will I slay my brother *Jacob*," Gen.

xxvii, 36–41. Rebekah, also, was deprived of the society of her darling son, whom "she sent away for one year," as she fondly imagined, "until his brother's fury should turn away," Gen. xxvii, 42–44; but whom she saw no more; for she died during his long exile of twenty years, though Isaac survived, Gen. xxxv, 27. Thus was "she pierced through with many sorrows." Jacob, also, had abundant reason to say, "Few and evil have been the days of the years of my pilgrimage," Gen. xlvii, 9.

JAD-DU'A, a high priest of the Jews, who went in his pontifical robes, accompanied by his brethren, to meet *Alexander* the Great, when he was advancing toward Jerusalem intending to destroy it. Alexander was so struck with the appearance of the priest, that he forbore all hostilities against Jerusalem, prostrated himself before Jaddua, and granted many privileges to the Jews, about 341 B. C.

JAH, one of the names of God, contracted from Jehovah, which we meet with in the composition of many Hebrew words.

JAM'BRES, a magician, who opposed Moses in Egypt.

JAMES. Two persons by this name are mentioned in the list of the apostles; the first was the son of Zebedee, and own brother of John, Mark iii, 17. He was present at the transfiguration of our Lord, and was put to death by Herod Agrippa the elder, about A. D. 44, Acts xii, 2.

The other James was the son of *Alpheus*, and called James *the Less*, Mark xv, 40, to distinguish him from the other; perhaps he was lower in stature. His mother was sister to the Virgin Mary. He was consequently cousin german to Christ, and is therefore termed his *brother*, Gal. i, 19, i.e., his *kinsman*, or near relation. On account of his distinguished piety he was called the *Just*. He was honoured by an interview with Christ soon after his resurrection, 1 Cor. xv, 7. He appears to have presided at the council of the apostles which was convened in Jerusalem, A. D. 49. He is said to have been stoned to death by the Jews, A. D. 62; and most learned men agree in placing his epistle in the year 61. The persons to whom this epistle was addressed were the Hebrew Christians, who were in danger of falling into the sins which abounded among the Jews of that time.

James the less was a person of great prudence and discretion, and was highly esteemed by the apostles and other Christians. Such, indeed, was his general reputation for piety and virtue, that, as we learn from Origen, Eusebius, and Jerome, Josephus declared it to be the common opinion, that the sufferings of the Jews, and the destruction of their city and temple, were owing to the anger of God, excited by the murder of James.

JAN'NES and JAMBRES, two magicians, who resisted Moses in Egypt, 2 Tim. iii, 8. As these names are not found in the Old Testament, the apostle probably derived them from tradition. They are often mentioned by Jewish writers.

JAPHETH, the first son of Noah, Gen. x, 21, whose posterity are described occupying chiefly the western and northern regions, Gen. x, 2–5; this accords well with the etymology of the name, which signifies *widely spreading*; and how wonderfully did Providence enlarge the boundaries of Japheth! His posterity diverged eastward and westward; from the original settlement in Armenia, through the whole extent of Asia, north of the great range of Taurus, distinguished by the general names of Tartary and Siberia, as far as the Eastern Ocean: and in process of time, by an easy passage across Behring's Straits, the entire continent of America; and they spread in the opposite direction, throughout the whole of Europe, to the Atlantic Ocean; thus literally encompassing the earth, within the precincts of the northern temperate zone; while the enterprising and warlike genius of this hardy hunter race frequently led them to encroach on the settlements, and to dwell in "the tents of Shem," whose pastoral occupations rendered them more inactive, peaceable, and unwarlike.

JASHER, *upright*, "book of *Jasher*," Josh. x, 3, i. e., the annals of the Jewish nation; a book of national songs or narratives, so called, as containing narratives respecting men of an upright character. That this was a poetical book, is apparent, both from the poetical character of the passage here quoted, in which the parallelism of numbers cannot be mistaken; and also from the fact, that in 2 Sam. i, 18, this same book is referred to, as containing the elegy of David over Saul and Jonathan. In all probability, it was a collection formed by degrees of poems in praise of theocratic heroes; for the same in the original is elsewhere employed to designate the true supporters of the theocracy.

JASPER, a precious stone of various colours, as brown, red, blue, green, which occurs abundantly in the deserts of Egypt; the colour is pretty deep, but the lustre is inconsiderable; and when stripes of green, yellow, and red occur on the same gem, it is called *striped jasper;* mostly employed in the formation of seals, and when well polished is a very beautiful stone. See PRECIOUS STONES.

JA'VAN, was the fourth son of Japheth, and the father of all those nations which were included under the name of Grecians, or Ionians, as they were invariably called in the east. Javan is the name used in the Old Testament for Greece and the Greeks.

JAVELIN, a kind of long dart, or light spear, thrown as a missile weapon at the enemy.

JEALOUSY, suspicions of infidelity, especially as applied to the marriage state. *God's jealousy* signifies his concern for his own character and government, with a holy indignation against those who violate his laws and offend against his majesty. "Whose name is *jealous*," Exod. xxxiv, 14; he is impatient of a rival, and the severe avenger of defection from himself. And the word is frequently used to express the vindictive acts of dishonoured love, Psa. lxxix, 5, "To provoke to *jealousy* or *emulation*," Rom. xi, 11–14, i. e., cause one to set a right value upon his privileges, by bestowing like privileges on others; also, to provoke God to *jealousy* or anger, by rendering to idols the homage due to him alone, 1 Cor. x, 22.

JEBUS, the ancient name of Jerusalem among the Canaanites, Judg. xix, 10.

JEBUSITES, a Canaanitish tribe, who inhabited Jerusalem and the neighbouring mountains; they were subdued by David, but still existed in the time of Ezra, Ezra ix, 1; put for the city itself, Josh. xv, 8; also poetically in later times for the inhabitants of Jerusalem, Zech. ix, 7.

JED'U-THUN, a Levite of Merari's family, and one of the four great masters of music belonging to the temple. The name is also put for his descendants, *the Jeduthanites*, who also were musicians, and is found in the title of several psalms, 2 Chron. xxxv, 15.

JE-HOSH'-A-PHAT, a king of Judah, 914–889 B. C., son of Asa, 1 Kings xxii, 41; from him the valley between Jerusalem and the Mount of Olives received its name, Joel iii, 2–12. This valley, running from north to south, is deep and narrow: through the middle of it flows the *Kedron*, which is dry during the greatest part of the year.

JEHOVAH, the name of the Supreme Being among the Hebrews; it is derived from a word which signifies *to be*, *to exist*; and is designed to express *the real existence of the one true God*, in opposition to the false deities; the eternal, immutable, who will never be other than the same. The later Hebrews, from several centuries before the Christian era, either misled by a false interpretation of certain laws, Exod. xx, 7; Lev. xxiv, 11–16, or following out some ancient superstition, regarded this name as too sacred to be uttered, as the ineffable name which they scrupled even to pronounce.

JEHU, a king of Israel, who destroyed the family of Ahab, 884–856 B. C. He was hostile to idolatry, but of great cruelty, 2 Kings ix, 10.

JEHOVAH-JIREH, (*Jy'-reh*,) *The Lord will provide*; a name which Abraham gave to the place where he had been on the point of slaying his son, and in allusion to his answer of Isaac's question, Gen. xxii, 14; see verse 8.

JEPHTHAH, a judge of the Israelites, celebrated for the rash vow which he made respecting his daughter, Judg. xi. In verse 31st, it is said, "Then it shall be that whatsoever cometh forth of the doors of my house to meet me, when I return in peace from the children of Ammon, shall surely be the Lord's; and I will offer it up for a burnt-offering." Dr. Clark says this passage may be translated according to the most accurate Hebrew scholars thus: *I will consecrate it to the Lord, or I will offer it for a burnt-offering*, i. e., if it be a thing fit for a burnt-offering, it shall be made one; if fit for the service of God, it shall be consecrated to him. That conditions of this kind must have been implied in the vow is evident enough; to have been made without them, it must have been the vow of a heathen or a mad man. If a dog had met him, this could not have been made a burnt-offering; and if his neighbour or friend's wife, son, or daughter, had been returning from a visit to his family, his vow gave him no right over them. From verse

39th, it appears evident that Jephtha's daughter was not sacrificed to God, but *consecrated to him in a state of perpetual virginity;* for the text says *she knew no man,* for this was a statute in Israel; viz. that persons thus dedicated, or consecrated to God, should live in a state of unchangeable *celibacy.* On this point, the remarks of Dr. Hales are of great weight.

That Jephthah could not possibly have sacrificed his daughter, according to the vulgar opinion, founded on incorrect translation, may appear from the following considerations : 1. The sacrifice of children to Moloch was an abomination to the Lord, of which in numberless passages, he expresses his detestation; and it was prohibited by an express law, under pain of death, as " a defilement of God's sanctuary, and a profanation of his holy name," Lev. xx, 2, 3. Such a sacrifice, therefore, unto the Lord himself, must be a still higher abomination. And there is no precedent of any such under the law in the Old Testament. 2. The case of Isaac, before the law, is irrelevant ; for Isaac was not sacrificed ; and it was only proposed for a trial of Abraham's faith. 3. No father, merely by his own authority, could put an offending, much less an innocent child to death, upon any account, without the sentence of the magistrates, Deut. xxi, 18-21, and the consent of the people, as in Jonathan's case 4. The Mishna, or traditional law of the Jews, is pointedly against it : " If a Jew should devote his son or daughter, his man or maid servant, who are Hebrews, the devotement would be void ; because no man can devote what is not his own, or of whose life he has not the absolute disposal."

These arguments appear to be decisive against the sacrifice ; and that Jephthah could not even have devoted his daughter to celibacy against her will, is evident from the history, and from the high estimation in which she was always held by the daughters of Israel, for her filial duty, and her hapless fate, which they celebrated by a regular anniversary commemoration four days in the year, Judges xi, 40. We may, however, remark, that, if it could be more clearly established that Jephthah actually immolated his daughter, there is not the least evidence that his conduct was sanctioned by God. Jephthah was manifestly a superstitious and ill-instructed man ; and, like Samson, an instrument of God's power, rather than an example of his grace.

JEREMI'AH, a celebrated prophet, of the sacerdotal race, being one of the priests that dwelt at Anathoth, about three miles north of Jerusalem. Jeremiah appears to have been very young when he was called to the exercise of the prophetical office, from which he modestly endeavoured to excuse himself by pleading his youth and incapacity; but being overruled by the Divine authority, he set himself to discharge the duties of his function with unremitted diligence and fidelity, during a period of at least forty-two years, reckoned from the thirteenth year of Josiah's reign. He was a man of unblemished piety and conscientious integrity; a warm lover of his country, whose misery he pathetically deplores; and so affectionately attached to his countrymen, notwithstanding their injurious treatment of him, that he chose rather to abide with them, and undergo all hardships in their company, than separately to enjoy a state of ease and plenty, which the favour of the king of Babylon would have secured to him.

The idolatrous apostacy, and other criminal enormities of the people of Judah, and the severe judgments which God was prepared to inflict upon them, but not without a distant prospect of future restoration and deliverance, are the principal subject matters of the prophecies of Jeremiah; excepting only the forty-fifth chapter, which relates personally to Ba'ruch, and the six succeeding chapters, which respect the fortunes of some particular heathen nations.

As to the style of Jeremiah, says Bishop Lowth, this prophet is by no means wanting either in elegance or sublimity, although, generally speaking, inferior to Isaiah in both.

Jeremiah survived to behold the sad accomplishment of his darkest predictions. He witnessed all the horrors of the famine, and, when that had done its work, the triumph of the enemy. He saw the strong holds of the city cast down, the palace of Solomon, the temple of God, with all its courts, its roofs of cedar and of gold, levelled to the earth, or committed to the flames; the sacred vessels, the ark of the covenant itself, with the cherubim, pillaged by profane hands. What were the feelings of a patriotic and religious Jew at this tremendous crisis, he has left on record in his unrivalled elegies. See *Lamentations.* He followed the remnant of the Jews on their retiring into Egypt, where he is said to have been put to death by his profligate countrymen, 583 B. C.

JERICHO, a celebrated city in the tribe of Benjamin, about twenty miles E. N. E. from Jerusalem, and five from the Jordan, situated at the foot of the mountains which border the valley of the Jordan and the Dead Sea. It was destroyed by Joshua, Josh. vi, 26; but was afterward rebuilt, 1 Kings xvi, 34, and became the seat of the schools of the prophets. The land around Jericho was exceedingly fertile, abounding in palm trees and roses;

hence called *the city of palm trees*, Déut. xxxiv, 3. Its site is now occupied by an inconsiderable village called *Richa*, consisting of fifty or sixty miserable Arab houses. The road from this place to Jerusalem is through a series of rocky defiles, and the surrounding scenery is of the most gloomy and forbidding aspect. The whole road being infested with robbers, is held to be the most dangerous in Palestine; this circumstance marks the admirable propriety with which our Lord made it the scene of his beautiful parable of the good Samaritan, Luke x, 30, 31.

JER-O-BO'AM, the son of Ne'bat and Ze-ru'ah, was born at Zer'e-da, in the tribe of Ephraim, 1 Kings xi, 26. He is the subject of frequent mention in Scripture, as having been the cause of the ten tribes revolting from the dominion of Re-ho-bo'am, and also of his having "made Israel to sin," by instituting the idolatrous worship of the golden calves at Dan and Bethel, 1 Kings xii, 26–33. He seems to have been a bold, unprincipled, and enterprising man, with much of the address of a deep politician about him. He reigned 975–954 B. C.

2. JEROBOAM, the second of that name, was the son of Jehoash, king of Israel. He succeeded to his father's royal dignity, 825 B. C., and reigned forty-one years. Though much addicted to the idola-

trous practices of the son of Ne'bat, yet the Lord was pleased so far to prosper his reign, that by his means, according to the predictions of the Prophet Jonah, the kingdom of the ten tribes was restored from a state of great decay, into which it had fallen, and was even raised to a pitch of extraordinary splendour. The Prophets Amos and Hosea, as well as Jonah, lived during this reign.

JERUSALEM, *dwelling of peace*. This celebrated city, the capital of Palestine, was the seat of true religion under the Jewish theocracy, and also the chief scene of our Saviour's ministry, and the central point from which his Gospel was promulgated. Hence it is often called *the Holy City*; and even among the Arabs of the present day, its current name is *El Kods, The Holy*. It is situated near the middle of Palestine, among the mountains, nearly forty miles distant from the Mediterranean, and some twenty-five from the Jordan and Dead Sea, (in lat. 31° 50′ N.) It lay on the confines of Judah and Benjamin, mostly within the limits of the latter; but was reckoned to the former. Its most ancient name was *Salem*, Gen. xiv, 18; Psa. lxxiii, 3; then Jebus, as belonging to the Jebusites. David first reduced it, 2 Sam. v, 6–9, and made it the capital of his kingdom; whence it is also called the city of David. It was destroyed by the Chaldeans, 2 Kings xxiv, 25, but rebuilt by the Jews on their return from exile; and at a later period Herod the Great expended large sums in its embellishment.

The city was built chiefly on three hills : *Sion* on the south, which was the highest, and contained the citadel, the palace, and the upper city, called by Josephus *the upper marketplace; Moriah*, on which the temple stood, a lower hill on the north-east quarter of Sion, and separated from it by a ravine; *Acra*, lying north of Sion, and covered by the lower town; the most considerable portion of the whole city. Jerusalem was bounded on three sides by valleys, the valley of Jehoshaphat on the east, Hinnom on the south, and the Gihon or Raphaim on the west. Those on the east and south are very deep; on the north side there was a steep declivity.

After the destruction of Jerusalem by the Romans, about A. D. 70, they endeavoured to root out its very name and nature as a sacred place, from the hearts and memories of the Jewish nation. In A. D. 136, the Emperor Adrian caused all the remaining buildings to be demolished, and erected a new city, which he called *Aelia Capitolina;* and it was only in the beginning of the fourth century, after Constantine had embraced Christianity, that the name Jerusalem was again restored. This city once had the population of a million; but it does not now exceed fifteen thousand. It occupies an irregular square, of about two miles and a half in circumference. In the time of Christ, about four miles and an eighth. It may be roughly stated to be about a mile in length and a half a mile in breadth. The plan of Jerusalem, which we have placed opposite, is that given by Dr. Jowett, who published Researches in the Holy Land, in 1823–4, and who had an ample opportunity for testing its correctness. The neighbouring country is destitute of attraction, and desolate, being girded all round by naked blue rocks and cliffs, without water, without level ground, without any of the common recommendations of a country. The name is used metaphorically for the Jewish Church, i. e., the former or Mosaic dispensation, Gal. iv, 25 ; also the latter or Christian dispensation; the Redeemer's kingdom, of which the spiritual or New Jerusalem is the seat, Gal. iv, 26.

JESH-U'RUN, a poetical name given to the collective body of Israelites, apparently expressive of affection and tenderness.

JESSE, the father of King David, who was a shepherd of Bethlehem, and of humble birth ; hence David was often called by his enemies in contempt *son of Jesse*, 1 Sam. xx, 27. *Stem* of Jesse is put poetically for the family of

David; and *root* of *Jesse*, i. e., a sprout or shoot from the root, for the Messiah, Isa. xi, 1–10.

JESUS, the same with the Hebrew word *Joshua*, which signifies *Jehovah his help;* or, according to Gesenius, *whose help is Jehovah*. The name of three persons in the New Testament.

1. *Christ*, the Saviour of the world. See below.

2. *Joshua*, the successor of Moses, and leader of Israel, Acts vii, 45; Heb. iv, 8.

3. *Jesus*. surnamed Justus, a fellow-labourer with St. Paul, Col. iv, 11.

On our Lord's character as a *teacher*, many striking and just remarks have been made by different writers, not excepting infidels, who have been carried into admiration by the overwhelming force of evidence.

" When our Lord is considered as a *teacher*, we find him delivering the most sublime truths with respect to the Divine nature, the duties of mankind, and a future state of existence; agreeable in every particular to the wisest maxims, showing that he lived and died for the most important purposes conceivable. He makes no display of the high truths which he utters; but speaks of them with a wonderful simplicity and majesty. He revives the moral law, carries it to perfection, and enforces it by peculiar motives. All his precepts, when rightly explained, are reasonable in themselves and useful in their tendency.

" If from the matter of his instructions we pass on to the *manner* in which they were delivered, we find our Lord usually speaking as an authoritative teacher. He is often sublime; and the beauties interspersed throughout his discourses are equally natural and striking. He is remarkable for an easy manner of introducing the best lessons from incidental objects and occasions. Difficult situations, and sudden questions of the most artful kind, serve only to display his superior wisdom, and to confound his adversaries. Instead of showing his boundless knowledge on every occasion, he restrains it, and prefers utility to the glare of ostentation.

" He sets an *example* of the most perfect piety to God, and of the most extensive benevolence and the most tender compassion to men. His fortitude is exemplary, in enduring the most formidable evils and sufferings: his patience is invincible; his resignation entire. Truth and sincerity shine throughout his whole conduct. He shows obedience to his parents; he respects authority, religious and civil; and he evidences his regard for his country. Never was a character at the same time so commanding, resplendent, pleasing, and venerable. There is a peculiar contrast in it between an awful greatness, and the most conciliating loveliness. There is something so extraordinary, so perfect, and so godlike in it, that it could not have been thus supported throughout by the utmost stretch of human art, much less by men confessedly unlearned and obscure." We may add, that such a character must also have been *divine*. His virtues are human in their class and kind, so that he was our "example ;" but they were sustained and heightened by that divinity which was impersonated in him, and from which they derived their intense and full perfection.

A great deal has been written concerning the form, beauty, and stature of Jesus Christ. Some have asserted, that he was in person the noblest of all the sons of men. The truth probably is, that all which was majestic and attractive in the person of our Lord, was in the *expression* of the countenance, the full influence of which was displayed chiefly in his confidential intercourse with his disciples : while his general appearance presented no striking peculiarity to the common observer.

JEWEL. This word does not in Scripture mean a precious stone : but a peculiar property or treasure, or whatever may be stored up, in consequence of its superior estimation.

JEWS, a name originally applied to the descendants of Judah, which soon included

under it the Benjamites. After the Babylonish captivity, the term Jews was extended to all the descendants of Israel who retained the Jewish religion, whether they belonged to the two or to the ten tribes, whether they returned into Judea or not. The history of this singular people is recorded in the sacred books of the Old Testament ; it will therefore be more useful to fill up the chasm between the close of the historical books there contained and the coming of our Lord by the following history.

When the kingdom of Judah had been seventy years in captivity, and the period of their affliction was completed, Cyrus (536 B. C.) issued a decree, permitting all the Jews to return to their own land, and to rebuild their temple at Jerusalem. Though the decree issued by Cyrus was general, a part only of the nation took advantage of it. The number of persons who returned at this time was forty-two thousand three hundred and sixty, and seven thousand three hundred and thirty-seven servants. They were conducted by Ze-rub'babel and Joshua. Darius, the successor of Cyrus, confirmed this decree, and favoured the re-establishment of the people. But it was in the reign of Artaxerxes that Ezra obtained his commission, and was made governor of the Jews in their own land, which government he held thirteen

15

years: then Nehemiah was appointed with fresh powers, probably through the interest of Queen Esther; and Ezra applied himself solely to correcting the canon of the Scriptures, and restoring and providing for the continuance of the worship of God in its original purity. The first care of the Jews, after their arrival in Judea, was to build an altar for burnt-offerings to God; they then collected materials for rebuilding the temple; and in the beginning of the second year after their return, they began to build it upon the old foundations. The Samaritans did all in their power to impede the work. The temple, after a variety of obstructions and delays, was finished and dedicated, in the seventh year of King Darius, 515 B. C., and twenty years after it was begun. Though this second temple, or, as it is sometimes called, the temple of Zerubbabel, who was at that time governor of the Jews, was of the same size and dimensions as the first, or Solomon's temple, yet it was very inferior to it in splendour and magnificence; and the ark of the covenant, the shechinah, the holy fire upon the altar, the urim and thummim, and the spirit of prophecy, were all wanting. At the feast of the dedication, offerings were made for the twelve tribes of Israel, which seems to indicate that some of all the tribes returned from captivity; but

by far the greater number were of the tribe of Judah, and therefore from this period the Israelites were generally called Jews, and their country Judea.

The Scriptural history ends at this period, 430 B. C., and we must have recourse to uninspired writings, principally to the books of the Maccabees, and to Josephus, for the remaining particulars of the Jewish history, to the destruction of Jerusalem by the Romans. Judea continued subject to the kings of Persia about two hundred years; but it does not appear that it had a separate governor after Nehemiah. From this time it was included in the jurisdiction of the governor of Syria, and under him the high priest had the chief authority. Alexander entered Palestine 328 B. C., showed respect to the Jewish high priest, Jaddu'a, and granted the Jews an exemption from tribute every sabbatical year. See JADDUA.

After the death of Alexander, 323 B. C., Ptol'e-my So'ter, son of Lagus, king of Egypt, made himself master of Judea by a stratagem: he entered Jerusalem on a Sabbath day, under pretence of offering sacrifice, and took possession of the city without resistance from the Jews, who did not on this occasion dare to transgress their law by fighting on a Sabbath day.

After the Jewish nation had been tributary to the kings of Egypt for about a hundred years, it became subject to the kings of Syria. They divided the land, which now began to be called Palestine, into five provinces, three of which were on the west side of the Jordan, namely, Galilee, Samaria, and Judea, and two on the east side, namely, Trach-o-ni'tis and Pe-ræ'a; but they suffered them to be governed by their own laws, under the high priest and council of the nation. In the series of wars which took place between the kings of Syria and Egypt, Judea, being situated between those two countries, was, in a greater or less degree, affected by all the revolutions which they experienced, and was frequently the scene of bloody and destructive battles. The evils to which the Jews were exposed from these foreign powers, were considerably aggravated by the corruption and misconduct of their own high priests, and other persons of distinction among them. To this corruption and misconduct, and to the increasing wickedness of the people, their sufferings ought indeed to be attributed, according to the express declarations of God by the mouth of his prophets. An-ti'o-chus E-piph'a-nes took the city, 170 B. C., plundered the temple, and slew or enslaved great numbers of the inhabitants, with every circumstance of profanation and of cruelty which can be conceived. For three years and a half, the time predicted by Daniel, the daily sacrifice was taken away, the temple defiled and partly destroyed, the observance of the law prohibited under the most severe penalties, every copy burned which the agents of the tyrant could procure, and the people required to sacrifice to idols, under pain of the most agonizing death. At length the moment of deliverance arrived. Mattathias, a priest, 167 B. C., eminent for his piety and resolution, and the father of five sons, equally zealous for their religion, encouraged the people by his example and exhortations, " to stand up for the law;" but being very old when he engaged in this important and arduous work, he did not live to see its completion. At his death, his son, Judas Maccabæus, succeeded to the command of the army; and having defeated the Syrians in several engagements, he drove them out of Judea, and established his own authority in the country; and from that time the Maccabæan princes continued to be high priests. Aristobulus was the first of the Maccabees who assumed the name of king. About forty-two years after, a contest arising between the two brothers, Hyr-ca'nus and Aristobulus, the sons of Alexander Jaddæus, relative to the succession of the crown, both parties applied to the Romans for their support, 63 B. C. Pompey considered this as a favourable opportunity for reducing Palestine under the power of the Romans; and therefore, without deciding the points in dispute, marched his army into Judea, and besieged and took possession of Jerusalem. He appointed Hyrcanus high priest, but would not allow him to take the title of king. Several years after, An-tig'o-nus, the son of Aristobulus, with the assistance of the Parthians, while the empire of Rome was in an unsettled state, deposed his uncle Hyrcanus, 41 B. C., seized the government, and assumed the title of king.

Herod, by birth an Id-u-me'-an, but of the Jewish religion, immediately set out for Rome, and prevailed upon the senate to appoint him king of Judea. Armed with this authority, he returned, and began hostilities against Antigonus. About three years after, he took Jerusalem, and put an end to the government of the Maccabees or Asmonæans, after it had lusted nearly a hundred and thirty years. Herod considerably enlarged the kingdom of Judea, though it continued tributary to the Romans. He repaired the temple of Jerusalem at a vast expense, and added greatly to its magnificence.

At this time there was a confident expectation of the Messiah among the Jews; and indeed, a general idea prevailed among the heathen, also, that some extraordinary conqueror or deliverer would soon appear in Judea. In the thirty-sixth year of the reign of Herod, while Augustus was emperor of Rome, the Saviour of mankind was born, according to the word of prophecy. Herod, misled by the opinion, which was then common among the Jews, that the Messiah was to appear as a temporal prince, and judging from the inquiries of the wise men of the east, that the child was actually born, sent to Bethlehem, and ordered that all the children of two years old and under should be put to death, with the hope of destroying one whom he considered as the rival of himself, or at least of his family. He was soon after smitten with a most loathsome and tormenting disease, and died, a signal example of divine justice, about a year and a quarter after the birth of our Saviour, and in the thirty-seventh year of his reign, computing from the time he was declared king by the Romans. See HEROD.

After the banishment of Archelaus, Augustus sent Publius Sulpitius Qui-ri'nus, who, according to the Greek way of writing that name, is by St. Luke called Cyrenius, president of Syria, to reduce the countries over which Archelaus had reigned, to the form of a Roman province. The power of life and death was now taken out of the hands of the Jews, and taxes were from this time paid immediately to the Roman emperor. Justice was administered in the name and by the laws of Rome : and it may be remarked that, at this very period of time, our Saviour, who was now in the twelfth year of his age, being at Jerusalem with Joseph and Mary upon occasion of the passover, appeared first in the temple in his prophetic office, and in the business of his Father, on which he was sent, sitting among the doctors of the temple, and declaring the truth of God to them. After Co-po′ni-us, Ambivius, Annius Rufus, Valerius Gratus, and Pontius Pilate, were successively procurators ; and this was the species of government to which Judea and Samaria were subject during the ministry of our Saviour. Herod Antipas was still tetrarch of Galilee, and it was he to whom our Saviour was sent by Pontius Pilate.

Several of the Roman governors severely oppressed and persecuted the Jews; and at length, in the reign of Nero, and in the government of Florus, who had treated them with greater cruelty than any of his predecessors, they openly revolted from the Romans. Then began the Jewish war, which was terminated, after an obstinate defence, and unparalleled sufferings on the part of the Jews, by the total destruction of the city and temple of Jerusalem, by the overthrow of their civil and religious polity, and the reduction of the people to a state of the most abject slavery. Since that time the Jews have nowhere subsisted as a nation.

JEWS, *Calamities of the.* All history cannot furnish us with a parallel to the calamities and miseries of the Jews : rapine and murder, famine and pestilence, within ; fire and sword, and all the terrors of war, without. Our Saviour wept at the foresight of these calamities ; and it is almost impossible for persons of any humanity to read the account without being affected. The predictions concerning them were remarkable, and the calamities that came upon them were the greatest the world ever saw. See Deut. xxviii, xxix ; Matt. xxiv. Now, what heinous sin was it that could be the cause of such heavy judgments ? Can any other be assigned than that which the Scripture assigns, "They both killed the Lord Jesus and their own prophets, and persecuted the apostles," 1 Thess. ii, 15 ; and so filled up their sins, and wrath came upon them to the utmost ? It is hardly possible to consider the nature and extent of their sufferings, and not conclude their own imprecation to be singularly fulfilled upon them : "His blood be on us, and on our children," Matt. xxvii, 25. The Romans, under Ves-pa′-si-an, invaded the country, and took the cities of Galilee, Cho-ra′zin, Beth-sai′da, Ca-per'na-um, &c., where Christ had been especially rejected, and murdered numbers of the inhabitants. At Jerusalem the scene was most wretched of all. At the passover, when there might have been two or three millions of people in the city, the Romans surrounded it with troops, trenches, and walls, that none might escape. The three different factions within murdered one another. Titus did all in his power to persuade them to an advantageous surrender, but they scorned every proposal. The multitudes of unburied carcasses corrupted the air, and produced a pestilence. The people fed on one another; and even ladies, it is said, boiled their suckling infants, and ate them. After a siege of six months, the city was taken. They murdered almost every Jew they met with. Titus was bent to save the temple, but could not: six thousand Jews who had taken shelter in it were all burned or murdered. The outcries of the Jews, when they saw it, were most dreadful: the whole city, except three towers, and a small part of the wall, was razed to the ground, and the foundations of the temple and other places were ploughed up. At Jerusalem alone, it is said, one million one hundred thousand perished by sword, famine, and pestilence.

The long protracted existence of the Jews as a separate people, is not only a standing evidence of the truth of the Bible, but is of that kind which defies hesitation, imitation, or parallel. Were this people totally extinct, some might affect to say, that they never had existed; or, that if they had existed, they never practised such rites as were imputed to them; or, that they were not a numerous people, but merely a small tribe of ignorant and unsettled Arabs. The care with which the Jews preserve their sacred books, and the conformity of those preserved in the east with those of the west, as lately attested, is a satisfactory argument in favour of the genuineness of both; and farther, the dispersion of the nation has proved the security of these documents; as it has not been in the power of any one enemy, however potent, to destroy the entire series, or to consign the whole to oblivion.—*Watson.*

JEZEBEL, the modern *Isabella;* the impious and idolatrous queen of Ahab king of Israel, infamous for her cruel persecution of the prophets, 1 Kings xviii, 4; put in the New Testament as an emblem of false and idolatrous teachers, Rev. ii, 20.

JEZREEL, a city in the tribe of Issachar; the royal residence of Ahab and his successors. Whence the *blood of Jezreel,* Hos. i, 4, is the blood shed there by the sons of Ahab and Jehu. Near the city was the great valley or *plain of Jezreel*, afterward called, according to the Greek pronunciation of the word, *Esdrelon.* This plain expands itself between the Jordan and Mount Carmel, computed by Dr. Jowett to be about fifteen miles square, making allowances for irregularities, and for its running out on the west toward Mount Carmel, and on the east toward the Jordan. Although it bears the name of *plain*, yet it abounds with hills, which in viewing it from the adjacent mountains sink into nothing; there are also many springs in this plain, and also brooks, which flow down into the Kishon from the mountains. It is now almost desolate; although exceedingly fertile, and capable of supporting many thousands of inhabitants;—a place well adapted to battles, and has been the scene of many conflicts, and is still a favourite field among the Arabs in their frays. Here Barak, descending with his ten thousand men from Mount Tabor, defeated Sisera, with his "nine hundred chariots of iron," Judges iv. Here Josiah, king of Judah, fell, fighting against Necho, king of Egypt, 2 Kings xxiii, 29. And here the Midianites and the Amalekites, who were "like grasshoppers for multitude, and their camels without number as the sand of the sea," encamped, when they were defeated by Gideon, Judges vi. The river Kishon flows through it.

JOAB, David's chief military officer, and son of his sister Zerui'ah; one of the greatest and most valiant generals of his time, but also the most cruel, revengeful, and imperious of men. See 1 Kings ii, 28–34.

JOASH, the king of Israel, who went to visit Elisha on his death-bed, and wept over the dying prophet, saying, "O my father, my father, the chariot of Israel, and the horsemen thereof," 2 Kings xiii, 14; i. e., thou art to Israel better than all its horses and chariots for defence and protection; a sentiment which conveys the highest idea of his respect and estimation of Elisha.

JO-AN'NA, the wife of Chuza, Herod's steward, was one of those women who, having been cured by our Saviour, followed him as disciples, and ministered to his necessities, Luke viii, 3.

JOB, *ill treated*, an Arabian chief of *Uz*, or Ausitis, distinguished for wealth, and also for piety and virtue; but tried of God with the heaviest calamities. That Job was a real, and not a fictitious character, may be inferred from the manner in which he is mentioned in the Scriptures, Ezek. xiv, 14. Now since Noah and Daniel were unquestionably real characters, we must conclude the same of Job. See also James v, 11. It is scarcely to be believed that a divinely inspired apostle would refer to an imaginary character as an example of patience, or in proof of the mercy of God. But, besides the authority of the inspired writers, we have the strongest internal evidence from the book itself, that Job was a real person; for it expressly specifies the names of persons, places, facts, and other circumstances usually related in true histories.

The next point is the age in which Job lived. One thing is generally admitted with respect to the age of the book of Job, namely, its *remote antiquity*. Grotius thinks the events of the history are such as cannot be placed later than the *sojourning of the Israelites in the wilderness*. Bishop Warburton, in like manner, admits them to bear the marks of high antiquity. As to the country in which he lived, see *Uz*.

His disease was probably a species of black leprosy, endemic (*peculiar*) in Egypt, called by physicians *eliphantï'asis*, from the dark scales with which the skin is covered, and the swelling of the legs like an elephant. The different parts of the book of Job are so closely connected together, that they cannot be detached from each other. The exordium prepares the reader for what follows, supplies us with the necessary notices concerning Job and his friends, unfolds the scope, and places the calamities full in our view as an object of attention. The conclusion, again, has reference to the exordium, and relates the happy termination of Job's trials; the dialogues which intervene flow in regular order.

Archbishop Magee supposes it to have been originally written by Job, and subsequently transcribed by Moses; who having applied it to the use of the Jews, and given it the sanction of his authority, it thenceforth became enrolled among the sacred writings. It has been quoted by almost every Hebrew writer, from the age of Moses to that of Malachi. In its form, this poem approximates to the Mekama, or philosophical discourses of the Arabian poets. Without the exordium the reader would be utterly ignorant who Job was, who were his friends, and the cause of his being so grievously afflicted. Without the discourse of Elihu, Job xxxii–xxxvii, there would be a sudden and abrupt transition from the last words of Job to the address of God, for which Elihu's discourse prepares the reader. And without the conclusion, we should remain in ignorance of the subsequent condition of Job. Hence it is evident that the poem is the composition of a single author.

JO'EL, the second of the twelve lesser prophets. It is impossible to ascertain the age in which he lived; but it seems most probable that he was contemporary with Hosea. No particulars of his life or death are certainly known. His prophecies are confined to the kingdom of Judah. The style of Joel is perspicuous and elegant, and his descriptions are remarkably animated and poetical.

JOHN *the Baptist*, the son of Zachariah, and the forerunner of Christ. This prophet was distinguished in some sense above all others. He was called to a very singular work; his ministry formed an epoch in the history of the church, the connecting link between the two dispensations; it finished the legal and brought in the evangelical. The most extraordinary events began with his baptism, and continued till Christ was taken up into heaven. His peculiar office was to announce the Saviour of the world as then present in it. His character and course were extraordinary and different from all others. He was indifferent alike to the charms of pleasure, the allurements of pomp, the smiles of power, and the frowns of greatness. The forms and fashions of the world made no impression on his mind, and left no traces. He was austere in his manner, abstemious in his food, and rustic in his apparel, Matt. iii, 4. By the authentic historian Josephus, he is spoken of in terms of the highest encomium. It is remarkable that he was the only prophet who was himself the subject of prophecy, Isa. iv, 3.

As his course was short, so was his end violent and tragical. He fell a martyr to his fidelity, and the artifices of an intriguing woman. Having rebuked Herod on account of his incestuous intercourse with his brother's wife, he was sacrificed to her resentment, Matt. xiv, 3–12. Herod Antipas ordered him into custody in the castle of Macherus, where he remained a long time. He was put to death about the end of A. D. 31, or early in 32.

JOHN *the Apostle*, called also *the divine*, that is, the *theologian*, as maintaining the divine nature and attributes of Christ in the beginning of his gospel, son of Zebedee and Salo'me, a fisherman; he had a boat and nets and hired servants, Mark i, 20, and followed his occupation on the sea of Galilee; a brother to James the Greater. It is believed that St. John was the youngest of the apostles. Our Saviour had a particular friendship for him; and he describes himself by the name of *that disciple whom Jesus loved*. Peter, James, and *John*, were chosen to accompany our Saviour on several occasions, when the other apostles were not permitted to be present, Luke viii, 51; Matt. xvii, 1, 2; xxvi, 36, 37. That he was treated by Christ with greater familiarity than the other apostles, is evident from St.

Peter desiring him to ask Christ who should betray him, when he himself did not dare to propose the question, John xiii, 24. He seems to have been the only apostle present at the crucifixion, and to him Jesus, just as he was expiring upon the cross, gave the strongest proof of his confidence and regard by consigning to him the care of his mother, John xix, 26, 27. St. John continued to preach the Gospel for some time at Jerusalem: he was imprisoned by the Sanhedrim, first with Peter only, Acts iv, 1, &c., and afterward with the other apostles, Acts v, 17, 18.

The time of his leaving Judea is unknown. Dr. Macknight thinks he remained till he saw Jerusalem encompassed with armies, and showed other signs of approaching destruction. He then fled into Asia, and coming at length to Ephesus, he fixed his ordinary abode in that city. In the reign of Domitian, who persecuted the Church, John, it is said, was carried to Rome about the year 95, where he was plunged into boiling oil, without being hurt, and afterward exiled to Patmos, a small, sterile island in the archipelago, where he remained some time instructing the inhabitants in the faith of Christ, and where he wrote his *Revelations*. Domitian being killed A. D. 96, his successor Nerva recalled all who had been banished; and John returned to Ephesus

A. D. 97, being about ninety years of age; at this place he wrote his Gospel, to confirm the divinity of the Son in opposition to heretics, who had endeavoured to corrupt the Christian doctrine, some sixty-four years after our Saviour's death. He wrote also three epistles—time when, and place where, are uncertain, and died a natural death, in the third year of the Emperor Trajan, answering to A. D. 100; and, if Lampe's opinion is well founded, that John was born in the same year with his Master, he must have been *a hundred years old* when he died.

JOHN, surnamed *Mark*, the companion of Paul and Barnabas, and writer of the gospel which bears his name.

JO'NAH, son of A-mit'tai, born at Gath-hepher, in Galilee. He is generally considered as the most ancient of the prophets, and is supposed to have lived 840 B. C. The book of Jonah is chiefly narrative, the style is simple and perspicuous; and his prayer, in the second chapter, is strongly descriptive of the feelings of a pious mind under a severe trial of faith, Matt. xii, 41.

JONATH, found in the title of 56th Psalm, *Jonath-elem-rechokim*, i. e., the silent dove among strangers, meaning perhaps the people of Israel in exile. See Psa. lxxiv, 19. Probably the inscription of a song or poem, to the tune or measure of which this psalm was to be sung.

JONATHAN, the son of Saul, a prince of an excellent disposition, and in all varieties of fortune a sincere and steady friend to David. The death of Jonathan was lamented by David, in one of the noblest and most pathetic odes ever uttered by genius consecrated by pious friendship, 2 Sam. i, 19–27.

JOPPA, now called *Jaffa*, a celebrated and very ancient city and seaport of Palestine, on the Mediterranean, about forty-five miles W.N.W. of Jerusalem, and thirty south of Cesare'a. The present town is situated on a promontory, jutting out into the sea, about 150 feet above its level, having on all sides picturesque and varied prospects. On the north are the flowery meads of Sharon ; on the east the hills of Ephraim and Judah raise their towering heads ; on the south spreads out a fertile plain, reaching as far as Gaza ; and on the west is the open sea. A few years ago it contained, according to an American traveller, from 10,000 to 15,000 inhabitants ; but since that time it has been destroyed by an earthquake, and nearly all buried in the ruins.

JORDAN, now called *El Sheriat*, i. e., the ford, the largest and most celebrated river of Palestine. It rises under the eastern ridge of Mount Lebanon, called Anti-libanus, and flows in a direc-tion almost constantly south. After a course of about fifteen miles, it passes through the lake or marsh of Merom ; and after flowing about the same distance farther, falls into the Lake of Tiberias. Leaving this lake, it flows through a fertile valley of considerable width into the Dead Sea, receiving in its course some minor streams. Its whole length is about 130 or 140 miles. Between these two seas, the average breadth of Jordan is from sixty to eighty feet, and its depth about ten or twelve, yet fordable in many places during the summer months ; in one place Mr. Stevens saw an Arab wading across it. It has double banks, i. e., those of its usual channel, and others at the distance of forty or fifty rods on each side. The low ground within the higher banks is overgrown with reeds and trees, affording a covert for numerous wild beasts. The stream of the Jordan is rapid, and its waters muddy. It is subject to floods, which sometimes, though not often, rise above its usual channel, and overflow the space within its higher banks, Josh. iii, 15. This happens in March, 1 Chron. xii, 15.

It will be recollected that the Jordan runs everywhere through a valley, in most places narrow, and shut in by parallel ranges of mountains. These mountains in two places expand so as to form circular, or rather elliptical basins of considerable extent; of which the northern is occupied by the Lake of Tiberias, and the southern by the Dead Sea, in which the Jordan now terminates. South of the Dead Sea, however, the same ranges of mountains again approach, and continue parallel to each other, enclosing between them a deep and·broad valley of sand, called toward the north *El Ghor*, an Arab word ·for any marshy ground, and toward the south *El Araba*, which extends in a direction nearly S.S.W. to the eastern or Elanitic Gulf of the Red Sea, at Akaba. This valley is obviously a continuation of the valley of Jordan; through which, in all probability, in very ancient times, before·the Dead Sea was formed on the plains of Jordan, that river discharged its waters into the Elanitic Gulf. The length of this valley between the two seas is about 110 English miles in a direct line. It was by this valley that the treasures of Ophir were probably transported to the warehouses of Solomon.

The pride of Jordan, Zech. xi, 3; in the translation of Jer. xlix, 19, it is the *swelling* of Jordan. This is a poetical expression for its green and shady banks, clothed with willows, tamarisks, and cane, in which lions make their covert.

The phrase *beyond Jordan*, in the books of Moses and in Joshua, sometimes means the *west;* but after the Hebrews had taken possession of the country, the term signified the country on the *east* of the river.

JOSEPH, *he will add*, a son of Jacob, the youngest except Benjamin, sold by his brothers into Egypt, and afterward advanced to the highest honours. It is sometimes used for the *ten tribes*, the kingdom of Ephraim, and sometimes for the whole *nation of Israel*, Zech. x, 6; Amos vi, 6, *tribe of Joseph*, Rev. vii, 8, compare verse 6, is the half tribe of Ephraim. The history of Joseph seems to have been left for its moral uses, and that it should afford, by its inimitable simplicity and truth to nature, a point of irresistible internal evidence of the truth of the Mosaic narrative.

2. JOSEPH, the husband of Mary, the mother of our Lord. His age and other circumstances of his life, excepting what are related in the gospels, are uncertain. It is thought that he died before Jesus entered upon his pub lic ministry.

3. JOSEPH of Arimathea, a member of the Jewish Sanhedrim, a disciple of Jesus, who assisted at his burial, Luke xxiii, 50, 51; John xix, 38.

JOSHUA, the minister and armour-bearer of Moses, afterward his successor, and the leader of the Israelites, the son of Nun. He was born A. M. 2460, and was about eighty-four years of age when he received the command to pass over Jordan. His piety, courage and disinterested integrity are conspicuous throughout his whole history.

The book of Joshua was probably written by himself, and is probably a continuation of Deuteronomy. It begins where that ends, immediately after the death of Moses, and concludes with Joshua's death, at the age of 110 years, 1443 before the Christian era. The last five verses giving an account of his death, were added by one of his successors.

JOSIAH, king of Judah 642–611 B. C. The restorer of the Mosaic law. He was slain at Megiddo in battle with Necho, king of Egypt, 2 Chron. xxxiv, 33. The mourning of the people on the death of this prince passed into a proverb, Zech. xii, 11.

JOT refers to the smallest letter in the Hebrew alphabet, and *tittle* to the *apex* or point at the angle of some, which distinguished them from others of similar form. In Matt. v, 19, our Lord means, that the smallest part of the law shall not be abolished.

JOTHAM, Gideon's youngest son, distinguished for having spoken the *oldest*, and perhaps the *best* fable extant, Judges ix, 7. The fable is beautiful for the simplicity of its language and structure, for the eloquence and severity of the appeal which it makes

to the Shechemites, and the boldness of the man who dared thus to address the murderers of all his father's house.

JOURNEY, *a march* from one place to another; a day's journey was sometimes greater and sometimes less, varying from twenty to thirty miles. The eastern method of reckoning by hours is very uncertain. As a general rule, an hour's distance may be assumed to be the space which a horse or mule will walk over in that time, i. e., from *three to three and a half miles.* "A Sabbath day's *journey*," Acts i, 12, according to the rabbinic limitation, is 1,000 paces, equal to about seven and a half furlongs, nearly one mile. This measure is a sort of Jewish invention, founded on Exod. xvi, 39. There were two principal routes from Palestine into Egypt; the one was along the shores of the Mediterranean from Gaza to Pelusium, and the other by the way of the Elanitic Gulf and Mount Sinai. The oriental merchants travelled in company, as is common in the east at the present day. "The troops of Tema looked, the *companies* of Sheba waited for them," Job vi, 9, i. e., the caravans. A travelling company of this kind is now called a *caravan*, which is an Arabic word, meaning *a company of men travelling together.* See MERCHANT.

JUBAL, a son of La'mech, the inventor of musical instruments, Gen. iv, 21.

JUBILEE, supposed to mean *when a triumph is sounded;* a joyful occasion which occurred every fiftieth year, so called from *the sounding of trumpets* on the tenth day of the seventh month (Tizri, and about the autumnal equinox) by which it was announced to the people. According to the Mosaic law, in this year all lands which had been sold returned to their first possessor, and all slaves were to be set free. It is called *the year of release,* Deut. xv, 9, because all debts were to be remitted. This law was mercifully designed to prevent the rich from oppressing the poor, and reducing them to perpetual slavery. Moses intended, as much as possible, to preserve the liberty of persons, a due proportion of fortune, and the order of families; as well as that the people should be bound to their country, their lands and inheritances, and cherish an affection for them; jubilees were not regarded after the exile.

JUDAH, the fourth son of Jacob; also the tribe descended from him, the bounds of which are described, Josh. xv.

After the secession of the ten tribes, the name of Judah was given to one of the two subsequent kingdoms, comprising the tribes of Judah and Benjamin; and also a portion of Simeon and Dan, having Jerusalem for its metropolis.

The other kingdom was called *Israel,* and sometimes *Ephraim,* Hosea vi, 4. After the carrying away of the ten tribes, and after the exile, the name *Judah, Judea,* was applied to the whole country of the Israelites, Hag. i, 14.

JUDAS, surnamed Iscariot, i. e., the man of Kerioth, an apostle, and the traitor who betrayed our Lord. He seems previously to have been dishonest, John xii, 6, though he enjoyed the confidence of the other apostles. There are some difficulties concerning the manner in which Judas died. We are informed in Matt. xxvii, 5, that he hung himself; we are farther informed in Acts i, 18 "that he fell headlong, burst asunder in the midst, and all his bowels gushed out." These two statements exhibit the appearance of being not altogether harmonious. The most easy and natural reconciliation of them, however, is this: having hanged himself, and remaining till putrescence had taken place, and the cord perhaps breaking, or being cut off by those who found him, he fell with such violence as to dash out his bowels.

JUDE, or **JUDAS,** an apostle, called also *Thaddeus* and *Lebbeus,* brother of James the Less, and brother, i. e., kinsman or cousin of our Lord, Gal. i, 19. The only account we have of him in particular, is that which occurs, John xiv, 21–23.

Dr. Lardner supposes that

his epistle was written about the year 66.

JUDEA, strictly the territory of the tribe of Judah, extending from the Dead Sea to the Mediterranean, and abounding in lime-stone hills, but usually employed in a wider sense. In the time of David, it denoted that portion of the country which belonged to the tribes of Judah and Benjamin, 2 Sam. v, 5. So after the secession of the ten tribes, it was applied to the dominions of the kingdom of Judah, including the tracts belonging to Judah and Benjamin, and also part of that which appertained to the tribes of Dan and Simeon. Hence it became at length a general name for the southern part of Palestine ; while the northern part was called Galilee, and the middle Samaria. After the captivity, as most of the exiles who returned were of the kingdom of Judah, the name Judea (Judah) was given generally to the whole of Palestine west of Jordan, Hag. ii, 2. Under the Romans, in the time of Christ, Palestine was divided into Galilee, Samaria, and Judea, John iv, 45 ; which last included the whole southern part west of the Jordan, and constituted a portion of the kingdom of Herod the Great. It then belonged to Archelaus, but was afterward made a Roman province dependant upon Syria and governed by procurators.

To JUDGE. 1. To form and give an opinion after separating, and considering the particulars of a case.

2. *To govern, to rule,* as connected with the power of judging, since to dispense justice was the part of kings and chief magistrates. The ideas of ruling and judging are closely allied in oriental language ; hence to punish, i. e., also to protect the cause of any one, to defend his right, to see that he obtains justice. " He *judged* the cause of the poor and needy," Jer. xxii, 16.

To vindicate, to avenge, by punishing one's enemy. " The Lord shall *judge* his people," Heb. x, 30. " Know ye not the saints shall *judge,*" i. e., rule the world ? It is supposed that Paul had in his mind the promise of our Lord to the apostles of their " sitting on thrones, and *judging* the twelve tribes of Israel," Matt. xix, 28, i. e., the saints shall be intrusted with the government and regulation of the whole world.

JUDGES, leaders and chief magistrates of the Israelites from Joshua to Samuel, who led out the people to war against their enemies, and after having delivered them from the oppression of the neighbouring nations, exercised during the peace the office of ruler and judge, Judg. ii, 16–18. Othniel was the first, Deborah and Barak, Gideon, Jephthah, Samson, and Samuel, were the most remarkable. The Apostle

Paul says, that the period during which Israel was governed by judges, was about 450 years, Acts xiii, 20. These judges might appropriately enough be called the supreme executive, exercising all the rights of sovereignty, with the exception of enacting laws and imposing taxes. "They were honoured," says Dr. Jahn, "but they bore no external badges of distinction; they were distinguished, but they enjoyed no special privileges themselves, and communicated none to their posterity; they subserved the public good without emolument, that the state might be prosperous, that religion might be preserved, AND THAT GOD ALONE MIGHT BE KING IN ISRAEL." It ought to be observed, however, that not all the judges ruled the whole nation. Some of them presided only over a few separate tribes.

THE BOOK OF JUDGES contains the history of the persons mentioned in the preceding article. "That the greater part of the book of Judges," says Rosenmuller, "is the production of one writer, is proved in chap. ii, 8–23, which appears to be the sum of the first part, i. e., to chap. xvii. It is supposed to have been written by the Prophet Samuel. The latter part, from chap. xvii, contains an account of the introduction of idolatry among the Israelites, and the consequent corruption of religion and manners among them; for which God gave them up into the hands of their enemies."

JUDGMENT. 1. The decision of a judge, 1 Kings iii, 28. 2. Justice, Matt. xxiii, 23; Luke xi, 42. 3. A legal decision, "to execute *judgment*," John v, 27; Jude 15. To sentence to punishment; hence it denotes afflictions and chastisements, 1 Pet. iv, 17. 4. The divine law, the religion of Jehovah as developed in the Gospel, Exod. xxi, 1; Psa. xiv, 7, 20; see Matt. xii, 18. The laws which the Messiah was to publish. 5. An opinion, 1 Cor. vii, 40; "Joined in the same *judgment*," touching all the grand truths of the Gospel, 1 Cor. i, 10. 6. Controversy, 1 Cor. vi, 4. The term is used in Matt. v, 21, 22 for a court of justice, *a tribunal, judges*, i. e., the smaller tribunals established in the cities of Palestine, subordinate to the Sanhedrim, compare Deut. xvi, 18; 2 Chron. xix, 5. According to the rabbins, they consisted of twenty-three judges; but Josephus expressly says the number was seven.

JUDGMENT DAY, is that important period which shall terminate the present dispensation of grace toward the fallen race of Adam, put an end to time, and introduce the eternal destinies of men and angels, Acts xvii, 31; Matt. xxv, 31–46.

But "it is appointed unto

men once to die, and after death the *judgment.*" These two events are inseparably linked together in the Divine decree, and they reciprocally reflect importance on each other. Death is, indeed, the terror of our nature. Men may contrive to keep it from their thoughts, but they cannot think of it without fearful apprehensions of its consequences. It was justly to be dreaded by man in his state of innocence; and to the unrenewed man it ever was, and ever will be, a just object of abhorrence. The Gospel of Jesus Christ, which has brought life and immortality to light, is the only sovereign antidote against this universal evil. To the believer in Christ, its rough aspect is smoothed, and its terrors cease to be alarming.

Were death all that we have to dread, death might be braved. But after death there is a judgment; a judgment attended with circumstances so tremendous as to shake the hearts of the boldest of the sons of nature. Nothing of terror or magnificence hitherto beheld,—no glory of the rising sun after a night of darkness and of storm,—no convulsions of the earth,—no wide irruption of waters,— no flaming comet dragging its burning train over half the heaven, can convey to us an adequate conception of that day of terrible brightness and irresistible devastation. Creation then shall be un-

created. "The heavens shall pass away with a great noise, and the elements shall melt with fervent heat; the earth also, and the works that are therein, shall be burnt up," 2 Peter iii, 10. "The Lord shall be revealed from heaven in flaming fire," 2 Thess. i, 7, 8, arrayed in all the glory of his Godhead, and attended by his mighty angels, Matt. xvi, 27. "All that are in the grave shall hear his voice, and shall come forth," John v, 28, 29. Earth and sea shall give up the dead which are in them. All that ever lived shall appear before him, Rev. xx, 12, 13. The judgment shall sit; and the books shall be opened, Dan. vii, 10. The eye of Omniscience detects every concealment by which they would screen from observation themselves, or their iniquity. The last reluctant sinner is finally separated from the congregation of the righteous, Psa. i, 5; and inflexible justice, so often disregarded, derided, and defied, gives forth their eternal doom! But to the saints this shall be a day of glory and honour. They shall be publicly acknowledged by God as his people; publicly justified from the slanders of the world; invested with immortal bodies; presented by Christ to the Father; and admitted into the highest felicity in the immediate presence of God for ever.

JUDGMENT HALL. See PRETORIUM.

16

JUNIPER, a well known shrub, of the cedar family, bearing berries of a bluish colour, and of a warm pungent taste. But the Hebrew word probably means the *genista*, or Spanish broom, as it is called; a shrub growing in Spain, Palestine, and Arabia, with yellowish flowers, and a bitter root, which is sometimes eaten by the poor, Job xxx, 4, in times of scarcity and famine. The psalmist seems to mention the *coals* of this wood as affording the fiercest fire of any matter that he found in the desert, Psa. cxx, 4.

JUPITER, the supreme god of the heathen mythology, who had power over all the rest. They supposed that Jupiter and Mercury most frequently assumed the human form. "*Jupiter* which was before their city," Acts xiv, 13, i. e., whose temple was in front of the city.

JUSTICE, the virtue which consists in giving to every one what is his due; practical conformity to the laws and principles of rectitude in the dealing of men with each other. Justice is *distributive* or *communicative*. *Distributive justice* belongs to magistrates or rulers, and consists in distributing to every man that right or equity which the laws and principles of equity require. *Communicative justice* consists in fair dealing in trade and mutual intercourse between man and man.

JUSTIFICATION. 1. The act of justifying, or showing to be just or conformable to law.

2. Remission of sin, and absolution from guilt and punishment. St. Paul clearly uses justification and forgiveness as synonymous terms, Rom. iv, 5–8. Here the justification of the ungodly, the imputation of righteousness, the forgiveness of iniquity, and the covering and non-imputation of sin, are phrases which express the very same blessing under different views.

On the ground of works, i. e., of perfect obedience, and therefore of merit, none can be justified because all are sinners. If any then are justified at all, it must be of *grace;* but this grace, although freely bestowed, and without any just claims on the part of the sinner, is still *not unconditionally* bestowed. *Faith* in Him who died to save sinners is requisite to prepare one for the reception of pardon; and he who is justified in this way as a consequence of his faith, is still justified in a manner altogether gratuitous. But (1.) the justification of a sinner does not in the least degree alter or diminish the evil nature and desert of sin. For we know "it is God," the holy God, "that *justifieth*." And he can never regard sin, on any consideration, or under any circumstances, with less than perfect hatred. The penalty is remitted, and the obligation to suffer that penalty is dissolved; but it is still naturally due, though graciously remitted. Hence appear the propriety and duty of continuing to confess and lament even pardoned sin with a lowly and contrite heart. (2.) The account which has been given of justification sufficiently points out the error of many of the Roman Catholic divines, and of some mystic theologians, who seem to suppose that to be justified is to be, not reckoned righteous, but actually made righteous, by the infusion of a sanctifying influence, producing a positive and inherent conformity to the moral image of God. This notion confounds the two distinct though kindred blessings of justification and regeneration. The former, in its Scriptural sense, is an act of God, not in or upon man, but for him, and in his favour. (3.) The justification extends to all past sins; that is, to all guilt contracted previously to that time at which the act of justification takes place. In respect of this, it is, while it remains in force, a most full, perfect, and entire absolution from wrath. "All manner of sin" is then forgiven. The pardon which is granted is a "justification," not merely from some things, from many things, from most things, but "from all things," Acts xiii, 39. God does not justify us, or pardon our innumerable offences, by degrees, but at once. (4.) Another remark, which it may not be unnecessary to make, is, that justification, however effectual to our release from past guilt, does not terminate our state of probation. It is not irreversible, any more than eternal. As he who is now justified was once condemned, so he may in future come again into condemnation, by relapsing into sin and unbelief, although at present "accepted in the Beloved." That justification may for our sin be reversed, appears from our Lord's parable of the two debtors, in which one who had obtained the blessing of forgiveness is represented as incurring the forfeiture of it by the indulgence of an unforgiving spirit toward his fellow-servant, Matt. xviii, 23-35. Let us therefore "watch and pray, that we enter not into temptation."

2. The immediate results of justification are (1.) The restoration of amity and intercourse between the pardoned sinner and the pardoning God. For, "being *justified* by faith, we have peace with God,' and, consequently, unforbidden access to him. (2.) Adoption of the persons justified into the family of God, and their consequent right to eternal life of body and soul, Rom. viii, 17. (3.) With these is inseparably connected another, of the utmost value and importance; namely, *the habitual indwelling of the Holy Spirit.* Of this indwelling the

immediate effects are, *tranquillity of conscience,* Rom. viii. 15, 16 : *power over sin;* a prevailing desire and ability to walk before God in holy obedience : *and a joyous hope of heaven.*

3. To have a complete view of the method by which justification and all its consequent blessings are attained, we must consider (1.) The originating cause is the grace, the free, undeserved, and spontaneous love of God toward fallen man. But God is wise, and holy, and just, as well as merciful and gracious. And his wisdom determined, that, in order to reconcile the designs of his mercy toward sinners with the claims of his purity and justice, those designs should be accomplished only through the intervention of a Divine Redeemer, Rom. i, 5. (2.) Our Lord Jesus Christ is the sole meritorious cause of our justification. All he did and all he suffered in his mediatorial character may be said to have contributed to this great purpose. For what he did, in obedience to the precepts of the law, and what he suffered, in satisfaction of its penalty, taken together, constitute that mediatorial righteousness, for the sake of which the Father is ever well pleased in him. Now, in this mediatorial righteousness all who are justified have a saving interest. It is not meant that it is personally imputed to them in its formal nature or distinct acts; for against any

such imputation there lie inseparable objections both from reason and from Scripture. But the collective merit and moral effects of all which the Mediator did and suffered are so reckoned to our account when we are justified, that, for the sake of Christ and in consideration of his obedience unto death, we are released from guilt, and accepted of God. (3.) As to the instrumental cause of justification, the merit of the blood of Jesus does not operate necessarily so as to produce our pardon as an immediate and unavoidable effect, but through the instrumentality of faith. The faith by which we are justified is present faith, faith actually existing and exercised. We are not justified by tomorrow's faith foreseen; for that would lead to the Antinomian notion of justification from eternity, a notion which to mention is to confute. We are not justified by yesterday's faith recorded or remembered; for that would imply the opinion that justification is irreversible. The justification offered in the Scriptures is a justification upon believing, in which we are never savingly interested until we believe, and which continues in force only so long as we continue to believe. On the whole, it may be said that the faith to which the privilege of justification is annexed, is such a belief of the Gospel, by the power of the Spirit of God, as leads us to come to Christ, to receive Christ, to trust in Christ, and to commit the keeping of our souls into his hands, in humble confidence of his ability and his willingness to save us. See FAITH.

To JUSTIFY, is, 1. To show or prove to be *just*, or conformable to law or duty.

2. *To pardon* and clear from guilt, to accept as righteous on account of the merits of the Saviour.

3. To cause another to appear comparatively innocent or less guilty than one's self, Ezek. xvi, 15.

4. To do justice to one's character, by acknowledging and declaring him to be free from all imputation of blame. God was *justified* in or by the Spirit, 1 Tim. iii, 16. Wisdom is justified, Luke vii, 35, acknowledged and honoured by her real followers.

JUST PERSONS. 1. Those who act *alike* to all, who practise even-handed justice, *impartial*; spoken of judges or kings who dispense justice and defend the righteous.

2. The upright, virtuous, also good in a general sense; including the idea of *innocent*, Matt. xxvii, 19–24; including also the idea of *mild, clement, kind.* "Joseph, being a *just man*," Matt. i, 19.

3. It is spoken especially of those whose hearts are right with God, *pious, godly*, Matt. xiii, 49.

KADESH, or more fully, *Kadesh-barnea; barnea* signifies *field*, or *plain of wandering;* like the Arabic *El Ty;* a city in the desert south of the Dead Sea, supposed to be in the great valley of *El Ghor.* This city was of sufficient importance to give its name to the tract of desert country which lay around it, Psa. xxix, 8. There is a deep valley of sand from five to eight miles wide, running between two parallel ridges of mountains, from the south part of the Dead Sea to the eastern gulf of the Red Sea. The only place where this valley is interrupted is about eight or ten miles distant from the Dead Sea, where a sand cliff from sixty to eighty feet high traverses the valley like a wall. The north part of the valley is called *El Ghor*, and is supposed by Burkhardt to be the *Kadesh-barnea* of Scripture, whence the Israelites sent forth their spies, Num. xiii, 26; and the south part is called *El Araba.*

KADMONITES, a Canaanitish tribe on the east of the Jordan, about Mount Hermon.

KEDAR, *dark skin;* a son of Ishmael, Gen. xxv, 13; also an Arabian tribe descended from him. These people live in tents. It is not possible to show the place of their habitation, because they often change it, Song i, 5.

KEDRON, a small brook which, rising near Jerusalem, runs through the valley on the east of the city, between it and the Mount of Olives. This brook is stated by Pococke to have its rise a little way farther to the north, but its source does not appear to have been ascertained. Like the Ilissus, it is dry at least nine months in the year; its bed is narrow and deep, which indicates that it must formerly have been the channel for waters that have found some other and probably subterranean course. The course of the brook is along the valley of Jehoshaphat, to the southwest corner of the city, and then winding between rugged and desolate hills, it runs to the Dead Sea.

KENITES, a people who dwelt west of the Dead Sea in mountains and rocks almost inaccessible. See Balaam's address to them, Num. xxiv, 21: "Strong is thy dwelling-place, and thou puttest thy nest in a rock." They extended themselves into Arabia, for Jethro was a Kenite, and out of regard to him all his tribe who submitted to the Hebrews were suffered to live in their own country; the rest in all probability fled to the Amalekites, 1 Sam. xv, 6.

KERCHIEF, a head-dress, a cloth to cover the head; the Hebrew word has more latitude, signifying *quilts, coverlets*, Ezek. xiii, 18.

KE-TU'RAH, the wife whom Abraham took after the death of Sarah, whose sons Abraham settled east in Arabia Deserta.

KEY, an instrument for locking and unlocking, used in a figurative sense as a symbol of *power* or authority. Keys were anciently *crooked*, and from their weight and inconvenient form carried on the shoulders, Isa. xxii, 22, as we see our reapers carrying their sickles. "*Keys* of the kingdom," Matt. xvi, 29, is the *power* of opening e shutting, of admitting to or excluding from the kingdom of God. Peter, as an inspired apostle, was appointed to open the new dispensation, by preaching salvation to all who should repent and believe, and to declare infallibly the laws of the Gospel; and this he did both to the Jews and to the Gentiles, by making the first converts among them, Acts ix. But that the power was not conferred on Peter exclusively of the rest of the apostles, is clear from Christ's own words, Luke xxii, 24–26. "The power of remitting and retaining sins," which was promised to all the apostles, may be interpreted of their being enabled, by inspiration, to declare whose sins, according to the tenor of the Gospel, are to be forgiven, and whose sins are not to be forgiven.

The key of knowledge, Luke xi, 52, is the means of attaining to true knowledge in respect to the kingdom of God.

The key of death and hell, is the power to bring to the grave, or to deliver from it to appoint to life or to death, Rev. i, 18.

KICK, to strike with the heel, used in the proverbial expression, *to kick against the goads,* Acts ix, 5. The goad is a rod or staff, with an iron point, for urging on horses, oxen, &c. To kick against such an instrument, is to offer vain and rash resistance.

KID, the young of the goat. Among the Hebrews, the kid was reckoned a great delicacy; and appears to have been served for food in preference to the lamb.

KIDNEYS, situated in the lower part of the back, enveloped in a coat of the purest fat; and therefore supposed to be the best part in the body of the animal. Hence used to point out the finest wheat, the most excellent species both for seed and bread, Deut. xxxiv, 14.

KID'RON. See KEDRON.

KINE, the old plural of *cow, kine of Bashan,* are by a metaphor put for the voluptuous females of Samaria, Amos iv, 1. Sometimes translated *heifer;* and occurs frequently as an emblem of a state, Hosea x, 11.

KING, one who exercises royal authority and sovereignty. In a more general and lower sense, it is used as a title of distinguished honour for a *viceroy, prince, leader, chief,* &c. Thus Herod the Great and his successors had the title of *king,* but were dependant for the name and power on the Romans. Herod Antipas, though he is called king, Matt. xiv, 9, was in fact only a *tetrarch,* verse 1. Besides, we find in Joshua, that almost every town in Canaan had its king, xii, 9–24; and we know that the territories of these towns must have been very inconsiderable. Moses was called *king in Jeshurun,* Deut. xxxiii, 5: he was the chief and guide of his people, fulfilling the duties of a king, though not such in the same sense as David or Solomon. Tropically, the word is applied to Christians as about to reign with Christ over the nations, Rev. v, 10. See REIGN.

The following catalogue of the Jewish kings may be regarded as approximating to a correct chronology.

Of the whole Nation.

	Began to reign B. C.	Years Reigned.
Saul	1091	40
David	1051	40½
Solomon	1010	40
Rehoboam	971	1

Of Judah alone.	Began to reign B. C.	Years Reigned.	*Of Israel alone.*	Began to reign B. C.	Years Reigned.
Rehoboam	972	16	Jeroboam	971	22
Abijam	954	3	Nadab	950	2
Asa	951	41	Baasha	949	24
Jehoshaphat	910	25	Elah	926	2
Jehoram	885	4	Zimri	925	7
Ahaziah	881	1	Omri	925	12
Interval	880	6	Ahab	914	22
Joash	874	40	Ahaziah	893	2
Amaziah	835	29	Jehoram	892	12
Uzziah, or Azariah	806	32	Jehu	880	28
Jotham	754	16	Jehoahaz	852	17
Ahaz	738	16	Joash, or Jehoash	835	16
Hezekiah	722	29	Jeroboam II.	819	41
Manasseh	694	55	Zachariah	778	10
Amon	639	2	Shallum	768	1 m
Josiah	637	31	Menahem	767	10
Jehoahaz	606	¼	Pekaiah	757	2
Jehoiakim	606	11	Pekah	755	20
Jehoiakin	594	¼	Interval	734	9
Zedekiah	594	11	Hoshea	725	9
Captivity	583		Captivity	716	

KINGDOM. 1. *Reign*, i. e., the exercise of kingly power, Matt. vi, 13; Heb. i, 8.

2. *Dominions of a king, a realm,* i. e., a people and territory under kingly rule, Matt. iv, 8.

3. All the expressions, kingdom of *God, Christ, heaven,* and *David,* as the ancestor and type of the Messiah, Mark xi, 10, are synonymous, and signify *the divine spiritual kingdom, the glorious reign of the Messiah,* or the community of those who, united by his Spirit under him as their head, rejoice in the truth, and live a holy life in love and in communion with him. This spiritual kingdom has both an internal and external form. As internal, it already exists and rules in the hearts of all Christians, and is therefore present. "The *kingdom* of God is within you," Luke xvii, 21, i. e., its seat is in your hearts and affections, not external; see also Rom. xiv, 17. As external, it is either embodied in the visible church of Christ, and in so far is present and progressive; or it is to be perfected in the coming of the Messiah to judgment, and his subsequent spiritual reign in bliss and glory, Matt. xiii, 43, in

which view it is future. But these different aspects are not always distinguished; the expression often embracing both the internal and external sense, and referring both to its commencement in this world and its completion in the world to come, Matt. v, 3–10; Col. i, 13. The idea of this kingdom has its basis in the prophecies of the Old Testament, where the reign of the Messiah is described as a golden age, when the true religion, and with it the Jewish theocracy, should be re-established in more than pristine purity, and universal peace and happiness prevail, Dan. ii, 44; vii, 14. All this was doubtless to be understood in a spiritual sense; and so the devout Jews of our Saviour's time appear to have received it; as Zacharias, Luke i, 67; Simeon, ii, 25; Anna, ii, 36; Joseph, Luke xxiii, 50, 51. But the Jews at large gave to these prophecies a temporal meaning, and expected a Messiah who should come in the clouds of heaven, and, as a king of the Jewish nation, restore the ancient religion and worship, reform the corrupt morals of the people, make expiation for their sins, free them from the yoke of foreign dominion, and at length reign over the whole earth in peace and glory. "Children of the *kingdom*," Matt. viii, 12, are the Jews, who thought the Messiah's reign was destined only for them. But in another place, Matt. xiii, 38, they are the true citizens of the kingdom of God. "The *kingdom* of God cometh not with observation," Luke xvii, 20, i. e., not so that its progress may be watched with the eyes.

KINGS, *Book of*. The first book commences with the death of David, 1014 B. C., and comprises the history of 126 years to the death of Jehoshaphat king of Judah. The second book continues the history of the kings of Israel and Judah, through a period of 300 years, to the destruction of the city and temple of Jerusalem by Nebuchadnezzar. These two books are compiled out of public and private records made by the various kings, scribes, and prophets mentioned in them; and there is strong reason to believe that *Ezra*, a learned and very inquisitive scribe, who lived during the captivity and after it, was the author of these compilations.

KINGS' WAY, Num. xx, 17, supposed to be the large rocky uneven valley *El Ghoeyr*, which is twelve miles wide at the eastern extremity, and descends toward the west into the *El Ghor*, where it is narrower. This valley is famous for the excellent pasturage produced by its numerous springs; and it has in consequence become a favourite place of encampment for all the Bedouins of the adjacent mountains. This was perhaps the "*kings' way*," by which Moses, aware of the difficulty of forcing a passage, requested permission of the Edomites to pass, on condition of leaving the fields and vineyards untouched, and of purchasing provisions and water from the inhabitants. But Edom refused, and "came out against him with much people and a strong hand."

KIR, *wall*, or *fortress*, Isa. xv, 1; a fortified city in the territory of Moab, now called *Kerek*, or *Karak*, which also signifies a *fortress*, situated on a steep lime-stone hill, some thirty-six miles north of due east from the southern extremity of the Dead Sea. From this hill the prospect extends even to Jerusalem, and overlooks the whole surrounding country. The name is also applied to the whole district. The same is called in Jer. xlviii, 31, *Kir-heres*, the *brick fortress*.

KISHON, Judges v, 21, a stream which takes its rise from a spring near the foot of Mount Tabor on the east. Its course is at first southerly; and after passing through the great plain, (*Jezreel*,) and being increased by the accession of many small streams, it reaches the foot of Carmel at the south-west corner of the plain, then flows to the north-west into the Bay of Ptolema'is, a short distance south of Acre.

KISS, *a love token*, as given in salutation, which has been practised among all nations. The ancient oriental, and especially the *Persian* mode of salutation was, between persons of equal rank to kiss each other on the lips; when the difference of rank was slight, they kissed each other on the cheek; when one was much inferior, he fell on his knees, and touched his forehead to the ground, or prostrated himself, kissing at the same time his hand toward the superior. See Job xxxi, 27; hence kissing the feet, hands, and lips of idols, was to perform the rites of worship in the most submissive manner, 1 Kings xix, 18. The Jews considered the *kiss* to be an expression of friendship, 2 Sam. xx, 9. Our Lord says to Simon, Luke vii, 45, "Thou hast given me no *kiss*," meaning that he had not expressed such affection to him as the woman had done who kissed his feet. This manner of expressing friendship to each other, the disciples of Christ adopted and practised in their religious assemblies, Rom. xvi, 16. This the apostle calls the *kiss* of charity, 1 Pet. v, 14, to distinguish it from the treacherous kiss of Joab and Judas; being given as an expression of that sincere, chaste, spiritual love which Christians owe to one another. "Righteousness and peace *kiss* each other," Psa. lxxxv, 10, (in the other member of the sentence, *are met together*,) i. e., are mutually connected, happiness follows upon righteousness.

KITE, a rapacious bird of the hawk kind, whose forked tail distinguishes it from all other birds of prey. Hence unclean, Lev. xi, 14.

KO'HATH, the second son of Levi, and father of Amram. Kohath's family was appointed to carry the ark and sacred vessels of the tabernacle, while the Israelites marched through the wilderness, Num. iv, &c.

KORAH, a Levite, who conspired against Moses, Num. xvi, 1, and offered strange fire, i. e., fire not consecrated, fire not taken from the altar. In verses 9, 10, which follow, is a command to Aaron and his sons that they should drink neither wine nor strong drink when they go into the tabernacle of the congregation, lest they should die there. The connection of the whole would seem to show that these offenders were under the influence of intoxicating liquors, when they offered strange fire before the Lord.

The *sons of Korah, Korahites,* a family of Levites, and singers in the time of David, in all probability the descendants of Korah, and to whom ten of the Psalms are attributed. In style they differ very sensibly from the Psalms of David; and they are some of the most exquisite of all the lyric compositions which the book of Psalms contains.

LAMA, a Hebrew word which signifies *why, wherefore.*

LAMECH, a son of Methusael, a descendant of Cain, and the first to misuse the arms invented by his son Tubal Cain, who was the first smith on record, and who taught how to make warlike instruments and domestic utensils out of brass and iron. His address to his wives is probably the oldest piece of poetry in the world. The following would seem to be a more appropriate translation of a part of it: "I have slain a man who wounded me; a young man who smote me." It is not to be understood that Lamech had slain two persons; it is merely the repetition of poetic parallelism, Gen. iv, 19–24.

LAMENTATIONS *of Jeremiah,* were intended as a pathetic description of the desolation of Judah and Jerusalem during the Babylonian captivity, Lam. iv, 22. The Lamentations are written in metre, and consist of a number of plaintive effusions, composed after the manner of funeral dirges. Tenderness and sorrow form the general character of these elegies; and an attentive reader will find great beauty in many of the images, and great energy in some of the expressions.

LAMP, a vessel for the burning of oil by means of a wick. The houses in the east were, from the remotest antiquity, lighted with lamps; and hence it is so common in Scripture to call every thing which enlightens the body or mind, which guides or refreshes, by the name of a *lamp*. To extinguish the light in an apartment, is a convertible phrase for total destruction; and nothing can more properly and emphatically represent the total destruction of a city than the extinction of the *lights*, Job xxi, 17; xviii, 5, 6. A burning lamp is, on the other hand, the chosen symbol of prosperity; a beautiful instance of which occurs in the complaint of Job, xxix, 2, 3.

A lamp despised, Job xii, 5, is one thrown aside because it ceases to give light; the emblem of a man once in high consideration, but now vile and contemned.

LANGUAGE is the expression of thought, either by articulate sounds, or by symbols; and this is one of the noblest traits of man, as distinguished from all other terrestrial beings. Language is undoubtedly the gift of God, as the most authentic history of our race, the book of Genesis, shows us that man possessed the power of employing language, and actually used that power, from the earliest period after his formation.

Many learned men are of the opinion that the Hebrew was the original language, which continued the language of the whole earth for nearly 2000 years, or until about a century after the flood. It was then that the tower of Babel was erected; and, for the purpose of confounding that presumptuous enterprise, God caused a confusion of languages, so that the various tribes should be incapable of understanding each other, and of course incapable of prosecuting their plans.

LANTERN. The word occurs, John xviii, 3. They came thus furnished to apprehend our Lord, lest he should escape through the darkness of the night.

LATTICE, any work of wood or iron made by crossing laths, rods, or bars, and forming open squares like *net work*. Hence the net work windows, *windows of narrow lights*, 1 Kings vi, 4, which are still usual in the chambers of eastern houses, Judges v, 28. These lattices or bars being let into the walls or beams, could not be opened and shut at pleasure. Also *Balustrade*, lattice work, which surrounds the roofs, 2 Kings i, 2.

LA-O-DI-CE'A, the chief city of Phrygia, in Asia Minor, situated on the river Lycus, not far to the south of Colosse and Hierapolis, with which it was destroyed by an earthquake about A. D. 65; but was rebuilt by Marcus Aurelius. Its three theatres, and the immense circus, which was capable of containing upward of thirty thousand spectators, the spacious remains of which (with other ruins buried under ruins) are yet to be seen, give proof of its ancient wealth and population; and indicate too strongly, that in that city where Christians were re-buked, without exception, for their lukewarmness, there were multitudes who were lovers of pleasure more than lovers of God. Its own tragedy may be briefly told. It was lukewarm, and neither cold nor hot; and therefore it was loathsome in the sight of God. And it has been blotted from the world. It is now as desolate as its inhabitants were destitute of the fear and love of God.

LAPWING, a species of snipe, about the size of a pigeon, found in Europe in large flocks; but according to the Septuagint and Vulgate, the *hoopoe* is intended—a beautiful crested bird, which is solitary and migratory, and sometimes called the marsh cock.

LAVER, a wash basin, made of brazen ornaments, and placed in the tabernacle for the use of the priests, Exod. xxx, 18. Solomon had one made of vast size, supported by twelve brazen oxen, and placed near the entrance of the temple, which was called the *molten sea*, 1 Kings vii, 22. It was nearly fifteen feet in diameter and eight deep, and had cocks for the convenience of drawing off the water into basins.

LAW signifies a rule by which actions are to be determined, and is either natural or positive; the former is founded on the unchange-able nature of things, and is therefore immutable; the latter is founded on the circumstances in which rational creatures may happen to be placed, and is therefore changeable. The former is called moral, the latter ritual.

1. The term *law* is sometimes taken in general, without reference to a particular people or state, Rom. iv, 15.

2. It is sometimes applied to the whole Mosaic code or body of laws.

3. To the *particular* laws, *statutes*, or *ordinances*, given by Moses, whether *moral*, *ceremonial*, or *political*. The moral law relates to the heart and conduct of men, Rom. vii, 7; the ceremonial to external religious rites, as purification and sacrifice, John vii, 23; and political to civil rights and duties, John vii, 51.

4. Law frequently signifies *divine revelation in general.* Thus the oracles of God, with which the Jews were intrusted, have the name of *law* often given to them, Psa. xix, 7; John x, 34, with a particular reference to the preceptive part. But when the Jewish Scriptures are distinguished into parts, as Luke xxiv, 44; *the law* in that division denotes *the Penta-teuch*, or *five books of Moses:* farther, because the *covenant* with Abraham is one of the

greatest of the ancient oracles of God, and is in substance the *Gospel covenant;* it is called in some passages *the law,* as Rom. ii, 25, 26. In like manner, *the Gospel* is sometimes called *the law.* It is called *the perfect law,* to distinguish it from the law of Moses, which made no man perfect either in respect of holiness or pardon, Heb. vii, 19; whereas the Gospel makes men perfect in both. It is also called *the law of liberty,* 1. Because it delivers men from the slavery of their lusts, and restores the dominion of reason and conscience in their minds, which is true liberty. 2. Because it has freed the Jews from the law of Moses, which was a yoke of bondage they were not able to bear. 3. Because it delivers all true believers from the punishment of sin. 4. Because it assures us that in the eye of God all men are on a level, and equally entitled to the privileges of the Gospel. 5. Because it forbids the acceptance of persons in judgment, James ii, 12. *Law* also signifies the law of nature, Rom. iii, 20, which being written on men's hearts, they are said on that account to be *a law unto themselves.*

Lastly, *law* is used in a metaphorical sense for any thing which hath the *force and strength of a law,* " as the law of sin," " the law of death ;" *works of the law* are the works which the law requires.

LAWYER, a person learn-ed in the law of Moses, particularly the oral or traditionary law ; one devoted to the study and explanation of the Scriptures. The *lawyers* belonged to the sect of the Pharisees. See SCRIBE.

LEAD, a heavy metal, and one of the six well known to the ancients, Num. xxxi, 22. It is soft and inelastic, and has a bluish grey colour ; and when recently cut, a strong metallic lustre. We are informed that writing with an iron style or pen on rolls of *lead* was of high antiquity, and came into practice next after writing on the bark and leaves of trees, and was used in recording public transactions, Job xix, 24.

LEAF. The bright fresh colour of the leaf of a tree, or plant, shows that it is richly nourished by a good soil. Hence it is emblematical of prosperity. On the contrary, a faded leaf becomes a fit emblem of adversity and decay, Jer. xvii, 8 ; Isa. lxiv, 6.

LEASING, falsehood, lies, Psa. iv, 2.

LEAST, superlative of *less,* least in magnitude, in number, and quantity, Luke xvi, 10 ; in rank or dignity, Matt. ii, 6 ; and in weight or importance, Matt. v, 19.

LEAVEN, *fermented* or *sour dough.* Hence as leaven causes to ferment and turn sour, it is spoken proverbially, 1 Cor. v, 6 ; *a little leaven leavens the whole mass,* i. e., a few bad men corrupt a multitude ; taken also for *corrupt-*

ness, perverseness of life, doctrine, and heart. The word is applied by Christ, Luke xii, 1, to the hypocrisy of the Pharisees ; a vice which secretly puffed up their minds, and strangely spread itself through their hearts and actions, so as to taint and spoil the very best of their duties. The Jews were commanded to put away all leaven, both old and new, before they ate the passover, as being an emblem of wickedness, which ʼsours and corrupts the mind, as leaven does the lump into which it is put, if it remain long unbaked. *Old leaven* signifies wicked *persons*, and wicked *practices*. The incestuous Corinthian is called *the old leaven*, 1 Cor. v, 7, because he was not a new offender, but had continued long in the bad practice for which he was to be cast out ; or, as his crime was *whoredom*, it is called *old leaven*, because the Corinthians in their heathen state had been much addicted to that vice.

LEBANON, *white.* The celebrated lime-stone mountains on the confines of Syria and Palestine, consisting of two lofty parallel ridges, of which the western one is called by way of excellence *Lebanon ;* while the eastern ridge, which is higher, and in part covered with *eternal snows*, Jer. xviii, 14, bears the name of *Anti-libanus ;* and in its southern part that of Hermon. But the Hebrews do not make this distinction of names, denominating both summits by the name of *Lebanon.* These mountains are particularly striking to the traveller approaching both from the Mediterranean on the west, and the desert on the east. On either side, he first discovers, at a great distance, a clouded ridge, stretching from north to south, as far as the eye can see ; the central summits of which are capped with clouds, or tipped with snow. This is Lebanon, which is often referred to in Holy Writ for its streams, its timber, and its wines ; and at the present day the seat of the only portion of freedom of which Syria can boast.

Mr. Fisk describes these mountains in the following manner :—" You would perhaps like to know how Mount Lebanon looks. It is not, as I used to suppose, one mountain, but a multitude of mountains thrown together, and separated by very deep narrow valleys, which seem to have been made merely for the sake of dividing the hills. There are more trees on Mount Lebanon than on the hills of Judea ; yet there is nothing which the Americans would call a forest. Most of the trees where I have been are either pines or fruit trees. I have not yet seen the cedars. The roads are *bad, worse,* and *worst ;* steep and rocky, I presume, beyond any thing you ever saw in Vermont or any where else. I generally ride a mule or an ass ; and it is often literally riding up and down stairs for a considerable distance together. These mountains present a variety of the most rude, sublime, and romantic scenery." Anciently on these mountains grew cedars, of which there remain (1824) about 300, and some of them of great size and antiquity. Every thing about this tree has a strong balsamic odour; and hence the whole grove is so pleasant and fragrant, that it is delightful to walk in it. This is probably the *smell of Lebanon* spoken of in Song iv, 11; Hos. xiv, 6. In the summer, snow is often brought down into the neighbouring cities and mingled with the drink of the inhabitants, in order to render it more cool and refreshing, Prov. xxv, 13.

The cedar of Lebanon has, in all ages, been reckoned as an object of unrivalled grandeur and beauty in the vegetable kingdom. It is, accordingly, one of the natural images which frequently occur in the poetical style of the Hebrew prophets; and is appropriated to denote kings, princes, and potentates of the highest rank.

The stupendous size, the extensive range, and great elevation of Libanus; its towering summits capped with perpetual snow, or crowned with fragrant cedars; its olive plantations; its vineyards, producing the most delicious wines; its clear fountains, and cold-flowing brooks; its fertile vales, and odoriferous shrubberies—combine to form in Scripture language, "the glory of Lebanon," Isaiah xxxv, 2.

LEEK, a bulbous, well known vegetable, like the onion. It has been cultivated in Egypt from a very early period.

LEES, dregs, or sediment of wine, which remains at the bottom of the vessel. By keeping wine standing on the *lees* its strength and colour are preserved. "Wines on the *lees*," Isa. xxv, 6, i. e., good old wine purified by the *lees* settling to the bottom. "To rest upon one's *lees*," Zeph. i. 12, is to be hardened in sin, to live a life of indifference.

LEGION, the largest division of troops in the Roman army, consisting of thirty bands or six thousand men, though varying greatly in numbers at different periods. It is taken for an indefinitely great number, e. g., of angels, Matt. xxvi, 53, of demons, Mark v, 9.

LEMUEL, a king, mentioned Prov. xxxi, 1–4, otherwise unknown, probably not an Israelite, perhaps an Arabian, to whom the moral maxims from verse 2–9 are directed.

LENTIL, a kind of pulse, resembling small beans, and crooked in the same manner, used chiefly by the poor. This formed a reddish or chocolate coloured dish, which is called *red pottage*, Gen. xxv, 29, 30.

LEOPARD, a fierce animal, of the cat kind, found chiefly in Senegal, remarkable for its spotted skin, by which only it is sensibly distinguished from the panther, and also for its cruelty, insidiousness, and activity, Jer. v, 6; Hos. xiii, 7; Hab. i, 8. It is said to be extremely cruel to man—all which properties seem to be alluded to in the emblematic beast mentioned, Rev. xiii, 1, 2.

LEP′ER, a person afflicted with the leprosy. The law excluded such from society; banished them into the country, and to places uninhabited, Lev. xiii, 45, 46; and even kings under the disease were expelled their palaces, and deprived of their government, 2 Chron. xxvi, 20.

LEPROSY, a contagious disease, which exhibits itself on the skin, Lev. xiii, 42–45, appearing in dry, white, thin scales, or scabs, either on the whole body or on some part of it, and usually attended with violent itching, and other pains. The eastern leprosy was a most filthy and loathsome distemper, highly contagious, so as to infect and seize even garments and houses, and by human means incurable, at least so deemed by the Jews, 2 Kings v, 7. This disease formerly existed in warm climates, but is not now very common. It is, however, among the Arabs, and generally over the east. At Scio, *Howard* found a hospital for patients labour-

17

ing under this malady. It contained 120 persons lodged in separate rooms. The leprosy has ever been considered as a lively emblem of the moral taint or corruption of the nature of every man, as the sacrifices which were to be offered by the healed leper prefigured the *Lamb of God that taketh away the sin of the world.*

LET is frequently used to signify *to hinder, retard,* to interpose obstructions.

LETTERS, marks for the purpose of expressing sounds used in writing. Few subjects have given rise to more discussion than the origin of alphabetic characters. But the author and the era of this discovery are both lost in the darkness of remote antiquity. Even the nation to which the invention is due cannot now be ascertained.

Writing and reading were familiar to Moses and the Israelites when the law was given, and must have long previously existed among them, and, probably, among the Egyptians of the same age too; which is much earlier than any of those monuments bearing hieroglyphical characters reach. We have given sufficient reason to conclude that Job lived at an earlier period still, and as he expresses a wish that his words should be written in a book, and engraven on the rock, the knowledge of reading as well as writing must have been pretty general in his country, or the book and the inscription could not have been a testimony of his faith and hope to his countrymen, as he passionately desired it to be. Here, too, it is to be observed, that in the early Mosaic history we have not the least intimation of writing by pictures or symbols, nor any that the art of writing had been revealed from heaven in the days of Moses, preparatory to the giving of a written law, and the introduction of inspired books for the religious instruction of the people. We must trace it up higher; though whether of Divine revelation, or human invention, cannot certainly be determined. Its importance was assuredly worthy of the former; and if this was not done by particular revelation, doubtless we may reasonably and piously ascribe it to a Divine suggestion.

2. Sacred literature, or a knowledge of the Scriptures, John vii, 15.

3. Paul uses the term letter to signify the literal sense and external ceremonies of the law, Rom. ii, 29. "The oldness of the *letter*," Rom. vii, 6, means the outward service of God. Paul places the *letter* in opposition to the Spirit, and by distinguishing between the *Spirit* and the *letter* of the law of Moses, he intimates that the rites enjoined in that law were typical, and had a spiritual or moral meaning, as Moses also expressly declared to the Jews, Deut. xxx, 6; Lev. xxvi, 41. The Prophet Jeremiah likewise represents circumcision as emblematical, chap. iv, 4; consequently all the other rites of the law were so likewise.

LE-VI'A-THAN, the *crocodile*, an amphibious animal of the lizard genus. of the largest kind, Job xli, 1. The description of leviathan suits no animal but the *crocodile*. The crocodile is a natural inhabitant of the Nile, and other Asiatic and African rivers; of enormous voracity and strength, as well as fleetness in swimming; attacks mankind and the largest animals with most daring impetuosity; when taken by means of a powerful net, will often overturn the boats that surround it; has, proportionally, the largest mouth of all monsters whatever; moves both its jaws equally, the upper of which has not less than forty, and the lower than thirty-eight sharp, but strong and massy teeth; and is furnished with a coat of mail, so scaly and callous as to resist the force of a musket ball in every part except under the belly. Indeed, to this animal the general character of the leviathan seems so well to

LEVITE, one of the posterity of Levi, son of Jacob, spoken in the Old Testament of the descendants of the

heads of which were Gershom, Kohath, and Merari, Num. iii, 17. They were appointed by the Mosaic law to be the *ministers* and *servants* of the priests, and to perform the *menial offices* of the temple; they studied the law, and were the ordinary judges of the country, but subordinate to the priests, Num. viii, 5-7.

LE-VITI-CUS, the third book of the Pentateuch; so called because it treats principally of the Levites. It also gives an account of the priests, and seems to contain little more than the history of what passed during the *eight days* employed in consecrating Aaron and his sons to the priesthood, which took place 1490 B. C.

LIBERTINE, *a freedman.* The *Libertines* are mentioned in Acts vi, 9; these were probably Jews, who having been carried as captives to Rome, and then *freed* by their masters, had settled down as residents in that city, i. e., as Roman *freedmen.* Philo expressly affirms that a large section of the city beyond the Tiber was occupied by Jews of this character. Tacitus, a celebrated Latin historian, also relates that, under Tiberius, 4,000 *freedmen* were at once transported to Sardinia.—*Robinson.*

LIBERTY, as opposed to servitude and slavery, denotes the condition of a man who may act independently of the will of another. Spiritual liberty consists in freedom from the curse of the moral law; from the servitude of the ritual; from the love, power, and guilt of sin; from the dominion of Satan; from the corruptions of the world, from the fear of death, and the wrath to come.

LIBYA, a region of Africa west of Egypt, along the coast of the Mediterranean, and extending back indefinitely into the desert. *Cyrene* was its chief city, in which, and in other cities of this province, dwelt many Jews, Acts ii, 10.

LIE, a *lie* is that which is spoken with an intention to deceive. Any thing *deceptive, fallacious,* which deludes with false hopes, as *idols,* Psa. xl, 4; Amos ii, 4; *a false oracle,* Ezek. xiii, 6-8. The apostle speaks of "changing the truth of God into a *lie.*" Idols are fitly called "*a lie,*" being false representations of the Deity. They are also called "*lying vanities,*" Psa. xxxi, 6; and every image of an idol is termed *a teacher of lies,* Hab. ii, 18. "We have made *lies* our refuge," Isa. xxviii, 15, i. e., we have placed our confidence in the delusive promises of false prophets, or in the assistance of idols which cannot save their deluded votaries. By implication, a *lie* is falsehood toward God, i. e., *wickedness, ungodliness;* so *to make a lie,* is to practise wickedness, or perhaps *idolatry.*

LIEUTENANTS, the governors or viceroys of large provinces among the ancient Persians, possessing both civil and military power, and being in the provinces the representatives of the sovereign, whose state and splendour they also rivalled. But parts or subdivisions of these provinces were under *deputies*, sometimes called "governors over every province," Esth. iii, 12; ix, 3.

LIFE, the vital principle, also the season or time which one lives, 1 Cor. xv, 19. The Hebrews regarded life as a journey, a pilgrimage on the face of the earth, Psa. xxxix, 12. The traveller, as they supposed, when he arrived at the end of his journey, which happened when he died, was received into the company of his ancestors who had gone before him, Gen. xxv, 8; Heb. xi, 13–15. Reception into the *presence of God* at death is asserted only in two passages of the Old Testament, Hag. ii, 23; Eccl. xii, 7. *Spiritual life* consists in union with God, influenced by a principle of grace, which leads to activity in his service. *Eternal life* is not barely the perpetuity of being; but that *bliss* and *glory* which springs from the presence of God, and the fulfilment of his precious promises. *Life* is put absolutely for the source of all life, John i, 4. It also signifies manner of life, conduct, in a moral respect, Rom. vi, 4; *life of God*, i. e., which God requires, a *godly* life,

Eph. iv, 18. "A man's *life* consisteth not in the abundance of the things which he possesseth," Luke xii, 5. By *life*, our Lord obviously means man's true interest, and that, he teaches us, consists not in worldly abundance, but being *rich toward God*, i. e., endowed with those things which form the treasure of the soul, and will remain its treasure after death.

LIGHT. The nature of light is yet unknown; according to some, it is an emanation from luminous bodies, and consists of inconceivably minute particles, which are too subtle to exhibit the common properties of matter, travel in straight lines with immense velocity, and produce the sensation of light, by passing into the eye, and striking against the expanded nerve of vision, the retina. Others ascribe its effects to the vibration or undulations of a subtle, ethereal medium, universally present in nature, the pulses of which, in some way excited by luminous objects, pass through space and transparent bodies, and give rise to vision by impressing the retina in the same way as pulsations of air impress the nerve of hearing, and produce the sensation of sound. Its motion is extremely quick, and is said to move about ten millions of miles in a minute. The term *light* is much used in Scripture: 1. For artificial light, a luminous body, as a lamp or torch, Acts xvi, 29. 2. Natural light, as the sun, moon, and stars. 3. For the *mind, conscience,* 'The *light* that is in thee," Matt. vi, 23. Light is used as the emblem of *welfare, prosperity, happiness.* The Lord is called the *light of Israel,* as the author and source of prosperity and happiness to them, Isa. lx, 1–3. *The light of the countenance* signifies the *cheerful, agreeable* look of persons who are *pleased,* in opposition to the gloomy, forbidding mien of those who are displeased. "Light being the purest of all material substances," says Macknight, "and that which, by means of the eye, conveys to the mind pleasures more grateful and more various than those communicated by the other senses; it is fitly used metaphorically to denote knowledge and virtue. Wherefore, when we are told that God is *light,* it signifies not only that he is infinite in knowledge, and possessed of all moral perfection, without the least mixture of evil; but that the contemplation of his nature and perfections is as pleasant to the minds of his rational creatures as light is to the eye." By metonymy, it is used for the *author* and *dispenser* of moral and spiritual light; *a moral teacher,* but especially *Jesus* the great teacher and Saviour of the world, who brought life and immortality to light in his Gospel. "Armour of *light,*" Rom. xiii, 12; the Christian virtues, which for their excellence and beauty may be compared to a *robe of light,* or such dress as is fit for the children of light to wear. *Armour* being used for any equipage of the body, may signify clothes, dress, &c. "The *light* of his cloud is lightning," Job xxxvii, 15.

LIGHTNING, Job xxviii, 26, a flash of electricity passing from one cloud to another, or from the clouds to the earth. Sometimes the earth and atmosphere appear to make a mutual exchange of their surplus electricity. When this subtle fluid is equally diffused, it remains in a state of quiescence; but when this equilibrium is destroyed by some cause not perhaps fully understood, then the bodies which have it in a degree less than others attract it, and it moves with such astonishing rapidity as to rend the stoutest oaks, and tear in pieces the strongest buildings. Dr. Franklin was the first man who was bold enough to make an experiment on the clouds, and to draw down the lightning from the sky. He supposed that lightning and electricity were identically the same, and determined to ascertain by direct experiment the truth of his bold conjecture. Having constructed a kite, by stretching a large silk handkerchief over two sticks in the form of a cross, on the first appearance of an approaching storm, in June 1752, he went into a field, accompanied by his son, to whom alone he had imparted his design. Having raised his kite, and attached a key to the lower end of the hempen string, he insulated it, by fastening it to a post by means of silk, and waited with intense anxiety for the result. When Franklin was about to despair of success, his attention was caught by the bristling up of some loose fibres on the hempen cord : he immediately presented his knuckle to the key, and received an electric spark! The rain now fell in torrents, and wetting the string, rendered it conducting in its whole length, so that electric sparks were now collected from it in great abundance. But, in 1753, Professor Richman, of St. Petersburgh, was killed while making a similar attempt.

LIGN ALOES. The same as ALOES, which see.

LIG'URE, a precious stone of a deep red colour, with a considerable tinge of yellow. See PRECIOUS STONES.

LILY, a well known and beautiful flower, of a great variety of species, the most beautiful of which are found in eastern countries, and are often mentioned by travellers. It furnished Solomon with a variety of images in his Song, and with graceful ornaments in the fabric and furniture of the temple, see Matt. vi, 28.

LIME, *the protoxide of calcium*, a well known white, brittle, earthy substance, which is obtained by exposing carbonate of lime, i. e., Iceland spar, marble, or shells to a strong red heat, so as to expel the carbonic acid. It has a powerful affinity for water, and the combination forms a white bulky hydrate, which is composed of twenty-eight parts by weight of lime, and nine of water. The process of slaking lime consists in forming this *hydrate*, and the hydrate itself is the common *slaked lime;* during this process, a large quantity of heat is disengaged, and, if done in the dark, light will be seen. The heat is caused by the condensation of the water, which enters into a chemical combination with the lime, forming the hydrate above mentioned. Lime is dissolved very sparingly by water; and it is a singular fact, that it is more soluble in cold than in hot water. Thus on heating water which contains lime in solution, a deposition ensues on the sides of the vessel. The prophet speaks of " burning human bones into *lime*," Amos ii, 1. Bones are composed of the *phosphate* and *carbonate* of lime and animal matter, and when heated to redness in an open vessel, a white substance remains, mostly the phosphate of lime.

LINE, a cord used for measuring land, as land is measured with us by a *chain,* Ezek, xl, 3; Amos vii, 17; Psa. lxxviii, 55. The word is accordingly used, by a figure of speech, for the *por-*

tion measured out and assigned to any one; the *lot* or *heritage* itself, Psa. xvi, 6. Hence used metaphorically for *law, rule.* "*Line* upon *line,*" Isa. xxviii, 10. It seems to be used also for the *cord* or *string* of a musical instrument; and hence *sound*, Psa. xix, 4.

LINEN, the cloth made from flax, a well known plant. A most precious stuff was made from this plant, distinguished for its fineness and beauty, and worn by kings, priests, and other persons of high rank and honour, Esth. i, 6, and viii, 15. Flax was cultivated very extensively in Egypt, both for the oil which was expressed from its seeds, and for the manufacture of linen. It is mentioned in Exod. ix, 31, as one of the large and important crops smitten down by the plague of hail. It was also an article of foreign commerce. Solomon made large and regular importations of it, 1 Kings x, 28; so Prov. vii, 16, "Fine *linen* of Egypt." The manufacture of this article was of a very early date, and the wearing of it a matter of courtly use and luxury in the days of Joseph, Gen. xli, 42. Also a cloth manufactured from the produce of the *cotton tree.* The pods of this shrub, which grow as large as pigeons' eggs, turn black when ripe, and divide at the top into three parts; the cotton is as white as snow, and with the heat of the sun,

swells to the size of a hen's egg. The Scriptures speak of cotton sometimes where the English version has *fine linen*, e. g., Exod. xxv, 4. This cloth, which is still found wrapped around mummies, appears to have been about of the texture and quality of the modern cotton sheeting; certainly not finer. Garments of cotton, varied in colour according to the tint of the material; white are mentioned, Rev. xix, 8; and they were sometimes dyed of a purple or crimson colour, Luke xvi, 19. See PURPLE.

LINTEL, the upper part of a door way, Exod. xii, 7, 22.

LION, a large beast of prey, for his courage and strength called the king of beasts. This animal is produced in Africa, and the hottest parts of Asia. It is found in the greatest numbers in the scorched and desolate regions of the torrid zone, in the deserts of Zahara and Billdulgerid, and in all the interior parts of the vast continent of Africa. In these desert regions, from whence mankind are driven by the rigorous heat of the climate, this animal reigns sole master. His disposition seems to partake of the ardour of his native clime. Inflamed by the influence of a burning sun, his rage is tremendous, and his courage undaunted. Happily, indeed, the species is not numerous, and is said to be greatly diminished.

The length of the largest lion is between eight and nine feet, the tail about four, and its height about four feet and a half. The female is about one-fourth less, and without a mane. As the lion advances in years, his mane grows longer and thicker. The hair on the rest of the body is short and smooth, of a tawny colour, but whitish on the belly. Its roaring is loud. When heard in the night it resembles distant thunder, and is one of the most terrible sounds in nature; but it becomes still more dreadful when it is known to be a sure prelude of destruction to whatever living creature comes in his way; for the lion does not usually set up his horrid roar till he beholds his prey, and is just going to seize it. This fact is referred to in the Bible, Amos iii, 4; Isa. v, 29; Judg. xiv, 5. Its cry of anger is much louder and shorter. The attachment of a lioness to her young is remarkably strong. For their support she is more ferocious than the lion himself; makes her incursions with greater boldness; destroys, without distinction, every animal that falls in her way, and carries it reeking to her cubs. When much disturbed or alarmed, she will sometimes transport her young, which are usually three or four in number, from one place to another in her mouth; and, if obstructed in her course, will defend them to the last extremity. The habits of the lion and the lioness afford many spirited and often sublime metaphors to the sacred writers.

The word is also used for *a cruel adversary, a persecutor,* 2 Tim. iv, 17, where some understand *Nero,* others *Satan,* and others again, as denoting an escape from the greatest dangers; in which sense it is used in Psa. xxii, 21. Some suppose that the apostle would not give so disrespectful an appellation to Nero. "The *Lion* of the tribe of Judah," Rev. v, 5, is a powerful deliverer; compare Jer. xlix, 19; the Messiah, in allusion to Jacob's prophecy, Gen. xlix, 9.

LIP. Because the lip is one of the chief instruments of speaking, it signifies *language;* it is also used for *talk, words, discourse.*

Lying lips, Prov. x, 18, i. e., a man of falsehood and deceit.

Burning lips, Prov. xxvi, 23, are words expressing ardent affection.

Calves of the lips, Hos. xiv, 2. The apostle translates this phrase, Heb. xiii, 15, "The fruit of our *lips.*" Praise and thanksgiving to God uttered by the lips.

LITTER, a vehicle formed of shafts supporting a bed between them, in which a person may be borne by men or by a horse, Isa. lxvi, 20.

LIVER is called in Hebrew *heavy,* as being the heaviest of the viscera; just

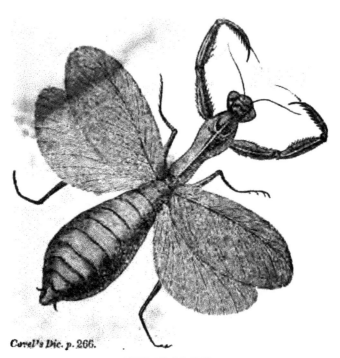

Carel's Dic. p. 266.

AFRICAN LOCUST.

as the *lungs*, which are the lightest, are in our language called the *lights*. This important organ is situated in the side below the right breast. " My *liver* is poured out upon the earth," Lam. ii, 11 ; an expression for the severest mental suffering. The inspection of the liver was a method of divination much practised by the Chaldeans and other heathen nations, Ezek. xxi, 21.

LIVING, spoken of natural life and existence as opposed to death or non-existence, and implying always some duration, as the *living God*, in opposition to idols which are dead. " *Living* sacrifice," Rom. xii, 1 ; the constant, in opposition to the interrupted sacrifice of slaughtered victims. " The *living* stone," 1 Pet. ii, 4, is *Christ* as the corner stone of the Church ; not inactive and dead, but living and efficient. This temple, of which he is the foundation, is built of *living men*. (See verse 5.) *Living water*, i. e., the water of running streams and fountains, opposed to that of stagnant cisterns, pools, marshes, &c., John iv, 10, 11.

LOCUST. The above is an accurate engraving of the African locust, which was brought from Africa by Mr. Seys, the American missionary, and about one-third less than the original. Its body and legs are yellow, and the wings of a dirty white. Locusts are one of the most terrific scourges of oriental countries, Exod. x, 12. See one of the most striking descriptions of the ravages of this insect, Joel ii, 1–11. They form themselves into large and numerous swarms, and fly in the air like a succession of clouds, forming many compact bodies, of several hundred yards square. Burckhardt, who had long resided in Arabia, says, when for the first time he saw a swarm of locusts, they so completely covered the surface of the ground that his horse killed numbers of them at every step, while he had the greatest difficulty in keeping from his face those that rose up and flew about. In the year 1813 they devoured the whole harvest from Berber to Shendy in the black countries ; and in the spring of that same year, he saw whole flights of them in Upper Egypt, where they are particularly injurious to the palm trees. These they strip of every leaf and green particle ; the trees remaining like skeletons with bare branches.

In Arabia, the locusts are known to come invariably from the East ; and the Arabs accordingly say, that they are produced by the waters of the Persian Gulf. The province of Nedjd is particularly exposed to their ravages ; they overwhelm it sometimes to such a degree, that having destroyed the harvest, they penetrate by thousands into the private dwellings, and devour whatever they can find, even the leather of the water vessels. It has been observed that those locusts that come from the East are not considered so formidable, because they only fix upon trees, and do not destroy the seed; but they soon give birth to a new brood, and it is the young locusts before they are sufficiently grown to fly away that consume the crops. According to general report, the locusts breed as often as three times in the year. The Bed'ouins who occupy the peninsula of Sinai, are frequently driven to despair by the multitudes of locusts, which constitute a land plague and a most serious grievance. These animals arrive by way of Akaba (therefore from the East) toward the end of May, when the Pleiades are setting, according to observations made by the Arabs, who believe that the locusts entertain a considerable dread of that constellation. They remain there generally during a space of forty or fifty days, and then disappear for the rest of the year.

Some few are seen in the course of every year, but great flights every fourth or fifth year; such is the general course of their unwelcome visits. Since the year 1811, however, they have invaded the peninsula every successive season for five years in considerable numbers.

All the Bedouins of Arabia, and the inhabitants of the towns in Nedjd and Hedjar, are accustomed to eat the locusts. "I have seen," says our traveller, "at Medinah and Tayf locust shops, where these animals were sold by measure. In Egypt and Nubia they are only eaten by the poorest beggars. The Arabs, in preparing locusts as an article of food, throw them alive into boiling water, with which a good deal of salt has been mixed; after a few minutes, they are taken out and dried in the sun; the head, feet, and wings are then torn off, the bodies are cleansed from the salt and perfectly dried; after which process, whole sacks are filled with them by the Bedouins. They are sometimes eaten broiled in butter; and they often contribute materials for a breakfast, when spread over unleavened bread with butter. It may here seem worthy of remark, that among all the Bedouins with whom he was acquainted in Arabia, those of Sinai alone do not use the locust as an article of food.

LODGE, a *hut* or *shed*, also a *hanging bed, hammock,* suspended from trees, in which travellers sleep, and also the keepers of gardens and vineyards, for fear of wild beasts while watching the fruits of those places; such as cucumbers, melons, and grapes, Isa. i, 8.

LOG, a Hebrew measure for things liquid, containing five-sixths of a pint.

LOINS, the lumbar region, the lower region of the back, around which the girdle is bound, and on which burdens are sustained, Gen. xxxvii, 34. The orientals, in order to run or labour with more ease, were accustomed to gird their long flowing garments close about them. Hence to have the *loins* girded, is to be in readiness, prepared for any action, Luke xii, 35. "The *loins* of the mind girded," 1 Pet. i, 13, is a bold but most expressive metaphor, to signify *the faculties of the mind prepared* for exerting themselves properly. Our minds must not be overcharged at any time with surfeiting and drunkenness; our affections must be placed on proper objects, and in a just degree; and our passions must all be under the government of our reason, Eph. vi, 14.

LOOKING GLASS, a mirror, plate glass, composed of sand and alkali in their purest state, and the composition on the back side is made of quicksilver and tin; but as glass was unknown to the ancients, (see GLASS,) tablets or plates of polished metal were used by the Hebrew women as mirrors, Exod. xxxviii, 8; Job xxxvii, 18; and were carried about by them in the manner of other nations, being mostly of a round form, and furnished with a handle, Isa. iii, 23.

LOOSE. See BIND.

LONG-SUFFERING, slowness to anger or to punish, forbearance, patient endurance.

LORD. 1. Means the owner of any thing, and one who has a person or thing under his control, and subject to his disposal; as a vineyard, Matt. xx, 8; a family, Mark xiii, 35; Gen. xviii, 12; a servant. It is also used of God, as the owner and governor of the world, "the *Lord* of the whole earth," Josh. iii, 13; and of Christ, as the supreme "Head over all things to the Church," Eph. i, 22. When the word *Lord* occurs in the Old Testament, printed in small capitals, it always stands for the Hebrew word *Jehovah*.

2. An honorary title of address to nobles and others to whom honour and reverence are due. It was addressed to Abraham by the children of Heth, Gen. xxxiii, 11; used by the woman of Samaria to our Saviour, John iv, 11; and by the man full of leprosy, Luke v, 12.

In respectfully addressing a person, the Hebrews, instead of the second personal pronoun *thou*, were accustomed to say, *My Lord;* and instead of the first person, *thy servant, thy handmaid*, "My *lord* asked his servants," i. e., thou didst ask us. In a style of still stronger adulation, this mode of speaking is also used in the case of an absent person, Gen. xxxii, 4.

LORD'S DAY. The first day of the week, observed as the Christian Sabbath instead of the seventh, because on it Jesus Christ rose from the dead, and made repeated visits to his disciples. It was on this day that the Holy Ghost descended on the apostles and first Christians. We find St. Paul preaching at Troas on this day when the disciples came to break bread, Acts xx, 7. The directions which he gave the Corinthians plainly allude to their religious assemblies on the first day of the week, 1 Cor. xvi, 2. And this day ever since has been kept as a Sabbath all over the Christian world.

LORD'S SUPPER, an ordinance instituted by our Saviour in place of the passover, and immediately after celebrating that rite for the last time with his disciples. At that feast, the Jews commemorated the deliverance of their own nation from the bondage of Egypt; this was designed to commemorate the infinitely more important deliverance of all mankind from the bondage of sin. *Jesus took the bread,* the bread which the master of the family used to divide among them after they had eaten the passover. He *said*, this bread *is*, i. e., *signifies*, or *represents* my body; according to the style of the sacred writers, thus, Genesis xl, 12, "the three branches are three days;" thus, Gal. iv, 24, St. Paul speaking of Sarah and Hagar, says, "These *are* the two covenants." Thus, in the grand type of our Lord, Exod.

xii, 11, God says of the paschal lamb, "This the *Lord's passover*." Now Christ, substituting the holy communion for the passover, follows the style of the Old Testament, and uses the same expressions the Jews were wont to use in celebrating the passover. "To eat this bread unworthily," 1 Cor. xi, 27, is to eat it as those Corinthians did, in aff *irreverent manner*, without regarding either him that appointed it, or the design of its appointment. Such shall be guilty of profaning that which represents the body and blood of the Lord. "Let a man examine himself." 1. Whether he comes to this service to keep up the memory of Christ. 2. Whether he is moved to do so by a grateful sense of Christ's love in dying for men. 3. Whether he comes with a firm purpose of doing honour to Christ, by living in all respects conformably to his precepts and example.

LO-RU-HA'MAH, *not obtaining mercy*, a symbolical name given by Hosea to his daughter, Hos. i, 6.

LOT, the son of Abraham's brother, the ancestor of the Ammonites and Moabites, who are therefore called *the children of Lot*, Deut. ii, 9. Respecting his wife, whether grieving for the loss of her property, or inwardly censuring the severity of the Divine dispensation, or whether moved by unbelief or curiosity, cannot now be known; but, looking back, she became a pillar of salt, Gen. xix, 26. Our Lord warns his disciples to remember Lot's wife in their flight from Jerusalem, and not to imitate her tardiness, Luke xvii, 32.

LOT, any thing used in determining chances, Prov. xviii, 18. The ancient manner of casting lots, was either in some person's lap, i. e., the fold or bosom of a garment, or into an urn, or some other vessel in which they might be shaken before they were cast or drawn. Hence it signifies that which falls to one by *lot ; a portion, inheritance,* Judges i, 3. Metaphorically, *destiny,* as assigned to men from God, Psa. xvi, 5.

LOVE, *to breathe after, to long for, to desire.* 1. To regard with strong and distinguished affection, and when referred to superiors, includes the idea of duty, respect, veneration : to love and serve with fidelity, Matt. vi, 24; xxii, 37.

2. To regard with favour, good will, benevolence, Luke vii, 5; John x, 17; sometimes the effects of benevolence are expressed, as, *thou shalt love thy neighbour.*

3. Spoken of things, to delight in, Luke xi, 43.

The love of God or Christ, signifies the love which God or Christ *exercises* toward Christians ; and also that love of which God or Christ is the *object* in the hearts of Christians.

Love of the truth, means true love, i. e., the true and real benefits conferred by God through Christ, 2 Thes. ii, 10. "The *love* of God is shed abroad in the heart," Rom. v, 5, i. e., the Divine conviction of God's love to us, and that love to God, which is both the earnest and the beginning of heaven.

LOWER PARTS *of the earth* are, 1. *Valleys,* which are lower than the hills, Isa. xliv, 23. 2. *The grave,* which is sometimes called the deep, Psa. lxiii, 9; Eph. iv, 9. 3. Poetically, any hidden place, Psa. cxxxix, 15.

LUCIFER, *Light giver.* This is the Latin name of the planet *Venus ;* so called from its *splendour,* when it appears in the morning before sunrise and ushers in the day. It is therefore expressly called *Son of the morning.* The only place where the word occurs in the Bible is Isa. xiv, 12; and is there most evidently applied to the king of Babylon—perhaps assumed by him. A brilliant star, and especially the morning star, is often put as the emblem of an illustrious prince, Num. xxiv, 17; and this meaning is in some measure confirmed by verse 13 : "I will exalt my throne above *the stars* of God." Some have understood the passage as referring to Satan ; and, from this circumstance, the name *Lucifer* has been since applied to him.

LUD, the son of Misraim, whose residence was in Af

rica; but in what particular part of that continent is not known.

LUKE, a physician, Col. iv, 14; the author of the gospel which bears his name, and of the Acts of the Apostles. He had more learning, it seems, than fell to the lot of the other evangelists; his language is more varied, copious, and pure. His gospel most probably was written in Greece, about the year 63 or 64, and the Acts of the Apostles soon after. Luke was deservedly beloved of the Apostle Paul. He was not only an intelligent and sincere disciple of Christ, but the apostle's affectionate and faithful friend, as appears from his attending him in several of his journeys through the Lesser Asia and Greece. He likewise accompanied him when he carried the collections to the saints in Judea, where, during the apostle's two years' imprisonment at Jerusalem and Cesarea he abode, and no doubt was present at his trials before Festus and Felix, and heard the speeches which he hath recorded in his history of the Acts. And when the apostle was sent a prisoner to Italy, Luke accompanied him in the voyage, and remained with him in Rome until he was released. Last of all, this excellent person was with the apostle during his second imprisonment in the same city; on which occasion, when his other assistants deserted him through fear, Luke abode with him and ministered unto him, 2 Tim. iv, 11. It is supposed that he died a natural death; but at what time or in what place is not known.

LUNATIC, *moon struck;* one afflicted with the *epilepsy,* the symptoms of which were supposed to become more aggravated with the increasing *moon.* This disease, in the New Testament and elsewhere, is ascribed to the influence of *demons,* Matt. xvii, 15, 18. See UNCLEAN SPIRITS.

LUST consists in impure desires inwardly cherished; *lewdness,* Rom. i, 24; but the word has also a more general signification in the Bible, viz., unlawful or sinful desires in general; desires which are fixed on sensual objects, as pleasures, profits, honours, &c. It also means the object of impure desire, that which is lusted after, John viii, 44.

LYC-A-O'NI-A, a region in the interior of Asia Minor, on the south of Galatia. It was adapted to pasturage; and its cities, Iconium, Derbe, and Lystra, are mentioned in the travels of St. Paul, Acts xiv, 6. The Lycaonians spoke a peculiar dialect, which some regard as corrupted from the Greek.

LYCIA, (*Lish'e-a,*) a province on the south-west coast of Asia Minor. Of its cities, only *Patara* and *Myra* are mentioned in the New Testament..

LYDDA, a large village, about twelve or fourteen miles from Joppa, toward Jerusalem, Acts ix, 32.

LYSTRA, a city in the southern part of Lycaonia, in Asia Minor, now called *Latik*. The apostle speaks of his persecutions in this city as known to Timothy, who was a native of the place, 2 Tim. iii, 10, 11; he might have been present on ·that occasion, and one of those who stood round about him when *he revived*, Acts xiv, 20.

MA'ACHA, called sometimes *Beth Ma'acha*, a city and region at the foot of Mount Hermon, north-east of the sources of the Jordan, not far from Geshur, a district of Syria, 2 Sam. x, 6–8.

MACEDONIA, Acts xvi, 9, a country lying north of Greece proper; bounded on the north by Moesia; on the east by Thrace and the Egean Sea; on the south by Thessaly and Epirus; and on the west by the Adriatic and Illyria. It was the original kingdom of Philip, and Alexander the Great, and was afterward subdued by the Romans, who divided the country into four districts, (see THESSALONICA;) and afterward they divided the whole of Greece into two great provinces, Macedonia and Achaia. Macedonia continued a Roman province for nearly 600 years, when it was conquered by the Turks, and is still subject to them.

Among its chief cities were Philippi and Thessalonica.

MADIAN, the same as *Midian*.

MAD, to be *furious, raging;* this epithet is applied, 1. To those who are insane or deprived of reason, Acts xxvi, 24. 2. To persons who so speak and act, as to seem to others to be out of their senses, John x, 20; Acts xii, 15. 3. To those whose reason is depraved and overruled by angry passions, Acts xxvi, 11.

Sinners are *mad*, because they are not under the influence of reason and conscience. "They *madly* trust in idols," Jer. l, 38; David's *madness*, 1 Sam. xxi, 13, 14, is, by many, supposed not to have been *feigned*, but real epilepsy, or falling sickness. It is urged in support of this opinion, that the troubles which David underwent, might very naturally weaken his constitutional strength; and that the force he suffered in being obliged to seek shelter in a foreign court, would disturb his imagination in the highest degree.

MAG, *Magus*, pl.. *Magi;* the name for priests and wise men among the Medes, Persians, and Babylonians. *Rab-mag*, Jer. xxxix, 3; Prince Magus, chief of the magi. See WISE MEN.

MAG'DALA, a place on the western shore of the Lake of Gennesaret, south of Capernaum, and a few miles north of Tiberias, near Dal-

18

manutha. Burckhardt found here a miserable village, still called *El Madjdel*, Matt. xv, 39.

MAGICIAN, one skilled in the science of magic, and who uses sorcery, enchantment, and the secret operations of natural causes; and *pretends*, in consequence of them, to exert supernatural powers. As early as the time of Joseph, there appeared in Egypt persons of this description; a class of Egyptian priests, skilled in the sacred writing, or hieroglyph'ics. We find that these persons were held in much honour as interpreters of dreams, Gen. xli, 8; and, in the history of Moses, we find them making *attempts* at miracles, Exod. vii, 11–18. Two of these workers of miracles the Jews agree in calling Jannes and Jambres, 2 Tim. iii, 8.

MAGOG, a son of Japheth, Gen. x, 2; also the name of a region, and of a great and powerful people; perhaps an assembly of nations, dwelling in the extreme recesses of the north, who are to invade the Holy Land at a future time, Ezek. xxxviii, 39. Nearly the same people seem to be intended as were comprehended by the Greeks under the name of *Scythians*. Their king is called *Gog*.

MAHALATH, supposed by some to be the name of a wind instrument of music, similar to the flute. Gesenius says, *a stringed instrument*. Occurs in the title of the Psalms liii and lxxxviii.

MA-HA-NA'IM, *hosts;* (according to Gen. xxxii, 2, camps, or hosts of angels;) a town beyond Jordan, on the confines of the tribes of Gad and Manasseh, near the brook Jabbok, afterward assigned to the Levites, 2 Sam. ii, 29.

MAHER, a word which occurs in the name given to one of the sons of the Prophet Isaiah, by way of prediction, Isa. viii, 3. MAHER-SHALLEL-HESH-BAZ, *haste to the spoil, quick to the prey.* The prophet observes, that his children were for signs and wonders, and that this name was evidence of the fact.

MAIMED, implies the loss of a limb or member—*crippled*, especially in the hands, Matt. xviii, 8.

MALACHI, the last prophet of the Old Testament, who prophesied about 400 years before Christ, while Nehemiah was governor of Judea, after his second coming from the Persian court. He was also contemporary with *Socrates*, the most celebrated philosopher of antiquity.

MALICE, ill-will in the mind, a wicked desire or intention of doing harm to others in a fraudulent and deceitful manner.

MALLOWS, a plant very useful in medicine, from its emollient qualities. The plant referred to in Job xxx, 4, is supposed to be or'ach, or *sea purslain;* a marine plant, the leaves of which were eaten by the poor, both raw and boiled, as a substitute for spinage.

MAMMON, a Chaldee word, signifying *riches, wealth, property;* that in which one *trusts,* called "*Mammon* of unrighteousness," Luke xvi, 9, i. e., worldly riches, because they are often the instruments of sin, and are acquired too often by unrighteous means. By riches, we may make ourselves instrumental *in* blessing and saving sinners, and thereby secure their friendship, Luke xvi, 9.

MAMRE, an Amorite, who made a league with Abraham, Gen xiv, 3; also the name of a grove of oaks near Hebron, Gen. xxiii, 19.

MAN, the human race; sometimes only a *person,* an individual of the human race.

To speak after the manner of men, is to speak in accordance with human views, to illustrate by human examples or institutions, to use a popular mode of speaking, Rom. iii, 5.

"The inward *man,*" Rom. vii, 22, is the mind; the rational man, called the *hidden man of the heart,* to which is opposed the external visible man.

The old man, the former unrenewed disposition of heart; and *the new man* is the disposition which is created and cherished by the religion of Jesus, Eph. iv, 22–24. "Put on the new *man.*" The dispositions of the mind are in Scripture compared to clothes, for two reasons: 1. Because they render persons beautiful or ugly, according to their nature. 2. Because they may be put off or on at pleasure.

Man of God, is a minister or messenger of God; one devoted to his service.

"The *man* of sin," 2 Thess. ii, 3. Although in the singular number, and with the article prefixed, it may, according to the Scripture idiom, denote a multitude, and even a succession of persons arising one after another. The character of this man of sin is given in verse 4; the meaning of which is, that the wicked teachers of whom the apostle speaks, will first oppose Christ, by corrupting the doctrine of the Gospel concerning him; and, after that, they will make void the government of God and of Christ in the Christian Church, and the government of the civil magistrate in the state, by arrogating to themselves the whole spiritual authority which belongs to Christ, and all the temporal authority belonging to princes and magistrates.

MANAS'SEH, *who causes to forget.* See Gen. xli, 51.

1. The son of Joseph adopted by Jacob, Gen. xlviii, 1, born 1714 B. C. For the territories of the tribe of Manasseh, which were partly beyond and partly on this side the Jordan, see Josh. xiii, 29–32.

2. The fifteenth king of Judah, who reigned 699–644

years B. C., son of Hezekiah, and notorious for his idolatry, superstition, and cruelty toward the pious, 2 Kings xxi, 1-18.

MANDRAKE, a plant similar to the *Belladonna*, or deadly night-shade, with a root like a beet, which anciently was supposed to possess magical virtues; white and reddish blossoms, and with yellow fragrant apples, Song vii, 13, which ripen from May to July, Gen. xxx, 14; and which are called *poma amatoria*, or love apples. To these apples, the orientals to this day ascribe the power of exciting to love.

MANNA, the miraculous food of the Israelites in the desert. See Exod. xvi, 12-36. Josephus relates, that in his day, manna was still found around Mount Sinai; and the same fact has also been abundantly ascertained by modern travellers. The modern manna, *manna Arabica*, differing some from *common manna*, is a sweet resin, similar to honey, consisting wholly of mucilaginous sugar, which in the desert of Sinai, and some other oriental regions, exudes in summer before sunrise, chiefly from the leaves of the *tamarisk*, or *tarfa*. This the Arabs collect, and regard it as the greatest dainty which their country affords. But the quantity is very trifling, not amounting, according to Burckhardt, to more than five or six hundred pounds each year. It has been ascertain-ed, within the last ten or twelve years, first by English naturalists, and more fully by Ehrenberg, that the manna flows out from the leaf in consequence of the puncture of an insect nearly allied to the *Cimex* genus. That this vegetable manna, however, could not have been the manna of the Israelites, is sufficiently obvious; unless we regard it as having been miraculously increased — a supposition which involves as great an exertion of miraculous power as the direct bestowment of a different substance. See Num. xi, 8. It is very likely that nothing of the kind had ever been seen before, Deut. viii, 3, 16; and by a pot of it being laid up in the ark, nothing of the kind ever appeared after the miraculous supply had ceased. It was called "bread of heaven," and "food of angels," perhaps as intimating its superior quality, Psa. lxxxviii, 24, 25.

"The hidden *manna*," Rev. ii, 17, is the full enjoyment of the kingdom of heaven. Some suppose this alludes to the pot of manna, which was laid up in the ark of the covenant in the holy of holies; others, to the Jewish tradition, that the ark with the pot of manna was hidden by order of King Josiah, and will again be brought to light in the reign of the Messiah.

MAN-SLAYER, one that has taken away the life of a human being, either accidentally or wilfully.

Covel's Dic., p. 277.

MANDRAKE.

MAN-STEALER, a kidnapper; one who steals men to make them slaves, or to sell them into slavery, Deut. xxiv, 7. They who make war for the inhuman purpose of selling the vanquished as slaves, as is the practice of the African princes, are really *man-stealers*. And they who, like the African traders, encourage that unchristian traffic, by purchasing the slaves whom they know to be thus unjustly acquired, are partakers in their crime.

MAON, a town in the tribe of Judah near the south Carmel, west of the Dead Sea, 1 Sam. xxiii, 24, 25; and xxv, 2. But in Judges x, 12, mention is made of an Arabian tribe, called *Maonites*. In 2 Chron. xxvi, 7, they are again mentioned as the *Mahunims*, joined with the Arabians properly so called. As a trace of this ancient people, we may probably regard the city of *Maon*, situated eastward from Wady Mousa, and not far from *Mount Hor*, on the great route of the Syrian caravans.

MARAH, *bitterness*; a bitter or brackish fountain or well, in the peninsula of Sinai, Exod. xv, 22, 23. Most probably, as Burckhardt supposes, the same which is now called *Bir Howara*, on the western gulf of the Red Sea, about fifty-six miles southeast of Suez. The water of this Bir or well is so bitter, (perhaps containing Epsom salts, the sulphate of mag-

nesia,) that men cannot drink it; and even camels, if not very thirsty, refuse to taste it. There is no other road of three days' march in the way from Suez to Sinai, nor is there any other well absolutely bitter on the whole of this coast. In moving with a whole nation, the march may well be supposed to have occupied three days.

MARANATHA, *Aramæan*, *the Lord will come*, viz. to judgment; a form of threatening, cursing, or anathematizing among the Jews. "May the Lord come quickly to take vengeance of thy crimes," 1 Cor. xvi, 22. See ACCURSED.

MARBLE, carbonate of lime; a valuable kind of limestone, of a texture so hard and compact, and of a grain so fine, as readily to take a beautiful polish. It is dug out of quarries in large masses, and is much used in buildings. Marble is of different colours, black, white, &c.; and is sometimes elegantly clouded and variegated.

MARK, whose Hebrew name was John; the writer of one of the four gospels, the son of a certain Mary, at whose house the apostles and first Christians often assembled, Acts xii, 12; the nephew of Barnabas, Col. iv, 10; the companion of Paul and Barnabas on their first journey, and of Barnabas on his second, in opposition to Paul, Acts xv, 39. At a later period, however, we find him again in Paul's company, 2 Tim. iv, 11. According to the fathers, he was also for a considerable time closely connected with Peter, and was interpreter to him when he preached among the Greeks. Though not an apostle, he did not write without apostolic authority. On the contrary, he was under the direction of the Apostle Peter, who affectionately called him his son, 1 Pet. v, 13. This is stated by the entire series of church fathers, during the second and third centuries, with perfect unanimity in the main; and the statement is corroborated by the case of Luke, which was exactly similar. On this account, the gospel of Mark was considered as originating with Peter; and such individuals as were particularly attached to this apostle, used Mark in preference to all others. He wrote his gospel, according to Horne, between the years 60 and 63, at the city of Rome, which was then the capital of the known world. Quotations from the ancient prophets, and allusions to Jewish customs, are as much as possible avoided; and such explanations are added as might be necessary for Gentile readers at Rome; thus, when Jordan is first mentioned in this gospel, the word *river* is prefixed, Mark i, 5; the oriental word *corban* is said to mean a gift, Mark vii, 11; *the preparation* is said to be the day before the Sab-

bath, Mark xv, 42; and defiled hands are said to mean unwashed hands, Mark vii, 2; and the superstition of the Jews upon that subject is stated more at large than it would have been by a person writing at Jerusalem.

MARK, a brand, as pricked or burned in upon the body. The slaves were branded with a hot iron, not only as a punishment for their offences, but to distinguish them in case they should run away. Soldiers were branded in the hand, but slaves in the forehead. In the same manner, it was customary to mark the votaries of some of the gods. Hence the beast, Rev. xiii, 1, had upon its head the name of *blasphemy*; and the worshippers of the beast, verse 16, had a "mark on their right hand," or "on their foreheads," whereby they were known to be their worshippers. In like manner, the servants of God have "his name on their foreheads," Rev. xxii, 4. The apostle, in allusion to these customs, calls the scars of the wounds which he received when stoned and left as dead on the street of Lystra, "the *marks* of the Lord Jesus in his body," Gal. vi, 17.

MARKET, a public place, or broad street in a city or town, where provisions and other things were exposed for sale. Among the ancients, markets were places of public resort, where assemblies and public trials were held.

The labourers who wanted employment were found in the market-place, Matt. xx, 3. See Acts xvi, 19; and xvii, 17.

MARRIAGE. This was regarded by the Jews as a sacred obligation, and celibacy was accounted a great reproach. No formalities appear to have been used by the Jews, at least none were enjoined upon them by Moses. In joining man and wife together, mutual consent followed by consummation was deemed sufficient. The manner in which a daughter was demanded in marriage is described in the case of Shechem, who asked Dinah, the daughter of Jacob, in marriage, Gen. xxiv, 6–12. There was indeed a previous espousal or betrothing, which was a solemn promise of marriage made by the man and woman each to the other, at such a distance of time as they agreed upon, Deut. xx, 7. Among the Jews, and generally throughout the East, marriage was considered a sort of purchase, which the man made of the woman he desired to marry. The nuptial solemnity continued seven days, Judges xiv, 12, and was celebrated with great festivity and splendour. The parable of the ten virgins in Matt. xxv, gives a good idea of the customs practised on these occasions. The happiness of the Messiah's kingdom is represented under the figure of a nuptial feast, Rev. xix, 7.

The public use of marriage institutions consists, according to Archdeacon Paley, in their promoting the following beneficial effects:—1. The private comfort of individuals. 2. The production of the greatest number of healthy children, their better education, and the making of due provision for their settlement in life. 3. The peace of human society, in cutting off a principal source of contention, by assigning one or more women to one man, and protecting his exclusive right by sanctions of morality and law. 4. The better government of society, by distributing the community into separate families, and appointing over each the authority of a master of a family, which has more actual influence than all civil authority put together. 5. The additional security which the state receives for the good behaviour of its citizens, from the solicitude they feel for the welfare of their children, and from their being confined to permanent habitations. 6. The encouragement of industry. See DIVORCE and BRIDE.

MARROW, an oily inflammable substance, which, during life, is a fluid of a whitish or yellowish colour, filling the cavity of the bones, to moisten and render them less liable to break, Job xxi, 24; and figuratively put for the richest and best part of a thing, Isa. xxv, 6.

MAR'S HILL, or *Hill of*

Mars, a hill in Athens, with an open place, where sat the court of the Areopagus, the supreme tribunal of justice, instituted by Solon, one of the seven wise men of Greece, who died 558 B. C. So called, because justice was said to have been pronounced there against *Mars*, the fabulous god of war. Our translators have entirely spoiled the narrative of the historian in Acts xvii, 19, 22, as *Mar's Hill* is *A-re-op'a-gus* translated; and as both signify the same place, the same rendering ought to have been preserved in both verses. See A-RE-OP'A-GUS.

MART, a place of sale or traffic.

MARTYR, *witness*, one who by his death bears witness to the truth, Acts xxii, 20.

MARY, the name of several females mentioned in Scripture. 1. The mother of Jesus. 2. Of Magdala, Luke viii, 2. The general impression that she was an unchaste woman, is entirely without foundation. She was probably in good circumstances, and of unblemished character. 3. The mother of James the Less and Joses, sister to our Lord's mother, and wife of Alpheus or Cleophas, John xix, 25. 4. A sister of Lazarus and Martha. 5. Mother of John, surnamed Mark, Acts xii, 12. 6. And a Christian female at Rome, Rom. xvi, 6.

MASCHIL, (*Mas-kil*,) a participle in Hebrew, signify-ing *he that instructs*, occurs as the title of thirteen Psalms, where it means a *song, poem.* The origin of this use of the word is uncertain; the most probable opinion is, that the word means an *instructive* song; but this does not accord with the character of all the Psalms which are thus designated. It is therefore supposed that this specific word came afterward to be applied to other and different kinds of song than those which are instructive. Gesenius says, that in Arabic, *instruction* is used for poetry in general.

MASON, a man whose occupation is to lay bricks and stones. From the history of the temple, and the ruins of Tadmor and Persep'olis and other places, it appears that the art was in as great perfection in ancient days as at present. The most noted were the masons of Tyre, 2 Sam. v, 11.

MATTHEW, the author of the gospel; he bore also the name of Levi, Matt. ix, 9; Mark ii, 14; the son of a certain Alpheus, of whom we know nothing farther. Of the history of Matthew very little is known in addition to the accounts in the New Testament. After our Saviour called him from his station as receiver of customs, he followed him with fidelity, and was one of the twelve whom Jesus sent forth. His labours as an apostle, however, seem to have been wholly confined to Palestine. The time when his gospel was written is quite uncertain. The most probable opinion is, that it was written in Judea for the benefit of the Hebrew Christians, about A. D. 37.

MAZ'ZA-ROTH denotes the *twelve signs of the zodiac*, a broad circle in the heavens, comprehending all such stars as lie in the path of the sun and moon.

MEAS'URE, that by which any thing is measured, or adjusted, or proportioned, Prov. xx, 10; Micah vi, 10. Tables of Scripture measures of length and capacity are found at the end of this volume.

MEAT does not mean *flesh* only, which is the usual acceptation of the word, but food in general, or whatever is eaten for nourishment. *Solid food* of flesh or vegetables, 1 Cor. iii, 2. *Meat-offering* is always a vegetable and never an animal offering. It might now be rendered *meal-offering*. The burnt and peace-offerings which were made of animals fit for food, and on which the offerers feasted in the court of the tabernacle, is called *meat*, Heb. xiii, 9. So likewise when the heathen offered sacrifices of such animals as were fit for food, a part of the carcass was burnt on the altar, a part was given to the priest, and on the remainder the offerers feasted with their friends, either in the idol's temple or at home. Sometimes, also, a part was sent as a present to such as they wished to oblige; and if the sacrifice was large, a part of it was sold in the public market. To these idolatrous feasts the heathens often invited the Christians of their acquaintances in Corinth; and some of the brethren there, desirous of preserving the friendship of their neighbours, accepted these invitations. They knew an idol was nothing in the world; and therefore their partaking of the sacrifice, even in the idol's temple, could not be reckoned a worship of the idol. See 1 Cor. viii, 8–13.

The word *meat* is used metaphorically for *sustenance, nourishment*. My *meat*, John iv, 34, i. e., that by which I live, in which I delight. The spiritual *meat*, 1 Cor. x, 3, is the *manna* as an emblem of spiritual nourishment or instruction, and given in a miraculous manner.

MEDE, an inhabitant of Media. "Darius the *Median*," Dan. v, 31. This was Cyaxares II., the son and successor of Astyages, and uncle of Cyrus, who held the empire of Media between Astyages and Cyrus 569–536 B. C., yet so, that Cyrus was his *colleague* and *viceroy*, and with whom he was associated in the taking of Babylon.

MEDIA, a country east of Assyria, lying between the Caspian Sea on the north, and Persia on the south, extending on the north and west to Armenia. It was incorporated with the kingdom of

Persia; hence the annals of the Medes and Persians are mentioned together, Esther x, 2, and comprised the following provinces of modern Persia, Shirvan, Adserbijan, Ghilan, Masanderan, and Irak Adjami. It covered a territory larger than that of Spain, lying between 30 and 40 degrees of north latitude, and was one of the most fertile and earliest cultivated among the kingdoms of Asia. Among the magi, the priests of their religion, is reckoned Zoroaster, as a reformer, or rather as the restorer of the ancient religion of light, who rendered himself famous by his deep and acute researches in philosophy, and whose disciples have maintained themselves in Persia and Judea even to the present day. The ancient metropolis of Media was Ec-bat'ana, Ezra vi, 2; the summer residence of the Persian kings, situated on the spot afterward and now occupied by Hamedan, the chief city of the Parthians. Into this country the ten tribes, who composed the kingdom of Israel, were transplanted in the captivity.

MEDIATOR, one who intervenes between two parties. 1. As an interpreter, a mere medium of communication, as, e. g., Moses, Gal. iii, 19, 20. 2. As a *reconciler*, intercessor. This Mediator is the man Christ Jesus, 1 Tim. ii, 5, who is appointed by God to make atonement for the sins of men by his death, and who, in consequence of that atonement, is authorized to intercede with God in behalf of sinners, and empowered to convey all his blessings to them. In this sense, there is but one mediator between God and man, and he is equally related to all. He is called, Heb. ix, 15, "the *mediator* of the new testament or covenant," i. e., the Gospel dispensation; the Divine promises conditioned on obedience. 1. "Because," says Macknight, "he procured this new covenant for mankind, in which the pardon of sin is promised; for, as the apostle tells us, his death, as the sacrifice for sin, is the consideration on account of which the pardon of the transgressions of the first covenant is granted. 2. Because of the new covenant having been *ratified* or confirmed, Heb. vi, 17, as well as procured, by the death of Christ, he is fitly called the *mediator* of that covenant. 3. Jesus, who died to procure the new covenant, being appointed by God the high priest thereof, to *dispense its. blessings*, he is on that account also called, Heb. viii, 6, 'the *mediator* of that better covenant.'"

"The inspired writers," says Mr. Watson, "declare that there was an efficacy in what he did and suffered for us beyond mere instruction and example. This they declare with great variety of expression: that 'he suffered for sins, the just for the unjust,' 1 Pet. iii, 18 ; that 'he gave his life a *ransom*,' Matt. xx, 28 ; Mark x, 45 ; 1 Tim. ii, 6 ; that 'we were bought with a price,' 2 Pet. ii, 1 ; Rev. xiv, 4 ; 1 Cor. vi, 20 ; that 'he redeemed us with his blood,' 'redeemed us from the curse of the law, being made a curse for us,' 1 Pet. i, 19 ; Rev. v, 9 ; Gal. iii, 13 ; that 'he is our advocate, intercessor, and propitiation,' Heb. vii, 25 ; 1 John ii, 1, 2 ; that 'he was made perfect through sufferings ; and being thus made perfect, he became the *author* of salvation,' Heb. ii, 10 ; v, 9 ; that 'God was in Christ, reconciling the world to himself, not imputing their trespasses unto them,' 2 Cor. v, 19 ; Rom. v, 10 ; Eph. ii, 16 ; and that 'through death he destroyed him that had the power of death,' Heb. ii, 14. Christ, then, having 'thus humbled himself, and become obedient to death, even the death of the cross ; God, also, hath highly exalted him, and given him a name which is above every name ;' hath commanded us to pray in his name ; constituted him man's advocate and intercessor ; distributes his grace only through him, and in honour of his death ; hath given all things into his hands ; and hath committed all judgment unto him ; 'that at the name of Jesus every knee should bow,' and 'that all men should honour the Son even as they honour the Father,'

Phil. ii, 8–10 ; John iii, 35 ; v, 22, 23."

MEDITATE, to think closely and seriously on any thing, Psa. i, 2.

MEEKNESS, a calm, serene temper of mind, not easily ruffled or provoked ; a disposition that suffers injuries without desire of revenge ; implies the absence of all irascible and malignant passions, and is the fruit of regenerating grace. "*Meekness* of wisdom," James iii, 3 ; a beautiful expression, insinuating that true wisdom is always accompanied with meekness or the government of the passions. "The meekness of wisdom," and the "beauty of holiness," are expressions of the same kind, formed to represent the excellency of these qualities.

MEGIDDO, a fortified city of Manasseh, situated within the borders of the tribe of Issachar, pretty well ascertained to be in the western or south-western part of the great plain of Esdralon, and formerly a royal city of the Canaanites. Here a famous battle was fought between Nech'o and King Josiah, in which the latter was defeated and mortally wounded. See 2 Kings xxiii, 39. "The waters of *Megiddo*," Judges v, 19, is the brook of Kishon.

MELCHIZEDEK, *righteous king* ; a king of Salem, which is the ancient name of Jerusalem, Psa. lxxvi, 2 ; and a patriarchal priest of the true God, cotemporary with

Abraham, Gen. xiv, 18–20. It was common among the ancients for the king to be priest also; thus uniting the two highest honours among men in his own person. The Jewish kings did not do thus so long as the race of David was upon the throne, because the priesthood was confined to the tribe of Levi. But the Maccabees did it. Among foreign nations this was very common. In reference to this double honour, Peter calls Christians *a royal priesthood,* 1 Pet. ii, 9; and John in Rev. i, 6, says, that Christ has made his followers *kings and priests,* i. e., he has prepared for them a *kingdom,* and constituted them *priests unto God.* It is said, Heb. vii, 6, that "*Melchizedek's* descent is not counted;" because, being a Canaanite, and not standing in the public genealogical registers, as belonging to the family of Aaron, he was a priest, not by right of sacerdotal descent, but by the grace of God. In the same sense, he was said to be *without father and mother,* i. e., recorded in the sacred genealogies; or, perhaps, whose father and mother were not of the kingly or priestly rank. His priesthood, therefore, is of a higher and more ancient order than that of Aaron. *Having neither beginning of days nor end of life,* i. e., whose time of birth or death is not related, or rather who, as high priest, has no limited time assigned for the commencement and expiration of his office.

ME-LI'TA, now called *Mal'ta,* an island in the Mediterranean, between Africa and Sicily, twenty miles in length and twelve in breadth, formerly reckoned a part of Africa, but now belonging to Europe.

There was another small island of the same name in the Asiatic *Gulf,* on the coast of Illyricum, now called *Mileda,* which some have thought to be the place of St. Paul's shipwreck; but its position does not accord with the account of the subsequent voyage to Puteoli; nor can we well suppose a vessel bound from Alexandria to Puteoli to have wintered in this island, Acts xxviii, 11.

MELODY, a succession of sounds so regulated and modulated as to please the ear. Melody differs from *harmony,* as it consists in the agreeable succession and modulation of sounds by a single voice; whereas *harmony* consists in the accordance of different voices or sounds. *To make melody in the heart,* is to praise God with a thankful and joyful disposition, ascribing to him the honour due to his name, Eph. v, 19. See Amos v, 23.

MELON, Num. xi, 5, supposed to be the *water melon,* which is cultivated on the banks of the Nile. This fruit is eaten in abundance during the season, even by the richer sort of people; but the com-

A CARAVAN

Caravan is an Arabic word meaning *a company of men travelling together* either as merchants or pilgrims. It is also used in *Persia* with the same sense, and applies more particularly to journeys made in Arabia, Nubia, Syria, and Persia. The proportion of horses and other animals observed in the large caravans is as follows: when there are five hundred elephants, they add one thousand dromedaries, and two thousand horses: and the escort is composed of four thousand men on horseback. The Syrian caravan, as it is called, has been the most numerous and the best regulated: according to Burckhardt, who saw it at Mecca in 1814, it consisted of more than fifteen thousand camels. They generally travel well armed, to defend themselves from the attacks of the wandering Arabs, and other robbers.

mon people, on whom Providence has bestowed nothing but poverty and patience, scarcely eat any thing else, and account *this* season the best time in the year. The juice of the fruit serving them for drink, they have therefore less occasion for water. This explains the Israelites regretting the want of the melon in the barren *parched* wilderness.

MEM'PHIS, a city of Egypt, Hos. ix, 6; elsewhere called *Noph*, Isa. xix, 13, whose ruins, though of small extent, are found on the west bank of the Nile, about fifteen miles south of old Cairo, near which are the celebrated pyramids.

MENE, *numbered*. At a feast which Belshazzar gave to his courtiers, where he profaned the sacred vessels of the Lord's house, there appeared on the wall a form like a hand writing these words: "*Mene, mene, tekel, upharsin,* Dan. v. 25,—all passive participles in the Chaldean language; *u* in the last word is the copulative conjunction *and*, and *in* the plural termination. The sentence signifies *numbered, weighed, and divided,* and is supposed to have been written in the *old Hebrew* character, which we now call the *Samaritan,* and which the Chaldeans could not read, verse 8. But had they possessed the power to read these words, they would not have been able to ascertain their pro-

phetic import. But Daniel explained this ill-boding inscription to the king.

MERCHANT, a trader; one who trades to foreign countries by sea or land on a large scale; a wholesale dealer. Merchants in the East transported their goods upon camels, animals which are patient of thirst and fatigue, and easily supported in the deserts. As all the great spaces between towns in the eastern countries are infested with Arabs or banditti, who frequently commit robbery and murder, merchants are accustomed to associate together in companies, more or less numerous, according to the nature of the ease, sometimes to the number of 2,000, for the purpose of mutual convenience and protection. A company of this kind is called a *caravan. The troops of Tema,* Job vi, 19, are travelling merchants or caravans; so also was the *company of Ishmaelites which came from Gilead, going down into Egypt,* Gen. xxxvii, 25. Our Saviour went with such a company to Jerusalem, Luke ii, 44. Every caravan had a leader to conduct it through the desert, who was acquainted with the direction of the route, and with the cisterns and fountains. (See the *engraving*.) These he was able to ascertain, sometimes from heaps of stones, Jer. xxxi, 21; sometimes by the character of the soil; and, when other helps failed him,

19

by the stars, Num. x, 29–32. A cloud in the form of a pillar answered all these purposes for the Israelites when wandering in the wilderness.

MERCURIUS, *a false god* in heathen mythology; the son of Jupiter and Maia; the messenger of the gods; the patron of eloquence, learning, and traffic, Acts xiv, 12.

MERCY, active pity, as referring to the afflicted, or to a person in unhappy circumstances. It implies not merely a feeling of the evils of others, which we call *sympathy*, but also an active desire of removing them. *The mercy of God* includes blessings of every kind. *To remember mercy* is to give a new proof of mercy and favour to Israel, in allusion to God's ancient mercies to that people, Psa. xxv, 6. The expression, "I will have *mercy* and not sacrifice," Matt. xi, 13, signifies, as its connection indicates, that God is pleased with the exercise of mercy rather than with the offering of sacrifices: though sin has made the latter necessary.

MERCY SEAT. The lid or cover of the ark, which was pure gold, Exod. xxv, 17, 21. It had two cherubs of gold placed at each end, stretching their wings toward each other. The high priest was accustomed once a year to sprinkle upon this the blood of an expiatory victim. It was over this that the Divine glory was seen, i. e., a supernatural excessive brightness; and hence God was supposed to be seated on it as his throne, and from it to dispense his mercy when atonement was made for the sins of the people by sprinkling it with blood.

MERIBAH, *strife.* This was a fountain flowing from the rock in the desert of Sin, on the western gulf of the Red Sea, Exod. xvii, 7. Dr. Shaw feels confident that he has discovered this extraordinary *rock* west of Sinai, in *Rephidim*, a block of granite marble, about six yards square, lying tottering, as it were, and loose in the middle of the valley, and seems to have formerly belonged to Mount Sinai, which hangs in a variety of precipices all over this plain. Moses smote the rock, and the water came forth in such abundance as to form a brook; and this is said to have been *like a river*, Psa. lxxviii, 16; cv, 41. Accordingly the river from the rock followed them, 1 Cor. x, 4. As Horeb was a high mountain, there may have been a descent to the sea; and the Israelites during the thirty-seven years of their journeying from Mount Sinai, may have gone by those tracts of country in which the waters from Horeb *could follow them*, till in the thirty-ninth year of the exodus they came to Ezion Geber, Num. xxxiii, 36; but in the fortieth year of the exodus, leaving that place to go into Canaan, by the east

THE EASTERN COUNTRIES, as mentioned by MOSES.

BLACK SEA

ASIA MINOR

ARMENIA

CAPPADOCIA

CILICIA

Tarsus

Mt. Mesha

Mt. Ararat

Pison R.

Gihon R.

Tigris R.

Havila

Hadebsab or Chebarus R.

GREAT SEA

Cyprus

SYRIA

ARAM or of Padan Aram

ARAM of or Palmyra

Hamath

Tiphsah

Antioch

Rehoboth

Arvad

Pethor

Damascus

Kenath

CANAAN

JERUSALEM

EGYPT

Mouth of the Nile

Longitude East 40 from London

Scale of Miles

ASSYRIA

Mt. Rezeph of Mount Latmos

NINEVEH or Ur

Phraortis

ELLASAR

BABYLON or BABEL

CHALDEA

SHINAR

Rehoboth R.

Pethor

MEDIA

Halach R.

Habor

Haran R. Habor

Ecbatana

PERSIA

Shushan Cuthah or Cutha

ELAM of or NOD

Ulai

Land of Nod

Persian Gulf

CASPIAN SEA

EGYPT

border of Edom; they no sooner entered the desert, which is *Kadesh*, than they were distressed a second time; water was brought from a rock in the wilderness of Zin, which was their thirty-third station. See Num. xx, 1–13. This was also called *Meribah*.

MEREDOCK, an idol of the Babylonians, probably the planet *Mars*, to which, as the god of blood and slaughter, as well as to Saturn, the ancient Semitic nations offered human sacrifices.

MEROM, Josh. xi, 5, a lake or marsh at the foot of Mount Lebanon, in a high region of country, through which the Jordan flows. In summer, this lake for the most part is dry, and covered with shrubs and grass; but in the spring, when the water is highest, it is about seven miles long, and three and a half broad.

MEROZ. Of the history or site of this city there is no trace whatever; we may suppose it to have lain in the territories of Issachar, or Napthali, in the neighbourhood of the *Kishon;* and its inhabitants were cursed for after having an opportunity to destroy the flying Caananites, they neglected to improve it, Judges v, 23.

MESHECK, i. e., the *Moschi*, a barbarous people inhabiting the Moschian mountains between Iberia, Armenia, and Colchis, Psa. cxx, 5, usually coupled with the neighbouring Tubal, Ezek. xxxviii, 2, 3; xxxix, 1.

MESHA is supposed to be the region around Bassora, between Selucia and the Persian Gulf, Gen. x, 30. The opposite coast is probably the western part of Yemen, along the Eastern Gulf of the Red Sea. The range of high and mountainous country between these borders, Moses calls *a mount of the east*, or eastern mountains, in reference either to Palestine or to Yemen, i. e., Sephar.

MES-O-PO-TA′MI-A, *between the rivers.* The fertile tract of country lying between the rivers Euphrates and Tigris, from near their sources to the vicinity of Babylon, Acts vii, 2, and celebrated in Scripture as the first dwelling of men after the deluge. The Hebrew name was *Padan-aran*, Gen. xxviii, 2; it now belongs to the Turkish dominion, comprised in the modern Persia under the name of *El Djezirat*, i. e., the peninsula.

MESSIAH, *the Anointed;* a Hebrew word of the same signification as the Greek word *Christ;* spoken of the Jewish high priest, Lev. iv, 16. The *Lord's anointed*, (in the Hebrew Messiah,) a name of honour given to the Jewish kings, as being consecrated by anointing, and therefore most holy. But the word most eminently denotes THE CHRIST, the Saviour of mankind, Dan. ix, 25, 26; that prince who was anointed, not with material, but with mystical oil; the graces and influences of the Holy Spirit, which were poured out without measure upon him, John iii, 34, i. e., was not measured and occasional like that of prophets and apostles, but ever abundant and constant. The Jews expected the Messiah would be their deliverer from civil bondage, and raise them as a nation to great power. Hence they rejected the meek and lowly Jesus, and put him to shame and death. They were disappointed and offended, because his kingdom was not of this world, and promised no privileges to them in distinction from the Gentiles. The whole Scriptures abound with evidence that they were and are under a gross delusion; and the Christian church is looking with deep interest for the time when the veil shall be taken from their eyes; when they shall look on Him whom they have pierced, and mourn; and when they shall receive him as the long-promised and long-expected Messiah.

ME-THU'SE-LAH, a patriarch before the flood, and grandfather of Noah, Gen. v, 21. He was born A. M. 687, and died A. M. 1656, being the very year of the deluge, at the age of 969, the greatest age to which any mortal man ever attained.

MICAH, the sixth among the twelve minor prophets, and who is supposed to have lived about 750 B. C. He was commissioned to denounce the judgments of God against both the kingdoms of Judah and Israel for their idolatry and wickedness. The style of Micah is nervous, concise, and elegant, often elevated and poetical, but sometimes obscure from sudden transitions of subject.

The prophecy contained in the fifth chapter, is, perhaps, the most important single prophecy in all the Old Testament, and the most comprehensive respecting the personal character of the Messiah, and his successive manifestations to the world. It carefully distinguishes his human nativity from his Divine nature and eternal existence; foretells the casting off the Israelites and Jews for a season; their ultimate restoration; and the universal peace which should prevail in the kingdom and under the government of the Messiah.

MICHAEL, *who as God!* There are said to be seven archangels, i. e., chief angels Rev. viii, 2, who stand immediately before the throne of God, Luke i, 19, and who have authority over other angels, Rev. xii, 7. *Michael* is one of the number, and the patron of the Jewish nation before God, Dan. x, 13; xii, 1. "By the body of Moses," Jude 9, about which the devil disputed with Michael, we may understand his *dead body*, which he contended should be buried publicly on pretence of doing honour to Moses; but his intention was to give the Israelites an opportunity of raising his body and worshipping it. But Michael, knowing his intention, rebuked the devil in the words mentioned by Jude; and to prevent the Israelites from committing idolatry, buried Moses' body so privately that none of the Israelites ever knew where his sepulchre was.

MICHTAM occurs in the title of several psalms. The most probable sense of the word is *inscription:* perhaps what might be inscribed a *triumphal song.* But whether it is intended to designate the *music* or the *subject* of it no one can tell with certainty; yet from the fact that all the psalms, six in number, which bear this title, (Psa. vi, lvi–lx,) are, in one form or another, *psalms of victory,* or triumphal songs, we may regard it as designed to show that such is the subject matter of the psalms.

MIDDLE WALL, spoken in a figure of the *Mosaic law,* as separating the Jews and Gentiles, and making the Jews exclusively the people of God, Eph. ii, 14, probably in allusion to the wall between the inner and outer courts of the temple, Rev. xi, 1, 2. The apostle observes, that God has broken down the wall; hath abolished the law which could be performed nowhere but in the temple of Jerusalem, and that by prescribing under the Gospel a spiritual form of worship, which may be performed everywhere, he hath joined Jews and Gentiles in one Church, and made them all one people of God. Now this happy union could not have taken place if the law of Moses had been continued. For the most important acts of the worship of God being limited to the temple at Jerusalem, the greatest part of the Gentiles could not come thither to worship with the Jews.

MIDIAN, an Arabian tribe descended from Abraham, Gen. xxv, 2, whose territories seem to have extended from the eastern shore of the Elanitic Gulf, where Josephus and the Arabian geographers place the town *Midyan,* to the region of Moab and to the vicinity of Mount Sinai, Exod. iii, 1; xviii, 5. Sometimes the Midianites appear to be reckoned among the Ishmaelites, Gen. xxxvii, 25, 36; but elsewhere they are distinguished from them. "The day of *Midian,*" Isa, ix, 4, is the victory gained over Midian; see Judges vii. "The curtains of *Midian,*" Hab. iii, 7. *Curtains* means the curtains of a *tent,* and sometimes used for the tent itself, Jer. xlix, 29; Song i, 5; and, figuratively, for the inhabitants of a place.

MIGDOL, *tower;* a place near the Red Sea, Exod. xiv, 2, which Stuart thinks is *Bir Suez,* (Beer Suez,) i. e., the well of *Suez*, about three miles west from the city. There is here a copious spring, strongly fortified in modern times, in order to secure the privilege of water for Suez. The water is brackish, but serves for drinking; if now we may suppose that this was a watering place 3400 years ago, and even then perhaps defended by a *tower*, it would correspond entirely to *Migdol*, between which and the sea the Israelites encamped. It is so assumed by Niebuhr, and he is followed by most critics; although it must be of course a matter of conjecture.

MILDEW, spots on cloth or paper, which are known to be plants similar to moss, whose seed and mode of propagation are not well ascertained. In the Bible, it signifies that disease in grain which causes it to turn yellow and wither away, Amos iv, 9; mildew is united with *blasting*. When grain has reached about a cubit in height, it is frequently so injured by cold winds and frost that it does not ear. This effect thus produced upon the grain is called *blasting*, Gen. xli, .

MILE, *a thousand*. The Roman *millaire*, or mile, contained 1000 paces, whence its name. It is usually estimated at 1611 yards, while the English mile contains 1760.

MILETUS, a maritime city in the southern part of Ionia, on the confines of Caria, a few miles south of the Meander, in Asia Minor. It was celebrated for a temple of Apollo, and as the birthplace of *Thales*, one of the seven wise men of Greece. A few ruins now mark its probable site near a village called *Palat*, Acts xx, 15, 17; 2 Tim. iv, 20.

MILK, a well known nourishing food, drawn principally from cows. It consists of three distinct parts, the *cream*, *curd*, and *whey*, into which, by repose, it spontaneously separates. Cream collects upon its surface, and by agitation, as in churning, the butter, which is an *animal oil*, is separated and brought into a solid form. During the process an acid is generated, which gives the buttermilk a sour taste. After the cream has separated, the milk soon becomes sour, and gradually forms into a solid *curd*, and a limpid fluid which is *whey*. This coagulation may be produced at pleasure, either by adding acid, or by means of *rennet*. *Butter* in the translation of Judges v, 25, as well as in most of the instances where the word occurs, is thought to be improper. The parallelism obviously requires that it should designate something *liquid*; perhaps *curdled milk*, as Gesenius has it, or *cream*. We know that sour or thick milk is a common or favourite beverage of the Arabs; and Niebuhr also informs us that they make use of *cream*, which they call *chei-*

Covel's Dic.   p. 296.

ANCIENT MODE OF GRINDING.

mak. There is, therefore, no strong objection to adopting either of these words in this place. *To suck the milk of nations* is a poetical expression, the same as to make their riches one's own, to get possession of their wealth, Isa. lx, 16. Milk is put as the emblem of pure spiritual nourishment, or of Christian instruction in general, 1 Pet. ii, 2; and for the *first elements* of Christian instruction, Heb. v, 12, 13. "A land flowing with *milk* and honey," Josh. v, 6, means a country of extraordinary fertility, affording every thing which is needed for the support and comfort of life. The phrase *wine and milk*, Isa. lv, 1, denotes all spiritual blessings and privileges.

MILLS. The mills used by the Hebrews are still common in the East. They were composed of two circular stones, two feet in diameter, and half a foot thick, of which the lower was fixed, and the upper was turned around upon it, having a hole in the middle for receiving the grain. The grinding was mostly done by hand, by female slaves, Exod. xi, 5; and though exceedingly laborious, was usually accompanied by song. This illustrates the prophetic observation of our Saviour, "Two women shall be grinding at the *mill*," Matt. xxiv, 41. "When the sound of the grinding is low," Eccl. xii, 4. This expression alludes to the noise by the hand mills in which the eastern nations daily grind their grain. See Jer. xxv, 10; Rev. xviii, 22. Job says, "Let my wife grind for another," Job xxxi, 10, i. e., be his mill-wench, his abject slave and *concubine.* See Isa. xlvii, 2. The necessity of baking bread every day in the warm climate of the East makes it necessary to grind daily at the mills; hence no man was allowed by the law to take the millstone as a pledge, Deut. xxiv, 6; for without his mill, there being no public ones, he would have been in a bad situation. Grain was frequently pounded also in a mortar, to which Solomon alludes, Prov. xxvii, 22.

MILLET, *a thousand;* a species of grain, of which several kinds are cultivated in Italy, Syria, and Egypt. It is used partly as green fodder and partly for the grain, which is of a dark tawny colour, and is employed for bread, pottage, &c. It is called *millet*, as if one stalk bore a thousand seeds, Ezek. iv, 9. Niebuhr informs us that there is a kind of millet used in the East, called *durra*, which, made into bread with camels' milk, butter, or grease, is almost the only food eaten by the common people in Arabia; but he says he found it so unpalatable that he would have preferred plain barley bread, which furnishes the reason of its being appointed as a part of the hard fare of Ezekiel.

MIL'LO, *rampart;* a part or suburb of Jerusalem; supposed to have been a deep valley which was filled up, and on which was a royal palace, built by Solomon, 2 Sam. v, 9; 2 Kings xii, 20.

MINISTER, an attendant, who serves under the direction of any one, as Joshua, Exod. xxiv, 13; John Mark, Acts xiii, 5. The minister of the synagogue was appointed to keep the book of the law, to observe that those who read it, read it correctly, &c., Luke iv, 20. Ministers were *servants,* not menial, but honourable; those who explain the word, and conduct the *service of God,* 1 Cor. iv, 1. The *holy angels* who, in obedience to the Divine commands, protect, and benefit the godly, are all ministers, beneficial ministers, to those who are under their charge, Psa. civ, 4.

MINNITH, a place east of Jordan, in the territory of the Ammonites, Judges xi, 33. From hence wheat was brought to the Tyrian market, Ezek. xxvii, 17.

MINSTREL, one who sings and plays on a musical instrument, 2 Kings iii, 15. The Hebrews hired women to weep and mourn, and also persons to play on instruments at their funerals. Persons in years, it is said, were carried to their graves by sound of trumpet, and younger people by the sound of flutes. In Matt. ix, 23, we observe a company of players on the flute at the funeral of a girl twelve years of age.

MINT, a well-known herb.

MIRACLE, *a wonder, prodigy;* an event or effect contrary to the established constitution or course of things, or a deviation from the known laws of nature, i. e., a supernatural event. Miracles can be wrought only by Almighty power, as when Christ healed lepers, saying, "*I will; be thou clean.*" No miracles are related in the Scripture to have been wrought, says Mr. Horne, in confirmation of falsehood; the magicians of Egypt did not perform any miracle. All they did, as the narrative of Moses expressly states, was to busy themselves in their enchantments; by which every man knows miracles cannot be accomplished. The witch of Endor neither wrought nor expected to work any miracle, being herself terrified at the appearance of Samuel, who was sent by God himself. The proper effect of miracles is to mark *clearly* the Divine interpositions; and the Scripture intimates this to be their design; for both Moses and the prophets, Christ and his apostles, appealed to them in proof of their Divine mission. The *variety* and *number* of Christ's miracles were very great. About forty are narrated at length; and one of the historians informs us that a much greater number were wrought, John xxi, 25, and their design was *important* and *worthy* of their author.

The following classification of our Saviour's miracles may be found convenient and useful :—

1. *Those which relate to human sustenance.*

Miracle.	Place.	Record.
Water turned into wine, .	Cana, . .	John ii, 5–11.
Two draughts of fishes, .	Sea of Gali-lee, . .	Luke v, 1–11. John xxi, 1–14.
Five thousand fed, . . .	Decapolis, .	Matt. xiv, 15–21.
Four thousand fed, . . .	Do. . .	Matt. xv, 32–39

2. *Those which relate to his curing diseases.*

The nobleman's son, . .	Cana, . .	John iv, 46–54.
Peter's wife's mother, . .	Capernaum,	Mark i, 30, 31.
A centurion's servant, . .	Do. . .	Matt. viii, 5–13.
Diseased cripple at Bethesda,	Jerusalem,	John v, 1–9.
Canaanite's daughter, . .	Near Tyre,	Matt. xv, 22–28.

The pathetic expostulation of this woman has not its equal in the Gospel history.

3. *Those which relate to cures performed on demoniacs.*

An unclean spirit, . . .	Capernaum,	Mark i, 23–26.
The two from the tombs, .	Gadara, .	Matt. viii, 28–34.
The dumb demoniac, . .	Capernaum,	Matt. ix, 32.
The blind and dumb, . .	Do. .	Matt. xii, 22.
The boy cured, ...	Tabor, . .	Matt. xvii, 18.

4. *Those which relate to the removal of various infirmities.*

Sight restored to two men,	Capernaum,	Matt. ix, 29.
A withered hand cured, .	Judea, . .	Matt. xii, 10.
Man deaf and dumb cured,	Decapolis,.	Mark vii, 31.
Blind man cured, . . .	Bethsaida, .	Mark viii, 22.
Man born blind cured, .	Jerusalem, .	John ix.
Two restored to sight, . .	Jericho, . .	Matt. xx, 30.
The ear of Malchus healed,	Gethsemane,	Luke xxii, 50.
Man sick of the palsy cured,	Capernaum,	Matt. ix, 1–8.
Leper healed, ...	Do. .	Mark i, 40–45.
Ten lepers cleansed, . .	Samaria, .	Luke xvii, 11–19.

5. *Miracles upon inanimate subjects.*

Tempest calmed, . . .	Sea of Galilee,	Matt. viii, 23–27
Money found in fishes mouth,	Do.	Matt. xvii, 27.
Walking on the sea, . .	Do.	Matt. xiv, 25.
Blasting of the fig tree, .	Olivet, . .	Matt. xxi, 18.

6. *Those which exhibit his power to raise the dead.*

Widow's son, ...	Nain, . .	Luke vii, 11–17.
Jairus's daughter, . . .	Capernaum,	Matt. ix, 18–25.
Lazarus, ...	Bethany, .	John xi.

How long miracles were continued in the Church, has been a matter of dispute. It is plain, that it may have been exercised in different countries, and may have remained, without any new communication of it, throughout the first, and a considerable part of the second century. Of the time at which several of the apostles died, we have no certain knowledge. St. Peter and St. Paul suffered at Rome about A. D. 66, or 67 ; and it is fully established that the life of John was much longer protracted, he having died a natural death, A. D. 100, or 101. Supposing that the two former of these apostles imparted spiritual gifts till the time of their suffering martyrdom, the persons to whom they were imparted might, in the course of nature, have lived through the earlier part of the second century ; and if John did the same till the end of his life, such gifts as were derived from him might have remained till more than the half of that century had elapsed.

MIRIAM, the sister of Moses, a prophetess ; she might have been some ten or twelve years of age when she watched Moses exposed on the banks of the Nile.

MITE, a Jewish coin of small value, and equal to about two *mills*, or the fifth part of one cent, Luke xii, 59. See MONEY.

MITRE, an ornament for the head ; anciently it was a *turban*, which consisted of a cap, and of a sash of fine linen or silk wound round the bottom of the cap. This is the usual head-dress of Turks and Arabs, and other eastern nations to this day. It is used for the turban of the high priest, Exod. xxviii, 4.

MITYLE'NE, the celebrated capital of Lesbos, which is one of the largest islands in the Archipela'go, Acts xx, 14. It was the birthplace of Alceus, the lyric poet, and Pittacus, one of the seven wise men of Greece.

MIZ'PAH, or MIZPEH, *watch tower, lofty place;* the name of several towers and cities in elevated situations.

MOAB, *water of a father*, i. e., his seed or progeny. See Gen. xix, 30–38 ; a people, Jer. xlviii, 11–13 ; and a region, verse 4. Now called Karrak, from its chief city. The Moabites were a tribe related to the Hebrews. Previous to the exodus, after expelling the original inhabitants, called *Emims*, Gen. xiv, 5 ; Deut. ii, 11, they possessed themselves of the region on the east of the Dead Sea and the Jordan, as far north as the river Jabbok. But the northern, and indeed the finest and best portion of the territory, viz. that extending from the Jabbok to the Arnon, which now goes under the name of *Belka*, had passed into the hands of the Amorites, a Canaanitish tribe, who set up there one of their kingdoms, with Heshbon for its capital, Num. xxi, 26. Hence at the time of the exodus, the valley and the river Arnon constituted the *northern* boundary of Moab, Judges xi, 18. The valley and stream *El Ahsa*, which flows into the southern extremity of the Dead Sea, is supposed to be the *south* border between Moab and Edom. As the Hebrews advanced in order to take possession of Canaan, they did not enter the proper territory of the Moabites, Judges xi, 18, but conquered the kingdom of the Amorites, which now bears the name of *Belka*, and which had formerly belonged to Moab; whence the western part lying along the Jordan opposite Jericho, frequently occurs under the name of the "*Plains*, or *land of Moab*," Deut, i, 5; xxxiv, 1, 8.

MOCK, to deride any one by imitating his voice or mode of speaking; to laugh at in scorn or contempt. Ishmael's mocking Isaac consisted probably in some species of ridicule which he used at the feast of his weaning, Gen. xxi, 9. The children *mocked* Elisha on his way from Jericho to Bethel, by saying, "Go up thou bald head," 2 Kings ii, 23; that there was something in being *bald*, which was made a subject of ridicule and reproach on this occasion and at this place, is sufficiently plain. The contempt here expressed was in all probability connected with the hatred which the idol-atrous parents of that period, and their children with them, bore toward the prophets of the true God; in particular toward Elijah, and Elisha his bosom friend. Such derision as the victims of persecution experienced, Heb. xi, 36, is called *cruel mocking*.

The word is used in the sense of *to delude, deceive*, Matt. ii, 16; hence spoken of impostors and false prophets, Jude 18.

MODERATION, means meekness under provocation, readiness to forgive injuries, equity in the management of business, candour in judging of the character and actions of others, sweetness of disposition, and the entire government of the passions, Phil. iv, 5.

MOLOCH, or MOLECH, *king;* an idol of the Ammonites, to which the Hebrews also at various times sacrificed human victims during their wanderings in the desert, and afterward in the valley of Hinnom. The same idol is also called MELCHOM, *their king*, Zeph. i, 5. The Rabbies describe the statue of Moloch as of brass, in the form of the human body, but with the head of an ox. It was hollow within, was heated from below, and the children to be immolated were placed in its arms. Similar to this was also the statue of *Saturn* among the Carthaginians, a nation living on the shore of the Mediterranean, in Africa. Hence both Moloch and the Carthaginian Saturn probably represent the *planet Saturn*, to which the Semitic nations sacrificed human victims. This same idol is also called *Milcom*, 1 Kings xi, 5.

MONEY. This anciently consisted of bars or pieces of silver, weighed out and not coined. They only considered the purity of the metal, and not the stamp. The weight was sometimes ascertained by means of an instrument, answering to the modern *steel-yards*. Merchants were accordingly in the habit of carrying about with them balances and weights in a sort of pouch or bag, Prov, xvi, 11 ; and fraudulent ones carried false weights, called the *balance of deceit*, Hos. xii, 7. Till the captivity, then, the Jews had no coins ; the shekel being properly a weight, and all the money being reckoned by weight, and not by tale. In the time of the Maccabees silver coins were first struck, 1 Maccabees, xv, 6, with the inscription *shekel of Israel*, which was worth sixty-two cents. See SHEKEL.

Gerah, a bean, used as the smallest weight and coin of the Hebrews, equivalent to the twentieth part of a shekel, Exod. xxx, 13. Most probably the Hebrews, like the Greeks and Romans, made use of the seeds or beans of the carob tree for this purpose, as the moderns sometimes do of barleycorns ;

whence the term *grain* for the smallest weight.

The *tribute money*, Matt. xvii, 24, was a silver coin, equal to the Jewish half shekel. This makes it equivalent to about twenty-eight cents ; a yearly tribute to the temple paid by every Jew, Exod. xxx, 13.

The most ancient coin of which we have a knowledge is the *daric ;* a Persian coin of pure gold, called in our translation *dram*. It was common also among the Jews while they were under the Persian dominion, 1 Chron. xxix, 7 ; Ezra ii, 69. The dram was equal in value to about $3 25. The *stater*, a coin in circulation among the Greeks, and, in our translation, called *a piece of money*, Matt. xvii, 27, was equal to about sixty-six two-third cents ; but was probably current among the Jews as equivalent to the *shekel*.

The *assarion* was a brass coin, equal to one-tenth of the denarius, i. e., to nearly one cent and a half, used in the New Testament to denote the most trifling value, like our *mite* or *farthing*, Matt. x, 29. It ought to be remarked, that silver and gold anciently were more scarce than at present, and consequently of greater value—about as *ten* to *one*. In Acts xix, 19, it was a matter of question whether the *pieces of silver* mean the Jewish *shekel*, which could make the sum about $28,000, or whether it stands for the dram or denarius, which would reduce the sum to about $7,000. In either case, we must take into account the very high price of ancient books in general; and especially of those prepared by the magicians.

A MONEY-CHANGER is a bro-*ker, an exchanger,* who deals in money or exchanges. The annual tribute of each Jew to the temple was a half shekel, and this the money-changers, sitting in the outer court of the temple, furnished to the people as they came up, in exchange for Greek and Roman coins. They also received money on deposite at interest, in order to loan it out to others at a higher rate, Matt. xxv, 27.

MONTH, i. e., *a lunar month;* it was customary among the Hebrews to reckon by *moons.* The lunar changes, without doubt, were first employed in the measurement of time. After their departure from Egypt, there existed among them two modes of reckoning the months of the year; the one *civil,* and the other *sacred.* The beginning of the *civil* year was *Tisri,* from the new moon of October to that of November; the *sacred* year commenced with *Nisan,* the new moon of April. Months anciently had no separate names, except *Ni'san,* which was called *A'bib,* i. e., *green ears,* so called because grain at that time was in the *ear.* The return of the *new moon* was ascertained by observation, and announced by the sounding of the silver trumpets, Num. x, 10. After the Babylonish captivity, the Hebrews continued the names of the months as they found them among the Chaldeans and Persians.

Names of the Hebrew Months.

Civil.	Sacred.		
7	1	Ni'san, from the new moon of April,	Neh. ii, 1.
8	2	Zif, or Zin, ...	May, 1 Kings vi, 1.
9	3	Si'van, ...	June, Esth. viii, 9.
10	4	Tam'muz, ...	July.
11	5	Ab, ...	August.
12	6	E'lul, ...	Sept., Neh. vi, 15.
1	7	Tis'ri, or E-than'im, . .	Oct., 1 Kings viii, 2.
2	8	Bul, (to rhyme with dull)	Nov., 1 Kings vi, 38.
3	9	Chisleu (kis'lu,) . . .	Dec., Neh. i, 1.
4	10	Te'beth, ...	Jan., Esth. ii, 16.
5	11	Se'bat, ...	Feb., Zech. i, 7.
6	12	A'dar, ...	March, Esth. iii, 7.
		Nisan was formerly called *Abib,* .	Exod. xiii, 4.

MOON, the lesser light, Gen. i, 16, revolving around the earth at the distance of 240,000 miles, and reflecting the light of the sun. Hence the Jewish dispensation is compared to the moon, Rev. xii, 1. It was the bright moonlight night of the world, and possessed a portion of the glorious light of the Gospel. Among the orientals in general, and the Hebrews in particular, the worship of the moon was more extensive, and more famous than that of the sun, Deut. iv, 19; xvii, 3. The Greeks worshipped the moon under the name of *Diana*.

MOREH, *teacher*, a Canaanite, like Mamre; whence the "plain," and "oaks of Moreh," not far from Shechem, so called from their owner, Deut. xi, 30. "The hill of *Moreh*," teachers' hill, in the valley of Jezreel, Judg. vii, 1.

MORNING, the dawn, daybreak, from the breaking forth of the light, used for *early*, *soon*, *speedily*, Psa. v, 4; also metaphorically, for the dawn of prosperity and happiness, Job xi, 17; poetically, there are ascribed to the morning *wings*, Psa. cxxxix, 9, expressive of the swiftness with which the dawn moves onward. *Son of the morning* is *Lucifer*, the morning star, Isa. xiv, 12.

MOR'DECAI, a Jew of the tribe of Benjamin, living in the metropolis of Persia, the foster-father of Esther, and afterward chief minister of state, Esth. ii, 5. Probably he was very young when taken into captivity.

MORIAH, one of the hills of Jerusalem, on which Solomon built the temple. *Land of Moriah* is the region around the mount, its vicinity, Gen. xxii, 2. According to Gesenius, the word signifies *chosen of Jehovah*, an appropriate name for a place of sacrifice, or a sanctuary.

MOSERA, Deut. x, 6, is supposed to lie near the foot of Mount Hor, perhaps on the elevated open plain from which the mountain rises. All writers agree in placing the sepulchre of Aaron upon the summit of Mount Hor, where it is still preserved and venerated by the Arabs.

MOSES, *drawn out*, i. e., from the water. See Exod. ii, 10; the great leader, legislator, and prophet of the Israelites; the son of Amram, 1 Chron. vi, 3, of the tribe of Levi. He is the author of the Pentateuch, or first five *books* of the Bible, which has been regarded by almost all nations as the most ancient history and code of laws which have come down to our times. The narrative of his life and actions occupies the last four books of his Pentateuch.

Moses was educated at the court of Egypt, as the son of Pharaoh's daughter, and brought up in all the learning and wisdom of the Egyptians. Here he appears to have stayed nearly forty years, till one day, having killed one of the oppressors of his Hebrew brethren, he was obliged to flee for his life to the land of Midian, in the peninsula of Sinai, where, entering into the service of the priest or prince of that country, he married his daughter, and guarded the flocks of his father-in-law for forty years. At the conclusion of this time, God gave him a commission to conduct the Israelites from Egypt to Canaan; and he faithfully discharged the trust reposed in him. He forgot himself and his own secular interest, with that also of his family, and laboured incessantly to promote God's honour and the people's welfare, which on many occasions he showed were dearer to him than his own life. Moses was in every respect *a great man;* for every virtue which constitutes greatness was concentrated in his mind, and fully displayed in his conduct. He always conducted himself as conscious of his own integrity, and of the guidance and protection of God, under whose orders he constantly acted. He left Egypt, having an eye to the recompense of reward in another world: he never lost sight of this great object, and was therefore neither discouraged by difficulties, nor elated by prosperity. Though his confidence in God was never shaken, yet his life was a life of trial and distress,

20

occasioned by the obstinacy and baseness of the people over whom he presided; and he died in their service, leaving no other property but his tent behind him. Of the spoils taken in war, we never read of the portion of Moses. He had none—he wanted none—his treasure was in heaven, and his heart was there also. His moral character is almost immaculate; that he offended Jehovah at the waters of *Meribah,* there can be no doubt. By Num. xx, 12, it appears that Moses, as well as Aaron and others, indulged a spirit of *unbelief.* Hence "he spoke unadvisedly with his lips," Psa. cvi, 33, and "did not sanctify the Lord in the midst of the children of Israel," Deut. xxxii, 49–52. It was for this that he was excluded from the promised land.

The following remarks upon the veracity of Moses, as a writer, have the merit of compressing much argument into few words:—"1. There is a *minuteness* in the details of the Mosaic writings which bespeaks their truth; for it often bespeaks the eye-witness, as in the adventures of the wilderness; and often seems intended to supply directions to the artificer, as in the construction of the tabernacle. 2. There are *touches of nature* in the narrative which bespeak its truth, for it is not easy to regard them otherwise than as strokes from the life; as where 'the mixed multitude,' whether half-castes or Egyptians, are the first to sigh for the cucumbers and melons of Egypt, and to spread discontent through the camp, Num. xi, 4; as the miserable exculpation of himself, which Aaron attempts, with all the cowardice of conscious guilt, 'I cast into the fire, and there came out this calf:' the fire, to be sure, being in the fault, Exod. xxxii, 24. 3. There is a *simplicity* in the manner of Moses, when telling his tale, which bespeaks its truth : no parade of language, no pomp of circumstance even in his miracles—a modesty and dignity throughout all. 4. There is a *candour* in the treatment of his subject by Moses, which bespeaks his truth ; as when he tells of his own want of eloquence, which unfitted him for a leader, Exod. iv, 10 ; his own want of faith, which prevented him from entering the promised land, Num. xx, 12 ; the idolatry of Aaron his brother, Exodus xxxii, 21 ; the profaneness of Nadab and Abihu, his nephews, Lev. x ; the disaffection and punishment of Miriam, his sister, Num. xii, 1. 5. There is a *disinterestedness* in his conduct which bespeaks him to be a man of truth ; for though he had sons, he apparently takes no measures during his life to give them offices of trust or profit ; and at his death he appoints, as his successor, one who had no claims upon him, either of alliance, of clanship, or of blood. 6. There are certain *prophetical* passages in the writings of Moses which bespeak their truth ; as, several respecting the future Messiah, and the very sublime and literal one respecting the final fall of Jerusalem, Deut. xxviii."

MOTE, *something dry;* any small dry particle, as of chaff or wood, used as the emblem of *lesser faults,* or small infirmities, opposed to a *beam,* Luke vi, 41, which is used figuratively for a great *fault* or *vice;* a Jewish proverb applied by our Saviour.

MOTH, *the cloth worm,* of a shining silver colour ; an insect which flies by night, and of which there are many kinds. It is first enclosed in an egg among cloth, whence it issues a worm, and feeds upon its habitation. After a time, it quits this worm state, to assume that of the complete insect, or moth.

"Crushed before the *moth,*" Job iv, 19, is a vivid image of the frailty of men, that the moth, insignificant and harmless as it appears to be, has power to crush them.

MOTHER, used for a *step-*mother, Gen. xxxvii, 10 ; has often also a wider sense, *a grandmother,* or any female ancestor. It expresses inti mate *relationship,* close alli ance, Job xvii, 14. A *nation* or *people,* as opposed to the children, i. e., individuals born of it, Hos. iv, 5.

It also signifies a *mother city,* metropolis, i. e., any

large and important city, although not the capital, 2 Sam. xx, 19. Tropically a city, as the parent or source of wickedness and abominations, Rev. xvii, 5. Deborah calls herself a *mother in Israel*, Judges v, 7, in the sense of *benefactress;* just as distinguished men are termed *fathers* in general, or *fathers of their country*, Job xxix, 16. .

MOUNTAIN occurs very frequently; often as a *mountainous tract* or region, Gen. ¬iv, 10, the mountainous part of Judah, Josh. xv, 48. *Mount Ephraim* lay almost in the middle of the Holy Land, east of Joppa, in the territory of that tribe. Palestine, being mountainous, is called a *holy mountain*, Isa. lvii, 13. The Hebrews frequently gave to mountains the epithet *eternal*, because they are ever the same from the creation.

The mountains of Palestine were anciently places of refuge to the inhabitants when defeated in war, Gen. xiv, 10; and modern travellers assure us that they are still resorted to for the purpose of shelter. The rocky summits found on many of them, appear to have been not unfrequently employed as altars, on which sacrifices were offered to Jehovah, Judg. xiii, 19. Mount Olivet is called Mount of Corruption, 2 Kings xxiii, 13, on account of the idols there worshipped. Proverbially, *to remove mountains*, is to accomplish great and difficult things, 1 Cor. xiii, 2.

MOURNING, the grief of the orientals formerly, on an occasion of death, was, as it is to this day in the East, very extreme. As soon as a person dies, the females in the family, with a loud voice, set up a sorrowful cry. They continue it as long as they can, without taking breath; and the first shriek of wailing dies away in a low sob. After a short space of time, they repeat the same cry, and continue it for eight days. Every day, however, it becomes the less frequent and less audible. The Hebrews hired women to weep and moan, and also persons to play on instruments of music at their funerals. Persons in years were carried to their graves by the sound of trumpets, as Servius says, and younger people by the sound of flutes. In Matt. ix, 23, we observe a company of players on the flute at the funeral of a girl of twelve years of age. All that met a funeral procession, or a company of mourners, out of civility were to join them, and to mingle their tears with those who wept. Paul alludes to this custom, Rom. xii, 15; and our Saviour, Luke vii, 32.

The shaving of the head is a familiar custom in mourning for the dead, Jer. xvi, 6, as well as in general calamities of the country, Amos viii, 10; the orientals thereby deprived themselves of the finest ornament of the body; and taking off ornaments, lies at the bottom in all mourning usages. A bald head is a special dishonour, 2 Ki. ii, 23.

MUFFLER, a female ornament to cover the face, Isa. iii, 19.

MULE, the offspring of the horse and ass. There is no probability that the Jews bred mules, because it was forbidden to couple animals of different species together, Lev. xix, 19. But they were not forbidden to use them, 2 Sam. xiii, 29. The animal is remarkably hardy, patient, and sure-footed, living ordinarily twice as long as a horse. Mules are much used in Spain and South America for transporting goods across the mountains. So also in the Alps they are used by travellers among the mountains, where a horse would hardly be able to pass with safety. Even the kings and most distinguished nobles of the Jews were accustomed to ride upon mules, 2 Sam. xiii, 29. Of one passage where the word *mule* occurs, Gen. xxxvi, 24, Gesenius says, by a groundless conjecture from the context, some of the rabbins and modern versions render it *mules;* but it should be rendered *warm springs*, such being actually found in the region in question on the eastern shore of the Dead Sea.

MUNITION, materials used in war for defence, or for annoying an enemy. In the Bible, it means a stronghold, a fortified city, Nah. ii, 1; compare 2 Chron. xi, 11.

MURDER, the deliberate killing of a human being; a vice which is said to have been exceedingly frequent at Rome. But the Jews regarded this as one of the most abominable crimes. In case of the inadvertent killing of another, provision was made for the protection of the offender by cities of refuge; but for this crime there was no pardon: the city of refuge, and even the altar, furnished no asylum, nor might money be taken in satisfaction. See Exod. xxi, 14; xxviii, 29; Num. xxxv, 30–34. Murder was always punished with death; and the kinsman of the murdered person might kill the murderer with impunity.

MURMURING, uttering complaints in a low voice privately; the expression of complaint, or sullen discontent; *without murmuring*, i. e., cheerfully, Phil. ii. 14.

MURRAIN, a deadly and infectious disease among cattle, Exod. ix, 3.

MUSIC is probably nearly coeval with our race, or, at least, with the first attempts to preserve the memory of transactions. The first mention of stringed instruments precedes the deluge. About 550 years after the deluge, or 1800 B. C., according to the common chronology, both vocal and instrumental music

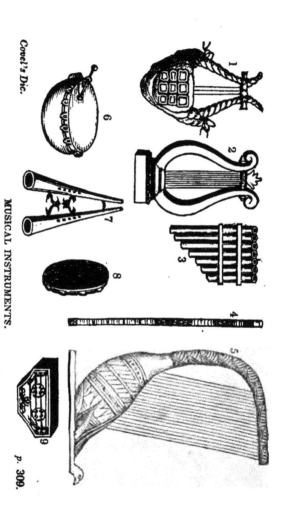

Covel's Dic.

MUSICAL INSTRUMENTS.

p. 309.

1. Original, or Tortoise-shell Harp of Apollo. 2. Harp of Apollo. 3. Pipe of Pan. 4. Pipe or Flute.
5. Theban Harp. 6. Cymbal. 7. Trumpet. 8. Timbrel. 9. Sackbut.

are spoken of as things in general use, Gen. xxxi, 26, 27.

The Hebrews insisted on having music at marriages, on anniversary birthdays, on the days which reminded them of victories over their enemies, at the inauguration of their kings, in their public worship, and when they were coming from afar to attend the great festivals of their nation, Isa. xxx, 29. In the tabernacle and the temple the Levites were the lawful musicians; but on other occasions any one might use musical instruments who chose. It should be remarked, however, that neither music nor poetry attained to the same excellence after the captivity as before that period. There were women singers as well as men in the temple choir.

THE MUSICAL INSTRUMENTS of the Hebrews were divided into three classes: the *stringed, wind,* and *percussion.* 1. The *neginoth,* which occurs in the title of some of the psalms, signifies those instruments which are furnished with strings. The use of the stringed instruments of music is very ancient; but their names, and sometimes even their forms, have been very much changed. From an examination of the drawings made of the ruins of ancient Egypt, we find that its inhabitants had three different kinds: those of the harp, those of the lyre, and of the guitar. The harp differs from the lyre, by being open on one side, as the Theban *harp.*

Of what the strings consisted cannot perhaps be ascertained to complete certainty. Probably they were made of the inner bark of trees, of the sinews of animals, and, in more modern times, of metal. 2. The *nehiloth* occurs in the title to the fifth Psalm, and signifies *wind instruments;* as different kinds of trumpets and flutes, which are nearly the modern instruments of those names. Flutes and pipes are found among all nations, even the most uncivilized; the *cornet* was an instrument of this kind, resembling a horn, now but little known. 3. And instruments of percussion, which are made to give forth their sounds by being struck either with the hand, or a stick, such as drums and bells. The cymbals were instruments for accompanying music, and not unlike those now used in the band. Bells were anciently worn by horses trained for war, to accustom them to noise, Zech. xiv, 20.

MUSTARD, perhaps the common mustard which often grows in the ·fertile soil of Palestine to a very considerable size. Dr. Clarke says, that some soils, being more luxuriant than others, and the climate much warmer, raise the same plants to a size and perfection far beyond what a poorer soil and a colder climate can possibly do. Some suppose it another species of plant; but whatever might have been the species, it is clear from our Lord's custom of taking his illustration from familiar objects, that he spoke of a plant which was remarkable, among his hearers, for the smallness of its seeds, and of such a size as to afford shelter for the birds of the air. The expression, "a grain of *mustard* seed," Matt. xvii, 20, is a proverbial phrase for *the least*, the smallest particle.

MYRA, one of the six principal cities of Lycia, on the south-west coast of Asia Minor, Acts xxvii, 5.

MYRRH, a bitter aromatic gum, procured from a tree growing in Arabia, and especially in Abyssinia. This tree, which has not been certainly known till very recently, is small and thorny, about eight feet high, covered with a whitish gray bark, and leaf like an olive. The gum distils in tears spontaneously, or by incisions made twice a year; was highly prized by the ancients, and used in incense and perfumes. *The sweet-smelling* and *pure* myrrh, or *stacte*, Song v, 5; Exod. xxx, 23, is the myrrh which distils of itself from the tree, and therefore the more highly prized.

MYRTLE, a beautiful evergreen tree, growing wild throughout the southern parts of Europe, north of Africa, and the temperate parts of Asia; furnished with leaves like those of the box, but much less, and more pointed: they are soft to the touch, shining, smooth, of a beautiful green, and have a sweet smell. The flowers grow among the leaves, and consist of five white petals, disposed in the form of a rose: they have an agreeable perfume, and ornamental appearance. The myrtle is mentioned in Scripture among lofty trees, not as comparing with them in size, but as contributing with them to the beauty and richness of the scenery, Isa. xli, 19.

MYSIA, the north-west province of Asia Minor, and at this day a beautiful and fertile country. The Mysian cities, Assos, Pergamos, and Troas, are mentioned in the New Testament, Acts xvi, 7.

MYSTERY, a profound secret; something kept cautiously concealed, and into which one must be instructed before it can be known; something of itself not obvious, and above human insight. In the New Testament, spoken of *facts, doctrines, principles,* &c., not fully revealed; but only obscurely or symbolically set forth. To the apostles it was *given to know the mysteries of the kingdom of heaven,* i. e., in a deeper and more perfect manner than they were made known to others, Matt. xiii, 11. *Mystery* often conveys the idea of something important or awfully sublime.

NA'A-MAN, general of the army of Ben'ha-dad, king of Syria, mentioned 2 Kings v.

He appears to have been a Gentile idolater; but being miraculously cured of his leprosy by the power of the God of Israel, and the direction of his Prophet Elisha, he renounced his idolatry, and acknowledged this God to be the only true God, 2 Kings v, 15, and promised, for the time to come, that he would worship none other but Jehovah, verse 17. He also requested the prophet that he might have two mules' load of earth to carry home with him from the land of Israel, most probably intending to build an altar with it in his own country; which seems, indeed, to be implied in the reason with which he enforces his request, verses 17, 18. He consulted the prophet, whether it was lawful for him, having renounced idolatry, and publicly professed the worship of the true God, still, in virtue of his office, to attend his master in the temple of Rimmon, in order that he might lean upon him, either out of state, or perhaps out of bodily weakness; because, if he attended him, as he had formerly done, he could not avoid bowing down when he did. To this the prophet returns no direct answer; making no other reply than, "Go in peace;" putting it, probably, upon his conscience to act as that should dictate, and not being willing to relieve him from this trial of his recent faith.

NA'DAB, son of Aaron, and brother to A-bi'hu. He offered incense to the Lord with strange, that is, *common fire*, and not with that which had been miraculously lighted upon the altar of burnt-offerings. The connection of the whole would seem to show pretty plainly that these offenders were under the influence of *intoxicating liquor*, Lev. x; see especially verses 8, 9, 10.

NA'HUM is supposed to have been a native of a village in Galilee, and to have been of the tribe of Simeon. It is generally allowed that he delivered his predictions between the Assyrian and Babylonian captivities, and probably about 715 B. C. They relate solely to the destruction of Nineveh by the Babylonians and Medes, and are introduced by an animated display of the attributes of God. Of all the minor prophets, none seems to equal Nahum in sublimity, ardour, and boldness. His prophecy forms an entire and regular poem.

NAIL. The nail of Jael's tent, with which she killed Sisera, was formed for penetrating earth, or hard substances, when driven by sufficient force, as with a hammer. A nail of this sort is the large pin of iron or wood with which they fastened to the ground the cords of their tents. It also includes the spikes or nails fixed in the walls of the house, upon which were hung the moveables and utensils in common use, Ezek. xv, 3. The care with which they fixed the nails may be inferred from the promise of the Lord to Eliakim, Isa. xxii, 23. He shall be strong enough to support whatever is suspended on him. This illustrates an allusion of the Prophet Zechariah, chap. x, 4. The house of Judah, which is *timid*, like a flock of sheep, the Lord hath made as martial as a horse trained to battle ; and out of him shall come the strong nail, or pikenead, i. e., *a prince*, on whom the care and welfare of the state depends. The same person is also called the corner, i. e., *corner stone*, on whom the state is founded.

NAIN, a town of Galilee, situated, according to Eusebius, about two miles south of Mount Tabor, near Endor, Luke vii, 11.

NAKEDNESS, without clothing ; spoken also of one who has no outer garment, and is clad only in the *tunic*, which fitted close to the body, John xxi, 7. It signifies, as in English, *half naked*, i. e., *poorly clad*, destitute as to clothing ; implying penury and want, Matt. xxv, 36. Figuratively spoken of the soul as disencumbered of the body in which it had been clothed, 2 Cor. v, 3. Metaphorically, any thing uncovered, open, manifest, Heb. iv, 13. "The *nakedness* of the land," Gen. xlii, 9–12, is the exposed part, where it is unfortified, easy of access.

NAME. 1. The proper appellation of a person. 2. It implies *authority*, or *the power of his name*, Acts iii, 16. To come or do any thing in one's name, i. e., using his name ; as his messenger or representative, by his authority or sanction. 3. It implies *character, dignity*, ., *name and dignity*, honourable appellation, title. "He who receives a prophet in the *name*," i. e., character of a prophet, *as* a prophet, Matt. x, 41. 4. *Name* is used emphatically, as the name of God or Christ ; a periphrase for God or Christ himself, in all his being, attributes, and relations. 5. Name often signifies *fame* or *renown* ; *a good name* is a good reputation, Eccl. vii, 1 ; *name after death*, memory, as in the phrase *blot out one's name*, i. e., utterly to destroy a people or city, so that their name and memory shall perish, Deut. ix, 14. In the following passages it seems to be used for *a monument*, in memory of any person or event, 2 Sam. viii, 13 ; Isa. iv, 13. *The name of the Lord* is the *renown*, or *good fame* of God ; his estimation among mankind, in the phrase *for his name's sake*, i. e., as vindicating his good name, in accordance with his name and character, that his glory and honour might not be obscured. The inhabitants of the East very frequently change their names, and sometimes do it for very slight reasons. This accounts for the fact of so many persons' having two names in Scripture, Judges vi, 30–33; vii, 1; 2 Sam. xxiii, 8. Kings and princes very often changed the names of those who held offices under them, particularly when they were elevated to some new station, and crowned with additional honours, Gen. xli, 45; xvii, 5; xxxii, 28; 2 Kings xxiii, 34; xxiv, 17; Dan. i, 6, 7; John i, 42. Hence a name, *a new name*, occurs tropically, as a token or proof of distinction and honour in the following among other passages, Rev. ii, 17.

NAPHTALI, *my wrestling*, see Gen. xxx, 8; a son of Jacob by Bilhah, and patriarch of the tribe of that name, the limits of which are described, Josh. xix, 32–39. "*Naphtali* is a hind let loose, he giveth goodly words," Gen. xlix, 21. Instead of *let loose*, Gesenius translates *stretched out*, and explains them as *slender* in *growth;* Robinson translates *shot up*, and gives a similar explanation, i. e., grown up in a *slender* and *graceful* form. A fine woman is compared to the roe or hind, Prov. v, 19; and also swift-footed heroes, 2 Sam. ii, 18. Such are to be the descendants of Naphtali; they are also to give *goodly words*, i. e., the tribe is to be distinguished for its orators, prophets, poets; and perhaps also for its singers.

NAPKIN, in common usage, a *towel;* a cloth used for wiping the hands. In the Bible, *a sweat cloth*, a handkerchief, John xi, 44.

NARCISSUS, *a flower;* the name of a man who is supposed to have been the freedman and favourite of the Emperor Claudius, Rom. xvi, 11.

NATHANAEL, *given of God*, of the same signification as *Theodore*, a disciple of Christ; supposed to be the same with the Apostle Bartholomew, John i, 46, &c., where he was seen under the fig tree, probably for the purpose of devotional retirement.

NATURAL. 1. That which pertains to nature, or is produced by it. "The *natural* body," 1 Cor. xv, 44, having breath and animal life opposed to the *spiritual body*, which has the nature of a spirit. 2. When spoken of the soul, it signifies *animal*, i. e., pertaining to the animal or natural mind and affections, swayed by the affections and passions of human nature, not under the influences of the Holy Spirit. *The natural man* is one who makes the faculties of his animal nature, his senses, passions, and his natural reason darkened by prejudices, the measure of truth and the rule of his conduct, without paying any regard to the discoveries of revelation.

NATURE, natural source, or origin, *birth, descent*, Gal. ii, 15; the natural constitution of any person; the innate disposition, qualities, &c.; in a moral sense, the native mode of thinking, feeling, acting, as unenlightened by the influence of Divine truth, Eph. ii, 3. It is used by analogy, once of the Divine moral nature, 2 Pet. i, 4, "Partakers of the Divine *nature*," i. e., regenerated in heart and disposition.

It signifies a *natural feeling* of decorum, a native sense of propriety, e. g., in respect to national customs, in which one is born and brought up, 1 Cor. xi, 14; "doth not your own *natural* feeling teach you," &c. See HAIR. It was the national custom among both Hebrews and Greeks for men to wear the hair short, and the women long.

The word also signifies the *order and constitution* of nature. Hence, according to nature, *natural*; contrary to nature, *unnatural*; Rom. xi, 24.

NAZARENE, an inhabitant or native of Nazareth; but also implying *reproach*, from the contempt in which that city was held, Matt. ii, 23; once used of Christians as the followers of Jesus, Acts xxiv, 5.

NAZARETH, a small city in Lower Galilee, just north of the great plain of Esdraelon, and about midway between the lake of Tiberias and the Mediterranean. It lies at the foot of a hill and on the side facing the east and south-east, along a small valley or basin, entirely shut in by hills, except a narrow rocky gullet toward the south leading to the great plain. Here is now shown the supposed place where the men of the city were about to cast Jesus down from the precipice, Luke iv, 29.

NAZARITE, *consecrated*; a species of ascetics among the Hebrews, who bound themselves by a vow to abstain from certain things. See the law, Num. vi, 12; compare Amos ii, 12; once it signified *a prince* as consecrated to God, Lam. iv, 7.

Perpetual Nazarites, as Samson and John the Baptist, were consecrated to their Nazariteship by their parents, and continued all their lives in this state, without drinking wine or cutting their hair. The institution is involved in much mystery; and no satisfactory reason has ever been given of it. This is certain, that it had the approbation of God, and may be considered as affording a good example of self-denial in order to be given up to the study of the law, and the practice of exact righteousness.

NEAPOLIS, a city and port of Macedonia, on the Egean coast, a few miles E.S.E. of Philippi, now called *Napoli*, Acts xvi, 11.

NEBO, a mountain in the confines of Moab, not far from the northern extremity of the Dead Sea. On a summit of a ridge of this mountain called Pisgah, which commands a view of the whole of Canaan, Moses surveyed the promised land, and "was gathered to his people," Deut. xxxiv, 1. The name seems to have been borrowed from the god *Nebo*, Isaiah xlvi, 1, who probably was worshipped there. And this idol is supposed to represent the planet *Mercury*, which the Chaldeans and ancient Arabs worshipped as the celestial *scribe*, who records the succession of events.

NEBUCHADNEZ'ZAR, son and successor of Nabopolassar, who succeeded to the kingdom of Chaldea 605 B. C. Some time previously to this his brother had made him associate in the kingdom, and sent him to recover Carchemish, which had been taken from him four years before by Necho, king of Egypt. Nebuchadnezzar, having been successful, marched against the governor of Phen-ic'i-a, and Jehoi'a-kim, king of Judah, who was tributary to Necho. He took Jehoiakim, and put him in chains in order to carry him captive to Babylon; but afterward left him in Judea, on condition of paying a large tribute. He took away several persons from Jerusalem; among others Daniel, Han-a-ni'ah, Mish'a-el, and Az-a-ri'ah, all of the royal family, whom the king of Babylon caused to be carefully instructed in the language and in the learning of the Chaldeans, that they might be employed at court, Dan. i.

In the mean time, Nebuchadnezzar, being at Babylon in the second year of his reign, had a mysterious dream, in which he saw a statue composed of several metals, the interpretation of which was given by Daniel, and procured his elevation to the highest post in the kingdom. In the same year, as Dr. Hales thinks, in which he had this dream, he erected a golden statue in the plains of Dura.

Jehoiachin having revolted, Nebuchadnezzar besieged him in Jerusalem, forced him to surrender, and took him, with his chief officers, captive to Babylon, with his mother, his wives, and the best workmen of Jerusalem, to the number of 10,000 men. Among the captives were Mordecai, the uncle of Esther, and Ezekiel the prophet. He took also all the vessels of gold which Solomon made for the temple and the king's treasury, and he set up Mattani'ah, Je-hoi'a-chim's uncle by his father's side, whom he named Zed-e-ki'ah. This prince continued faithful to Nebuchadnezzar nine years: being then weary of subjection, he revolted, and confederated with the neighbouring princes. But in the eleventh year of Zedekiah, 588 B. C., the city was taken. The king of Babylon condemned him to die, caused his children to be put to death in his presence, and then bored out his eyes, loaded him with chains, and sent him to Babylon, 2 Kings xxv, 5–7.

Three years after the Jewish war Nebuchadnezzar besieged the city of Tyre, which siege held thirteen years. The city of Tyre was taken in the year 752 B. C. The Lord gave up to them Egypt and its spoils. Nebuchadnezzar made an easy conquest of it, enriched himself with booty, and returned in triumph to Babylon, with a great number of captives. Being now at peace, he applied himself to the adorning of Babylon with magnificent buildings.

About this time Nebuchadnezzar had a dream of a great tree, loaded with fruit. A year after, as he was walking on his palace at Babylon, he says, " *Is not this great Babylon, which I have built for the house of the kingdom, by the might of my power, and for the honour of my majesty?*" And scarcely had he pronounced these words, when he became insane, which so altered his imagination, that he fled into the fields and assumed the manners of an ox. After having been seven years in this state, God opened his eyes, his understanding was restored to him, and he recovered his royal dignity. Nebuchadnezzar died 562 B. C., after having reigned forty-three years.

NEB-U-ZAR'A-DAN, a general of Nebuchadnezzar's army, and the chief officer of his household, 2 Kings xxv, 20.

NECH'O, king of Egypt, son and successor of Psammeticus. He carried his arms to the Euphrates, where he conquered the city of Carchemish. Josiah, king of Judah, being tributary to the king of Babylon, opposed Nech'o, and gave him battle at Megiddo, where he received the wound, of which he died; and Necho passed forward, without making stay in Judea. On his return, he halted at Riblah, in Syria; and sending for Jehoahaz, king of the Jews, he deposed him, loaded him with chains, and sent him into Egypt. Then coming to Jerusalem, he set up Eliakim or Jehoakim in his place, and exacted the payment of one hundred talents of silver and one talent of gold; but he did not retain his conquests above four years. The king of Babylon, pursuing his victory, brought under his dominion the whole country between the river Euphrates and Egypt, except Judea. Thus Necho was again reduced within the limits of his own country.

NECK, "laying down their *necks*," Rom. xvi, 4; a proverbial expression, which denotes the undergoing of the greatest perils, in allusion to the custom of placing on blocks the necks of criminals whose heads are to be cut off. The passage in Job xv, 26, will admit of a better translation. "He runneth up on him with his *neck*," i. e., erect, proudly, stiff-necked, a well-known gesture of pride, *with the thick bosses of his bucklers. The boss* of a shield or buckler is the exterior convex part. The passage is a metaphor drawn from soldiers who join their shields together, and so rush forward upon the enemy.

NECROMAN'CER, *one who divines by the dead;* a sorcerer, or conjurer, who pretends to call up the dead by means of incantations and magic formulas, in order that they may give response as to doubtful or future things. And hence we find that they are coupled in the same passage, Deut. xviii, 11, with *enchanters.* They themselves uttered the communications which they pretended to receive from the dead. They doled them out syllable by syllable, sometimes muttering in a low tone, and sometimes peeping like a chicken. See Isa. viii, 19; xxix, 4. Among the ancients, this power of ventriloquism was often misused for this purpose; pretending also by such means to procure the assistance of the prince of the power of the air. But as all such pretensions, whether true or false, were not only a forsaking of God, but a setting up of his creatures against him, they were expressly forbidden to his people, and that under pain of death : for those who attributed to the dead a knowledge of future events, which belongs to God alone, virtually disclaimed his allegiance, Lev. xx, 26, 27. But besides these highly criminal incantations, it appears from Psa. lviii, 5, and other passages, that they had a method, as some of the Easterns still have, of charming serpents by sounds, so as to render them tractable and harmless. See ADDER.

NEESINGS, an old word for *sneezing,* Job xli, 18.

NEGINOTH, a word which occurs in the titles of some of the psalms, and signifies *stringed instruments of music,* such as are played on by the fingers. See Psa. iv, once Psa. lxi. *Neginah,* the construct form of the Hebrew noun instead of the absolute.

NE-HE-MI'AH professes himself the author of the book which bears his name, in the very beginning of it, and he uniformly writes in the first person. He was of the tribe of Judah, and was probably born at Babylon during the captivity. He was so distinguished for his family and attainments as to be selected for the office of cup-bearer to the king of Persia, a situation of great honour and emolument. He was made governor of Judea, upon his own application, by Artaxerxes Lon-gim'a-nus; and his book, which anciently was joined to that of Ezra, gives an account of his appointment and administration through a space of about thirty-six years, to 420 B. C., at which time the Scripture history closes.

NEHILOTH, a word designating wind instruments of music, such as *pipes* or *flutes,* Psa. v, the title.

NEHUSHTAN. The superstitious people having made an *idol* of the serpent which Moses set up in the wilderness, Hezekiah caused it to be burned, and in derision gave it the above name; meaning, perhaps, *a little brazen thing,* 2 Kings xviii, 4.

NEIGHBOUR, one who lives near to us, generally a *fellow-man;* any other member of the human family, Matt. xxii, 39; a fellow-countryman, one of the same people or country, Acts vii, 27 : compare ver. 24, 26 ; and one of the same faith, a fellow-Christian, Rom. xv, 2. By the beautiful parable of the good Samaritan, Luke x, 29, our Lord has taught us to comprehend in the term *every man,* so that our enemies are not excepted.

NERGAL, an idol of the Cuthites, 2 Kings xvii, 30; probably the planet *Mars,* which was ever the emblem of bloodshed, as the light of the planet is reddish.

NERO, a Roman emperor, mentioned only in the spurious subscription, 2 Tim. iv, 23.

NETH'IN-IMS, *the given, the devoted;* the name of the Hebrew servants of the temple, or temple slaves, who were, under the Levites, in the ministry of the temple, to perform the meanest and most laborious services therein, in supplying wood and water. At first the Gibeonites were appointed to this service. Josh. ix, 27.

NEW MOON, the first day of the lunar month, which was a festival to the Hebrews, 1 Sam. xx, 5. This was not ascertained by astronomical calculation, but by the moon's first appearance ; for Moses regulated his chronology by the aspect of the earth, i. e., the situation of the earth and moon, and the return of the seasons.

NICODEMUS, a Pharisee, and one of the members of the Jewish Sanhedrim, who came to Jesus by night, probably as a serious, though timid inquirer, John iii, 1. He afterward avowed himself a disciple of Christ, John xix, 39.

NICOLAITANS, the followers of Nicolas, Rev. ii, 6, 15. Many suppose this to be an heretical sect, sprung from some leader of that name. Dr. Robinson thinks a more probable supposition is, that the appellation is not here derived from a proper name, but is used symbolically, and refers to the same persons who are said, in Rev. ii, 14, *to hold the doctrine of Balaam,* since the Greek word *Nicholas* corresponds to the Hebrew Balaam, and signifies *to overcome, seduce a people.* The allusion then would be to false and seducing teachers like Balaam ; and refers more particularly, perhaps, to those who opposed the decree of the apostles in Acts xv, 29.

NICOP'OLIS, a city of Thrace, now *Nickopi,* on the river Nessus, which was here the boundary between Thrace and Macedonia; and hence the city is sometimes reckoned to the latter, Tit. iii, 12. There were other cities of this name.

NIGHT. The ancient Hebrews began their artificial day in the evening, and ended it the next evening; so that the night preceded the day, whence it is said, "*evening and morning.*" They allowed twelve hours to the night, and twelve to the day. Metaphorically used for a time of moral and spiritual darkness, the opposite of Gospel light and day, Rom. xiii, 12. Hence *children of the night* are those who walk in the darkness of ignorance, and perform only works of darkness, 1 Thess. v, 5. *Night* is put for the time of *affliction, adversity, calamity,* Psa. xvii, 3; Isa. xxi, 11, 12. In the last passage, some suppose, the word *teaching* being implied, it is asked by the prophet, *What of the night* hast thou to teach? or what of the night still remains? It is also put for the time of death. "One *night* remains for all," John ix, 4. *In* or *by the night* is sometimes employed to express sudden, unexpected destruction, Job xxvii, 20; xxxiv, 25; "as a thief in the *night,*" 2 Pet. iii, 10. "Because thieves commonly break into houses in the night time," says Macknight, "and occasion great fear to those who are within. Any sudden, unexpected event, especially such as occasioned terror, was com-
21

pared by the Hebrews to the coming of a thief in the night. The suddenness, therefore, and unexpectedness of the coming of the *day of the Lord,* and the terror which it occasions to the wicked, are the circumstances in which it will resemble the coming of a thief, and not that it will happen in the night time."

NIGHT-HAWK, a bird resembling the whippoorwill, and generally supposed to be the same. They are, however, different birds. The night-hawk is often seen on summer evenings, with his long wings flying high in the air, uttering a frequent plaintive cry, and frequently sweeping downward with a rapid, and almost perpendicular descent to catch the flies and gnats on which it lives, Lev. xi, 16.

NIMROD, *rebel,* son of Cush, founder of the kingdom of Babylon, Gen. x, 8, 9.; hence *land of Nimrod* is Babylonia, Micah v, 5. "He was *a mighty one in the earth,*" Gen. x, 8, 9, i. e., he was the first who, excelling in bodily strength, exercised authority among men. Others render the sentence, he was the first tyrant in the earth; the first who robbed men of their freedom. *A mighty hunter,* doubtless the leader of a band, who, in hunting wild beasts, and other similar exercises prepared themselves for war. *Before the Lord,* i. e., *very powerful.* To Nimrod is im puted the invention of idolatrous worship paid to men.

NINEVEH, *dwelling of Ninus;* the ancient capital of the Assyrian empire. It was situated on the eastern bank of the Tigris, opposite the modern Mosul, where there still exists a village called *Nunia.* The city is supposed to have been built by Nimrod. See ASSYRIA. It is styled in the book of Jonah "*a great city,*" i, 2; and "*an exceeding great city, of three days' journey,*" iii, 3; three days' journey has reference to the *circuit* of the city, rather than to its length. Diod'orus mentions that the circuit of Nineveh was 480 stadia, which make somewhat more than fifty-four miles; allowing the stadium to be, according to Robinson, 604½ feet. He describes the walls as 100 feet high, sufficiently broad to admit of three chariots being driven abreast. On the walls were 1,500 towers, each 200 feet high, regarded as impregnable. Nahum ii, 8, says, that "*Nineveh* was of old like a pool of water," signifying by this expression the vast multitudes that flowed into her gates. It is asserted in Jonah iv, 11, that in Nineveh, "there were more than sixscore thousand persons who could not discern between their right hand and their left hand," i. e., who had not come to the exercise of their reasoning powers; see Deut. i, 39; reckoning such a fifth part, would give 600,000 for the whole population; the same number which Pliny attributes to Seleucia near Babylon. This population shows that a great part of the city must have been left open and unbuilt.

The threatened overthrow of Nineveh within three days was, by the general repentance and humiliation of the inhabitants, from the highest to the lowest, suspended for near two hundred years, until "their iniquity came to the full;" and then the prophecy was literally accomplished, in the third year of the siege of the city, by the combined Medes and Babylonians, about 606 B. C.

The utter and perpetual destruction and desolation of Nineveh were foretold: "The Lord will make an utter end of the place thereof. Affliction shall not rise up the second time. She is empty, void, and waste," Nahum i, 8, 9; ii, 10; iii, 17–19. "The Lord will stretch out his hand against the north, and destroy Assyria, and will make *Nineveh* a desolation, and dry like a wilderness. How is she become a desolation, a place for beasts to lie down in," Zeph. ii, 13–15.

Such an utter ruin in every view has been made of it; and such is the truth of the Divine predictions!

NI'SAN, the first month of the Hebrews, beginning with the new moon of April, called in the Pentateuch *Abib.* See MONTH. The name

Ni'san was introduced only since the time of Ezra, and the return from the exile.

NISROCH, an idol of the Ninevites. According to etymology, the name would signify *eagle*, or *great eagle*. Among the ancient Arabs, also, the eagle occurs as an idol, 2 Kings xix, 37.

NITRE. This is not the common nitre or saltpetre, which has no effect when combined with an acid, but the native impure carbonate of soda; a mineral alkali, which abounds in many parts of Asia, and is procured from certain lakes in Egypt, west of the Delta of the Nile, called the Lakes of Natron. Hence this substance is denominated by the Germans na'tron, or Egyptian nitre, which, combined with oil, is still used as soap, Jer. ii, 22. When vinegar is poured upon this article, an effervesance or violent commotion takes place, which will illustrate Prov. xxv, 20.

NO, or No-Ammon, the Egyptian *Thebes*, or *Diospolis;* the ancient and splendid metropolis of Upper Egypt, founded by Cadmus, who invented sixteen letters of the Greek alphabet, 1432 B. C. It-was sixteen miles in circuit, situated on both banks of the Nile, near 300 miles south of Cairo, and celebrated for the multitude and splendour of its temples, obelisks, and statues. In the time of the Prophet Nahum, see chap.

iii, 8, it was already destroyed, before Nineveh, probably by the Assyrians. The name signifies *dwelling of Ammon*, because it was the chief seat of the worship of *Jupiter Ammon*, the supreme god of the Egyptians, and held by the Greeks and Romans to be the same with their *Jupiter*. On Egyptian monuments he is usually depicted with a human body, and the head of a ram. He was worshipped in temples of the utmost splendour at Meroe, and in an oasis of the Lybian desert, whither Alexander the Great made an expedition; but the chief seat of his worship was at *Thebes*. The god himself is only once referred to in the Bible, Jer. xlvi, 25. The English translators have here incorrectly translated the original word Ammon by a *multitude.*

NOAH, celebrated for having been preserved from the deluge, which occurred 1656 years from the creation of man, or 2348 B. C. Noah lived after the deluge 350 years; and, according to common opinion, he divided the earth among his three sons. To Shem he gave Asia, to Ham Africa, and to Japheth Europe.

NOB, a city within sight of Jerusalem, on the north.

NOBLE, *well born*, of high rank. *Noblemen* are men of rank and power, Luke xix, 12.; used also metaphorically, *noble minded, generous;* which, in the mind of an oriental, is closely connected with liberality in giving.

NOD, *flight, wandering;* hence the proper name of the region to which Cain fled, Gen. iv, 16.

NOPH, generally believed to be the same with *Memphis.*

NUMBERS. This fourth book of Moses is so called, because the first three chapters contain the numbering of the Hebrews and Levites, which was performed separately, after the erection and consecration of the tabernacle. It includes also the history of the Israelites during their journey in the wilderness; though most of the transactions here recorded took place in the second and thirty-eighth years. It appears from chap. xxxvi, 13, to have been written by Moses in the plains of Moab.

NUTS, *walnuts* and *almonds* are common in Palestine. There is also a very rich species of nuts called *pistacia nuts,* resembling almonds in appearance and taste; but they are of a much better flavour, and more valued by the orientals. They grow in clusters on a tree which resembles the *terebinth,* or turpentine tree; a small tree with heavy crooked limbs, somewhat resembling the walnut in foliage, indigenous to Syria and the neighbouring parts of Asia. These nuts become ripe in October, and form a considerable article of commerce, Gen. xliii, 11.

OAK, a well-known, strong, durable tree: groves of this tree were esteemed proper places for religious services; hence the tree was sacred to Jupiter. It was common among the Hebrews to sit under oaks, Judges vi, 11; 1 Kings xiii, 14. The famous oracle of Dodona in modern Greece stood among oaks.

OATH. This is a solemn appeal to God for the truth of our assertions and the sincerity of our promises; and he who swears either expressly or by implication, invokes upon himself the judgments of God, if he speak falsely. The form of swearing has in all ages been various; consisting, however, for the most part, of some bodily action. Among the Jews, the custom was *to hold up the right hand toward heaven,* Psa. cxliv, 8; Rev. x, 5. This form is sometimes used in this country. Among the Jews, also, an oath of fidelity was taken by the servant's *putting his hand under the thigh of his master,* Gen. xxiv, 2. As the oath was an appeal to God, Deut. vi, 13, the taking of a false oath was deemed a heinous crime; and perjury, accordingly, is forbidden in the decalogue, Exod. xx, 7. *Stuart* translates the passage thus: " *Thou shalt not utter the name of Jehovah, in respect to a falsehood,*" i. e., thou shalt not take a false oath, thou shalt not call God as a witness to that which is not true. Says Mr. Way

Covel's Dic.,   *p.* 325.

PISTACHIA NUT.

and, "Oaths are frequently forbidden in the New Testament, and we are commanded to use *yes* for our affirmative, and *no* for our negative; for the reason, that '*whatsoever is more than these cometh of evil, or of the evil one,*'" Matt. v, 34–37; and yet it is thought, from an observation made by Paul, Heb. vi, 16, that both promissory oaths concerning things lawful and in our power, and oaths for the confirmation of things doubtful, *when required by proper authority, and taken religiously*, are allowable under the Gospel.

O-BA-DI'AH. The age in which this prophet lived is very uncertain. Some think that he delivered his prophecy about 585 B. C., soon after the destruction of Jerusalem by Neb-u-chad-nez'zar. His book, which consists of a single chapter, is written with great beauty and elegance, and contains predictions of the utter destruction of the Edomites, and of the future restoration and prosperity of the Jews.

OFFEND, *to vex, displease;* to cause dislike or anger. To *be offended in* or *at* any one, is to be so displeased at his character, words, conduct, as to desert and reject him, Matt. vi, 11.

The word has another signification, *to cause to offend, to lead astray, to lead into sin,* i. e., to be a stumbling block, or the occasion of one's sinning, Matt. v, 29. One is so offended who is *led astray,* or *into sin,* and so falls away from the truth, Matt. xiii, 21.

OFFERINGS, *oblations;* those things which are presented in Divine worship.

Burnt-offerings, or sacrifices in which the victims were wholly consumed, were expiatory, and more ancient than any others, and were, for that reason, held in special honour: and we accordingly find that they were offered sometimes for the whole people; as the morning and the evening sacrifices; and sometimes by an individual for himself alone, either from the free impulse of his feelings, or in fulfilment of a vow, Psa. li, 19; lxvi, 13, 14. The victims were bullocks of three years old, goats and lambs of a year old, turtle doves, and young pigeons. A libation of wine was poured out upon the altar.

Drink-offerings, consisting of wine, flour, and oil.

Meat-offerings. These, like the drink-offerings, were appendages to the sacrifices. They were of thin cakes or wafers. In some instances they were offered alone.

Heave-offerings. So called from the sacrifice being lifted up toward heaven, in token of its being devoted to Jehovah.

Peace-offerings. Bullocks, heifers, goats, rams, and sheep, were the only animals sacrificed on these occasions, Lev. iii, 1–17; vii, 23–

27. These sacrifices, which were offered as an indication of gratitude, were accompanied with unleavened cakes, covered with oil, by pouring it upon them; with thin cakes or wafers, likewise unleavened, and besmeared with oil; also with another kind of cakes, made of fine meal, and kneaded with oil. The priest, who sprinkled the blood, presented one of each of these kinds of cakes as an offering, Lev. vii, 11–14, 28–35. The remainder of the animal substance and of the cakes was converted by the person who made the offering into an entertainment, to which widows, orphans, the poor, slaves, and Levites, were invited.

Sin-offerings were for expiation of particular sins, or legal imperfections, called therefore sin-offerings : the first sort were for sins of ignorance or surprise. The other sort of sin-offerings were for voluntary sins ; but as to the more capital violations of the moral law, as murder, adultery, or the worship of idols, no expiatory sacrifice was admitted.

Trespass-offerings were not required of the people as a body. They were to be offered by individuals, who, through ignorance, mistake, or want of reflection, had neglected some of the ceremonial precepts of Moses, or some of those natural laws, which had been introduced into his code, and sanctioned with the penalty of death.; and who were subsequently conscious of their error.

Wave-offering. It was so called, because it was waved up and down, and toward the east, west, north, and south, to signify, that he to whom it was offered was Lord of the universe, the God who fills all space, and to whom all things of right belong. See SACRIFICES.

OG, supposed to mean *long necked*, king of Bashan, famous for his gigantic stature, Num. xxi, 33.

OIL, i. e., *olive oil*, commonly called sweet oil ; a nutritious substance, of a pale or greenish yellow colour, with scarcely any smell, and a bland slightly sweetish taste. This oil is the product of the *olive*, and obtained by first bruising the olives, and then submitting them to pressure. Sometimes the oil was expressed by treading them, Mic. vi, 5. Oil was anciently used for lamps, Matt. xxv, 8 ; for wounds, and anointing the sick ; and mixed with spices for anointing in token of honour, Luke vii, 46. The Jews were accustomed not only to anoint the head at their feasts, in token of joy, but also both the head and feet of those whom they wished to distinguish by peculiar honour. In case of sick persons, and also of the dead, they anointed the whole body, Psa. civ, 15 ; Mark vi, 13. *Beaten oil*, Exodus xxvii, 20, is said to be such as flowed from the

Covel's Dic.   p. 330

OLIVE BRANCH AND FRUIT.

olives when merely pounded in a mortar, and not put into a press; hence the purest and finest oil.

Oil of gladness, Psa. xlv, 7, means *perfumed*, or *odoriferous oil*, which was exhibited and used on occasions when there was much festivity and gladness; and here used as an emblem of the highest honour. A joyful occasion would be the coronation season of King Messiah, when the most precious and costly oil would be used to anoint him for his office. " *Oil* out of the flinty rock," Deut. xxxii, 13, i. e., from olives growing among rocks.

OINTMENT, *spiced oil*, described Exod. xxx, 34; see Psa. cxxxiii, 2. The holy anointing oil.

OLIVE TREE. This valuable tree is usually from fifteen to twenty feet in height, and grows at present in all the countries bordering on the Mediterranean. It has a solid erect stem, with numerous straight branches, covered with a grayish bark. The leaves, which stand opposite to each other on short footstalks, about three inches in length, resemble those of the willow, of a dull green colour on their upper surface, whitish and almost silvery beneath. The tree has a beautiful appearance, remaining green in winter. The flowers are disposed in clusters, the fruit of the tree, *the olive*, which is pleasant to the palate, has a pericarp, containing a very hard *nut* of similar shape. See *Engraving*.

It flourishes about two hundred years, and even while it is living, young olives spring up around it, which occupy its place when dead; the young sprouts are called *plants*, Psa. cxxviii, 3. The olive branch, from the most ancient time, was used as the signal of peace. The *oleaster*, or *wild olive tree*, bears no fruit, and is therefore contrasted by Paul with the cultivated or good olive, Rom. xi, 17, 24.

OLIVES, or OLIVET, the high lime-stone ridge, lying about two-thirds of a mile east of Jerusalem, parallel to the city, and separated from it by the valley of the Cedron; it was formerly planted with olive trees, of which few remain. Perhaps not more than fifty can be found upon it. Although the hill is not high, there is a splendid view on its summit toward the east; in the distance are seen the Dead Sea and the course of the Jordan, which falls into it, and the ruins of Jericho on the left; and so commanding is the view of Jerusalem afforded in this situation, that the eye roams over all the streets and around the walls, as if in the survey of the plan or model of the city. This mount has three summits, ranging from north to south, and about a mile in length; from the middle of, which our Saviour ascended into heaven. See PLAN OF JERUSALEM.

"It is truly a curious and interesting fact," adds a learned traveller, "that, during a period of little more than two thousand years, Hebrews, Assyrians, Romans, Moslems, and Christians, have been successively in possession of the rocky mountains of Palestine; yet the olive still vindicates its paternal soil, and is found, at this day, upon the same spot which was called by the Hebrew writers Mount Olivet, and the Mount of Olives, eleven centuries before the Christian era," 2 Sam. xv, 30.

OMEGA, the last letter of the Greek alphabet, used poetically for the *last*, as the writer himself explains it, Rev. xxii, 13. *First* and *last*, some understand in the same sense as *eternal*; others, the source and sum of all things.

OMER, a Hebrew measure for things dry; a little more than *five pints*.

ON, in Ezek. xxx, 17, written *Aven*, called also by the Hebrews, probably as a translation of the Egyptian name, Beth-shemesh, i. e., *house of the sun*, Jer. xliii, 13; by the Greeks Heliop'olis, *city of the sun*; an ancient Egyptian city, which stood on the eastern bank of the Nile, a few miles north of Memphis; and was celebrated for the worship and temple of the sun, and for its obelisks, some of which remain to the present day.

ONES'IMUS, a slave of Phil-e'mon, converted under St. Paul's preaching at Rome, and sent back by him to Philemon with an epistle, Col. iv, 9; Philem. 10.

ON-E-SIPH'O-RUS, a Christian at Ephesus, 2 Tim. i, 16.

ONION, a well-known garden plant, with a bulbous root. Onions and garlics were highly esteemed in Egypt; and not without reason, this country being admirably adapted to their culture. "Whoever has tasted onions in Egypt," says Hasselquist, "must allow that none can be had better in any part of the world; here they are *sweet*, in other countries they are nauseous and strong."

ONYCHA, Exod. xxx, 34. The *Blatta Byzantina*; the turbinated or spiral *shell* of a species of muscle, which, when burned, emits *a musky odour*, and whose fish yields a purple die. The name *blatta*, cockroach, seems to be given to this shell from the colour, as being of a dark hair colour, like that of the common cockroach. It is found in the lakes of India, where the *nard* grows, (see SPIKENARD,) which is the food of this fish, and makes its shell so *aromatic*. The best is said to be white, and found in the Red Sea. But the present name, *Byzantina*, is taken from those which are found about Constantinople.

ONYX, *the nail*, or *banded agate*; a gem exhibiting two or more colours, disposed in parallel bands or zones. It was obviously of high value, from the uses made of it, being placed in the breastplate, and from its being named with other highly valuable substances, Job xxviii, 16. See PRECIOUS STONES.

OPHEL, *hill*, a mound or height, on the eastern part of Mount Sion, surrounded and fortified by a separate wall, 2 Chron. xxxiii, 14; Neh. xi, 21.

OPHIR, a celebrated region, abounding in gold, which the seamen of Solomon, in company with the Phenicians, were accustomed to visit, taking their departure from the ports of the Elanitic Gulf, and bringing back every three years gold, precious stones, and algum trees, i. e., sandal wood, 2 Chron. viii, 18; ix, 10; especially, 1 Kings x, 22, where *Ophir* is to be understood, although not expressly mentioned. *The gold of Ophir* is frequently mentioned in the Old Testament. As to the geographical situation of this place, there is the greatest diversity of opinion among interpreters. Yet, among modern writers, the best seem to hesitate only between two regions, viz., *India* and some part of *Arabia*. From the articles imported, the port from which the ships sailed engaged in the trade, and the time required for the performance of the voyage, it seems far more probable that this place was situated somewhere in the *East Indies*;

but the precise spot cannot now be ascertained.

ORACLE, the inner sanctuary of Solomon's temple, also called *holy of holies*, whence Jehovah spake and gave forth his orders and directions. *Oracles* also mean any kind of Divine response or communication. "The *oracles* of God," Heb. v, 12, are the ancient revelations contained in the writings of Moses and the prophets.

Among the heathen, the term *oracle* is usually taken to signify an answer, generally couched in very dark and ambiguous terms, *supposed* to be given by demons of old, either by the mouths of their idols, or by those of their priests, to the people, who consulted them on things to come; probably invented in imitation of the responses given by Jehovah to the priests of ancient days. *Oracle* is also used for the demon who gave the answer, and the place where it was given.

ORCHARD, a place planted with fruit trees. The word so translated came to the Hebrews from the language of Eastern Asia, where it was applied to the pleasure gardens and parks, with wild animals around the residence of the Persian monarchs, Song iv, 13.

ORDAIN signifies *to appoint, set, constitute*, Rom. xiii, 1. In Acts xiii, 48, the original word signifies *to order, arrange, appoint, dispose, determine*: "As many as were ordained to eternal life believed;" i. e., as many as were *fixed*, or *resolved*, or *determined* upon eternal life: or, as Mr. Henry says, "As many as *were disposed* to eternal life, as many as *had a concern* about their eternal state, and *aimed to make sure* of eternal life, believed in Christ." The original word is not once used in Scripture to express *destiny* or *predestination* of any kind. The writer does not say *foreordained*. He is not speaking of what was done from eternity, but of what was then done through the preaching of the Gospel.

ORDINANCES, Exodus xviii, 20, as used by the sacred writers, the term signifies prescribed laws, rules, or appointments of God's government.

ORGAN, a wind instrument of music, invented by Jubal, Gen. iv, 21. It may be called the ancient shepherds' pipe, corresponding most nearly to the *pipe of Pan* among the Greeks, the origin of which is lost in the remote ages of antiquity. It consisted at first of only one or two, but afterward of about seven pipes made of reeds, and differing from each other in length. See cut, MUSICAL INSTRUMENTS.

O-RI'ON, one of the brightest constellations or clusters of stars of the southern hemisphere. The orientals appear to have conceived of this constellation under the figure of an impious giant, bound upon the sky; whence Job xxxviii, 31. "Canst thou loose the bands of *orion?*" or, as the constellation appears about the middle of November, some suppose that the ancients associated with it *frost*, figuratively represented as *bands*, which no human power can dissolve.

ORNAMENTS. The Hebrews, like the Babylonians, carried a staff merely for ornament, and not for any positive benefit, Exod. xii, 11. The dress of the ladies in the East was always expensive, Num. xxxi, 50; and how apt they were to indulge themselves in *finery*, we learn from the prophet's description of the dress of the Jewish ladies in his time. See Isa. iii, 16–24.

They had ornaments for the head, *veils* which hung down from the eyes over the face, called in the English version *mufflers*, Isa. iii, 19.

They also wore *cauls*, or nettings, i. e., caps of network, ver. 18; and also *amulets*, or superstitious ornaments suspended from the neck or the ears, called *earrings*; these earrings were of ten gems and precious stones, or plates of gold or silver, on which certain magic formulas were inscribed. Likewise from costly necklaces were often hung *bottles of perfumes*, called in the translation, Isa. iii, 20, *tablets*, filled with amber and musk. Also *crescents*, or little moons of silver and gold, were suspended this

Covel's Dic.   p. 336.

THE OSTRICH.

way, translated, ver. 18, *round tires like the moon.* The Jewish women wore rings upon their fingers, and also rings or *bands* of gold and other materials around the ankles, and short chains attached to them, so as to compel them to take short and mincing steps; compare ver. 20 with 16. Moreover, the Hebrew women *painted* their eyes with a *paint* called by the ancients *stibium,* which was the ore, i. e., the sulphuret of antimony; they also used a powder commonly prepared from lead ore and zinc, which they mixed with water, and spread upon the eyelids in such a way that the white of the eye might appear more white by being surrounded with a black margin. See Ezek. xxiii. 40.

OSEE, same as HOSEA.

OSPREY, a species of eagle.

OS'SI-FRAGE, *bone-breaker;* a name given to a kind of eagle, from its habit of breaking the bones of its prey, after it has eaten the flesh.

OSTRICH. This is the largest of birds; the height is usually seven feet, but the back is only four, and the neck and head are about three feet long. Their eggs are very large, some of them measuring above five inches in diameter, and weighing twelve or fifteen pounds. The plumage, which is unlike that of other birds, is generally white and black, though some

22

of them are said to be gray. The ostrich is rendered incapable of flying, not only by the peculiar structure of her wings, but by her enormous size. It is a native only of the torrid regions of Africa and Arabia, and aptly called by the ancients, *a lover of the deserts;* shy and timorous in no common degree, she retires from the cultivated field into the deepest recesses of the Sahara. When the ostrich is provoked, she sometimes makes a fierce, angry, and hissing noise, with her throat inflated and her mouth open; when she meets with a timorous adversary that opposes but a faint resistance to her assault, she cackles like a hen. But in the silent hours of the night she assumes a quite different tone, and makes a very doleful noise, and groans as if she were in agony. "On the least noise," says Dr. Shaw, "or trivial occasion, she forsakes her eggs, or her young ones; to which, perhaps, she never returns. The Arabs often meet with a few of the little ones no bigger than well-grown pullets, half starved, straggling and moaning about like so many distressed orphans for their mother. In this manner the ostrich may be said to be hardened against her young ones, as though they were not hers; her labour in hatching and attending them so far being in vain, without fear or the least concern of what becomes of them afterward. This want of affection is also recorded, Lam. iv, 3, 'The daughter of my people is become cruel, like *ostriches* in the wilderness;' that is, by apparently deserting their own, and receiving others in return."

Notwithstanding the stupidity of this animal, its Creator hath amply provided for its safety, by endowing it with extraordinary swiftness, and a surprising apparatus for escaping from its enemy. They, when they raise themselves up for flight, "laugh at the horse and his rider." They afford him an opportunity only of admiring at a distance the extraordinary agility and the stateliness likewise of their motions, the richness of their plumage, and the great propriety there was in ascribing to them an expanded, quivering wing.

OUCHES, *bezels*, or *sockets* in which gems are set.

OUTER, Matt. viii, 12, "*Outer* darkness," i. e., far remote from the light and splendour of the feast within. See verse 11, put for the infernal regions, or Tartarus; the farthest dark prison, as the image of the place of punishment, Matt. xxv, 30.

OVEN, a place for baking food. Perhaps the most common form of the oven was a large round pot of earthen or other materials, two or three feet high, narrowing toward the top; this being first heated by a fire made within, the dough or paste was spread upon the outside to bake, thus forming thin cakes. Another form was an excavation in the earth, about three feet in diameter, and five or six feet deep, as we may suppose from those which still exist in Persia. The bottom is paved with stones; when the oven is sufficiently hot, the fire is taken away; the cakes are placed upon the stones, and the mouth of the oven is shut. Sometimes a whole sheep is thus baked or roasted in them. The inhabitants of the East to this day, fuel being scarce, make use of *dry straw*, *withered herbs*, and *stubble*, to heat their ovens, Matt. vi, 30.

OWL. There are several varieties of this species, all too well known to need a particular description. They are nocturnal birds of prey, and have their eyes better adapted for discerning objects in the evening or twilight than in the glare of day.

OX. This animal is smaller in oriental countries than among us, and has a certain protuberance on the back directly over the fore feet. They were chiefly useful in agriculture, and were employed, two yoked together, in drawing carts and ploughs. See Num. vii, 7, 8; 1 Kings xix, 19; but the Nomades, i. e., those who lead a wandering life, frequently make use of them to transport goods on their backs, as they do on camels. The bull or ox is used figuratively for powerful, fierce, insolent enemies,

Covel's Dic.   p. 340.

PALM-TREE.

Psa. xxii, 12. The Egyptians had a particular veneration of this animal; they paid divine honours to it; and the Jews are supposed to have imitated them in their worship of the golden calves. The *wild ox*, mentioned Deut. xiv, 5, is supposed by Gesenius to be a species of *deer*, of a reddish colour, as the root signifies, with serrated horns, which are cast every year; probably the *fallow deer*.

PACATIANA, the western part of Phrygia, as divided by the Romans; occurs only in the spurious subscription, 1 Tim. vi, 22.

PA'DAN-A'RAM, a compound word, which signifies *plain of Syria*, i, e., Mesopotamia, with the desert on the west of the Euphrates; a level region, opposed to the mountainous tract along the Mediterranean, Gen. xxxi, 18. See MESOPOTAMIA.

PALESTINA, or PALESTINE, taken in a limited sense, denotes the country of the Philistines, Exod. xv, 14; a tract of country on the south-west coast of Syria, west and south-west of Canaan: but taken in a more general sense, it signifies the whole land of Canaan, as well beyond as on this side of Jordan, though frequently it is restrained to the country on this side that river: so that in latter times the words *Judea* and *Palestine* were synonymous.

PALM TREE, called. by Linnæus one of the princes of the vegetable kingdom. The palm is a lofty tree, sometimes rising to the height of 100 feet, consisting of a straight scaly trunk, whose centre is not solid, like other trees, but filled with pith, around which is a tough bark; and as the tree grows old, this bark hardens and becomes ligneous. It is destitute of limbs; but crowned with a spreading evergreen tuft of elongated leaves. The leaves, when the tree has grown to a size for bearing fruit, are six or eight feet long, are very broad when spread out, and are used for covering the tops of houses; also for making baskets, bags, mats, and brushes. The fruit, which is called *date*, grows below the leaves in large clusters, and is a great article of food in oriental countries. They grow on small stems at the angles formed by the stock of the tree and the branches, and become ripe in August, September, and October. The tree, as Dr. Shaw was informed, is in its greatest vigour about thirty years after it is planted, and continues in full strength seventy years longer; bearing all this while, every year, about three or four hundred pounds' weight of dates. Hence from its long and useful life, it is made the emblem of the righteous man, Psa. xcii, 12-14. The tree is regarded by the orientals above all others as the most excellent and noble. The *palm* was anciently very abundant in Palestine, particularly all around Jericho, which was thence called *the city of Palms*, Deut. xxxiv, 3. Hence on Jewish and Roman coins, the palm sometimes appears as the emblem of Palestine. The boughs, called also *palms*, were borne in the hands, or strewed in the way on seasons of rejoicing, Rev. vii, 9.

PALMER WORM, Joel i, 4; *a palmer* is a pilgrim, a palmer worm, i. e., a pilgrim worm, so called from its not being confined to any one species of plant; but the Hebrew word is supposed to refer to a destructive species of insect, of the locust tribe; the *creeping* locust without wings.

PALSY, a nervous disease, known by the loss or diminution of the power of voluntary *motion*, and sometimes of *sensation*, in one or several parts of the body. One species of this disease in oriental countries is a fearful malady, and by no means unfrequent, and very powerful. See Matt. viii, 6.

PAMPHYLIA, a district of Asia Minor, bounded north by Pisidia, east by Cilicia, south by a part of the Mediterranean, here called the Sea of Pamphylia; of its cities only *Perga* is mentioned in the New Testament, Acts xiii, 13.

PANNAG, Ezek. xxvii, 17. Gesenius says, *a kind of pastry*, or *sweet cake*.

PAPER, first invented in the time of Alexander the Great, and then made of the inner rind of the *papyrus*; a species of rush, which the ancients procured exclusively on the banks of the Nile. For the description of this plant, see RUSH.

Paper was first made of cotton about the year A. D. 1000, and of linen about A. D. 1300. Gesenius says, the *paper reeds*, mentioned Isa. xix, 7, should be translated *naked places*, i. e., without trees; spoken here of the meadows or grassy places on the banks of the Nile.

PAPHOS, a maritime city of Cyprus, near the western extremity; the station of a Roman proconsul or governor, Acts xiii, 6, 13. Near seven miles from the city was a celebrated temple of Venus; hence called *the Paphian goddess*.

PARABLE signifies sometimes *a figurative* or *dark saying*; one which is obscure, and full of hidden meaning. Matt. xiii, 35; but generally a short discourse, usually a narrative, under which something else is figured, or in which the fictitious is employed to represent and illustrate the real. Or it may be regarded exactly in the light of what we call *putting a case*, when a case is supposed with a design to teach and enforce something else. Such are the parables of our Saviour; they are ingenious comparisons, taken from the ordinary affairs of men, and used to illustrate the things of God. This was a favourite mode of teaching among all Eastern nations, especially the people of Palestine. It was the language of their sages and learned men; hence Solomon considers nothing is more insupportable than to hear a fool speaking parables, Proverbs xxvi, 7.

Some parables in the New Testament are supposed to be true histories, as the "*rich man and Lazarus*," the "*good Samaritan*," and the "*profligate son*." In reading the parables no attempt should be made to explain *every term;* for many parts belong to the ornament, to the filling up of the story, and are often introduced to complete the narrative. The *scope* is to be chiefly regarded, the *leading circumstances* which the author introduces to illustrate his subject, and not the words taken severally.

PARADISE, a word which seems to have had its origin in the languages of Eastern Asia, signifying *a land elevated and cultivated:* applied to the *pleasure gardens* and *parks,* with wild animals around the country residences of the Persian monarchs and princes, planted with grass, herbs, trees, for use and ornament. Hence the name has been given, by way of eminence, to the *garden of Eden,* where our first parents were placed; also to the place where the spirits of the just after death reside in felicity till the resurrection, as appears from our Lord's words to the penitent thief, Luke xxiii, 43; the same place is called Acts ii, 27, *Hades,* or *the invisible world,* or *world of the dead;* yet, Rev. ii, 7, heaven seems to be called the *paradise of God.*

PARAN signifies, according to Gesenius, *a region abounding in caverns;* a desert region, lying between Palestine and the peninsula of Sinai on the south, and between the valley *El Ghor* on the east, and the desert of Egypt on the west. It includes the present desert called *El Ty,* which, Burckhardt says, is the most barren and horrid tract of country he had ever seen; black flints covered a chalky or sandy ground, and in most places without any vegetation. The tree which produces the gum-arabic grows in some spots, and the tamarisk is met with here and there; but the scarcity of water forbids much extent of vegetation; and the hungry camels are obliged to go in the evening for whole hours out of the road, in order to find some withered shrubs upon which to feed. During ten days' forced marches, [from the El Ghor to Cairo,] he passed only four springs or wells, of which one only, at about eight hours east of Suez, was of sweet water. The others were brackish and sulphurous.

MOUNT PARAN, Hab. iii, 3,

was perhaps the chain on the west of the El Ghor, as *Seir* was on the east, or perhaps the mountains on the southern border of the desert toward the peninsula.

PARCHED occurs in Isa. xxxv, 7; *the parched ground,* which Gesenius translates, the mirage *shall become a lake.* The *mirage* is a phenomenon frequent in the deserts of Arabia and Egypt, and also occasionally seen in the southern parts of Russia and France. It consists in this: the flat surface of the desert presents the appearance of *water,* so that the most experienced travellers are sometimes deceived; and while he is all anxiety to arrive at it, it recedes as a new horizon discovers itself. The optical deception is so strong, that the shadow of any object on the horizon is apparently reflected as in water. Hence light is thrown upon the above words; the desert which presents the appearance of a lake shall be changed into a real lake.

PARCHMENTS. This word means books written on parchment, as the art of printing was not discovered till A. D. 1430. See BOOK.

Paul says to Timothy, 2 Tim. iv, 13, "Bring with thee the *books,* but especially the *parchments.*" By *books,* it is understood books made of the *papyrus.* See RUSH. Perhaps the apostle had notes, memoranda, and first draughts of writings executed on papy-

rus sheets, and some which were more carefully revised and finished on *parchments.*

PARTHIAN, Acts ii, 9, spoken of Jews born or living in Parthia. Parthia Proper was a large region of Persia, described as bounded north or north-west by Hyrcania; east by Asia; south by Carmania Deserta; and west by Media, and wholly surrounded by mountains. In the later period of the Roman republic, the Parthians extended their conquests, and became masters of a large empire. They were esteemed the most expert horsemen and archers in the world; and the custom of discharging their arrows while in full flight is peculiarly celebrated by the Roman poets.

PARTITION, "The middle wall of *partition,*" Eph. ii, 14; referring to the Mosaic law as separating the Jews and Gentiles; probably in allusion to the wall between the inner and outer courts of the temple.

PARTRIDGE, Jer. xvii, 11. The partridge often fails in her attempts to bring forth her young. To such disappointments she is greatly exposed from the position of her nest on the ground, where her eggs are often spoiled by the wet, or crushed by the foot. So he that broods over his ill-gotten gains will often find them unproductive; or, if he leaves them, as a bird occasionally driven from her nest, may be despoiled of their possession.

PASSION. It signifies, 1. *Suffering*, Acts i, 3. 2. *Infamous passion* or *lusts*, Rom. i, 26, to which those are given up whom God abandons to their own desires.

PASSOVER, *a passing over, sparing, immunity* from punishment and calamity. This great sacrifice and festival was instituted in commemoration of God's *sparing* the Hebrews, when he destroyed the first-born of the Egyptians; it was celebrated on the 14th day of the month *Ni'san*, which began with the new moon of April at sunset, i. e., at the moment when the new or 14th day began; for the institution and particular laws of this festival, see Exod. xii; Lev. xxiii; and Num. ix. The later Jews made some additions; in particular, they drank at intervals during the paschal supper four cups of wine, the third of which was called *the cup of benediction.* See 1 Cor. x, 16; and Matt. xxvi, 27. In the New Testament, *passover* is spoken,

1. Of *the paschal lamb*, i. e., a lamb or kid of a year old, slain as a sacrifice. According to Josephus, the number of lambs provided at Jerusalem in his time was 256,500; which were slain between the ninth and eleventh hour, i. e., from three to five o'clock in the afternoon, before the evening or commencement of the 14th day of Ni'san.

2. *The paschal supper, the festival of the passover*, on the eve of the 14th of Ni'san, which was also the commencement of the seven days' festival of unleavened bread. The word sometimes means *the paschal supper alone*, and sometimes in a wider sense it includes also *the seven days of unleavened bread*, i. e., the days in which they were to eat unleavened bread; hence the feast is so called, Matt. xxvi, 17.

The paschal lamb was an illustrious type of Christ, who became a sacrifice for the redemption of a lost world from sin and misery. Hence Christ is called "our passover;" and the "Lamb of God," without "spot," by the "sprinkling of whose blood" we are delivered from guilt and punishment; and faith in him is represented to us as "eating the flesh of Christ," with evident allusion to the eating of the paschal sacrifice.

PATARA, a maritime city of Lycia, Acts xxi, 1.

PATH, metaphorically the manner of life and conduct in which one walks; so a false way is false and deceitful conduct, Psa. cxix, 104; *the way of the Lord* is the way of life pleasing to God. Wicked people are said to have paths full of *snares*.

When a man walks from place to place in the dark, he may be glad of a *light* to assist in directing his *steps*; so the word of God is a light to guide those in their course of piety and duty who otherwise might wander, or be at a loss for direction.

PATHROS, the domestic proper name for *Upper Egypt*, distinguished from *Egypt*, which denotes, in its more limited sense, *Lower Egypt*. See Ezek. xxix, 14, where Pathros is called the native land of the Egyptians.

PATIENCE. This virtue consists in bearing all kinds of afflictions meekly and quietly, in the hope, whether of reward or deliverance. It differs from courage in this, that it is exerted under the actual suffering of evil; whereas courage is exerted in encountering evil, with a view to avert it. Afflictions are essential to the cultivation of patience, Rom. v, 3; they afford to the afflicted an opportunity of exercising patience, and they suggest considerations which naturally lead the mind to that virtue.

PATMOS, a small rocky island in the Ægean Sea, about eighteen miles in circumference; which, on account of its dreary and desolate character, was used by the Roman emperors as a place of confinement for criminals. To this island St. John was banished by the Emperor Domitian; and here he had his revelation, recorded in the Apocalypse.

PATRIARCH, the father and founder of a family or tribe, as Abraham, Heb. vii, 4; the sons of Jacob as heads of the twelve tribes, so of David as the head of a family, Acts ii, 29.

PATTERN. 1. The form or model after which any thing is made. Thus the visionary tabernacle shown to Moses in the mount is called the *type*, or *pattern*, because he was to make the material tabernacle exactly like it, Heb. viii, 5.

2. Spoken of a person as a type, bearing the form and figure, i. e., as having a certain resemblance in relations and circumstances. Thus, Rom. v, 14, Adam is called the *type* (*figure*) of Christ, who on that account is called the second Adam. See FIGURE.

PAUL, the apostle of the Gentiles, originally called *Saul*. He was of the tribe of Benjamin, and of purely Hebrew descent, Phil. iii, 5; but born at Tarsus in Cilicia, Acts xxi, 39, where his father enjoyed the rights of Roman citizenship, of which privilege Paul several times availed himself, e. g., Acts xvi, 37, xxii, 27. At Tarsus, which was a celebrated seat of learning, he probably gained that general acquaintance with Greek literature, which appears in his writings, and which was so important to him as a teacher of the Gentiles, or nations of Greek origin. His Jewish education was completed at Jerusalem, where he devoted himself to the severest discipline of the Pharisaic school, under the instruction of Gamaliel, Acts xxii, 3; compare v, 34. According to the custom of learned Jews, he appears also to have learned a trade, viz., that of a tent-maker, by which he afterward often supported himself, Acts xviii, 3 ; xx, 34.

Paul, in the fierceness of his Jewish zeal, was at first a bitter adversary of the Christians ; but after his miraculous conversion, he devoted all the powers of his ardent and energetic mind to the propagation of the Gospel of Christ, more particularly among the Gentiles. His views of the pure and lofty spirit of Christianity, in its worship and in its practical influence, appear to have been peculiarly deep and fervent ; and the opposition which he was thus led to make to the mere rites and ceremonies of the Jewish worship, exposed him to the hatred and malice of his countrymen. On their accusation, he was put in confinement by the Roman officers ; and after being detained for two years or more at Cesare'a, he was sent to Rome for trial, having himself appealed to the emperor. Here he remained in partial imprisonment two whole years, Acts xxviii, 30. Later accounts, mostly traditionary, relate that he was soon after set at liberty ; and that after new journeys and efforts in the cause of Christ, he was again imprisoned, and at last put to death by order of Nero.

The following chronological table of the principal events in his life, may be of use in directing and assisting inquiries into this most interesting portion of history.

	A. D.
Paul's conversion, . .	36
Escapes from Damascus,	39
Sent with Barnabas to Jerusalem to carry alms, ...	45
First missionary journey, Acts xiii, 14, commencing	45
Sent to consult the apostles, Acts xv, 1, . .	53
Second missionary journey, in which he finds Aquila at Corinth, Acts xviii, 2, ...	54
After being brought before Gallio, he departs for Jerusalem the fourth time, Acts xviii, 21, ...	56
Winters at Nicopolis, and then goes to Ephesus, ...	57
After a residence of two years or more at Ephesus, departs for Macedonia, ...	59
Goes the fifth time to Jerusalem, where he is . imprisoned, Acts xx, 21, ...	60
Arrives at Rome, after wintering in Malta, .	63
The history in Acts concludes, and Paul is supposed to have been set at liberty, . . .	65
Probable martyrdom of Paul and Peter, . .	65

The chronology of *Hug* is adopted, which is highly probable, yet *entire* certainty is not to be expected.

The following is *Hug's* arrangement of his epistles, with the places where they were written, and the date :—

Epistles.	Places.	Date.
1 Thessalonians,	Corinth,	54
2 Thessalonians,	do.	55
Titus,	Ephesus,	56
Galatians,	do.	57
1 Corinthians,	do.	59
2 Corinthians,	Macedonia,	59
1 Timothy,	do.	59
Romans,	Corinth,	60
Ephesians,	Rome,	61
2 Timothy,	do.	61
Colossians,	do.	61
Philemon,	do.	61
Philippians,	do.	{ end of 61 or beginning of . . 62
Hebrews,	do.	beginning of . . 62

PAVEMENT. The tesselated pavement of Mosaic work, i. e., floors most curiously inlaid, with variously coloured stones, or square tiles, disposed in a great variety of ornamental forms. Many of these remain in different countries to the present day. The Romans were particularly fond of them. Suetonius relates that Julius Cæsar, in his military expeditions, took with him pieces of marble ready fitted, in order that whenever he encamped, they might be laid down in his prætorium or *tent*.

PAVILION, (*Pa-vil'yun*,) a *tent*, designed chiefly for a general, or king.

PEACE is a word generally used for quiet and tranquillity, public or private; but often for prosperity and happiness of life. The Hebrew word *shalom*, usually translated *peace*, means, properly, *health*, *prosperity*, *welfare*. It is the same as the *salam* of the modern Arabs, and is, in like manner, used in salutations.

PEACOCK, a bird distinguished by the length of its tail, and the brilliant spots with which it is adorned; which displays all that dazzles in the sparkling lustre of gems, and all that astonishes in the rainbow. The peacock is a bird originally of India; thence brought into Persia and Media. From Persia it was gradually dispersed into Judea, Egypt, Greece, and Europe, 1 Kings x, 22.

PEARL. This substance is the production of a shell fish of the *oyster kind*, found mostly in the *East Indies* near Ceylon, an island in the Indian Ocean. They are of a brilliant sparkling white, and

Covel's Dic p. 360.

PELICAN.

in general perfectly round, formed of the same material as the inner shell, viz., the *carbonate of lime*, and consist of coats, similar to an onion. The largest are of the size of a small walnut; but these are very rare. The worth of the pearl is in proportion to its magnitude, roundness, fine polish, and clear lustre. Dr. Clarke saw one that formed the body of a Hindoo idol, more than an inch in length, and valued at more than $1500. The formation of these beautiful gems is one of the wonders of nature. The pearl oysters are found in clusters on rocks, at the depth of seventy feet on an average. They are obtained by diving, and this is done by a class of persons trained to the business. See Job xxviii, 18.

PELICAN, Lev. xi, 18, a very remarkable water bird. The one which I saw in the Zoological Institute, New-York, I judged to be four or five times larger than a goose. Its colour is a grayish white, except the upper part of its breast, which is a light yellow, and the middle of the back feathers are blackish. From the point of the bill, which was a little hooked, to the opening of the mouth, it measured seventeen inches. The bill was two and a half inches wide, and had under it a lax membrane, forming a sort of bag or pouch, which it could draw up at pleasure; and, at a little distance, resembled buckskin, both in its colour and texture, and capable of holding, I should say, five quarts of water. When empty, this pouch is not seen; but when filled, its great bulk and singular appearance may easily be conceived. Its voice resembles that of the goose, only much coarser. The pelican is slow of flight; and when it rises to fly, performs it with difficulty and labour. When they have raised themselves about thirty or forty feet above the surface of the sea, they turn their head with one eye downward, and continue to fly in that posture. As soon as they perceive a fish sufficiently near the surface, they dart down upon it with the swiftness of an arrow, seize it with unerring certainty, and store it up in their pouch. They then rise again and fish as before.

In feeding its young, the pelican squeezes the food deposited in its bag into their mouths, by strongly compressing it upon its breast with the bill; an action, says Shaw, which might well give occasion to the received tradition and report, that the pelican, in feeding her young, pierced her own breast, and nourished them with her blood. The annexed engraving will give you a good idea of a pelican when it is about to take its food.

PEN, from *penna*, a quill; because this well-known instrument for writing is usually made of the quill of a large bird. But *reeds* were anciently employed for this purpose, split and shaped to a point like our quills; and when it was necessary to write upon hard materials, as tables of wood or stone, the pen was made of iron, and sometimes tipped with *diamond*, Jer. xvii, 1, properly *a style*.

PENI'EL, *face of God;* a place beyond Jordan, near the ford on the brook Jabbok. See the origin of the name, Gen. xxxii, 32.

PENNY is put in the English translation for the Greek *drachma*, and the Roman *denarius*, both of which were equal in value to about fourteen cents. As this was a single coin, perhaps we should do well, in translating, to express it by one of our own, as near to it in value as possible; say, for instance, *a shilling*. Something like this is absolutely necessary, in Rev. vi, 6. As the passage now stands, it indicates great plenty; whereas it was intended to express a most distressing scarcity; *a measure*, i. e., a pint *of wheat for a shilling*.

PENTECOST, *fiftieth*, one of the three great Jewish festivals, in which all the males were required to appear before God; so called, because celebrated on the *fiftieth* day, counting from the second day of the festival of unleavened bread, or passover, i. e., seven weeks after the 16th day of Ni'san, Deut. xvi, 9; hence called *the feast of weeks*,

verse 10. It was a festival of *thanks* for the harvest, which began directly after the passover; and hence called *the day of the first fruits*, Num. xxviii, 26; and also for the law given from Mount Sinai, the fiftieth day after the exodus from Egypt. Josephus relates that, in his day, great numbers of Jews resorted from every quarter to Jerusalem to keep this festival. It was on the feast of pentecost that the Holy Ghost descended in the miraculous manner related Acts ii.

PEOR, a mountain in Moab, probably one of the summits of the Pisgah ridge, Num. xxiii, 28. ' *Beth-peor* is the temple of Peor; where the worship of Baal-peor was conducted, Deut. xxxiv, 6. See BAAL-PEOR.

PERDITION, utter ruin; spoken of the second death, i. e., eternal exclusion from the Messiah's kingdom, and subjection to eternal punishment for sin. *Son of perdition* is a Hebrew form of expression, signifying one devoted or exposed to perdition, 2 Thess. ii, 3.

PERFECTION, properly what has reached its *end;* hence *complete, full, wanting in nothing*. Thus fruit grown to *maturity* is in its perfection. The young man in the Gospel said, *What* LACK *I yet?* Jesus said unto him, If thou wilt be *perfect*, i. e., if thou wilt be *complete*, so that nothing shall be wanting, or *no lack* in thee, renounce the world, and become a spiritual man, Matt. xix, 20, 21.

Christian perfection is maturity in the Christian graces, the attainment of *full age;* see Eph. iv, 13: it is that participation of the Divine nature, which excludes sin from the heart, and fills it with love to God and man.

There is no such perfection in this life as implies freedom from *ignorance,* or *mistake,* or *temptation.*

Adamic perfection extends to the whole man; but Christian perfection extends chiefly to the *will,* or *bent of the mind,* leaving the understanding ignorant of ten thousand things, and the " body dead because of sin." But, whatever *mistakes,* or *errors,* or *faults;* whatever improprieties of speech or behaviour, may exist in Christians, so long as the *whole bent of the mind, the affections and desires,* is turned toward God, to "do the things that are pleasing in his sight," they do not sin, according to the Gospel. See Gen. xvii, 1; Deut. xviii, 13; Rom. xii, 2; 2 Cor. vii, 1; James i, 4; John xvii, 23; Col. iv, 12. It is certain that no *unclean thing* shall ever " enter the New Jerusalem:" we must, then, be saved from our sins in *this life,* or *in* death, or *after* death; but not *after* death, for if we die in our sins, where Christ is we can never come: nor *in* death, for as death cannot separate us from the love of God, so neither can it bring this love

23

into our hearts. It is the blood of Christ alone, applied by the eternal Spirit, that can cleanse us from sin, and bring us into the glorious liberty of the sons of God.

PERGA, the metropolis of Pamphylia, situated on the river Cestus; nearly seven miles from its mouth, and celebrated for a splendid temple of Diana, Acts xiii, 14.

PERGAMUS, now called *Bergamo,* a celebrated city of Mysia. It was situated near the river Caicus, about sixty miles north of Smyrna, and was the metropolis of the powerful kingdom of Pergamus, which was so famous under several of its kings, called *Attalus.* The kings of this race collected here a noble library of 200,000 volumes, which was afterward given by Mark Antony to Cleopatra, and added to the library at Alexandria. Here also *parchment* was first perfected; hence called in Latin *Pergamena.* At Pergamus was also a celebrated and frequented temple of Esculapius, who was the god of medicine, usually represented under the image of a serpent; whence probably the allusion in Rev. ii, 13. The celebrated physician Galen was a native of this place.

PERISH signifies *to die,* and also *to be lost for ever.* The destruction by which God will punish the wicked is not extinction of being. Their bodies will not be annihilated, for they will " rise to the resurrection of damnation," Dan. xii, 2; and their souls shall eternally exist, "where their worm dieth not, and the fire is not quenched," Mark ix, 43–50.

PER'IZ-ZITES, *inhabitants of the plain;* a Canaanitish tribe expelled by the Israelites, dwelling in the mountains of Judah, Joshua xvii, 15. This fact need not militate against the etymology above proposed, since their former seat may have been in the plains, Gen. xiii, 7.

PERSECUTION is the sufferings of Christians on account of their religion. The establishment of Christianity was opposed by the powers of the world, and occasioned several severe persecutions against Christians, during the reigns of several Roman emperors. The steady and uniform opposition made by the Christians to heathen superstition could not long pass unnoticed. Their open attacks upon Paganism made them extremely obnoxious to the populace, by whom they were represented as a society of atheists, who, by attacking the religious constitution of the empire, merited the severest animadversion of the civil magistrate.

PERSIA, (*Per'she-a,*) an ancient kingdom of Asia, bounded on the north by Media, on the east by Carma'ni-a, on the south by the Persian Gulf, and on the west by Su-si-a'na. The Persians became very famous from the time of Cyrus, the founder of the Persian monarchy. Their ancient name was Elamites; and in the time of the Roman emperors they went by the name of Parthians: but now Persians. See CYRUS.

PESTILENCE, or *plague,* generally is used by the Hebrews for all epidemic or contagious diseases. The prophets usually connect together sword, pestilence, and famine, being three of the most grievous inflictions of the Almighty upon a guilty people.

PETER, *a rock, stone;* the later Hebrew CEPHAS, *a rock;* the surname of Simon, one of the apostles, son of Jonas, and brother of Andrew, a fisherman of Bethsaida, Matt. xvi, 18. He afterward lived at Capernaum, and was married, Mark i, 30; compare ver. 21. This name was given him by Jesus at their first interview, John i, 43, probably on account of the boldness and usual firmness of his character. He was of an ardent but unequal temperament; at one time expressing unbounded devotedness to Jesus, and then denying him, Matt. xxvi, 33, 70. Although the first to preach the Gospel directly to the Gentiles, Acts xv, 7, 14, yet he wavered in respect to the introduction of Jewish observances among them, for which he was openly reproved by Paul, Gal. ii, 11. In later years, he is said to have gone abroad, and to have preached the Gospel in the

Parthian empire, whence probably his first epistle was written; the time is unknown. A still later legendary account makes him to have been the first bishop of Rome, and to have suffered martyrdom in that city along with Paul, (67 A. D.)

The honours and powers granted to St. Peter by name were conferred equally on all the disciples. For no one will say that Christ's Church was built upon St. Peter singly: it was built on the foundation of all the apostles and prophets, Jesus Christ himself being the chief corner stone. As little can any one say that the power of binding and loosing was confined to St. Peter, seeing it was declared afterward to belong to all the apostles, Matt. xviii, 18; John xx, 23. To these things add this, that as St. Peter made his confession in answer to a question which Jesus put to all the apostles, that confession was certainly made in the name of the whole; and, therefore, what Jesus said to him in reply was designed for the whole without distinction; excepting this, which was peculiar to him, that he was to be the first who, after the descent of the Holy Ghost, should preach the Gospel to the Jews, and then to the Gentiles—an honour which was conferred on St. Peter in the expression, "I will give thee the keys," &c.

PE'THOR, a city of Meso-

potamia, of which the Prophet Balaam was a native, Num. xxii, 5.

PHARAOH, *the king*, as the word signifies in the Egyptian language, OURO, meaning *king;* and P or PH being the article, the common title of the ancient Egyptian kings down to the time of the Persian invasion, about 525 B. C., as Ptolemy was after that time. It often stands simply like a proper name, Acts vii, 10.

PHARISEE, *the separate*, one of the sect of the Pharisees. This was a powerful sect of the Jews, in general opposed to the Sadducees, first mentioned by Josephus as existing under Hyrcanus, about 130 B. C., and already in high repute. They were rigid interpreters of the Mosaic law, and exceeding strict in its ceremonial observances; but often violated the spirit of it by their traditions and strained expositions, Matt. xxiii, 13. They also attributed equal authority to the traditional law or unwritten precepts, relating chiefly to external rites, as ablutions, fastings, prayers, alms, and the avoiding of intercourse with Gentiles, publicans, &c. Matt. ix, 11; xxiii, 2; Mark vii, 3; Luke xviii, 11. Their professed sanctity and adherence to the external ascetic forms of piety, gave them great favour and influence with the people. They believed with the Stoics, that all events are controlled by fate; but yet did not wholly exclude the liberty of the human will. They held to the separate existence of spirits and of the soul, and believed in the resurrection of the body; both of which the Sadducees denied, Acts xxiii, 8. They are said to have admitted the transmigration of souls; but this was only partially the case, since they merely held that the souls of the just pass into other human bodies. Our Saviour is often represented as denouncing the great body of the Pharisees for their hypocrisy and profligacy, Luke xvi, 14; yet there were doubtless exceptions, and individuals among them appear to have been men of probity and even of genuine piety, e. g., Gamaliel, Acts v, 34; Simeon, Luke ii, 25; Joseph of Arimathea, Luke xxiii, 51; and Nicodemus, John vii, 50; xix, 39.

PHAR'PAR. See ABANA.

PHEBE, an almoner in the church at Cenchrea. St. Paul had a particular esteem for this holy woman. It is thought she carried the epistle to Rome, which he wrote to the church of that city, in which she is so highly commended, Rom. xvi, 1, 2.

PHENICIA, a narrow tract of country on the east of the Mediterranean, about eighty miles long and twelve broad, between Palestine and Syria; according to Greek and Roman writers, terminating on the north at the river Eleu'the-rus, opposite the little island Aradus; and extending on the south as far as to Dora, or even to Pelusium; though according to the Scriptures, all the country south of Tyre belonged to the Hebrew jurisdiction. The chief cities were Tyre and Sidon. Phenicia may be considered as the birthplace of commerce, if not also of letters and the arts. It was a Phenician who introduced into Greece the knowledge and the use of letters. Phenician workmen built the temple of Solomon; Phenician sailors navigated his ships; Phenician pilots directed them; and before other nations had ventured to lose sight of their own shores, colonies of Phenicians were established in the most distant parts of Europe, Asia, and Africa; but the most famous of all their colonies was that of *Carthage.*

PHILADELPHIA, so called from its founder *Philadelphus,* king of Pergamus, a city of Lydia, in Asia Minor, about twenty - seven miles south-east of Sardis, and seventy, in nearly the same direction, from Smyrna. It has, however, retained a better fate than most of its neighbours. *Philadelphia is still erect, a column in a scene of ruins.* It has about a thousand Christian inhabitants, chiefly Greeks, who have five churches, with a resident bishop, and inferior clergy.

PHIL-EMON was an inhabitant of Colosse; and from

the manner in which he is addressed by St. Paul in his epistle to him, it is probable that he was a person of some consideration in that city. St. Paul seems to have been the means of converting him to the belief of the Gospel, Philemon 19. We learn from this epistle itself, that it was written when St. Paul was a prisoner, and when he had hope of soon recovering his liberty, Philemon 1, 22; and thence we conclude that it was written toward the end of his first confinement at Rome, A. D. 62. This epistle has always been deservedly admired for the delicacy and address with which it is written; and it places St. Paul's character in a very amiable point of view.

PHILIP, the name of four persons mentioned in the New Testament.

1. One of the twelve apostles, a native of Bethsaida, John i, 44.

2. The evangelist, one of the seven primitive deacons at Jerusalem, but residing afterward at Cesare'a, Acts xxi, 8. After the death of Stephen, he preached the Gospel at Samaria, Acts viii, 5. It was he also who baptized the Ethiopian treasurer, Acts viii, 38.

3. The tetrarch of Batanea. See Luke iii, 1. He was son of Herod the Great, by his wife Cleopatra, and own brother of Herod Antipas; at his death, his tetrarchy was annexed to Syria. From him

the city *Cesarea Philippi* took its name.

4. The first husband of Herodias, also a son of Herod the Great, by Mariamne, the daughter of Simon, the high priest. He led a private life, having been disinherited by his father, Matt. xiv, 3.

PHIL-IP'PI, one of the chief cities of Mac-e-do'ni-a, lying on the north-west of Ne-ap'o-lis, and taking its name from Philip, the celebrated king of Macedon, by whom it was repaired and beautified. In process of time it became a Roman colony, and was celebrated for the defeat of Brutus and Cassius. It was the first place at which St. Paul preached the Gospel upon the continent of Europe, A. D. 51. As the apostle tells the Philippians that he hoped to see them shortly, Phil. ii, 24, and there are plain intimations in his epistle of his having been some time at Rome, Phil. i, 12; ii, 26, it is probable that it was written A. D. 62, toward the end of his confinement.

PHILISTINES, the people who inhabited the plain of the Mediterranean, west and south-west of Canaan, and between Jaffa and Gaza, about forty miles long and fifteen broad. Gesenius says the conjecture is not improbable that the Philistines sprang from the Island of *Crete*, called in Scripture *Caphtor*, Jer. xlvii, 4; Amos ix, 7, which was inhabited by a colony of the Egyptians. The time of their coming to Palestine is unknown; but they were a powerful people in that place even in Abraham's time, (A. M. 2083.) They are not enumerated among the nations devoted to extermination. Joshua, however, did not hesitate to give their land to the Hebrews, and to attach them by command from the Lord, because they possessed various districts promised to Israel. But these conquests must have been ill maintained, since under the judges, at the time of Saul, and at the beginning of the reign of David, the Philistines had their kings and their lords. Their country to the north of Gaza is very fertile; and, long after the Christian era, it possessed a very numerous population and strongly fortified cities.

It now partakes of the general desolation common to it with Judea and other neighbouring states. While ruins are to be found in all Syria, they are particularly abundant along the sea coast, and the land of the Philistines.

PHILOSOPHY, literally, *the love of wisdom;* but, in modern acceptation, philosophy is a general term, denoting an explanation of the reasons of things; or an investigation of the causes of all phenomena, both of mind and of matter. When applied to any particular department of knowledge, it denotes the collection of general laws or principles under which all the subordinate phenomena, or facts relating to that subject, are comprehended. Thus that branch of philosophy which treats of God is called *theology;* that which treats of nature is called *physics,* or *natural philosophy;* that which treats of man is called *logic,* and *ethics* or *moral philosophy;* that which treats of the mind is called *intellectual,* or *mental philosophy,* or *metaphysics.*

A knowledge of the animal, vegetable, and mineral kingdoms, or the science of natural history, was always an object of interest. We are informed that Solomon himself had given a description of the animal and vegetable kingdoms, 1 Kings iv, 33. Traces of philosophy, strictly so called, that is, the system of prevailing moral opinions, may be found in the book of Job, in the thirty-seventh, thirty-ninth, and the seventy-third Psalms; also in the books of Proverbs and Ecclesiastes, but chiefly in the apocryphal book of Wisdom and the writings of the son of Sirach.

But, in the New Testament, philosophy signifies the Jewish theology, or theological learning pertaining to the interpretation of the law and other scriptures, and to the traditional law of ceremonial observances, Col. ii, 8; compare verse 16, and 1 Tim. vi, 20.

A PHILOSOPHER is an inquirer after knowledge natural and moral, in things human and Divine; spoken in the New Testament of Greek philosophers, Epicureans, and Stoics, who spent their time in inquiries and disputations respecting moral science, Acts xvii, 18.

PHRYGIA, an inland province of Asia Minor, bounded north by Bithynia and Galatia; east by Cappadocia and Lycaonia; south by Lycia, &c. In early times Phrygia seems to have included the greater part of Asia Minor. The cities of this province mentioned in the New Testament are Laodicea, Hierapolis, and Colosse. *Antioch of Pisidia* was also within its limits, Acts ii, 10.

PHUT, an African people, the same as *Maurita'nia*, which forms the modern kingdom of *Fez* and *Morocco*, in which country Pliny also mentions a river *Phut*, Ezekiel xxvii, 10.

PHY-LAC'TER-IES are little scrolls of parchment, in which are written certain sentences of the law, enclosed in leather cases, and bound with straps of leather on the forehead and on the left arm. The making and wearing of these phylacteries, as the Jews still do in their private devotions, is owing to a misinterpretation of those texts on which they ground the practice, namely, God's commanding them "to bind the law for a sign on their hands, and to let it be as frontlets be-

tween their eyes," &c., Deut. vi, 8. The command ought to be understood metaphorically, as a charge to remember it, and to meditate upon it; as when Solomon says, "Bind them about thy neck, write them upon the table of thy heart," Prov. iii, 1, 3; vi, 21. It seems the Pharisees used to *make broad their phylacteries;* which we may suppose they did from pride and hypocrisy, as pretending thereby an extraordinary regard for the precepts of the law. See FRONTLETS.

PHYSICIANS are mentioned first in Gen. l, 2. The Egyptians carried their sick into the temples of *Serapis;* the Greeks into those of *Esculapius.* In both of these temples there were preserved written recipes of the means by which various cures had been effected. With the aid of these recorded remedies, the *art of healing* assumed, in the progress of time, the aspect of a science. There is ample evidence that the Israelites had some acquaintance with the internal structure of the human system, although it does not appear that dissections of the human body for medical purposes were made till as late as the time of Ptolemy. The probable reason of King Asa's not seeking help from God, but from the physicians, as mentioned 2 Chron. xvi, 12, was, that they had not at that period recourse to the simple medicines which nature offered, but to certain superstitious rites and incantations; and this, no doubt, was the ground of the reflection which was cast upon him.

PI-HA-HI'ROTH, doubtless an Egyptian name, *the place of green grass or sedge;* perhaps the modern *Suez.* The situation of this place is described as between *Migdol* (Bir-Suez) and the Red Sea, Exod. xiv, 2, i. e., *Suez,* or near to that place. In Num. xxiii, 7, the Hebrews are said to have encamped *before* this and Migdol. Of course both towns must have been within the view of their encampment; and Baal-Zephon lay *before* or *toward the east,* i. e., north-east of Pihahi'roth, where the ruins of Colsum now are situated.

PILATE, i. e., *Pontius Pilate;* the fifth Roman procurator, or governor of Judea; the fourth was Valerius Gratus, who was succeeded by Pilate about A. D. 26. He is represented, both by Philo and Jo-se'phus, as a man of an impetuous and obstinate temper, and, as a judge, one who used to sell justice, and, for money, to pronounce any sentence that was desired. The same authors make mention of his rapines, his injuries, his murders, the torments that he inflicted upon the innocent, and the persons he put to death without any form of process. Philo, in particular, describes him as a man that exercised an excessive cruelty during the whole time of his government; who disturbed the repose of Judea, and was the occasion of the troubles and revolt that followed. Pilate continued in office about ten years; and being hated both by Jews and Samaritans for the caprice and cruelty of his administration, he was accused by them before *Vitellius,* then president of Syria, and sent by him to Rome to answer to these complaints before the emperor. Tiberius was dead before the arrival of Pilate; and the latter is said to have been banished by Caligula to Vienna, in Gaul, and there to have died by his own hand, about A. D. 41. The extreme reluctance of Pilate to condemn Christ, Matt. xxvii, 17–25, considering his merciless character, is signally remarkable, and still more his repeated protestations of the innocence of his prisoner; although, on occasions of massacre, he made no scruple of confounding the innocent with the guilty. But he was unquestionably influenced by the overruling providence of God to make the righteousness of his Son appear as clear as the noonday, even when condemned and executed as a malefactor.

PILGRIM, properly one who is going forward to visit a holy place, with design to pay his solemn devotions there; but, in Scripture, it means *a sojourner,* a temporary resident among any people; one who lives in another country without the rights of a citizen, Heb. xi, 13.

PILLAR, a column raised to support a building. *The pillars of heaven* are the lofty mountains, upon which heaven, spread out like an arch above the earth, seems to rest, Job xxvi, 11. The earth also is represented as founded upon a similar basis, Job ix, 6; a *pillar* of cloud, Exod. xiii, 21; a cloud, the form of which resembled a pillar, not like other clouds spread out horizontally, but extending from the earth upward like a pillar. See Judges xx, 40. That this was the same as the *pillar of fire*, or fiery pillar, is rendered quite probable by Exod. xiv, 20, where the same cloud affords light to the Hebrews by night, and darkness to the Egyptians, i. e., that part of this cloudy pillar which was toward the camp of the Israelites was luminous; while it only increased the darkness to those who were in an opposite direction. By day the same cloud appears to have afforded a shade to shelter from the burning rays of the sun; and also to have guided the way of the caravan.

St. Paul represents the Christian Church as the *pillar* and basis of the truth, 1 Tim. iii, 15, and the sum and substance of the Gospel, as an inscription engraven on that pillar, for the purpose of luminous exhibition to the world, see verse 16.

Pillar is used figuratively, for *any firm support;* e. g., for persons of authority and influence in the Church, Gal. ii, 9.

PILLAR OF SALT. See SALT.

PILLED, Gen. xxx, 37; the same with *peeled.*

PILLOW, *a cushion for the head or arm.* The prophet speaks of "sewing pillows to arm holes." There is here, probably, an allusion to the easy indulgence of the great, Ezekiel xiii, 18; see Amos vi, 4.

PINE TREE, a well-known tree of the nature of the fir.

PINNACLE, a part of a building elevated above the main building. "The *pinnacle* of the temple," Luke iv, 9, was probably the *apex* or *summit* of Solomon's porch, which Josephus describes as being exterior to the temple on the east side, and built up to the giddy height of 600 or 700 feet from the foundation in the valley of the Cedron below.

PIPE, 1 Cor. xiv, 7; a wind instrument of music, consisting of a long perforated tube of wood or metal. Pipes and flutes are found among all nations, even the most uncivilized. The New Zealanders, and the inhabitants of the South Sea Islands, had them when first discovered. The pipe, probably, had anciently a general resemblance to the flageolet.

PISGAH, a mountain

ridge, in Moab, over against Jericho; probably a part of Mount Nebo, and not far from the northern part of the Dead Sea, Deut. xxxiv, 1, and at whose base are several fine springs of water, Deut. iv, 49.

PISIDIA, a district of Asia Minor, lying mostly on Mount Taurus, between Pamphylia, Phrygia, and Lycaonia. Its chief city was Antioch, Acts xiii, 14.

PISON, a river issuing from the garden of Eden, and flowing around the land of Havilah, i. e., Colchis, Gal. ii, 11. This is supposed by Stuart and others to be the *Phasis*, a river of Colchis, which runs into the east end of the Black Sea.

PIT, a cistern or reservoir; cisterns were sometimes hewn in stone, prepared in those regions where they have few springs, for the purpose of preserving rain water for travellers and cattle; and when without water, they were often used as *prisons*, Zech. ix, 11. Into such a pit Joseph was cast, Gen. xxxvii, 20.

The word also means a deep hole in the earth, covered very slightly with boughs or shrubs, upon which bait is placed for the purpose of entrapping wild beasts, Ezek. xix, 8. It also signifies a sepulchre, the grave, where the dead are described as "those who go down to the *pit*," Psa. xxviii, 1; and "to the stones of the *pit*," Isa. xiv, 19, i. e., who are laid in

costlier sepulchres, hewn in the rock. "The sides of the *pit*," Isa. xiv, 15, are the *recesses* of the sepulchre.

The bottomless pit is the prison of demons and the souls of wicked men, Rev. ix, 1. See SEPULCHRE.

PITCH, a tenacious oily substance, drawn chiefly from pines and firs. In the Bible, it is supposed to be a mineral production. See SLIME.

PITHOM, a city of Lower Egypt, on the eastern bank of the Nile, Exod. i, 11.

PLAGUE, spoken chiefly of pestilential and fatal diseases, Num. xiv, 37, and of the judgments sent from God.

PLAINS, a low, level country, as opposed to mountains, e. g., that in which Babylon was situated. There was also a plain lying at the foot of Hermon around the sources of the Jordan, called the *valley of Lebanon*, Josh. xii, 7. The *plain of Jordan*, or *region round about*, Matt. iii, 5, includes the shore of both sides of the Jordan, from the Lake Genesareth to the Dead Sea. Its breadth from west to east is thirteen miles; and modern travellers make the length about fifty-six, This plain or valley is called *El Ghor*, and comprehends the *Dead Sea*; hence called "sea of the *plain*," Deut. iv, 49, extending south to the Elanitic Gulf. See JORDAN.

PLANETS, *wanderers*, so called from changing their places in the heavens, being sometimes stationary and sometimes retrograde. They shine by reflecting the light of the sun around which they revolve. Five of them, viz., *Mercury, Venus, Mars, Jupiter,* and *Sa'turn,* were discovered long before the invention of the telescope, (A. D. 1590.) They appear brighter and larger than the fixed stars ; the other five are scarcely visible to the naked eye. The word occurs but once in the Bible, 2 Kings xxiii, 5, where Gesenius translates it *lodgings,* and understands by it *the twelve signs of the Zodiac,* which the Hebrews regarded as the *lodgings* of the sun during the twelve successive months, and offered them idolatrous worship.

PLEIADES, (*Ple'yadz,*) a cluster of stars, consisting of seven large ones, commonly called the *seven stars,* closely conglomerated with others, which are smaller, Job ix, 9. They appear about the middle of April ; and hence are associated with the return of spring, the season of sweet influences.

POETS. The Hebrew poets were men inspired of God ; and among them we find kings, lawgivers, and prophets. Paul gives a pagan poet, whose name was Epimen'ides, the title of prophet, Tit. i, 12, because, among the heathen, poets were thought to be inspired by Apollo. The apostle quotes the poet Ara'tus, a native of his own city, *Cilicia,* Acts xvii, 28 ; see Col. vii, 54.

POISON is any substance which, when taken into the stomach in small quantities, or otherwise introduced into the system, produces changes in the body deleterious to the health, and even destructive to life, by means not mechanical. Many poisons operate chemically, corroding the organized fibre, destroying the form and connection of the parts, causing inflammation and mortification. To this class belong most of the poisons of the mineral kingdom, as arsenic and corrosive sublimate. Others operate more, by a powerful action upon the nerves, and a rapid destruction of their energy. To this class belong prussic acid, opium, hemlock, belladonna, &c. David speaks of *animal* poison, Psalm lviii, 5. *The poison of serpents ;* and the prophet of *vegetable poison,* Hosea x, 4 ; *the gall of asps,* Job xx, 14, is put for their *poison,* which the ancients falsely supposed to lie in the gall. It appears that the art of *poisoning arrows* was very ancient in Arabia ; see Job vi, 4. And we are told that the Africans were obliged to *poison their arrows,* in order to defend themselves from the wild beasts with which their country was infested. This poison, Pliny tells us, was incurable. The Indians of South America, it is said, apply also a very powerful poison, called the *wourali* poison, to the heads of their arrows, with which they shoot their game. It destroys life very quickly, without corrupting or imparting any bad quality to the flesh.

POLL, Num. iii, 47. When used as a noun, *poll* means a head ; and, when used as a verb, it means to cut the hair from the head, 2 Sam. xiv, 26.

POL'LUX, a protecting deity of mariners in ancient times, Acts xxviii, 11, whose *image* was placed either at the prow or stern of the ship.

POMEGRANATE, i. e., *the granate apple*. This tree grows wild in Syria, Palestine, and Egypt. It is low, with a straight trunk, and at a little distance from the ground ; shoots out into a multitude of branches ; the flowers are large, and of a brilliant red ; the fruit it bears is about the size of a large apple, of a tawny brown, beautiful to the eye, and pleasant to the palate ; and is encircled at the upper part with something resembling a crown. It is covered with a thick astringent coat, containing abundance of seeds, each enveloped in a distinct rind, like those of the orange, Deut. viii, 8 ; Song iv, 13. - Artificial pomegranates made to resemble natural ones were used as ornaments, Exod. xxviii, 33 ; 1 Kings vii, 18.

POMMEL, a knob or ball ; in the Bible *a globe*, or *bowl*, as an ornament on the tops or capitals of columns, 2 Chr. iv, 12 ; 1 Kings vii, 41.

PONTUS, the north-eastern province of Asia Minor, bounded north by the **Black** Sea, east by Colchis, south by Cappadocia, and west by Paphlagonia, Acts ii, 9. The kingdom of Pontus became celebrated under Mithridates the Great, who waged a long war with the Romans, in which he was at last defeated by Pompey, and his kingdom made a Roman province. Aquila, Paul's companion, was of this province, Acts xviii, 2.

POSTS signifies in the Bible *runners, couriers*, referring to the mounted couriers of the Persians, who carried the royal edicts to the provinces, Esth. iii, 13. Cyrus, or according to He-rod-o'tus, Xerxes was the first to establish relays of horses and couriers, at certain distances, on all the great roads, in order that the royal letters and messages might be transmitted with the greatest possible speed. The public couriers had authority to press into their service men, horses, ships, or any thing which came in their way, and which might serve to hasten their journey. Hence the word *posts* is said to be derived from the Latin *positus*(placed,) because horses were placed at certain distances to transport letters or travellers. This is the origin of one of the most effective instruments of civilization.

POTSHERD, a broken fragment, or a piece of an earthen vessel.

POTTAGE, *broth*, or any

Cowel's Dic.   p. 365.

POMEGRANATE.

dish of food made by boiling.

POTTER, a maker of
earthen vessels, Jer. xviii, 3.

POTTER's FIELD, the land
that was bought with the
money for which Judas sold
our Saviour, Matt. xxvii, 7, 10,
and which he returned. ·See
A-CEL'DA-MA.

POUND. In the New
Testament a silver coin, equal
to $16¼. It varied, however,
in different countries.

Sometimes the word *pound*
signifies *a weight*, which was
equal to about twelve ounces
avoirdupois, John xii, 3.

PRAISE. In the ordinary
Scripture use of the term, it
denotes an act of worship,
and is often used synony-
mously with thanksgiving. It
is called forth by the contemplation of the character and
attributes of God, however
they are displayed; and it
implies a grateful sense and
acknowledgment of past mercies. Expressions of praise
abound in the Psalms of David in almost every variety
of form and beauty; and the
nature of the duty, as well as
the proper manner of its performance, may be best ascertained by a diligent study of
his language and spirit, Psa.
xxxiii, 1.—*Union Dic.*

PRAYER has been well
defined, the offering up of our
desires unto God, Phil. iv, 6.

1. Prayer is in itself a becoming acknowledgment of
the all-sufficiency of God, and
of our dependance upon him.
It is his appointed means for
the obtaining of both temporal
and spiritual blessings. He
could bless his creatures in
another way: but he will be
inquired of, to do for them
those things of which they
stand in need, Ezek. xxxvi,
37. It is the act of an indi
gent creature, seeking relief
from the fountain of mercy.

2. All acceptable prayer
must be offered in faith, or a
believing frame of mind. "If
any man lack wisdom, let him
ask of God, who giveth to all
men liberally, and upbraideth
not, and it shall be given him.
But let him ask in faith, nothing wavering—for let not
the wavering man think that
he shall receive any thing of
the Lord," James i, 5–7. "He
that cometh unto God must
believe that he is, and that he
is a rewarder of them that
diligently seek him," Heb. xi,
6. It must be offered in the
name of Christ, believing in
him as revealed in the word
of God, placing in him all our
hope of acceptance, and exercising unfeigned confidence
in his atoning sacrifice and
prevalent intercession.

3. Prayer is to be offered for
"things agreeable to the will
of God." So the apostle says:
"This is the confidence that
we have in him, that, if we
ask any thing according to
his will, he heareth us; and
if we know that he hear us,
whatsoever we ask, we know
that we have the petitions that
we desired of him," 1 John v,
14, 15.

4. All this must be accom-

panied with confession of our sins, and thankful acknowledgment of God's mercies. These are two necessary ingredients in acceptable prayer. " I prayed," says the Prophet Daniel, " and made confessions." Sin is a burden of which confession unloads the soul. Thanksgiving is also as necessary as confession ; by the one, we take shame to ourselves ; by the other, we give glory to God. By the one, we abase the creature ; by the other, we exalt the Creator. In petitioning favours from God, we act like dependant creatures ; in confession, like sinners ; but in thanksgiving, like angels.

The reason on which this great and efficacious duty rests seems to be, the preservation in the minds of men of a solemn and impressive sense of God's agency in the world, and the dependance of all creatures upon him. Perfectly pure and glorified beings, no longer in a state of probation, and therefore exposed to no temptation, may not need this institution ; but men in their fallen state are constantly prone to forget God ; to rest in the agency of second causes, and to build upon a sufficiency in themselves. It is then equally in mercy to us, as in respect to his own honour and acknowledgment, that the Divine Being has suspended so many of his blessings, and those of the highest necessity to us, upon the exercise of prayer. And those who bow to the authority of the Scriptures will see, that the duty of praying for others rests upon the same Divine appointment ; for there is the same reason to conclude that our prayers may benefit others, as any other effort we may use. It can only be by Divine appointment that one creature is made dependant upon another for any advantage, since it was doubtless in the power of the Creator to have rendered each independent of all but himself. Whatever reason, therefore, might lead him to connect and interweave the interests of one man with the benevolence of another, will be the leading reason for that kind of mutual dependance which is implied in the benefit of mutual prayer. He who believes the Scriptures, will, however, be encouraged by the declaration, that " the effectual fervent prayer of a righteous man," for his fellow-creatures, " availeth much." It is a part of the Divine plan, as revealed in his word, to give many blessings to man independent of his own prayers, leaving the subsequent improvement of them to himself. They are given in honour of the intercession of Christ, man's great " advocate ;" and they are given, subordinately, in acceptance of the prayers of Christ's Church, and of righteous individuals.—*Watson.*

PREACHER, one who addresses a public assembly.

and imparts instruction respecting the Divine will. From the earliest associations for the worship of God, religious truth has been imparted to mankind through the instrumentality of preachers. Noah "was a *preacher* of righteousness," 2 Pet. ii, 5.

Moses was a most eminent prophet and preacher, raised up by the authority of God, and by whom, it was said, came the law, John i, 17. This great man had much at heart the promulgation of his doctrine; he directed it to be inscribed on pillars, to be transcribed in books, and to be taught both in public and private by word of mouth, Deut. iv, 9; vi, 9; xvii, 18; xxvii, 8; xxxi, 19. He himself set the example of each; and how he and Aaron preached, we may see by several parts of his writings. The first discourse was heard with profound reverence and attention; the last was both uttered and received with raptures, Exod. iv, 31; Deut. xxxiii, 7, 8, &c.

Moses had not appropriated preaching to any order of men: persons, places, times, and manners, were all left open and discretional. Many of the discourses were preached in camps and courts, in streets, schools, cities, villages; sometimes with great composure and coolness; at other times with vehement action and rapturous energy; sometimes, in a plain, blunt style; at other times, in all

24

the magnificent pomp of eastern allegory. These men were highly esteemed by the pious part of the nation; and princes thought proper to keep seers and others who were scribes, who read and expounded the law, 2 Chron. xxxiv, 29, 30; xxxv, 15.

When the Jews were carried captive into Babylon, the prophets who were with them inculcated the principles of religion, and endeavoured to possess their minds with an aversion to idolatry; and, to the success of preaching, we may attribute the reconversion of the Jews to the belief and worship of one God; a conversion that remains to this day. The Jews had almost lost, in the seventy years' captivity, their original language. Formerly, preachers had only explained subjects: now they were obliged to explain words; words which, in the sacred code, were become obsolete, equivocal, or dead. Houses were now opened, not for sacrificing, for this was confined to the temple; but for moral and religious instruction, as praying, preaching, reading the law, Divine worship, and social duties. These houses were called synagogues: the people repaired thither for morning and evening prayer; and on Sabbaths and festivals, the law was read and expounded to them. We have a short but beautiful description of the manner of Esra's first preaching, Nehemiah viii.

From this period to that of the appearance of Jesus Christ, public preaching was universal; synagogues were multiplied, vast numbers attended, and elders and rulers were appointed for the purpose of order and instruction.

The most eminent preacher that arose before the appearance of Jesus Christ was John the Baptist. Let the reader charm and solace himself in the study and contemplation of the character, excellency, and dignity of this Divine teacher, as he will find them delineated in the evangelists.

The apostles copied their Divine Master. They formed multitudes of religious societies, and were abundantly successful in their labours. They confined their attention to religion, and left the schools to dispute, and politicians to intrigue. The doctrines they preached they supported entirely by evidence; and neither had nor required such assistance as human laws or worldly policy, the eloquence of schools, or the terror of arms, could afford them.

PRECIOUS STONES, or *gems*; these are crystalized mineral substances, frequently referred to in the Bible, and remarkable for their *hardness, brilliancy, scarcity*, and *colour*. It is this last property, heightened by the lustre of the stone, which principally strikes the beholder. By lustre is meant the quantity of light which the mineral is capable of reflecting. The ancients, deceived by the external appearance, classified the stones according to their colours; but modern mineralogy rejects this false classification and establishes one upon the chemical properties of the stone. Thus *quartz*, for example, constitutes one of the most abundant of minerals. It often occurs in the state of silex, or common sand; and very frequently in the form of regular crystals. Any mineral substance is a crystal whose component particles are so arranged as to give the mineral a particular shape, having flat sides and regular angles, and appearing as though it had been formed by art. The most common form of *quartz* is a six-sided prism, terminated by six sided pyramids. When this crystal is of uniform density perfectly transparent, i. e., objects are distinctly seen through it, and colourless, it occupies a distinguished place in the collections of amateurs, under the name of *rock crystal*, (see Rev. iv, 6,) which the ancients believed was water congealed to that hardness by intense and long continued cold. Hence the word *crystal*, which signifies *ice*. But this mineral is often coloured by the oxide of iron, mangenese, nichel, &c., forming a class of gems called "oxidental gems."

When coloured *violet*, it is called *omethyst*; when red, it is called *rose quartz*; when yellow, it is called the *Indian topaz*. This gem the ancients seem to have distinguished by the name of *chrysolite*. The colouring matter of the amethyst is the oxide of manganese. *Jasper* also is a species of quartz, distinguished by its opacity and by the darkness of its colours. It is found in Egypt; and, Thomson says, seems to consist of silica, united to a small quantity of the peroxide of iron. *Chalcedony*, when pure, consists of silex, with a small quantity of water, which enters into the composition of all crystaline bodies, differing from quartz merely in the way in which the particles have been united together. The lustre is dull, or only glimmering; the hardness, of course, is the same as that of quartz; alternate layers of brown and opaque white chalcedony constitute the *onyx*; when the colour is a deep brownish red, or by transmitted light, *blood-red*, the stone is termed *sardine*, more commonly known by the name of *cornelian*. Alternate layers of sardine, or cornelian and milk-white chalcedony constitute *sardonyx*.

Agate is a compound mineral, consisting of alternate layers of chalcedony and quartz, and the lowest in value of all the precious stones.

Chrysoprasus, or chrysoprase, is from two Greek words, which signify *gold* and *leek*. It resembles in all respects the *chalcedony*, **except** in colour, in which it resembles the juice of the *leek*, but with somewhat of a golden tinge; and hence its name. Its colouring matter is the oxide of nickel.

The *ligure* is supposed to be the modern *opal*, which is a beautiful white gem, of the silicious family.

Alumina, alumine, or pure clay enters into the composition of a class of gems called " oriental gems." Alumina is one of the most abundant productions of nature; it is found in every part of the globe, and occasionally *crystalized*. This is the *sapphire*, and one of the most beautiful gems with which we are acquainted. The pure colourless sapphire is composed of alumina, nearly pure. This name, however, is appropriated to the blue variety of this mineral; when red, it is called *ruby*; when yellow, *topaz*; when green, *emerald*; and, when violet, *amethyst*. These genera are harder than any other minerals except the diamond, and more commonly found in primary rocks as granite, or in loose sands. The finest crystals come from the Uralian mountains, Kamschatka, and South America. The *blue sapphire* is brought from Ceylon, and has been found six inches in length, valued at £3000 sterling, over $13,000. It is cut by means of diamond dust, and admits of the highest degree of lustre. A sapphire of ten carats' weight is worth fifty guineas. Among the crown jewels of France is a sapphire weighing 166 carats.

The *ruby*, a beautiful red sapphire, is coloured by the chromic acid, and is more highly esteemed than any other variety of the sapphire. A crystal weighing four carats (one carat is four grains) has been valued at half the price of the diamond of the same size. It seldom exceeds half an inch in length; but two splendid crystals of this gem are said to be in the possession of the king of Arracan, with a diameter of about an inch. The finest specimens occur in the Copeland mountains, in the kingdom of Ava.

Topaz, so called from an island in the Red Sea, in which the gem was anciently found. It is of a golden or orange colour; and besides alumina, it contains silicia and fluoric acid.

Under the word *emerald*, the ancients appear to have comprehended all gems of a *fine green colour*. The green sapphire called *emerald* is extremely rare, found in the kingdom of Cambay.

Our *emerald* contains a substance called *glucina;* a white powdered earth, which has neither taste nor smell; and when combined with an acid, form a salt of a sweetish taste. Hence the name *glucina*, which signifies *sweet*. This substance is found only in three rare minerals; the beryl, emerald, and another mineral lately found in Peru, South America.

The *emerald* and *beryl* are varieties of the same species, and are distinguished merely by their colour. The bright green variety is called *emerald*, while all the pale varieties are denominated *beryl*. These gems consist of alumina silica and glucina, above described. The colouring principle the emerald is the *oxide of chrome*, and in the beryl a small quantity of iron. The ancients procured their emeralds chiefly from Upper Egypt, about twenty miles from the Red Sea, in Mount Zalara. A splendid specimen of the emerald, in the possession of Mr. Hope, of London, weighing but six ounces, cost £500 sterling, over $2,200.

Chrysolite consists of silex, magnesia, and a small quantity of the protoxide of iron; the colour is green, of various shades. Perfectly crystalized specimens are brought from Constantinople; but as the name signifies *golden stone*, which the ancients applied to any yellow gem, their chrysolite is supposed to be the modern hyacinth, or jacinth, which is of a deep golden, or amber colour. This gem is composed of silex, and zircon, coloured by the oxide of iron. Sometimes found in the sands of rivers; it is thus found in Ceylon. None of these gems are bright, except some of the red tints.

Garnet. The precious garnet consists of silex, alumina, lime, iron, and sometimes nanganese; the colour is always *red.* It occurs in the greatest perfection in Ceylon and Greenland. The large proportion of iron contained in it does not impair its transparency. It is the *carbuncle* of the ancients, though some suppose it to be what they termed the *hyacinth.*

Lapis lazuli, a splendid mineral of a rich azure blue colour; the ancient sapphire. It contains particles of iron pyrites, which have been mistaken for gold. Hence it is described by Theophrastus as sprinkled with gold. About one half of this gem is *silex;* it contains alumina, lime, potash, and soda, and also a small portion of magnesia, oxide of iron, and sulphuric acid, brought from China; has been seen regularly crystalized only in a few instances.

The *diamond* is pure crystalized carbon; heated to redness in the open air, it is entirely consumed. When exposed to the direct rays of the sun, or to candlelight, especially when cut, it exhibits a most beautiful play of colours; the lustre is splendid, and of a peculiar kind. Though harder than any other substance in nature, it is not difficult to break it by a blow. A diamond of one carat is said to be worth £8 sterling, and to increase in value according to the square of the weight. The largest diamond known to exist was in the possession of the great mogul. It is about the size and form of half of a hen's egg.

The one purchased by the Empress Catharine II., of Russia, is without flaw or fault of any kind, and resembles a pigeon's egg flattened. The *engraving* and setting of precious stones was an art quite familiar to the Egyptians. See Exodus xxviii, 11–21. And because no tool can be found to engrave the hardest substance in nature, it is supposed that the diamond was unknown in the days of Moses.

PREDESTINATE. This word occurs four times in the Scriptures, and signifies to determine, appoint, or decree any thing beforehand. In Eph. i, 5, it refers to God's predetermination to bestow on the Gentiles the blessings mentioned in that place. Dr. Macknight says, the Jews were sons, because they sprang from Isaac, who was called God's son, on account of his supernatural birth. They had this appellation likewise, because they were God's visible Church and people. Hence *the adoption* is mentioned as one of their national privileges, Rom. ix, 4; wherefore *the adoption of sons*, to which believers are predestinated through Christ, is their being delivered from the power of Satan, and made members of the Church of God by faith, and their being raised at the end of the world to live with God, their Father, in heaven for ever. Because the Jews denied that the privilege of *election* and *adoption* belonged to the Gentiles, the apostle in this chapter strenuously maintained their title to these privileges in common with the Jews.

The subjects of predestination mentioned in Romans viii, 29, are those who *believe*. As God justifies or pardons those who believe, and admits persevering believers to final glory, so all such *are the subjects of his predetermination. God does not predetermine that *certain persons* shall believe and obey ; but he predetermines that those who *believe and obey* shall enjoy the pardon of sin and final glory.

PREPARATION. The word in the New Testament is used in the Jewish sense, for the day or hours which precede the Sabbath ; the *eve* of the Sabbath, or any other festival, when preparation was made for the celebration, Matt. xxvii, 62. " Feet shod with *preparation*," Eph. vi, 15. Robinson translates, *shod as to your feet with readiness, alacrity, in behalf of the Gospel*, i. e., let your feet be ever ready to go forth to preach the Gospel.

PRESBYTERY, *eldership*; the body of officers in the primitive church, to whom were committed the direction and government of individual churches, 1 Tim. iv, 4.

PRESENCE. The presence of the Lord is that luminous cloud with which the Lord will be surrounded when he comes to judge the world. But, in the Old Testament, it is termed *the face of God*. See 2 Thess. i, 9. This glory, or fiery shining cloud, appeared to the patriarchs, when the Deity was pleased to make them sensible of his presence. In particular, this glory appeared to Moses in the bush, and on Mount Sinai at the giving of the law. Hence he is said to have conversed with God *face to face*, Exod. xxxiii, 11. It accompanied the Jews in their journeyings from Egypt, and through the wilderness, in the form of a pillar of fire. On these occasions its brightness was softened by the cloud which attended it. When it appeared to Saul on the road to Damascus, it shone with a brightness above that of the sun. But in its greatest splendour it cannot be looked on with mortal eyes. Hence it is called, 1 Tim. vi, 16, the light which no man can approach.

PRE-TO'RI-UM, Mark xv, 16, a place or court where causes were heard by the pretor, or any other chief magistrate. This place might be termed in English the *court house.*

PREVENT, *to hinder ;* this is now its only signification ; but when our translation was made, it had a meaning which it now has in every part of the Bible, i. e., *to anti-*

espats; to get before another in a race or journey. See 1 Thess. iv, 15.

PRIDE, thinking highly of ourselves, and looking with disdain upon others. This word is often connected with the accessory notion of impiety, ungodliness; as elsewhere gentleness and humility include also the idea of piety, Jer. xlviii, 29.

PRIEST, a general name for the minister of religion. The priest under the law was, among the Hebrews, a person consecrated and ordained of God to offer up sacrifices for his own sins and those of the people, Lev. iv, 5, 6. The priesthood was not annexed to a certain family till after the promulgation of the law of Moses. Before that time the first-born of every family, the fathers, the princes, the kings were priests. But after the Lord had chosen the tribe of Levi to serve him in his tabernacle, and the priesthood was annexed to the family of Aaron, then the right of offering sacrifices to God was reserved to the priests alone of this family—God having reserved to himself the first-born of all Israel, because he had preserved them from the hand of the destroying angel in Egypt, by way of exchange or compensation accepted of the tribe of Levi for the service of the tabernacle, Num. iii, 41. Of the three sons of Levi, Gershon, Kohath, and Merari, the Lord chose the family of Kohath,

and out of this the house of Aaron, to exercise the functions of the priesthood. All the rest of the family of Kohath, even the children of Moses and their descendants, remained of the order of mere Levites. See LEVITES.

The posterity of the sons of Aaron, namely, El-e-a'zar, and Ith'a-mar, Lev. x, 1-5; 1 Chron. xxiv, 1, 2, had so increased in number in the time of David that they were divided into twenty-four classes, which officiated a week at a time, alternately. Sixteen classes were of the family of Eleazar, and eight of the family of Ithamar. Each class obeyed its own ruler. The class *Jojarib* was the first in order, and the class *A-bi'a* was the eighth, Luke i, 5; 1 Chron. xxiv, 3-19. This division of the priesthood was continued as a permanent arrangement after the time of David, 2 Chron. viii, 14; xxxi, 2; xxxv, 4, 5. Indeed, although only four classes returned from the captivity, the distinction between them, and also the ancient names, were still retained, Ezra ii, 36-39.

Aaron, the high priest, was set apart to his office by the same ceremonies with which his sons the priests were, with this exception, that the former was clothed in his robes, and the sacred oil was poured upon his head, Exod. xxix, 5-9.

It was not customary for

the priests to wear the sacerdotal dress, except when performing their official duties, Exod. xxviii, 4, 43; Ezekiel xlii, 14; xliv, 19.

The ordinary priests served immediately at the altar, offered sacrifices, killed and flayed them, and poured the blood at the foot of the altar, 2 Chron. xxix, 34; xxxv, 11. They kept a perpetual fire burning upon the altar of burnt sacrifices, and in the lamps of the golden candlestick that was in the sanctuary; they prepared the loaves of show-bread, baked them, and changed them every Sabbath-day. Every day, night, and morning, a priest, appointed by casting lots at the beginning of the week, brought into the sanctuary a smoking censer, and set it upon the golden table, otherwise called the altar of perfumes, Luke i, 9.

The term priest is most properly given to Christ, of whom the high priests under the law were types and figures, he being the high priest especially ordained of God, who, by the sacrifice of himself, and by his intercession, opens the way to reconciliation with God, Heb. viii, 17; ix, 11-25. The word is also applied to every true believer who is enabled to offer up himself "a spiritual sacrifice acceptable to God through Christ," 1 Pet. ii, 5; Rev. i, 6. But it is likewise improperly applied to Christian ministers, who have no sacri-

fices to offer; unless, indeed, when it is considered as contracted from *presbyter*, which signifies an elder, and is the name given in the New Testament to those who were appointed to the office of teaching and ruling in the Church of God.

PRISON. To prisons is compared whatever tends to restrict liberty, and to render one disgraced and wretched. It also denotes *hell*, the bottomless pit, as the prison of demons, and the souls of wicked men, Rev. xx, 7.

Christ went and preached by the *ministry of Noah*, and by the *influence of the Holy Spirit*, to the spirits that are *now* in prison, though not in prison when Christ preached to them, 1 Pet. iii, 19.

PRIS-CIL'LA, a Christian woman, well known in the Acts, and in St. Paul's epistles.

PRIZE, that reward which was bestowed on victors in the public diversion of the Greeks; such as a wreath, chaplet, garland, 1 Cor. ix, 24. Metaphorically, it is spoken of the rewards of virtue in a future life, Phil. iii, 14. The crowns for which the Greeks contended in the games were, for the most part, made of the leaves of trees, which, though evergreens, soon withered. Some of the crowns were of the *wild olive*, some of *laurel*, some of *pines*, and some of *smallage*, or *parsley*. The honours, likewise, of which these crowns were the pledges, by length of time lost their agreeableness, and at last perished, being all confined to the present life: but the *crown of life* is infinitely better—it never fails, 1 Cor. ix, 25. Hence *running* is a comparison drawn from the public races and applied to Christians, as expressing strenuous effort in the Christian life and cause.

PROFANE, applied anciently to persons not consecrated, or to the uninitiated among the heathen, who were not allowed to be present at the sacred services. Profane things are common, unholy, unsanctified things, 1 Tim. iv, 7; "a *profane* person," Heb. xii, 16, is one who treats sacred things with contempt, who despises spiritual blessings, and who, in the whole of his behaviour, shows that he has no sense of God nor of religion; and therefore is ranked among the most atrocious sinners. To profane a thing is to degrade it from a sacred to a common use. "The priests *profane* the Sabbath," Matt. xii, 5, i. e., put it to what might be called a common use, by slaying and offering up sacrifices, and by doing the service of the temple as on common days. See Num. xxviii, 9.

PROMISES. The apostles called the promises of the Gospel *great*, 2 Pet. i, 4, because the things promised are the grandest that can be conceived by the human mind: such as the pardon of sin, the favour of God, the return of Christ, the resurrection of the dead, the judgment, &c. He likewise calls them *precious*, because of their efficacy to make us partakers of the Divine nature; a possession more precious than all the riches in the universe. Sometimes *promises* signify the *things* which are promised; see Heb. xi, 13, 39, where the persons mentioned by the apostle lived in expectation of some *future* good, *of some promised blessing*. They habitually, by faith, looked forward to something which they did not attain in the present life.

PROPHECY, a foretelling of future events, *prediction*; but including also from the Hebrew the idea of prophetic revelations, declarations, exhortations, and warnings, uttered by the prophets while acting under Divine influence, as ambassadors of God, and interpreters of his mind and will. In 1 Tim. i, 18, and iv, 14, *prophecy* seems to refer to the prophetic revelations or directions of the Holy Spirit, by which persons were designated as officers and teachers in the primitive church. See *Robinson*, Acts xiii, 2; comp. 1 Cor. xiv, 24, 31, with verse 30.

The word also signifies that prophetic spiritual gift which was imparted to the primitive teachers of the Church, 1 Cor. xii, 10.

Prophesying is the exercise of the prophetic office, the

acting as an ambassador of God, and the interpreter of his mind and will, Rev. xi, 6.

In the Old Testament, in several instances, it signifies *to shout, to sing sacred songs, to praise God,* while under a Divine influence. This is spoken of Saul, and of the sons of the prophets. See *Gesenius,* and compare 1 Chr. xxv, 1, 2, 3, with 1 Sam. xix, 20-24.

The distinction between the prophecies of Scripture and the oracles of heathenism is marked and essential. In the heathen oracles we cannot discern any clear and unequivocal tokens of genuine prophecy. Far from attempting to form any chain of prophecies, respecting things far distant as to time or place, or matters contrary to human probability, and requiring supernatural agency to effect them, the heathen priests and soothsayers did not even pretend to a systematic and connected plan. They hardly dared, indeed, to assume the prophetic character in its full force, but stood trembling, as it were, on the brink of futurity, conscious of their inability to venture beyond the depths of human conjecture. See ORACLES. The Scripture prophecies, on the other hand, constitute a series of Divine predictions, relating principally to one grand object of universal importance, the work of man's redemption, and carried on in regular progression through the patri-

archal, Jewish, and Christian dispensations, with a harmony and uniformity of design, clearly indicating one and the same Divine Author. They speak of the agents to be employed in it, and especially of the great agent, the Redeemer himself; and of those mighty and awful proceedings of Providence as to the nations of the earth, by which judgment and mercy are exercised with reference both to the ordinary principles of moral goverament, and especially to this restoring economy, to its struggles, its oppositions, and its triumphs. They all meet in Christ, as in their proper centre.

The advantage of this species of evidence belongs then exclusively to our revelation. Heathenism never made any clear and well-founded pretensions to it. Mohammedanism, though it stands itself as a proof of the truth of Scripture prophecy, is unsupported by a single prediction of its own.

The objection which has been raised to Scripture prophecy, from its supposed obscurity, has no solid foundation. There is, it is true, a prophetic language of symbol and emblem; but it is a language which is definite and not equivocal in its meaning, and as easily mastered as the language of poetry, by attentive persons. This, however, is not always used. The style of the prophecies of Scripture very often differs in nothing from the ordinary style of the Hebrew poets ; and, in not a few cases, and those too on which the Christian builds most in the argument, it sinks into the plainness of historical narrative.

The two great ends of prophecy are, to excite expectation before the event, and then to confirm the truth by a striking and unequivocal fulfilment ; and it is a sufficient answer to the allegation of the obscurity of the prophecies of Scripture, that they have abundantly accomplished those objects among the most intelligent and investigating, as well as among the simple and unlearned, in all ages. It cannot be denied, for instance, leaving out particular cases which might be given, that by means of these predictions the expectation of the incarnation and appearance of a Divine Restorer was kept up among the people to whom they were given, and spread even to the neighbouring nations ; that as these prophecies multiplied, the hope became more intense ; and that at the time of our Lord's coming, the expectation of the birth of a very extraordinary person prevailed, not only among the Jews, but among other nations. This purpose was then sufficiently answered, and an answer is given to the objection. The second end of prophecy is to confirm the truth by the subsequent event. See those which are exclusively appli-

cable to our Saviour and were accomplished in him, Gen. xlix, 10 ; Isa. lii, liii ; Dan. vii, 13, 14 ; Micah v, 2 ; Zech. ix, 9 ; Mal. iii, 1.

PROPHET, one who speaks from a Divine influence, under inspiration, whether as foretelling future events, or as exhorting, reproving, threatening individuals or nations, i. e., as the ambassador of God and the interpreter of his will to men. See 1 Cor. xiv, 3. With the Jewish use of the word *prophet*, there was also necessarily connected the idea that he spoke not his own thoughts, but what he received from God ; retaining, however, his own consciousness. This is evident from Exod. vii, 1 : " I have made thee a god to Pharaoh : and Aaron thy brother shall be thy *prophet*," i. e., in your intercourse with Pharaoh, thou, as the wiser, shalt act, as it were, the part of God, and suggest to thy brother what to say ; while thy brother, as more fluent of speech, shall be to thee as a prophet, and utter what he receives from thee ; compare chap. iv, 16. The idea of prophet is also frequently taken in a wider sense, so as to include any friend of God to whom God makes known his will ; as Abraham, Gen. xx, 7 ; and the patriarchs, Psa. cv, 15. There was a class of instructers or preachers in the primitive Church, called *prophets*, who were next in rank to the apostles, and be-

fore the teachers, 1 Cor. xii,
28. It would seem that *prophet* indicated *one who taught
by inspiration*, and only so far
as inspiration prompted and
enabled him to teach. In the
strict sense of the word, it
was an office created and
sustained by miraculous gifts.
But *teacher* appears to have
been an ordinary stated
teacher; one who was so by
official station, and who taught
according to the degree of
religious knowledge which he
possessed. There were also
frequently among the Israelites *false prophets*, who pretended to have inspiration
from God, flattered the ears
of the people with bland promises, and were therefore
severely rebuked by the true
prophets. See, for example,
Jer. xiv, 13, 14. The word
prophet is used for a *poet,
minstrel*, spoken of the Greek
poet Epimenides, Tit. i, 12.
Poets were held to be in-
spired of the muses. The
above poet may well be called prophet, the interpreter of
the gods, one who explains
obscure oracles, since he was
reckoned among the seven
wise men of Greece, and was
sent for by Solon to aid in
the preparation of his laws.

Sons of the prophets were
those who were educated for
the prophetic office, and were
disciples or pupils of the prophets, and were thereby qualified to be *public teachers*,
which seems to have been
part of the business of the
prophets on the Sabbath days

and festivals, 2 Kings iv, 23,
somewhat like ministers of
the present day. Isaiah, Jeremiah, Ezekiel, and Daniel
are called the greater prophets, from the size of their
books, and the extent and
importance of their prophecies. The others are called
the minor or lesser prophets.
The following is the *order*
and *time* in which the prophecies were written, according
to Mr. Horne, which probably
is nearly correct:—

Jonah,	. . .	856	.	784
Amos,	. . .	810	.	785
Hosea,	. . .	810	.	725
Isaiah,	. . .	810	.	749
Joel,	. . .	810	.	660
Micah,	. . .	758	.	699
Nahum,	. . .	720	.	698
Zephaniah,	.	640	.	609
Jeremiah,	. .	628	.	586
Habakkuk,	.	612	.	598
Daniel,	. . .	606	.	534
Obadiah,	. .	588	.	583
Ezekiel,	. .	595	.	536
Haggai,	. .	520	.	518
Zechariah,	.	520	.	518
Malachi,	. .	434	.	397

The classification of the
prophets by Mr. Horne assigns
the first eight to the period
before the Babylonian captivity; the five next to a period
near to and during the captivity; and the last three after
the return of the Jews from
Babylon.

PROPHETESS. 1. Used for
an ambassadress from God;
one who speaks and acts from
Divine influence, Judges iv,
4; compare Rev. ii. 20

2. Spoken of a female friend of God; one who lives in communion with him, to whom God reveals himself by his Spirit, Luke ii, 26. Just as Abraham is called a prophet, Gen. xx, 7.

3. A poetess, female minstrel, Exod. xv, 20.

PROPITIATION. To propitiate is to appease, to atone, to turn away the wrath of an offended person. In the case before us, the wrath turned away is the wrath of God; the person making the propitiation is Christ; the propitiation offering or sacrifice is his blood. All this is expressed in most explicit terms in the following passages:—"And he is the *propitiation* for our sins," 1 John ii, 2. "Herein is love, not that we loved God, but that he loved us, and sent his Son to be the *propitiation* for our sins," 1 John iv, 10. "Whom God hath set forth to be a *propitiation* through faith in his blood," Rom. iii, 25.

This is in strict accordance with Eph. i, 7, "We have redemption through his blood, the remission of sins." It is only by his blood that Christ reconciles us to God.

It sufficiently proves that there is not only no implacability in God, but a most tender and placable affection toward the sinning human race itself, and that the Son of God, by whom the propitiation was made, was the free gift of the Father to us. This is the most eminent proof of his love, that, for our sakes, and that mercy might be extended to us, "he spared not his own Son; but delivered him up freely for us all." Thus he is the fountain and first moving cause of that scheme of recovery and salvation which the incarnation and death of our Lord brought into full and efficient operation. The true questions are, indeed, not whether God is love, or whether he is of a placable nature; but whether God is holy and just; whether we, his creatures, are under law or not; whether this law has any penalty, and whether God, in his rectoral character, is bound to execute and uphold that law. As the justice of God is punitive, (and if it is not punitive, his laws are a dead letter,) then is there wrath in God; then is God angry with the wicked; then is man, as a sinner, obnoxious to this anger; and so a propitiation becomes necessary to turn it away from him. Nor are these terms unscriptural; they are used in the New Testament as emphatically as in the Old; though the former is, in a special sense, a revelation of the mercy of God to man. John declares that, if any man believeth not on the Son of God, "the wrath of God abideth upon him;" and St. Paul affirms, that "the wrath of God is revealed from heaven against all ungodliness and unrighteousness of men."— The day of judgment is, with reference to the ungodly, said to be "the day of wrath;" God is called "a consuming fire;" and, as such, is the object of "reverence and godly fear."

Let men talk ever so much or eloquently of the pure benevolence of God, they cannot abolish the facts recorded in the history of human suffering in this world as the effects of transgression; nor can they discharge these fearful comminations from the pages of the book of God. These cannot be criticised away; and if it is "Jesus who saves us from this wrath to come," that is, from those effects of the wrath of God which are to come, then, but for him, we should have been liable to them. That principle in God from which such effects follow, the Scriptures call wrath; and they who deny the existence of wrath in God deny, therefore, the Scriptures.

It by no means follows, however, that this wrath is a passion in God; "because we make the design of punishment not to be the satisfaction of anger as a desire of revenge, but to be the vindication of the *honour* and *rights* of the offended person by such a way as he himself shall judge satisfactory to the ends of his government." See *Watson* and ATONEMENT.

PROSELYTE, properly "one who comes to another country or people;" *a stranger, sojourner;* in the New Testa- ment, a convert from Paganism to Judaism, Matt. xxiii, 15. The same are called *the devout,* and men *fearing God,* Acts xiii, 16, 50.

The rabbins distinguish two kinds of proselytes, viz., *proselytes of right,* i. e., complete, perfect proselytes, who embraced the Jewish religion in its full extent, and enjoyed all the rights and privileges of Jewish citizenship. See Exod. xii, 48.

And also *proselytes of sojourning,* called also *proselytes of the gate,* i. e., foreigners dwelling among the Jews, who, without being circumcised, conformed to certain Jewish laws and customs, especially those which the rabbins call the "seven precepts of Noah," viz., to avoid blasphemy against God, idolatry, homicide, incest, robbery, resistance to magistrates, and the eating of blood or things strangled. They frequented the synagogues with the Jews, and although they were at liberty to offer sacrifices to God in any place, they preferred visiting the temple of Jerusalem, and offered sacrifices through the priests.

PROVENDER, *fodder, meslin,* for camels or asses, made up of various kinds of grain, as wheat, barley, vetches, and the like, all mixed together, and thus sown or given to cattle, Job vi, 5; perhaps chopped straw, barley, and beans, such as they still use for fodder in the East.

PROVERBS, short aphorisms, and sententious, moral, and prudential maxims, usually expressed in numbers, or antithesis, as being more easily remembered, and of more use than abstruse and methodical discourses.

The Proverbs of Solomon, on account of their intrinsic merit, as well as of the rank and renown of their author, were collected into one volume, and constitute the book in the sacred canon entitled, "The Proverbs of Solomon, the son of David, king of Israel." One portion of the book, from the twenty-fifth chapter to the end of the twenty-ninth, was compiled by the men of Hezekiah, as appears from the title prefixed to it. They were persons, however, as we may reasonably suppose, well qualified for the undertaking, who collected what were known to be the genuine proverbs of Solomon, from the various writings in which they were dispersed, and arranged them in their present order. Whether the preceding twenty-four chapters, which, doubtless, existed in a combined form previous to the additional collection, were compiled by the author, or some other person, is quite uncertain.

PSALM. A psalm is properly *a song sung to the music of the lyre, a lyric poem.* The *Psalms* deserve the name of lyric on account of their character as works of taste. The essence of lyric poetry is the immediate expression of feeling; and feeling is the sphere to which most of the Psalms belong. Pain, sorrow, fear, hope, joy, confidence, gratitude, submission to God; every thing that moves and elevates the soul is expressed in these hymns. Most of them are the warm outpouring of the excited, susceptible heart; the fresh offering of inspiration and elevation of thought, while only a few seem like the colder productions of artificial imitation, and a few others are simply forms of prayer, temple hymns, and collections of proverbs. Among all the books of the Bible, there is, perhaps, no one so rich in piety as the Psalms. It is the great fountain and source of *religious experience;* and on this account worthy of very special attention in all inquiries into the history of religion. They are the productions of different persons, but are generally called the *Psalms of David,* because a great part of them were composed by him, and David himself is distinguished by the name of the Psalmist. We cannot now ascertain all the Psalms written by David, but their number probably exceeds seventy; and much less are we able to discover the authors of the other Psalms, or the occasions upon which they were composed. A few of them were written after the return from the Babylonian captivity.

It is supposed they were collected into one book by Ezra, without any regard to chronological order.

Dr. Robinson says, that many of the *inscriptions* cannot well be genuine; and therefore the others become suspicious. We cannot rely upon any one when it does not accord with the contents of the Psalm; perhaps mostly out of the exile, or not long after it. Some have classified the Psalms according to their contents, viz., 1. Hymns in praise of Jehovah. These express thoughts of the highest sublimity in respect to God, e. g., Psa. civ. 2. Temple hymns; sung at the consecration of the temple, the entrance of the ark, or intended for the temple service; so also *pilgrim songs*, sung by those who came up to worship in the temple, e. g., the so called *songs of degrees*, Psa. cxxii. 3. Religious and moral songs of a general character, containing the poetical expression of emotions and feelings, Psa. xvi. 4. Elegiac Psalms, i. e., lamentations, Psalms of complaint; generally united with prayer for help, e. g., Psa. lii. 5. Odes to kings, patriotic hymns, e. g., Psa. xlv, and lxii. 6. Historical Psalms, in which the ancient history of the Israelites is repeated in a hortatory manner, e. g., Psa. lxxviii.

PSALTERY, an instrument of music used by the Hebrews, supposed to be that species of lyre which is fre-

quently found on ancient monuments, and in connection with the statues of Apollo, called the *harp of Apollo;* the form of which is represented by Fig. 1. and 2. See MUSICAL INSTRUMENTS.

PTOLEMAIS, a maritime city of Palestine belonging to Galilee, on the bay north of Mount Carmel, Acts xxi, 7; same as *Accho.*

PUBLICAN, *a toll-gatherer, a collector of customs.* The *office* of collector among the Greeks and Romans was usually sold out; and among the Romans, the purchasers were chiefly of the equestrian order, or at least persons of wealth and rank, like Zaccheus, one of the principal receivers, since he is called *chief among the publicans,* Luke xix, 2. But these had sub-contractors, or employed agents, who collected the taxes and customs at the gates of cities, in seaports, on public ways, bridges, &c. These, too, were called *publicans;* and in countries subject to the Roman yoke they were objects of hatred and detestation; so that none but persons of the lowest rank and worthless character were likely to be found in this employment. And, besides, the Jews looked upon them as the instruments of their subjection to the Romans, to whom they generally held it sinful for them to submit. They considered it as incompatible with their liberty to pay tribute to any foreign power, Luke xx, 22; and those of their own nation that engaged in this employment they regarded as *heathens*, Matt. xviii, 17. It is even said, that they would not allow them to enter into their temple or synagogues, nor to join in prayers, nor even allow their evidence in a court of justice; nor would they accept of their offerings in the temple.

It appears by the Gospel that there were many publicans in Judea at the time of our Saviour.

PUBLIUS, a wealthy inhabitant of Malta, Acts xxviii, 7, 8.

PUL, (rhymes with *dull*,) king of Assyria, about 774–759 B. C., 2 Kings xv, 19. He was the first monarch of that nation who invaded Israel, and began their transportation out of their own country.

PULSE, a term applied to those grains or seeds which grow in pods, as beans, peas, and vetches.

PUNISHMENT. Corporal punishment among the Hebrews may be limited to one kind, viz., the infliction of blows with a rod, or scourging, Deut. xxv, 23; the dignity or high standing of the person who had rendered himself liable to this punishment, could not excuse him from its being inflicted. It is practised at the present day in the East; with this difference, however, that the stripes were formerly inflicted on the

back, but now on the soles of the feet.

The more recent Jews, from their great fear, lest, from any circumstance, the stripes might exceed the number prescribed, fixed it at thirty-nine instead of forty, which were inflicted in their synagogues, Matt. x, 17. Criminals who had committed homicide were punished, as we may learn, as far back as Gen. ix, 6, with *death*. But the mode in which the punishment was inflicted is not there stated. The execution devolved on the brother or other nearest relation of the person whose life had been taken away. In case he did not slay the guilty person, he was considered *infamous*. *Stoning* was a mode of effecting the punishment of death, authorized by the laws of Moses. *Stoning* was practised likewise among many other ancient nations, Josh. vii, 25; John viii, 7. The process was commenced by the witnesses themselves, whose example was followed, and the punishment rendered complete by the people, Deut. xvii, 7.

PUNON, a city of Idumea, between Petra and Zoar, celebrated for its mines, Num. xxxiii, 42.

PUR, a Persian word, which signifies *lot, a die;* explained Esther iii, 7. The *festival of Purim* was celebrated by the Jews in memory of the events recorded in the book of Esther, on the four

25

teenth and fifteenth days of the month *Adar*.

PURITY. See HOLINESS.

PURIFY, to render pure; in a moral sense, to reform, James iv, 8. "To *purify one's self*," John xi, 55, is to prepare one's self *by purification* for the sacred festivals; which was done among the Jews by visiting the temple, offering up prayers, abstaining from certain kinds of food, washing the clothes, bathing, shaving the head, &c. It also signifies *to live like one under a vow of abstinence*, i. e., like a Nazarite, Acts xxi, 24, 26; xxiv, 18. The Jews were accustomed, when under a vow of this kind, to abstain for a certain time from the better sorts of food, to let their hair grow, to keep themselves from all pollution, &c. And when this time had expired, they were freed from the obligation of their vow by a particular sacrifice.

PURPLE, a precious colour obtained from a species of shell-fish or muscles, found on the coasts of the Mediterranean, which yields a reddish purple die, much prized by the ancients.

Purple is also any thing died with purple, as purple clothes or robes, worn by persons of rank and wealth, Luke xvi, 19. The purple robe put on our Saviour, John xix, 2, 5, is explained by a Roman custom, the dressing of a person in the robes of state, as the investiture of office. In Acts xvi, 14, Lydia is said to be "a seller of *purple*." Mr. Harmer styles purple the most sublime of all earthly colours, having the gaudiness of red, of which it retains a shade, softened with the gravity of blue.

PUT, Nahum iii, 9, was an African tribe, probably dwelling near Carthage.

PATE'O-LI, now called *Puzzuoli*, a maritime town of Italy, on the northern shore of the Bay of Naples, not far distant from the latter city. It was a favourite place of resort for the Romans, on account of the adjacent mineral waters and hot baths; and its harbour was defended by a celebrated mole, the remains of which are still to be seen. Here Paul landed on his way to Rome, Acts xxviii, 13.

PYGARG. This is properly the name of a species of eagle, but is applied in Deut. xiv, 5, to a quadruped, apparently a species of gazelle or antelope.

QUAIL. This beautiful bird is nearly allied to the partridge, differing only in being smaller, and having a more delicate beak, shorter tail, and no spur on the legs. Its note is very similar to the words "*Bob White*," accompanied with a whistling sound. Scarcely any of the feathered tribe appear to have so strong local attachments as the American quail; but the quail of Europe and Asia is a bird of passage. It is spread over the whole of the old world, and they are found in immense flocks on the coast of the Mediterranean and Red Seas.

When God by a miracle brought such vast quantities to the camp of the Israelites, it is said they were "two cubits high upon the face of the earth," Num. xi, 31. We may consider the quails as *flying* within two cubits of the ground; so that the Israelites could easily take as many of them as they wished while flying within the reach of their hands or their clubs; and it is in this that the miracle consists, that they were brought so seasonably to this place, and in so great a number, as to furnish food for above a million of persons for more than a month.

QUATERNION, *four together*, a detachment of four men, the usual number of a Roman night-watch, relieved every three hours, Acts xii, 4. Peter was therefore guarded by four men at a time, two within the prison and two before the doors, making in all sixteen men.

QUEEN, the king's wife, 2 Kings x, 13, also the king's *mother.* This sets in its proper light the interference of the "queen," in the story of Belshazzar, Dan. v, 10, who, by her reference to former events, appears not to have been any of the wives of the king; neither indeed could any of his wives have come to that banquet. See Esther iv, 16. As the sun was called *the king*, so the moon was called the QUEEN OF HEAVEN, found only in Jer. vii, 18; and xliv, 17-25. This *goddess*, which the Israelitish women worshipped, is either *the moon*, or *Astarte*, i. e., the planet *Venus.* The worship of this deity was common in Palestine before its occupation by Moses. Hence the command to cut down the groves, Exod. xxxiv, 13, which were consecrated to her.

QUENCH, *to put out*, extinguish a fire, in 2 Samuel xiv, 7, "*Quench* my coal which is left;" *a coal*, as being kept in order to preserve fire, is put for the last hope or scion of a race or family; and to *quench the coal*, destroy the family from among the people; so likewise David was regarded as the light of the nation, by which all Israel was guided, 2 Sam. xxi, 17.

Quench is also taken figuratively, and signifies *to damp, to hinder, to repress;* to prevent any thing from exerting its full influence, 1 Thess. v, 19.

QUICK, a word which we have retained from the *Saxon*, our ancient mother tongue, and signifies *living.* By the *quick and the dead*, Acts x. 42, we are to understand all that shall be found *alive* at the day of judgment, and all that shall have *died* previously.

QUICKSANDS, Acts xxvii, 17; sand banks drawn together by currents of the sea, dangerous to navigation.

Two gulfs with quicksands on the northern coast of Africa were particularly famous among the ancients; one was between Cyrene and Leptis, and the other near Carthage.

QUIT, to be free from an obligation or oath, Josh. ii, 20. It is used in another sense, when Christians are commanded to "quit themselves like men," 1 Cor. xvi, 13. They were not to act like children tossed about with every wind of doctrine, but like good soldiers to act the firm and manly part.

QUIVER, a box or case for arrows, which was slung over the shoulder in such a position that the marksman could draw out the arrows when wanted; the small part of the quiver being downward, Gen. xxvii, 3.

RAAMSES, the same as *Rameses.*

RABBI, a Hebrew word, the same as *doctor, teacher, master,* a title of honour in the Jewish schools, continued also in modern times. This was introduced as a title into the Jewish schools under a threefold form, viz., *Rab,* as the lowest degree of honour; *Rabbi,* i. e., *my master,* of higher dignity; and *Rabboni,* q. d., *my great master,* the most honourable of all; which was publicly given to only seven persons, all of the school of Hillel, and of great eminence. It was on this account, it should seem, that the blind man gave this title to Christ, Mark x, 51; being convinced that he was possessed of Divine power, and worthy of the most honourable distinctions. And Mary Mag-da-le'ne, when she saw Christ after his resurrection, "said unto him, Rabboni," John xx, 16, that is, my rabban, like *my lord* in English; for rabbon is the same with rabban, only pronounced according to the Syriac dialect.

RABBAH, *great city,* the capital of the Ammonites, situated beyond Jordan, near the source of the Arnon, Deut. iii, 11; where the brave Uriah lost his life by a secret order of his prince, 2 Sam. xi, 17. It is now called Ammon, and is about fifteen miles south-east of *Szalt,* a strong town of Syria, where extensive ruins are found.

RABSHAKEH, a military chief under Sennacherib, 2 Kings xviii, 17.

RACA, a Syriac word, which properly signifies *empty, vain, beggarly, foolish,* and which includes in it a strong idea of contempt. Our Saviour pronounces a censure on every person using this term to his neighbour, Matt. v, 22. Lightfoot assures us that, in the writings of the Jews, the word *raca* is a term of the utmost contempt, and that it was usual to pronounce it with marked signs of indignation.

RACHAB, Matt. i, 5, most probably the same with Rahab, of Jericho; for Naasson, the father of Salmon, was the leader of the tribe of Judah at the breaking up from Mount Sinai, (Num. x, 14; compare verse 11, and on,) and therefore Salmon, his son, the husband of Rachab, would be cotemporary with the fall of Jericho, about forty years later.

RACHEL, *ewe-lamb*, the younger wife of Jacob, and mother of Joseph and Benjamin. The Prophet Jeremiah (xxxi, 15) introduces Rachel, whose sepulchre seems to have been not far from Ramah, (Gen. xxxv, 19; 1 Sam. x, 2,) as bewailing the captivity of her descendants, i. e., of Ephraim, as the representative of the ten tribes. A similar use is made of her name by the Evangelist Matthew, (ii, 18,) where she is supposed to renew her lamentations at the slaughter of so many of her descendants as fell under the barbarous edict of Herod.

RAHAB. 1. A poetical name for Egypt, Isa. li, 9. 2. The *harlot*, so called on account of her former way of life. But after she believed in the true God, it is reasonable to think she amended her manners, as well as repented of the lie by which she deceived the king of Jericho's messengers. For that faith in the true God which made her hazard her life in receiving and concealing the spies, must, when she attained to more knowledge, have wrought in her a thorough reformation. See James ii 25.

RAIMENT. The dress of oriental nations, to which the inspired writers often allude, has undergone almost no change from the earliest times. Their stuffs were fabricated of various materials; but wool was generally used in their finer fabrics; and the hair of goats, camels, and even of horses, was manufactured for coarser purposes, especially for sackcloth, which they wore in time of mourning and distress. Sackcloth of black goats' hair was manufactured for mournings; the colour and the coarseness of which being reckoned more suitable to the circumstances of the wearer than the finer and more valuable texture which the hair of white goats supplied. This is the reason why a clouded sky is represented, in the bold figurative language of Scripture, as covered with sackcloth and blackness, the colour and dress of persons in affliction. The beauty of their clothes consisted in the fineness and colour of the stuffs; and it seems the colour most in use among the Israelites, as well as among the Greeks and Romans, was white, not imparted and improved by the dier's art, but the native colour of the wool, Eccles. ix, 8. See COLOUR. Blue was a colour in great esteem among the Jews, and other oriental nations.

The Jewish nobles and courtiers, upon great and solemn occasions, appeared in scarlet robes, died, not as at present with madder, with cochineal, or with any modern tincture, but with a shrub, whose red berries give an orient tinge to the cloth; sometimes they wore purple, the most sublime of all earthly colours, says Mr. Harmer, having the gaudiness of red, of which it retains a shade, softened with the gravity of blue. The children of wealthy and noble families were dressed in vestments of different colours. This mark of distinction may be traced to the patriarchal age; for Joseph was arrayed, by his indulgent and imprudent father, in a coat of many colours. A robe of divers colours was anciently reserved for the king's daughters who were virgins; and in one of these was Tamar, the virgin daughter of David, arrayed, when she was met by her brother.

In the east, where the people are by no means given to change, the form of their garments continues nearly the same from one age to another. The greater part of their clothes are long and flowing, loosely cast about the body, consisting only of a large piece of cloth, in the cutting and sewing of which very little art or industry is employed. They have more dignity and gracefulness than ours, and are better adapted to the burning climates of Asia. From the simplicity of their form, and their loose adaptation to the body, the same clothes might be worn, with equal ease and convenience, by many different persons. The clothes of those Philistines whom Samson slew at Askelon required no altering to fit his companions; nor the robe of Jonathan, to answer his friend. The arts of weaving and fulling seem to have been distinct occupations in Israel, from a very remote period, in consequence of the various and skilful operations which were necessary to bring their stuffs to a suitable degree of perfection; but when the weaver and the fuller had finished their part, the labour was nearly at an end: no distinct artisan was necessary to make them into clothes every family seems to have made their own. Sometimes, however, this part of the work was performed in the loom; for they had the art of weaving robes with sleeves all of one piece: of this kind was the coat which our Saviour wore during his abode with men. The loose dresses of these countries, when the arm is lifted up, expose its whole length: to this circumstance the Prophet Isaiah refers: " To whom is the arm of the Lord revealed?" that is, uncovered: who observes that he is about to exert the arm of his power?

The ancient Jews very seldom wore any covering upon the head, except when they were in mourning, or worshipping in the temple, or in the synagogue. To pray with the head covered was, in their estimation, a higher mark of respect for the majesty of Heaven, as it indicated the conscious unworthiness of the suppliant to lift up his eyes in the Divine presence. Their legs were generally bare ; and they never wore any thing upon the feet but soles fastened in different ways, according to the taste or fancy of the wearer. It may be observed, that to make presents of changes of raiment, Gen. xlv, 22, has always been common among all ranks of orientals. The perfuming of raiment with sweet-scented spices or extracts is also still a custom, which explains the smell of Jacob's raiment. A coat or robe of many colours, such as Jacob gave to Joseph, is also a mark of distinction.

RAIN. The descent of water in drops from the clouds, or the water thus falling. When it falls in very small particles, we call it mist, and fog is composed of particles so fine as to be not only indistinguishable, but to float or be suspended in the air. We read in James v, 7, of the *early and latter rain*, the *former* in the climate of Palestine, where rains come in regular course, falling in the first, and the *latter* in the last part of the year. *The early rain* falls from the middle of October until the middle of December, and prepares the ground for receiving the seed.

The latter rain falls in the months of March and April, before the harvest, Deut. xi, 14.

From the middle of April, which is the time of harvest, to the middle of September, there is neither rain nor thunder, Prov. xxvi, 1 ; 1 Sam. xii, 17. Sometimes in the latter half of April, i. e., the beginning of the harvest, a cloud is perceived in the morning, which, as the sun rises, gradually disappears, Hosea vi, 4. But in the month of May, June, July, and August, not a cloud is seen, and the earth is not wet, except by the dew, which is, therefore, everywhere used as the symbol of the Divine benevolence, Job xxix, 19 ; Mic. v, 7. If at this season of the year fire get among the dry herbs and grass, a wide conflagration ensues, Psalm lxxxiii, 14 ; Jer. xxi, 14. See CANAAN.

RAINBOW, Gen. ix, 13, a bow or an arch of a circle, consisting of all the colours formed by the refraction and reflection of rays of light from drops of rain or vapour, appearing in the part of the hemisphere opposite to the sun. When the sun is at the horizon, the rainbow is a semicircle.

RAM, *a battering ram*, Ezek. iv, 2. This was a warlike machine, used for making a breach in the walls of cities, constructed of a long beam of strong wood, usually oak, armed with a mass of heavy metal, in the shape of a ram's head, and suspended by ropes, in equilibrium, so that a comparatively small force would impel it with vast effect against a fortification.

RAMAH. See Arimathea.

RAMESES, an Egyptian city, probably the chief city of the land of Goshen, built, or at least fortified, by the labour of the Israelites, the same as *Hero-op'olis*, which is about forty miles from Suez, and near the canal connecting that city with the Nile. The word appears also to be given to the whole province, where the Israelites dwelt; *Rameses* is the Egyptian name, while *Goshen* would seem to be the Hebrew appellation. See Gen. xlvii, 11.

RAMOTH, a famous city in the mountains of Gilead. It is often called *Ramoth-Gilead.* The city belonged to the tribe of Gad. It was assigned for a dwelling of the Levites, and was one of the cities of refuge beyond Jordan, Josh. xx, 8; xxi, 38.

RANSOM, the *fine* or price which is paid for the setting free of a captive or slave. "Christ gave his soul a ransom for many," Mark x, 45, i. e., as a ransom for the deliverance of many, especially from the consequences of sin and guilt. See Redemption.

RAVEN, a sagacious and beautiful bird, often domesticated, and capable of being taught, distinguished from the common crow by being somewhat larger, and the bill a little curved. The *blackness* of the raven is proverbial, Song v, 11. It feeds on carrion, and is therefore unclean.

REBEKAH, the sister of Laban, and wife of Isaac. The circumstances of her marriage constitute one of the most simple and beautiful passages of sacred history. See Gen. xxiv. She died before Isaac, and was buried in Abraham's tomb, Gen. xlix, 31. See Jacob.

RECEIPT (*resee't*) occurs in the passage, *at the receipt of custom,* Matt. ix, 9. The *toll* or *custom-house,* the collector's *office,* built in the most public places, where taxes were received which were paid for the maintenance and expenses of the state. See Publican.

RECHABITES, the descendants of Rechab, 2 Kings x, 15, 23, who were bound by a vow ever to follow the nomadic life, i. e., shepherds of the desert, wandering about without any fixed habitation. These people are to be reckoned with the proselytes to the Jewish nation. They entered the promised land with the Hebrews, dwelt in the tribe of Judah about the Dead Sea, and were distinguished from the Israelites by their retired life, and by their dislike of cities and houses.

Rechab, their founder, established a rule for his posterity, that they should possess neither land nor houses, but should live in tents ; and should drink no wine nor strong drink. In obedience to this rule, the Rechabites continued a separate but peaceable people, living in tents, and removing from place to place, as circumstances required. When Judea was invaded by Nebuchadnezzar, they fled to Jerusalem for safety, where it pleased God, by the Prophet Jeremiah, to exhibit them to the wicked inhabitants of Jerusalem, as an example of constancy in their obedience to the mandates of an earthly father, Jer. xxxv, 2–19. They still exist in the mountainous tropical country of the northeast of Medina, in Arabia, distinct, free, and practising exactly the institutions of the man whose name they bear, and of whose institutions they boast. This is a remarkable instance of the exact fulfilment of a minute and isolated prophecy.

RECONCILIATION signifies, 1, *restoration* to the Divine favour. The state of mankind by nature is that of enmity, dissatisfaction, and disobedience ; but by the sufferings and merit of Christ they are reconciled to God, i. e., brought into that state in which pardon is offered to them, and they have it in their power to render themselves capable of that pardon, viz., by laying down their enmity. Signifies, 2, the *means* by which sinners are recon-ciled and brought into favour with God, viz., the *atonement*, *expiation*, Dan. ix, 34 ; Heb. ii, 17.

" If the casting away of them be the reconciling of the world," Rom. xi, 15, i. e., be the means, occasion of reconciling the world to God. Grotius observes that, in heathen authors, men's being reconciled to their gods is always understood to signify appeasing the anger of their gods. Condemned rebels may be said to be reconciled to their sovereign, when he, on one consideration or another, pardons them ; though perhaps they still remain rebels in their hearts against him. And when our Lord ordered the offender to go and be reconciled to his offended brother, Matthew v, 23, 24, the plain meaning is, that he should go and try to appease his anger, obtain his forgiveness, and regain his favour and friendship, by humbling himself to him, asking his pardon, and satisfying him for any injury that he might have done him. In like manner God's reconciling us to himself by the cross of Christ is a reconciliation that results from God's graciously providing and accepting an atonement for us, that he might not inflict the punishment upon us which we deserve, and the law condemned us to ; but might be at peace with us, and receive us into favour on Christ's account.

RECORDER, i. e., a historiographer, the king's annalist, one of the high officers of the Hebrew kings, whose duty it was to record the events of the king's reign, and especially what took place near his person. The same officer is mentioned as existing in the Persian court, both ancient and modern, 1 Kings iv, 3.

REDEEMER, one who redeems, or ransoms, who, in the Old Testament, was the next of kin, *nearest kinsman*, translated sometimes revenger, Numbers xxxv, 19–21, who, by the Mosaic law, had a right to redeem an inheritance; and who was also permitted to vindicate or avenge the death of his relation, by killing the slayer, if he found him out of the cities of refuge. He was a type of Him who was to redeem man from death and the grave, to recover for him the eternal inheritance, and to avenge him on Satan, his spiritual enemy and murderer. Spoken of God, who redeems and delivers men, Isa. xlix, 7. "I know that my *Redeemer* liveth," i. e., God himself, who will deliver me from these calamities.

REDEMPTION signifies, 1, *deliverance*, on account of a ransom paid; spoken of the deliverance from the power and consequence of sin which Christ procured for man by laying down his life as a ransom. "The redemption that is in Christ Jesus," Rom. iii, 24. This passage designates the Author of our deliverance, viz., him who paid the ransom and procured our freedom; when we were the slaves and captives of sin and Satan, and exposed to the wrath of God, Rom. i, 18.

Throughout the whole of this glorious doctrine of our redemption there is in the New Testament a constant reference to *the redemption price*, which is declared to be the *death of Christ*. "The Son of man came to give his life a ransom for many," Matt. xx, 28. "Who gave himself a *ransom* for all," 1 Tim. ii, 6. "In whom we have redemption through his blood," Eph. i, 7. "Ye were not redeemed with corruptible things, as silver and gold, but with the precious blood of Christ," 1 Peter i, 18, 19. That deliverance which constitutes our redemption by Christ is not, therefore, a gratuitous deliverance, granted without a consideration, as an act of mere prerogative; the *ransom*, the *redemption price*, was exacted and paid; one thing was given for another, the precious blood of Christ for captive and condemned men.

2. Simply *deliverance*, the idea of a ransom being dropped. The *redemption* of our body, Rom. viii, 23, i. e., its redemption from a state of frailty, disease, and death; so of the soul from the body as its prison, Eph. iv, 30.

RED SEA, an extensive gulf of the Indian Ocean, dividing Arabia from the opposite coast of Africa. This sea is connected with the ocean by the Straits of *Bab-el-mandel*, an Arabic word, which signifies the *gate of tears*, derived from the danger which was supposed to attend the passage. The sea extends in a north-west direction to the Isthmus of Suez, where it approaches within sixty miles of the Mediterranean. Its length is about 1400 miles; breadth, where greatest, about 200. The northern extremity of the Red Sea is divided into two gulfs, which enclose the Peninsula of Mount Sinai; the western is called sometimes the Gulf of Suez, and the eastern the Gulf of Akaba, (See SINAI.) The northern end of this gulf is connected with the southern extremity of the Dead Sea by the great valley, called toward the north, El Ghor, and toward the south, El Araba.

The western gulf is remarkable for the passage of the Israelites in their journey from Egypt to Canaan. Dr. Robinson, Stuart, and other learned writers, contend that this took place at, or in the vicinity of, the modern city of Suez. Here this arm is *now* almost three quarters of a mile broad, although the gulf has evidently retired from its ancient limits, perhaps by its being filled up with sand.

The circumstances, then, of the miraculous passage were these :—Hemmed in, as they were, on all sides, the Israelites began to despair of escape, and to murmur against Moses, Exod. xiv, 11, 12. Jehovah now directed Moses to stretch out his rod over the sea; "and the Lord caused the sea to flow—by a strong east wind all that night, and made the sea dry, and the waters were divided. And the children of Israel went into the midst of the sea upon the dry (ground;) and the waters were a wall unto them on their right hand and on their left," Exod. xiv, 21, 22. It would follow that the Israelites, who were probably all night upon the alert, entered on the passage toward morning. "The Egyptians pursued and went in after them," and "in the morning watch" the Lord "troubled the host of the Egyptians;" and Moses stretched out his hand over the sea, and the sea returned to his strength, when the morning appeared, and the Egyptians fled against it,—and the waters returned, and covered all the host of Pharaoh," &c., xiv, 23–28. Some suppose that the Israelites set off from the vicinity of the Nile, at or near Bassetin, a little above Cairo ; and passed to the southward of the Mokattam Mountain, through a wady, or series of wadys, called Wady Tia, which terminates at the Red Sea, in the Wady Bedea, or Touarek. But there are insuperable objections to this hypothesis, growing out of what has been already adduced. First, the distance from the Nile, as above hinted, which cannot be less than from eighty to one hundred miles. Secondly, the breadth of the sea, which is here from fifteen to twenty miles across, and which, therefore, such a multitude could not have traversed in a small part of a night, as we have seen, was probably the case with the Israelites. Thirdly, as the Lord effected the division of the waters by means of a strong east or northeast wind, acting probably with the ebb of the tide, the passage could have taken place at no point where such a wind would not naturally have produced this effect. At Suez, we have seen, this would have been the case; but at Bedea, or the point in question, no such effect could have been produced by it.

It is singular, that previous to the time of Niebuhr, almost all commentators, both ancient and modern, had united in fixing upon Bedea, or some point still lower down, as the place of passage; chiefly, it would seem, on the ground, that the broader the sea, the greater the miracle. Niebuhr supposed for a time that he was the first to regard Suez as the point of passage, until he found that Le Clerc had in general terms made the supposition; and that Eusebius also had affirmed that the Israelites passed through the sea at *Clysma*. It is no less singular, that since the time of Niebuhr all travellers and scientific men who have visited the spot, have united, in general, in the same opinion as to the place of passage.

REED, a plant with a jointed hollow stalk, growing in wet or marshy grounds. (See Job xl, 21.) The flag, the common cane, and bamboo are species of the reed. Fishing poles, canes, and rods are formed of it, Matt. xxvii, 48, used as an emblem of frailty. *A bruised reed*, Matt. xii, 20, is a reed broken together so as to have flaws or cracks, but not entirely broken off, used as the representation of the bodily or mental infirmities and afflictions of men, quoted from Isa. iv, 2, 3.

REFUGE. 1. Shelter or protection from danger or distress, Isa. xxvii, 15. 2. That which shelters, or protects from danger, distress, or calamity; a *strong hold* which protects by its strength, or a *sanctuary* which secures safety by its sacredness; any place inaccessible to an enemy, Psa. ix, 9; civ, 18.

CITIES OF REFUGE, among the Israelites, certain cities appointed to secure the safety of such persons as might undesignedly spill the blood of a fellow-creature. A law which authorizes a *blood-avenger*, i. e., required a brother, or other nearest relation of the slain, to kill the guilty person, or be considered *infamous*, may indeed be necessary where there is no other tribunal of justice; but as soon as there is such a one, it ought to cease. To change a law, however, or practice of long standing, is a matter of no little difficulty. Moses, therefore, left it as he found it, but he endeavoured, nevertheless, to prevent its abuses. To this end he appointed *cities of refuge*, three on each side of Jordan. He took care also that roads reaching to them in straight lines should be laid out in every direction, which were to be distinguished in some way from other streets.

Any one who had been the cause of death to another might flee into one of these cities, and, on examination, if he were found guilty, he was delivered up to the *avenger of blood*. But otherwise he was not to depart from the city into which he had fled till the death of the high priest; after which the right of revenge could not be legally exercised, Num. xxxv, 6–15. This custom still exists in full force among the modern Bedouins.

REGENERATION. 1. A new birth; that work of the Holy Spirit by which we experience a change of heart. It is expressed in Scripture by being born again, John iii, 7; born from above; being quickened, Eph. ii, 1; by Christ being formed in the heart, Gal. iv, 19; by our partaking of the Divine nature, 2 Peter i, 4. The efficient cause of regeneration is the Divine Spirit.

That man is not the author of it, is evident from John i, 12, 13; iii, 4; Eph. ii, 8, 10. The instrumental cause is the word of God, James i, 18; 1 Pet. i, 23; 1 Cor. iv, 15. The change in regeneration consists in the recovery of the moral image of God upon the heart; that is to say, so as to love him supremely, and serve him ultimately as our highest end, and to delight in him superlatively as our chief good. In a word, it is faith working by love that constitutes the new creature, the regenerate man, Gal. v, 6; 1 John i, 1–5. Regeneration is to be distinguished from our justification, although it is connected with it. Every one who is justified is also regenerated; but the one places us in a new *relation*, and the other in a new moral *state*. 2. *Regeneration* signifies the complete external manifestation of the Messiah's kingdom; when all things are to be delivered from their present corruption, and restored to spiritual purity and splendour, Matt. xix, 28. Dr. Campbell translates the passage thus: "At the renovation, when the Son of man shall be seated on the glorious throne, ye, my followers, sitting also upon twelve thrones, shall judge." We are accustomed, says he, to apply the term solely to the conversion of individuals; whereas its relation here is to the general state of things. The principal completion will be at the general resurrection, when there will be, in the most important sense, a renovation or regeneration of heaven and earth, when all things shall become new.

REHOBOAM, the son and successor of Solomon, who reigned in Juda, 975–958 years before Christ. The indiscretion of this prince caused ten of the tribes to revolt, and thus occasioned the founding of the kingdom of Israel, 1 Kings xii, 1; xiv, 21.

REIGN signifies to possess, and to exercise dominion; spoken of God as vindicating to himself his regal power, Rev. xi, 17. Figuratively, *to be exalted to an elevated and glorious condition*, spoken of Christians who are to reign with Christ, i. e., enjoy the high privileges, honours, and felicity of the Messiah's kingdom, Rom. v, 17. So of Christians on earth, to enjoy the honour and prosperity of kings, 1 Cor. iv, 8. Also, to have dominion, to prevail, to be predominant, as, e. g., death, Rom. v, 14, 17; sin and grace, verse 21.

REINS, *the kidneys* or *loins*, from their *retired* situation in the body, and their being *hid* in fat, they are often used figuratively for the *inmost mind*, the seat of the desires and passions, Rev. ii, 23; Jer. xi, 20.

RELIGION, *piety*, the worship of God, with the practice of all moral duties, James i, 27. By a usual figure, a part of religion is put for the whole. It is supposed that the apostle likens religion to a gem, whose perfection consists in its being clear, i. e., without flaw or cloud.

REMEMBRANCE occurs in the titles of Psalms xxxviii and lxx.

To bring to remembrance, especially before God. An expression commonly understood to refer to those sorrows in memory of which David composed the Psalms designated by it, or as implying that Jehovah would remember David, and help him.

REMPHAN, Acts vii, 43, the same as *chiun*, a name for the planet *Saturn*. Remphan is the Egyptian or Coptic name for the same planet, quoted from Amos v, 26. Here this prophet calls this god both a *star* and a *king*; as in fact Saturn was both a planet and the king or idol deity, who was otherwise called *Moloch*, (which see,) and worshipped by the offering up of human sacrifices to him. The Egyptians consecrated to Saturn the seventh day of the week; hence our word *Saturday*, i. e., Saturn's day.

REPENTANCE. 1. A change of mind or purpose. " He found no place of *repentance*," Heb. xii, 17, i. e., *change of mind* in his father Isaac, who had given the blessing to Jacob. The writer evidently does not mean to say that Esau found no place of repentance in himself; com pare Gen. xxvii, 34, 37. 2. In a religious sense, *penitence*, implying pious sorrow for unbelief and sin, and a turning from them unto God and the Gospel of Christ, Matt. iii, 8. This is called "repentance toward God," as therein we turn from sin to him; and "repentance unto life," as it leads to spiritual life, and is the first step to eternal life, Acts iii, 19; xi, 18; xx, 12. 3. God is said to repent, Gen. vi, 6, because the ancients used the same language in respect to God, which they employed when speaking of one another; and there is some point of analogy, when God is said to *repent*; the meaning is, that he acts in a manner analogous to that in which men act when they repent, i. e., he *changes* the course which he was pursuing.

REPETITION, *vain repetitions*, Matt. vi, 7, were particular expressions in prayer, which the Jews were accustomed to repeat a certain number of times. But all repetitions in prayer are not *vain*; for our Saviour himself prayed *thrice*, saying the same words; and St. Paul, through his earnestness, was led to pray thrice that "his thorn in the flesh might depart from him;" and if he used not exactly the same words, the import of his prayer must have been each time the same. But *vain repetition* is the use of *empty words*, and repeating the same over and over, think-

ing that they shall be heard for their *much speaking*.

REPHAIM. The sons of *Rephah*, a giant, 1 Chron. viii, 37; an ancient Canaanitish tribe beyond the Jordan, celebrated for their gigantic stature, Gen. xiv, 5.

The valley of Raphaim, or *the giants*, was south-west of Jerusalem, toward the country of the Philistines, Joshua xv, 8.

REPHIDIM. This station of the Israelites is, by universal consent, placed south-west of Sinai. It could not be far from this place, because God ordered Moses to go from thence to the rock of Horeb, to give the people water, Exod. xvii, 6. And this same water seems to have served the Israelites, not only in this encampment, and in that of Mount Sinai, but also in other encampments. This miracle happened in the second month after the departure from Egypt. See Me-RIBAH.

REPROBATE, in the language of modern times, is one who is excluded from the possibility of salvation by an absolute decree of God; one who is delivered over to perdition; but nowhere in Scripture is the word used in that sense, but signifies, 1. Not enduring proof or trial, properly spoken of metals not of standard purity or fineness; disallowed, rejected, Jer. vi, 30. 2. Figuratively, worthy of condemnation or execration, Rom. i, 28; 2 Cor. xiii, 5, 6, 7.

3. *Worthless*, good for nothing, abandoned in sin, and lost to virtue, Tit. i, 16.

REST, *a resting*, place of rest, fixed abode, dwelling, see Psalm xxxii, 14, where God is represented as searching through the earth, and selecting Zion as his dwelling place. It also signifies the *fixed* and *quiet* abode of the Israelites in the promised land after their wanderings, Heb. iii, 11. "My *rest*," i. e., the rest which I have promised, quoted from Psa. xcv, 11. Hence used figuratively for the *quiet abode* of those who shall dwell with God in heaven, in allusion to the rest of the Sabbath, which shows the nature of the rest, Heb. iv, 9. It will resemble the rest of the Sabbath, both in its employments and enjoyments. For therein the saints shall rest from their work of trial, and from all the evils they are subject to in the present life, and shall recollect the labours they have undergone, the dangers they have escaped, and the temptation they have overcome : and by reflecting on these things, and on the method of their salvation, they shall be unspeakably happy.

Matrimony is called *rest*, Ruth iii, 1. The word is used of those who quietly wait for any thing, as the martyrs, who *rest a little season*, Rev. vi, 11, i. e., take rest, enjoy repose ; the idea of previous exertion, anxiety, or suffering being included.

RESTITUTION. 1. The act of returning to a person some right or thing of which he has been unjustly deprived, Exod. xxii, 1–6. 2. *Restoration to a former state*, Acts iii, 21. "The time of the *restitution* of all things," i. e., the Messiah's future kingdom ; the same as the *time of reformation*, Heb. ix, 10, i. e., the time of a new and better dispensation under the Messiah ; compare Isa. lxvi, 22 ; lxv, 17, alluding to that peaceful enjoyment and bliss which are called *times of refreshing*, Acts iii, 19 ; when all things shall be adjusted, or restored to a state of tranquillity and order, as after wars and tumults.

RESURRECTION, the rising again from the state of the dead ; spoken of the future and general resurrection which shall take place at the end of all things. This is to be of the same body. It is true that some philosophers teach the questionable doctrine that the body changes its substance as it passes through different periods of life. It is not the same body, say they, but a similar body that shall be raised again. But unless the same body which is laid in the grave is the subject of the change from death to life, the term resurrection would be absurd. For God to give us a new body, one which the spirit never inhabited, would not be a resurrection, but a new creation. The resurrection of the dead is exclusively the doctrine of the Bible, and must be admitted to be a great mystery, which nothing but the occurrence of the fact can unfold. It is expressly taught both in the Old and New Testament, and without any nice distinctions, Job xix, 25; Psa. xvi, 10; Isa. xxvi, 19; Dan. xii, 2; Acts xxiv, 15.

As to the difficulties which have in all ages been urged against the resurrection of the same body, from the scattering of its parts, and their supposed conversion into others, it is even manifest to reason that a being of almighty power, who is always changing lifeless, inorganic matter into the living bodies of vegetables, animals, and men, is able to prevent every combination and change in the world of matter which could frustrate his design, Heb. xi, 35.

It is said, that "they might obtain a *better resurrection;*" plainly, a · *better* than that which had just been mentioned, viz., a resurrection to life in the present world merely; as in the examples of the children mentioned in 1 Kings xvii, and 2 Kings iv. It was not the hope of such a resurrection—the hope of merely regaining the present life, and being again subject to death as before—which led the martyrs to refuse liberation, but a resurrection to a life of immortal happiness and glory. "Why are they then baptized for the dead?" 1 Cor. xv, 29,

26

i. e., why baptized into a belief of the resurrection of the dead, if in fact the dead rise not? why expose ourselves to so much danger and suffering in hope of the resurrection of the dead?

REUBEN, *provided for my affliction,* Gen. xxix, 22; the eldest son of Jacob, though deprived of his birth-right, Gen. xlix, 4, and head of the tribe of like name. For the location of this tribe beyond Jordan, see Num. xxxii, 33; Josh. xiii, 15.

REVELATION, disclosure, manifestation, e. g., of that which becomes manifest by the event, Rom. ii, 5, when God's judgment shall be revealed, i. e., in the great day of judgment. In Eph. i, 17, "the spirit of revelation" is a spirit which can fathom and unfold the deep things of God; spoken of future events, Rev. i, 1, where it makes part of the title of the book.

THE BOOK OF REVELATION. This book belongs in its character to the prophetical writings, and stands in intimate relation with the prophecies of the Old Testament. This circumstance has surrounded the interpretation of this book with difficulties which no interpreter has yet been able fully to overcome. To explain it perfectly, says Newton, is not the work of one man, or of one age; but, probably, it never will be clearly understood till it is all fulfilled.

It was written by John, the

beloved apostle, in the Isle of Patmos, whither he was banished by Domitian, between the years A. D. 95 and 97.

REVELLING, a carousing, or merry-making after supper; the guests often sallying into the streets, and going through the city with torches, music, and songs, in honour of Bacchus, Gal. v, 21; the same as *rioting*, Rom. xiii, 13.

REVENGE, Jer. xv, 15; the return of an injury, from a desire of hurting the object. It is also taken in a good sense for hatred and just censure of sin; and simply *to punish*, 2 Cor. x, 6; the same in the Bible as *avenge*, i. e., to do justice to, to maintain one's right, to defend one's cause, Luke xviii, 5; also to make penal satisfaction, Rom. xii, 19; so to take vengeance of, to punish, Rev. vi, 10.

REVERENCE, a respectful, submissive disposition of mind, arising from affection and esteem, from a sense of superiority in the person reverenced.

REVEREND, a title of respect given to the clergy; but in the Bible it signifies *deserving reverence*, august, fearful, Psa. cxi, 9.

REVIVE, to gather new life, to show additional vigour, Rom. vii, 9; also *to live again*, Rom. xiv, 9. " *Revive* thy work," Hab. iii, 2, cause it to live, accomplish it.

RHEGIUM, a city on the coast, near the south-west extremity of Italy, now Rheggio, opposite Messina, in Sicily, Acts xxviii, 13.

RHODES, Acts xxi, 1, a celebrated island in the Mediterranean Sea, lying off the coast of Caria in Asia Minor, forty miles long and fifteen broad. The capital has the same name; and over the mouth of the harbour stood the famous Colossus, a statue of bronze, 105 feet high, reckoned one of the seven wonders of the world, but which was thrown down by an earthquake fifty-six years after its erection, some 240 years B. C.

RIBLAH, a city in the northern borders of Palestine, in the district of Hamath, through which the Babylonians, both in their irruptions and departures were accustomed to pass, 2 Kings xxiii, 33. Traces of it would seem to be extant in the town *Rebla*, situated some thirty miles south of Hamath, on the Orontes, and mentioned by Buckingham in his travels.

RICHES in Greek signifies *an abundant year*, and the Hebrew word for riches signifies *enough*, to live at ease, to live in comfort; one referring to the source, and the other to the effects of wealth. Hence *rich* often means *happy*, prosperous, wanting nothing, 2 Cor. viii, 9; Rev. iii, 17. The word is used by a figure as a source of power and influence, in ascriptions, Rev. v, 12.

Riches of God or Christ are the abundant gifts and blessings imparted from him, Eph.

iii, 8; also *richness*, *abundance*; *riches of glory*, Rom. ix, 23, is the abundant, pre-eminent glory of God, as displayed in his beneficence.

RIGHTEOUSNESS, justice, holiness. The righteousness of God is the essential perfection of his nature; sometimes it is put for his justice. The righteousness of Christ denotes, not only his absolute perfection, but is taken for his perfect obedience unto death, and his suffering the penalty of the law in our stead. The righteousness of the law is that obedience which the law requires. The righteousness of faith is the justification which is received by faith. He shall be called "the Lord our *righteousness*," Jer. xxiii, 6. The interpretation of this passage seems to be plain and obvious. When Christ is called *light* and *life*, and *way* and *truth*, the abstract nouns, *light*, *life*, &c., are employed as designations of the qualities of an agent; and in this way characterize that agent himself. Thus *light* means he who gives light or instruction; *life* means he who imparts life, or the author of spiritual life; *way* means he who shows or points out the way; *truth* means he who exhibits or discloses saving truth. So in the case before us, *the Lord our righteousness* means the author of it, he who gives or bestows or confers justification or pardoning mercy.

RIGHT HAND, among the Hebrews, as also among the Greeks and Romans, was the side of good omen; compare Matt. xxv, 33–46; and hence denotes *good fortune*, *prosperity;* so in the proper name *Benjamin*, Gen. xxxv, 18. To sit on the right hand of the king is the highest place of honour, e. g., spoken of the queen, 1 Kings ii, 19; Psa. xlv, 9; also of the favourite of the king and minister of the kingdom, Psa. cx, 1. See HAND.

RIMMON, the name of several towns in Palestine. Also an *idol* of the Assyrians, 2 Kings v, 18.

RINGS. The antiquity of rings appears from Scripture and from profane authors. The Israelitish women wore rings, not only on their fingers, but also in their nostrils and their ears. St. James distinguishes a man of wealth and dignity by the ring of gold on his finger, James ii, 2. At the return of the prodigal son, his father orders him to be dressed in a new suit of clothes, and to have a ring put on his finger, Luke xv, 22. The ring was used chiefly to seal with, and Scripture generally assigns it to princes and great persons, Esther iii, 10. The patents and orders of these princes were sealed with their rings or signets, an impression from which was their confirmation. The ring was one mark of sovereign authority. Pharaoh gave his ring to Joseph, as a token of authority, Gen. xli, 42. See ORNAMENTS.

RING-STREAKED, *banded*, i. e., marked with bands or stripes, Gen. xxx, 35.

RIVER. The Hebrews give the name of "the river," without any addition, sometimes to the *Nile*, sometimes to the *Euphrates*, and sometimes to *Jordan*. It is the tenor of the discourse that must determine the sense of this vague and uncertain way of speaking. They give also the name of river to brooks and rivulets that are not considerable. The name of river is sometimes given to the sea, i. e., the current or tide of the sea, Hab. iii, 8. *Rivers of Babylon*, the Euphrates with its canals, Psa. cxxxvii, 1. *Rivers*, in the plural, refers sometimes to the branches and canals of the Nile, Psa. lxxviii, 44. The word is also used for *abundance*, Job xxix, 6; Psa. xxxvi, 8.

ROBE, an upper garment, which was fuller and longer than the common one, reaching to the feet, but without sleeves. It was worn by women, 2 Sam. xiii, 18; by men of birth and rank, called *mantle*, Job i, 20; by kings, 1 Sam. xxiv, 5, 12; by priests, xxviii, .4; and especially by the high priest, under the eph'od, Exod. xxviii, 31. It is described by Josephus as not made of two pieces, but was one entire long garment, of blue cloth, woven throughout, having no seams on the sides

or shoulders: compare John xix, 23.

ROCK. In times of danger the people retired to rocks, and found refuge against sudden irruptions of their enemies. Thus the Benjamites secured themselves in the rock *Rimmon*, Judges xx, 47. It appears that rocks are still resorted to in the East as places of security; and we may remark, also, that before the invention of gunpowder, fastnesses of this kind were, in a manner, rendered absolutely impregnable. By a metaphor, God is said to be a rock, as affording refuge and protection to Israel, Deut. xxxii, 18, 37. *The rock where they took refuge.*

By another metaphor drawn from a quarry, it is put for the founder of a people, Isa. li, 1. Figuratively, a man of firmness and energy, one like a rock, Matt. xvi, 18. *A rock of offence* is Christ, as the occasion of destruction to those who reject him, Rom. ix, 33. *Rocks of the wild goats* are situated in the deserts of Engedi, 1 Sam. xxiv, 2.

ROD. 1. Branches of trees (see Gen. xxx, 37) used for beating or striking in chastisement, Prov. x, 13.

The rod of God, Job xxi, 9, is the rod with which *he* chastises, i. e., the calamities which he inflicts; and *rod of iron*, Psa. ii, 9, is put for *stern dominion.*

2. A shepherd's staff or *crook*, Psa. xxiii, 4, by which

Covel's Dic. p. 406.

ROE, OR GAZELLE.

he guides, restrains, and controls his *sheep*.

3. Figuratively used for a *portion*, which is measured off by a *rod*, Jer. x, 16.

Staff is nearly allied to a rod. *The staff of his shoulder*, i. e., which threatened blows, Isa. ix, 3. To break the staff of bread is to cause a famine of bread, i. e., of the *strengthener* of the heart, as it is elsewhere called, Psa. civ, 15. See also Gen. xviii, 5.

ROE, or *Roe-buck*, a species of deer, but there is little doubt that the animal intended in the Bible is the *gazelle*, a species of antelope, which is between the deer and the goat. It is about two feet and a half in height, of a reddish-brown colour, with the belly and feet white, has long naked ears, and a short tail. The horns are black, about twelve inches long, and bent like a lyre. It goes in large flocks, is easily tamed, though naturally very timid; and its flesh is reckoned excellent food. They are mostly confined to Asia and Africa, inhabiting the hottest regions of the old world. These animals are of elegant form, remarkable for their mild and brilliant eyes, &c.; they are active and astonishingly swift, running with vast bounds, and springing or leaping with surprising elasticity. Both the Hebrews and the Arabs make much of the beauty of the gazelle, and use it as the emblem of every thing that is elegant and beauti-

ful. See the annexed engraving.

ROMANS, natives or inhabitants of the city of Rome. It is also used for persons who possessed the privileges attached to the citizenship of Rome. See Acts xxii, 25. Paul, who pleads this privilege, was not actually a Roman by having been born at Rome, or in Italy: the Roman laws forbade that a Roman citizen should be bound, or scourged, or beaten with rods. And if any man falsely claimed the privilege of one, he was severely punished. The Romans took the city of Jerusalem three times : first, by the arms of Pompey, 63 B.C.; by Sosius, 37 B. C. ; and by Titus, A. D. 70, when both the city and temple were destroyed. They took from Judea the privilege of being a kingdom, and of having kingly government, i. e., reduced it into a province, first after the banishment of King Archelaus, son of Herod the Great, A. D. 16; and this continued to A. D. 37.

PAUL'S EPISTLE TO THE ROMANS was written at Corinth, A. D. 57. The Roman Church was composed partly of converted heathens, and partly of Jewish Christians. The grounds of dissension among them were, on the one hand, the national pride of the Jew, and his attachment to the Mosaic institutes, the observance of which he deemed necessary to salvation. This made him unwilling to believe that the Gentile could be admitted to equal privileges with the Jew in the kingdom of the Messiah, without being proselyted to the Jewish religion. On the other hand, the Gentile disregarded the prejudices of the Jews, and was wounded at the claim of superiority which they seemed to make. The apostle in his épistle meant to establish some great and geeral principles of Christiani-y, and also to apply them to .he state of the Church at Rome. That he intermingles with general truths many things which are local, is almost a matter of course in an epistle to a particular Church.

ROME. Acts xxviii, 16. The capital of the Roman empire, and once the metropolis of the world, is situated on the river Tiber, in Italy. It was built by Romulus, 750 years before Christ, and though at first it occupied a single hill of less than a mile in extent, it included in the days of its glory seven (some say fifteen) hills, and covered a territory twenty miles in circumference, and had a population of two or three millions. It had 150,000 houses, besides the mansions of the nobility; and it had 420 temples crowded with pagan deities. The city was given up to the grossest idolatry and superstition, while in arts and arms she was decidedly the mistress of the world. This was the state of Rome at the birth of Christ. Judea form-ed a part of her immense empire, and many Jews were resident in the city. At what time the Christian religion was introduced is uncertain; probably soon after the day of Pentecost, Acts ii, 10. We know that as early as A. D. 64, eight or ten years after a church was established there and addressed by Paul, Rom. i, 8; xvi, 19, the Emperor Nero commenced a furious persecution against its members, which the Emperor Domitian renewed, A. D. 81, and the Emperor Trajan carried out with implacable malice, (A. D. 97–117.) Seasons of suffering and repose succeeded each other alternately until the reign of Constantine, (A. D. 325,) when Christianity was established as the religion of the empire.

The modern city is celebrated not only for its own magnificence and splendour, but for the ruins of its former greatness. It is called the great school of painters, statuaries, and architects; and the lovers of the arts from all quarters of the globe are found at all times within her walls, or on a pilgrimage thither. In 1830 Rome contained nearly 150,000 inhabitants, among whom were 35 bishops and archbishops, 1490 priests, 1983 monks, 2,390 nuns, and 10,000 Jews, who occupy a particular section of the city. The majestic ruins, the grandeur of the churches and palaces, the religious customs, the boundless treasures of antiquity and art, and the recollections of what Rome once was, may well produce the highest degree of excitement in the mind of the traveller to that renowned city. *Union Dic.*

ROOF. Many of the large houses in the east were square, and enclosed a square area or court. This is the place where it is supposed our Saviour preached, Mark ii, 2. In verse 4 it is said, "They uncovered the *roof;*" perhaps they removed the awning which was drawn over the *court.* See HOUSE.

ROOT, used figuratively for the bottom, the lowest part of any thing, e. g., for a mountain, Job xxviii, 9; also for the cause or ground of controversy, Job xix, 28; used poetically for *fixed dwelling, abode,* Judg. v, 14, just as nations, taking up their abode in a land, are said to be planted in it, to take root in it, Amos ix, 15.

Also, the cause or source of any thing, 1 Tim. vi, 10; retaining the figure of a root, see Romans xi, 16, 17, 18, where Paul makes Abraham and the Jewish people *the root* from which the Gospel dispensation, with its blessings, has sprung, into which root and stem the Gentiles are ingrafted. Also, *a shoot, sprout,* springing from the root, Isa. liii, 2; used metaphysically *sprout of Jesse,* i. e., the Messiah, Isa. xi. 10, the offspring of Jesse, a descendant. "The root and

offspring of David," signifies that he is the life and strength of the family of David, as its offspring; that family being raised and preserved for the sole purpose of giving birth to the Messiah, Rev. xxii, 16.

"A *root* that beareth gall and wormwood," Deut. xxix, 18, is intended to characterize those who turn from the worship of the true God to that of idols. *Root of bitterness,* Heb. xii, 15, is applied to any person of an unholy life and deleterious example.

ROSE is the pride of the garden for elegance of form, glow of colour, and fragrance of smell. Tournefort mentions fifty-three kinds, of which the Damascus rose and the rose of Sharon are the finest. The beauty of these flowers is too well known to be insisted on; and they are at this day much admired in the east, where they are extremely fragrant. A traveller in Persia describes two rose-trees full fourteen feet high, laden with thousands of flowers, in every degree of expansion, and of a bloom and delicacy of scent that imbued the whole atmosphere with the most exquisite perfume, Isa. xxxv, 1, 2

RUBY, a precious stone of a rose-red colour, and of great beauty and value, Job xxviii, 18. It is a species of sapphires. See PRECIOUS STONES.

RUDIMENTS, Col. ii, 8, the same word is elsewhere

translated *elements*, signifying the component parts of the physical world, 2 Peter iii, 10; spoken of philosophers, and especially of the Jewish religion, in contrast with Christianity, the same as *the mere rudiments.* See ELEMENTS.

RUE, Luke xi, 24, a small shrubby plant common in gardens. It has a strong, unpleasant smell, and a bitterish, penetrating taste; but is not a native of this country.

RUSH, or BULRUSH. This is the famous Egyptian reed called the *papyrus.* It grew formerly in great quantities on the banks of the Nile, and in pools of stagnant water left by the Nile after its inundation. See Job viii, 11. See BULRUSH.

The roots of this plant are tortuous, the stem triangular, rising to the height of twenty feet, tapering gradually toward the extremity, which is surmounted by a flowing plume. The Egyptians made from it garments, shoes, baskets, vessels of various kinds, and especially *boats* or *skiffs.* So, Exod. ii, 3, we read of an "ark or skiff of bulrushes," i. e., *the papyrus,* Isa. xviii, 2. The most useful and valuable part of the papyrus, however, was its delicate rind or bark, which was used for paper. To prepare it for this purpose, the several coatings of which the stem is composed were carefully separated and spread out upon a table, artfully matched and pressed together, and moistened with water, which, dissolving the glutinous juices of the plant, caused them to adhere closely together. They were afterward pressed, and then dried in the sun, and thus rendered fit for paper.

RUST, a substance composed of oxygen combined with a metal, and forming a rough coat on its surface. The word is used in the Bible for any foul matter contracted. "Your gold and silver is cankered: and the rust of them shall be a witness against you," James v, 3. The circumstance of the gold and silver being rusted, i. e., tarnished, is mentioned to show that they had not been properly used, but covetously hoarded; and by a strong poetical figure the rust, i. e., the tarnish of their gold and silver, is represented both as a witness against them, and an executioner to destroy them. It will bear witness to their covetousness, and punish them by raising the most acute pain in their conscience, *as it were fire.*

RUTH. The book of Ruth is so called from the name of the person, a native of Moab, whose history it contains. Ruth had a son called Obed, who was the grandfather of David, which circumstance probably occasioned her history to be written, as the genealogy of David, from Pha'rez, the son of Judah, from whom the Messiah was to spring, is here given. We

p. 411.

PAPYRUS, OR RUSH.

are nowhere informed when Ruth lived ; but as King David was her great-grandson, we may place her history about 1250 B. C. This book was certainly written after the birth of David, and probably by the Prophet Samuel. The story related in this book is extremely interesting ; a pleasing digression from the general thread of the sacred history.

A simplicity of narrative so sweet and unstudied reigns through the book as to ensure its credibility. Particulars in relation to manners, and the spirit of the actors in the scene, are pointed out with such accuracy as greatly to delight the reader.

RYE, a well-known grain, of a quality inferior to wheat. Gesenius says the Hebrew signifies a species of grain like wheat, with a smooth or bold ear, as if shorn ; the modern *spelt* or German wheat, Exod. ix, 32.

SABACHTHANI, a Chaldean word, *thou hast forsaken me*, Matt. xxvii, 46 ; quoted from Psa. xxii, 1.

SAB'A-OTH, a Hebrew word, signifying *hosts* or *armies*. By this phrase we may understand the host of heaven, or the angels and ministers of the Lord ; or the stars and planets, which, as an army ranged in battle array, perform the will of God ; or, lastly, the people of the Lord, both of the old and new covenant, which is truly a great army,

of which God is the Lord and commander, Rom. ix, 29.

SABBATH, *rest, a lying by from labour ;* the seventh day of the week, kept originally by a total cessation from all labour, even to the kindling of a fire ; but apparently without any public solemnities, except an addition to the daily sacrifice in the tabernacle, and the changing of the show-bread, Exod. xx, 8 · but, see Lev. xxiii, 3, the custom of reading the Scriptures in the public assemblies and synagogues appears to have been introduced after the exile, Luke iv, 16.

It is wholly a mistake, that the Sabbath, because not re-enacted with the formality of the decalogue, is not explicitly enjoined upon Christians, and that the testimony of Scripture to such an injunction is not unequivocal and irrefragable. The Sabbath was appointed at the creation of the world, and sanctified, or set apart for holy purposes, "for man," for all men, and therefore for Christians ; since there was never any repeal of the original institution. To this we add, that if the moral law be the law of Christians, then is the Sabbath as explicitly enjoined upon them as upon the Jews. But that the moral law is our law, as well as the law of the Jews, a few passages of Scripture will prove as well as many. Our Lord declares that he "came not to destroy the law and the prophets, but to fulfil." I take it, that by "the law," he meant both the moral and the ceremonial; ceremonial law could only be fulfilled in him, by realizing its types; and moral law, by upholding its authority. That the observance of the Sabbath is a part of the moral law, is clear from its being found in the decalogue, the doctrine of which our Lord sums up in the moral duties of loving God and our neighbour; and for this reason the injunctions of the prophets, on the subject of the Sabbath, are to be regarded as a part of their moral teaching.

Another explicit proof that the law of the ten commandments, and consequently the law of the Sabbath, is obligatory upon Christians, is found in the answer of the apostle to an objection to the doctrine of justification by faith: "Do we then make void the law through faith?" Rom. iii, 31; which is equivalent to asking, Does Christianity teach that the law is no longer obligatory on Christians, because it teaches that no man can be justified by it? To this he answers, in the most solemn form of expression, "God forbid; yea, we establish the law." Now, the sense in which the apostle uses the term, "the law," in this argument, is indubitably marked in Rom. vii, 7: "I had not known sin but by the law; for I had not known lust, except the law had said, Thou

shalt not covet;" which, being a plain reference to the tenth command of the decalogue, as plainly shows that the decalogue is "the law" of which he speaks. This, then, is the law which it established by the Gospel; and this can mean nothing else but the establishment and confirmation of its authority, as the rule of all inward and outward holiness. Whoever, therefore, denies the obligation of the Sabbath on Christians, denies the obligation of the whole decalogue.

Now, though there is not on record any Divine command issued to the apostles, to change the Sabbath from the day on which it was held by the Jews to the first day of the week; yet, when we see that this was done in the apostolic age, and that St. Paul speaks of the Jewish Sabbaths as not being obligatory upon Christians, while he yet contends that the whole moral law is obligatory upon them, the fair inference is, that this change of the day was made by Divine direction. It is, indeed, more than inference that the change was made under the sanction of inspired men; and those men, the appointed rulers in the Church of Christ; whose business it was to "set all things in order," which pertained to its worship and moral government. We may, therefore, rest well enough satisfied with this—that as a Sabbath is obligatory upon us, we act under apostolic authority for observing it on the first day of the week, and thus commemorate at once the creation and the redemption of the world.

The same portion of time which constituted the seventh day from the creation could not be observed in all parts of the earth; and it is not probable, therefore, that the original law expresses more than that a seventh day, or one day in seven, the seventh day, after six days of labour, should be thus appropriated, from whatever point the enumeration might set out, or the hebdomadal cycle begin. For if more had been intended, then it would have been necessary to establish a rule for the reckoning of days themselves, which has been different in different nations; some reckoning from evening to evening, as the Jews now do, others from midnight to midnight, &c. So that those persons in this country who hold their Sabbath on Saturday, under the notion of exactly conforming to the Old Testament, and yet calculate the days from midnight to midnight, have no assurance at all that they do not desecrate a part of the original Sabbath, which might begin, as the Jewish Sabbath now, on Friday evening, and, on the contrary, hallow a portion of a common day, by extending the Sabbath beyond Saturday evening. Even if this were ascertained, the differences of latitude and longitude would throw the whole into disorder; and it is not probable that a universal law should have been fettered with that circumstantial exactness, which would have rendered difficult, and sometimes doubtful, astronomical calculations necessary in order to its being obeyed according to the intention of the Lawgiver.

Thus that part of the Jewish law, the decalogue, which, on the authority of the New Testament, we have shown to be obligatory upon Christians, leaves the computation of the hebdomadal cycle undetermined; and, after six days of labour, enjoins the seventh as the Sabbath, to which the Christian practice as exactly conforms as the Jewish. It is not, however, left to every individual to determine which day should be his Sabbath, though he should fulfil the law so far as to abstract the seventh part of his time from labour. It was ordained for worship, for *public* worship; and it is therefore necessary that the Sabbath should be uniformly observed by a whole community at the same time. The Divine Legislator of the Jews interposed for this end, by special direction as to his people. The first Sabbath kept in the wilderness was calculated from the first day in which the manna fell; and with no apparent reference to the creation of the world. By apostolic authority, it is now fixed to be held on the first day of the week ; and thus one of the great ends for which it was established, that it should be a day of "holy convocation,"is secured, Acts xx, 7 ; 1 Cor. xvi, 2.

Sabbaths are taken sometimes for all the Jewish festivals, Lev. xix, 3, 30; Col. ii, 16 ; because they were times of sacred *rest*.

The Sabbatical year was celebrated among the Jews every seventh year, when the land was left without culture, Exodus xxii, 10. God appointed the observation of the Sabbatical year, to preserve the remembrance of the creation of the world, to enforce the acknowledgment of his sovereign authority over all things, and in particular over the land of Canaan, which he had given to the Israelites, by delivering up the fruits to the poor and the stranger. It was a sort of tribute, or small rent, by which they held the possession. Besides, he intended to inculcate humanity upon his people, by commanding that they should resign to the slaves, the poor, and the strangers, and to the brutes, the produce of their fields, of their vineyards, and of their gardens. In the Sabbatical year all debts were remitted, and the slaves were liberated, Exod. xxi, 2; Deut. xv, 2.

SABEANS, the inhabitants of the country SHEBA, or Arabia Felix, abounding in frankincense, spices, gold, and precious stones, Isa. lx, 6; Psa. lxxii, 15; celebrated also for their traffic, Joel iv, 8 ; but in Job i, 15, the name seems to stand for Arabians, or Arab robbers, driving off plunder in the vicinity of *Uz*, or *Ausitis*. The genealogical tables in Genesis enumerates three persons of the name ; 1, a grandson of Cush, and son of Raamah, Gen. x, 7 ; 2, a son of Joktan, verse 28, which accords with the Arabic tradition ; 3, a grandson of Abraham by Keturah, xxv, 4. In the first and last of these instances *Sheba* is coupled with Dedan, his brother. Gesenius supposes that there were at least two Arabic tribes of this name, the one in South Arabia, and the other dwelling in the northern Arabian desert, near the Persian Gulf, and the mouths of the Euphrates. See SHEBA.

SACKBUT, a wind instrument of music, used for the bass, resembling a trumpet, and so contrived as to be capable of being drawn out to different lengths, as the acuteness or gravity of the sound requires. The Hebrew word occurs only in Daniel, and is supposed by Gesenius and others to signify a stringed instrument. Pfeiffer, a German author, says it was furnished with four strings, and had an acute sound ; but by degrees it obtained a greater number of strings, which were touched with the fingers. Some suppose that it was of that form represented by figure 9. See cut on page 109.

SACKCLOTH, a coarse black cloth, commonly made of hair, Rev. vi, 12, and used for sieves and strainers, for sacks, and for mourning garments; in the latter case it was worn instead of the ordinary garments, or bound around the loins, or spread under a person on the ground. It was also the garment of ascetics and prophets, Isa. xx, 2. It was in truth *a sack*, which was thrown over the person, and extended down to the knees, but which, nevertheless, had arm holes for the admission of the arms.

SACRIFICE. A sacrifice is that which is offered directly to God, and is in some way destroyed or changed, which is done, as far as respects the flesh employed in the sacrifice, by *burning* it, and as far as concerns the libation, by *pouring it out*. It differs from an oblation in this: in a *sacrifice* there must be a real change or destruction of the thing offered; whereas an *oblation* is but a simple offering or gift. It is not improbable, although nothing is expressly said to this effect, that God taught our first parents by the death of animals, whose skins were used as clothing, not only what they themselves deserved on account of their sins, but also gave them to understand that animals should be slain, in order to remind them of guilt and punishment. Perhaps the idea recurred to

them of itself, when first called upon to witness the sudden and violent death of animals. If, however, these views be incorrect, if it were the fact that sacrifices were of merely *human origin*, they, nevertheless, had a meaning. They, in this case, resulted from, and were the indications of a grateful and reverential state of mind toward God, and were the means of acknowledging God in a solemn manner, as the great and universal Ruler, and as the source and sustainer of life, as well as all other things.

The sacrifices, in which animals were slain, were all symbolical, or had a meaning. The Divine promises were confirmed by them, and the Hebrews, on the other hand, imparted, in this way, new sacredness to the engagements which they had made to continue true to their religion: and were thus excited to new desires after piety of feeling and rectitude of conduct.

But very many of the Hebrews were disposed to go farther than this, and to attribute an inherent efficacy to the sacrifices in themselves considered, and to trust in the multitude of victims, with whatever mind they might be offered. This error is very frequently condemned, and in very decided terms.

That this symbolic substitution, however, of victims in place of transgressors,

27

prefigured a true substitution in the person of Jesus Christ, seems to have been known but to very few of the prophets. See Isa. liii. But although the people did not originally understand this particular meaning of the sacrifices, they were prepared to receive it at last.

Hence the death of violence which *Jesus* suffered is everywhere termed in the New Testament a SACRIFICE; for expressions of this kind are not mere allusions, such as occur in Rom. xii, 1; Phil. ii, 17; but they indicate a *real* sacrifice in the person of Christ, which the sacrifices of the Old Testament prefigured, as is expressly stated in Heb. ix; x, 10–14, and elsewhere.

The word sacrifice signifies, 1, the act and rite of sacrificing, Matt. ix, 13; 2, by a figure the thing sacrificed, *victim*, the flesh of victims, part of which was burned on the altar, and part given to the priests, see Lev. ii, iii; Mark ix, 49; 3, it is spoken of service, obedience; praise offered to God, *offering, oblation*, Phil. iv, 18. So Paul speaks of the *sacrifice of praise*, Heb. xiii, 15.

A *living sacrifice* may signify *an excellent one;* sacrifices being made only of animals brought alive to the altar, the living, active powers of their bodies were to be continually offered, or devoted to God; or in other words, they were to offer a *living,* enduring, lasting sacrifice,

not a sacrifice once for all by self-immolation.

SACRILEGE, the crime of robbing temples, Romans ii, 22.

Since the captivity, the Jews have always expressed the greatest abhorrence of idolatry; but still they withheld the tithes and offerings which God required of them, Mal. iii, 8–10, and robbed him of due honour, worship, and obedience.

SADDUCEES, a sect of the Jews. Some derive the name from the Hebrew word TZADAK, *the just;* the Talmudists refer it to a certain person whose name was *Sadok*, who, according to them, lived about three centuries before Christ, and was the founder of the sect. The Sadducees rejected all traditions and unwritten laws, which the Pharisees prized so highly, and held the Scriptures to be the only source and true rule of the Jewish religion. They denied the existence of angels and spirits, as well as an overruling providence, Acts xxiii, 8, and held that the soul of man dies with the body, rejecting, of course, the idea of a future state of rewards and punishments.

In their lives and morals they were more strict than the Pharisees; and although their tenets were not generally acceptable among the common people, yet they were adopted by many of the higher ranks.

It does not appear that they merely received the Pentateuch, and rejected all the other books of the Old Testament; for we find in the disputes of the Talmud, a work which contains the doctrines and morality of the Jews, that the Sadducees are not only attacked from the other books of the Old Testa, ment besides the Pentateuch-but they draw arguments from them in their own defence.

Descendants of the Sadducees are apparently the modern *karaim*, who reside in Crimea, a peninsula of the southern part of Russia.

SAFFRON, the *crocus*, Song iv, 14, a perennial plant, generally cultivated in gardens, of a deep colour, and a peculiar aromatic smell. It is a native of Greece and Asia Minor, where it has been cultivated from the earliest ages of antiquity.

SAINT signifies *that which is clean*, or *free from defilement*; and as this is assumed of all who profess the Christian name, the saints are *Christians*; those who are purified and sanctified by the influences of the Spirit. It is sometimes appropriated to the *spiritual men* in the Christian Church who were inspired with the knowledge of the Gospel, Col. i, 26.

SAL'AMIS, once a famous city in the Isle of Cyprus, opposite to Seleucia, on the Syrian coast. Here St. Paul preached, A. D. 44, Acts xiii, 5. The ruins of this place were visited in 1835 by two American missionaries. Very little of the ancient tower is now standing.

SALEM, *peace*, the ancient name of Jerusalem, Heb. vii, 1, 2.

SALIM. The situation of this place, where John baptized on the Jordan, is unknown, John iii, 23.

SAL'MON, son of Nahshon, married Rahab, by whom he had Boaz, Ruth iv, 20, 21; Matt. i, 4. He is named the father of Bethlehem, because his descendants peopled that place.

SALMONE, the name of a promontory which forms the eastern extremity of the Isle of Crete, Acts xxvii, 7.

SAL-O'ME, the wife of Zebedee, and mother of St. James the greater, and St. John the evangelist, Matthew xxvii, 56; and one of those holy women who used to attend upon our Saviour in his journeyings, and to minister to him. She was the person who requested of Jesus Christ that her two sons, James and John, might sit on his right and left hand when he should enter upon his kingdom, having then but the same obscure views as the rest of the disciples; but she gave proof of her faith when she followed Christ to Calvary, and did not forsake him even at the cross, Mark xv, 40; Matt. xxvii, 55, 56.

SALT is spread in great abundance throughout nature;

great quantities of it are held in solution by the water of the ocean. It is found crystallized in immense masses, called *fossil* or *rock salt*. This kind generally contains a large proportion of clay or other earthy matter, and is liable from exposure to become insipid, as Mr. Maundrell found in his journey to Jerusalem. He tells us that in the Valley of Salt, on the side toward Gibul, from a small precipice, formed by the continual taking away of the salt, he broke out a piece, of which the part that had been exposed to the sun, rain, and air, though it contained sparks and particles of salt, had entirely *lost its savour*, while that part next the rock still retained, as he found, its saltness. Salt which had thus become insipid might be used for the purpose of repairing roads; or " cast out to be trodden under foot," Matt. v, 13. "Wherewith shall it be salted," *how can it be itself preserved or recovered?* Among the orientals salt is the symbol of inviolable friendship; *a covenant of salt*, accordingly, means an everlasting or perpetual covenant, 2 Chron. xiii, 5, i. e., most solemn and sure. The word in Mark ix, 49, is used metaphorically, every one shall be *seasoned*, tried *with fire*, i. e., the wicked with eternal fire, (verses 47, 48 ;) while every Christian shall be tried, perfected by suffering, so as to become acceptable in the sight of God; just

as every victim is prepared for sacrifice by being sprinkled with salt; compare Lev. ii, 13.

It also signifies *wisdom* and *prudence*, both in words and actions, Mark ix, 50. "Ye are the *salt* of the earth," Matt. v, 13, i. e., ye are those who, by your instructions and influence, are to render men wiser and better ; just as salt imparts to food a more acceptable flavour. See Col. iv, 6. Although *salt* in small quantities may contribute to the fertilizing of some kinds of stubborn soil, yet according to the observations of *Pliny*, " all places where salt is found are barren, and produce nothing." The effect of salt where it abounds on vegetation is described by *burning*, Deut. xxix, 23. So a *salt land* is the same as the " parched places in the wilderness," and is descriptive of barrenness, Jer. xvii, 6. Hence the ancient custom of sowing an enemy's city, when taken, with salt, in token of perpetual desolation, Judges ix, 45.

Pillar of salt, a stone of fossil salt, having the figure of a column, such, says Genius, as are occasionally found near the Dead Sea, Gen. xix, 26.

Valley of salt, 2 Sam. viii, 13, is supposed to be the northern part of the great valley *El Ghor*, which leads south from the Dead Sea ; or perhaps some smaller valley or ravine opening into it near the Dead Sea. The whole of this region is strongly impregnated with salt, as appears from the reports of travellers.

SALT SEA, the sea into which the Jordan pours its waters, and which occupies the place where once stood the cities of the plain, in the vale of Siddim, Gen. xiv, 3. As the Jordan before the celebrated destruction of this plain discharged itself in the same place that it now does, the conclusion is a necessary one, that the sea which then existed was subterranean. It was covered with a crust of earth, which was sustained by the asphaltus, a pitchy, bituminous substance, which arises from the lake to this day, and floats on its surface, Isaiah xxxiv, 9, 10. Hence it has obtained the name of the Lake Asphaltites. This statement is confirmed by Gen. xiv, 10, where mention is made of *slime pits*, through which the asphaltus or bitumen penetrated from the subterranean water. The lake is said to be sixty-seven miles from north to south, and seventeen in its greatest breadth from west to east. But Mr. Legh, who visited the lake in 1818, and who had a prospect of the whole extent of it from an eminence, says, "that its length has been greatly overrated, and that it cannot exceed *forty miles*." Common sea-water is bitter and saline, and its fixed constituents amount to about three per cent.; (three pounds in 100;)

but the water of this sea contains one-fourth of its weight of solid matter! It is clear and limpid, but has a peculiarly bitter, saline, and pun gent taste. Hence called the *Salt Sea*, Num. xxxiv, 12. No plants grow in the immediate vicinity of the lake, where every thing is dull, cheerless, and inanimate; whence it is supposed to have derived the name *Dead Sea*.

Our Arab guides, says the above named traveller, had endeavoured to alarm us as to the consequences of bathing in these pestiferous waters; but we made the experiment, and found that though two of our party were unable to swim, they were buoyed up in a most extraordinary manner. The sensation perceived immediately upon dipping was, that we had lost our sight; and any part of the body that happened to be excoriated smarted excessively. The taste of the wa ter was bitter, and intolerably saline. The lake is enclosed, except on the north-west by ranges of broken and barren hills, on the south by El Ghor, and has, apparently, no outlet; the sand on the beach is of a dirty dark brown. It has been computed that the Jordan discharges into it upward of six millions of tons daily. Yet there is never any perceptible variation in the height of its waters. Some have conjectured the possibility of a subterraneous communication with the Red Sea; others are of opinion that the daily evaporation is sufficient to carry off all the waters discharged into it, which is a simple solution of the difficulty.

From the extremity of the Dead Sea, (according to Mr. Banks and his companions,) a sandy plain or flat extends southward between hills, and on a level with the sea, for the distance of eight or ten miles, where it is interrupted by a sandy cliff, from sixty to eighty feet high, which traverses the valley like a wall, forming a barrier to the waters of the lake when at their greatest height. Beyond this cliff the valley is prolonged without interruption to Akaba. It is skirted on each side by a chain of mountains; but the streams which descend from these are in summer lost in their gravelly beds before they reach the valley below; so that the lower plain, or bottom of the great valley, is in summer entirely without water, which alone can produce verdure in the Arabian deserts, and render them habitable.

SALUTATION, the act of showing to a person some outward token of love or respect. The forms of salutation that prevailed among the ancient Hebrews implied the wish or invocation of every good, 1 Sam. xv, 13. This of course is more emphatic than the mode of salutation which merely asks after one's welfare. See Ruth ii, 4; Judges xix, 20.

Oriental salutations were attended with various gestures and inflections of the body; the ceremony of grasping hands and kissing, and the interrogations respecting each other's health, and frequently repeated on the same occasion, necessarily consumed much time. Hence the caution, 2 Kings iv, 29; Luke x, 4. The prohibition in this last passage was probably designed to secure the close and undivided attention of the apostles to the work before them, and to prevent loss of time or waste of thought on mere matters of form and ceremony.

SALVATION, *safety, deliverance, preservation* from danger or destruction.

1. Taken generally for a temporal deliverance or security, Heb. xi, 7; hence *welfare, prosperity*, Phil. i, 19; and by implication, *victory*. See 1 Sam. xiv, 45; Rev. vii, 10.

2. In the Christian sense, it is deliverance from punishment and misery as the consequence of sin, and admission to eternal life and happiness in the kingdom of Christ the Saviour, Luke i, 77. "*Salvation* is of the Jews," i. e., deliverance by a Messiah, John iv, 22; and, figuratively, a source or bringer of salvation, Saviour, Acts xiii, 47.

3. The Christian religion; the full phrase would seem to be *the word of this salvation*, which is found in Acts xiii, 26. "How shall we escape"

with impunity if we neglect the Christian religion with all its promised blessings and tremendous threats, Heb. ii, 3; see also verse 4. The word *neglect* is plainly emphatic in this connection, and means to treat with *utter disregard* or *contempt*; such as would be implied in an apostacy. •

SAMARIA, Acts viii, 5; a celebrated city, near the middle of Palestine; perhaps forty miles north of Jerusalem, built ·by Omri, king of Israel, on a mountain or hill of the same name. It was the metropolis of the kingdom of Israel or the ten tribes; and after being several times destroyed and restored, it was enlarged and beautified by Herod the Great, and named by him *Sebaste*, in honour of Augustus. It is now an inconsiderable village, still called Sebaste. See 1 Kings xvi, 24.

By a figure of speech, the word is put for the inhabitants, Acts viii, 14. In a wider sense, it signifies *the region of Samaria;* the district of which Samaria was the chief city, lying between Judea and Galilee or the plain of Esdralon.

SAMARITAN, an inhabitant of the city or country of Samaria; spoken in the New Testament of the descendants of a people sprung originally from an intermixture of 'the ten tribes with the heathen colonists sent into the country by Shalmaneser, 2 Kings xvii, 24. This mixed people, although they retained the books of Moses; and although priests were sent to teach them the Jewish religion, soon fell away into gross idolatry, and were regarded almost as Gentiles by the Jews, even before the exile, 2 Kings xvii, 26–41. When the Jews, after their return from exile, began to rebuild Jerusalem and the temple, the Samaritans also laid claim to a descent from Ephraim and Manasseh, and requested permission to aid the Jews in their work; but this being refused, they turned against them and calumniated them before the Persian kings, Ezra iv, and Neh. iv. They afterward erected a temple on Mount Ger'izim, in allusion to Deut: xxvii, 11, 12, and there instituted sacred rites in accordance with the law of Moses. From these and other circumstances, the natural hatred between the Jews and Samaritans was continually fostered and augmented; the name Samaritan became to the Jews a term of reproach, and intercourse with them was carefully avoided; see John iv, 9; viii, 48. The temple on Ger'izim was destroyed by Hyrcanus about 125 B. C. But the Samaritans still held the mountain as sacred, and the proper place of national worship, John iv, 20, 21. The same is the case with the small remnant of the Samaritans existing at the present day;

who still go three times a year from Naplous, the ancient Sychar, to worship on Mount Ger'izim. The Samaritans, like the Jews, expected a Messiah, John iv, 25 ; and many of them became the disciples of Jesus ; compare John iv, 39 ; Acts ix, 31. See an interesting account of the modern Samaritans in Calmet, p. 810.

SAMOS, Acts xx, 15 ; an island of the Ægean Sea, near the coast of Lydia, in Asia Minor, thirty-two miles long, and twenty-two broad. It was celebrated for the worship of Juno and for its valuable pottery. It was the birthplace of Pythagoras, and the burial-place of Lycurgus.

SAMOTHRACIA, an island in the north-east part of the Ægean Sea, above the Hellespont, with a lofty mountain, Acts xvi, 11. It was anciently called *Samos ;* and to distinguish it from the other Samos, the name of *Thracia* was added. The island was celebrated for the mysteries of Ceres and Proserpine, and was a sacred asylum ; now called *Samondrachi.*

SAMSON, *sunlike,* a judge of Israel, famous for his great strength. He was born, according to Hales, about 1200 B. C. See Judges xiii, 24. His extraordinary achievements are particularly recorded in Judg. xiv–xvi. "Faith" is attributed to him by St. Paul, Heb. xi, 32, though whether he retained it to the end of his life may be doubted.

He is not inaptly called by an old writer, "a rough believer."

SAMUEL, *heard of God,* or *name of God ;* the son of Elkanah and of Hannah, was born 1151 B. C. He was an eminent inspired prophet, historian, and the seventeenth and last judge of Israel ; and died in the ninety-eighth year of his age, two years before Saul. To Samuel are ascribed the book of Judges, that of Ruth, and the first book of Samuel. Samuel began the order of the prophets, which was never discontinued till the death of Zechariah and Malachi, Acts iii, 24. From early youth to hoary years, the character of Samuel is one on which the mind rests with veneration and delight. See his history in 1 Sam.

SANBALLAT, the name of the sat'rap or governor of the king of Persia, in Samaria, Neh. ii, 10. He endeavoured by every means of force and fraud to hinder Nehemiah in the work of rebuilding the temple, Neh. vi, 1–9.

SANCTIFICATION, that work of God's grace by which we are *renewed after the image of God, set apart* for his service, and enabled to die unto sin and live unto righteousness. Sanctification comprehends all the graces of *knowledge, faith, repentance, love, humility, zeal, patience,* &c., and the exercise of them in our conduct toward God or man, Gal. v, 22–24. Sanctification in this world must be complete; the whole nature must be sanctified, all sin must be utterly abolished, or the soul can never be admitted into the glorious presence of God, Heb. xii, 14; 1 Peter i, 15; Rev. xxi, 27; yet the saints, while here, are in a state of spiritual warfare with Satan and his temptations, with the world and its influence, 2 Cor. ii, 11; 1 John ii, 16.

SANCTIFY. In the Old Testament, to sanctify often denotes to *separate from a common to a holy purpose;* to *set apart* or *consecrate* to God as his special property, and for his service. Our Lord also uses this term when he says, "For their sakes I *sanctify* myself," John xvii, 19; that is, I *separate* and *dedicate* myself to be a sacrifice to God for them, "that they also may be *sanctified* through the truth;" that is, that they may be *cleansed* from the guilt of sin. Hence St. Paul speaks of "the blood of bulls and goats, and the ashes of a heifer sprinkling the unclean, as *sanctifying* unto the purifying of the flesh," Heb. ix, 13. These things were in reality of no more worth or value; they were merely typical institutions, intended to represent the blessings of the new and better covenant, those "good things that were to come;" and therefore God is frequently spoken of in the prophets as despising them, namely, in any other view

than that for which his wisdom had ordained them, Isa. i, 11–15; Psa. l, 8, 9; li, 16. But that dispensation is now at an end; under the New Testament the state of things is changed, for now "neither circumcision availeth any thing, nor uncircumcision, but a new creature." The thing signified, namely, *internal purity and holiness,* is no less necessary to a right to the privileges of the Gospel, than the observance of those external rites was to the privileges of the law.

SANCTUARY usually means *a holy place;* and in a general sense, it may be taken for the whole temple, Heb. ix, 1, called *worldly,* i. e., material, pertaining to this world, of a terrestrial nature, in opposition to the one which is made without hands. See verses 11, 24; compare Psa. xx, 2. It also signifies that spacious apartment of the temple in which the various articles of sacred furniture were placed which are mentioned, Heb. ix, 2.

The term is also applied to any place appointed for the public worship of God, Psa. lxxiii, 17; to heaven, where God and his holy angels dwell, Psa. cii, 19; and in allusion to the Jewish sanctuary, whose brazen altar protected petty criminals; a place of refuge and shelter is called *a sanctuary,* Isa. viii, 14.

SANDALS, Mark vi, 9. The sandals or shoes of the orientals were in ancient times, and are still at the present day, merely soles of hide, leather, or wood, fastened to the bottom of the feet by straps.

The business of untying and carrying the sandals being that of a servant, the expressions of the Baptist, "whose shoes I am not worthy to bear," "whose shoe latchet I am not worthy to unloose," was an acknowledgment of his great inferiority to Christ, and that Christ was his Lord. To pull off the sandals on entering a sacred place, or the house of a person of distinction, was the usual mark of respect. They were taken care of by the attendant servant. At the doors of an Indian pa-go'da, there are as many sandals and slippers hung up as there are hats in our places of worship.

SAPPHIRE, a precious stone, remarkable for its beauty and splendour, next in hardness and value to the diamond, mostly of a blue colour, in various shades, Exod. xxiv, 10. See PRECIOUS STONES.

SA'RAH, *princess, noble lady;* the wife of Abraham, and his sister, as he himself informs us, by the same father, but not the same mother, Gen. xx, 12. See ABRAHAM.

SARDINE, the same as *Sardius;* a precious stone of a blood-red, or sometimes of a flesh colour, more commonly known by the name of *cornelian,* Rev. iv, 3; and xxi, 20. See PRECIOUS STONES.

SARDIS, the metropolis of Lydia, in Asia Minor, situated at the foot of Mount Tmolus, on the banks of the river Pactolus, celebrated for its wealth and voluptuous debauchery, Rev. iii, 1–4.

SARDONYX, a precious stone, exhibiting a milk-white variety of the onyx or chalcedony, intermingled with shades, or stripes of sardian or cornelian, i. e., alternate bands of red and white, Rev. xxi. 20. See PRECIOUS STONES.

SAREPTA, a Phenician town, on the shore of the Mediterranean, midway between Tyre and Sidon, Luke iv, 26.

SATAN, a Hebrew word, which signifies *adversary;* he is sometimes called *the devil,* i. e., *the accuser,* by way of eminence; the prince of the fallen angels, Matt. ix, 34. According to the later Hebrew, he acts as the accuser and calumniator of men before God, Job i, 7, 12; Zech. iii, 1, 2; Rev. xii, 9, 10; seduces them to sin, 1 Chron. xxi, 1, and is the author of evil, both physical and moral, by which the human race is afflicted. See SPIRIT, *unclean.*

In the New Testament, the devil appears as the constant enemy of God, of Christ, of the Divine kingdom, of the followers of Christ, and of all truth; full of falsehood and malice, and exciting and seducing to evil in every possible way, Matt. i, v, viii, xi; John xiii, 2; a *child of the devil* or of *Satan*, is one like Satan, an enemy of God and man, John viii, 44; Acts xiii, 10. See DEVIL.

SATYRS, rural deities of Greek mythology; the Hebrew word in the singular signifies *hairy, rough, a he-goat;* in the plural *wood demons*, resembling he-goats, supposed to live in deserts; poetically introduced by Isaiah, as dancing among the ruins of Babylon, Isa. xiii, 21; xxxiv, 14, signifying that the place shall become a wild and an uncultivated waste.

SAUL, *asked, desired;* the Jewish name of the Apostle Paul, Acts ix, 4; also the name of the first king of the Israelites, from the tribe of Benjamin, who was anointed 1091 B. C., 1 Sam. i, 2, seq. He reigned forty years, but exhibited to posterity a melancholy example of a monarch, elevated to the summit of worldly grandeur, who, having cast off the fear of God, gradually became the slave of jealousy, duplicity, treachery, and the most malignant and diabolical tempers. His behaviour toward David shows him to have been destitute of every generous and noble sentiment that can dignify human nature; and it is not an easy task to speak with any moderation of the atrocity and baseness which uniformly mark it. His character is that of a wicked man, "waxing worse and worse;" but, while we are shocked at its deformity, it should be our study to profit by it, which we can only do by using it as a beacon to warn us, "lest we also be hardened through the deceitfulness of sin."

SAVIOUR, a deliverer, preserver, who saves from danger or destruction, and brings into a state of prosperity and happiness, spoken of Jesus as the Messiah, Luke ii, 11.

SCALL, the *scab, mange,* in the head and beard, Lev. xiii, 30; a kind of leprosy, which frequently causes the hair to fall off from the part thus affected.

SCARCELY, with difficulty, hardly.

SCARLET. This colour, which was very much admired, the ancients obtained from a certain insect, (*coccus ilicis* of Lin.,) which adheres with its eggs to the leaves of a species of oak, and is related to the cochineal, found on a species of *cactus* growing in Mexico. The word is used for *scarlet* cloths or garments, Prov. xxxi, 21. Scarlet was the favourite colour of the wealthy and noble, Dan. v, 16 It was very deep, and sometimes called *crimson*, 2 Chron. ii, 14.

The Hebrew word in this place is *carmil*, which, Gesenius says, was adopted from the Persian *kerne*, a worm; hence the German *cramoisi carmesin*, and English *crimson*. In the lamentation of David over Saul and Jona than, the daughters of Israel are invoked to "weep over Saul, who had clothed them with *scarlet*," 2 Sam. i, 24. The idea implied is, that under Saul the land had attained to such a degree of wealth and prosperity that elegance and splendour of dress were within the reach of all.

SCATTERED ABROAD, James i, 1, alluding to the state of dispersion in which many of the Jews lived after the captivity in Chaldea and Persia; but more especially in Egypt, Syria, and Asia Minor. See 1 Pet. i, 1. In John vii, 35, *the dispersed* are the Jews dwelling either among the Gentiles generally, or among nations that use the Greek language, i. e., *the Greeks*. See Psa. cxlvii, 2.

SCEPTRE, the staff or wand of office. The sceptre of King Saul was *a spear*, 1 Sam. xviii, 10; xxii, 6; but generally the *sceptre* was a wooden rod or staff, which was not much short of the ordinary height of the human form, and was surmounted with an ornamental ball on the upper extremity, as may still be seen in the ruins of Persep'olis. This sceptre was either overlaid with gold, or, according to the representation of Homer, was adorned with golden studs and rings.

If we endeavour to seek for the origin of this ensign of royal authority, we shall find the first suggestion of it either in the pastoral staff that was borne by shepherds, or in those staves which, at the earliest period, were carried by persons in high rank, merely for show and ornament, Num. xvii, 6, 7. A sceptre is used figuratively for the royal dignity and authority, and a righteous sceptre for a just government, Gen. xlviii, 10; Amos i, 5, 8; Psa. xlv, 6.

SCEVA, (*Se'vah*,) a Jew residing at Ephesus, who had been a chief priest, Acts xix, 14.

SCHISM, 1 Cor. xii, 25, (*Sizm*,) from *schisma, a rent*. In its general meaning, it signifies division or separation; and, in particular, on account of religion. Schism is properly a division among those who stand in one connection or fellowship; but when the difference is carried so far that the parties concerned entirely break off all communion and intercourse one with another, and form distinct connections for obtaining the general ends of that religious fellowship which they once cultivated, it is undeniable there is something different from the schism spoken of in the New Testament. This is a separation from the body. Dr. Campbell shows that the word schism in Scripture does not usually signify an open separation, but that men may be guilty of schism by such an alienation of affection from their brethren as violates the internal union in the hearts of Christians, though there be no error in doctrine, not separation from communion.

SCIENCE is religious *knowledge*, as the word is used in the Bible. In 1 Cor. xii, 8, we find *the word of knowledge* mentioned, by which is meant that kind of inspiration which gave to the apostles and superior Christian prophets the knowledge of the true meaning of the Jewish Scriptures. Pretending to possess · this inspiration, the false teachers dignified their misinterpretations of the ancient Scriptures with the name of science or knowledge. The apostle very properly termed these interpretations *oppositions of science*, 1 Tim. vi, 20, because they were framed to establish doctrines contrary. to the Gospel; and also affirmed that ·this knowledge was falsely called *science*. They were not inspired with the knowledge of the true meaning of the Scriptures, but *falsely* pretended to that gift.

SCHOOL, *leisure, rest;* freedom from labour and business. In the New Testament, a place where persons being at *leisure* from bodily labour and business, attended to the improvement of the mind, and where the teacher and his disciples held discussions and disputations. See Acts xix, 9.

SCHOOLMASTER was usually a slave or freedman, to whose care the boys of a family were committed, who trained them up, instructed them at home, and accompanied them to the public schools. They were generally persons of rigid manners. It is used, figuratively, of the Mosaic law, Gal. iii, 24, 25, which was designed to train us up for Christ, and this it does by showing us the need we have of his atonement; and its ceremonies all point to him.

SCORNER, a *mocker, scoffer;* a frivolous and an impudent person, who sets at naught and scoffs at the most sacred precepts and duties of religion, piety, and morals, Prov. ix, 7, 8.

Peter speaks of *scoffers*, 2 Pet. iii, 3, who were *impostors*, false prophets.

The evil of scoffing at the doctrines and promises of the Gospel may be learned from Psa. i, 1, where scoffing at religion is represented as the highest stage of impiety.

SCORPION, a large insect, sometimes several inches long, shaped somewhat like a lobster, and furnished with a sting at the extremity of its tail. Scorpions are found only in hot countries, where they lurk in decayed buildings and among the stones of old walls. It is exceedingly irritable, striking immediately whatever happens to disturb them; and the sting is venomous, producing inflammation and swelling; but is rarely fatal, unless through neglect, Luke x, 19. The wound of a scorpion is said to be of the most painful kind.

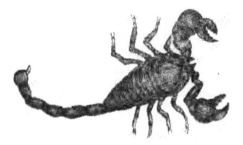

'The word *scorpion* also signified a kind of scourge, armed with sharp iron points or nails, used as an instrument of punishment by those who had no relentings of heart, especially by cruel masters in the punishment of their slaves, 1 Kings xii, 11. But the application of such an instrument was not sanctioned by the laws of Moses.

SCOURGE, or WHIP. This punishment was very common among the Jews, Deut. xxv, 1-3. There were two ways of giving the lash; one with whips, made of ropes' ends, or straps of leather; the other with rods, or twigs. St. Paul informs us, that at five different times he received thirty-nine stripes from the Jews, 2 Cor. xi, 24, namely, in their synagogues, and before their courts of judgment. For, according to the law, punishment by stripes was restricted to forty at one beating. But the whip with which these stripes were given, consisting of three separate cords, and each stroke being accounted as three stripes, thirteen strokes made thirty-nine stripes, beyond which they never went. He adds, that he had been thrice beaten with rods, namely, by the Roman lictors, or beadles, at the command of the superior magistrates.

SCRIBES, *writers*, in the Jewish sense, the king's scribe or secretary of state, 2 Sam. viii, 17, who committed to writing not only the edicts and sayings of the king, but every thing of a public nature that related to the kingdom; and whose business it was likewise to present to the king in writing an account of the state of affairs. *Military secretaries*, who had charge of the enrolment and muster-rolls, 2 Kings xxv, 19.

In the later books, and in the New Testament, *a scribe* signifies one skilled in the Jewish law, an interpreter of the Scriptures, *a lawyer*. The Scribes had the charge of transcribing the sacred books, of interpreting difficult passages, and of deciding in cases which grew out of the ceremonial law. Their influence was of course great; and since many of them were members of the Sanhedrim, we often find them mentioned with elders and chief priests. They are also called *lawyers*; compare Mark xii, 28, with Matt. xxii, 35. Hence, by implication, *one instructed*, *a scholar*, a learned teacher of religion, Matt. xiii, 52.

SCRIP, a bag, or sack of leather, in which shepherds and travellers carried their provisions, 1 Sam. xvii, 40.

SCRIPTURE, a word which signifies *writing*, and refers to the writings of the Old Testament, see John v, 39; but in 2 Peter iii, 16, the writings of Paul and other apostles are called *Scriptures*. Hence, the word includes now both the *Old* and *New* Testaments; the former contains the revelation of the Divine will before the birth of Christ, and the latter comprises the inspired writings of the evangelists and apostles.

THE OLD TESTAMENT. The writings of the Old Testament were published in separate books, and at different periods, through the space of about a thousand years. They were collected into one volume, it is generally supposed, by *Ezra*, soon after the return of the Jews from Babylon, or about 500 B. C.

Division and date. The following is the division of the Old Testament, and the order of time in which the books were written, according to many critics.

1. *Pentateuch.*

Books.	Chap.	Date.
Genesis, . .	59	B.C. 1491
Exodus, . .	40	. 1491
Leviticus, . .	27	. 1490
Numbers, . .	36	. 1451
Deuteronomy,	34	. 1451
2 Samuel, . .	24	. 1018
1 Kings, . .	22, 1–11	1002
	22, 11	897
2 Kings, . .	25	. 590
1 Chronicles, .	29	. 1015
2 Chronicles, .	36 1–9	1004
	36, 10	623

2. *Historical Books.*

Joshua, . . .	24	. 1427
Judges, . . .	21	. 1406
Ruth, . . .	4	. 1312
1 Samuel, . .	31	. 1055
Ezra, . . .	10	. 457
Nehemiah, . .	13	. 434
Esther, . . .	10	. 509

3. *Doctrinal Books.*

Job, ...	42	uncertain
Psalms, . . .	150	do.
Proverbs, . .	31	. 1000
Ecclesiastes, .	12	. 975
Song, . . .	8	. 1013

4. *Prophetical,*

Containing the four greater, with Lamentations, and the twelve minor prophets. See PROPHETS.

Greek translation. The books of the Old Testament were mostly written in Hebrew, and, after the Hebrew had ceased to be spoken, they were translated into Greek; and this translation, which was made at Alexandria some 280 years before Christ, was called the *Septuagint*, from a Latin word signifying *seventy*, either because a company of seventy elders were employed in the work, or because it was approved by the Jewish council or Sanhedrim, which consisted of seventy or seventy-two persons. This version, though originally made for the use of the Egyptian Jews, gradually acquired the highest authority among the Jews of Palestine, who were acquainted with the Greek language, and subsequently also among Christians.

NEW TESTAMENT. This work was written in Greek, and fully unfolds the history and doctrines of our Divine Redeemer, and the way of salvation through him.

I. THE HISTORICAL BOOKS.

Gospels.	Places.	A. D.
Matthew (Hebrew) }	Judea	{ 37 or 38
—— (Greek) }		61
Mark	Rome	between 60 and 63
Luke (Gospel)	Greece	63 or 64
—— (Acts of the Apostles) }		
John	Ephesus	97 or 98

II. THE EPISTLES OF PAUL.

Epistles.	Places.	A. D.
1 Thessalonians	Corinth	52
2 Thessalonians	Corinth	52
Galatians	Corinth	{ At the close of 52 or early in 53
1 Corinthians	Ephesus	56
Romans	Corinth	{ About the end of 57 or beginning of 58
2 Corinthians	{ Macedonia (perhaps from Philippi) }	58
Ephesians	Rome	61
Philippians	Rome	{ Before the end of 62 or beginning of 63
Colossians	Rome	62
Philemon	Rome	{ About the end of 62 or early in 63
Hebrews	{ Italy (perhaps from Rome) }	{ About end 62 of or begin. 63
1 Timothy	Macedonia	64
Titus	Macedonia	64
2 Timothy	Rome	65

III. THE CATHOLIC OR GENERAL EPISTLES.

Epistles.	Places.	A. D.
James	Judea	61
1 Peter	Rome	64
2 Peter	Rome	about the beginning of 65
1 John	{ Unknown (perhaps Ephesus) }	{ 68 or early in 69
2 and 3 John	Ephesus	{ 68 or early in 69
Jude	Unknown	64 or 65
The Revelation		96 or 97

Quotations. The sacred writers of the New Testament have in many instances quoted from the Hebrew Scriptures; yet they have very frequently made their citations from the Septuagint, because it was generally known and read; and as the apostles wrote for the use of communities, whose members were ignorant of Hebrew, it was necessary on that account that they should refer to the Greek version. But where this materially varied from the meaning of the Hebrew Scriptures, they either gave the sense of the passage cited in their own words, or took as much of the Septuagint as was necessary, introducing the requisite alterations.

Quotations Classified. 1. Passages quoted which are said to be fulfilled in the *literal* sense, as, for example, Acts iii, 25.

2. Passages which are fulfilled, not in a literal, but in a *spiritual* sense. The Scripture is therefore said to be *fulfilled* when that is accomplished in the antitype which is written concerning the type. Thus, in John xix, 36, we read, these things were done that the *scripture should be fulfilled,* " A bone of him shall not be broken." These words, which were originally written of the paschal lamb, Exod. xii, 46, are said to be fulfilled in Christ, who is the *antitype* of that lamb.

3. Numerous passages of the Old Testament are cited and applied by the writers of the New Testament to an occurrence which happened in their time, merely on account of *correspondence and similitude.* These citations are not prophecies, though they are said sometimes to be fulfilled. This method of explaining Scripture by the way of *illustration* will enable us to solve many difficulties relating to the prophecies. Similar instances are to be found in some classic authors.

4. Passages are frequently quoted *merely in the way of allusion,* and hence the words which they borrow express their own meaning, and not the precise meaning of the passage alluded to. Thus, Deut. xxx, 12–14, which was originally written concerning the law, is by St. Paul accommodated to the Gospel, Rom. x, 6–8, with proper variations and explanations.

Chapters and verses. The dividing of the Old Testament into chapters is attributed to Cardinal Hugo de Sancto Caro, who lived about the middle of the thirteenth century, and who did it for convenience of reference in a Latin concordance he was preparing. He also subdivided the chapters into smaller sections, distinguishing them by the first seven letters of the alphabet. The introduction of verses into the Hebrew Bible was first made in 1661, by Athias, a Jewish printer, at Amsterdam: and from him the division of verses has been adopted in all copies of the Bible in other languages. The introduction of points or stops, to mark the sense, is a gradual improvement, commenced by Jerome, in the fourth century, and continued and improved by succeeding critics.

The verses at present found in the New Testament were invented by Robert Stephens, a learned printer, who first introduced them into his edition of the New Testament, published in 1551.

This division into verses is very convenient; but it must not govern the sense, for there are several instances in which the sense is injured, if not destroyed, by an improper division. See 1 Pet. i, 4, 5.

Very often the chapter breaks off in the midst of a narrative; and if the reader stop because the chapter ends, he loses the connection.— See Isa. ix, 8; x, 4; Gal. i, 23: ii, 1.

English translation. Shortly after the accession of King James to the throne, in 1603, several objections being made to the English Bible then in use, the king, at the conference held at Hampton Court, in the following year, commanded that a new version should be undertaken, and fifty-four men of distinguished learning and piety were appointed to this important labour. Only forty-seven engaged in the work. They divided themselves into six companies, and entered upon their labour in 1607, and completed it in 1610. It was then revised by a committee of six of the translators, and finally reviewed by Bishop Bilson and Dr. Smith. This translation was first printed in 1611, and is the common English translation which is universally adopted wherever the English language is spoken. Of all modern versions this is undoubtedly the most accurate and faithful. Its style is simple, harmonious, and energetic; and what is of no small importance, use has made it familiar, and time has rendered it sacred.

SCURVY, Leviticus xxii, 22, a disease of a putrid nature, which prevails more in cold than in warm climates, and among those who live on putrescent salted animal food, and who neglect cleanliness and exercise.

SCYTHIAN, a name in ancient geography which is applied sometimes to a people, and sometimes to all the Nomadic tribes that had their seat on the north of the Black Sea and Caspian, stretching indefinitely eastward into the unknown regions of Asia; having much the same latitude as the modern names *Mongols* and *Tartars,* and, like them, synonymous with *barbarian,* Col. iii, 11.

SEA. The Hebrews gave the name of sea to all great collections of water, to great lakes or pools. In Isa. xi, 15 these words particularly apply to the Nile at the Delta. *The Hinder Sea*, Zech. x, 8, i. e., the Western, the Mediterranea Sea. The *Salt Sea* is called *Eastern Sea*, and *Sea of the Desert. Abundance of the sea*, Deut. xxxiii, 19, signifies riches of the sea, the riches of maritime nations, and those beyond the sea, obtained by commerce and voyages.

Am I a sea? i. e., Am I, like the sea, untamed? Job vii, 12.

The word is used figuratively for the *Brazen Sea*, i. e., the great laver in the court of the priests before Solomon's temple, 1 Chron. xviii, 8, containing 2000 baths, i. e., 468 barrels ; but when playing as a fountain, and when all its parts were filled for that purpose, they, together with the sea itself, *received* 3000 baths, or 702 barrels ; thus is reconciled 1 Kings vii, 26 with 2 Chron. iv, 5.

SEAL, probably a stone engraved with some motto. The ancient Hebrews wore their seals or signets in rings on their fingers, or in bracelets on their arms, as is now the custom in the east; and sometimes suspended upon the breast by a string, to which allusion is made in Song viii, 6 ; sometimes merely the name of the owner, and at other times an additional sentence was engraved upon the signet. If a door or box was to be sealed, it was first fastened with some ligament, over which was placed some clay, or wax, which then received an impression from the seal or signet.

The word *seal* signifies not only the seal itself, with its inscription, but the figure that is made by the seal when impressed on some soft substance, as upon letters or books, and which is done for the sake of privacy and security, Rev. v, 1 ; or as a mark or token of genuineness, Rev. ix, 4 ; and so of a motto, i. e., the motto around the seal, the inscription, 2 Tim. ii, 19, figuratively a *token, pledge, proof*, 1 Cor. ix, 2.

To seal up is to close and make fast, as with a seal, or signet; e. g., letters, books, so they may not be read, 1 Kings xxi, 8 ; hence, figuratively, to secure to any one, to make sure, to deliver over safely, Rom. xv, 28.

SEARED, to sear, to cauterize, to brand with a hot iron, 1 Tim. iv, 2 ; " having the conscience *seared*," i. e., having the marks, stigma, of their guilt burned upon their own consciences ; others understand the passage as expressing the effect of sin, by which the conscience becomes hardened and stupified, so as to be insensible to the most enormous guilt and fearful threatening of punishment.

SEAT. The seat upon which the orientals sit is a divan, or a very low sofa, with arms, stuffed cushions, and costly ornaments. Upon the divans, as well as upon the floor, or ground, they sit, with the legs bent under, and crossed in a half kneeling posture.

Seat sometimes signifies an assembly of persons and sitting together, Psa. i, 1.

To sit in Moses' seat, Matt. iii, 2, figuratively, is to occupy his place as an expounder of the law.

SEBA, a country and people descended from Cush, Gen. x, 7, and which seems to have been *Meroe*, a province of *Ethiopia*, distinguished for its wealth and commerce, surrounded by the two arms or branches of the Nile, and with a metropolis of the same name; of which the ruins are still found, not far from the town of Shendy. The Sabeans were remarkable for their stature, Isaiah xlv, 14.

SEBAT, Zech. i, 7, same as *Shebat*. See MOTH.

SEED. The only important sense of this word is the figurative. It is taken for a germ of the Divine life, the inner man, as renewed by the Spirit of God, 1 John iii, 9. It is also taken for *children, posterity.* Christians from the Gentiles are called the *seed* of Abraham, because they imitate his faith, and, like him, believe implicitly in the Divine declarations, Gal. iii, 29.

Sometimes it means *a remnant,* a few survivors, like seed kept over from a former year, Rom. ix, 29.

SEED-TIME, the time of sowing, which in Palestine is from the middle of October to the middle of December.

SEEING. *To see God* is sometimes meant the actual vision of the Divine presence, or the light in which God dwells, Exod. xxiv, 11; elsewhere spoken of those who worship in the temple, Psa. lxiii, 2; so to behold the face of God is metaphorical, the same as to enjoy his favour, to find him propitious, the figure being drawn from the practice of kings, who admit to their presence only those whom they favour, Psa. xvii, 15.

Spoken especially, and as the usual word, for what is presented by a Divine influence to the prophet's mind, either in visions, properly so called, or in revelations, oracles, " the burden which Habakkuk saw," i. e., which was divinely presented to his mental vision, revealed to him; and those who proclaim false revelations are said to *see lies*, Zech. x, 2.

Hence, a *vision* is a revelation from God, Divine communication, 1 Samuel iii, 1; and

SEER is the more ancient name for prophet, according to 1 Sam. ix, 9, from his foresight of the future.

By a bold metaphor *seeing* is ascribed to the roots of a plant which feel the stones, i. e., meet with, strike upon, the stones, Job viii, 17.

SEEK, *to seek after God* is to turn to him, to strive humbly and sincerely to follow and obey him, Acts xvii, 27. Seeking denotes the constant employing of one's thoughts to obtain the object of one's desires, to strive after with the idea of earnestness and anxiety, Matt. vi, 33 ; though it sometimes means only *to desire, to wish*, Luke xi, 54.

SE'IR, *hairy*, a chief of the Horites, Gen. xxxvi, 20.

Also that range of mountains which stretches from the southern extremity of the Dead Sea southward to the Elanitic Gulf, on the east of the El Ghor and El Araba. The northern part of these mountains is now called *Dje-bal*, the middle *El Shera*, and the southern *Hesma*.

Eastward of this mountainous tract, which seems in general not to be more than from eight to twelve miles broad, lies the great Arabian Desert. The mountains, as seen from the Ghor, appear to have a very considerable elevation; but, as seen from the eastern plain, they look only like low hills, the desert being upon a much higher level than the Ghor. The highest of the mountains of Hesma, near Akaba, has been estimated at about 3250 feet above the sea. This region was first inhabited by the Horites, Deut. ii, 12 ; then by Esau, Gen. xxxii, 3, and his posterity. This mountainous country may possibly have derived its name from the Horite *Seir ;* but Gesenius prefers to render the word as an appellative, the *Shaggy Mountains*, i. e., clothed, and as it were bristling with trees and forests.

SELA, *rock*, Isa. xvi, 1, the same as the Greek *Petra*, which also signifies *rock ;* hence, " Let the inhabitants of the *rock* sing," Isa. xlii, 11. The capital city of the Idumeans, situated on the east side of the Ghor, some thirty or forty miles south of the Dead Sea, in a deep valley, surrounded by lofty rocks, so that, indeed, a great part of the dwellings were hewn out in the rock itself. This place seems to be first mentioned in Judges i, 36. See also 2 Kings xiv, 7. The above are the only obvious notices of *Petra* contained in the Scriptures. Pliny states that the city called Petra is in a hollow, somewhat less than two miles in circumference, surrounded by inaccessible mountains, with a stream running through it. Diodorus mentions it as a place of trade, with caves for dwellings, and strongly fortified by nature. In the red sandstone, says Burckhardt, of which the vale consists, there are found more than 250 sepulchres, which are entirely hewn out of the solid rock, generally with architectural ornaments, in the Grecian style. The entrance to this celebrated place is from the east through a very narrow pass, between eight and fifteen feet wide, and from two to three miles long, environed on both sides by enormous high walls of rock, varying from four to seven hundred feet in height. Ruins of this ancient city still exist under the name of *Wady Mousa*, Valley of Moses.

This city appears to have been coeval with the birth of commerce; and there is indubitable evidence that it was a flourishing emporium seventeen centuries before the Christian era; but its remarkable character and history have been but recently disclosed.

SELAH, *silence! pause!* Such, says Gesenius, seems to be the most probable meaning of this musical note, or term. Its use seems to have been, in chanting the words of the psalm, to direct the singer *to be silent, to pause a little,* while the instruments played an interlude or symphony. It stands usually in the middle of a psalm, at the close of a certain section. Thus it serves to divide the psalm. It is very rarely to be found in the middle of a verse, Psa. lv, 19; Hab. iii, 3, 9.

SELEUCIA, a city of Syria, situated west of Antioch, on the sea coast near the mouth of the Orontes, Acts xiii, 4.

SENATE, a council of elders, "the council and senate of the children of Is-rael," Acts v, 21, means either *the Sanhedrim,* EVEN *the whole senate of Israel,* or else it here stands for the elders of Israel in general; i. e., persons of age and influence, who were invited to sit with the Sanhedrim, the same as *the elders of Israel,* Acts iv, 8.

SENNACHERIB, king of Assyria, son and successor of Shal-man-e'ser. He began his reign 710 B. C., and reigned only four years. He was murdered in the temple of Nisroch by his sons A-dram'-me-lech and Sha-re'zer, and was succeeded by his other son, Esar-haddon, 2 Kings xix, 37.

SENIR, the same as *She-nir.* See Deut. iii, 9.

SEPH-AR-VA'IM, a city of the Assyrian empire, whence colonists were brought into the territory of Samaria, probably *Sipphara* in Mesopotamia, situated on the Euphrates, 2 Kings xvii, 24.

SEPULCHRES, the sepulchres or burial places of the poor Hebrews were mere excavations in the earth, such as are commonly made at the present day in the East; but sepulchres for persons who sustained a higher rank were often caverns, Gen. xxiii, 9, or were hewn by art out of rocks, or in the sides of hills, in various forms and sizes, sometimes with several compartments, the interior of which, the farthest removed from the first entrance, were deeper than the others, and were approached by a flight of descending steps, Psalm lxxxviii, 6.

Sepulchres were closed either by stone doors, or by flat stones placed against the mouth of them; and the entrance was often decorated with ornaments and whitewashed. The object of this last practice was, by a timely warning, to prevent those who came to the feast of the passover, from approaching them, and thus becoming contaminated, compare Matthew xxiii, 27; Luke xi, 44. Sepulchres were commonly situated beyond the limits of cities and villages, Luke vii, 12; Matt. viii, 28. The Mosaic law respecting defilements by means of dead bodies, seems to render it necessary that they should not be located within them; and this practice is continued to the present day in the East. *Ye build*, i. e., ye adorn or build up, renew *the sepulchres* of the prophets, Luke xi, 47.

They often decorated the sepulchres with garlands and flowers, or by adding columns or other ornaments. See Matt. xxiii, 29. See BURIAL.

SERAPHIM, plural of *seraph*, an order of angels who attend upon Jehovah, furnished with six wings, Isa. vi, 2, 6. Some render it, by *burning*, i. e., *shining angels*; but Gesenius says, it is better to understand by it, *princes, nobles* of heaven.

SERGEANTS, Acts xvi, 35, 36, officers in the Roman government who attended on the magistrates of cities and colonies, to execute their orders. They carried before them a bundle of rods, and were appointed to inflict the punishment of scourging and beheading upon criminals.

SERGIUS PAULUS, Acts xiii, 7, a Roman governor in command at Cyprus, the *proconsul*, i. e., an officer sent by the senate, who only exercised a civil power, and for one year. He was a *prudent*, i. e., discerning, intelligent, sagacious man, (for so the word signifies,) and was converted under the preaching of Paul and Barnabas.

SERPENT. The serpent is the known emblem of sagacity, in Egypt, and through the eastern world, but for what reason I cannot say. Serpents in general are remarkable for their *acute eyeing* of objects; hence, a *serpent's eye* became a proverb among the Greeks and Romans, who applied it to those who viewed things sharply and acutely. Our Lord also uses the serpent as an emblem of wisdom or cunning, e. g., in a good sense, Matt. x, 16; and in a bad sense, xxiii, 33.

Three hundred species are known, the largest of which are, indeed, terrific in their power and venom. About one-sixth of all the species known are venomous.

The devil is called *the serpent*, and *the old serpent*, Rev. xii, 9, probably in allusion to his subtlety and malice, as also to the fact that in tempting our first parents to disobey God, he employed a serpent, or assumed the form of one, 2 Cor. xi, 3. In Isa. xiv, 29, mention is made of the *fiery flying serpent*. It is supposed to be called *fiery* from the burning inflammation caused by its bite, or perhaps from its fiery colour. As to their *flying*, if we might depend on the testimony of the ancients, a cloud of witnesses might be produced who speak of *flying or winged serpents*. But Mr. Parkhurst says, I do not find that any of them affirm they actually saw such *alive* and *flying*. Admiral Anson in his voyage also speaks of the flying serpents that he met with at the Island of Quibo, but which were without wings. But I apprehend that the *flying serpent* is a species named the *arrow* or *dart snake*, so called from its *darting* and *springing*, in the manner of the rattlesnake.

The word *serpent* is put for the constellation of the serpent or dragon in the northern quarter of the heavens, Job xxvi, 13.

THE BRAZEN SERPENT was the figure of one which Moses caused to be put on the top of a pole, Num. xxi, 9; compare John iii, 14.

SERVANT, one devoted to the service of another, one who is subject to the will and control of another; of course it may import a station or condition which is in itself high or low, honourable or dishonourable, according to the state or rank of the master. A servant of any common man is a *slave*; at least the word in its strict sense would import this. But the servants of a king may be courtiers of the highest rank, who count this title a matter of honour.

1. The word *servant* is spoken of *a slave*, one who renders involuntary service, Gen. xvii, 23; 1 Cor. vii, 21; 1 Tim. vi, 1. "*Servant* of *servants*," Gen. ix, 25, is the lowest, meanest servant. "Taking the form of a *servant*," Phil. ii, 7, i. e., appearing in an humble and despised condition.

2. It also signifies one who renders voluntary service, implying obedience, devotedness. See Matt. xviii, 23. That the servant spoken of in this passage was a voluntary servant is plain from this; he was afterward appointed to be sold to pay his debt, which would have been of no benefit to the master had he been a *slave*; and therefore already the property of his owner. See John xv, 15; 1 Cor. vii, 23.

The word *servants* is often spoken of the true followers and worshippers of God, as Dan. vi, 21: "O Daniel, *servant* of the living God."

It is used also for *an agent from God*, sent to perform any service. Often there is connected with the term the idea of a *familiar servant*, chosen and beloved of God for his piety and approved fidelity. Very often the two ideas of a pious worshipper of God, and of an ambassador sent from God, appear to have coalesced, e. g., in the passages which relate to Abraham and Moses, and particularly in those where Israel or Jacob, i. e., the people of Israel, is addressed by this honourable and endearing appellation, as Isa. xli, 8, 9. Still, it is the *pious* Israelites who are here especially meant, i. e., those truly worthy of the name, Isa. xliii, 10. In this sense it is applied directly to the Messiah, Zech. iii, 8. In all the passages respecting the *servant of God* in the chapters of the last part of Isaiah, he is represented as the intimate friend and ambassador of God, as aided by the Divine Spirit, and as about to restore the tribes of Israel and become the teacher of other nations. In addressing superiors, the Hebrews, from modesty or humility, were accustomed to call themselves *servants*, and those whom they addressed *lords*. See Dan. x, 17. In the East, during a meal, the servants stand with silence and respectful demeanour before the master of the house, receiving his tokens and obeying his orders. By eastern custom the commands of the master are communicated chiefly by signs, and these are regarded with singular earnestness and attention. This illustrates the words of the psalmist, Psa. cxxiii, 2. Hence also the expressiveness of the phrase, " to stand before the Lord," i. e., *to serve him.*

SETH, the third son of Adam, born in the year 130, Gen. v, 3.

SEVEN. As from the beginning this was the number of days in the week, so it has even in Scripture a sort of emphasis attached to it, and is very often used as a round number, Ruth iv, 15; Prov. xxvi, 16.

God created the world in the space of *seven* days, and consecrated the *seventh* day to repose. Every *seventh* year is also consecrated to the rest of the earth, by the name of a Sabbatical year; as also the *seven times seventh* year is the year of jubilee. *Seven* years of plenty, and *seven* of scarcity. *Seven* trumpets; seven priests that sounded them, seven days to surround the walls of Jericho, Josh. vi, 4, 6, 8. In the Revelation are the seven Churches, seven candlesticks, seven spirits, seven stars, seven lamps, seven seals, seven angels, seven phials, seven plagues.

In like manner, *seven times*, or *sevenfold*, means *often*, abundantly, completely, and *seventy times seven*, Matt. xviii, 22, is a frequent general expression for any large number; compare Gen. iv, 24.

SHADOW. The privation of light by an object interposed between a luminary and the surface on which the shadow appears. A shadow is often extreme!y swift, as that of a bird flying, which very rapidly appears and disappears from observation: human life is compared to this, 1 Chron. xxix, 15.

Job says, "All my members are as a *shadow*," i.e., scarcely a shadow of me remains, Job xvii, 7.

The word is used for a *covering, shelter*, which affords shade and protection; then for *protection, defence*, usually preserving the figure of a shade, Psa. xvii, 8. "Make thy *shadow* as the night," Isa. xvi, 3, i. e., afford a refuge from the burning heat as at night.

The shadow of death, the thickest darkness, and imminent danger, such as exists in the tomb, total and frightful. Though I may be placed in circumstances apparently most hopeless and distressing, "I will fear no evil," Psa. xxiii, 4. The apostle uses the word *shadow*, as related to *image*, Heb. x, 1. The former is an *imperfect sketch, a mere outline*, (as we say,) *a slight representation* or *resemblance*; the latter is a picture or image filled out or completed, and made in all its minute parts to resemble the original. "The law presented only an imperfect sketch, and not a full representation of good things to come."

SHAHAR, *dawn, morning;* the word occurs in the title to the twenty-second psalm: the other word, *aijeleth*, sig-

nifies *a hind ;* the phrase *hind of the dawn* probably stands for the morning sun scattering his first rays upon the earth; just as the Arabian poets call the rising sun the *gazelle.* The words seem to be the title of some other poem or song, to the measure of which this psalm was to be sung or chanted.

SHALMANESER, a powerful king of Assyria, 734–716 B. C., by whom the ten tribes were carried into exile 722 B. C. He was succeeded by his son Sennacherib. Some suppose that *Shalman*, Hosea x, 14, is the same with Shalmaneser.

SHAMBLES, *a meat market ;* a place where all kinds of provisions are exposed for sale, 1 Cor. x, 25.

SHARON, a level tract of Palestine, along the Mediterranean, between Cesare'a and Joppa, celebrated for its rich fields and pastures, Isa. xxxv, 2; Song ii, 1.

SHAVING. The custom of shaving the head as a token of deep affliction is very ancient, Job i, 20. It seems, however, to have been generally significant of repentance and humiliation for sin, or of bondage and reproach. See Jer. xlviii, 37.

SHEAF, a bundle of grain. "To take the *sheaf* from the hungry," Job xxiv, 10, is to deprive the poor of bread.

SHEBA was situated toward the southern part of Arabia, at a distance from the coast of the Red Sea.

The queen who visited Solomon, and made him presents of gold, ivory, and costly spices, was most probably the mistress of this region; hence called queen of the south, Matt. xii, 42; and the tradition of her visit to Solomon has maintained itself among the Arabs, who call her Balkis, and affirm that she became the wife of Solomon, 1 Kings x, 1.

SHECHEM, or SYCHEM, Acts vii, 16; a city among the mountains of Ephraim, situated between Mount Ebal and Mount Gerizim, Gen. xxxiii, 18. It is about thirty miles north of Jerusalem and six south of Samaria. It afterward received the name of *Sychar*, John iv, 5, probably but a like sounding by-name, given by the Jews in contempt to this place as the seat of the Samaritan worship. As such, it might be a Hebrew word, which signifies *falsehood*, or from a word nearly of the same sound, which signifies *a drunkard*.

It was called by the Romans *Flavia Neapolis*, whence the modern name *Nablus*, or *Naploos*. About a mile from the city is *Jacob's well*.

The ancient Shechem was given to the Levites, and was one of the cities of refuge, Josh. xx, 7. It was destroyed by Abimelech, Judg. ix, 45, but rebuilt by Jeroboam, and made the seat of his kingdom, 1 Kings xii, 1, 25. At a later period it became the metropolis of the Samaritans, and the seat of their worship, John iv, 20, 21. At present it is an inconsiderable village, and inhabited by the few remaining descendants of the ancient Samaritans. The place is very rich in pastures, and well watered. Few spots in Palestine are superior to it.

SHEEP. The sheep is a well-known animal. The benefits which mankind owe to it are numerous. Its mildness and inoffensiveness of temper strongly recommend it to human affection and regard; and have designated it the pattern and emblem of meekness, innocence, patience, and submission. It is a social animal. The flock follow their leader, who frequently displays the most impetuous courage in their defence. There are two varieties of sheep found in Syria. The first, called the "Bidoween sheep," differs little from the large breed among us, except that the tail is somewhat longer and thicker. The second is much more common, and is more valued on account of the extraordinary bulk of its tail, which has been remarked by all the eastern travellers. Jahn says they are about four feet long, and five inches thick. A reference to this part is made in Lev. iii, 9; where the fat and the tail were to be burned on the altar of sacrifice. Docility, timidity, and liability to wander, all which are among the characteristics of this animal, are often figuratively employed by the sacred writers, as 2 Chron. xviii, 16; Isa. liii, 67; Matt. ix, 36.

SHEKEL was properly and only a *weight;* it was used especially in weighing gold and silver, which then passed as current money among the Hebrews, Gen. xxiii, 15, 16. The smallest weight among them was the *gerah,* which signifies a *grain, berry, bean.* Most probably the Hebrews, like the Greeks and Romans, made use of the seeds or beans of the carob tree for this purpose, as the moderns sometimes do of barley corns; whence the term *grain* for the smallest weight, and twenty *gerahs* are equivalent to one *shekel,* Exod. xxx, 13, or about ten pennyweights, i. e., the half of an ounce.

Two kinds of shekel are distinguished, the shekel of the sanctuary, and the king's shekel, 2 Sam. xiv, 26; but which of these was the heavier cannot be known.

The hair of Absalom was weighed with the king's weight. The heaviest head of hair that has been found in England weighed *five ounces.* Absalom's, we may well suppose, could not have weighed more than ten. This supposition would lead us to the conclusion, that the king's shekel did not amount to more than one-tenth of the other. But Dr. Clarke supposes that the text is not in its original form, and that a mistake has crept into the numeral letters, which would make it seven ounces and a half.

SHEM, the second son of Noah, from whom (Gen. x, 22–30) are derived the *Semitic* nations, i. e., the nations of western Asia; the Persians, Assyrians, Arameans, Hebrews, and part of the Arabs. The languages of these nations are still called the Shemitish, or Semitic languages, including the Chaldee, Syriac, Arabic, Ethiopic, &c., which are all radically the same.

SHEMINITH, *octave;* a key in music; a word denoting the lowest and gravest notes of the scale, sung by men, the modern *bass,* 1 Chro. xv, 21. It is opposed to ALAMOTH, a *virgin,* the *treble,* verse 20; *with psalteries on Alamoth,* i. e., after the manner of virgins, with the female voice, the same as our *treble,* while "*Mattathiah played with harps* on the *Sheminith,*" verse 21, the bass, so as to *excel,* to lead the song, i. e., govern, regulate the singing.

SHENIR, same as *Senir,* which see.

SHEPHERD, one who tends herds or flocks. The care of sheep was among the earliest and most respectable employments, Genesis iv, 2; Exod. iii, 1; 1 Sam. xvi, 11. Shepherds of the present day wander about without any fixed habitation. They despise or neglect all other business but that of tending their flocks; still they are not mean and uncultivated, but are polite, powerful, and magnanimous. Such were Abraham, Isaac, Jacob, and their posterity also, till they conquered the land of Canaan.

It is said that the shepherds of Judea gave each lamb, as we do our dogs, a distinct name, and that they promptly obeyed the voice of the shepherd, coming and going daily at his call.

These shepherds occupy almost the same position in the deserts every year; in the vicinity was erected a sort of watch-house, from which the approach of enemies could be discovered afar off, called in Micah iv, 8, *tower of the flock.*

In the Bible kings are called *shepherds*, Ezek. xxxiv, 7–10; and for the same reason *shepherd* was applied to God, who was the king of the Hebrews; and as the shepherd is to his flock, so he was the guide and protector to his people, Psa. xxiii, 1–4.

In the New Testament the name is applied to Jesus, as the great Shepherd, who watches over and provides for the welfare of the Church, his flock, Matt. xxvi, 31, quoted from Zech. xiii, 7.

The use of the word to denote religious teachers was received and transmitted in the Christian Church, and they are spoken of as *pastors,* Eph. iv, 11, i. e., shepherds, the spiritual guides of the churches.

SHEW-BREAD, the twelve loaves which were set out every week before the Lord in the sacred tabernacle. The table on which this bread was arranged was three feet long, and one and a half wide, and one and a half high, and covered over with laminæ of gold, Exod. xxv, 23. They were placed one above another in two piles, and changed every Sabbath by the priests.

SHIBBOLETH, *an ear* of grain; a word which the Gileadites used as the test of an Ephraimite. The Ephraimites could not, from disuse, pronounce the Hebrew letter *shin;* therefore they said Sibboleth instead of Shibboleth, Judges xii, 6.

SHIELD. See ARMOUR. *Jarchi* says, "Shields were made of tanned hides, and were anointed with oil in order to render them smooth," as also to make them more compact and firm, and to prevent their breaking and being injured by the wet; compare Isa. xxi, 5, where the prophet, announcing the sudden attack of Cyrus, makes the watchmen exclaim to the princes of Babylon, "Arise, *anoint the shield!*" as a preparation for instant fight. Shields made wholly of brass were very uncommon; it was sometimes the case, nevertheless, that they were covered with thin plates of brass, and even of silver and gold, 1 Kings x, 16, 17.

SHIGGAION, *elegy, song,*

occurs in the title of the seventh psalm, and the plural form of the word in Hab. iii, 1.

SHILOH, *rest, quiet, tranquillity ;* such, says Gesenius, seems to be the meaning of the word in the difficult passage, Gen. xlix, 10. The sceptre shall not depart from Judah until *rest* shall come, and the nations obey him, i e., Judah. Judah shall not lay aside the sceptre of a leader until he shall have subdued his enemies and obtained dominion over many nations ;— referring to the expected kingdom of the Messiah, who was to spring from the tribe of Judah. Others take the word as concrete, i. e., *pacificator, prince of peace.*

SHILOH, a city in the tribe of Ephraim, situated on a mountain to the north of Bethel, where the sacred tabernacle remained for a long time, Josh. xviii, 1 ; said to be twenty-five miles north of Jerusalem.

SHINAR, the most ancient name of the country around Babylon, Gen. x, 10. Afterward Babylon and Babylonia became its common appellation. This region is situated between the Tigris, which bounds it on the east, and the Euphrates, which bounds it on the west. It is an extensive plain, interrupted by no hill or mountain, consisting of a fatty brownish soil ; and, from the descriptions of the ancients, fertile almost without parallel, and

subject to the annual inundations of the rivers. Isaiah (xxi, 1) calls this land *the desert of the sea.* This we may regard as a poetical expression, derived from the circumstance, that before the erection of dikes and mounds by Semir'amis, the whole of this flat region was often overflowed, and thus actually resembled, and might with propriety be called *a sea.*

SHIP, in the Bible, signifies a *sailing vessel,* whether large or small. Sometimes spoken of a vessel of considerable tonnage, Num. xxiv, 24 ; and *gallant,* i. e., a large ship, Isa. xxxiii, 21 ; and in the gospels, of the small fishing vessels on the Sea of Galilee. The most complete description of an ancient ship is that furnished by the Prophet Ezekiel (chap. xxvii) when comparing the commercial city of Tyre to one of those magnificent constructions by means of which she carried on her commerce. "*Ships* of Tarshish," Isa. xxiii, 1, were ships employed by the Tyrians in voyages to and from Tarshish ; also all large merchant ships, although sailing to other and different countries, Psa. xlviii, 7. A galley is a low flat-built vessel, navigated with oars and sails, and used particularly in the Mediterranean, Isa. xxxiii, 21.

SHISHAK, a king of Egypt, cotemporary with Jeroboam, 1 Kings xi, 40. He is supposed to be the Sesanchosis of Manetho, about 970 B. C., the first who is mentioned by his proper name.

SHITTIM, a valley in Moab, on the borders of Palestine, Joel iii, 18.

SHITTIM WOOD. The wood of the *shittah tree*, Isa. xli, 19, supposed by Gesenius to be the wood of the *acacia ;* a large tree growing in Egypt and Arabia, from which is obtained our *gum-arabic ;* its bark is covered with large black thorns ; the wood is exceedingly hard, and when old resembles ebony.

"The acacia tree," says Dr. Shaw, "being by much the largest and most common tree in these deserts, Arabia Petræa, we have some reason to conjecture that the shittim wood was the wood of the acacia; especially as its flowers are of an excellent smell, for the shittah tree is joined with the myrtle and other fragrant shrubs."

SHOES. To what has been said under *sandals*, I will add, the poor sometimes went barefoot ; the more rich and honoured never, except in case of mourning, 2 Sam. xv, 30. In transferring a possession or domain, it was customary *to deliver a shoe*, Ruth iv, 7, as in the middle ages a glove ; hence the action of throwing down a shoe upon a region or territory was a symbol of occupancy, Psa. lx, 8, "over Edom will I cast out my *shoe*," i. e., I will possess, occupy it, claim it as my own ; hence a man *without shoes* was a proverbial expression, implying the reproach of prodigality, Deut. xxv, 9.

The *shoe latchet*, the strap which fastens the shoe or sandal to the foot, Gen. xiv, 23, or a pair of shoes, Amos ii, 6, is put for any thing of little value, worthless.

SHOSHANNIM. See SHUSHAN.

SHOULDER, the part on which burdens are carried. "The government shall be upon his *shoulder*," Isa. ix, 6; like a burden laid upon him, and borne by him.

SHRINE, a case in which sacred things are deposited. But the *silver shrines of Diana*, mentioned Acts xix, 24, were miniature copies of the temple of Diana at Ephesus, containing a small image of the goddess. Such shrines of other gods were also common, made of gold, silver, or wood, and were purchased by pilgrims and travellers, probably as memorials, or to be used in their devotions.

SHULAMITE, a maiden who is celebrated in the book of Canticles vi, 13, an inhabitant of *Shunem*, which, Eusebius says, was also called *Shulem*.

SHUNEM, a city in the tribe of Issachar, probably the *Shulem* of Eusebius, some four or five miles south of Mount Tabor, 1 Sam. xxviii, 4.

SHUR, a city on the confines of Egypt and Palestine, Gen. xxv, 18. Most probably *Shur* occupied the site of the

modern *Adjeroud*, called elsewhere *Etham*, and from which
the desert around the head of
the Arabian Gulf was named.
This desert in one place is
called *the desert of Shur*, Exod.
xv, 22; but in Num. xxxiii, 8,
the wilderness of Etham, now
called *Djofar*. It is sufficiently known that a wide tract of
mere sandy desert encircles
the Red Sea in this place;
and that for three days after
the Israelites had crossed the
Red Sea, they continued to
travel in this wilderness on
the borders of the sea.

SHUSAN, the ancient
capital of Susiana, and of all
Persia, in which the Persian
monarchs held their winter
residence, Dan. viii, 2. It
was situated on the Eulæus
or Choaspes, probably on the
spot now occupied by the
village *Shush*; but others suppose its site is now occupied
by the village *Susten*.

SHUSHAN, *a lily; Shushan-
eduth*, Psa. lx, title; a musical instrument, probably so
called from its resemblance
to a lily. To the common
lily several kinds of trumpets
and pipes may be said to
have a resemblance; but to
the Mortagon lily, or Turk's
cap, the cymbal approaches
the nearest; and indeed the
name of cymbal was at a later
period sometimes given to
th.s flower. Hence *shushan-
eduth*, Gesenius renders *pipe
of song*, a lyric pipe; *shoshannim*, Psa. lxxx, title, has the
same signification.

SHUT, a word used in
respect to a *door*, Matt. vi, 5;
and *heaven*, i. e., the windows
of heaven, so that no rain can
fall, Luke iv, 25. " To *shut*
up the kingdom," Matt. xxiii,
13, is wilfully to prevent men
from entering. It is used
also of the authority to exclude or admit, Rev. iii, 7, 8.
" To *shut* up one's bowels
from any one," i. e., not to let
one's compassion flow out, to
be hard-hearted, 1 John iii,
17.

SICHEM, Gen. xii, 6, the
same as *Shechem*.

SIDDIM, Gen. xiv, 3, the
plain of the cities Sodom and
Gomorrah, now occupied by
the Dead Sea.

SIDON, Acts xxvii, 3, a
celebrated city and port of
Phenicia, and one of the most
ancient cities in the world;
as it is supposed to have been
founded by Sidon, the eldest
son of Canaan, which will
carry it up to above two thousand years before Christ. Its
inhabitants appear to have
early acquired pre-eminence
in arts, manufactures, and
commerce; and from their
superior skill in hewing timber, by which must be understood their cutting it out and
preparing it for building, as
well as the mere act of felling
it, Sidonian workmen were
hired by Solomon to prepare
the wood for the building of
his temple. Add to this, they
were, if not the first ship-
wrights and navigators, the
first who ventured beyond
their own coasts, and in those
early ages engrossed the great-

est part of the then commerce of the world. The natural result of these exclusive advantages to the inhabitants of Sidon was, a high degree of wealth and prosperity; and content with the riches which their trade and manufactures brought them, they lived in ease and luxury, trusting the defence of their city and property, like the Tyrians after them, to hired troops: so that to live in ease and security, is said in Scripture to be after the manner of the Sidonians. In all these respects, however, Sidon was totally eclipsed by her neighbour and rival, Tyre; whose more enterprising inhabitants pushed their commercial dealings to the extremities of the known world, raised their city to a rank and power and opulence unknown before, and converted it into a luxurious metropolis, and the emporium of the produce of all nations.

At present the name of the place is *Saide*. It is a trading town of some importance. The harbour is rendered comparatively useless, however, by sand bars, and the town itself is badly built, and very dirty. The inhabitants are called Sidonians, Deut. iii, 9; and, according to Mr. Goodell, the American missionary, about 3000, of whom one half he supposes Mussulmans.

SIGN is the token of any thing in itself not visible or discernible, e. g., the token of a covenant, as circumcision, Rom. iv, 11, or that by which the character and truth of any person or thing is known, 2 Cor. xii, 12.

The word sign also signifies a supernatural event or act, *a miracle*, by which the power and presence of God are manifested, either directly, or through the agency of those whom he sends. The apostle says, 1 Cor. xiv, 22, that " tongues are for a *sign*," i. e., a token to the unbelieving of God's presence and power; compare verse 25: or perhaps a sign of the Divine displeasure; compare verse 21. The *sign* of Jonah is the sign which God wrought in the case of Jonah, Matt xii, 39.

Isaiah says, viii, 18, " Behold I and the children whom the Lord hath given me are for *signs* and for wonders in Israel," i. e., through the names Divinely given us, which are all of good omen, God has made us types of future things to prefigure future deliverance and prosperity; compare xx, 3; Ezek. iv, 3.

The sign of a ship, Acts xxviii, 11, commonly a picture or image on the prow, and distinguished from the figure of the tutelar god of the ship upon the stern, though sometimes they are both the same.

SIGNET, Exod. xxviii, 11, an instrument for sealing, a sealing ring. See SEAL.

SIHOR, 1. *The river of Egypt*, Numb. xxxiv, 5, a

29

small river on the confines of Egypt and Palestine.

2. The river *Nile*, Isa. xxiii, 3; Jer. ii, 18. The whole course of this river, which is very direct, from Elephantine to the Mediterranean, is not far from 1,000 miles. The fertile and well-inhabited portion of Egypt lies on both banks of the Nile ; the valley of which from the eastern to the western mountains which enclose it, averages in Middle and Upper Egypt not more than from five to fifteen miles in width. Rain in these regions seldom falls, and the soil owes all its vegetative power to the waters of this river. See EGYPT.

SILAS, contracted from *Silvanus*, a distinguished Christian teacher, the companion of Paul in his journeys in Asia Minor and Greece. The former name is found only in the Acts ; the latter only in the Epistles, 2 Cor. i, 19 ; Acts xv, 22.

SILK, an article drawn from the bowels of a worm which lives on the mulberry tree. It is not mentioned at a very early period; see Ezek. xvi, 10, 13. Silk was first brought into Greece after Alexander's conquest of Persia, and came into Italy during the flourishing times of the Roman empire ; but was long so dear in all these parts as to be worth its weight in gold. At length the Emperor Justinian, who died in the year 365, by means of two monks, whom he sent into India for that purpose, procured great quantities of silk worms' eggs to be brought to Constantinople, and from these have sprung all the silk worms and all the silk trade that have been since in Europe.

SIL'OAH, Neh. iii, 15, the same as *Siloam*, elsewhere called *Gihon*, 1 Kings i, 33.

SILOAM, *sent*, a fountain in the valley by Jerusalem, John ix, 7. It is apparently the same with that called *Siloah*, or *Shiloah*, Neh. iii, 15. Ancient tradition and the testimony of all travellers unite in placing the fountain of *Siloam* on the south-eastern part of Jerusalem, near the foot of Mount Zion, having Moriah on the north. Here, at the present day, a fountain issues from the rock, at first twenty feet or more below the surface of the ground, in to a reservoir, to which there is a descent by two flights of steps ; from this place it makes its way several rods under the mountain, and then appears again as a beautiful rill winding its way down into the valley toward the south-east ; the water is soft, of a sweetish taste, and pleasant. Several modern critics assign the location of Siloam to the south-western side of Mount Zion, in the valley which runs northward from the upper part of the valley of Hinnom. This opinion is founded chiefly on two passages of Josephus, which may indeed be so understood, but not necessarily ; and no traveller makes mention of any fountain on this side of the city.

SILVER. This metal was known to the ancients, Gen. xxiii, 15. It frequently occurs noticed in silver mines, and also in combination with gold. It is very soft when pure, so that it may be cut with a knife, and in that state does not rust by exposure to air and moisture.

The silver cord, Eccl. xii, 6, is supposed to refer to the *spinal marrow*, from its coming out of the head with all its nervous branches ; that *cord* which regulates the motions of every part of the body, and which is denominated *silver* on account of its resplendent whiteness, like that of silver.

SIMEON, *a hearing with acceptance ;* the son of Jacob, born of Leah's handmaid, Gen. xxix, 33 ; the progenitor of the tribe of the same name. The cities of this tribe were within the territory of Judah, and are enumerated Joshua xix. "*Simeon* and Levi are brethren," Gen. xlix, 5, i. e., true brethren, not only by birth, but also in disposition. Also a pious Jew, by this name, took the infant Jesus in his arms and blessed him in the temple, Luke ii, 25. He is supposed by many to be the same with Shammai, mentioned by Josephus, and also in the Talmud as the father of *Gamaliel.*

SIMON, an apostle ; the same as Simon the Canaanite : perhaps the same with Simon the brother of James and Jude, Matt. xiii, 55. He was called *Zelotes,* Luke vi, 15, which appears to be the signification of the word *Canaanite,* probably from his having been one of the *Zelotes.* See ZELOTES.

SIMON MAGUS was a native of Gittum, a town in Samaria. Concerning the time of his birth, and of his first rising into notice, little can now be known. The only cotemporary document which mentions him is the Acts of the Apostles ; and we there read, that, when Philip the deacon preached the Gospel in Samaria after the death of Stephen, "there was a certain man called Simon, which beforetime in the same city used sorcery, and bewitched the people of Samaria, giving out that himself was some great one ; to whom they all gave heed, from the least to the greatest, saying, This man is the great power of God. And to him they had regard, because that of long time he had bewitched them with sorceries," Acts viii, 9–11. According to Mr. Watson's calculation, the death of Stephen happened in the same year with the crucifixion of our Lord ; and it appears from the passage now quoted, that Simon's celebrity had begun some time before. We are then told that "Simon himself believed also ; and when he was baptized, he continued with Philip, and wondered, beholding the miracles and signs which were done," Acts viii, 13. I need not mention how he shortly fell away from the faith which he had embraced, and how St. Peter rebuked him for thinking that the gift of God might be purchased for money, Acts viii, 20; but I would observe, that some of those persons who insist upon the fact that Simon was not a Christian, appear to have forgotten that he was actually baptized. For a time, at least, he believed in Jesus Christ; and part of this belief he appears always to have retained; that is, he always believed that Jesus Christ was a being more than human, who came from God. If these events happened, as I have supposed, within a short time of our Lord's ascension, the fathers had good reason to call Simon Magus the parent of all heresies; for he must then have been among the first persons, beyond the limits of Jerusalem who embraced the Gospel; and we might hope that there was no one before him who perverted the faith which he had professed.

SIN. 1. The transgression of the law, or want of conformity to the will of God, 1 John iii, 4; aberration from a prescribed law or rule of duty.

2. The word *sin* is spoken of *that* in which one sins, the *cause* or *occasion* of sin, as idols, Deut. ix, 21. The apostle says, "Is the law *sin* ?" Rom. vii, 7. *Sin* from the necessity of the case must here mean the cause of sin. So Micah i, 5, "What is the *transgression* of Jacob? Is it not Samaria ?" i. e., what is the cause of Jacob's transgression?

3. It sometimes signifies *sin-offering*. There are many passages in the Old Testament where it has this signification, as Hos. iv, 8, "They eat up the *sin* of my people." In the New Testament, likewise, the word sin has the same signification, 2 Cor. vi, 21; Heb. xiii, 11.

4. *The penalty due to sin*, i. e., the punishment or consequences of it, Heb. ix, 26, 28. Hence *calamity*, *misfortune*, Isa. xl, 2; see Prov. x, 16, where it is opposed to *life*.

"The *sin* unto death," 1 John v, 16, according to Clarke and others, means a case of transgression, particularly of grievous backsliding from the life and power of godliness, which God determines to punish with *temporal death*; while, at the same time, he extends mercy to the penitent soul. The *disobedient prophet*, 1 Kings xiii, 1–32, is, on this interpretation, a case in point. So Paul told the Corinthians who had been guilty of great irregularities in the celebration of the Lord's Supper, 1 Cor. xi, 30, "For this cause many of you are sick, and some are dead." *The sin not unto death* is any sin which God does not choose thus to punish. We may believe that when John directed *any one* who saw his brother sinning a sin not unto death, to ask God to give him life, he did not mean any ordinary Christian, but any spiritual man who was endowed with the gift of healing diseases; (1 Cor. xii, 9;) and that the brother for whom the spiritual man was to ask life, was not every brother who had sinned, but the brother only who had been punished for his sin with some mortal disease; but who having repented of his sin, it was not a sin unto death; and that the *life* to be asked for such a brother was not eternal life, but a miraculous recovery from the mortal disease under which he was labouring.

The unpardonable sin is, according to some, the ascribing to the devil the miracles which Christ wrought by the power of the Holy Ghost. This sin, or blasphemy, as it should rather be called, many Scribes and Pharisees were guilty of, who, beholding our Lord do his miracles, affirmed that he wrought them by Beelzebub, the prince of devils, which was in effect, calling the Holy Ghost Satan, a most horrible blasphemy; and, as on this ground they rejected Christ, and salvation by him, their sin could certainly have no forgiveness, Mark iii, 22-30. No one, therefore, could be guilty of this blasphemy, except spectators of Christ's miracles. See Blasphemy.

SIN, Ezek. xxx, 15, 16; *Pelusium*, a city situated in the marshes, at the north-eastern extremity of Egypt, in a tract now entirely covered by the sea.

The Desert of Sin lies westward of Mount Sinai, on the coast of the Gulf of Suez, Exod. xvi, 1.

SIN-Money, 2 Kings xii, 16, money sent by persons at a distance with which to buy the required offerings; and as there was usually some surplus, it was the perquisite of the priests, and was called *sin-money*, or *sin-offering money*, Num. xviii, 9.

SINAI, (*Si'na*,) a mountain, or rather a cluster of mountains, from six to eight hundred feet in height, in the Arabian peninsula, between the two gulfs of the Red Sea, celebrated as the place where the Mosaic law was given. The particular mountain or summit, which probably bore the name of *Sinai*, is now called *Djebel Mousa*, Mount of Moses. At its foot is a convent of Catholic monks, situated in a narrow valley. Directly behind the convent, toward the south-west, the mountain rises with a steep ascent; and after three quarters of an hour, there is a small plain or lower summit, called *Dejbel Oreb*, or Mount Horeb, where the law is also said to have been given, Deut iv, 15; compare Exod. xxiv, 16

From hence a still steeper ascent of a half an hour leads to the peak of the mountain. On the W. S. W. of Djebel Mousa lies Mount St. Catharine, still higher, and separated from the former by a narrow valley. Mr. Carne remarks, "From the summit of Sinai you see only innumerable ranges of rocky mountains. One generally places, in imagination, around Sinai extensive plains, or sandy deserts, where the camp of the hosts was placed, where the families of Israel stood at the doors of their tents, and the line was drawn around the mountain, which no one might break through on pain of death. But it is not thus, save the valley by which we approach Sinai, about half a mile wide and a few miles in length; and a small plain we afterward passed through—there appear to be few open places around the mount."

The same writer says farther on, "We had not the opportunity of making the tour of the whole of the region of Sinai; yet we traversed three sides of the mountain, (the east, west, and north,) and found it everywhere shut in by narrow ravines, except on the north, in which direction we had first approached it. Here there is, as before observed, a valley of some extent, and a small plain, in the midst of which is a rocky hill. These appear to have been the only places in which the Israelites could have stood before the mount; because, on the fourth (or south) side, though unvisited, we could observe from the summit only glens or small rocky valleys, as on the east and west." See the *Map*, p. 000.

The whole peninsula, which is formed by the two branches of the Red Sea, whose extremities are 125 miles apart, is a wild and desolate region. It would seem, as one says, as if it had once been an ocean of lava; and that while its waves were literally running mountain high, it was commanded suddenly to stand still. It is composed of bare rocks and craggy precipices, among which narrow defiles and sandy valleys are interspersed. There is little vegetation; many of the plains are covered with loose flints and pebbles, and others are sandy. The few plants and shrubs that are to be found are such as love a dry sandy soil, or such as contrive to draw nourishment from the fissures of the rocks, or from a thin mixture of clay, which may be found in some parts of the soil. Rain rarely falls in this wilderness, and fountains of springs of water are exceedingly rare. In the central part of this peninsula stands the group of the Sinai mountains. This group Mr. Burckhardt describes as composed almost entirely of granite, forming a rocky wilderness of an irregular circular shape, intersected by many narrow valleys, and from thirty to forty miles in diameter. It contains the highest mountains of the peninsula, whose shagged and painted peaks, and steep and shattered sides, render it clearly distinguishable from all the rest of the country in view. It is upon this high region of the peninsula that the fertile valleys are found, which produce fruit trees. They are principally to the west and south-west of the convent, at three or four miles' distance.

Water, too, is always found in plenty in this district; on which account it is the place of refuge of all the Bedouins, when the low country is parched up. This is the spot which was selected for the encampment of the Israelites, who remained here nearly a year; for there seems little doubt that this upper country or wilderness formed exclusively the desert of Sinai, so often mentioned in the account of their wanderings. See Exod. xvi, 1. This region is about 260 miles from Cairo, which is a journey of ten days.

SINCERITY, 2 Cor. i, 12; honesty of mind or intention, opposed to double-mindedness or deceit. But in the Scriptures sincere signifies pure, without mixture, properly, to such a degree as to bear examination in the full splendour of the solar rays.

SINGLENESS OF HEART, a simple intention of doing right, without looking any farther.

SINIM. Gesenius understands by this term *the Chinese*; see Isa. xlix, 12, where the context implies a remote country, situated in the eastern or southern extremity of the earth. This very ancient and celebrated people was known to the Arabians and Syrians by the name of Sin or Tchin. And a Hebrew writer might well have heard of them, especially if sojourning in Babylon, the metropolis, as it were, of all Asia. Others who reject this application of the name to the Chinese, understand *the inhabitants of Sin*, i. e., Pelusium, and consequently the *Egyptians*.

SION, the mountain usually called Hermon, Deut. iv, 48; also the same as *Zion*. Rev. xiv, 1. See ZION.

SISTER, in the style of the Hebrews, has equal latitude as brother. It is used not only for a sister by natural relation from the same father and mother, but also for a sister only by the same father or by the same mother, or a near relation only. Sarah is called sister to Abraham, Gen. xii, 13; xx, 12. In the gospels, the brothers and sisters of Jesus Christ are his cousins, children of the sisters of the holy virgin, Mark vi, 3.

It signifies also an ally, a confederate city or state, Ezek. xvi, 46. Metaphorically, sister is used for any thing with which we are intimately connected, as Prov.

vii, 4, " Say unto wisdom, Thou art my *sister*."

It is also used as a term of endearment addressed to a spouse, Song iv, 9.

SIVAN, Esther viii, 9, the third month of the Hebrew year, from the new moon of June to the new moon of July. See MONTH.

SLAVE, Rev. xviii, 13. Slavery existed and prevailed before the deluge, Gen. ix, 25. Moses, therefore, although he saw the evils of slavery, was not in a condition to abolish it, and it would not have been wise for him to have made the attempt; compare Gen. xvii, 12.

Men lost their freedom in ancient times in many ways

1. *By captivity in war*, Deut. xx, 14. Some suppose this to have been the origin of slavery.

2. *By debts*, when they were so large that the debtor was unable to pay them, 2 Kings iv, 1; Isa. l, 1; Matt. xviii, 25.

3. *By theft*, when the thief was not able to pay the amount of the property which he had taken, Exod. xxii, 3.

4. *By man-stealing*. Moses enacted laws of very great severity against this crime; but they were restricted in their operation to those who had by violence made a slave of a free Hebrew, Exod. xxi, 16; Deut. xxiv, 7.

5. *By being the children of slaves*. See Gen. xiv, 14; xvii, 23.

6. *By purchase*. We may infer from Exod. xxi, 32, that the medium price of a slave was thirty shekels, i. e., fifteen ounces of silver; and by an examination of Lev. xxvii, 1–8, form a probable opinion as to the difference of the value of a slave in the different periods of his life.

SLEEP, that state of the body in which there is no voluntary motion or consciousness, and in which the senses are not exercised. The term is taken either for the repose of the body, or for the sleep of the soul, which is supineness, indolence, stupidity; or for the sleep of death, Jer. li, 39. " Awake, thou that *sleepest*, and arise from the dead, and Christ shall give thee light," Eph. v, 14. Here St. Paul speaks to those that were dead in sin and infidelity. St. Peter says of the wicked, " Their damnation *slumbereth* not," 2 Pet. ii, 3, i. e., God is not asleep, he will not forget to punish them in his own due time.

SLIME. The word translated slime signifies the asphaltus, or Jews' pitch; a gummy, inflammable, mineral substance, which breaks with a smooth shining surface, usually of a dark brown colour, not unlike common pitch. It boils up in the manner of boiling pitch, from subterranean fountains not far from Babylon, also near the Dead Sea, and at its bottom: afterward it hardens in the sun. The fragments of this substance scattered over the ruins of Babylon are black, shining, and brittle, somewhat resembling pit coal in substance and appearance. It is collected even on the surface of the Dead Sea, which is thence called *Lake Asphaltites*, Gen. xiv, 10. It was used by the ancients for mortar, for the calking of boats, and for the embalming of the dead, Gen. vi, 14; xi, 3.

SLINGS. See ARMOUR.

SMYRNA, an Ionian city, situated at the head of a deep gulf on the western coast of Asia Minor, still known as a commercial place, though greatly fallen from its ancient wealth and power. It was anciently frequented by great numbers of Jews. This city at present contains a population of about 130,000 inhabitants.

Our Lord, by the mouth of John, addresses the angel or pastor of the church in this place, Rev. ii, 8–10, who is thought to have been *Polycarp*, the martyr, who was put to death A. D. 166.

SO, one of the Ethiopian kings, who reigned over Upper Egypt, about 722 B. C., 2 Kings xvii, 4.

SOAP is composed of an *alkali*, combined with oil, and used for the washing and scouring of garments, Jer. ii, 22, and also for the refining of metals, Mal. iii, 2. The ancients obtained their alkali from the ashes of various plants, and also used *natron*, which has powerful alkaline properties similar to potash. See NITRE.

SOBRIETY is commonly taken for the opposite to intemperance; it is taken also for moderation, modesty, and freedom from any inordinate passion.

SODERING, Isa. xli, 7; joining separate things or parts of the same thing by a metallic substance in a state of fusion; the same as *soldering*.

SOD'OM, the capital city of the Pen-tap'o-lis, which for some time was the residence of Lot. The history of its destruction is given in the book of Genesis.

Vines of Sodom, which were probably degenerated and inferior, are put Deut. xxxii, 32, as the emblem of a degenerated state; compare the opposite, Jer. ii, 21.

Judges of Sodom, i. e., unjust and corrupt judges, Isa. i, 10.

SODOMITE, 1 Kings xiv, 24, signifies properly one *consecrated*, especially to *Astarte*, or *Venus*, prostituting chastity in honour of her.

SOJOURNING, a residence in a foreign land, without the right of citizenship; spoken metaphorically of human life, 1 Pet. i, 17.

SOLOMON, *pacific*, the tenth son of David, 2 Sam. iii, 5; 1 Chron. iii, 5; born of Bathsheba, the successor of his father, and the third king of the Hebrew nation; he reigned 1015–975 B. C. He is celebrated through the world for his wealth, splendour, and wisdom. See *first book of Kings*. Solomon during his reign enjoyed a profound peace throughout his dominions; Judah and Israel lived in security; and his neighbours either paid him tribute, or were his allies; he ruled over all the countries and kingdoms from the Euphrates to the Nile, and his dominions extended even beyond the former; he had abundance of horses and chariots of war; he exceeded the orientals, and all the Egyptians, in wisdom and prudence; he was the wisest of mankind, and his reputation was spread through all nations. He composed or collected three thousand proverbs, and one thousand and five songs. See also 1 Kings iv, 29–34. There was a concourse of strangers from all countries to hear his wisdom, and ambassadors from the most remote princes.

Solomon began to build the temple in the fourth year of his reign, and the second after the death of David; four hundred and eighty years after the exodus from Egypt. He employed in this great work seventy thousand proselytes, descendants of the ancient Canaanites, in carrying burdens, fourscore thousand in cutting stones out of the quarries, and three thousand six hundred overseers of the works; beside thirty thousand Israelites in the quarries of Libanus. The temple was completed in the eleventh year of Solomon, so that he was but seven years in performing this vast work. The dedication was made the year following, 1003 B. C.

Solomon afterward built a palace for himself, and another for his queen, the king of Egypt's daughter. He was thirteen years in finishing these buildings, and employed in them whatever the most exquisite art, or the most profuse riches could furnish. The palace in which he generally resided was called the house of the forest of Lebanon; probably because of the great quantity of cedar used in it. He fitted out a fleet at E'zion-Ge'ber, and at Elath, on the Red Sea, to go to Ophir. Hiram, king of Tyre, furnished him with mariners, who instructed the subjects of Solomon. They performed this voyage in three years, and brought back various curiosities, 2 Chron. ix, 21. About the same time, the queen of Sheba came to Jerusalem, attracted by the great fame of the king.

Solomon was one of the richest, if not the very richest of all princes that have ever lived; and the Scripture expressly tells us he exceeded in riches and wisdom all the kings of the earth, verse 13. But the latter actions of his life disgraced his character.

Solomon died after he had reigned forty years, 975 B. C. He might be about fifty-eight years of age; for he was about eighteen when he began to reign. Of all the ingenious works composed by Solomon, we have nothing remaining but his Proverbs, Ecclesiastes, and the Canticles; that is, every literary monument respecting him has perished, except the inspired history which registers his apostacy, and his own inspired works, which, in all the principles they contain, condemn his vices.

SON. 1. In its primary and literal sense, it means *a masculine descendant* of any one. But the word son, like those of father and brother, is employed by the Hebrews in various other and wider senses.

2. It often means *offspring, posterity*, near or remote.

3. *A subject vassal* yielding obedience to a king or lord as to a father, 2 Kings xvi, 7.

Son is the same as a *foster son;* one educated as a son, Exod. ii, 10; also a *pupil, disciple*, since teachers were regarded and obeyed as in the place of parents, and were also addressed by the title of father. Hence " *sons* of the prophets," 1 Kings xx, 35.

Children of Zion denote the *natives* of that place; those born and brought up there. " *Children* or *men* of the East," Judges vi, 3, are the inhabitants of the Arabian desert, which lies eastward of Palestine, and extends to the Euphrates.

This arises from the more general idiom, by which whatever is done in any place or time is ascribed to that place or time itself. " The *sons* of Arcturus," Job xxxviii, 32; the three beautiful stars in the tail of the *Great Bear;* a splendid constellation of the northern hemisphere.

Children of pride, Job xli, 34, i. e., the larger beasts of prey, as the lion, so called from their proud gait.

The Son of man, Dan. vii, 13, is a proper name for *the Messiah*. It is used by Jesus of himself; but it is applied to him by no other person, except once by Stephen, Acts vii, 56. It would seem to refer not so much to his human nature, as to the fact of his being the Messiah, who is described as coming from heaven in a human form, John iii, 13; vi, 62; see John xii, 34, where the *Son of man* and *Christ* are interchanged. By using this name of himself before his judges, Jesus openly professed himself to be the Messiah, and was so understood by all present, Matt. xxvi, 64, 65; Luke xxii, 69–71.

Angels are called *sons of God*, for the like reason that men are, viz., because God is their creator and benefactor; and especially, because they bear a high resemblance to God. See Job i, 6; Dan. fii, 25.

But the phrase *Son of God* is applied to Christ to designate the high and mysterious relation which subsisted between him and God the Father; by virtue of which he was in his complex person, "the brightness of his glory, and the express image of his person," Heb. i, 3; and "the image of the invisible God," Col. i, 15. In this respect, *Son of God* is rather a name of *nature* than of office; for it is predicated of the high and glorious *image, resemblance, similitude.* which the Son exhibits of the Father, he being the *brightness* of his glory; so that what Jesus said to Philip is true, viz, "He that hath seen me, hath seen the Father," John xiv, 9.

SONG, "a new song," i. e., a nobler, loftier strain, Rev. xiv, 3. *Song of songs*, i. e., the most beautiful of songs; compare the phrase, *the heaven of heavens.* i, e., the highest heaven, 1 Kings viii, 27, as the title of a book, Song i, 1, which, however, could hardly proceed from the author, this epithet contains an encomium similar to "song of loves," Psa. xlv, title.

In 1 Kings iv, 32, we read that Solomon composed 1005 songs; but we have only remaining this one.

SOOTHSAYING, foretelling future events without Divine aid; uttering responses as from an oracle, Acts xvi, 16. See NECROMANCER.

SORCERY, Acts viii, 9, the use of magical arts, by which magicians pretended to predict future events, cure diseases, and work miracles.

SOREK, the Hebrew name of a fine and noble species of grape vine. The grapes are said to be small, partially round, dark-coloured, with the stones soft, and scarcely perceptible. The English version gives the word by *choice, noble*, Gen. xlix, 11; Isa. v, 2; Jer. ii, 21.

Also the name of a valley between Askelon and Gaza, where Delilah dwelt, probably so called from its vineyards, Judges xvi, 4.

SOUL. This word is equivocal. It is taken, 1. For a living person. When God formed the body of man out of the dust, Gen. ii, 7, he "breathed into his nostrils the breath of life, and man became a living soul," that is, *a living being.* The phrase "*souls of men*," Rev. xviii, 13, is supposed to mean female slaves, in distinction from the preceding word *bodies*, which is masculine, and rendered in our translation *slaves*. 2. For the affections and desires, or appetites, Gen. xxxiv, 3; Deut. vi, 5. 3. For that spiritual, reasonable, and immortal substance or principle in man, capable of thinking and reasoning, which distinguishes him from the brute creation, and in which chiefly consists his resemblance to God, Gen. i, 26.

The immortality of the soul is a fundamental doctrine of revealed religion,

Matt. x, 28. The ancient patriarchs lived and died persuaded of this truth; and it was in hope of another life that they received the promises. When Balaam desired that his death might be like that of the just, (Num. xiii, 10,) he must have meant in the hope and expectation of a happy resurrection, 2 Tim. i. 10.

Another decisive proof that the Israelites believed in the immortality of the soul, is found in their persuasion, that the souls of the dead sometimes appeared after their decease, as Samuel appeared to Saul, 1 Sam. xxviii, 13–15. When the apostles saw Christ walking on the sea, they took him for an apparition, Matt. xiv, 26; and after his resurrection, he referred to this current belief, Luke xxiv, 39.

SOWING. The sowing "beside all waters," mentioned by Isaiah, seems to refer to the sowing of rice, which is done on low grounds flooded, and prepared for sowing by being trodden by oxen and asses, mid-leg deep. Thus, they send "forth thither the feet of the ox and the ass."

SPAIN included the modern Spain and Portugal, and was a province of the Roman empire. It was the place of many Latin writers; and many Jews appear to have settled there, Rom. xv, 24.

SPAN, Exod. xxviii, 16, a measure of length from the end of the thumb to the end of the little finger, or three palms—about nine inches.

SPARROW, a little bird everywhere known.

SPEAR, a wooden staff, surmounted with an iron point, used by the ancients in fighting. The spear was never shorter than eleven cubits, nor longer than twenty-four. See ARMOUR.

SPICES, aromatic substances, vegetables fragrant to the smell and pungent to the taste, such as myrrh and aloe, John xix, 40.

SPIDER, an insect well known, remarkable for the thread which it spins, with which it forms a web of curious texture, but so frail that it is exposed to be broken and destroyed by the slightest accident, the thinness and frailty of which are strikingly emblematical of a false hope, Job viii, 14, and the schemes of wicked men, Isa. xlix, 5.

SPIKENARD, a plant belonging to the grasses, and in India, whence the best sort comes, it grows as common grass, in large tufts close to each other, in general from three to four feet in height. So strong is its aromatic principle, which resides chiefly in the husky roots, that when trodden upon, or otherwise bruised, the air is filled with its fragrance. This plant was highly valued among the ancients, and the ointment manufactured from it was the favourite perfume used at baths and feasts. It was very costly; in our Saviour's day, a "pound of it might be sold for more than three hundred pence," i. e., for upward of forty dollars, John xii, 3; Mark xiv, 5. Like other unguents and perfumes, the ointment was carried in a box or vase, made of any materials, as gold, glass, and alabaster, a variety of the gypsum, differing some from the alabaster of modern times. These vases often had a long narrow neck, the mouth of which was sealed; so that when the woman is said to break the vase, verse 3, we are to understand only the extremity of the neck, which was thus closed.

SPIRIT. 1. That spiritual, thinking, and reasoning substance, which is capable of eternal happiness, Num. xvi, 22; Acts vii, 59.

2. The term spirit is also often used for an *angel*, a *demon*, and a *ghost*, or soul separate from the body, Luke xxiv, 39; Heb. i, 14; 1 Sam. xvi, 14.

3. Add to this, spirit is sometimes put for the *disposition* of the heart or mind, 1 Pet. iii, 4.

4. The Holy Spirit, the third person in the Holy Trinity. In the New Testament this spirit is everywhere represented as in intimate union with God the Father and Son, as proceeding from, and sent forth by them, as possessing the same attributes, and performing the same acts with God the Father and the Son. Among the passages in which being, *intelligence*, and *agency* are predicated of the spirit, are the following, Matt. xxviii, 19; 1 Cor. xii, 4, 5, 6. Same *Spirit*, same *Lord*, same *God*, 2 Cor. xiii, 14; 1 Pet. i, 2; Jude 20; 1 John v, 7.

The Holy Spirit is represented as the author of revelations to men, as communicating a knowledge of future events, Acts x, 19; 1 Tim. iv, 1; John xiv, 17, 26.

Spirit of God often means that *Divine energy or power*, that *inspiration* which results from the immediate agency of the Spirit, Luke iv, 1; compare iii, 22; see John iii, 34. "God giveth not the *Spirit* by measure unto him," i. e., the Divine influence, energy, resting upon Christ, was not measured and occasional, like that of prophets and apostles, but ever abundant and constant.

Sometimes the *human spirit* or life is called *spirit of God*, Job xxvii, 3, as being breathed into man from God, and again returning to God, Eccl. xii, 7.

Discerning of spirits, 1 Cor. xii, 10, is a critical faculty of the mind quickened by the Holy Spirit, consisting not only in the power of discerning who was a prophet and who was not, but also of distinguishing in the discourses of a teacher what proceeded from the Holy Spirit, and what did not.

SPIRITUAL, any thing that pertains to the nature of spirits; any thing that pertains to or proceeds from the Holy Spirit.

Spiritual persons are those who are enlightened by the Spirit, enjoying the influences, graces, and gifts of the Holy Spirit, 1 Cor. ii, 13.

A *spiritual body*, 1 Cor. xv, 44, i. e., having the nature of a spirit, of so fine a texture that it will be supported without animal life, merely by the presence of our rational spirit.

Spiritual gifts are miraculous powers, 1 Cor. xii, 1.

Spiritual songs, Eph. v, 19; songs composed in the spirit on spiritual and religious subjects.

The *law* is spiritual, because it is according to the mind and will of the Spirit, Rom. vii, 14.

Spiritual is also spoken of things in a higher and spiritual sense, i. e., not literal, not corporeal, including also a reference to the Holy Spirit, 1 Cor. x, 3, 4.

SPONGE, a species of submarine plant, composed of capillary fibres, which are hollow and implicated in a curious manner, and surrounded by thin membranes, which arrange them into a cellular form. This structure, no less than the constituent matter of sponge, renders it capable of imbibing a great quantity of fluid, and upon a strong pressure, to part with it again. Drink could easily be conveyed in this way where cups could not be used, Matt. xxvii, 48.

STACTE, Exod. xxx, 34, the purest kind of gum myrrh, that which flows from the tree spontaneously.

STANDARD, or *ensign* of war. This was a long pole fixed into the earth. A flag was fastened to its top, which was agitated by the wind, and seen at a great distance, Jer. iv, 6, 21; Ezek. xxvii, 7. In order to render it visible as far as possible, it was erected on a lofty mountain, and was in this way used as a signal to assemble soldiers.

STAR. Under the name of stars, the ancient Hebrews comprehended all the heavenly bodies, constellations and planets; in a word, all the luminaries, the sun and moon excepted. The number of the stars was looked upon as infinite. And the psalmist, to exalt the power and magnificence of God, says, that he numbers the stars and calls them by their names.

Jesus is the *morning star*, which is the symbol of majesty and glory, Rev. xxii, 16.

Wandering stars or *meteors* are false and impious teachers, Jude 13. The Jews called their teachers *stars*, and teachers in the Christian Church are represented under the emblem of stars, Rev. i, 20; ii, 1. Therefore *stars* or *meteors*, which have irregular motions, are proper emblems of those who are unsettled in their principles, and irregular in their behaviour.

The *day star* is put as emblematic of the dawn of spiritual light and happiness upon the benighted mind, 2 Pet. i, 19.

STAY, Isa. iii, 1, a support of any kind, e. g., food and drink; also the chief persons of the nation on whom the people lean, verses 2, 3.

STEWARD, an overseer, a house manager, one who had authority over the servants or slaves of a family, to assign their tasks and portions; with which was also united the general management of affairs and accounts; such persons were themselves usually slaves, Luke xii, 42. But free persons appear also to have been thus employed, Luke xvi, 1, 3, 8; compare verses 3, 4.

The word is used figuratively of the apostles and other teachers, as ministers of the Gospel, 1 Cor. iv, 1.

STEPHEN, Acts vi, 5, 6, the first martyr. He is always put at the head of the seven deacons; and it is believed he had studied at the feet of Gamaliel. He was an example of the majesty and meekness of true Christian heroism, and as the first, so also the pattern of all subsequent martyrs. His Christian brethren forsook not the remains of this holy man; but took care to bury him, and accompanied his funeral with great mourning, Acts viii, 2.

STOCKS, a wooden block or frame with holes, in which the feet, and sometimes the hands and neck of prisoners, were confined, Job xiii, 27.

STOICS, a sect of heathen philosophers, Acts xvii, 18. Their distinguishing tenets were, that matter, in its original elements, is also underived and eternal; and is by the powerful energy of the Deity impressed with motion and form: that though God and matter subsisted from eternity, the present regular frame of nature had a beginning originating in the gross and dark chaos, and will terminate in a universal conflagration, which will reduce the world to its pristine state: that from this chaotic state, however, the world will again emerge by the energy of the efficient principle; and gods, and men, and all forms of regulated nature be renewed and dissolved in endless succession. According to the general doctrine of the stoics, all things are subject to a stern irresistible fatality, even the gods themselves. Some of them explained this fate as an eternal chain of causes and effects; while others describe it as resulting from the Divine decrees—the fiat of an eternal providence. Considering the system practically, it was the object of this philosophy to divest men of their passions and affections. They taught, therefore, that a wise man might be happy in the midst of torture; and that all external things were to him indifferent. Their virtues all

STORK.

Cowl's Dic.

arose from themselves; and self-approbation was their great reward.

STOMACHER, an ornament or support to the breast, worn by females, Isa. iii, 24.

STONE. Our Lord is compared in the New Testament to a foundation cornerstone, in two different points of view. 1. As this stone lies at ●● foundation, and gives support and strength to the building, so Christ, or the doctrine of a Saviour, is called *a foundation*, Eph. ii, 20, because this doctrine is the most important feature of the Christian religion, and is the foundation of all the precepts given by the apostles and other Christian teachers. Farther, as the corner stone occupies an important and honourable place, Jesus is compared to it, 1 Pet. ii, 6, because God has made him distinguished, and has advanced him to a dignity and conspicuousness above all others.

But in Psalm cxliv, 12, corner-stones signify the corner *columns* of a palace; Gesenius translates it, *that our daughters may be as corner columns finely sculptured*, in allusion probably to the columns representing female figures, so common in Egyptian architecture.

Christ is also called *a stone of stumbling*, 1 Pet. ii, 7, i. e., he is the occasion of destruction to the Jews, since they took offence at his person and character, and thus rejected their spiritual deliverer. See LIVING.

"I will lay thy stones with *fair colours*," Isa. liv, 11, i. e., I will use fair colours as *cement* in building up the walls.

"And he became as *stone*," 1 Sam. xxv, 37, i. e., stiff, rigid like stone; a heart of stone is a hard, obdurate heart, Ezek. xi, 19; also a heart of firm undaunted courage, Job xli, 24.

Once stone means the *ore* of a metal, Job xxviii, 2.

"*Stones* of the sanctuary," Lam. iv, 1, i. e., holy gems, figuratively for the nobles of the people, in allusion to the gems on the breastplate of the high priest.

A game was practised in Palestine, so late as the time of Jerome, which consisted in lifting *a stone;* the one who could lift it higher than all the rest was the victor, Zech. xii, 3.

White stone, or pebble, occurs in Rev. ii, 17, and is supposed to refer to the black and white stones which were anciently used in voting, viz., the white for approval or acquittal, and the black for condemnation.

STORK, a bird similar to the crane, only more corpulent, and remarkable for the tenderness which it manifests toward its parents; never, as is represented, forsaking them, but feeding and defending them in their decrepitude. Hence its name, which signifies natural affection.

The stork is a bird of passage, Jer. viii, 7, and migrates to southern countries in August, and returns in the spring. The psalmist says, "The fir trees are her house," civ, 17. In the climate of Europe she commonly builds her nest on some high tower, or on the top of a house; but in Palestine, where the coverings of the houses are flat, she builds in high trees. The stork has the beak and legs long and red; it feeds on serpents, frogs, and insects, and therefore placed by Moses among unclean birds, Lev. xi, 19. Its plumage would be wholly white; but that the extremities of its wings, and some small part of its head and thighs, are black.

STRAIT, Luke xiii, 24, a narrow gate.

STRANGE, something foreign, of another country and people; hence *a stranger* is one who is not an Israelite, Exod. xxx, 33; with this is often connected the accessory idea of an *enemy*, a *barbarian*, Isa. xxix, 5; Hos. vii, 9.

A strange god is the domestic god of another people, foreign to the Hebrews, Psa. xliv, 20; lxxxi, 9.

A strange woman is the wife of another, spoken especially in respect to unlawful intercourse with her; and hence an *adultress, prostitute,* Prov. ii, 16.

Strange is sometimes unlawful; strange fire, i. e., unlawful, profane, opposed to the sacred fire, Lev. x, 1.

Also, figuratively, *strange* signifies new, unheard of, Isa. xxviii, 21.

STRANGLED, Acts xxi, 25; things strangled, that is, strangled meat; the flesh of animals killed by strangling, without shedding their blood.

STRONG DRINK, any intoxicating liquor, whether wine, Num. xxviii, 7, or more usually, as prepared or distilled from grain, fruit, honey, dates, &c., Luke i, 15. The Egyptians prepared a strong drink from barley.

STRONG-HOLD, *a fortress*, a place of security and defence; spoken of a fortified city, or one enclosed with a wall for safety, as Jerusalem. In Zech. ix, 12, we are to understand the *Messiah*, who is referred to in all the preceding context.

SUCCOTH, *tents*, or *tent place*, Exod. xii, 37. Whether there was any town of this name in ancient times is uncertain, as no remains of such a one in the desert are found at the present time on the routes from the Nile to Suez. Nothing more is necessary than to suppose Succoth to be an ordinary *encamping place*, between Rameses and Suez, for those who took the direct route, i. e., about twenty miles from each.

Also a town in the tribe of Gad, on the east of the Jordan, Judges viii, 5. "I will *mete* out," measure as with a line, "the valley of Succoth," Psa. lx, 6, i. e., to my victorious troops, who shall become its inhabitants.

Succoth-benoth, tents of the daughters; the place which the Babylonian colonists in Samaria are said to have made for their idols, 2 Kings xvii, 30. It is generally understood to mean the *tents* in which their daughters prostituted themselves.

SUCKLING, *a sucking child*, Psa. viii, 2. The action of sucking is performed by the child's making a vacuum in its mouth, which extracts the air from the pores of the nipple, and the milk is consequently ejected from the breast by the unresisted elasticity of the air within. This wise contrivance shows the intelligence and power of the Creator.

SUMMER. The warm season in Palestine corresponds to the whole of our spring and summer months. During that part of the year which is called the summer, extending from the middle of June to the middle of August, the heat is so severe that the effect of it is felt through the night, and the inhabitants sleep under the open sky.

SUN, *under the sun* on earth, an expression frequent in the book of Ecclesiastes, as i, 3, *before the sun*, i. e., in the sunshine, Job viii, 16. *In the sight of the sun*, i. e., the sun being, as it were, present, and looking on, 2 Sam. xii, 11. "The *sun* hath looked upon me," Song i, 6, i. e., hath scorched me, made me dark and swarthy. The sacred writers, to represent a great public calamity, speak of the sun as being obscured, Isa. xiii, 10. To express the long continuance of any thing glorious, it is said, it shall continue as long as the *sun*. Christ is compared to the sun, because he came to give light to the world.

SUPERSTITIOUS. This word is generally used in a bad sense; but in the New Testament it is used in a good sense, and signifies *religiously disposed;* spoken of the Athenians, Acts xvii, 22, who were addicted to the worship of invisible powers; compare Acts xxv, 19.

SUPPER was the chief meal of the Jews, and also of the Greeks and Romans, taken at or toward evening, and often prolonged into the night, Mark vi, 21.

THE LORD'S SUPPER, 1 Cor. xi, 20, was instituted by our Lord, after he had supped with his apostles, immediately before he went out to be delivered into the hands of his enemies. Jesus, having fulfilled the law of Moses, by eating the paschal supper with his disciples, proceeded after supper to institute a rite, which, to any person that reads the words of the institution without having formed a previous opinion upon the subject, will probably appear to have been intended by him as a memorial of that event which was to happen not many hours after, Luke xxii, 19, 20. He took the bread which was then on the table, and the wine, of which some had been used in sending around the cup of thanksgiving; and by saying, "This is my body, this is my blood, do this in remembrance of me," he declared to his apostles that this was the representation of his death by which he wished them to commemorate that event. The Apostle Paul, not having been present at the institution, received it by immediate revelation from the Lord Jesus; and the manner in which he delivers it to the Corinthians, 1 Cor. xi, 23–26, implies that it was not a rite confined to the apostles who were present when it was instituted, but that it was meant to be observed by all Christians till the end of the world. "As often as ye eat this bread, and drink this cup, ye do show the Lord's death till he come."

There is a striking correspondence between this view of the Lord's Supper, and the circumstances attending the institution of the feast of the passover. Like the Jews, we have the original sacrifice: "Christ our passover is sacrificed for us," and by his substitution our souls are delivered from death. Like the Jews, we have a feast in which that sacrifice, and the deliverance purchased by it, are remembered; and his disciples in all ages, when they receive the bread, keep a feast of thanksgiving. To Christians, as to Jews, this is "a rite to be much observed unto the Lord," in all generations. To Christians, as to Jews, the manner of observing the rite is appointed. To both it is accompanied with thanksgiving.

The Lord's Supper exhibits, by a significant action, the characteristical doctrine of the Christian faith, that the death of its author was a voluntary sacrifice, so efficacious as to supersede the necessity of every other; and that his blood was shed for the remission of sins. By partaking of this rite his disciples publish an event most interesting to all the kindreds of the earth; they declare that, far from being ashamed of the suffering of their Master, they glory in his cross; and while they thus perform the office implied in that expression of the apostle, "Ye do show forth the Lord's death," they at the same time cherish the sentiments by which their religion ministers to their own consolation and improvement.

SURETY, in common speech, is one who gives security for another. Thus Judah became security to Jacob for the safety of Benjamin in his journey to Egypt, Gen. xliii, 9. In Heb. vii, 22, it is plain that the word is equivalent to that of *mediator*.

SWADDLING, *swathing*, binding in tight clothes; to wrap a new-born child in bandages, Luke ii, 7, 12.

SWALLOW, a bird too well known to need description.

SWAN, a large water fowl, white, and somewhat resembling a goose. But the meaning of the Hebrew word is not known.

SWEARING. See OATH.

SWINE. In impurity and grossness of manners, this animal stands almost unrivalled among the order of quadrupeds; and the meanness of his appearance corresponds to the grossness of his manners. He has a most indiscriminate, voracious, and insatiable appetite.

It was avarice, a contempt of the law of Moses, and a design to supply the neighbouring idolaters with victims, that caused whole herds of swine to be fed on the borders of Galilee. Whence the reason is plain of Christ's permitting the devils to throw the swine headlong into the Lake of Gen-es'a-reth, Matt. viii, 32. The term is applied to those who are wallowing in the mire of sin, Matt. vii, 6. The sense is, "*Give not to dogs lest they turn about and rend you, cast not to swine lest they trample them under their feet*," i. e., generally proffer not good and holy things to those who will spurn and pervert them.

SWORD. The sword in use among the Hebrews appears to have been short, and kept in a sheath, which accounts for such expressions as *to draw the sword*, Exod. xv, 9. It was polished to such a degree, as to render it exceedingly splendid; and in reference to this circumstance, is used figuratively for *lightning*, Psa. vii, 12; Gen. iii, 24. Also sword is attributed to God, which the strong imagination of the Hebrew poets represent as if drunk with blood, Deut. xxxii, 41, 42.

Farther, this well-known instrument is often used for *war*, instead of the weapon to which it gives employment, Lev. xxvi, 33. Language of reproof, of severe threats or commination, or of condemnation, is, by the sacred writers, called the *sword*, or *rod of the mouth*, Isa. xi, 4; xlix, 2; and Paul says, that the word of God is "sharper than any two-edged *sword*," Heb. iv, 12, i. e., has a more efficient power to inflict wounds than a sword with two edges; his words *cut*, as it were, like a sharp sword. *To bear the sword* is to have the power of life and death, Rom. xii, 4.

SYC'A-MINE. See next article.

SYCAMORE, "the fig mulberry." This tree in size and figure resembles the mulberry tree, and is very frequent in Egypt and the level parts of Palestine, 2 Cor. i, 15; ix, 27. Its body is large and its branches numerous; by means of which it is easy of ascent, Luke xix, 4, 5, and always green. Its fruit, which does not spring from the branches and among the leaves, but from the trunk itself, resembles the fig, but is indigestible; it is not, therefore eaten, except for want of something better. It is frequently called the *syca-mine*, Luke xvii, 6.

SYCHAR and SYCHEM, Acts vii, 16 ; John iv, 5 ; the same as *Shechem*.

SY'ENE, a city on the Nile, in the southern extremity of Egypt, situated directly under the tropic of cancer, now called Assouan, Ezek. xxix, 10.

SYN'A-GOGUE, *an assembly*, Rev. ii, 9 ; iii, 9 ; and by metonymy used for the place of assembling. During the Babylonish captivity, the Jews, who were then deprived of their customary religious privileges, were wont to collect around some prophet or other pious man, who taught them and their children in religion, exhorted to good conduct, and read out of the sacred books, Ezek. xx, 1 ; Neh. viii, 18. These assemblies, or meetings, became, in progress of time, fixed to certain places, and a regular order was observed in them. Such appears to have been the origin of synagogues. By "all the *synagogues* in the land," Psa. lxxiv, 8, we may understand, all the sacred places of assembly, as Ramah, Bethel, Gilgal, &c., distinguished as seats of the prophets, and as high places. In the time of the apostles there were synagogues wherever there were Jews. They were built in imitation of the temple of Jerusalem, with a court and porches, as is the case with the synagogues in the East at the present day. In the centre of the court is a chapel, supported by four columns, in which, on an elevation prepared for it, is placed the book of the law, rolled up. This, on the appointed day, is publicly read. The uppermost seats in the synagogue, that is, those which were nearest the chapel where the sacred books were kept, were esteemed peculiarly honourable, Matt. xxiii, 6 ; James ii, 3. In each synagogue a discipline was established for the support of purity of manners ; and punishments were sometimes inflicted on notorious transgressors of the law. Thus we read of Saul scourging men and women in the synagogues.

The persons who were employed in the services and government of the synagogue, in addition to the persons who read and translated the Scriptures, were, 1. "The ruler of the synagogue," who presided over the assembly, and invited readers and speakers, unless some persons who were acceptable voluntarily offered themselves, Luke viii, 41 ; xiii, 14, 15. 2. "The ministers or servants of the synagogue," Luke iv, 20 ; whose business it was to reach the book of the law to the person who was to read it, and to receive it back again, and to perform other services.

We do not find mention made of public worship in the synagogues, except on the

Sabbath. When an assembly was collected together for worship, the services began, after the customary greeting, with a doxology. A section was then read from the Mosaic law. Then followed, after the singing of a second doxology, the reading of a portion from the prophets. Acts xv, 31; Luke iv, 16, The sections which had been read in the Hebrew were rendered by an interpreter in the vernacular tongue, and the reader or some other man then addressed the people, Luke iv, 16; Acts xiii, 15. It was on such occasions as these that Jesus, and afterward the apostles, taught the Gospel. The meeting, as far as the religious exercises were concerned, was ended with a prayer, to which the people responded, Amen, when a collection was taken for the poor.

It is affirmed, that in the city of Jerusalem alone there were no less than four hundred and eighty synagogues. Every trading company had one of its own, and even strangers built some for those of their own nation. Hence, we find synagogues of the *Cyrenians*, *Alexandrians*, *Cilicians*, and *Asiatics*, appointed for such as came up to Jerusalem from those countries, Acts vi, 9.

SYRACUSE, now called *Syracusa*, the celebrated capital of Sicily, situated on the eastern coast, with a capacious harbour. It was the birthplace and residence of Archimedes, Acts xxviii, 12, and contains now about 18,000 inhabitants.

SYRIA, Matt. iv, 24, a large country of Asia, lying, in the widest acceptation of the name, between Palestine, the Mediterranean, Mount Taurus, and the Tigris; thus including Mesopotamia. The region around Damascus, which is a beautiful plain, including probably the valley between the ridges of Libanus and Anti-Libanus, is called in Scripture *Syria of Damascus*, 2 Sam. viii, 5; and by Strabo *Cœle-Syria*, i. e., Hollow Syria.

At the time of the Jewish exile, Syria with Palestine was subject to the empire of Babylon; and later, to the Persian monarchs and Alexander the Great. After the death of the latter, Babylon and Syria became a powerful kingdom under the dominion of the Seleucidæ, monarchs of the Seleucian family, of which, at a later period, Antioch was the capital. Syria was subdued by Pompey as far as the Euphrates, and made a Roman province, including also Phenicia and Judea.

In the time of Christ, it was governed by a proconsul, to whom the procurator of Judea was amenable. See Luke ii, 2; Acts xxi, 3.

SYRO-PHENICIAN, referring to the Syro-Phenician woman, i. e., a Phenician of Syria, probably in distinction from the Phenicians of Libya,

TAB 474 TAB

or the Carthaginians, Mark vii, 26. This country is called the coasts of Tyre and Sidon, Matt. xv, 21, 22. See PHENICIA.

TAANACH, a royal Canaanitish city, which is supposed to lie a short distance east or south-east of Megiddo, Joshua xii, 21.

TABERNACLE, *a tent;* the sacred tent of the Hebrews in which the ark was kept; the seat of the Jewish worship before the building of the temple. The ark, however, was separated from the tabernacle long before this period, and was kept in Jerusalem, while the tabernacle itself remained in Gibeon; see 2 Chron. i, 3, 4, 13; compare 2 Sam. vi, 17.

This building was constructed with extraordinary magnificence in every part, according to the express instruction of Jehovah, and evidently with a typical design, Heb. ix, 1–8. The value of the gold and silver only used for the work, amounted, according to the best calculation, from Exod. xxxviii, 24, 25, to more than $810,000.

The tabernacle, as you will see by the engraving, was of an oblong form, thirty cubits long, i. e., forty-five feet, ten broad, and ten in height, i. e., fifteen feet. The rear, which is the west, and the two sides, were enclosed with boards; but on the east end, which was the entrance, there were no boards but only five pillars of shittim wood, whose ornaments and tops were overlaid with gold, and between which, to close the entrance, was suspended a richly embroidered curtain. Over the top was thrown a gorgeous fabric, of various materials, the connection and disposition of which, as well as of the other parts of the covering, are described with the utmost minuteness, Exod. xxvi, 1–30.

'his sacred structure was divided into two apartments by means of four pillars, whose tops are seen in the cut, and on these pillars was hung a curtain, formed of the same materials as the one placed at the entrance. This was called the *second veil,* Heb. ix, 3; the first division was called the *holy place,* or *sanctuary,* or the *first tabernacle;* the second division was the *second tabernacle,* or the *most holy place,* or the *holiest of all,* Heb. ix, 2–8.

The tabernacle stood in the west part of an open space called the *court,* which was also of an oblong form, one hundred and fifty feet in length by seventy-five in breadth, Exod. xxvii, 18, situated due east and west.

It is observable that neither the *holy* nor the *most holy place* had any window. Hence the need of the candlestick in the first one for the service that was performed therein; and the darkness of the other would create reverence. In the *holy place* was the *altar*

TABERNACLE.

Covel's Dic.

COURT OF THE TABERNACLE.

TAB 477 TAB

of incense placed in the middle ; the *candlestick* was on the south, and the *table of the shew-bread* on the north side of the altar ; the *most holy place* contained the ark, with its golden cherubim. This court was surrounded with pillars of brass or copper, supposed to be eight feet high, and placed at the same distance from each other, and on rods of silver, which reached from one pillar to another, were suspended curtains, made of linen. These pillars, on the east and west ten, and on the north and south twenty in number, were without doubt made of the ACACIA, (*Shittim*,) the most durable kind of wood.

Within this enclosure stood the *altar of burnt-offerings*, and between this and the tabernacle the *brazen laver*, corresponding to the molten sea, 1 Kings vii, 23, in its shape resembling an urn. It contained water for washing the hands and feet of the priests, when they were about to enter the sanctuary. The tabernacle was so constructed as to be taken to pieces and put together again as occasion required. It was finished on the first day of the first month of the second year after the departure out of Egypt, A. M. 2514. When it was set up, a dark cloud covered it by day, and a fiery cloud by night. Moses went into the tabernacle to consult the Lord. It was placed in the midst of the camp, and the Hebrews were ranged in order about it, according to their several tribes. When the cloud arose from off the tabernacle, they decamped ; the priests carried those things which were most sacred, and the Levites all the several parts of the tabernacle. Part of the tribes went before, and the rest followed after ; and the baggage of the tabernacle marched in the centre. The tabernacle was brought into the land of Canaan by Joshua, and set up at Gilgal. Here it rested till the land was conquered. Then it was removed to Shi′loh, and afterward to Nob. Its next station was Gib′e-a, and here it continued till the ark was removed to the temple.

"*Tabernacle* of witness," Acts vii, 44, is put for the "tent of the congregation," Exod. xxvii, 21 ; xl, 22 ; i. e., the sacred tent or tabernacle of the Hebrews. It is so called, either because God there met Moses, Exod. xxv, 22, or because the assemblies of the people were held before it.

The true tabernacle, Heb. viii, 2, means that which is spiritual, immutable, and eternal in the heavens ; and which, therefore, is called *true* or *real*, in distinction from the earthly tabernacle that was made by the hands of men, and was of materials earthly and perishable. The tabernacle in heaven is the *substance ;* that on earth, the *image* or *type*.

TAB 478 TAB

The tabernacle of David is used, metaphorically, for the *family* or royal line of David, fallen into darkness and decay, Acts xv, 16, as a house in ruins.

The word is used also for *the body*, as the frail and temporary abode of the soul, 2 Cor. v, 1.

Tabernacle of Moloch, Acts vii, 43, quoted from Amos v, 26; a tabernacle which the idolatrous Israelites constructed in the desert, in honour of Moloch, like that in honour of Jehovah; probably of a small size, so as to elude the notice of Moses.

FEAST OF TABERNACLES. The third great annual festival of the Jews, in which all the males were required to appear before God at the tabernacle or temple; the other two being the passover and pentecost, Deut. xvi, 16.

This festival was so called from the booths or tents of green boughs and leaves in which the people dwelt during its continuance, on the roofs of the houses, and in the courts and streets. It began on the 15th day of the seventh month Tisri, which commenced with the new moon of October, and was celebrated for eight days; partly as a memorial of the forty years' wandering in the desert, where the Israelites dwelt in booths, Lev. xxiii, 42, 43, and partly as a season of thanksgiving for the ingathering of the harvest; hence called *feast of ingathering*,

Exod. xxiii, 16. It was a season of rejoicing and feasting; particularly sacrifices were offered, and portions of the law read in public, Neh. viii, 18. To these the later Jews added a libation of water brought from the fountain Siloam, mixed with wine, and poured upon the altar. The eighth day is called the great day of the feast, John vii, 37. See FEASTS.

TABITHA signifies *gazelle*, as does also the corresponding Greek name *Dorcas*; the name of a female Christian, Acts ix, 36.

TABLE. See EATING. The word is used also for the little board on which the ancients used to write, Hab. ii, 2; Luke i, 63. (See BOOK.) And because the heart is ready to receive Divine truth, it is called a *table*, Prov. iii, 3; 2 Cor. iii, 3. "To serve *tables*," Acts vi, 2, signifies to make provision for those tables at which the poor were fed.

TABLES OF THE LAW. Those that were given to Moses upon Mount Sinai were written by the finger of God, and contained the decalogue or ten commandments of the law, as they are rehearsed in Exod. xx. The words which intimate that the tables were written by the finger of God always signify immediate Divine agency.

TABLETS, in common language, a small table; but in the Bible, Isa. iii, 20, it signifies smelling bottles, per-

TAB   479   TAD

fume boxes, filled with amber and musk, which the Jewish ladies wore suspended to the waist.

TABOR, Judges iv, 6, a mountain on the northern side of the plain of Jezreel, about fifty miles north of Jerusalem. It stands isolated and prominent above all the surrounding mountains. It is described, by Burckhardt and others, as resembling a cone with the point struck off; the sides of which are not so steep but that it may be ascended on horseback; the top presenting a level area of two furlongs in length and one in breadth. Its altitude is estimated at 3,000 feet, i. e., less than two-thirds of a mile. The sides are covered to the very top with forests of oak and wild pistachio-nut trees. On it are still to be seen the remains of fortifications, probably of the time of the crusades. The prospect from Mount Tabor is described by all travellers as one of the loveliest on earth. The eye wanders over the mountains and plains of Galilee, takes in the mountains of Ephraim, and rests on "the excellency of Carmel;" while immediately below is the wild plain of Esdraelon, (*Jezreel*,) spread out like a carpet, through which the Kishon is seen winding its way, and approaching gradually the base of Carmel.

"It is," says Pococke, "one of the finest hills I ever beheld, being a rich soil that produces excellent herbage, and is most beautifully adorned with groves and clumps of trees. The ascent is so easy that we rode up the north side by a winding road. Some authors mention it as nearly four miles high, others as about two : the former may be true, as to the winding ascent up the hill."

Plain of Tabor, 1 Sam. x, 3, was a grove of oaks, in the territory of Benjamin, two miles distant from Jerusalem.

TAB′RET, or *timbrel*, Gen. xxxi, 27, an instrument of music, which consisted of a circular hoop, either of wood or brass, some three inches wide, covered with a skin tensely drawn, and hung around with small bells. It was held in the left hand, and beaten to notes of music with the right. The ladies through all the East, even to this day, dance to the sound of the timbrel, Exod. xv, 20.

Under this word are also comprehended *triangles*, instruments of music struck in concert with drums, as in modern military music, 1 Sam. xviii, 6.

TACHE, a hook to which a loop or eye is fitted, Exod. xxvi, 6.

TAD′MOR, a city built by Solomon, 1 Kings ix, 18, afterward called Pal-my′ra; situated in a wilderness of Syria, upon the borders of Arabia, east of Damascus. Josephus places it two days' journey from the Euphrates and six days' journey from

Babylon. He says there is no water anywhere else in the wilderness, but in this place. At the present day there are to be seen vast ruins of this city. There was nothing more magnificent in the whole East. There are still found a great number of inscriptions, the most of which are Greek, and the other in the Palmyrenian character. The Palmyrenian inscriptions are entirely unknown, as well as the language and character of that country.

TAHAPANES, Jer. ii, 16, or TAHPANHES, Jer. xliii, 7, or *Tehaphnehes*, Ezek. xxx, 18; a city of Egypt, which the *seventy* render by *Taphne*, doubtless the same as *Daphne;* a strong city near Pelusium. To this city many of the Jews retired after the destruction of Jerusalem by the Chaldeans, taking with them the Prophet Jeremiah, Jer. xliv, 1.

TALENT, a weight equal to 3000 shekels of the sanctuary, as appears from Exod. xxxviii, 25, 26. For 603,550 persons being taxed at half a shekel each, they must have paid in the whole 301,775; now that sum is said to amount to 100 talents, and 1,775 shekels only; deduct the number of shekels stated in the text, viz., 1,775, and there will remain 300,000, which divided by 100, will leave 3000 shekels for each of these talents. According to Arbuthnot, a talent was equal to 113 lb. 10 oz. 1 dwt. 2 2-7 grs. troy weight. The common

Attic talent is usually estimated at about $1600; but the estimate of Arbuthnot is $860 25.

In the New Testament generally *a talent* is put for an indefinitely large sum of money, Matt. xxv, 15.

TAL'I-THA-CU'MI. The words are not pure Hebrew, but Syriac, and signify, "My daughter, arise," Mark v, 41.

TAMMUZ, a Syrian deity: the *Adonis* of the Greeks, for whom the Hebrew women also were accustomed to hold an annual lamentation in the fourth month, called *Tammuz,* beginning with the new moon of July, Ezek. viii, 14.

TARES, weeds injurious to grain; but in the New Testament it is spoken of a plant common in Palestine, which infests fields of grain, and resembles wheat in appearance, but is worthless, *bastard wheat,* Matt. xiii, 25.

TARGET, 1 Sam. xvii, 6, is a *shield;* but some suppose the word may be better translated by *javelin* or *dart,* as may be learned from Job xxxix, 23, where it is joined with a spear.

TARSHISH, supposed by Gesenius and Parkhurst to be a region in Spain, situated between the two mouths of the river *Gaudalquivir,* originally settled by the descendants of *Tarshish,* Gen. x, 4, and called after his name; and thence by the Romans *Tartessus.* From hence silver, iron, tin, and lead were brought to Tyre, Ezek. xxvii, 12, 25.

It was to this place that Jonah attempted to flee from the presence of the Lord, as being a place at a great distance both from Judea and Nineveh.

Ships of Tarshish mean large strong ships, fit to sail from Judea to Tarshish, or to undertake the like distant voyage ; this expression is used of ships going to *Ophir*, 1 Kings x, 20, and Parkhurst thinks that *Ophir* was sometimes called *Tarshish*, 1 Kings xxii, 48. We must conclude one of these two things ; either that there were two countries called *Tarshish*, one upon the ocean, and another upon the Mediterranean, or that ships of Tarshish in general signifies nothing else but ships able to bear a long voyage : large merchant ships, in opposition to the small craft intended for a home trade in navigable rivers.

TARSUS, a celebrated city, the capital of Cilicia in Asia Minor, situated on a fruitful plain through which flowed the river Cydnus, now called by the Turks *Kara-Su*, i. e., black water, from its depth. Tarsus was great and populous, and a celebrated seat of Greek philosophy and literature ; and from the number of its schools and learned men, was ranked by the side of Athens and Alexandria. The city was made free by Augustus. This seems to have implied the privilege of

being governed by their own laws and magistrates, with freedom from tribute, but not the right of Roman citizenship ; since the Roman tribune at Jerusalem ordered Paul to be scourged, though he knew him to be a citizen of Tarsus, but desisted after learning that he was a Roman citizen, Acts xxi, 39 ; xxii, 24, 27.

Tarsus is now a poor fallen place, inhabited by Turks, Greeks, and Armenians, belonging to the government of Cyprus.

TAVERNS occurs only in the phrase *The Three Taverns ;* the proper name of a small place on the Appian way, thirty-three Roman, a little over thirty English miles from Rome toward Brundusium, Acts xxviii, 15.

TEETH, "Gnashing of the *teeth*," Matt. viii, 12. The image is drawn from a person in a paroxysm of envy, rage, or pain ; compare Acts vii, 54.

Cleanness of teeth is a figurative expression for famine, Amos iv, 6 ; the phrase in Ezek. xviii, 2, signifies that the children suffer for the sins of their fathers.

TEIL TREE, Isa. vi, 13, the linden or lime tree, which grows in warm climates, bearing a species of acid fruit smaller than the lemon. But Gesenius renders it *a terebinth*, the turpentine tree, which is common in Palestine. It is long lived, and therefore often employed for landmarks, and in designating places. It is sometimes rendered *an oak.* Hence the word may be taken in a broader signification for any large and durable tree, Gen. xxxv, 4; Judges vi, 11.

TEKEL, Chald., participle passive, *weighed,* Dan. v, 27. See MENE.

TEKOA, 2 Sam. xiv, 2, a fortified city, situated on a slight eminence, south-eastward from Bethlehem, on the borders of the Great Desert, and from which the Dead Sea is also to be seen. Its ruins are still found, and retain the ancient name.

TEMA, a tract and people in the northern part of the Arabian Desert, adjacent to the Syrian Desert, so called from Tema, the son of Ishmael, Gen. xxv, 15, and still called by the Arabs Teima. *The troops of Tema* are the caravans, Job vi, 19.

TEMAN, the name of a city, region, and people, a few miles east from Petra, which sprung from Teman, the grandson of Esau, Gen. xxxvi, 11. Like other Arabs, the Temanites were celebrated for wisdom, Jer. xlix, 7.

The name *Theman,* or *Teman* signifies *what is on the right hand;* and hence, according to the Hebrew mode of designating the different points of compass, it means also the *south.* When, therefore, it is said in Hab. iii, 3, that "God came from *Teman,*" this may perhaps refer to the district of Teman above described, which was near to Mount Hor; or it more probably is put as a poetical designation for *the south* in general.

TEMPLE, the house of God; properly the temple of Solomon. David first conceived the design of building a house somewhat worthy of the Divine majesty, and opened his mind to the Prophet Nathan, 2 Sam. vii. God accepted of his good intentions, but refused him the honour. Solomon laid the foundation of the temple, 1011 B. C., completed it in 1003, and dedicated it in 1002,1 Kings viii, 2. There were two temples, namely, the first erected by Solomon; the second by Zerubbabel and Joshua the high priest: and this corresponds with the prophecy of Haggai, ii, 9, "That the glory of this latter house," the temple built by Zerubbabel, "should be greater than that of the former;" which prediction was uttered with reference to the Messiah's honouring it with his presence and ministry.

The FIRST TEMPLE is that which usually bears the name of Solomon; the materials for which were provided by David before his death, though the edifice was raised by his son. It stood on Mount Moriah, an eminence of the mountainous ridge in the Scriptures termed *Mount Zion,* Psalm cxxxii, 13, 14, which had been purchased by Araunah, or Ornan, the Jebusite, 2 Samuel xxiv, 23, 24; 1 Chron. xxi, 25. The plan and the whole model of this superb structure were formed after that of the tabernacle, but of much larger dimensions. It was surrounded, except at the front or *east end*, by three stories or chambers, each nearly eight feet square, which reached to half the height of the temple; and the front was ornamented with a magnificent portico, which rose to the height of 180 feet. The utensils for the sacred service were the same; excepting that several of them, as the altar, candlestick, &c., were larger, in proportion to the more spacious edifice to which they belonged. Seven years and six months were occupied in the erection of the superb temple of Solomon, by whom it was dedicated, with peculiar solemnity, to the worship of the Most High; who, on this occasion, vouchsafed to honour it with the *shechinah*, or visible manifestation of his presence. It retained its pristine splendour only thirty-three or thirty-four years, when Shi'shak, king of Egypt, took Jerusalem, and carried away the treasures of the temple; and after undergoing subsequent profanations and pillages, this stupendous building was finally plundered and burned by the Chaldeans under Neb-u-chad-nez'zar, 584 B. C., 2 Kings xxv, 8–17; 2 Chron. xxxvi, 17–20.

2. After the captivity, the temple emerged from its ruins, being rebuilt by Zerubbabel, but with vastly inferior and diminished glory, as appears from the tears of the aged men who had beheld the former structure in all its grandeur, Ezra iii, 12.

The SECOND TEMPLE was profaned by order of An-ti'o-chus E-piph'a-nes, 163 B. C., who caused the daily sacrifices to be discontinued, and erected the image of Jupiter O-lym'pus on the altar of burnt-offering. In this condition it continued three years, 1 Mac. iv, 42, when Judas Maccabeus purified and repaired it, and restored the sacrifices and true worship of Jehovah. Some years before the birth of our Saviour, the repairing and beautifying of this second temple, which had become decayed in the lapse of five centuries, was undertaken by Herod the Great, who for nine years employed eighty thousand workmen upon it, and spared no expense to render it equal, if not superior, in magnitude, splendour, and beauty, to any thing among mankind. Josephus calls it a work the most admirable of any thing that had ever been seen or heard of, both for its curious structure and its magnitude, and also for the vast wealth expended upon it, as well as for the universal reputation of its sanctity. But though Herod accomplished his original design in the time above specified, yet the Jews continued to ornament and enlarge it, expending the sacred treasure in annexing additional buildings to it; so that they might with great propriety assert, that their temple had been forty and six years in building, John ii, 20.

The second temple, originally built by Ze-rub'babel after the captivity, and repaired by Herod, differed in several respects from that erected by Solomon, although they agreed in others.

The temple erected by Solomon was more splendid and magnificent than the second temple, which was deficient in five remarkable things that constituted the chief glory of the first: these were, the *ark*, the *shechinah*, or manifestation of the Divine presence, in the holy of holies; the *sacred fire on the altar*, which had been first kindled from heaven; the *Urim* and *Thummim*; and the *Spirit of prophecy*. But the second temple surpassed the first in glory; being honoured by the frequent presence of our Divine Saviour, agreeably to the prediction of Haggai, ii, 9. Both, however, were erected upon the same site, a very hard rock, encompassed by a very frightful precipice; and the foundation was laid with incredible expense and labour. The superstructure was not inferior to this great work: the height of the temple wall, especially on the south side, was stupendous. In the lowest places it was 450 feet, and in some places even greater. This most magnificent pile was constructed with hard white stones of prodigious magnitude.

"How natural is the exclamation of the disciples, when viewing this immense building at a distance: 'Master, see what manner of stones, and what buildings are here!' Mark xiii, 1; and how wonderful is the declaration of our Lord upon this; how unlikely to be accomplished before the race of men who were then living should cease to exist! 'Seest thou these great buildings? There shall not be left one stone upon another that shall not be thrown down.' Improbable as this prediction must have appeared to the disciples at that time, in the short space of about thirty years after it was exactly accomplished; and this most magnificent temple, which the Jews had literally turned into a den of thieves, through the righteous judgment of God upon that wicked and abandoned nation, was utterly destroyed by the Romans, in the year 70, or 73 of the vulgar era, on the same month, and on the same day of the month, when Solomon's temple had been razed to the ground by the Babylonians!"

Both the first and second temples were contemplated by the Jews with the highest reverence. Of their affectionate regard for the first temple, and for Jerusalem, within whose walls it was built, we have several in stances in those psalms which were composed during the Babylonish captivity; and of their profound veneration for the second temple, we have repeated examples in the New Testament. They could not bear any disrespectful or dishonourable thing to be said of it. The least injurious slight of it, real or apprehended, instantly awakened all the choler of a Jew, and was an affront never to be forgotten, Matt. xxvii, 40.

It remains to be added that the Jews had a *band of men* who guarded the temple, John xviii, 3, 12. These were Levites, who performed the menial offices of the temple, and kept watch by night, Psa. cxxxiv, 1; 2 Kings xii, 9; 1 Chron. ix, 17-27. They were under the command of officers called *captains of the temple*. Some understand here a band of Roman soldiers; but these would rather have led Jesus directly to their own officers, and not to the chief priests; and besides, this was not a band of regularly armed troops; compare Matt. xxvi, 55; Luke xxii, 52.

TEMPTATION. 1. The soliciting of a person to sin, especially from Satan, Luke vi, 13, who with an ill intent puts his character to the test.

2. Used in a good sense; a *state of trial* into which God brings his people through adversity and affliction, in order to excite and prove their faith and confidence in him. See Gen. xxii, 1, 2. Hence tempt-

ations sometimes mean those *mighty works* of God intended to excite and prove the faith of his people, Deut. xxix, 3. On the contrary, *temptation of God by man is distrust*, complaint against him, doubting his power and aid. He puts the Divine patience, forbearance, goodness, &c., to a trial. It is difficult, speaking after the manner of men, to preserve a strict regard to these, Heb. iii, 8; compare verse 9.

"Lead us not into *temptation*," Matt. vi, 13, i. e., bring us not into a state of trial, lay not trials upon us. The Christian is, by all means, to rejoice when he falls into trials; because he who is found worthy obtains the crown of life, James i, 2, 12; but yet the Christian is not, on that account, to seek temptations; nay, in the consciousness of his weakness, he should pray to be constantly preserved from them, since he cannot answer for himself that he shall be found proof against their power. When temptations are absent, we should deprecate them; when present, bear them manfully, that we may show both modesty and fortitude; we are taught, therefore, not to be too confident in ourselves, nor to rush into temptation out of a spirit of defiance.

TEN TRIBES, or *Samaria*, was called Ephraim, because the tribe of Ephraim was the most important, and also because the family of Jeroboam, the first king, was of that tribe. They were transported by Shalmanezer into the northernmost province of Assyria, on the borders of Armenia, 2 Kings xvii, 6; xviii, 11.

"The ten tribes of Israel have been long considered as lost, or mingled with other nations; but in the Asiatic Researches, we learn that a people have recently been discovered in Afghanistan, or East Persia, (not very distant from the place where it is thought the captives were settled by Shalmanezer,) who, it is confidently believed, are the lost ten tribes of Israel. A considerable district of this country is called Hazareh, or Hazareth, which is probably the *Arsareth* mentioned in Esdras. (See 2 Esdras xiii, 40, 45.) It is said that this people have traditions of their origin; and the Persian historians, with whose empire they have always been connected, assert that the Afghans are descendants of the Hebrews. The names of their families, too, are distinguished by the very names of the Hebrew tribes, as Reuben, Simeon, &c. Their language, which has been examined by Mr. Vansittart, is, he says, manifestly of Hebrew origin. Dr. Buchanan, during his residence in India, investigated this subject, and was fully convinced, from many proofs which he obtained respecting this people, that they are the descendants of the lost Israelites. Among other circumstances mentioned by him, he says he asked the black Jews, a people in the south of India, where their brethren, the great body of the ten tribes, were to be found. They answered promptly, in the north, in the regions adjacent to Persia. That eminent scholar, Sir William Jones, whose residence in India gave him the best opportunities of information on this subject, has also given it as his opinion that the Afghans were descended from the Hebrews. St. Jerome, in the fifth century, writing his notes upon Hosea, has these words: ' Unto this day the ten tribes are subject to the kings of Persia, nor has their captivity ever been loosed.'

"Our limits will not allow us to adduce other authorities, which might be easily done; but we think sufficient has been said to show that the posterity of the ten tribes still exist in the countries to which they were carried in their first captivity."

TENTS, Gen. xxxiii, 7. At first no doubt tents were constructed of skins; but in the progress of years they were covered with various kinds of cloth, particularly linen. The Nomades of the East still use skins. The first tents which were made were undoubtedly round in their construction, and small in size; afterward they were made larger and oblong.

TENT-MAKER. St. Paul, according to the practice of

Covel's Dic   p. 497.

ARAB TENTS.

the Jews, who, however opulent, always taught their children some trade, appears to have been a tent-maker. This, however, is understood by some moderns to mean a maker of tent cloth. The fathers, however, say that he made military tents, the material of which was skins.

TENTH DEAL, Lev. xxiii, 17. *Deal* is the old English word for *part, tenth part*, i. e., of the ephah, which would make it about five pints and one tenth, grain measure.

TER'A-PHIM. It appears from all the passages in which this word is used, that they were domestic idols or family gods, Judges xvii, 5, translated in some places *images*, Gen. xxxi, 19. They seem to have had the human form and stature, 1 Sam. xix, 13; and it appears that responses were sought from them the same as from oracles, Ezek. xxi, 21. This is confirmed by 2 Kings xxiii, 24, where they are spoken of in connection with the arts of divination.

Perhaps it was also applied to the forms or instruments of astrology, and so might be found in possession of those who were not idolators.

TERTIUS, the name of Paul's amanuensis, Romans xvi, 22.

TESTAMENT, in common language, is an instrument in writing, called the *will*, by which a man determines what disposition shall be made of his property after his death; and a testator is one that makes such a will. Mr. Wesley says, "The original word also means a covenant. St. Paul takes it sometimes in the former, and sometimes in the latter sense, and sometimes includes both."

Jesus is called a testator, because he has freely bequeathed unto sinful men unsearchable riches of grace and glory. The term *New Testament* denotes that covenant dispensation, or institution of God, which Jesus ratified by his blood, Heb. ix, 16, 17; hence the title of the books which contain this covenant. See COVENANT.

TESTIMONY, a witnessing, evidence, or proof, Acts xiv, 3. The whole Scripture or word of God, which declares what is to be believed, practised, and expected by us, is called God's "testimony," and sometimes in the plural, "testimonies," Psa. xix, 7. The *two tables of stone* on which the law or ten commandments were written, which were witnesses of that covenant made between God and his people, and testified what it was that God had required of them, have the same title, Exodus xxv, 21; xxxi, 18.

TET'RARCH, a sovereign prince that has the fourth part of a state, province, or kingdom under his dominion, without wearing the diadem, or bearing the title of king. It is spoken in the New Testament only of *Herod Antipas*, Luke ix, 7.

THAMMUZ. See **Tammuz.**

THANKSGIVING, the act of acknowledging the mercies of God. (See **Praise.**) Whoever possesses any good without giving thanks for it, deprives him who bestows that good of his glory, sets a bad example before others, and prepares a recollection severely painful for himself, when he comes in his turn to experience ingratitude. Let only that man withhold thanksgiving who has no enjoyments for which to give thanks.

THANK-OFFERINGS, 2 Chron. xxix, 31 ; sacrifices offered to God with praise and thanksgiving : they were of the same kind with the *peace-offerings.*

THAT. In the sentence translated "that it might be fulfilled," and perhaps in the translation itself, there are two senses in which the word *that* (ἵνα) may be understood.

1. When employed in the sense of *in order that*, indicating the END *or reason why a thing is done.*

2. When it is used in the sense of *so that*, i. e., used in such a way as shows the *effect* or *event* of a thing. For an example, let us look at Matt. ii, 23, where we read that "Jesus dwelt in a city called Nazareth; *that* it might be fulfilled which was spoken by the prophets." Now if we say, *This took place* IN ORDER THAT *the prediction by Isaiah might be fulfilled*, this is representing the event as taking place merely for the purpose of fulfilling the prophecy. But if we say, This took place, so THAT the prediction by Isaiah might be fulfilled, then we merely affirm that the mode of the event was such that a fulfilment of prophecy was accomplished by it ; while at the same time, the event itself might have an unspeakably higher end in view.

It implies that something took place, not *in order that* a prophecy might be fulfilled ; not *in order* TO MAKE the event correspond to the prophecy, but *so that* the event DID correspond to it. In Matt. i, 22, it is said, " Now all this was done *that* it might be fulfilled," referring to Isa. vii, 14. Shall we say now that the Saviour was to be born merely that this prophecy might be fulfilled? Was it not rather to redeem a world in ruin than to accomplish the prediction of Isaiah? The *great* and *ultimate* end must be THE REDEMPTION OF MANKIND. The other was altogether *subordinate*, and merely *preparatory.* The passage must be understood as marking simply the event or result, *so that* the prophecy is fulfilled. " The law entered, *that* the offence might abound," Rom. v, 20. The apostle is not showing the reason *why* the law came in, but the *effect* or *consequence*, *so that* offence should abound.

THEATRE, a building erected for the exhibition of public shows, Acts xix, 29, 31.

The theatre which was introduced by Herod and his sons into Palestine was an edifice constructed–in such a manner as .to describe the larger part of a circle. The games were exhibited in that part of it where a line would have passed to enclose precisely a semicircle. In these places comedies and tragedies were acted ; assemblies of the people were held to hear harangues, to hold public consultations, and to receive ambassadors. Some of their exercises in truth were of a very bloody character ; criminals who had been condemned by the laws of the country, and enemies who had been captured in war, were compelled to fight till they lost their life, either with wild beasts or with one another.

THE-OPH'I-LUS, one to whom St. Luke addresses the books of his Gospel and Acts of the Apostles, which he composed, Acts i, 1 ; Luke i, 3. And the epithet of "most excellent," which is given to him, shows him to have been a man of great quality.

THES'SA-LO'NI-ANS, Christians of Thessalonica, to whom St. Paul sent two epistles. It is recorded in the Acts, that St. Paul, in his first journey upon the continent of Europe, preached the Gospel at Thessalonica, at that time the capital of Mace-donia, with considerable success ; but that after a short stay he was driven thence by the malice and violence of the unbelieving Jews. From Thessalonica St. Paul went to Be-re'a, and thence to Athens, at both which places he remained but a short time. From Athens he sent Timothy to Thessalonica, to confirm the new converts in their faith, and to inquire into their conduct. Timothy, upon his return, found St. Paul at Corinth. Thence, probably in A. D. 52, St. Paul wrote the First Epistle to the Thessalonians ; and it is to be supposed that the subjects of which it treats were suggested by· the account which he received from Timothy. It is now generally believed that this was written the first of all St. Paul's epistles, but it is not known by whom it was sent to Thessalonica. The Church there consisted chiefly of Gentile converts, 1 Thess. i, 9.

It is generally believed that the messenger who carried the former epistle into Macedonia, upon his return to Corinth, informed St. Paul that the Thessalonians had inferred, from some expressions in it, that the coming of Christ and the final judgment were near at hand, and would happen in the time of many who were then alive, 1 Thess. iv, 15, 17 ; v, 6. The principal design of the Second Epistle to the Thessalonians was to correct that error, and pre·

vent the mischief which it would naturally occasion. It was written from Corinth, probably at the end of A. D. 52.

THESSALO-NI'CA, now called *Saloniki*, a city of Macedonia, at the head of the Thermaic Bay. It was anciently called *Therma*, but was named by Cassander *Thessalonica* after his wife, the daughter of Philip. Under the Romans, it was the capital of one of the four divisions of Macedonia, and the usual station of a Roman prætor and quæstor. This last was a Roman officer who collected the revenues of the state. The Jews had here a synagogue, and it was to the Church gathered here that St. Paul wrote his epistles, Acts xvii, 1.

THEUDAS, an impostor who excited tumult among the Jews, Acts v, 36. He is probably to be placed during the interregnum after the death of Herod the Great, when Judea was disturbed by frequent seditions. Judas too, who came after him, Acts v, 37, appeared under Cyrenius and Coponius, A. D. 6-9. Josephus mentions another Theudas, an impostor, under Claudius, while Caspius Fadus was procurator of Judea, about A. D. 45.

THIGH. *Smiting on the thigh* is mentioned as a gesture of violent grief or indignation, Jer. xxxi, 19. The inscription upon the thigh, Rev. xix, 16, alludes to the custom of inscribing the names and deeds of conquerors on their garments. The name might be inscribed on the sword, which was girded on the thigh, or on that part of the dress which covered the thigh. Samson smote the Philistines; literally, *leg upon thigh*, Judges xv, 8, *hip and thigh*, i. e., he cut them in pieces, so that their limbs, their legs and thighs, were scattered one upon another— he totally destroyed them.

THOMAS, the apostle, called in Greek Didymus, which signifies *a twin*; but the place of his birth and the circumstances of his calling are unknown. See John xx, 24.

THORN, a general name for several kinds of prickly plants. These grow spontaneously in the fields and among ruins, and yield a troublesome and never failing crop.

A thorn in the flesh *is* something which excites severe and constant pain, probably some bodily infirmity, 2 Cor. xii, 7; compare verse 10.

THOUGHT. In Matt. vi, 25, the Greek word rendered "take no thought," is regarded as an unhappy translation; for simple thoughtfulness, and a moderated care, are both necessary to that prudent and industrious conduct by which, under God's blessing, our daily wants are appointed to be supplied. The idea is better expressed by *to be anxious, troubled*. Care becomes dangerous and sinful when it goes beyond the necessity of the case; when it is disproportionate to the temporary interests of the present life; when it leads to distrust in God; when it arises from want of submission to the lot he may be pleased to assign us; when it disturbs our minds, unfitting us for devotional exercises, and inducing the neglect of our spiritual concerns.

THOUSAND YEARS. By the reign of Christ and the saints for a thousand years on earth, "nothing more is meant than that, before the general judgment, the Jews shall be converted, genuine Christianity be diffused through all nations, and mankind enjoy that peace and happiness which the faith and precepts of the Gospel are calculated to confer on all by whom they are sincerely embraced." The state of the Christian Church will be, for a thousand years before the general judgment, so pure and so widely extended, that, when compared with the state of the world in the ages preceding, it may, in the language of Scripture, be called a resurrection from the dead. See two passages from St. Paul, in which a conversion from Paganism to Christianity, and a reformation of life, is called a "resurrection from the dead," Rom. vi, 13; Eph. v, 14.

THRESHING FLOORS, among the ancient Jews, were only, as they are to this day in the East, round level plots of ground in the open air, where the corn was trodden out by oxen. Thus Gideon's floor, Judges vi, 37, appears to have been in the open air; as was likewise that of Araunah the Jebusite; else it would not have been a proper place for erecting an altar and offering sacrifice. See FLOOR.

THRONE, Gen. xli, 40. This was a seat with arms and a back, and of so great height, as to render a *footstool* necessary, Psa. cx, 1. On this kings usually set to receive the homage of their subjects, or to give audience to ambassadors, where they appear with pomp and ceremony, and whence they dispense justice. The throne, the sceptre, the crown, are the ordinary symbols of royalty and regal authority.

THUMMIM, *truth.* See URIM.

THUNDER is a repercussion of the air violently separated by the lightning or electric spark: the loudest natural sound with which mankind are acquainted, and like many other surprising things, is expressed by an addition of the name of God; hence called "the voice of God;" "the *thunder* of his power," i. e., the whole compass of the Divine power, all the mighty deeds which can be predicated of God, Job xxvi, 14.

THY-A-TI'RA, a city of Lydia, in Asia Minor, and

the seat of one of the seven Churches in Asia. It was situated nearly midway between Per'ga-mos and Sardis, and is still a tolerable town, considering that it is in the hands of the Turks, and enjoys some trade, chiefly in cottons.

It is now called *Ak-hisar*, and contains a population of about 1,000 families, three or four hundred of which are composed of nominal Christians of the Greek and Armenian faith.

THYINE, (*Thine,*) *thyine wood*, Rev. xviii, 12, was an evergreen African tree, with aromatic wood, from which statues, according to Theophrastus, and costly vessels were made; but it is not agreed whether it was a species of cedar, savin, or lignum vitae, which latter constitutes the modern genus *thuja*, or *thyia*.

TIBERIAS, a city of Galilee, built by Herod Antipas, and named in honour of the Emperor Tiberius, now *Tabaria*. It is situated on the south-west shore of the Lake of Gennesareth, about an hour's distance from the place where the Jordan flows out, and about sixty miles from Acre, John vi, 23. The lake itself is hence sometimes called *the Sea of Tiberias*, John vi, 1. See GALILEE, *sea of*. The city was celebrated on account of the hot springs in its vicinity; and after the destruction of Jerusalem, it became a famous seat of Jewish schools and learning. It is now a small walled city, with only one gate of entrance, containing a great number of Christians.

TIBERIUS, the third Roman emperor, the son of Livia, and stepson of Augustus, who reigned A. D. 14–37. John the Baptist commenced preaching in the fourteenth year of his reign; and the crucifixion of Jesus took place three or four years later, Luke iii, 1.

TIMBREL, the same as the *tabrel*, which see.

TIME, opportunity or proper season for doing a thing; *a set time, certain season*, and that finite duration in opposition to eternity, Eccl. iii, 17. "To every thing there is a *season*," it endures only for a time, nothing is permanent. The word time is united with *chance*, Eccl. ix, 11, which signifies an event that falls upon any one without being expected or foreseen, translated in one place, *evil occurrent*, 1 Kings v, 4.

TIMOTHY, a young Christian of Derbe, the son of a Jewish mother and Greek father, selected by Paul as the chosen companion of his journeys and labours in preaching the Gospel, Acts xvi, 1, 3. He appears to have been with Paul at Rome, Heb. xiii, 23; but his later history is unknown.

The principal design of St. Paul's *First Epistle* to Timothy was to give him instructions concerning the management of the Church of Ephesus; and it was probably intended that it should be read publicly to the Ephesians, that they might know upon what authority Timothy acted.

That the *Second Epistle* to Timothy was written while St. Paul was under confinement at Rome, appears from the two following passages: "Be not thou therefore ashamed of the testimony of our Lord, nor of me his prisoner," 2 Tim. i, 8. "The Lord give mercy unto the house of On-e-siph'o-rus; for he oft refreshed me, and was not ashamed of my *chain*; but when he was at Rome, he sought me out very diligently, and found me," 2 Tim. i, 16, 17. The epistle itself will furnish us with several arguments to prove it could not have been written during St. Paul's first imprisonment; and, therefore, it was written during his second imprisonment, and probably in A. D. 65, not long before his death. It is by no means certain where Timothy was when this epistle was written to him. It seems most probable that he was somewhere in Asia Minor, since St. Paul desires him to bring the cloak with him which he had left at Troas, 2 Tim. iv, 13.

TIN, one of the six metals known to the ancients, Num. xxxi, 22, and also well known at the present day. Silver, of all the metals, suffers most from being mixed with tin, a very small quantity serving to make that metal as brittle as glass; and, what is worse, being with great difficulty separated from it again. "Hence we may see," says Parkhurst, "the propriety of Jehovah's denunciation by the prophet," Isa. i, 25, having at verse 22 compared the Jewish people to *silver*, he says at verse 25, "I will take away all thy *tin*," i. e., all the impure and spurious parts.

TIPHSAH, 1 Kings iv, 24. *Thapsacus*, a large and opulent city on the western bank of the Euphrates, situated at the usual point of passing that river.

TIRES. See ORNAMENTS.

TISHBITE, probably a native of *Tishbeh*, in the tribe of Naphtali, lying north or north-west of the Sea of Galilee, 1 Kings xvii, 1.

TITHE, *a tenth part*, spoken of the tithes which were received by the Levitical priesthood, and which, by the Jewish law, were to be paid both from the produce of the earth and from the increase of the flocks, Heb. vii, 8, 9.

We have nothing more ancient concerning tithes than what we find in Gen xiv, 20, that Abraham gave tithes to Melchisedec, king of Salem, of all the booty he had taken from the enemy. Jacob imitated this piety of his grandfather, when he vowed to the Lord the tithe of all the substance he might acquire in Meso-po-ta'mi-a; Gen. xxviii,

22. The Pharisees, in the time of Jesus Christ, to distinguish themselves by a more scrupulous observance of the law, did not content themselves with paying the tithe of the grain and fruits growing in the fields, but they also paid the tithe of the pulse and herbs growing in their gardens, which was more than the law required of them.

TITTLE. See JOT.

TITUS. It is remarkable that Titus is not mentioned in the Acts of the Apostles. The few particulars which are known of him are collected from the epistles of St. Paul. We learn from them that he was a Greek, Gal. ii, 3; but it is not recorded to what city or country he belonged. From St. Paul's calling him "his own son according to the common faith," Titus i, 4, it is concluded that he was converted by him; but we have no account of the time or place of his conversion. He is first mentioned as going from Antioch to the council at Jerusalem, A. D. 49, Gal. ii, 1, &c.; and upon that occasion St. Paul says that he would not allow him to be circumcised, because he was born of Gentile parents. During St. Paul's second imprisonment at Rome, Titus went into Dalmatia, 2 Tim. iv, 10; and after the apostle's death, he is said to have returned into Crete, and to have died there in the ninety-second year of his age; he is often called bishop of Crete by ec-clesiastical writers. St. Paul always speaks of Titus in terms of high regard, and intrusted him, as we have seen, with commissions of great importance. It is by no means certain from what place St. Paul wrote to Titus. It is concluded that the epistle was written after his first imprisonment at Rome, and probably in A. D. 64. The principal design of it was to give instructions to Titus concerning the management of the Churches in the different cities of the Island of Crete; and it was probably intended to be read publicly to the Cretans, that they might know upon what authority Titus acted.

TOB, a country of Palestine, lying beyond Jordan, in the northern part of the portion of Manasseh, Judg. xi, 3.

TO-BI'AH, an Ammonite, an enemy to the Jews. He was one of those who strenuously opposed the rebuilding of the temple, after the return from the captivity of Babylon, Neh. ii, 10; iv, 3. This Tobiah is called "the servant," or "slave," in some parts of Nehemiah; probably because he was of a servile condition. However, he was of great consideration in the land of the Samaritans, of which he was governor with Sanballat.

TOGARMAH, a northern region and people sprung from Gomer, i. e., the Cimmerians, and abounding in horses and mules. Most probably *Armenia*, which was *noted for* its horses, or at least a part of it. Such, too, is the tradition or opinion of the Armenians themselves, who claim *Torgom*, the son of Gomer, as the founder of their nation, and call themselves *the house of Torgom*, 1 Chron. i, 6.

TONGUE. This word is taken in three different senses. 1. For the organ of speech, James iii, 5. 2. For the language that is spoken in any country, Deut. xxviii, 49. 3. For good or bad discourses, Prov. xii, 18; xvii, 20.

To gnaw the tongue, Rev. xvi, 10, is a token of fury, despair, and torment.

To speak with *other* or *new tongues*, referred to Mark xvi, 17; and Acts ii, 4. The sense would seem to be, *to speak in other living languages*, which enabled the apostle immediately to preach the Gospel to other nations, without spending time in learning their language. Wherefore the apostle says, "Tongues are for a *sign* to them that believe not," 1 Cor. xiv, 22, i. e., to such strangers as understood the language in which they were addressed.

By the *tongues of angels*, 2 Cor. xiii, 1, the apostle meant the methods, whatever they are, by which angels communicate their thoughts to each other, and which must be a much more excellent language than any that is spoken by men.

Tongue, by a figure, is put for any thing resembling *a tongue* in shape, e. g., Acts ii,

3, *tongues as of fire*. The origin lies in the notion of licking, lapping, gliding over, and is applied especially to *flame*, which seems like a tongue to lick, i. e., to be lambent; "divide their *tongues*," i. e., cause dissension among them, Psa. lv, 10.

TOPAZ, Rev. xxi, 20, a transparent gem of a golden or orange colour; not the green topaz of Pliny, which seems to have been the modern chrysolite. See PRECIOUS STONES.

TOPHET, Jer. vii, 31. As to the etymology of the name, it is rendered "place to be spit upon," i. e., to be abhorred; but it seems to have borne this name with all, even among the idolaters themselves. Better, therefore, to regard *Tophet* as signifying *a place of burning*, especially dead bodies. By an easy metaphor, the Jews transferred the name to the place of punishment in the other world, the abode of demons and the souls of wicked men. See HINNOM.

TORMENTOR, *jailer*, a prison keeper, one who applies the torture. The word properly signifies *examiner*, one who has it in charge to examine by torture. Hence it came to signify *jailer*; for on such, in those days, was this charge devolved, Matt. xxviii, 34.

TORTURED, Heb. xi, 35. The word signifies scourged upon the *tympanum, drummed* to death, alluding to the *tym-*

32

panum or *drum*, an instrument of torture, a wooden frame; so called, probably, as resembling a drum in form, on which criminals were bound to be beaten to death.

TOWER, a building either round or square, raised to a considerable elevation, and consisting of several stories; intended properly for defence, as in the wall of a city, Luke xiii, 4.

The tower of Siloam is the tower in the wall of the city of Jerusalem, near Siloam. Hence used, metaphorically, of proud and powerful men, Isa. xxx, 25.

TOWER *of the flock*, a village near Bethlehem; hence put for the city Bethlehem itself, and figurative, for the royal line of David, Mich. iv, 8; same as the tower of *Edar*, Gen. xxxv, 21.

The word also means a *watch tower*, in which weapons of war are suspended, Song iv, 4.

Also a *lofty place*, whence one can see far and wide around, whether furnished with a watch tower or not, 2 Chron. xx, 24.

The word is used for the small *towers* or spires which are occupied by keepers of vineyards to defend them from thieves and from animals, such as dogs and foxes, Isa. v, 2; Song i, 6; ii, 15.

TOWER OF BABEL.   See BABEL.

TOWN CLERK, a public officer in the cities of Asia Minor, whose duty it seems to have been to preside in the senate, to enrol and have charge of the laws and decrees, and to read what was to be made known to the people, Acts xix, 35.

TRACH-O-NI'TIS, Luke iii, 1. This province was bounded on the north by the country of Damascus, on the east by the Arabian Desert, on the south by It-ure'a, and on the west by Bat-a-ne'a. It belonged rather to Arabia than Palestine; was a rocky province, and served as a shelter for thieves and depredators.

TRADITION, that which is handed down from age to age by oral communication. The Jews observed a multitude of such unwritten precepts which originated with their ancestors; and some of them, as they maintained, with Moses himself. They not only placed these traditions on an equality with the laws which were acknowledged to be Divine, but even esteemed them of still higher importance, Matt. xv, 2, 3, 6.

These traditions were collected and gathered into one body by Rabbi Judah Hakkodesh, about A. D. 190 or 220, lest they should be lost and forgotten, because of the dispersion of the Jews. This work is called the *Mishna*, i. e., the second law. About a century later, Rabbi Jochanan, who presided in the school of Palestine eighty years, wrote illustrations of the Mishna, and things supplementary to it, in the nature of commentary, which is called the *Gemara*, which signifies *completion*; and these two together, i. e., the *Mishna* and the *Gemara* constitute what is called the *Talmud*, a Hebrew word signifying *teaching*, or *traditional doctrine*.

There is another *Talmud* having the same *Mishna*, but a gemara composed by another hand, A. D. 400. This is called the *Talmud* of Babylon, because it was compiled in that city, and was chiefly prevalent among the Jews beyond the Euphrates. This work abounds with a multitude of fables and ridiculous stories.

In the writings of the apostles, *traditions* are those doctrines and precepts which persons divinely inspired taught as the doctrines and precepts of God, whether they taught them by word of mouth or by writing, 2 Thess. iii, 6; and no doctrines merit the name of *traditions*, in the Scripture sense of the word, but such as were taught by the apostles of Christ, or by other spiritual men who received them by immediate revelation from him, and hold a place in their writings. It would be hazardous to trust in any other, and might be considered as adding to the word of God. See Rev. xxii, 18.

TRANCE, a state in which the soul is unconscious of present objects, being wrapt into visions of distant or future things, Acts x, 10.

TRANSFIGURE signifies to change one's form or appearance. The word refers to that change which our Lord produced in his own body, when his face shone as the sun, and his garments became white as the light. The light with which he was invested appears to have penetrated his garments themselves, and to have arrayed his whole form with intense and dazzling splendour, Matt. xvii, 2-7.

This memorable transaction was designed to teach,—

That Jesus was invested with the *authority* which now passed away from Moses and the prophets. When the disciples were commanded by the voice from the cloud to *hear* HIM, it was thus solemnly enjoined upon them to take him for their SUPREME TEACHER; a plain allusion to the prophecy of Moses, Deut. xviii, 15. He had the supreme power to establish, explain, enlarge, and even to abrogate what was enjoined in the law and enforced by the prophets.

Rightly understood, therefore, the transaction must be considered as the solemn inauguration of our Lord in the presence of his three chosen disciples into the office of SUPREME LAWGIVER in the Church of God.

Subordinate to this general design, however, the transfiguration served other important purposes. It tended to support the faith of the disciples, which was to be

eply tried by his approach-
ig humiliation.

A sensible demonstration
was also given in the real
appearance of the two men
who had for so many ages
ceased to be inhabitants of
this world, of the immortality
of the soul. The presence
of Moses proved also, that
between death and the resurrection from the dead, the
disembodied spirit exists in
a state of consciousness and
vigour; and, as to the righteous, in a state of glory and
felicity. It furnished a proof
that the bodies of good men
shall be so *refined* and *changed,*
as, like Elias, to live in a state
of immortality.

TRANSGRESSION.
This word, by usage, is nearly or quite synonymous with
disobedience, Heb. ii, 3. It
literally means *going beyond,*
passing by any thing, and is
applied to a moral action.
Transgression and disobe-
dience, taken together, mean
every kind of offence against
the law.

TREASURE, any thing
laid up in store, or collected
together, as a treasure of corn,
of wine, of oil, of honey, Jer.
xli, 8; treasures of gold, silver, brass, Dan. xi, 43. Snow,
winds, hail, rain, waters, are
in the treasuries of God, Psa.
cxxxv, 7. "The wise men
opened their *treasures,*" Matt.
ii, 11; that is, their packets
or bundles, to offer presents
to our Saviour.

TREE. The trees in the
climate of Palestine put forth
their foliage in the month of
February; the amygdalus, the
earliest tree of the forest,
comprehending the *almond,*
the *peach,* and the *nectarine,*
is in bloom about the middle
of February. In Europe, the
almond tree is cultivated for
the sake of its beautiful rose-
coloured flowers, (not white;)
but in the countries that have
a long and hot summer, it
is for the *fruit* that it is esteemed.

The Hebrew word for al-
mond tree signifies *the waker,*
so called as being the earliest
of all trees to awake from
the sleep of winter, Jer. i, 11.
There is also here an allusion to the haste and ardour
thus implied; compare verse
12.

"The almond tree shall
flourish." Gesenius renders
the sentence: the almond is
spurned, rejected, i. e., by the
old and toothless man, although in itself a delicate and
delicious fruit, Eccl. xii, 5.
Others, less well, *the almond
tree shall flourish,* which they
refer to white hairs. See
ALMOND.

"The *green* and *dry tree,*"
may be regarded as emble-
matic of the righteous and the
wicked, compare Psalm i, 3,
because *a green tree* is one
which is vigorous and flourishing; and is, therefore, an
emblem of prosperity. "I
see men as *trees,*" Mark viii,
24, not distinctly, larger than
natural.

Tree of life, i. e., of long
life, of immortality, Gen. ii, 9.

The tree of which he that eateth shall live, and not die ; compare Gen. iii, 22.

"The *tree* of the knowledge of good and evil," i. e., knowledge of the difference or distinction between happiness and misery ; the eating of the fruit which was prohibited, occasioned man to know, by unhappy experience, the difference between a state of happiness and one of misery, Gen. ii, 17.

TRESPASS is a sin committed unintentionally, arising from ignorance or inadvertence, Matt. vi, 14. The word is used to denote the first transgression of Adam and Eve, Rom. v, 17. But *sins* signify those acts of disobedience which are committed deliberately and habitually, Eph. ii, 1.

TRIBE, a clan or class of people, spoken of the descendants of each of the sons of Jacob as a subdivision of the nation, Exod. xxviii, 21.

TRIBUTE, properly what is paid for public *ends*, for the maintenance and expenses of the state, rendered *custom*. There was another tax paid by each person whose name was taken in the census, Matt. xvii, 25.

The Hebrews acknowledged God alone for their supreme sovereign; whence Josephus calls their government a theocracy, or Divine government. They acknowledged the sovereign dominion of God by a *tribute*, or capitation tax, of half a shekel a head, which every Israelite paid yearly, Exod. xxx, 13.

TROAS, a city of Phryg'ia Minor, in Mysia, situated on the coast at some distance southward from the site of Troy, now *Eski-Stamboul*, Acts xvi, 8.

The name *Troas*, or the *Troad*, strictly belonged to the whole district around Troy.

TROGYLLIUM, a town and promontory on the western coast of Asia Minor, opposite Samos, at the foot of Mount Mycale, Acts xx, 15.

TROPH'I-MUS, a disciple of St. Paul, and an Ephesian by birth, Acts xxi, 29.

TROW, to believe ; to trust ; to think or suppose, Luke xvii, 9.

TRUMPET. This was a very ancient instrument. It was made of the horns of oxen. In progress of time rams' horns were employed for the same purpose. The Lord commanded Moses to make trumpets of beaten silver, Numb. x, 2, 3. These instruments were straight, eighteen inches in length, and at the larger extremity shaped so as to resemble the mouth of a small bell. These were sounded on different occasions. See Lev. xxv, 9, 10.

We are informed that at the giving of the law from Sinai, there was "the sound of a *trumpet*," Exod. xix, 19 ; probably the meaning is, a *voice like that of a trumpet*, i. e., very loud. In Deut. v,

23, it is called *a great voice;* in Deut. iv, 12, it is called *the voice of words,* i. e., articulate sounds; and in Deut. iv, 33, *the voice of God.* From comparing all these passages together, it seems evident that the meaning is, "an articulate voice loud like that of a *trumpet.*"

In like manner, at the descent of Christ from heaven, a great voice, called *the trump of God,* 1 Thess. iv, 16, will be made by the attending angels, as the signal for the righteous to come forth from their graves. And this noise being made at Christ's command, it is called by himself *his voice,* John v, 25. After the righteous are raised, the *trump* shall sound a second time; on which account it is called *the last trumpet.* And while it sounds, the righteous who are alive on the earth shall be changed.

TRUTH. 1. Conformity to the nature and reality of things, as evinced in the relation of facts, Mark v, 33, or that which is *true* in itself, purity from all error or falsehood. "I speak the words of *truth,*" Acts xxvi, 25.

2. The word signifies *the love of the truth,* as shown both in words and conduct, i. e., *veracity.* It is said of the father of lies, "there is no *truth* in him," i. e., he is a liar, and loves not the truth, John viii, 44. "In spirit and in *truth;*" with sincerity of heart, not with external rites, John iv, 23, 24.

3. But the word *truth* more especially means *Divine truth;* the faith and practice of the true religion; and called *truth,* either as being *true* in itself, and derived from the *true* God; or, as declaring the existence and will of the one true God, in opposition to the worship of false gods; hence *Divine truth, Gospel truth,* as opposed to heathen and Jewish fables, John i, 14, 17. Jesus is called *the truth,* i. e., the teacher of Divine truth, John xiv, 6. The Spirit of truth is the Spirit who declares or reveals Divine truth, 1 John iv, 6.

4. Finally, truth is *conduct* conformed to the truth; integrity, probity; a life conformed to the precepts of religion, John iii, 21.

TUBAL, Ezek. xxvii, 13, the *Tibareni* of the Greeks, a people dwelling near the Black Sea, on the west of the *Moschi.* See MESHECH.

TU'BAL-CAIN, son of La'mech the bigamist and of Zillah, Genesis ix, 29. The Scriptures tell us that he was the inventor of the art of forging and managing iron, and of making all kinds of iron work. There is great reason to believe that he was the Vulcan of the heathens.

TURTLE, a species of dove. This clean bird the Jews might offer in sacrifice. It was appointed in favour of the poor who could not afford a more substantial one, Lev. xii, 8; Luke ii, 24.

Jeremiah speaks of the turtle as a bird of passage, Jer. viii, 7, in which it differs from some of the species. And Solomon mentions the return of this bird as one of the indications of spring. "The voice of the *turtle* is heard in the land," Song ii, 12.

Turtle is used as a name of endearment for one beloved, Psa. lxxiv, 19. *Thy turtle dove*, i. e., the people dear to thee, and now afflicted and affrighted. See DOVE.

TUTOR, Gal. iv, 2; the same as SCHOOLMASTER, which see.

TYCHICUS, (*Tik'-e-kus*,) a disciple of St. Paul, whom the apostle often employed to carry his letters to the several Churches. He was of the province of Asia, and accompanied St. Paul when he made his journey from Corinth to Jerusalem, Acts xx, 4.

TY-RAN'NUS, Acts xix, 9. The generality conclude, that Tyrannus was a converted Gentile, a friend of St. Paul, to whom he withdrew.

TYRE, or TYRUS, Ezek. xxvi, 2, (*rock.*) The celebrated city of Phenicia, younger than Sidon, and not mentioned by Moses or Homer. Tyre was situated on the coast of the Mediterranean, about ninety miles north-west from Jerusalem, and eighteen miles south-west of Sidon. It was within the limits assigned to the tribe of Asher; but was never subdued by the Israelites, Josh. xix, 29. On the contrary, un-

der the reigns of David and Solomon, there was a close alliance of aid and commerce between the two nations, 2 Sam. v, 11; 2 Chron. ii, 3.

The ancient city lay on the continent, and the modern part upon an island opposite. It was long besieged by Salmanassar, and afterward for thirteen years by Nebuchadnezzar. (See Ezekiel, chapters xxvi, xxvii xxviii.) Whether it was actually captured by the latter, is matter of question among critics, since neither Josephus nor any Greek or Phenician writer asserts it; but see Ezek. xxvi, 7, and on. At any rate, Tyre appears to have come under the dominion of the Babylonians, and afterward under that of the Persians, in whose time the Tyrians furnished cedar for the second temple, Ezra iii, 7. Tyre was taken by Alexander the Great, after a celebrated siege, 332 years B. C. The ancient part of the city lying on the continent was destroyed in this siege, and *never again rebuilt.*

Under the Seleucidæ and the Romans, Tyre still retained its importance as a commercial city.

Strabo, a famous geographer in the time of Christ, describes it as situated wholly upon an island, and as flourishing in trade and commerce. In the fourth century, according to Jerome, it was still a place of great importance; and such it continued to be in the time of the crusades. The prophets of the Old Testament describe Tyre as full of wealth, pride, luxury, and vice; and denounce judgments against her for her idolatry and wickedness.

The city is now called *Sour*, (*Sur*,) containing about 4000 inhabitants, and has some commercial prosperity.

Pococke observes, " that there are no signs of the ancient city; and as it is a sandy shore, the face of every thing is altered, and the great aqueduct is in many parts almost buried in the sand."

ULAI, the river which is now called *Karah;* it flows south by Susa, in Persia, and falls into the Tigris, near its confluence with the Euphrates, Dan. viii, 2.

UNCLEAN SPIRITS, Luke viii, 29, *devils*, evil spirits subject to Satan. These were supposed, by popular belief, to wander in deserts and desolate places; see Matt. xii, 43, and also to dwell in the atmosphere; see Eph. ii, 2. They were thought to have the power of working miracles, but not for good; see Rev. xvi, 14; compare John x, 21; to be hostile to mankind, John viii, 44; to utter the heathen oracles, Acts xvi, 16, 17; and to lurk in the idols of the heathen, which are hence called *devils*, 1 Cor. x, 20; Rev. ix, 20; Deut. xxxii, 17.

They are spoken of by St. Paul and other inspired writers, as the authors of evil to mankind, both moral, (1 Tim. iv, 1, James ii, 19,) and also physical, viz., by entering into a person, thus rendering him a demoniac, and afflicting him with various diseases, such as melancholy, madness, epilepsy, &c. It is much disputed whether these writers believed the actual presence of evil spirits in the persons affected. It is supposed by some, not many, that they spoke of persons *possessed of devils*, in compliance with popular usage and belief; just as we now call a man a *lunatic*, without assenting to the old opinion of the influence of the moon. But a serious difficulty in the way of this supposition is, that the demoniacs everywhere at once address Jesus as the Messiah, e. g., Matt. viii, 29; Mark i, 24. Farther, Christ spake to them on various occasions, as distinct from the persons possessed by them, commanding them, and asking them questions, and receiving answers from them, or not suffering them to speak. They asked and obtained permission to enter the herd of swine, and precipitated them into the sea, Matt. viii, 31, 32. These circumstances can *never* be accounted for by any distemper whatever.

UNCTION, *an anointing with oil*, figuratively spoken of Christians, who are anointed with the gifts and graces of the Holy Spirit imparted to them, 1 John ii, 20.

UNDERGIRDING, Acts xxvii, 17, signifies girding a cable around the bottom and whole body of a ship, in order to strengthen it against the waves. Lord Anson mentions a Spanish man-of-war that was saved by throwing overboard one tier of guns, and taking six turns of a cable around the ship, by which the opening of the seams was prevented.

UNICORN, Job xxxix, 9, a wild and ferocious animal; it is represented as horned, and destroying men with his horns, Psa. xxii, 21; compare Deut. xxxiii, 17. This animal was frequent and well known in Palestine and the adjacent regions, being everywhere mentioned with other animals common to the country. "The species of animal here meant," says Gesenius, "is somewhat doubtful; but I do not hesitate to understand, with Schultens and De Wette, the *bos bubalus*, or *buffalo*," which differs from the bison, or American buffalo, chiefly in the shape of the horns and the absence of the dewlap. This animal is indigenous, originally, in the hotter parts of Asia and Africa, and also in Persia and Egypt. As, therefore, it existed in the countries all around Palestine, there is every reason to suppose that it was also found in that country, or at least in the regions east of the Jordan, and south of the Dead Sea, as Bashan and Idumea. This animal bears a similar relation to the ox, as the wild ass does to the domestic one. The real *unicorn*, i. e., an animal with *one horn*, described by Pliny, for a long time natural historians, especially since Buffon, have held to be fabulous; but a few years since one was said to have been discovered in the deserts of Thibet. But this cannot be the animal referred to in the Bible; since the unicorn, as described, resembles the horse much more than it does the ox; and is, in any case, an extremely rare animal. Whereas the animal in question was well known in the countries where the scenes of the Bible are laid.

UNKNOWN GOD. Eichhorn conjectures that there were standing at Athens various very ancient altars, which originally had no inscription, and which were afterward not destroyed, for fear of provoking the anger of the god to whom each had been dedicated, although it was no longer known who this god was. He supposes that the inscription upon them would properly signify, to "an *unknown* god."

So much at least is certain, that such an altar existed at Athens, both from Paul's assertion and the testimony of Greek writers.

But the attempt to ascertain definitely whom the Athenians worshipped under this appellation, must ever remain fruitless for want of sufficient data. The inscription afforded to Paul a happy occasion of proclaiming the Gospel; and those who embraced it, found indeed that the Being whom they had thus "ignorantly worshipped," was the one only living and true God.

UNTIMELY FIG, Rev. vi, 13, the winter fig, i. e., such as grow under the leaves and do not ripen at the proper season, but hang upon the trees during winter, Song ii, 13.

UPHARSIN. See MENE.

UPPER ROOM, Acts i, 13; the upper part of the house; a sort of guest chamber not in common use, where the Hebrews received company and held feasts, and where at other times they retired for prayer and meditation. The principal rooms anciently in Judea were those *above*, as they are to this day at Aleppo; the ground floor being chiefly made use of for their horses and servants.

UR, a city of Mesopotamia, the birthplace of Abraham, Gen. xv, 7. Traces of it, most probably, remain in the Persian fortress *Ur*, between Nesibis and the Tigris.

URIM and THUMMIM, *light and truth*, i. e., revelation and truth. The high priests of the Jews, we are told, consulted God in the most important affairs of their commonwealth, and received answers by the Urim and Thummim. What these were is disputed. It seems highly probable that they were no other than the *twelve precious stones* inserted into the high priest's breastplate, on which were engraven the names of the twelve tribes of Israel: see Exod. xxviii; compare verse 29 with 30.

1. He that compares these two verses attentively together, must see that the Urim and Thummim are the substance or matter upon which the names were engraven.

2. In the description of the high priest's breastplate, given Exod. xxxix, 8, &c., the Urim and Thummim are not mentioned, but the rows of stones are, and *vice versa*. In the description, Lev. viii, 8, the Urim and Thummim are mentioned by name, and the stones *not;* therefore, it is probable that the Urim and Thummim, and the precious stones, are only different names for the same things.

3. If the Urim and Thummim be not the same with the precious stones, then Moses, who hath so particularly described the most minute things relating to the high priest's dress, hath given us no description at all of this most splendid part of it, which seems highly improbable.

It seems probable, also, that the answer was given in an audible voice from the shekinah, or that brightness which always rested between the cherubims over the mercy seat; see 1 Samuel xxiii, 9–12.

USURY, in present usage, signifies *illegal interest*; but,

in the Bible, it means simply *interest*; the premium paid or stipulated to be paid for the use of money, Psa. xv, 5. As the law of nature does not forbid the receipt of moderate interest in the shape of rent, for the use of lands or houses, so neither does it prohibit it for the loan of money. When one man trades with the capital of another, and obtains a profit from it, he is bound in justice to return a part of it to his benefactor, who, in the hands of God, has been a second cause of "giving him power to get wealth." As the Jews had very little concern in trade, and so only borrowed in case of necessity; and as their system went to secure every man's paternal inheritance to his own family, they were allowed to lend money upon usury to strangers, Deut. xxiii, 20; but were prohibited to take usury from their brethren of Israel, at least if they were poor, Lev. xxv, 35–37.

UZ, the proper name of a region and tribe in the northern part of the Arabian Desert, between Palestine, Idumea, and the Euphrates, Job i, 1; compare verse 3; Jer. xxv, 20; see also Lam. iv, 21, where it is to be understood of Idumeans dwelling in Uz, whose origin is uncertain.

VAIL, or VEIL, *a curtain,* especially of the tabernacle and temple, of which there were two, viz., one before the external entrance, Exod. xxvi, 36, and the other before the holy of holies, separating it from the outer sanctuary, Exod. xxvi, 31, 32. Hence the veil of the temple may be either the outer or inner veil, Matt. xxvii, 51. Figuratively, *that within the veil,* Heb. vi, 19, is the inner sanctuary, holy of holies in the heavenly temple; compare verse 20; and x, 19.

This veil is emblematic of the body and death of Jesus; see Heb. x, 20.

Women were wont to cover their faces with veils in token of modesty, of reverence, and subjection to their husbands, Gen. xxiv, 65; 1 Cor. xi, 3, &c. In modern times, the women of Syria never appear in the streets without their veils. "The woman ought to have *power* on her head," probably "the emblem of power," i. e., a *veil* or *covering,* as an emblem of subjection to the power of a husband, a token of modest adherence to duties and usages established by law or custom; "because of the angels," (*messengers,*) lest *spies* or evil-minded persons should take advantage of any impropriety in the meetings of the Christians, 1 Cor. xi, 10.

VERMILLION, a bright, beautiful red colour, formed of the bisulphuret of mercury, Jer. xxii, 14. Perhaps this colour anciently was formed of *red ochre,* a species of clay deeply coloured by the oxyde of iron.

VESSEL is used for a boat or skiff, Isa. xviii, 2.

Also, figuratively, for the human body, as formed of clay, and therefore frail and feeble, and liable to be broken, 2 Cor. iv, 7. The body was called by the Greeks and Romans *a vessel*, because it contains the soul, and is its instrument, 1 Thess. iv, 4.

St. Peter calls the wife *the weaker vessel*, because she is weaker in body, and subject to more natural infirmities than men, 1 Pet. iii, 7.

Vessels of wrath, Rom. ix, 22, means vessels in respect to which wrath should be displayed, i. e., wicked men who deserve to be punished. The reason why the writer here makes use of *vessels*, may be found in the verses immediately preceding, where he has spoken of the *vessels* of the potter.

VIAL, Rev. xvi, 1, in the Bible, is not a vessel with a narrow mouth, such as we commonly call *a vial*, but one with a wide mouth, a bowl, which has more breadth than depth, similar to the censer, which has been called *fire-pan*, because it contained fire; and also incense-pan, because incense was put upon the fire within it. Hence we read that vials or bowls full of the wrath of God are poured out, for if they contained *fire*, that is a fit emblem of wrath; and burning embers may be described as *poured out* from a censer with great propriety.

VINE, or GRAPE VINE, a well-known plant that flou-

rishes most in warm countries, where its cultivation forms a part of husbandry.

Vines frequently grew to a great height, being supported by trees and props; hence we read of "sitting under one's own vine and fig tree," i. e., enjoying a prosperous and happy life, Micah iv, 4.

The vine of the earth, Rev. xiv, 18, 19, signifies the enemies of the Messiah, who are in a prosperous state, and who are to be cut off, as grapes are gathered and cast into the wine-press; compare Isa. lxiii, 2, 3; Lam. i, 15.

In John xv, 1, our Lord declares himself to be the "*true* vine," perhaps in opposition to the *carved* vines which were used, it is said, to adorn the temple, whose branches, tendrils, and leaves were of the finest gold, and whose stalks of the bunches were of the length of the human form.

The vintage in Syria commences about the middle of September, and continues till the middle of November. But grapes in Palestine, we are informed, were ripe sometimes even in June and July; then the first vintage was in August, referred to in Num. xiii, 20.

The treading of the wine-press was laborious, and not very favourable to cleanliness; the garments of the persons thus employed were stained with the red juice, and yet the employment was a joyful one. It was perform ed with singing, accompanied with musical instruments and shouting, Jer. xxv, 30 ; xlviii, 33.

A noble vine is put as an emblem of men of noble and generous dispositions, Jer. ii, 21 ; the same as the *choicest vine* ; Isa. v, 2. On the contrary, a strange vine, a vine of Sodom, stands for men of ignoble and degenerate characters, Deut. xxxii, 32.

VINEGAR is made in France, and was probably made in Palestine, by exposing weak wines to the air during warm weather, Prov. x, 26. A cheap poor wine, which, mixed with water, constituted a common drink among the Romans, especially for the poorer classes and soldiers, was called *vinegar*, Ruth ii, 14 ; Matt. xxvii, 48.

Robinson says sour wine, or vinegar mingled with myrrh or bitter herbs, was given to persons about to be executed in order to stupify them, Prov. xxxi, 6.

VINTAGE. See VINE.

VIOL, an instrument of music, of the same form as the violin, but larger. The musical instrument intended by the Hebrew word, is supposed to be a species of harp or lyre. Josephus describes this instrument as having *twelve strings*, and as played with the fingers, and not with a key. It is supposed that David refers to it, and that it sometimes had *ten* and sometimes *twelve* strings. See Psa. xxxiii, 2 ; cxliv, 9. It resembled in form a right-angled triangle, or the Greek delta inverted ▽ : chanting to sound of it, was to make like sounds with the voice, modulating the tones so as to correspond with the sounds of the instrument, Amos vi, 5.

VIPER, a species of serpent unknown in this country, so called from bringing forth its young alive ; but in this respect it does not differ from other venomous serpents. The viper is remarkable for its quick and penetrating poison, which, in hot countries, is one of the most dangerous poisons in the animal kingdom. So remarkable has the viper been for its venom, that the remotest antiquity made it an emblem of what is destructive. They were very commonly thought to be sent as executioners of Divine vengeance upon mankind, for enormous crimes which had escaped the course of justice. An instance of such an opinion as this we have in the history of St. Paul, Acts xxxviii, 3, 4.

The *cerastes*, or horned viper, is among the most deadly of the serpent tribe, and distinguished by two small horns, one over each eye. It is numerous in Egypt and Syria, so that it could not escape the notice and allusions of the sacred writers. It is reported of them that they hide themselves in holes adjacent to the highways, and in the ruts of wheels, in order more suddenly to spring upon passengers. The *cerastes* is supposed to be referred to Gen. xlix, 17. By the *cockatrice*, Michaëlis understands the horned *viper* or *cerastes*, Isa. lix, 5.

VIRGIN, one who has not known a man, Matt. i, 23. "Behold, a *virgin* shall bring forth a son," quoted from Isa. vii, 14, apparently referring, however, to the *youthful spouse* of the prophet; compare Joel i, 8. The sense of Matthew would be: Thus was fulfilled, in a strict and literal sense, that which the prophet spoke in a wider sense and on a different occasion.

In 1 Cor. vii, 36, 37, *his virgin* signifies his virgin daughter, marriageable, but unmarried.

Virgin also signifies *chaste, pure*, Rev. xiv, 4.

VIRTUE, good quality, excellence of any kind, whether of the earth or moral excellence.

Also, goodness of action, virtuous deeds, 2 Pet. i, 5.

VISION, in Scripture, generally signifies a *supernatural appearance*, either by dream or in reality, by which God made known his will and pleasure, Acts ix, 10, 13; xvi, 9; xxvi, 13.

VISION, a revelation from God, Divine communication, 1 Sam. iii, 1.

"Valley of *vision*," Isa. xxii, 5, i. e., Jerusalem as the seat and home of the Divine reve-

lations; compare Isa. ii, 3. The city was situated on the side of a valley.

TO VISIT. This word is often spoken of God, who is said to visit men, to inquire, as it were, into their situation, and afford them relief or aid, Acts xv, 14.

And sometimes he visits men in order to punish them, Psa. lxxxix, 32. Men should visit the sick or poor to assist or benefit them, Matt. xxv, 36.

VOCATION, Eph. iv, 1, in the New Testament, signifies *invitation*, especially to the kingdom of God and its privileges; that is, that Divine call by which Christians are introduced into the privileges of the Gospel. See CALLING.

VOLUME. See BOOK.

VOW. This word means a solemn religious promise, or covenant, by which one binds himself to do or abstain from certain things, depending on God for power to accomplish it. Hence vows were made with prayer, and paid with thanksgiving; see Num. vi, 2-21.

In case of indigent Nazarites, it was customary among the Jews for others to be at the expense of the sacrifice by which their vow was terminated, who thus became partners in their vow; see Acts xxi, 23, 24.

VULTURE, a species of eagle that lives on carrion; it seldom attacks living animals when it can find a supply from those that are dead. It is

distinguished by the nakedness of the head and neck,
which are without feathers.
Hence in all those places
where the eagle is said to be
bald, Micah i, 16; and also
represented as feeding on
dead bodies, some species of
vulture is probably intended,
Matt. xxiv, 28. In Job xxviii,
7, where this bird is represented as *keen-sighted*, Gesenius supposes the Hebrew
word to be a general term for
the *falcon* or hawk species.

WAGON. The Hebrew
word translated wagon, Gen.
xlv, 27, is derived from a root
signifying *to roll*, and means
simply *a vehicle on wheels*,
whether chariot or wagon,
for the transportation of goods
or persons; and may, for
aught we know, have included as many forms and kinds
as our word *car* or *carriage*.

WALK signifies *to live*, to
follow a way of life and conduct. Hence "to *walk* in the
counsel of the ungodly" is to
live and act as they do, Psa.
i, 1.
To walk in the ways of
the Lord is to follow his precepts, Deut. xix, 9.
"The wicked *walketh* with
a froward mouth," Prov. vi,
12, i. e., his life is a series
of falsehoods. "To *walk* in
darkness," 1 John i, 6, 7, is
to be misled by error. "In
the light," to be well informed. "By faith" is to expect
things promised or threatened, and to maintain a conduct

accordingly. To walk after
the flesh is *to* gratify fleshly
appetites. To walk after the
Spirit is to pursue spiritual
objects and cultivate spiritual
affections, to be spiritually
minded.
WALL. See PARTITION.
WAR, WARFARE, the at-
tempt to decide a contest or
difference between princes,
states, or large bodies of people, by resorting to extensive
acts of violence, or, as the
phrase is, by an appeal to
arms. The Hebrews were
formerly a very warlike nation. The books that inform
us of their wars display neither ignorance nor flattery;
but are writings inspired by
the Spirit of truth and wisdom. Their warriors were
none of those fabulous heroes or professed conquerors,
whose business it was to
ravage cities and provinces,
and to reduce foreign nations
under their dominion, merely
for the sake of governing, or
purchasing a name for themselves. They were common-
ly wise and valiant generals,
raised up by God "to fight
the battles of the Lord," and
to exterminate his enemies.
Such were Joshua, Caleb,
Gideon, Jephthah, Samson,
David, Josiah, and the Maccabees, whose names alone
are their own sufficient enco-
miums. Their wars were not
undertaken upon slight occasions, or performed with a
handful of people. Under Joshua the affair was of no less
importance than to make him-

self master of a vast country which God had given up to him; and to root out several powerful nations that God had devoted to an anathema; and to vindicate an offended Deity, and human nature which had been debased by a wicked and corrupt people, who had filled up the measure of their iniquities.

We may distinguish two kinds of wars among the Hebrews: some were of obligation, as being expressly commanded by the Lord; but others were free and voluntary.

Military fortifications were at first nothing more than a trench or ditch, dug around a few cottages on a hill or mountain, together with the mound, which was formed by the sand dug out of it; except, perhaps, there might have sometimes been an elevated scaffolding for the purpose of throwing stones with the greater effect against the enemy. In the age of Moses and Joshua, the walls which surrounded cities were elevated to no inconsiderable height, and were furnished with towers. The art of fortification was encouraged and patronized by the Hebrew kings, and Jerusalem was always well defended, especially Mount Zion. In later times the temple itself was used as a castle. The principal parts of a fortification were, 1. The wall, which, in some instances, was double and triple, 2 Chron. xxxii, 5.

2. Towers, which were erected at certain distances from each other on the top of walls, and ascended to a great height, terminated at the top in a flat roof, and were surrounded with a parapet, which exhibited openings similar to those in the parapet of the walls. 3. The walls were erected in such a way as to curve inward; the extremities of them, consequently, projected outward, and formed a kind of bastions. The object of forming the walls so as to present such projections was to enable the inhabitants of the besieged city to attack the assailants in flank. 4. The gates were at first made of wood, and were small in size. They were constructed in the manner of valve doors, and were secured by means of wooden bars. Subsequently they were made larger and stronger; and in order to prevent their being burned, were covered with plates of brass or iron. The bars were covered in the same manner, in order to prevent their being cut asunder; but it was sometimes the case that they were made wholly of iron. The bars were secured by a sort of lock, Psa. cvii, 16; Isa. xlv, 2.

The attack of the orientals in battle has always been, and is to this day, characterized by vehemence and impetuosity. In case the enemy sustain an unaltered front, they retreat, but it is not long before they return again with renewed ardour. It was the practice of the Roman armies to stand still in the order of battle, and to receive the shock of their opposers. To this practice there are allusions in the following passages : 1 Cor. xvi, 13 ; Eph. vi, 14.

WARD. 1. A prison ; the place where any one is watched, guarded, Gen. xlii, 17.

2. The persons themselves who are set to keep watch or guard. See Acts xii, 10.

WATCH, a part of the night, so called from the military watches. Among the ancient Hebrews there were only three night watches ; the FIRST was called the *first watch*, Lam. ii, 19, and continued till midnight ; the SECOND was called the *middle watch*, Judges vii, 17, and continued from midnight till the crowing of the cock ; the THIRD was called the *morning watch*, and continued till the rising of the sun, Exod. xiv, 24 ; 1 Sam. xi, 11. Later, and in the times of the New Testament, the night was divided into *four* watches, after the Roman manner.

The word *watch* signifies also *a guard of soldiers*, Matt. xxvii, 63, 66, referring to the guard of Roman soldiers at the sepulchre of Jesus. That this guard consisted of *Roman* soldiers is evident from the circumstances of the history.

Josephus informs us that it was usual with the Roman governors to order a *cohort* to mount guard in the porticoes of the temple at the solemn feasts. A cohort consisted of from 300 to 600 men ; and some of which, who were not then on duty, Pilate gave them leave to employ to watch the tomb. Mr. Watson says, there were sixty in number. I regret he does not state the source of his information.

WATCH-TOWER. See TOWER.

WATCHER, a name for the angels in the later Hebrew, as keeping watch over the souls of men, Dan. iv, 10, 14, 20.

WATER. Pure water is a transparent colourless liquid, which has neither smell nor taste. The purest, without having recourse to distillation, is obtained by receiving rain in clean vessels at a distance from houses, or by melting freshly fallen snow. Hence Job says, " If I wash myself with *snow-water*, and make my hands never so clean," Job ix, 30.

When joined with the name of a place, the word signifies waters situated near that place, a fountain, stream, torrent, lake, marsh, &c.

Living water, John iv, 10, 11, is the water of running streams and fountains, opposed to that of stagnant cisterns, pools, and marshes.

The term in John v, 3, refers to the medicinal waters of the fountain near Jerusalem ; and in John xix, 34, to the *watery fluid*, which is naturally found in the pericar-

33

drum, or membrane that encloses the heart.

In Rev. xiv, 2, we find the expression, " *The voice of many* WATERS," and followed by the sentence, " as the voice of thunder," i. e., a voice exceedingly loud. It is the waves of the sea, probably, to which the writer here alludes ; for there were no cataracts in Palestine that would have supplied him with an apposite idea. " To drink in iniquity like *water*," Job xv, 16, is to be wholly filled and overflowing with it ; compare xxxiv, 7. Poetically, water is the emblem of great abundance, plenty ; see Psa. lxxxviii, 17 ; Isa. xi, 9 ; and also of great and overwhelming dangers, Psa. xviii, 16. " He drew me out of *many waters ;*" compare xxxii, 6 ; Job xxvii, 20. Those who come out of the *waters* of Judah," Isa. xlviii, 1, are his offspring, " from the *fountain* of Israel," Psa. lxviii, 26. " The hearts of the people melted, and became as *water*," Joshua vii, 5, i. e., timorous, full of fluctuation and trembling ; opposite to this is a heart *firm as a stone*, Job xli, 24.

Water is an emblem of the vii,

tress which is enced by man want of it is indescribable. Park, the African traveller, tells us, that after several days of privation, he fell-asleep, and his fancy carried him to the banks of a clear and beautiful river, which he surveyed with transport ; and on eagerly hastening to quench his thirst, the effort awaked him to a dreadful disappointment. How happily does this illustrate Isa. xxix, 8. Hence *water* is used as an emblem of spiritual nourishment, as the doctrines and blessings of the Gospel, John iv, 14.

" *Stolen waters*" signify unlawful pleasures with strange women, Prov. ix, 17. The Israelites are reproached with having forsaken the fountain of living water, to quench their thirst at broken cisterns, Jer. ii, 13 ; that is, with having quitted the worship of God for the worship of false and ridiculous deities. See FOUNTAIN.

WATERSPOUTS, Psa. xlii, 7. This phenomenon has been thus described by those who have witnessed it. From a dense cloud a cone descends in the form of a trumpet, with the small end downward ; at the same time the surface of the sea under it is agitated and whirled around ; the waters are converted into vapour, and ascend with a spiral motion, till they unite with the cone proceeding from the cloud ; frequently, however, they disperse before the junction is effected. In the middle of the cone there is a vacant space, in which none of the small particles of water ascend; and in this, as well as around the outer edges of the waterspout, large drops of rain precipitate themselves. A notion has been entertained that they are very dangerous to a ship, owing to the descent at the instant of their breaking of a large body of water; but this does not appear to be the case, for the water descends only in the form of heavy rain.

WAY, 1. Is the path in which one walks; hence "the *way* of any one," is the way which he is wont to go or pass, e. g., the *king's way* is the public highway, the military road, Num. xx, 17. *One's way*; also Gen. xix, 2, is one's journey by the usual road.

Sometimes *way* includes a whole region or district, in or through which a way passes, as *the way*, i. e., the country *of the Gentiles*, Matt. x, 5. "The *way* of the sea," Matt. iv, 15, i. e., the region around the Sea of Galilee.

Figuratively, "Jesus is the *way*," John xiv, 6, i. e., he is the author and medium of access to God and eternal life.

2. *Way* signifies the mode or manner in which one walks or lives, the course which one follows, Prov. xii, 15. "The fruit of one's *way*," the good or evil resulting from his conduct, Prov. i, 31.

The way of God, or *the Lord*, is his mode of proceeding or acting, his counsels, Deut. xxxii, 4, or it is the way or conduct which God requires, and in which men ought to walk, Matt. xxii, 16.

The psalmist says, "Thou wilt show me the path of life," Psa. xvi, 11; that is, thou wilt raise my body from death to life, and conduct me to the place and state of everlasting happiness." All eastern potentates have their precursors and a number of pioneers to clear the road, by removing obstacles, and filling up the ravines and the hollow ways in their route. In the days of Mogul splendour, the emperor caused the hills and mountains to be levelled, and the valleys to be filled up for his convenience. This beautifully illustrates the figurative language in the approach of the Prince of peace, when "every valley shall be exalted, and every mountain and hill shall be made low, and the crooked shall be made straight, and the rough places plain," Isa. xl, 3–5.

Wayfaring man, is a traveller, *way marks* are columns or pillars which serve to mark out the way, Jer. xxxi, 21.

WEAN, Gen. xxi, 8, to reconcile a child to the want of the breast or any object of desire. The Jews probably weaned their children when they were thirty or thirty-six months old; compare 2 Chron. xxxi, 16, with 2 Mac. vii, 27; and the day on which the child was weaned was made a festival, Gen. xxi, 8.

WEAVER, Isa. xxxviii, 12. The combined arts of spinning and weaving are among the first essentials of civilized society, and we find both to be of very ancient origin. The frequent allusions to this art in the sacred writings tend to show that the fabrication of cloth from threads, hair, &c., is a very ancient invention. It has, however, like other useful arts, undergone a vast succession of improvements, both as to the preparation of the materials of which cloth is made, and the apparatus necessary in its construction, as well as in the particular modes of operation by the artist.

WEDDING GARMENT. See GARMENT.

WEEKS. A period of seven days, under the usual name of *a week*, is mentioned as far back as the time of the deluge, Gen. vii, 4, 10; viii, 10, 12; xxix, 27, 28. It must, therefore, be considered a very ancient division of time, especially as the various nations among whom it has been noticed, for instance, the Nigri in Africa, appear to have received it from the sons of Noah. In addition to the week of days, the Jews had three other seasons denominated *weeks*, Lev. xxv, 1-17; Deut. xvi, 9, 10.

1. *The week of weeks.* It was a period of seven weeks or forty-nine days, which was succeeded on the fiftieth day by the feast of *pentecost*, which signifies "fifty," Deut. xvi, 9, 10.

2. *The week of years.* This was a period of seven years, during the last of which the land remained untilled, and the people enjoyed a Sabbath or season of rest.

3. *The week of seven Sabbatical years.* It was a period of forty-nine years, and was succeeded by the year of *jubilee*, Lev. xxv, 1-22; xxvi, 34. See YEAR.

WEIGHTS. The Hebrews weighed all the gold and silver they used in trade. The *shekel* and *talent* are not denominations of money in gold and silver, but of certain *weights*. The "*shekel* of the sanctuary," Exod. xxx, 13, was probably the standard weight preserved in some apartment of the tabernacle or temple, and not a different weight from the common shekel, Ezek. xlv, 12.

The following are the Jewish weights reduced to troy weight:—

		lb.	oz.	ds.	g.
Gerah,	Exod. xxx, 13,	0	0	0	12
Bekah,	. . . . .	0	0	5	0
Shekel,	Gen. xxiv, 22,	0	0	10	0
Maneh,	. . . . .	2	6	0	0
Talent,	2 Sam. xii, 30,	113	10	1	2

The word *weight* conveys the idea of greatness, abundance, fulness. The apostle speaks of " an eternal *weight* of glory," 2 Cor. iv, 17, and elegantly joins together the two senses of a Hebrew word, which signifies both *weight* and *glory*.

The troubles we endure are even levity itself, if we compare them to the *intenseness*, the *fulness* of that glory, so solid and lasting, which shall be hereafter.

WELLS. When the pool, the fountain, and the river fail, the oriental shepherd is reduced to the necessity of digging wells; and, in the patriarchal age, the discovery of water was reckoned of sufficient importance to be the subject of a formal report to the master of the flock, who commonly distinguished the spot by an appropriate name. A remarkable instance of this kind is recorded by Moses, Gen. xxvi, 17, &c. To prevent the sand which is raised from the parched surface of the ground by the winds from filling up their wells, they were obliged to cover them with a stone, Gen. xxix, 3. In this manner the well was covered from which the flocks of Laban were commonly watered; and the shepherds, careful not to leave them open at any time, patiently waited till all the flocks were gathered together before they removed the covering, and then, having drawn a sufficient quantity of water, they replaced the stone immediately. The extreme scarcity of water in these arid regions entirely justifies such vigilant and parsimonious care in the management of this precious fluid, and accounts for the fierce contentions about the possession of a well, which so frequently happened between the shepherds of different masters, see Gen. xxi, 25.

Twice in the day they led their flocks to the wells; at noon, and when the sun was going down. To water the flocks was an operation of much labour, and occupied a considerable space of time. It was, therefore, an office of great kindness with which Jacob introduced himself to the notice of his relations, to roll back the stone which lay upon the mouth of the well, and draw water for the flocks which Rachel tended.

WHALE, the largest of all the inhabitants of the water. A late author supposes that the crocodile, and not the whale, is spoken of in Gen. i, 21. The word in Job vii, 12, must also be taken for the crocodile. It must mean some terrible animal, which, but for the watchful care of Divine Providence, would be very destructive. We are told, that, in order to preserve the Prophet Jonah when he was thrown overboard by the mariners, "the Lord prepared a great fish to swallow him up." What kind of fish it was is not specified; probably a *shark*, as sharks are common in the Mediterranean.

In the common translation of Matt. xii, 40, it is called a *whale*; but the Greek word signifies any large fish, a sea monster.

Although the whale is the largest of all known fish, its gullet is too small to permit the passage of a human body through it ; and therefore we cannot, without the supposition of an additional miracle, admit this to be the fish intended.

WHEAT, the principal and the most valuable kind of grain for the service of man, and is produced in almost every part of the world. Being called *corn* in England, where the Bible was translated, it is often so called in Scripture, Matt. xii, 1. Wheat grew in Egypt in the time of Joseph, as it now does in Africa, on several branches, coming up from one stalk, see Gen. xli, 5, each of which produced an ear.

This sort of wheat does not flourish in Palestine ; the wheat of Palestine is of a much better kind.

WHIRLWIND, Hab. iii, 14, a wind which rises suddenly from almost every point, is exceedingly impetuous and rapid, and imparts a whirling motion to dust, sand, water, and occasionally to bodies of great weight and bulk, carrying them either upward or downward, and scattering them about in different directions. Whirlwinds and water spouts are supposed to proceed from the same cause ; their only difference being, that the latter pass over the water, and the former over the land. Both of them have a progressive as well as a circular motion, generally rise after calms and great heats, and occur most frequently in warm latitudes. A water

spout has been known to pass, in its progressive motion, from sea to land, and, when it has reached the latter, to produce all the phenomena and effects of a whirlwind. There is no doubt, therefore, of their arising from a similar cause, as they are both explicable on the same general principles. In the imagery employed by the sacred writers, these frightful hurricanes are introduced as the immediate instruments of the Divine indignation.

WHITE, Rev. iv, 4, a favourite and emblematical colour in Palestine. Paul said to Ananias, *Thou whited wall*, i. e., thou hypocrite ; fair without and foul within, Acts xxiii, 3.

WHOREDOM, Gen. xxxviii, 24, chiefly spoken of a female, whether married or unmarried, and often used figuratively for *idolatry* ; the relation existing between God and the Israelitish people is everywhere shadowed forth by the prophets under the emblem of the conjugal union ; see Hosea i, 2 ; Ezek. xvi, 22, and therefore the people in worshipping other gods are compared to a harlot and adulteress.

The word is also used for any breach of fidelity toward God, e. g., of a murmuring and seditious people, Num. xiv, 33.

. Hence the *great whore*, Rev. xvii, 1, 5, is *Babylon*, probably pagan Rome, as being the chief seat of idolatry, and in this respect the successor of ancient Babylon.

WIDOW. Among the Hebrews, even before the law, a widow who had no children by her husband was to marry the brother of her deceased spouse. The law that appoints these marriages is recorded in Deut. xxv, 5. Two motives prevailed to the enactment of this law. The first was, the continuation of estates in the same family; and the other was to perpetuate a man's name in Israel. It was looked upon as a great misfortune for a man to die without an heir, or to see his inheritance pass into another family.

WILDERNESS, a region of forest, uncultivated by human beings, but in the Scriptures applied to the Arabian Desert, Gen. xvi, 7; a sterile, sandy region between Egypt and El Ghor, of which the different parts are distinguished by separate proper names, as *Paran, Shur, Sinai.* This desert is now called *El Tyh, the wanderings,* in which, according to the belief of Jews and Mohammedans, the Israelites wandered for several years, and hence its name. Burckhardt describes this desert as "the most barren and horrid tract of country he had ever seen; black flints cover the chalky or sandy ground, which in most places is without any vegetation. The tree which produces the gum arabic grows in small spots; and the tamarisk is

met with here and there: but the scarcity of water forbids much extent of vegetation, and the hungry camels are obliged to go in the evening for whole hours out of the road in order to find some withered shrubs upon which to feed. During ten days' forced marches he passed only four springs or wells, of which one only, about twenty-five miles from Suez, was of sweet water."

The *mountain deserts* are not of so dreary and unproductive a character; they are more adapted to pasturage, see Luke xv, 4; compare Matt. xviii, 12. These deserts obtain their names from the places near which they are situated. The wilderness of Judea was the south-eastern part of Judea, from the Jordan along the Dead Sea, which was mostly uninhabited, Matt. iii, 1; see Judges i, 16. The wilderness where Jesus was tempted was probably between the Mount of Olives and Jericho. See **DESERT.**

The term is used metaphorically for a region desolated by violence, Isa. xiv, 17.

Also for a place *naked,* Jer. ii, 31. "Have I been a *wilderness* unto Israel?" i. e., have I commanded them to worship me for naught; have I been barren, destitute of every thing toward them?

WILLING. "Thy people are *willing,*" Psa. cx, 3, i. e., are prompt for warlike service; compare Judges v, 2, 9.

WILL-WORSHIP, a worship of human invention, i. e., beyond what God requires; this is the just character of whatever worship is paid to angels, Col. ii, 23.

WILLOW, a well known tree which flourishes best in moist situations, and on the borders of streams; see Isa. xliv, 4, Psa. cxxxvii, 2, where the *Salix Babylonica,* the Babylonian willow, i. e., the common weeping willow, whose pendulous boughs are a fit emblem of grief and mourning, is to be understood. This species grows wild in Persia; and besides, has long been a favourite ornamental tree in *China.*

The brook of the willows, Isa. xv, 7, not improbably the *Et Ahsa,* a small stream on the east of the Dead Sea, which forms the southern border between Moab and Edom.

WIMPLE, Isa. iii, 22, a hood or veil; but in the Bible it is supposed to be a wide upper garment worn by women. By the circumstances of the story in Ruth, iii, 15, where the word is translated *veil,* it must have been of considerable size, perhaps a *mantle* or *cloak.*

WIND. The Hebrews acknowledge, as we do, four principal winds, north, east, south, and west, Ezek. xxxvii, 9, though it appears that the winds which most commonly prevail in Palestine are from the western quarter, more usually, perhaps, from the south-west. This statement is confirmed by the reports of intelligent travellers. A north wind not unfrequently arises, which, as in ancient days, is the sure harbinger of fair weather, Prov. xxv, 23.

But the *east wind* is the most vehement of all in western Asia and the adjacent seas, Job xxvii, 21; Jer. xviii, 17. It is represented, Gen. xli, 6; Jonah iv, 8, as scorching and withering plants and herbage, as blowing with great violence, Ezek. xxvii, 26; and also as a horrible tempest," Psa. xi, 6; this is a sultry and oppressive wind, blowing from the south-east, and prevailing only in the hot and dry months of summer. Coming thus from the Arabian desert, it seems to increase the heat of the season, and produces universal languor.

Mr. Smith, who experienced its effects during the summer at Beyrout, describes it as possessing the same qualities and characteristics as the sirocco which he felt at Malta, i. e., resembling a blast of burning steam from the mouth of an oven; in a few minutes those exposed to it find every fibre relaxed in an extraordinary manner. This wind is more or less violent, and of longer or shorter duration at different times, seldom lasting more than thirty-six or forty hours.

Many interpreters refer the *east wind* of the Scriptures to the wind called by the Arabs *simoom ;* but the former accounts of this wind have been much exaggerated. For a full account of it, see Robinson's Calmet, article WIND.

WINDOW. The windows in the East are large, extending almost to the floor. Persons sitting on the floor can look out at them. They are mostly confined to the interior court of the house; occasionally, however, the traveller sees a window which looks toward the street ; but it is closed by a lattice and not with glass, and thrown open only on the public festivities, Judges v, 28; Song ii, 9. In Solomon's portraiture of old age, *windows* signify the holes or openings for the eyes, Eccl. xii, 3.

Moses speaks of *windows*, sluices, flood-gates of heaven, which are open to let fall the rain, Gen. vii, 11.

WINE, the fermented juice of grapes. This juice, when newly expressed, and before it has begun to ferment, is called *must*, and, in common language, *sweet wine*. This, however, could not have been the new wine referred to by the Jews, Acts ii, 13, because there was no such wine in Judea so early as Pentecost, (May 23.) It must have been a peculiar kind, that which the prophet calls *sweet wine*, which distils spon-taneously from the grape, and which, it is said, the ancients had a method of preserving a long time. This was remarkably intoxicating. But Dr. Jahn says that *sweet wine* was manufactured from dried grapes, soaked in wine and pressed a second time, called also *new wine*. Perhaps this was the method of preserving it sweet. Among the Greeks and Romans, the sweet wine was most commonly in use ; and in preparing their wine, the ancients often inspissated it until it became of the consistence of honey, or even thicker. This was diluted with water previously to its being drank. But in the Scripture *mixed wine*, prov. xxiii, 30, is not wine diluted with water, but on the contrary, increased in strength by being mixed with *spices*, the same as *spiced wine*, Song viii, 2. Wine rendered more fragrant and palatable with aromatics. This was considered a great delicacy.

" *Wine* cheereth God and man," Judges ix, 13. This refers to the use which was made of wine in the libations which were presented to the Deity, and to the common use of it by men.

" *Wine* of God's wrath," Rev. xiv, 10, is the intoxicating cup which God in wrath presents to the nations, and which causes them to reel and stagger to destruction. This is called by Isaiah *the cup of trembling*, Isa. li 17; compare Jer. xxv, 15.

"*The wine of the wrath of her fornication*," i. e., a love potion, or potion adapted to excite love, with which a harlot seduces to fornication (idolatry,) and thus brings upon men the wrath of God, Rev. xviii, 3; compare Jer. li, 7.

WINE-BIBBER, Luke vii, 34, one who drinks much wine.

WINE-PRESS, Rev. xiv, 19. The presses consisted of two receptacles or vats, which were either built of stones and covered with plaster, or hewn out of a large rock. The upper receptacle called the vat, Joel iii, 13, as it is constructed at the present day in Persia, is nearly eight feet square and four feet high. Into this the grapes are thrown and trodden by five men. The juice flows out into a lower receptacle through a grated aperture near the bottom. The treading of the wine-press was laborious, and not very favourable to cleanliness; the garments of the persons thus employed were stained with the red juice, and yet the employment was a joyful one. It was performed with singing, accompanied with musical instruments, Isa. xvi, 10; Jer. xlviii, 33. Figuratively, vintage gleaning, and treading the wine-press, signified battles and great slaughters, Isa. lxiii, 1-3; Lam. i, 15.

WING, generally used in the plural; one having *wings* is a poetical expression for a bird, Eccl. x, 20. "*Wings* of the wind," Psa. xviii, 11, and "*wings* of the morning," Psa. cxxxix, 9, is a poetical figure expressive of the swiftness with which the winds and the dawn move onward. The word conveys also the idea of protection, defence, Ruth ii, 12. Wings are attributed to armies, Isa. viii, 8; hence "land shadowing with *wings*," signifies full of armies, Isa. xviii, 1.

WINTER, in Palestine, the rainy season, the seasons of rains and storms, extending from the middle of December to the middle of February, John x, 22. The snow, which is not then unfrequent, scarcely continues through the day, except on the mountains; the ice is thin, and melts as soon as the sun ascends to any considerable height. The roads are slippery, and travelling is both tedious and dangerous, Jer. xxiii, 12; Matt. xxiv, 20.

WISDOM. 1. Signifies practical wisdom, skill in the affairs of life, wise management, as shown in forming the best plans, and selecting the best means, including the idea of judgment and sound good sense, Acts vi, 3.

2. In a higher sense, it signifies deep knowledge, natural and moral; insight, learning in respect to things human and Divine, implying cultivation of mind and an

enlightened understanding, Matt. xii, 42.

"The *wisdom* of this world," 1 Cor. i, 20, was the learning and philosophy current among the Greeks and Romans in the apostolic age, which stood in contrast with the simplicity of the Gospel, and tended to draw away the minds of men from Divine truth; so the "*wisdom* of words," verse 17, is mere philosophy and rhetoric.

Wisdom in respect to Divine things is represented everywhere as a Divine gift, and so joined with purity of heart and life, 2 Pet. iii, 15. Wisdom is also insight imparted from God in respect to the Divine counsels, 1 Cor. ii, 6.

It is spoken by a figure of the author and source of this wisdom, 1 Cor. i, 30, as conjoined with purity of heart and life, James i, 5, 17.

Wisdom has been distinguished from knowledge thus: wisdom means the faculty of practical judgment; but knowledge, in the New Testament, is more particularly the theoretic, higher, deeper, experimental part of religion.

4. The word signifies *the Divine wisdom*, including the ideas of infinite skill, insight, knowledge, purity, Rom. xi, 33.

"*Wisdom* is justified of her children," Luke vii, 35, i. e., *Divine wisdom*, as revealed and manifested in Christ and his Gospel, is acknowledged and honoured by her real followers; compare chap. xi, 49.

The wide circle of virtues and mental endowments which the Hebrews comprised under this word, is best gathered from the history and character of those whose wisdom became proverbial among them, e. g., Solomon, 1 Kings v, 9, s. q., Daniel, Ezek. xxviii, 3; and the Egyptians, Acts vii, 22.

The seat of wisdom is placed by the Hebrews in the heart, Prov. xvi, 21.

WISE MEN, men of wisdom and learning. In Matt. ii, 1, the *magi*, i. e., priests and philosophers among the Persians, who devoted themselves to the study of the moral and physical sciences, and particularly cultivated astrology and medicine. See Num. xxiii, 7. As they thus acquired great honour and influence, they were introduced into the courts of kings, and consulted on all occasions. They also followed them in warlike expeditions; and so much importance was attached to their advice and opinions, that nothing was attempted without their approbation. The remarkable *star* which directed the wise men appears to have been a meteor in the middle of the air, which having been observed by them to be attended with miraculous and extraordinary circumstances, was probably taken for the star so long foretold by Balaam, Num.

xxiv, 17, i. e., a light that moved in the air before them, something like the pillar of cloud in the desert.

WIT, the old word for *know*, from which comes *wot*, the past tense, *knew*, Exod. xxxii, 1. "We do you *to wit*," 2 Cor. viii, 1, means *we make known* to you, we *inform* you. It is now used only in the infinitive mode, *to wit* meaning *namely, that is to say*, Rom. viii, 23.

WITCH is a woman, and *wizard* is a man, who, by a supposed compact with the devil practises sorcery, i. e., foretells future events, pretends to cure diseases, to call up or drive away spirits, or to disclose information beyond the reach of the natural powers. No sin is more severely denounced by a holy God, Exod. xxii, 18, who claims to himself the exclusive prerogative of revealing the future; and those who consult such wicked pretenders are partakers of their guilt, Gal. v, 20.

A famous pretender to this supernatural power lived at Endor. This woman neither wrought nor expected to work any miracle, being herself terrified at the appearance of Samuel, who was sent by God himself. See ENDOR.

WOLF. This animal in his general appearance resembles a large dog. He has, however, a fiercer and more savage aspect; the form of the animal also is thinner, and he has a gaunt, emaciated look. The European wolves usually lead a solitary life; but when urged by hunger, they unite together in packs, which at times even become dangerous to travellers. This wolf possesses such strength that it is able to carry off a sheep at full speed, and few dogs are able to attack it with success.

They are represented in the Bible as terrifying the flocks and prowling at night, Hab. i, 8; Gen. xlix, 27. "Benjamin shall *rave as a wolf*." In this passage a certain warlike disposition in this tribe is alluded to.

Figuratively, a wolf signifies a rapacious and violent person, wolf-like, Acts xx, 29.

WORD. Sometimes the Scripture ascribes to the *word of God* certain supernatural effects, and often represents it as animated and active: "He sent his *word* and healed them," Psa. cvii, 20. It also signifies what is written in the sacred books of the Old and New Testaments, Luke xi, 28; James i, 22; the Divine law which teaches and commands good things, and forbids evil, Psa. cxix, 101; and is used to express every promise of God, Psa. cxix, 25, &c., and prophecy or vision, Isa. ii, 1.

This term likewise occurs in the writings of St. John, i, 1. It here stands for the pre-existent nature of Christ, i. e., that spiritual and Divine nature spoken of in the Jewish writings before and about the time of Christ, under various names, as *wisdom*, Prov. viii, 12, 22, *son of man*, &c.; Dan. vii, 13. On this Divine *word* the Jews of our Saviour's time would appear to have had much subtle discussion; and therefore, probably, the apostle sets out with affirming, "In the beginning was the *Word*," and then also declares that this Word became flesh, and was thus the Messiah, verse 14.

The Unitarian comment is, "from the beginning of his ministry," or "the commencement of the Gospel dispensation;" which makes St. John use trifling truism, and solemnly tell his readers that our Saviour, when he began his ministry, *was in existence!* Almost immediately it is added, "All things were made by him;" which can only mean the creation of universal nature. *He*, then, who made all things, was prior to all things created; *he* was when they began to be, and therefore before they began to be; and, if he existed before all created things, he was not himself created, and was therefore eternal. Again, he is expressly called God; and he is said to be the Creator of all things, verse 3.

WORKS. "The *work* of the Lord" signifies the cause of Christ, the Gospel work, which he began and left to be continued by his disciples, 1 Cor. xv, 58.

The work of God is that work which God requires, duty toward him, John vi, 28.

So the "*works of the law*," are those works which are required by the law, or those which are conformable to the Mosaic moral law; so of course required by this law, Rom. iii, 25.

Works of faith, i. e., works springing from faith, combined with faith, 1 Thess. i, 2.

Good works signify virtuous actions in general, but especially charitable and beneficent actions, Matt. v, 16.

WORLD, the universe, Matt. xiii, 35; sometimes it means *the earth*, this lower world, as the abode of men, Mark xvi, 15.

The term is also taken for the inhabitants of the world, John iii, 16; and *men of the world* are *worldlings*, who have their portion in this life, as opposed to those who seek the kingdom of God, John xii, 31. Also the wealth and enjoyments of this world, this life's goods, Matt. xvi, 26.

This world means the present order of things, as opposed to the kingdom of Christ; and hence always with the idea of transientness, worthlessness, and evil, both physical and moral, the seat of cares, temptations, irregular desires, &c., John xii, 25.

World is figuratively spoken of any thing, for an aggregate congeries, an abundance, James iii, 6.

WORM, the general name

in Scripture for little creeping insects, especially such as are generated in putrid substances, Isa. xiv, 14.

"Their *worm* dieth not," Mark ix, 44. In allusion to Isa. lxvi, 24, the language of the prophet being applied to the place of punishment of the wicked.

The word is used, metaphorically, of a person feeble and despised, Psa. xxii, 7.

WORMWOOD, Deut. xxix, 18. From the passages of Scripture where this plant is mentioned, something more than the bitterness of its qualities seems to be intimated, and effects are attributed to it greater than can be produced by the wormwood of America. It may therefore mean a plant allied, perhaps, to it in appearance and in taste; but possessing more nauseous, hurtful, and formidable properties.

Indeed bitter herbs were commonly regarded as poisonous by the Hebrews; compare Rev. viii, 11, where the figure of waters thus converted into bitter poison, is drawn, perhaps, from Jer. xxiii, 15.

WORSHIP,-Matt. iv, 10, consists in paying a due respect, veneration, and homage to the Deity, under a sense of an obligation to him; and this is to be shown and testified by external acts, as prayers, thanksgivings, &c. The Scriptural obligation of public worship is partly founded upon example, and partly upon precept; so that no person who admits that authority can question this great duty without manifest and criminal inconsistency. The institution of public worship under the law, and the practice of synagogue worship among the Jews, from at least the time of Ezra, cannot be questioned; both of which were sanctioned by the practice of our Lord and his apostles. The preceptive authority for our regular attendance upon public worship, is either inferential or direct. The command to publish the Gospel includes the obligation of assembling to hear it. The name by which a Christian society is designated in Scripture is a Church; which signifies an assembly for the transaction of business; and in the case of a Christian assembly, that business must necessarily be spiritual, and include the sacred exercises of prayer, praise, and hearing the Scriptures. But we have more direct precepts, although the practice was obviously continued from Judaism, and was therefore consuetudinary. Some of the epistles of St. Paul are commanded to be read in the Churches. The singing of psalms, hymns, and spiritual songs is enjoined as the act of solemn worship to the Lord; and St. Paul cautions the Hebrews that they "forsake not the assembling of themselves together." The practice of the primitive age is also manifest from the epistles of St. Paul. The Lord's Supper was celebrated by the body of believers collectively ; and this apostle prescribes to the Corinthians regulations for the exercises of prayer and prophesyings " when they came together in the Church," i. e., to the assembly.

WOT. See WIT.

WRATH, a violent commotion of mind, especially as including desire of vengeance, punishment, and therein differing from *anger*. Anger is the passion begun, but wrath is the passion carried to its height, accompanied with a desire of punishment, and leading the enraged person to revile, and even to curse his adversary, Eph. iv, 31.

The wrath of God, Rom. ix, 22, speaking of him after the manner of men, the Divine displeasure or indignation, as implying utter abhorrence of sin and aversion to those who live in it.

Sometimes the phrase signifies the *punishment* of God. The most heavy and awful of all punishments, such as sinners deserve, and such as it becomes Divine justice to inflict, Romans ii, 5. See ANGER.

WRITING, Dan. v, 8, 25. In regard to alphabetic writing, all the ancient writers attribute the invention of it to some very early age, and some country of the East : but they do not pretend to designate precisely either the time or the place. They say, farther, that Cadmus introduced letters from Phenicia into Greece, if we may credit the Parisian Chronicle, B. C. 1519, that is, forty-five years after the death of Moses. An-ti-cli'des asserts, and attempts to prove, that letters were invented in Egypt fifteen years before Pho-ron'e-us, the most ancient king of Greece ; that is, four hundred and nine years after the deluge, and in the one hundred and seventeenth year of Abraham. On this it may be remarked, that they might have been introduced into Egypt at this time, but they had been previously invented by the Phenicians. Hence it is not at all wonderful that books and writings are spoken of in the time of Moses, as if well known, Exod. xvii, 14 ; xxiv, 4.

The materials and instruments of writing were, 1. The *leaves* of trees. 2. The *bark* of trees, from which, in the process of time, a sort of paper was manufactured. 3. A *table of wood*, Luke i, 63. In the East, these tables were not covered with wax as they were in the west ; or at any rate very rarely so. 4. *Linen* was first used for the object in question at Rome. Linen books were mentioned by Livy. Cotton cloth also, which was used for the bandages of Egyptian mummies, and inscribed with hieroglyphics, was one of the materials for writing upon. 5. The paper made from the reed pa-py'rus, which, as Pliny has shown, was used before the Trojan war. See RUSH. 6. The *skins* of various animals ; but they were poorly prepared for the purpose, until some improved methods of manufacture were invented at Pergamus, during the reign of Eumenes, about 300 B. C. Hence the skins of animals, prepared for writing, are called in Latin *pergamena*, in English parchment, to this day, from the city Pergamus. 7. *Tables of lead*, Job xix, 24. 8. *Tables of brass.* Of all the materials, brass was considered among the most durable, and was employed for those inscriptions which were designed to last the longest, 1 Macc. viii, 22 ; xiv, 27. 9. *Stones* or *rocks*, upon which public laws, &c., were written. Sometimes the letters engraved were filled up with lime, Exod. xxiv, 12. 10. *Tiles.* The inscriptions were made upon the tiles first, and afterward they were baked in the fire. They are yet to be found in the ruins of Babylon ; others of later origin are to be found in many countries in the East. 11. And the *sand* of the earth, in which the children in India to this day learn the art of writing, and in which Ar-chi-me'des himself delineated his mathematical figures. See BOOK.

YEAR, Deut. xiv, 22. The Hebrew word for year signifies *repetition*, as the repetition of the course of the sun, or of the seasons, as spring, harvest, summer, and winter. In ancient times, when it was thought that the sun moved round the earth, this period was called the *solar* year. The year of the Hebrews consisted of twelve months of thirty days each, (see Gen. vii,) except the twelfth, which was thirty-five, making the year to consist of 365 days. It is now ascertained by accurate astronomical observations that the year contains five hours and forty-nine minutes more, which in four years make one day, and added to February, occasions that year to be called *leap year*.

The Hebrews practised two modes of reckoning the months. The more ancient mode of reckoning was by beginning the year with *Tisri*, i. e., the first new moon in October, and was used only in civil and agricultural concerns. In other matters, they began the year with Ni'san, or the first new moon in April, because the Hebrews departed from Egypt on the fifteenth day of that month, Exod. xii, 2. This reckoning is used by the prophets.

While the Jews continued in the land of Canaan, the beginnings of their months and years were not settled by any astronomical rules or calculations, but by the actual appearance of the new moon. When they saw the new moon, they began the month. Persons were therefore appointed to watch for the first appearance of the moon after the change. As soon as they saw it, they informed the sanhedrim, and public notice was given by lighting beacons throughout the land, or blowing trumpets. See Month.

The Fallow Year. Agricultural labour among the Jews ceased every seventh year. Nothing was sown and nothing reaped; but whatever spontaneous productions there were, were left to the poor, the traveller, and the wild beast, Lev. xxv, 1-7; Deut. xv, 1-10. The object of this regulation seems to have been, among others, to let the ground recover its strength, and to teach the Hebrews to be provident of their income, and to look out for the future. It is true that extraordinary fertility was promised on the sixth year, but in such a way as not to exclude care and foresight. We are not to suppose, however, that the Hebrews spent the seventh year in absolute idleness: they could fish, hunt, take care of their bees and flocks, repair their buildings and furniture, manufacture cloths of wool, linen, and of the hair of goats and camels, and carry on commerce. Finally, they were obliged to remain longer in the tabernacle or temple this year, during which the whole Mosaic law was read, in order to be instructed in religious and moral duties, and the history of their nation, and the wonderful works and blessings of God, Deut. xxxi, 10-13.

Year of Jubilee. See Jubilee.

YESTERDAY is used to denote all time past, however distant. "Jesus Christ, the same yesterday, to-day, and for ever," Heb. xiii, 8. This sentence expresses the *past*, the *present*, and the *future*; and also implies *immutability*. Jesus Christ is always the same, and is always ready to aid his disciples.

YOKE, the carved piece of wood upon the neck of draught animals, which are coupled together, and by which they are fastened to a pole or beam, Deut. xxi, 3.

The word is often used figuratively, 1. As the emblem of servitude, 1 Tim. vi, 1. 2. For the Mosaic law, whose severe precepts and multitude of sacrifices brought the Jews into moral bondage, especially since they were aggravated by the tradition of the elders, Acts xv, 10; Gal. v, 1. 3. Hence by opposition, it signifies the precepts of Christ, Matt. xi, 29, 30; compare 1 John v, 3.

ZAC-CHE′US, chief of the publicans; that is, collector general of the revenues, Luke xix, 1, &c. This is all that is known concerning this person. See Publicans.

ZACHARIAH. 1. Same

34

as ZACHARIAS, a king of Israel, son of Jeroboam II., put to death by Shallum after a reign of six months, 773 B. C., 2 Kings xv, 8–11.

2. A prophet, who flourished after the exile, whose writings are preserved in the sacred canon, son of Barachias, and grandson of the Prophet Iddo, Ezra v, 1.

3. A person killed in the temple, Luke xi, 51. The allusion is probably to Zechariah, the son of Jehoida, (probably also called Barachias,) who was stoned by order of Joash, 2 Chron. xxiv, 20, 31. Others refer it to the Prophet Zechariah, but history gives no account of his death; several other persons bore this name.

ZAM-ZUMMIM, Deut. ii, 20. The name of a race of giants, the aborigines of the Ammonitish country; but extinct before the time of Moses. The same, perhaps, with the *Zuzim;* a name which occurs only in Gen. xiv, 5.

ZEAL. The original word, in its primary signification, means *heat;* such as the heat of boiling water. When it is figuratively applied to the mind, it means any *warm emotion* or *affection.* And when any of our passions are strongly moved on a religious account, whether for any thing good, or against any thing which we conceive to be evil, this we term religious zeal. But it is not all that is called religious zeal which

is worthy of that name. It is not properly religious or Christian zeal, if it be not joined with love. Phinehas is commended for having expressed much zeal against those wicked persons that violated the law of the Lord, Num. xxv, 11, 13. In Psalm lxix, 9, the psalmist says, "The *zeal* of thine house hath eaten me up;" my earnest desire to have all things duly ordered about thy worship, and my just displeasure and indignation at all abuses in it, have wasted my natural moisture and vital spirits, John ii, 17.

ZEBOIM, one of the cities in the vale of Siddim, destroyed with Sodom and Gomorrah, and covered by the Dead Sea, Deut. xxix, 23.

ZEBULUN, *habitation;* see Gen. xxx, 80. The proper name of the tenth son of Jacob, born of Leah; also the name of the tribe descended from him, the territory of which is described in Joshua xix, 10, s. q.

In the last words of Moses he joins Zebulun and Is'sachar together, Deut. xxxiii, 18, because of their affinity, and because their possessions lay near together.

These two tribes, being at the greatest distance north, should come to Jerusalem, *the mountain;* and it is said, verse 19, "they shall call the *people*," i. e., the Gentiles, with whom they had commerce, or such of the other tribes as dwelt in their way. "By the abundance of the sea," is meant the wealth obtained from the sea by traffic; "treasures hid in the sand," may refer to such precious things as gold, silver, pearl, coral, which are found in the sand, or the expression may refer to their enriching themselves by making *glass* of the sand found on their coasts. The river *Belus*, famous for its sand, of which alone glass was for a long time manufactured, was in the territory of Zebulun.

ZECHARIAH, the same as ZACHARIAH.

ZEDEKIAH, a king of Judah, who reigned 600–568 years B. C., to whom this name was given by Nebuchadnezzar instead of his former one, *Mattaniah*, 2 Kings xxiv, 17. He was the son of Josiah, and uncle to Jehoi'a-chin his predecessor, 2 Kings xxiv, 17–19. When Nebuchadnezzar took Jerusalem, he carried Jehoiachin to Babylon, with his wives, children, officers, and the best artificers in Judea, and put in his place his uncle Mattaniah, whose name he changed into Zedekiah, and made him promise, with an oath, that he would continue in fidelity to him, 2 Chron. xxxvi, 13. He was twenty-one years old when he began to reign at Jerusalem, and he reigned there eleven years. He did evil in the sight of the Lord, committing the same crimes as Jehoiakim; and regarded not the menaces of the Prophet Jeremiah, from the Lord; but hardened his heart. In the ninth year of his reign he revolted against Neb-uchad-nez'zar. Then Neb-uchad-nez'zar marched his army against Zedekiah, and took all the fortified places of his kingdom, except La'chish, A-ze'kah, and Jerusalem. He sat down before the latter on the tenth day of the tenth month of the holy year, which answers to our January. During the siege Zedekiah often consulted Jeremiah, who advised him to surrender, and pronounced the greatest woes against him if he should persist in his rebellion, Jer. xxxvii, 3–10. But this unfortunate prince had neither patience to hear, nor resolution to follow good counsels. In the eleventh year of Zed-e-ki'ah, on the ninth day of the fourth month, (July,) Jerusalem was taken, 2 Kings xxv, 2–4; Jer. xxxix, 2, 3. Zedekiah and his people endeavoured to escape by favour of the night; but the Chaldean troops pursuing them, they were overtaken in the plains of Jericho. He was seized and carried to Neb-uchad-nez'zar, then at Riblah, a city of Syria. The king, reproaching him with his perfidy, caused all his children to be slain before his face, and his eyes to be put out; and loading him with chains of brass, ordered him to be sent to Babylon, 2 Kings xxv, 4–7; Jer. xxxii, 4–7; lii, 4–11. Thus were accomplished *two prophecies* which seemed contradictory. Jeremiah had assured him that he should die in peace; that his body should be burned, as those of the kings of Judah usually were; and that they should mourn for him, saying, *Ah, lord!* Jer. xxxiv, 4, 5. The year of his death is not known.

ZE-LO'TES; a surname given to Simon the Canaanite, one of the apostles, Luke vi, 15. It signifies, properly, *one passionately ardent in any cause, a zealot.* He was probably so called from his having been one of the *zelotae*, a name applied, in the age of Christ, to an extensive association of private persons, who professed great attachment to the Jewish institutions, and undertook to punish without trial those guilty of violating them; under which pretext they frequently committed the greatest excesses and crimes.

ZEPH-A-NI'AH was the son of Cushi, and was probably of a noble family of the tribe of Simeon. He prophesied in the reign of Josiah, about 630 B. C. The style of Zephaniah is poetical; but it is not distinguished by any peculiar elegance or beauty, though generally animated and impressive.

ZE-RUB'BA-BEL in Matt. i, 12. ZOROBABEL, the leader of the first colony of the Jews that returned to their own country after the exile, Ezra ii, 2. He was the son of *Sa-la'thi-el,* and of the family of David.

Zerubbabel returned to Jerusalem long before the reign of Darius, son of Hystas'pes. He returned at the beginning of the reign of Cyrus, 532 B. C., fifteen years before Darius. He is always named first, as being the chief of the Jews that returned to their own country. He laid the foundations of the temple, Ezra iii, 8, 9; Zech. iv, 9; and restored the worship of the Lord, and the usual sacrifices. When the Samar'i-tans offered to assist in rebuilding the temple, Zerubbabel and the principal men of Judah refused them this honour, since Cyrus had granted his commission to the Jews only, Ezra iv, 2, 3.

ZIDON, Judges i, 31, the same as SIDON, which see. *Zidonians,* 1 Kings xvi, 31, is a name applied to all the inhabitants of the northern parts of Canaan dwelling around the skirts of Mount Lebanon, and called by the Greeks PHENICIANS, comprehending also the *Tyrians.*

ZIF, *brightness, beauty,* especially of flowers; hence the name of the second Hebrew month from the new moon of May to that of June, *the month of flowers,* 1 Kings vi, 1, 37.

ZIKLAG, the name of a city in the territory of Simeon, but at times subject to the Philistines, 1 Sam. xxx, 1.

ZIN, *a low palm tree,* a desert which lay around the

south-west shore of the Dead Sea, and extended south along the great valley *El Ghor*; but how far, we have no means of ascertaining. It constituted the north-east part of the great desert of *Paran*. In this desert was situated *Kadesh-Barnea*, see Num. xx, 1.

ZION, *sunny place*, or *sunny mount*, called in the New Testament *Sion*. *Zion* is the southernmost and highest of the hills on which Jerusalem was built; not the northernmost, as Lightfoot supposes.

It included especially the most ancient part of the city, with the citadel and temple, (Mount Moriah, on which the temple was built, being reckoned to Zion,) and was also called *the city of David*, see 2 Chron. v, 2.

By the poets and prophets, *Zion* is very often put for Jerusalem itself, Isa. x, 24; xxxiii, 14. Also for its inhabitants, Isa. xlix, 14; Psa. xcvii, 8.

The inhabitants are also called *daughters of Zion*, Isa. lxii, 11. But "*daughters of Zion*" are the females of Jerusalem, Isa. iii, 16, 17. "The Zion *of* the Holy One," i. e., sacred to him, Isa. lx, 14.

Sion occurs once in the Old Testament, Deut. iv, 48, for the mountain usually called Hermon.

ZOAN, or TANIS, one of the oldest cities of Lower Egypt, Num. xiii, 22, situated on the eastern shore of the second or Tanitic mouth of the Nile, within a few miles of the Lake *Tennis*. It was an extensive city even in later ages; and its ruins occupy an extensive space of country. Among these are obelisks of granite, a colossal statue of Isis, and fragments of buildings of great magnitude.

In Isaiah's time, it appears to be quite clear that Zoan was the place where the Egyptian court resided, Isa. xix, 11, i. e., one of the places of the royal residence, see verse 13; and probably the place where Moses wrought the Egyptian miracles, Psa. lxxviii, 12, 43.

Field of Zoan means the *region* or *territory* round about it.

ZOAR, *smallness*; compare Gen. xix, 20, a small town near the southern extremity of the Dead Sea, more anciently called *Bela*, Gen. xiv, 2.

ZU'ZIM. See ZAM-ZUM MIM.

45

THE END.

Lightning Source UK Ltd.
Milton Keynes UK
UKHW021344240119
336090UK00005B/423/P